american contributions to the ninth international congress of slavists

Vol. I
Linguistics

american contributions to the ninth international congress of slavists

KIEV, SEPTEMBER 1983

Vol. I
Linguistics

edited by
Michael S. Flier

Slavica

Slavica publishes a wide variety of books and journals dealing with the peoples, languages, literatures, history, folklore, and culture of the peoples of Eastern Europe and the USSR. For a complete catalog with prices and ordering information, please write to:

Slavica Publishers, Inc.
P.O. Box 14388
Columbus, Ohio 43214
USA

ISBN: 0-89357-112-1.

Each article copyright © 1983 by the author. All rights reserved.

Text set by Randy Bowlus at the East European Composition Center, supported by the Department of Slavic Languages and Literatures and the Center for Russian and East European Studies at UCLA with grants from the Joint Committee on Eastern Europe of the American Council of Learned Societies and Social Sciences Research Council and the Research and Development Committee of the American Association for the Advancement of Slavic Studies.

Printed in the United States of America.

CONTENTS

Preface 7

RONELLE ALEXANDER
Directions of Morphophonemic Change in Balkan Slavic: The
Accentuation of the Present Tense 9

ROBERT CHANNON
A Comparative Sketch of Certain Anaphoric Processes in Russian
and English 51

CATHERINE V. CHVANY
On 'Definiteness' in Bulgarian, English and Russian 71

JAMES FERRELL
Names with Stems ending in {l-} in Old Russian 93

MICHAEL S. FLIER
The Alternation $l \sim v$ in East Slavic 99

FRANK Y. GLADNEY
Did Slavic Develop Declension Classes? 119

ZBIGNIEW GOŁĄB
The Ethnogenesis of the Slavs in the Light of Linguistics 131

MARVIN KANTOR
The Second Old Slavonic Legend of St. Wenceslas: Problems
of Translation and Dating 147

EMILY KLENIN
The Genitive-Accusative as a Slavonicism in the Laurentian
Manuscript of 1377: The problem of text segmentation 161

HENRY KUČERA
A Semantic Model of Verbal Aspect 171

RADO L. LENCEK
From Language Interference to the Influence of Area in
Dialect-Geography 185

ROBERT MATHIESEN
The Typology of Cyrillic Manuscripts (East Slavic vs. South
Slavic Old Testament Manuscripts) 193

KENNETH E. NAYLOR
On Expressing "Definiteness" in the Slavic Languages and
English 203

JOHANNA NICHOLS AND JOE SCHALLERT
The Pragmatics of Raising in Old Russian and Common Slavic 221

DAVID F. ROBINSON
On Loanwords between Baltic and Slavic 247

A. SCHENKER
Главные пути лексических заимствований в славянских языках
(на материале чешского, польского и восточнославянских
языков X-XVI вв.) 255

WILLIAM R. SCHMALSTIEG
Morphological Considerations on the Balto-Slavic Problem 269

EDWARD STANKIEWICZ
The Collective and Counted Plurals of the Slavic Nouns 277

ALAN TIMBERLAKE
Compensatory Lengthening in Slavic, 2: Phonetic
Reconstruction 293

C. N. VAN SCHOONEVELD
Contribution to the Systematic Comparison of Morphological and
Lexical Semantic Structures in the Slavic Languages 321

DEAN S. WORTH
The "Second South Slavic Influence" in the History of the
Russian Literary Language 349

OL'GA YOKOYAMA
В защиту запретных деепричастий 373

Preface

The linguistics volume of *American Contributions to the Ninth International Congress of Slavists* represents the cooperative effort of a number of people whose labors merit special acknowledgment. I am grateful to Professors Catherine Chvany (Massachusetts Institute of Technology) and Alexander Schenker (Yale) for providing invaluable assistance in the selection and editing of the contributions submitted for consideration. Many of their comments and recommendations have been incorporated in the final version of the text. Special thanks are extended to Professor Dean S. Worth (UCLA), President of the American Committee of Slavists, for organizing the initial phase of the selection process and helping the Selection Committee and the Editor at every stage of editing and production; to Professor Kenneth E. Naylor (Ohio State), Secretary of the American Committee of Slavists, for keeping an accurate tally of the papers submitted and providing a clearinghouse for the distribution of papers and correspondence to members of the Selection Committee; and to Professor Charles E. Gribble (Ohio State), President and Editor of Slavica Publishers, Inc., for his technical advice and supervision of the final phases of production.

Special commendation must be given to Randy Bowlus (UCLA) for accomplishing with apparent ease the arduous task of converting a collection of typographically difficult manuscripts, charts and graphs into a finished book; to Mary Pottala and Celia Epstein of the UCLA Slavic Department staff for their efficient performance of all clerical duties connected with this volume; and to Professor Bariša Krekić, Director, and Vera Wheeler of the UCLA Center for Russian and East European Studies for making personnel and facilities available to our production staff. Finally, I wish to acknowledge the generous contribution of Professors Ronelle Alexander (Berkeley) and Zbigniew Gołąb (Chicago) in supplying superb cartographic representations for their respective articles.

In a volume of such diverse subject matter, the task of the Editor has been confined to making minor stylistic emendations and ensuring a degree of uniformity in matters of punctuation, citation and transliteration. With few exceptions, the format for footnotes and bibliographical reference has been left to the individual authors. I take this opportunity to thank each of them for their efficiency and cooperation in helping to bring this collaborative project to fruition.

Los Angeles Michael S. Flier
September, 1982

Directions of Morphophonemic Change in Balkan Slavic: The Accentuation of the Present Tense

Ronelle Alexander

0. *Introduction.* My goal in this contribution is to describe the distribution of existing types of accentuation within the present tense in Balkan Slavic dialects (sec. 1) and to present a hypothesis about the nature and direction of the changes which have produced the present system (sec. 2).[1] Since in the course of the paper I will argue that interaction between the accentual paradigms of the present and the aorist tenses was significant in the development of both paradigms, I will also outline the conclusions of a similarly organized investigation of the accentuation of the aorist (sec. 3). Finally, I will discuss accentual relationships between the two paradigms (sec. 4), and present general conclusions (sec. 5).

The original goals of this paper (as formulated with respect to the present tense alone) are similar to those of Gustavsson 1969, and the data base for the synchronic distributional statements made herein is composed more or less of the same sources.[2] In its aims, methodology and assumptions, however, the present work differs from Gustavsson 1969 (and from most diachronically oriented descriptions of accentual systems) in three important ways. First, the synchronic focus of this work is on linguistic geography, on the isoglosses defining the patterns of distribution of existing accentual types over the geographical expanse of Balkan Slavic.[3] An inventory of types is seen as but a preliminary step to the study of their distribution. This methodological principle assumes that the shape and direction of present isoglosses are directly correlated with the relative stages of productivity of different historical processes, and that this data needs to be integrated into any attempt at a hypothesis about the changes which have produced this distribution.

Second, the diachronic focus of this work is on processes, on the actual mechanisms of change, rather than on diachronic correspondences or on the reconstruction of the underlying proto-system. In many descriptions of language change, the goal is to provide a concise and elegant phrasing of the observable correspondences between the present system(s) and the proto-system; such formulations may or may not describe the actual mechanisms of change (which are unobservable). These statements of correspondences are then usually understood as hypotheses about the mechanisms and motivations of change. This study, however, proceeds from the assumption that one must separate *results* from *motivations,* and that one's hypotheses about the mechanisms of change must start from the latter and not from the former. A corollary of this assumption is that one must begin from an objective and reliable point of departure, and that one must not use one's own hypotheses about change (in the particular area) as the basis for the reconstructed proto-system. In the case of the present study, therefore, which is limited to a small area of Slavic dialects, it would not be justifiable to propose reconstructed forms solely on the basis of hypotheses suggested by the present distribution of phenomena within these dialects. Rather, I accept as a base point the reconstruction of Proto-Slavic (PSl) accentual paradigms as proposed by Stang (1957) and as modified and amplified by Dybo and Illič-Svityč (1963).[4] The temporal and spatial focus of the present study is exclusively South Slavic, however: the assumption is that the *changes,* the processes discussed herein, occurred after the migration of this Slavic group to the Balkans, and are motivated solely by relationships within this East South Slavic dialectal group.

Third, this study assumes three distinct types of change, as opposed to the two considered in most studies: 1) phonological change 2) morphological change and 3) morphophonemic change. The processes involved are, respectively, 1) reinterpretation of the distribution of distinctive elements within the sound chain, 2) reinterpretation of the correspondences between the distinctive formal elements of morphemes and their respective lexical or grammatical functions and 3) reinterpretation of the "convention" which determines the distribution of systematic phonological shifts which are not automatic but are rather bound to the expression of grammatical distinctions. The first two types of change are concerned with the distinctions defining individual elements, and are generally accepted as known, more or less understood types of language change. The typology of change in most studies stops here, however: that which is here called morphophonemic change is viewed in such studies as a combination of various of the processes of phonological (1) and morphological (2) change; the underlying assumption appears to be that morphophonology represents but a concise statement of the debris—what is "left over" when the various phonological and morphological changes have ceased to be productive.

This study, however, takes the explicit stand that morphophonology is a meaningful and distinct component of language structure, that it is perceived as such by speakers and learners of language, and that the elements of morphophonology are therefore subject to reformulation in their own terms (and not just in terms of phonology or morphology or of a random combination of the two). The elements of the morphophonological component of language are usually called "morphophonemic rules." I propose, however, at least with respect to accentual morphophonemics, the term "convention," to emphasize the fact that the relationships defined by it often function simultaneously on several different levels of a particular grammatical hierarchy (e.g., as will be specifically demonstrated in this paper, within the category of person, within the category of number [but subsuming all three persons], or within the category of simplex verbal forms [subsuming two or more "tenses"]).[5]

In terms of the processes of change involved, types 1 and 2 (phonological and morphological change) are concerned primarily with individual elements within the phonological or morphological systems of a language, while type 3 (morphophonemic change) is concerned exclusively with the set of *relationships* embraced and specified by particular morphophonemic conventions. The mechanisms involved in change type (3) are extension and curtailment, either in terms of the phonological or grammatical environment embraced or specified by the convention, or of the lexical items or word classes subject to the convention. The view that type 3 should be interpreted as distinct from types 1 and 2 presupposes, of course, the assumption that morphophonemic relations are separate, functioning elements of a linguistic system, capable themselves of reinterpretation by language learners. The claim of the present paper is that this assumption allows one achieve a deeper and better understanding of the processes of change, and to view the results of these changes not as the random, now presently codified remains of phonological and morphological change, but as a stage in a natural, integrated process of linguistic development which continues even today.

1.0 *Present tense—synchronic distribution.* The diversity of accentual types of the present tense in Balkan Slavic can be described in terms of two major variables. The first of these is the presence vs. the absence of an accentual opposition within the present tense (between the 1st singular and all other forms of the present); the distribution of this trait is discussed in 1.1 and schematized on map I. The second concerns the place of accent in forms of the present tense other than 1sg, and the distribution of stems with respect to various accentual types. This distribution is discussed in 1.2 and schematized in map II. There are also two additional accentual phenomena which affect smaller areas of Balkan Slavic, the accentuation of 1st and 2nd plural forms (discussed in 1.3 and included on map I) and the accentual relationship between aspectual pairs (discussed in 1.4 and shown on map II).

1.1 With respect to tense-internal accentual relationships, Balkan Slavic can be divided into two major groups—one in which the 1st singular form is opposed to all other forms (2-3sg, 1-3pl) by means of accent placement, and one in which the accent is columnar throughout the present tense, falling always either on the stem-initial syllable (*naprávа naprávіš, ispíšuvam ispíšuvaš*),[6] on the stem-final syllable (*továra továriš*), or on the suffixal/verbal classifier syllable (*naberá naberéš*). The opposition "1sg vs. other present tense forms" is always realized by means of absolute initial stress in the 1sg form vs. stress on any of the other syllables in the other forms, e.g. *náprava napráviš* (stem-initial), *nátovara natováriš* (stem-final) or *béra beréš, nábera naberéš* (suffixal).

This accentual opposition is found in a large area throughout south Balkan Slavic, stretching from its extreme eastern border westward up to and including eastern Macedonian dialects (area "A" on map I). Its northern limit in east and central Bulgaria is roughly the northern limit of the Rhodope mountains, and its northern limit in the west is the southeastern edge of Serbia, near the Bulgarian/Serbian/Macedonian border (southwest of Bosilegrad [8]).[7] In west-central Bulgaria, however, this area extends north as far as the Danube (near Orjaxhovo [46]), including Sofia [50] but excluding all areas west of Sofia, and including the larger Iskăr valley (the areas of Vraca [47], Bela Slatina [44] and Mihailovgrad [43]) but excluding the Danubian areas of Lom [45] and Vidin [41]. In extreme northwestern Bulgaria, it is found only in a small group of villages between Vidin and Belogradčik [44].[8] In general, the occurrence of this accentual opposition is limited to 1st and 2nd conjugations (i.e. the *e* and *i* conjugations). In some areas it is attested with 3rd conjugation verbs (the *a* conjugation); in these instances its occurrence is usually limited to perfective, prefixed verbs (e.g. *dókaram dokáraš*).[9] It is never found with 3rd conjugation derived imperfective verbs: one finds only forms such as *ispíšuvam ispíšuvaš*.[10]

There is thus a striking correlation between the shape of the 1sg desinence and the occurrence of the initial accent: in nearly all of the area where this accentuation is attested, the 1sg desinence in 1st and 2nd conjugations is *-a* (or the equivalent phonetic reflex of PSl *-ϱ), i.e. a vocalic desinence. Thus, to the geographical statement of distribution given above, one may add the statement that initial stress (i.e. the accentual opposition between 1sg and other present tense forms) is found only in those 1sg forms with vocalic desinences. The fact that original 3rd conjugation verbs are often attested with vocalic desinences and initial stress attests to the strength of this correlation cf. *zákopaa zakopáeš* (Gabare, near [44]),[11] *óglida ogledáš* (Sadovo, near [76]),[12] *útepa utépaš* (Pijanec area of Kjustendil [51]),[13] and *ódigra odígraš* (Berovo [28]).[14]

But initial stress in 1sg forms with the consonantal desinence *-m* is not unknown. It occurs in three different instances: 1) areas in which the consonantal desinence *-m* has been extended to all conjugational classes (this occurs primarily in certain Rhodope dialects, where the phonetic shape is often of the sort *berem*)[15] 2) areas in which the opposition has been extended to certain prefixed, perfective 3rd conjugation verbs (*dókaram dokáraš*, mentioned above) and 3) areas in which 1st and 2nd conjugation verbs are attested with both types of 1sg desinences, as in certain areas north of Goce Delčev [57], north of Batak [79], southeast of Smoljan [78] and west of Blagoevgrad [53]—both *dóveda* and *dóvedem*. The distribution of the last of these types (specified as type "X" on map I) is of special interest, for not all dialects with mixed desinences have extended the 1sg accentual opposition to all forms regardless of desinence shape. More frequently, the occurrence of the initial accentuation is limited to forms with vocalic desinences, while those with consonantal desinences have stem or suffixal stress, e.g., (in Kjustendil [51]) *dónesa* but *donesém*,[17] *náprava* but *naprávim* (this is called type "Y" on map I).[18] Indeed, a speaker will use the same verb twice in the same sentence, but with a shift in the desinence shape and accent placement; compare the following (the first from Kjustendil [51] and the second from Samokov [58]): *Četém pismoto pa mi milo da go čéta*[19] and *Koga da izléznem tam na snego, da izléznem na suoto, ne moga da ízlezna*.[20] Such differentiation is also attested in the larger Sofia area, where a geographical distributional statement can be made: vocalic desinences with initial accent are more common in the east, while consonantal desinences and non-initial accentuation are more common in the west.[21]

Most investigators, however, while conceding the significance of the correlation between accent placement and desinence shape, have concluded that the primary determinant of initial accent is prefixation and/or perfectivity. The fact that most of the verbs concerned have stem-initial stress throughout the present (and therefore exhibit this shift perceptibly only when prefixed, e.g., *práva práviš* vs. *náprava napráviš*), no doubt contributes to this interpretation. A number of examples, however, afford distinct evidence of the prefixed/perfective correlation. For instance, the differentiation between *zákaram* (with the initial accent) and *dokáruvam* (without it) in a number of dialects[22] attests to the aspectual distinction, while forms such as *pópatuvam* in Berovo [28][23] demonstrate the close tie between the prefix and the initial accent. Similarly, in the following two examples, it appears that it is a combination of prefixation and perfectivity which occasions the shift: *veséla veséliš* but *rázvesela razvesélišʹ* (attested southwest of Blagoevgrad [53])[24] and *rabóta rabótišʹ* but *pórabota porabótišʹ* (attested in Berovo [28]);[25] note that these two points are contiguous, separated only by the present Yugoslav/Bulgarian border. In Berovo, however, the shift occurs in another verb of the same type (polysyllabic *i*-stem) even without this condition: *tóvara továriš*. Indeed, the obstruent stems, attested throughout this area with suffixal stress in the present, demonstrate that prefixation/perfectivity is **not** a necessary condition for the occurrence of the shift, cf. *pléta pletéš*, etc., and other end-stressed imperfective such as *béra bereš* and *pía pieš*. At the same time, the majority of dialects in this area exclude *any* 3rd-conjugation verb, even if prefixed and perfective, from the shift, e.g., *odígram odígraš*.[27]

There are thus several factors relevant to the determination of initial stress in 1sg forms, and the exact interrelationship of these factors is unclear. What is clear, however, is that for 1sg present tense forms, there seems to have developed a general, overall correlation between prefixation, perfectivity, desinence shape and (in most of the area where the 1sg initial accent is known) place of accent, such that prefixed perfective verbs are associated with the vocalic desinence and absolute initial stress, while nonprefixed imperfective verbs are associated with the consonantal desinence and stem or suffixal stress. Thus, verbs of the type *prikážuvam*, even though prefixed, are in all areas imperfective, and occur in all areas with consonantal desinences and stem stress. The exact implementation of these variables must be defined with respect to individual dialects, however.[28]

1.2 Let us now examine the distribution of verbal stems according to accentuation of forms other than 1sg. Earlier, I identified three possibilities, stem-inital ([*na*]*práviš*, [*is*]*píšuvaš*),[29] stem-final ([*po*]*továriš*), and suffixal ([*po*]*sedíš*). For the purposes of the present discussion, however, I will speak merely of stem stress (accent on any syllable of the stem) vs. end stress (accent on the theme vowel/stem class marker—*i, e* or *a*). Further, I will classify verbal stems as follows:[30] i) obstruent stems ([pres] *pleteš, doneseš, pečeš* [aor] *plete, donese, peče*); ii) sonorant stems ([pres] *piješ, umreš, počneš* [aor] *pi, umre, poče*); iii) *n*-stems ([pres] *mineš, staneš* [aor] *mina, stana*); iv) *Ca*-stems ([pres] *pišeš, bereš, oreš* [aor] *pisa, bra, ora*); v) *i*-stems ([pres] *nosiš, učiš* [aor] *nosi, uči*); vi) *e*-stems ([pres] *letiš, goriš* [aor] *lete, gore*); vii) *Ča*-stems ([pres] *ležiš, klečiš* [aor] *leža, kleča*) and viii) *aj*-stems ([pres] *gledaš, karaš* [aor] *gleda, kara*).[31] Types (i)–(iv) are 1st-conjugation verbs; types (v)–(vii) are 2nd-conjugation and type (viii) is 3rd-conjugation.[32]

With respect to present tense accentuation as a whole, there are three clearly defined areas in Balkan Slavic, the west (1), the central (2) and the east (3), shown in map II. In area 1, which includes far southern Serbian dialects and most Macedonian dialects, all present tense forms are stem-stressed. In area 2, which includes the rest of southeastern Serbian dialects, all West Bulgarian dialects, and a small strip of easternmost Macedonian dialects, the distribution of present tense accent is roughly correlated with stem type: obstruent stems (i), *e*- (vi) and *Ča*- (vii) stems are regularly end-stressed, and all others are generally stem-stressed. In various regions throughout this area, certain other stems appear with end stress (such as *učíš* in Knjaževac [3],[33] *pijéš* in Bosilegrad [8][34] and *beréš* in Berovo [28][35]); the most common of these is the *beréš* type. Nevertheless, the occurrence of these must be specified according to local dialect. Finally, in area 3, which comprises the remainder of Bulgarian dialects, end stress appears regularly not only in types (i), (vi), (vii), but also in a wide number of stems scattered throughout other classes, e.g. (ii) *viéš,* (iii) *minéš,* (v) *pogubíš,* in Šumen (southeast of [64]).[36] The distribution is roughly that of standard Bulgarian, but must be exactly specified with respect to each local dialect. The important fact is that one can state a general rule only for stem classes type (i), (vi) and (vii); all other stems must be lexically marked for stress.[37]

The distribution of these types is shown on map II. Schematically, it may be summarized as follows:[38]

SUMMARY OF PRESENT TENSE ACCENTUATION IN BALKAN SLAVIC

Area	(1)	(2)	(3)
stem class			
(i)	(za)pléteš	*(za)pletéš*	*(za)pletéš*
(ii)	(po)píješ	(po)píješ	(po)píješ, *(na)vijéš*
(iii)	(za)míneš	(za)míneš	(po)gíneš, *(za)minéš*
(iv)	(na)píšeš	(na)píšeš	(na)píšeš, *(po)oréš*
(v)	(na)práviš	(na)práviš	(na)práviš, *(iz)učíš*
(vi)	(pri)létiš	*(pri)letíš*	*(pri)letíš*
(vii)	(po)léžiš	*(po)ležíš*	*(po)ležíš*

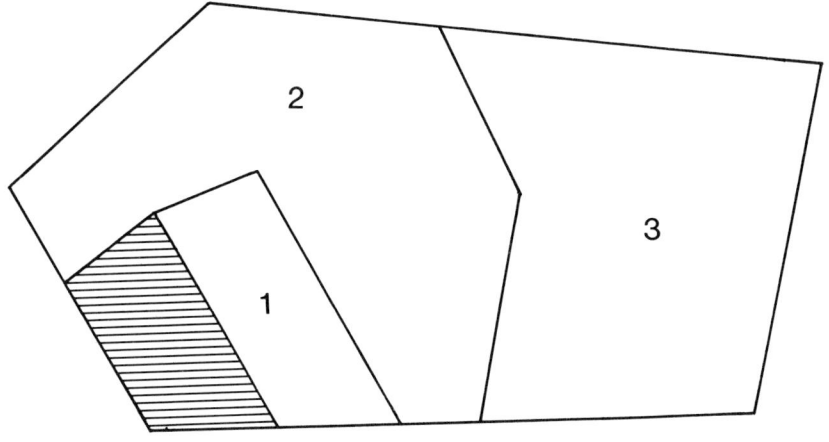

FIGURE 1.

Comparing areas 1, 2 and 3 on map II with area "A" on map I, one could identify those portions of 1, 2 and 3 in which 1sg forms carry initial stress as 1A, 2A and 3A, respectively (see fig. 2). Area 1A is quite small, covering only a few villages in southernmost Serbia to the southeast of Vranje [7] and a somewhat larger section of eastern Macedonia, primarily the area to the immediate west of Berovo [28] and Delčevo [25]. Area 2A, on the other hand, is quite large, including nearly all the Bulgarian and Macedonian dialects within area 2 (but excluding the Serbian ones). Area 3A is limited to the Rhodopes and Thrace. Schematically:[39]

SUMMARY OF 1sg PRESENT ACCENTUATION IN BALKAN SLAVIC

Area	1A	2A	3A
stem class			
(i)	dónesa/donésem**	dónesa	dónesem
	[donéseš]	dónesa/dónesem*	dónesa
		dónesa/*donesém***	[*doneséš*]
		[*doneséš*]	
(v)	náprava/	náprava	nápravem
	naprávim**	náprava/nápravim*	náprava
	[napráviš]	náprava/naprávim**	[napráviš]
		[napráviš]	
(vi)	príleta/	príleta	príletem
	prilétim**	príleta/príletim*	príleta
	[*prilétiš*]	príleta/*priletím***	[priletíš]
		[*priletíš*]	

* variant type X
** variant type Y

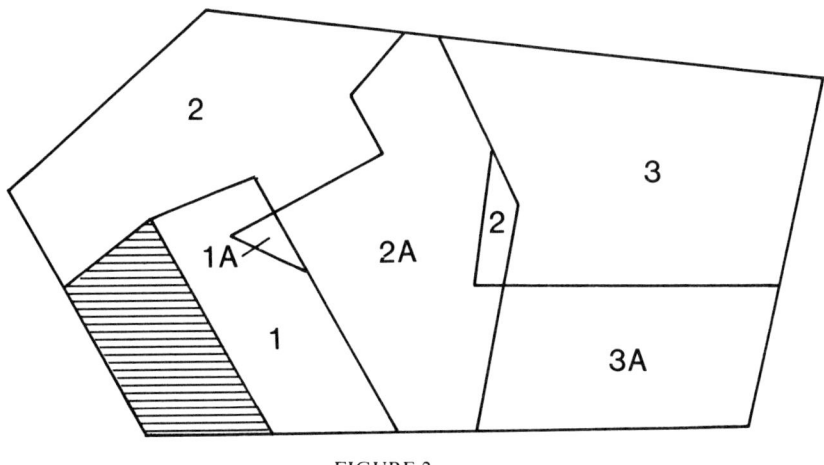

FIGURE 2.

1.3 In two small, non-contiguous portions of area 2 (depicted on map I, and designated as type "B"), certain of the end-stressed stems are found occasionally with accent on the final syllable of the desinence in 1st and 2nd plural forms, e.g., *sedimó sedité* or *donesemé doneseté*.[40] The occurrence of this accentuation is limited not only geographically but also lexically. In the first of these two areas, that located in the north, encompassing the eastern Serbian dialects around Knjaževac [3] and to the east of Aleksinac [1], and the western Bulgarian dialects south of Belogradčik [42] (2B-1 in Fig. 3), it is restricted almost exclusively to stems of type (vi), e.g., *sedimó*, and (vii), e.g., *ležimó*. In the other, that located in the south, embracing the areas around Kriva Palanka [24] in eastern Macedonian and Kjustendil [51] in western Bulgaria (2B-2 in Fig. 3), it also appears in certain obstruent stems, e.g., *donesemé* (i), in sonorant stems, e.g., *piemé* (ii), and stems of the type *raskovemé* and *poznaemé* (iv).[41] It is interesting that in the northern area (2B-1), this desinence-final accentuation is limited to verbs of the type (vi) and (vii) in all but the extreme western portion of this area.[42] In this corner of 2B-1 (the village Šarbanovac near Soko Banja), the distribution of desinence-final accentuation among stem classes is almost identical to that found in area 2B-2.[43]

A small part of area 2B-2 (near Kjustendil [51]) is located at the edge of area 2A. There, one finds paradigms of the sort *dónesa* (and *donesém*) *doneséš donesé donesemé* (and *doneséme*) *doneseté* (and *doneséte*) *donesát*. In fact, the correlation of these two phenomena is such that to the northwest of Kjustendil, where *donesém* (1sg) is the norm and *dónesa* a less frequent variant, *donesemé* (1pl) is also the norm and *doneséme* is the less frequently attested variant. To the southeast of Kjustendil, however, the reverse is the case: *dónesa* (1sg) and *doneséme* (1pl) are more frequent, while *donesém* (1sg) and *donesemé* (1pl) are variant forms.[44] Schematically, the distribution of accent type 2B is as follows:[45]

ACCENTUATION OF 1sg AND 1pl/2pl PRESENT IN BALKAN SLAVIC

Area	2	2B-1	2B-2	2A
stem class				
(i)	*(za)pletém*	*(za)pletém*	*(za)pletém*	pléta, zápleta
	(za)pletémo	*(za)pletémo*	*(za)pletemé*	*(za)pletéme*
(v)	(na)právim	(na)právim	(na)právim	práva, náprava
	(na)právimo	(na)právimo	(na)právime	(na)právime
(vi)	*(po)ležím*	*(po)ležím*	*(po)ležím*	léža, póleža
	(po)ležímo	*(po)ležimó*	*(po)ležimé*	*(po)ležíme*
			[norm]	[norm]
			— — — mixing — — —	

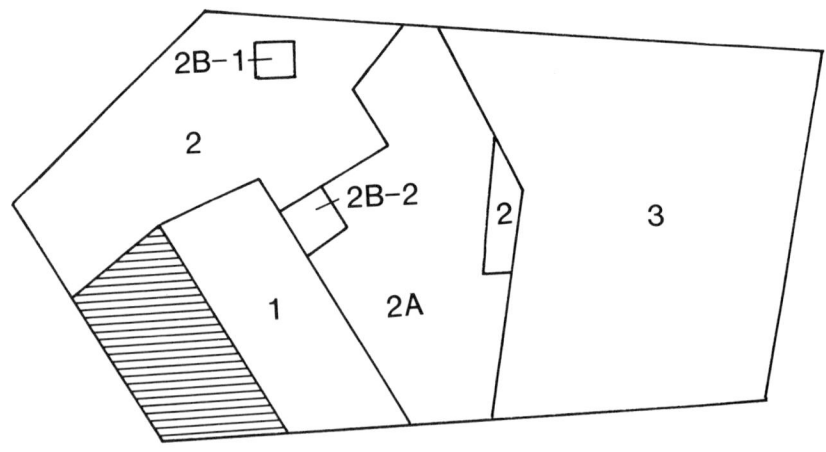

FIGURE 3.

1.4 Finally, there are two zones within area 2 of Balkan Slavic in which there is an accentual distinction between simple and prefixed forms of the same stem. Here, obstruent stems (type i) and e/ča stems (types vi–vii) are end-stressed in their simple forms only, and stem-stressed in their prefixed forms. This accentuation is labelled type "C" on map II, and occurs in two zones. The smaller of these zones is in the north (located to the immediate south of Priština [9][46] and called 2C-1 in Fig. 4), and the other is in the east (encompassing Kriva Palanka [24][47], Delčevo [25][48] and Berovo [28][49] in eastern Macedonia, and Kjustendil [51][50] and Blagoevgrad [53][51] in western Bulgaria, and called 2C-2 in Fig. 4). Although non-contiguous, both of these zones (see map II) straddle the border between areas 1 and 2; they can thus be considered transitional between the accentual systems characteristic of the larger areas 1 and 2. Schematically, the distribution is as follows:[52]

ACCENTUATION OF PREFIXED AND NONPREFIXED FORMS IN BALKAN SLAVIC

Area	1	2C	2
stem class			
(i)	(za)plétem	pletém, zaplétem	(za)plétem
(v)	(na)právim	(na)právim	(na)právim
(vii)	(pri)létim	letím, prilétim	(pri)letím

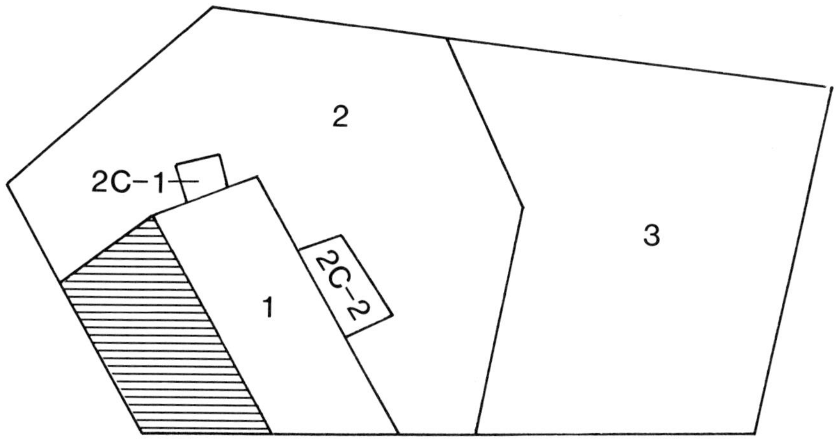

FIGURE 4.

2.0 *Present tense—diachronic interpretation*. The hypotheses presented in this section use as a base the reconstructed PSl present tense accentuation phrased in terms of accentual paradigms (a) (b) and (c).[53] In 2.1, I give a simplified sketch of the relevant points of this reconstruction. Subsequently, I propose a set of morphophonemic innovations which account for the distribution of accentual patterns depicted on map I (2.2) and on map II (2.3). Finally, in 2.4, I discuss the specifically morphophonemic character of these innovations. Since morphophonemics by its nature makes constant reference to both phonological and morphological elements, I will refer to factors both phonological and morphological. The innovations considered in this discussion, however, are specifically morphophonemic: they pertain to that component of linguistic structure which defines the phonological expression of grammatical relationships between members of a paradigmatic set. The motivation for most of the innovations discussed below is to be found in the grammatical relationship between prefixed/perfective and nonprefixed/imperfective forms. The sum of these innovations creates a morphophonemic convention defined primarily in terms of this opposition. The motivation for the remainder of the innovations discussed in this section, however, is morphologically based; the morphophonemic convention created by these innovations is defined in terms of verbal stem class markers.[54]

2.1 Each verbal stem in Proto-Slavic belonged to one of three accentual paradigms—(a), (b) or (c). Paradigms (a) and (b) were characterized by columnar stress, on the root syllable in (a) and on the theme vowel (which is in present Slavic languages now largely equivalent with the stem class marker) in (b). Paradigm (c) was mobile: accent fell on the final syllable of the desinence (or on a following enclitic) in some forms of the paradigm and on the initial syllable (or on a preceding proclitic) in others. The new mobility exhibited by stems of paradigm (b) in many Slavic languages (and represented in the reconstructions given below) is assumed to be due to various stress retractions carried out in late Common Slavic; it is assumed that the underlying PSl characteristic of this paradigm was columnar stress.[55]

In the examples given below, and in the ensuing discussion, I have regarded only stress placement as a distinctive prosodic feature, i.e. I have not taken tone and quantity distinctions into consideration. I have done this largely for simplicity of exposition and in no way mean it as a departure from the conception of PSl accentual paradigms established by Stang, Dybo and Illič-Svityč. While it is true that Balkan Slavic dialects have lost all former tonal and quantity oppositions—probably quite early in most dialects—a full diachronic treatment of Balkan Slavic accentuation must also take into account factors of tone and quantity; this is particularly true for western Balkan Slavic dialects, where the loss of these distinctions is assumed to be of a more recent date.[56] The following paradigms, therefore, must be seen as simplified versions of the actual reconstructed proto-system. Examples of types (i) and (v) are given below—original thematic presents with stem ending in obstruent, and original *i*-presents:[57]

PRESUMED PSl OBSTRUENT STEMS (TONE AND QUANTITY NOT SHOWN)

	1sg	3sg	2pl
(a)	*pádǫ	*pádetъ	*pádete
	*napádǫ	*napádetъ	*napádete
(b)	*mogǫ́	*móžetъ	*móžete
	*pomogǫ́	*pomóžetъ	*pomóžete
		[from earlier	[from earlier
		*(po)možétъ]	*(po)možéte]
(c)	*nésǫ	*nesétъ	*neseté
	*prínesǫ	*prinesétъ	*prineseté
		[from earlier	
		*(pri)nesetь̌]	

PRESUMED PSl *i*-STEMS (TONE AND QUANTITY NOT SHOWN)

	1sg	3sg	2pl
(a)	*stávljǫ	*stávitъ	*stávite
	*postávljǫ	*postávitъ	*postávite
(b)	*nošǫ́	*nósitъ	*nósite
	*donošǫ́	*donósitъ	*donósite
		[from earlier	[from earlier
		*(do)nosítъ]	*(do)nosíte]
(c)	*lómljǫ	*lomítъ	*lomité
	*pólomljǫ	*polomítъ	*polomité
		[from earlier	
		*(po)lomitь̌]	

The distribution of PSl stems among the three paradigms appeared to be relatively balanced in some stem classes (modern sonorant, *i, n-* and *Ca*-stems [types ii-v]), and quite restricted in others—for example, the great majority of modern obstruent stems (type i) and nearly all modern *e-* and *Ča*-stems (types vi-vii)[58] belonged to paradigm (c), while nearly all modern *aj*-stems (type (viii)) belong to paradigm (a).

2.2 Both the initial stress of 1sg forms in area "A" of Balkan Slavic, and the desinential stress of 1-2pl forms in area "B" Balkan Slavic can be seen as direct continuants of the accentuation of PSl paradigm (c). Indeed, the latter is attested in Balkan Slavic only in stems which originally belonged to paradigm (c); it thus appears to represent an archaism continued unchanged. This is corroborated by the shape of the isoglosses enclosing areas of type "B" which take the form of two unconnected "islands," normally indicative of a non-productive archaism.

The initial stress in 1sg forms, also inherited from paradigm (c), has been greatly extended, however, in a large part of south-central Balkan Slavic (area "A"). Likewise, the columnar stress of paradigm (a) has also been radically extended in another large part of Balkan Slavic (areas 1 and 2). Area 3 of Balkan Slavic, however, appears to have been largely unaffected by either of these innovations: there the original paradigm (c) accentuation, now widespread in area "A" was totally eliminated; and the original distribution of verbal stems with respect to accentual paradigms seems to have been more or less preserved, at least in relation to areas 1 and 2.

The motivation of these innovations is best seen if we examine them together. Consider first the non-prefixed forms of *i*-stem verbs (type (v)—the following proposals are meant to apply to types (ii)–(iv) as well; the remaining stem classes will be discussed below):

	1sg	3sg
(a)	*stávljǫ	*stávitъ
(b)	*nošǫ́	*nósitъ
(c)	*lómljǫ	*lomítъ

Only paradigm (a) has columnar stress; in the other two there is an accentual opposition between the 1sg form and the other forms of the paradigm. The levelling of paradigm (b) in the direction of paradigm (a) appears fairly straightforward: when all but one form of a paradigm appear with one shape and that one with another, it is not uncommon (other things being equal) for this shape to be extended to the unique form as well (a).[59] But in the areas concerned (1 and 2), it is obvious that the columnar stem stress of paradigm (a) has been uniformly extended to verbs of paradigm (c) as well.

What is the source of this innovation? We find a clue in the prefixed forms of the same verb type:

	1sg	3sg
(a)	*postávljǫ	*postávitъ
(b)	*donošǫ́	*donósitъ
(c)	*pólomljǫ	*polomítъ

If we assume that the levelling of paradigm (b) in the direction of (a) was carried out in prefixed stems as well (2)—in the same manner and with the same motivations as in nonprefixed stems—we are left with the forms of paradigm (c), in which the 1sg form is opposed to all other forms of the paradigm by stress placement. Here, it appears that the initial stress of the prefixed 1sg form (falling, of course, on the prefix morpheme) was interpreted as an overt marker of the perfective aspect and as such, extended to perfective verbs of all three paradigms (3).[60] As this accentual opposition became identified with verbs of the perfective aspect, columnar stress was generalized for their imperfective partners (4). Finally, as the 1sg form with accent on the prefix became the significant marker of perfective verbs, all prefixed forms of paradigm (c) but 1sg generalized the stem stress of the other two paradigms (5). Using the above reconstructed forms to represent paradigms (a), (b) and (c), respectively, we may exemplify these innovations as follows:

(1) *nošǫ̃ *nósitъ > *nóšǫ *nósitъ

(2) *donošǫ̃ *donósitъ > *donóšǫ *donósitъ

(3) {*postávljǫ *postávitъ > *póstavljǫ *postávitъ}
    {*donóšǫ *donósitъ > *dónošǫ *donósitъ}

(4) *lómljǫ *lomítъ > *lómljǫ *lómitъ

(5) *pólomljǫ *polomítъ > *pólomljǫ *polómitъ

As a result of the above innovations, the morphophonemic convention denoting a perfective verb thus became "initial stress [on the prefix] in 1sg vs. non-initial stress in all other forms." All the stages phrased above as individual instances of "*X > *Y" are to be understood as components of this single morphophonemic convention. The overall innovation was in the reinterpretation of the functional significance of this convention: its original functional significance was to mark a certain group of stems called "paradigm (c)." From this, it was transformed into a general convention marking perfective verbs of most stem classes (and all three inherited paradigms). Thus, while each of the individual instances noted above can be (and usually is) phrased in terms of morphological analogy within a single paradigm, the overall governing motivation nevertheless was the reinterpretation and extension of the morphophonemic convention embracing the larger set of paradigmatic relationships between perfective/prefixed and imperfective/nonprefixed verbs.[61]

The generalization of columnar stem stress instead of columnar end stress was supported in the western area of Balkan Slavic by an increasingly strong phonological restriction against accent in open final syllables. Indeed, in area 1, stem stress has been generalized in all verbal stems, regardless of aspect. In fact, the spread of the consonantal desinence (-*m*) to all 1sg forms in this area, as well as the absence of paradigm (c) accentuation from this area, suggest that the generalization of columnar stem stress in area 1 is largely unrelated to the distinction between prefixed and nonprefixed forms. Only in area 1A (the small Gornja Pčinja region of extreme southeast Serbia) are there traces of both these processes: columnar stem stress in nearly all imperfective verbs and an opposition of the sort *nápravu napráviš* in perfective verbs, when these are attested with the 1sg vocalic desinence.

In obstruent stems and *e/Ča* stems (types i, vi, vii), however, the distinction "initial stress in 1sg perfectives vs. columnar stem stress in imperfectives" did not develop. No doubt largely because of the overwhelming predominance of paradigm (c) membership among these stems, end stress was maintained in verbs of both aspects. Accentual relationships such as *béra beréš* in area 2A thus continue the inherited archaic accentuation of paradigm (c). Here, the only innovation was the extension of paradigm (c) accentuation to the few obstruent stems of paradigm (a).

2.3 The above hypothesized course of development accounts for the accentuation of the large area 2A. In the remainder of area 2 (southeastern Serbia and parts of western Bulgaria), we find stem stress in all verbs except types (i), (vi), (vii), but the absence of an accentual distinction between 1sg and other present tense forms. For certain portions of this area, we may presume that the above development indeed occurred, and that the 1sg initial stress was later eliminated by a more recent generalization of columnar stress throughout the paradigm of the present tense. The shape of the isogloss in central and northern West Bulgaria (cf. map I) strongly suggests that this was the case: the "indentation" shape encompassing the Trăn [48] and Breznik [49] areas, and the "erosion" shape around Lom [45], Vidin [41] and Belogradčik [42], leaving an "island" between the latter two points, are normal indicators of the gradual elimination of a once productive pattern. It is also significant that this area of erosion coincides largely with the spread of the consonantal desinence in 1sg to all verb stem classes. The presence of the variant accentual types 1A-Y (*dónesa* alongside *donésem*) and 2A-Y (*dónesa* alongside *donésém*) at the edges of this area is proof that the elimination of this trait is still in progress. Conversely, the presence of the variant type 2A-X (*dónesa* alongside *dónesem*) deep within the area of 2A suggest that the pattern is still productive in these areas, despite the spread of the consonantal desinence.

In the western section of area 2, however (the majority of southeast Serbian dialects), there is very little evidence suggesting that the initial accentuation of 1sg forms of paradigm (c) was ever identified as a marker of perfective presents. Rather, the generalization of columnar stress in most stems appears to be tied to the general phonological restriction against stress in open final syllables,[62] and the elimination of the distinctive initial stress of 1sg forms, to the spread of the consonantal desinence -*m* to all verbal stems. The tenacity of end stress in the present tense of types (i), (vi), (vii), in the western part of area 2 suggests that end stress has been generalized as a marker of these verbal classes. This was aided by the predominance in these stem classes both of paradigm (c) accentuation and of stems with short root vocalism (cf. here the correlation between short root vocalism and desinential stress, well attested in standard Serbo-Croatian and in many of its dialects;[63] the apparent relevance of this correlation with respect to the present tense accentuation of these stems is yet another indication that the loss of distinctive quantity in northwestern Balkan Slavic—the Torlak dialects of Serbo-Croatian—was a relatively recent event).

The accentuation of these stems (types i, vi, vii) constitutes the principal difference between areas 1 (where they are stem-stressed) and 2 (where they are end-stressed). The isogloss shape separating these two areas indicates that the accentuation of area 1 represents the presently innovative process, i.e., the total elimination of end stress in the present: the isogloss defining area 1 extends along the major lines of communication in western Balkan Slavic, the Vardar River in the south and the Južna Morava River in the north.[64] It is not surprising, therefore, that we should find transitional zones (type "C") where this innovation is in progress but has not yet been acomplished: it has spread to the perfective verbs but not yet to the imperfectives. Such a development is the logical extension of a correlation between columnar end stress in imperfective forms and alternating initial/non-initial stress in perfective forms. That is, even though the convention extending the accentuation *zápleta zapleteš* to all perfectives (marked by initial accent in the 1sg perfective form) is no longer productive, there is still a remnant of it in the correlation of non-end stress in perfectives vs. end stress in imperfectives. Here, then, two lines of development are seen—the older tendency to identify non-final stress with perfectives, and the newer, productive tendency to extend columnar stem stress to all present tense forms.[65]

2.4 Thus, the development of the present tense accentuation in the various areas of Balkan Slavic can be described in terms of the maintenance of the archaic state, the gradual spread of innovations, and the gradual elimination either of archaisms or of innovations which are no longer productive. Some of the innovations find their source in phonological change (such as the retraction of stress from open final syllables), and some in morphological change (such as the generalization of -*m* as the 1sg desinence). For most of the phenomena discussed herein, however, the overall motivation is morphophonological, directly related to the convention correlating phonological alternations with the grammatical, paradigmatic distinction they express. In other words, the extension of the accentual opposition between the 1sg present form and other forms of the present (the inherited paradigm (c) accentuation) is the logical result of the reinterpretation of that relationship as an expression of the perfective/imperfective distinction. This explains why (in the areas where it is attested with 3rd-conjugation verbs) it has been extended only to perfective stems (i.e., *dókaram* but *dokáruvam*): the convention marked by initial stress in 1sg was such a strong indicator of perfectivity that the existence of an imperfective marker such as *-uva-* blocked its extension to these verbs. Similarly, the concomitant extension of columnar stem stress in the imperfective forms, as well as the elimination of end stress in all perfective forms, is part of the same overall morphophonemic convention—the only stems which remain outside this convention in area 2 (types i, vi, vii) continue for the most part the archaic state. In this instance, we have a morphophonemic innovation which is morphologically rather than grammatically motivated—the primary correlate of end stress appears to be the morphological definition of these particular stem classes.[66] Indeed, many of the individual innovations involved in morphophonemic change—discussed above as particular curtailments, but often also referred to as analogical levellings—could be explained as individual instances of morphologically motivated change. When seen in the overall context of the grammatically motivated morphophonemic convention described above, however, it appears equally possible to view the several levellings as elements of a single, systemically motivated innovation, whose function is to strengthen the accentually marked distinction of perfective and imperfective verbs. Indeed, the majority of morphophonemic changes considered thus far (including the extension of stem stress only to prefixed forms of types (i), (vi), (vii)) appear to be functionally motivated, bound to the expression of grammatical relations, and to be related to a single morphophonemic convention with hierarchically ordered subdivisions.

3. *Accentuation of the aorist tense, summary.* Indeed, the most convincing support for this hypothesis is found not in the accentuation of the present tense itself, but in that of the aorist tense. The striking parallels in the distribution of tense-internal accentual types allow one not only to propose a similar diachronic interpretation, but also imply that interaction between the two tenses has been a significant factor in the development of the present situation. Therefore, before discussing the relationship between the two tenses, I will summarize briefly the synchronic distribution and diachronic interpretation of the accentuation of the aorist in Balkan Slavic.[67]

As in the present tense, there is an accentual opposition within the singular of the aorist tense in a large group of Balkan Slavic dialects: in all southern Serbian dialects and a few West Bulgarian dialects, the 2-3sg aorist forms carry absolute initial stress, and the other forms of the aorist have non-initial (usually end) stress, e.g., *napraví nápravi* (v); *pogledá pógleda* (viii); *priležá príleža* (vii); *donéso dónese* (i).[68] The area encompassed by this phenomenon is shown on map III; it is largely coterminous with the area where final *-x* has been lost. In all areas where the "2-3sg vs. other aorist" opposition is known, there is a clear correlation between aspect/prefixation and accentuation: the aorists of prefixed/perfective verbs consistently exhibit the opposition, while the aorists of nonprefixed/imperfective verbs display it only as a variant.[69] In the Bulgarian dialects where this accentuation is known at all, it is attested only in prefixed/perfective verbs (and, in some dialects, also in nonprefixed *n*-stems).[70]

With respect to the place of accent in aorist forms other than 2-3sg, the distribution is again similar to that of the present tense: in the southwestern-most dialects (area 1 on map IV), all aorist forms are end-stressed. To the north and east of this area (area 2), all aorist forms but those of obstruent stems—type (i)—are end stressed. Further to the east of this (area 3), all nonprefixed verbs of types (ii)—(viii), as well as prefixed verbs of types (vi)–(vii) (*e/ča*-stems), are end stressed. In the easternmost dialects (area 4), the occurrence of accent can be predicted only for type (i), which have stem stress, and types (vi)–(vii), which have end stress; for all other classes, the place of accent must be lexically specified. Schematically:[71]

Area	1	2	3	4
(i)	*(za)pletó*	(za)pléto	(za)plétox	(za)plétox
(v)	*(na)praví*	*(na)praví*	pravíx, naprávix	(na)právix, *(na)učíx*
(vii)	*(pri)ležá*	*(pri)ležá*	*(pri)ležáx*	*(pri)ležáx*

As in the present tense, the tense-internal accentual opposition continues the inherited PSl paradigm (c) accentuation.[72] The fact that the aspectual/prefixation parameter is significant in the distribution of both sets of accentual relationships, the tense-internal (seen on map III) and the general (seen on map IV) suggests a similarly motivated set of innovations.[73] The extension of the "2-3sg vs. other aorist" opposition throughout the lexicon, found in most dialects of Serbo-Croatian, appears to be connected primarily with quantity distinctions: where this opposition previously characterized only stems of paradigm (c), it is now found in the great majority of Serbo-Croatian verbs with short root vocalism.[74] The early loss of tone and quantity distinctions in southern and eastern Balkan Slavic is probably a factor in the total elimination of this opposition from these dialects. In northwestern Balkan Slavic, by contrast, the relatively recent loss of quantity oppositions led to the extension of this opposition to all stems.[75]

A concurrent innovation was the identification of this tense-internal opposition with the perfective aspect: as in the present tense, accent on the prefixal morpheme of a perfective verb began to be generalized as the mark of perfectivity. To strengthen this marking, columnar end stress began to be generalized as the marker of imperfective verbs. The absence of a clear isogloss with respect to this phenomenon in Serbian dialects (areas A and B) attests both to its relatively recent date and to its current productivity. In West Bulgarian dialects (areas C and D), by contrast, the results of this process are more clearly delineated: the accentual opposition is found only in prefixed/perfective verbs and in nonprefixed n-stems (where the grammatical notion of semelfactivity associated with the stem-marker n, and its similarity to the general notion of perfectivity, appears to have kept the opposition alive in this stem class).

With respect to aorist forms other than 2-3sg, the distribution of accentual types (seen in map IV) is quite similar to that of the present (seen in map II). Except for the elimination of the accentual mobility within paradigm (c), the easternmost region (area 4 on map IV) appears to have conserved the PSl distribution of stems among the accentual paradigms, such that accent placement must now be defined lexically for most stems. In area 3, the tense-internal opposition was likewise eliminated, and with it the means for an accentual manifestation of aspectual differentiation similar to that which developed in northwestern Balkan Slavic (areas A-B-C-D). Here, however, a complementary innovation arose: stem stress was generalized for prefixed/perfective forms and end stress for nonprefixed/imperfective forms. The underlying motivation for the two seemingly unrelated innovations, however, is the same: the association of one type of accentual paradigm with prefixed/perfective verbs and another with nonprefixed/imperfective verbs.

In areas 1 and 2, a more recent innovation is seen: the extension of end stress to the aorist of all verbs, regardless of the aspectual/prefixation parameter. The motivation for this interpretation will be identified below.

4. *Relationships between present and aorist tenses.* The striking similarities and complementarities in the distribution of the accentual types of the present and aorist tenses, which I have summarized above, have prompted me to propose in both instances a series of morphophonemic changes whose primary systemic motivation is the implementation of the distinction between perfective/prefixed and imperfective/nonprefixed verbs by means of accent placement. Together with morphophonemic changes whose primary motivation is morphological (the identification of an accentual pattern with a stem-class type), these appear to have produced the morphophonemic conventions which define the present distribution of present and aorist accentual types in Balkan Slavic.

Each of the two tense-internal accentual oppositions ("2-3sg aorist vs. other aorist"; "1sg present vs. other present") can be identified with a specific area of innovation. The first is centered roughly in northwestern Balkan Slavic, and the second in south-central Balkan Slavic. These two centers of innovation can, in turn, be identified with the genetic division "West South Slavic" (essentially Serbo-Croatian) and "East South Slavic" (essentially Bulgarian); and the changes I have discussed can be specifically linked with phonological and morphological changes characteristic of each of these areas. The most significant of these are (for Serbo-Croatian based dialects) the tendency to retract stress from open final syllables, the recent loss of [tone and] quantity distinctions, the generalization of the 1sg present desinence -*m* in all conjugational classes, and the loss of -*x*; and (for Bulgarian-based dialects) the early loss of tone and quantity distinctions, and the preservation of inherited phonological and morphological characteristics. The isogloss separating the area of the present tense-internal opposition from the aorist tense-internal opposition delineates clearly these two areas; indeed, the two phenomena are in almost exact complementary distribution. One, the aorist-internal opposition (depicted on map III), occurs throughout southeastern Serbia and reaches into western Bulgaria as far as Sofia and into extreme northwestern Bulgaria around Vidin; while the other, the present-internal opposition (depicted on map I), occurs in eastern Macedonia and throughout western and southern Bulgaria, but is absent precisely in the two areas of Sofia and Vidin. The formal, "mirror-image" relationship of the two accentual oppositions is just as striking as their geographical distribution: in each case, the 1sg form is opposed to the other two forms of the singular, and absolute initial stress is the distinctive marker of the opposition. In one opposition (present-internal), it is the 1sg form which carries the initial stress, while in the other (aorist-internal), it is the 2-3sg forms which carry the initial stress. This clear relationship of complementary distribution, both in form and in dialectal spread, suggests the existence of an overall Balkan Slavic constraint: a Balkan Slavic linguistic system may utilize tense-internal accentual oppositions to mark the morphological/grammatical distinction of prefixation/perfectivity in one tense or the other, but not in both. Stated in diachronic terms, when the inherited limitations on this kind of mobile accent (in PSl, it could occur only in paradigm (c) stems) were abolished, and the mobile accent was extended to stems of all three paradigmatic classes, new, specifically Balkan Slavic constraints arose: tense-internal mobility could be extended throughout the paradigmatic classes in one tense or the other, but not in both. The accentual systems depicted in maps I and III represent two Balkan Slavic solutions to this dilemma, the south-central (old East South Slavic) and northwestern (old West South Slavic), respectively.

East-central Macedonian dialects, however, are marked by the absence of *both* tense-internal oppositions. Here, we have the second striking instance of complementary distribution in the accentuation of present and aorist tenses in Balkan Slavic: a large area in which stem stress in the present is opposed to end stress in the aorist. That is, in addition to the tense-specific morphophonemic conventions discussed above, there also exists a morphophonemic convention embracing both present and aorist, implemented by stem stress in the present and end stress in the aorist. The area of this accentual opposition includes both the northwestern (West South Slavic) and southcentral (East South Slavic) areas defined above, and those east-central Macedonian dialects which remained outside the domain of the morphophonemic conventions associated with either of these tense-internal oppositions—thus, all dialects of Balkan Slavic with free, paradigmatically mobile accent.[76]

In terms of scope, this morphophonemic convention is superordinate to each of the tense-specific morphophonemic conventions: it defines the relationship between the present and the aorist in broad terms, and does not contravene relationships within each of these tenses in different areas. The area in which it is known can be termed the "core" area of Balkan Slavic. Schematically, this can be visualized as follows:

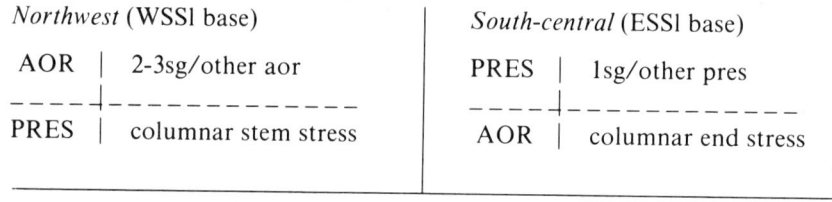

Synchronically, the distribution of the aorist/present morphophonemic convention can be defined in terms of three areas: AP-1 (southwestern Balkan Slavic), AP-2 (northwestern and west-central Balkan Slavic) and AP-3 (central Balkan Slavic). AP-1 is identical with area 1 on map IV, and includes those portions of area 1 from map II which are co-territorial with it. In this area, all verbs are subject to the aor/pres morphophonemic convention:

AP-1

	[3sg pres]	[3sg aor]
(stem class)		
(i)	zapléte	*zapleté*
(iii)	zamíne	*zaminá*
(iv)	napíše	*napisá*
(v)	naprávi	*napraví*
(vi)	priléti	*prileté*
(vii)	poléži	*poležá*

Area AP-2, situated to the north and east of AP-1, is identical with area 2 on map IV, and includes those portions of area 2 from map II which are co-territorial with it. Here, the aor/pres morphophonemic convention embraces all verbs except types (vi)–(vii). In type (i), however, its implementation is formally distinct from that of the remainder of the stem classes. Thus

AP-2

	[3sg pres]	[3sg aor]
(stem class)		
(i)	*pleté*	pléte
(iii)	míne	*miná*
(iv)	píše	*pisá*
(v)	právi	*praví*
(vi)	*letí*	leté
(vii)	*leží*	ležá

The opposition is present in perfective/prefixed forms also, but is partially obscured by the two tense-internal oppositions. In the plural paradigms, however it is clear:

AP-2

	[1pl pres]	[1pl aor]
(stem class)		
(i)	*zapletémo*	zaplétomo
(iii)	zamínemo	*zaminúmo*
(iv)	napíšemo	*napisámo*
(v)	naprávimo	*napravímo*
(vi)	*priletímo*	priletémo
(vii)	*poležímo*	poležámo

Area AP-3, situated to the immediate east of AP-2, is identical with area 3 on map IV, and includes those few portions of area 2 from map II which are co-territorial with it. Here, the aor/pres accentual opposition is found in the same verb classes as in AP-2, but is limited to nonprefixed/imperfective forms of all but type (i). Thus:

AP-3	nonprefixed/imperfective		prefixed/perfective	
(stem class)	[3sg pres]	[3sg aor]	[3sg pres]	[3sg aor]
(i)	*pleté*	pléte	*zapleté*	zapléte
(iii)	míne	*miná*	zamíne	zamína
(iv)	píše	pisá	napíše	napísa
(v)	právi	praví	naprávi	naprávi
(vi)	*letí*	leté	*priletí*	*prileté*
(vii)	*ležĺ*	ležá	*priležĺ*	*priležá*

In diachronic terms, the accentual patterns of areas AP-2 and AP-3 represent the combined results of the morphophonemic innovations discussed earlier in terms of the present and aorist as individual tenses. The accentuation of area AP-1, however, can only be described in terms of a morphophonemic convention embracing both present and aorist, which has been extended to all verbs regardless of stem class. That is, earlier innovations made in terms of aspectual relations within the individual tenses created an accentual situation which was subsequently interpreted as manifesting a relationship between present and aorist tenses. The isogloss defining the aor/pres accentual opposition clearly suggests that it is a recent, currently productive innovation: it is characterized by an innovating center (AP-1), from which the innovation has spread in successive waves. In the area of its furthest spread (AP-3), it embraces all nonprefixed verbs of classes other than types (vi)-(vii) (this statement is true of AP-2 and AP-1 as well). The second wave of this innovation, which has embraced only areas AP-2 and AP-1, has extended the opposition also to prefixed verbs of the same types. Finally, area AP-1 represents the third wave, the most thorough extension of this innovation: here it has been extended to all verbs. Schematically, we may visualize this as follows:

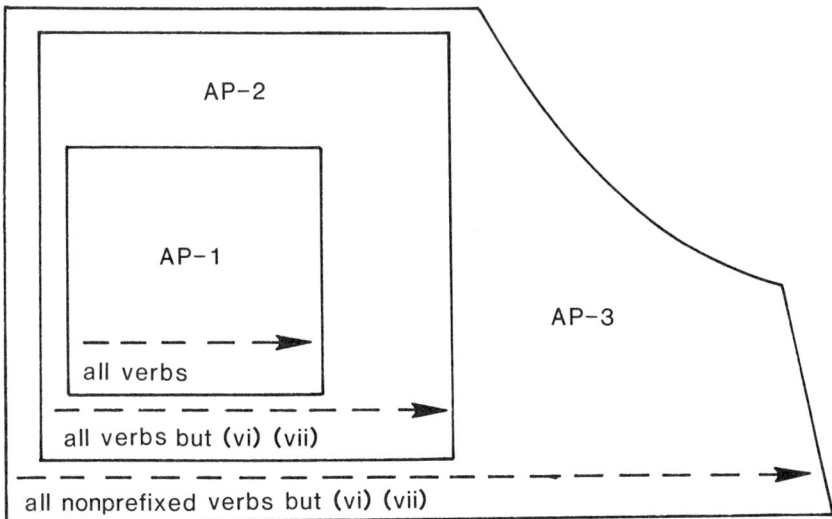

FIGURE 5.

Thus, whereas all areas *can* be described purely in terms of the tense-specific morphophonemic innovations summarized earlier, they can also be seen in terms of the supra-temporal morphophonemic convention just set forth. The fact that the accentual pattern in AP–1, clearly the innovative center for this aor/pres morphophonemic convention, can be properly motivated *only* in terms of this supra-temporal relationship, strongly suggests that it is the currently productive pattern throughout the portion of Balkan Slavic with free and paradigmatically mobile stress. Similarly, the tense-internal accentual oppositions discussed earlier can also be described purely in terms of tense-specific innovations. The overall distribution of these oppositions throughout Balkan Slavic, however, strongly suggests the existence of a supra-temporal morphophonemic constraint governing them both.

5. *Summary & conclusions.* I have proposed as a hypothesis a sequence of morphophonemic changes for Balkan Slavic in which I have identified several morphophonemic conventions, and associated each with a specific morphological or grammatical correlate. The most significant of these are prefixation/perfectivity vs. nonprefixation/imperfectivity, and the tendency to identify stress with morphological class markers.

I have also identified three different centers of innovation, the relative distribution of which can be schematized as follows:

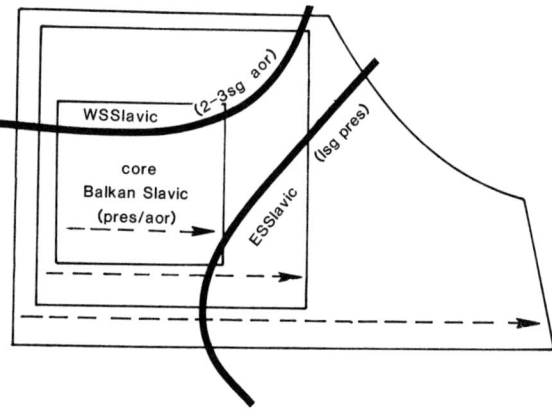

FIGURE 6.

The peripheral areas (northwestern and south-central areas) represent changes associated with the genetically-defined West South Slavic (WSSl) and East South Slavic (ESSl) dialectal bases, respectively; the clearest differentiating markers of these changes are the tense-internal accentual oppositions manifested by initial accent in certain persons of the singular in one of the two tenses. In the northwestern area (WSSl dialectal base), the marker is initial accent in 2-3sg aorist, while in the south-central areas (ESSl dialectal base), it is initial accent in 1sg present.

The "core Balkan Slavic" section, by contrast, represents changes associated with the core of the Balkan Slavic linguistic area. This area is defined—in cultural, linguistic-geographic rather than in genetic terms—as the result of intense convergence phenomena among those dialects of the Balkan Sprachbund which show close genetic relationship.[78] The significant characteristic of this area is the accentual opposition between the present and the aorist tenses.

The relative distribution of the isoglosses indicates their relative age: the northwest/south-central split represents an old, now stabilized differentiation (the inherited WSSl/ESSl distinction); while the Balkan Slavic innovating core, starting from a point between them, is gradually radiating out to embrace portions of both the northwest and the south-central areas. The identity of Balkan Slavic as a convergence area is thus represented iconically in the distribution of these isoglosses. Furthermore, the several isoglosses demonstrate dramatically both the processes of early differentiation due to historical separation (complementary innovations) and the processes of more recent, shared innovations due to subsequent contact under different historical circumstances. The fact that the core of the more recent innovations is located precisely in the area of most intense contact underscores the validity of the correlation between an isogloss and the historical processes it represents.

The primary aim of this study has been to demonstrate the existence of a morphophonemic component (particularly in Balkan Slavic), and its importance in historical Slavic dialectology (particularly in accentological studies). While it is clear that phonologically and morphologically defined processes have played a significant role in the complex of changes discussed here, only a morphophonemically based hypothesis can provide an integrated, systemically motivated description of the developmental processes which have produced the present distribution of accentual systems in Balkan Slavic, and which continue to reshape these systems, for only a system of interlocking morphophonemic conventions can account for the striking interdependence of the various phenomena discussed. In turn, the interconnected relationships of these accentual morphophonemic systems can best be described by assuming that the morphophonemic conventions of Balkan Slavic dialects are actively learned and commanded by speakers of these dialects, and reformulated by them in response to perceived shifts within the system of signified relationships. Morphophonemic conventions such as those discussed in this contribution appear to represent not only a straightforward statement of correspondences between systems of relationships, they also reflect intuitive judgments about structural facts which are deeply ingrained in these languages.

University of California, Berkeley

NOTES

[1] For a similarly constructed discussion of the imperative in Balkan Slavic, see Alexander 1978. The term "Balkan Slavic" refers to those South Slavic dialects spoken in Greece, Albania, Bulgaria, the republic of Macedonia within Yugoslavia, and the "Torlak" dialects of southeastern Serbia within Yugoslavia. The dialects of central and western Macedonia, although included in the area defined as Balkan Slavic, are nevertheless excluded from consideration in this paper, since in these dialects the accent is fixed with respect to the word boundary and plays no role in paradigmatic alternations. In the maps accompanying this paper the "fixed-accent" area is left blank; and in Figures 1-4, it is denoted by diagonal shading.

[2] Gustavsson 1969 refers to Balkan Slavic as "East South Slavonic"; in a subsequent work, however (1981:71n) he has accepted the term Balkan Slavic for this area. I will not re-list here source materials included in the bibliography to Gustavsson 1969 unless I make specific reference to the data in such sources.

[3] In his review of Gustavsson 1969, Ivić (1969:261) notes with regret Gustavsson's failure to discuss this data from the standpoint of linguistic geography, depriving his study thereby of a "harvest within easy reach." Part of my intention in the present study is to fill this gap.

[4] See also Dybo 1958, 1961, 1962, 1968, 1969, 1971. I consider these works by Stang, Illič-Svityč and Dybo to be the most reliable reconstructions of the Proto-Slavic state, because they both take into account all available Slavic data (both synchronic correspondences and diachronic, textual evidence drawn from various periods), and all functional levels of the assumed Proto-Slavic accentual system.

[5] That is, whereas in practice various morphophonemic relations are usually described as individual oppositions, there nevertheless appears to exist a deep-seated correlation between the functioning of morphophonemic shifts at these different levels, since learners and speakers of languages seem to process them simultaneously as separate elements and an integrated system. The term "morphophonemic convention" is meant to embrace both these possibilities. My usage of this term is thus more or less equivalent to the Russian term *akcentnaja krivaja*, as used by Popova, who defines it as follows (1974:58):

Akcentnaja krivaja: èto a) sočetanie raznyx konturov udarenija, svojstvennyx opredelennym slovoformam i xarakterizujuščix odno slovo v sovokupnosti vsex ego slovoform b) sočetanie funkcional'no i material'no toždestvennyx konturov udarenija (t.e. akcentnyx krivyx) v gruppe slov s odinakovoj akcentnoj xarakteristikoj.

I avoid the literal English translation of this term, "accentual curve", because of its phonetic connotations.

[6] Unless noted otherwise, paired examples in this section are 1st singular – 2nd singular, and are from southwestern Bulgarian dialects near Blagoevgrad.
[7] Numbers given in brackets after place names refer to their location on map V.
[8] The northwestern isogloss of this phenomenon is based primarily on Todorov 1939:333-337.
[9] For instance, in the Pijanec area of Kjustendil (Umlenski 1965:99).
[10] Ibid.
[11] Popov 1955:146.
[12] Georgiev 1907:434.
[13] Umlenski 1965:99.
[14] Gabor 1979:154
[15] Stojkov 1975, part 2:157 (commentary to map 200); Miletič 1912:62 and passim.
[16] Stojkov 1975, part 1: map 201.
[17] Umlenski 1965:101.
[18] The cartographic identification of these types was possible in such detail because of the inclusion in the Bulgarian dialect atlas, vol. 3 (Stojkov 1975) of a question devoted to this trait. Most of the cartography in this paper, however, is based on my own study of the dialectal sources (and in certain instances, on my own field data). The maps are thus as correct as I can make them, given the present state of published data and of my own field data.
[19] Umlenski 1965:101.
[20] Stojkov et al. 1955:280. Compare also the following: from Samokov [58]—*sósipa* but *sosípam* (ibid); from the neighboring area of Gorno Pole (northeast of Stanke Dimitrov [52])—*zavéžem* but *zákaža* (Kotova 1962:81-82); and from villages in extreme southern Serbia (southeast of Vranje [7])—*dónesu* but *donésem* (Alexander 1975:308f.).
[21] Popivanov 1940a:250,256.
[22] Although numerous investigators have mentioned this trait, I have not attempted to account for the distribution in 3rd conjugation verbs in cartographic terms. The extension of this opposition to 1st and 2nd conjugation verbs is more rarely mentioned, but must also be presumed to exist in at least some dialects, cf. Umlenski's statement that in Kjustendil stem stress, specifically non-initial stress, is an unambiguous mark of imperfective verbs, since the mark of perfective verbs is initial stress (1965:120). For illustration of this statement, he includes two examples with vocalic desinences (*izláza* and *donósa*) and eight examples with consonantal desinences (type *donósim*).
[23] Gabor 1979:202.
[24] Popova 1974:78-81.
[25] Gabor 1979:202.
[26] Ibid.
[27] These forms are attested southwest of Blagoevgrad (Popova 1974:83-85). Compare in this respect Kabasanov's data for the dialect of Momčilovci near Smoljan (1955:61), in which,

according to the investigator, [1sg forms of] prefixed perfective verbs are accented on the prefix and prefixed imperfective verbs on the root vowel, viz. *póbaxta* (pf) vs. *pobaxtávam* (impf), [where the accent in the imperfective form is in fact *not* on the root but on the imperfectivizing suffix], and—with more than one prefix—*isponábaxta, isponápija* (pf) vs. *ispobaxtávam, isponapívam* (impf). Here the accent in the perfective verbs is in fact *not* initial but appears to be bound to the prefix closest to the root morpheme. In this dialect, therefore, the accentuation of verbal forms appears to be determined more by morphological factors than by morphophonemic ones.

[28] The fate of such dialectal features in diaspora often provides interesting insight into such patterns of implementation. Compare, for instance, the Bulgarian dialect of Suvorovo (East Thracian base) in the USSR, where initial accent in 1sg forms is known only in *e/ča* stems with a liquid in the root (Bernštejn et al. 1953:137). It may be that this particular phonological characteristic of the root is the operative factor in the preservation of this accentual type (as suggested by Gustavsson 1969:39); but since no other stems from this group are cited, one cannot tell.

[29] The great majority of verbs with stem-initial accent also have stem-final accent, since the stem consists of only one syllable. The only systematically attested polysyllabic stems with stem-initial accent are derived imperfectives whose stems include aspect markers such as -*uva*-.

[30] The classification of stem types is based on information from both present and aorist stems. Thus, although the present tense forms *počneš* and *mineš* both terminate in -*neš*, the different in the aorist forms (*poče* vs. *mina*) dictates their membership in two separate classes. Similarly, the aorist forms *peče* and *poče* both terminate in -*če*, but the difference in the present tense forms (*pečeš* vs. *počneš*) demonstrates the stem-type distinction.

[31] All forms are 2nd singular and are taken from the dialectal area southwest of Blagoevgrad (after Popova 1974). When one makes regular phonetic or morphological adjustments (such as in the aorist of group [iii]—*minu* for *mina*), these forms can serve as "cover terms" for all of Balkan Slavic, since the distribution of verbal stems throughout these classes is more or less constant. Subsequent schematic charts use these cover terms with the understanding that the appropriate local dialectal forms can be recovered by making the necessary phonetic and morphological adjustments. The relevant factor in all discussions is, of course, the place of accent.

[32] I omit from the present discussion stems such as *igraj*- which in some dialects belong to the 1st conjugation and in others to the 3rd, e.g., *igraješ* vs. *igraš*.

[33] Belić 1905:537.
[34] Zahariev 1916:201.
[35] Gabor 1979:149.
[36] Popivanov 1940b:354.

[37] In fact, however, there seem to be a few dialects, such as that of Široka Lăka (near [80]) which *do* permit a stem-class specific distributional statement: all 3rd-conjugation verbs (i.e., *aj*-stems) are stem-stressed in the present, while all other stem classes are end-stressed in the present (Popova 1976). I am unable at present to specify the extent to which this accentual type has spread.

[38] Only 1st and 2nd conjugation verbs have been listed here, comprising types (i)–(vii). The accentuation of type (viii) verbs (3rd conjugation) is always characterized by columnar stress on one of the stem syllables; the choice of which stem syllable carries the accent is largely dependent on the presence or absence of specific imperfectivizing morphemes. All forms with end stress in this and other charts are printed in boldface italics. The sketch maps accompanying this and subsequent summary charts are schematic simplifications of the actual distribution shown on the corresponding scale maps provided in the appendix.

[39] Here only three verbs types are given. The accentuation of sonorant stems (ii), *n*-stems (iii) and *Ca*-stems (iv) is as that of *i*-stems (v); while the accentuation of *Ča*-stems (vii) is as that of *e*-stems (vi).

[40] The desinence -*mo* is characteristic of northwestern Balkan Slavic (Serbian dialects and certain bordering West Bulgarian and North Macedonian dialects), while the desinence -*me* is

characteristic of the rest of Balkan Slavic. For the determination of areas 2B-1 and 2B-2, the shape of the final vowel is irrelevant; the sole determining factor is whether or not this vowel is stressed. The vocalic shape of the forms given in the chart on p. 18 must thus be adjusted for the proper local dialectal realization.

[41] Umlenski 1965:75; Zahariev 1916:201; Kotova 1962:83; Vidoeski 1954:11.
[42] Alexander 1975:427f; Todorov 1936:355.
[43] Alexander 1975:428f.
[44] Umlenski 1965:73-75, 100-120.
[45] Here, type (i) includes also those stems of type (iv) which show this accentuation; type (vi) stands for type (vii) as well, and type (v) stands for all remaining types. 2nd plural forms have the same accentuation as 1st plural forms. 1st and 2nd plural forms with absolute end stress are marked with a line under the desinence.
[46] Alexander 1975:414.
[47] Vidoeski 1954:11.
[48] Kuševski 1958:89.
[49] Gabor 1979:201.
[50] Umlenski 1965:167.
[51] Stoilov 1905:212-214. Note, however, Popova's 1974 study of two villages (Padež and Lesko, located within the larger area studied by Stoilov), in which she found *no* evidence of this accentuation.
[52] Here again, type (vii) stands for type (vi) as well, and type (v) stands for all other stem types not depicted (ii, iii, iv and viii).
[53] The reconstructions in this section as well as those in section 4.1 below are based on Stang 1957, Dybo and Illič-Svityč 1963, and works cited in footnote 4.
[54] The integration of these two types of innovations into a unified theory of morphophonemic change is a task for the future. Here I will simply attempt to identify the factors at work.
[55] A discussion of the shifts which created the new accentual mobility of PSl paradigm (b) [*mogǫ́ *mǫ́žetь, *nošǫ́ *nósitь] is outside the scope of the present paper. This mobility was subsequently eliminated in all of Balkan Slavic.
[56] On the relative chronology of quantity loss in far western Balkan Slavic, see Ivić 1968-69:477-479, and Ivić and Alexander 1973.
[57] The accent of the 1st plural is as that of the 2nd plural; the accent of the 2nd singular, 3rd plural, and all forms of the dual is as that of the 3rd singular.
[58] Historically, these two belonged to the same class.
[59] Numbers in parentheses refer to the hypothesized individual innovations.
[60] It is also possible that reinterpretation (3) was made without the intermediate stage hypothesized as (2).
[61] Gustavsson's view of this composite innovation is the traditional one: he describes the spread of initial stress in 1sg to processes of analogy (1969:34). In his view, apparently, it is the loss of the distinction between paradigms with "fixed post-boundary stress" in all but the 1st sg (*izgoríš*) and those with "fixed pre-boundary stress" in all forms (*donósiš*) which has led to the extension of initial accent in the second type (1969:34-35). He does not feel it necessary to seek a motivation for this reinterpretation, even though he subsequently notes, in passing, that "the reason that only perfective prefixed *a*-presents [3rd conjugation–RA] acquire an initial stress is that with few exceptions prefixed *e*- and *i*-presents [1st and 2nd conjugations–RA] are perfective. By and large prefixion combined with the perfective aspect implies an initial stress" (1969:36). He cites as proof of this "tendency" the presence in Kjustendil of prefixed imperfectives such as those cited in note 25 above. He does not appear to have dealt with the systematic consequences of these correlations, however.
[62] Gustavsson rejects a phonologically based explanation for this shift (1969:22). Recent scholarship has shown, however (cf. the works cited in note 56 above), that the phonological

explanation is indeed valid in the great majority of cases. For further discussion, see Alexander 1975:543-546.

[63] See Stankiewicz 1979:147-158 for a discussion of this question.

[64] Cf. Belić 1905:286, and map II in the appendix to this paper.

[65] On the accentual relationship between prefixed and nonprefixed present tense forms, Gustavsson states: "The reason for the vacillation between post- and pre-boundary stress will not be dealt with in detail here" (1969:21), although in the same paragraph he mentions both "analogical transitions" and "rhythmic factors," and notes, in passing, that "it is also possible that the stress indicates a difference in function with regard to the verbal aspect" (ibid.).

[66] It is also likely that part of the motivation for the morphophonemic opposition which I have identified in aspectual (grammatical) terms is morphological: the presence vs. absence of a prefix may have played a considerable role in the innovations described in 2.2. In this instance, however, the morphological factor (prefixation) is very closely intertwined with the grammatical factor (aspect).

[67] The research summarized here is set forth in more detail in my forthcoming article "Directions of morphophonemic change in Balkan Slavic, the accentuation of the aorist tense."

[68] Examples are drawn from the dialect of Šarbanovac near Aleksinac [1] (Alexander 1975); see also Belić 1905 and Broch 1903.

[69] Belić 1905:575-580; Belić 1911:64-75; Alexander 1975:325-327. For a discussion of conflicting views on this problem, see Alexander 1975:354-363.

[70] Găbjov 1903:12; Gospodinkin 1921:11; C. Mladenov 1959:17.

[71] The accentuation of types (ii)–(iv) are as type (v); the accentuation of type (vi) is as type (vii). All forms are 1st singular.

[72] Specifically on the accentuation of the aorist of paradigm (c), see Dybo 1961, 1968, 1971.

[73] Indeed, Ivić hints at a possible correlation between the spread of the recessive accentuation in 1sg present and that in 2-3sg aorist in his review of Gustavsson 1969 (1972:261).

[74] Daničić 1925.

[75] Belić 1905:566, 571 and passim.

[76] In general, East Bulgarian dialects (area 4 on map IV) remain outside the domain of all of these morphophonemic conventions; accent in these dialects is free, but there is little or no paradigmatic mobility.

[77] The extent of area 1 on map IV constitutes a correction to the maps appended to earlier articles of mine (Alexander in press (b); in press (c)); I am able to draw this isogloss with greater precision thanks to the recent appearance of dialectal data previously unknown to me (specifically Peev 1979 and Gabor 1979).

[78] For more discussion of Balkan Slavic as a Sprachbund (language convergence area), see Alexander in press (d).

REFERENCES

Abbreviations

AC-8	*American Contributions to the Eighth International Congress of Slavists,* volume I: Linguistics and Poetics, ed. Henrik Birnbaum. Columbus, Ohio, 1978.
AUS	*Acta Universitatis Stockholmiensis* (Stockholm Slavic Studies).
BD	*Bălgarska dialektologija, proučvanija i materiali.* Sofia.
BDA	*Bălgarski dialekten atlas.* Sofia.
BI	*Bălgaristični izsledvanija, părvi bălgaro-skandinavski simpozium.* Sofia, 1981.
BV	*Balkanologische Veröffentlichungen.* Munich.
FS	*Folia Slavica.*
IIBE	*Izvestija na Instituta za bălgarski ezik pri BAN.* Sofia.
ISSF	*Izvestija na seminara po slavjanska filologija pri universiteta v Sofia.*
JF	*Južnoslovenski filolog.*
KSIS	*Kratkie soobščenija Instituta slavjanovedenija AN SSSR.*
LZ	*Literaturn zbor.* Skopje.
Mak	*Makedonistika.* Skopje.
MJ	*Makedonski jazik.* Skopje.
OLA	*Obščeslavjanskij lingvističeskij atlas, materialy i issledovanija.* Moscow.
PISKA	*Posebna izdanja.* Belgrade.
PSISBS	*Proceedings of the Second International Symposium on Bulgarian Studies.* Sofia.
SB	*Slavistische Beiträge.* Munich.
SbBAN	*Sbornik na Bălgarskata Akademija na Naukite.* Sofia.
SBJa	*Slavjanskoe i balkanskoe jazykoznanie, problemy morfologii sovremennyx slavjanskix i balkanskix jazykov.* Moscow.
SBK	*Schriften der Balkankommission, linguistische Abteilung.* Vienna.
SbNU	*Sbornik za narodni umotvorenija i narodopis.* Sofia.
SDZ	*Srpski dijalektološki zbornik.* Belgrade.
SJa	*Slavjanskoe jazykoznanie, doklady sovetskoj delegacii. V meždunarodnyj s"ezd slavistov (Sofia, sentjabr' 1963).* Moscow. 1963.
SMBD	*Stat'i i materialy po bolgarskoj dialektologii.* Moscow.
SSl	*Sovetskoe slavjanovedenie.* Moscow.
SSMA	Stankiewicz, Edward. *Studies in Slavic morphophonemics and accentology.* Ann Arbor, 1979.
TBD	*Trudove po bălgarska dialektologija.* Sofia.
VJa	*Voprosy jazykoznanija.*
VpamSS	*V pamet na profesor Stojko Stojkov, ezikovedski izsledvanija.* Sofia, 1974.
VSJa	*Voprosy slavjanskogo jazykoznanija.* Moscow.
ZFL	*Zbornik Matice Srpske za filologiju i lingvistiku.* Novi Sad.

References

Alexander, Ronelle
  1975 *Torlak accentuation* (*SB* Band 94).
  1978 "Pravci morfofonološke promene u balkanskoslavenskim dijalektima, akcentuacija imperativa," *AC-8,* 26-44.
  in press (a) "Directions of morphophonemic change in Bulgarian dialects," *PSIBS.*
  in press (b) "External and internal change in Balkan Slavic," *FS.*
  in press (c) "On the definition of Sprachbund boundaries, the place of Balkan Slavic," *BV.*

Belić, Aleksandar
1905 *Dijalekti istočne i južne Srbije* (*SDZ* 1).
1911 "O dijalekskom materijalu O. Broha u knjizi *Die Dialekte des südlichsten Serbiens,*" *SDZ* 2:1-104.
Bernštejn, S. B. et al.
1953 "Otčet o dialektologičeskoj ėkspedicii v bolgarskoe selo Suvorovo letom 1951 goda," *SMBD* 3:110-149.
Broch, Olaf
1903 *Die Dialekte des südlichsten Serbiens* (*SBK* 3).
Daničić, Djuro
1925 *Srpski akcenti* (*PISKA* 58).
Dybo, V. A.
1958 "O drevnejšoj metatonii v slavjanskom glagole," *VJa* 1958, 6:55-62.
1961 "Udarenie slavjanskogo glagola i formy staroslavjanskogo aorista," *KSIS* 30:33-38.
1962 "O rekonstrukcii udarenija v praslavjanskom glagole," *VSJa* 6:3-27.
1968 "Fragment praslavjanskoj akcentnoj sistemy (formy-enklinomena v aoriste i-glagolov)," *SSI* 1968, 6:66-77.
1969 "Srednebolgarskie teksty kak istočnik dlja rekonstrukcii praslavjanskogo udarenija (Praesens)," *VJa* 1969, 3:82-101.
1971 "Zakon Vasiljeva-Dolobko i akcentuacija form glagolov v drevnerusskom i srednebolgarskom," *VJa* 1971, 2:93-114.
Dybo, V. A. and V. M. Illič-Svityč
1963 "K istorii slavjanskoj sistemy akcentuacionnyx paradigm," *SJa* 70-87.
Găbov, P. K.
1903 Po govora v gr. Vidin," *SbNU* 19.
Gabor, Linda Ann
1979 *The morphology of the dialect of Berovo within the context of the Macedonian dialects.* Unpublished doctoral dissertation, Yale University.
Georgiev, Pop Srebru
1907 "Po govora na s. Češnegir Nova mahala, Stanimaško," *ISSF* 2:411-444.
Gospodonkin, D. I.
1921 "Trănčanite i trănskijat govor," *ISSF* 4:148-211.
Gustavsson, Sven
1969 *Accent paradigms of the present tense in South Slavonic. East and Central South Slavonic* (*AUS* 3).
1981 "Akcentuacija imperativa v balkanoslavjanskix dialektax," *BI*, 71-82.
Ivanov, Dimităr
1931 "Udarenite v Gevgelskija govor," *ISSF* 7:447-457.
1932 *Gevgelskijat govor.* Sofia.
Ivić, Pavle
1968-69 "Review of Koneski, Blaže, *Istorija makedonskog jezika*," *JF* 27:463-484.
1972 "Review of Gustavsson 1969," *ZFL* 15, 1:259-268.
Ivić, Pavle and Ronelle Alexander
1973 "Refonologizacija količestva v kačestvo glasnogo v odnom jugovostočnom serbskom govore," *OLA* 1973:18-21.
Kabasanov, Stojko
1955 "Govorăt na s. Momčilovci, Smoljansko," *IIBE* 4:5-101.
Kănčev, Ivan
1968 "Govorăt na selo Smolko, Pirdopsko," *BD* 4:5-160.
Kotova, N. V.
1962 "Sistema udarenija v govora rajona Gorno Pole," *SMBD* 10:45-90.

Kovačev, Stojan
 1968 "Trojanskijat govor," *BD* 4:161-242.
Kuševski, Metodi
 1958 "Delčevskiot gradski govor," *MJ* 9:67-108.
Manevik, T.
 1952 "Zabeleški za ovčepolskiot govor," *MJ* 3:188-199.
Miletič, Ljubomir
 1912 *Die Rhodopemundarten der bulgarischen Sprache* (*SBK* 10).
Mladenov, Canko
 1959 "Minalite vremena v brezniškija govor," *SMBD* 9:7-50.
Mladenov, Maksim
 1969 "Govorăt na Novo Selo Vidinsko," (*TBD* 6).
Peev, Kosta
 1979 "Dojranskiot govor," *Mak* 2:3-191.
Popivanov, G.
 1940a "Sofijskijat govor," *SbBAN* 34:209-326.
 1940b "Osobenosti na šumenskija govor (dopălnenie kăm opisanieto mu v "Das Ostbulgarische" na profesor L. Miletič)," *SbBAN* 34:329-468.
Popov, K.
 1955 "Govorăt na s. Gabare, Beloslatinsko," *IIBE* 4:103-176.
Popova, T. V.
 1974 "Morfonologičeskie čeredovanija glagola v odnom iz zapadnobolgarskix govorov," *OLA* 1972:45-90.
 1975 *Glagol'noe slovoizmenenie v bolgarskom jazyke, morfonologičeskij aspekt.* Moscow.
 1976 "Morfonologičeskaja xarakteristika glagol'nogo slovoizmenenija v jugovostočnom bolgarskom govore," *SBJa* 231-282.
Popova, T. V. and B. Velčeva
 1974 "Morfonologičnoto akcentno reduvane v glagolite ot II spreženie kato edin ot priznacite za dialektna topologičeska xarakteristika," *VpamSS*, 203-216.
Ralev, Lilo
 1977 "Govorăt na selo Bojnjagovo, Karlovsko," *BD* 8:3-199.
Stang, Christian
 1977 *Slavonic accentuation.* Oslo.
Stankiewicz, Edward
 1979 "The oxytonic accent of the present tense in Serbo-Croatian and other Slavic languages," *SSMA,* 147-158.
Stoilov, Hr. P.
 1905 "Udarenieto v gornodžumajskija govor," *ISSF* 1:183-216.
Stojčev, K. S.
 1915 "Tetevenski govor," *SbNU* 31.
Stojkov, Stojko
 1968 *Bălgarska dialektologija.* Sofia.
 1975 ed., *BDA,* vol. III: Jugozapadna Bălgarija.
Stojkov, Stojko and K. Kostov et al.
 1955 "Govorăt na s. Govedarci, Samokovsko," *IIBE* 4:255-320.
Todorov, Cvetan
 1936 "Severozapadnite bălgarski govori," (*SbNU* 41).
Umlenski, Ivan
 1965 "Kjustendilskijat govor," (*TBD* 1).
Vidoeski, Božo
 1954 "Severnite makedonski govor," *MJ* 5:1-30; 109-198.

Vidoeski, Božo
  1970   "Akcentnite sistemi vo makedonskite dialekti," *LZ* 17, 3:1-11.
Xristov, Georgi
  1955   "Govorăt na s. Nova Nadežda, Xaskovsko," *IIBE* 4:177-253.
Zahariev, Iordan
  1916   "Kjustendilsko graište," *SbNU* 32.

Map 1

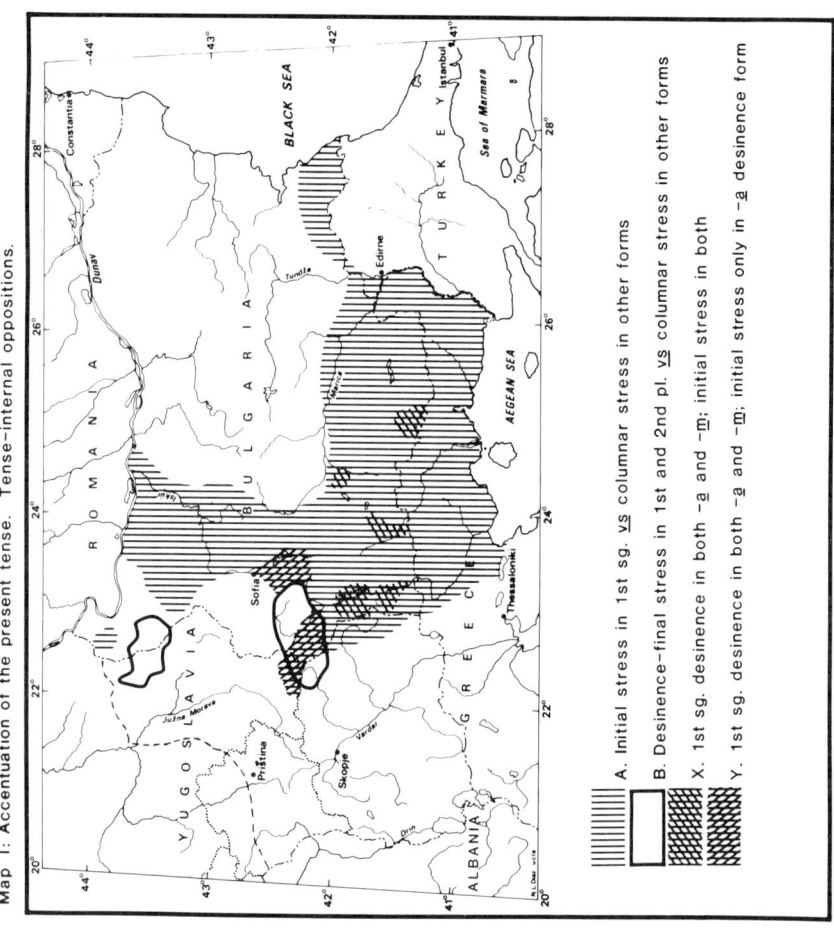

Map I: Accentuation of the present tense. Tense-internal oppositions.

A. Initial stress in 1st sg. vs columnar stress in other forms
B. Desinence-final stress in 1st and 2nd pl. vs columnar stress in other forms
X. 1st sg. desinence in both -a and -m; initial stress in both
Y. 1st sg. desinence in both -a and -m; initial stress only in -a desinence form

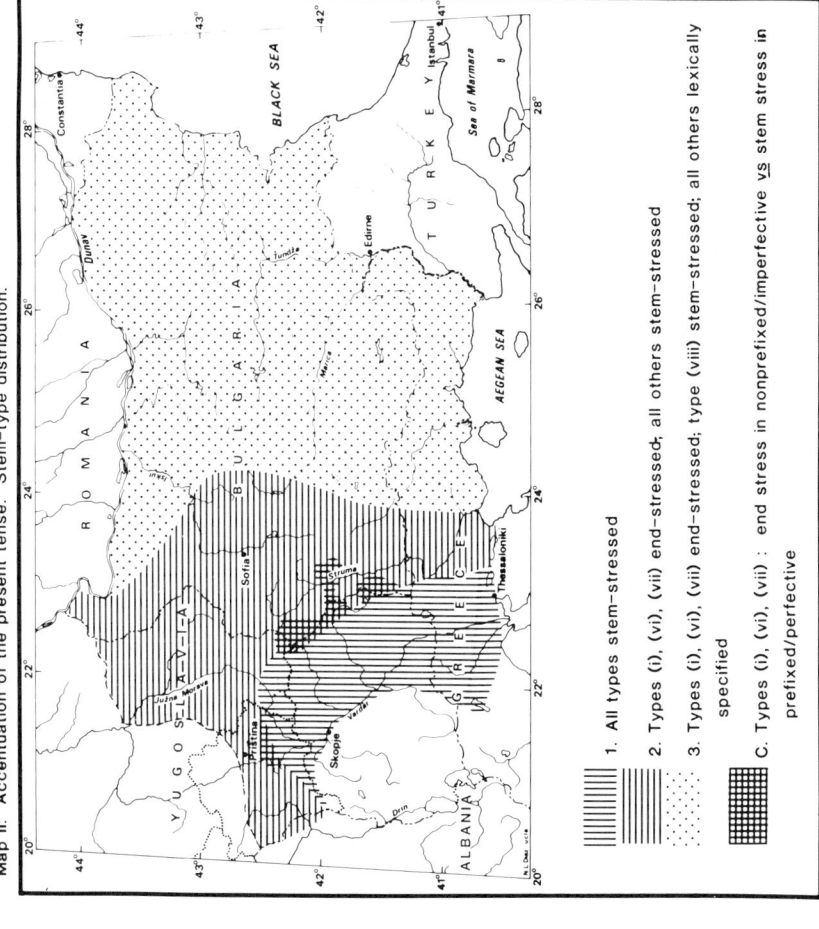

Map II: Accentuation of the present tense. Stem-type distribution.

1. All types stem-stressed
2. Types (i), (vi), (vii) end-stressed; all others stem-stressed
3. Types (i), (vi), (vii) end-stressed; type (viii) stem-stressed; all others lexically specified
C. Types (i), (vi), (vii): end stress in nonprefixed/imperfective vs stem stress in prefixed/perfective

Map III

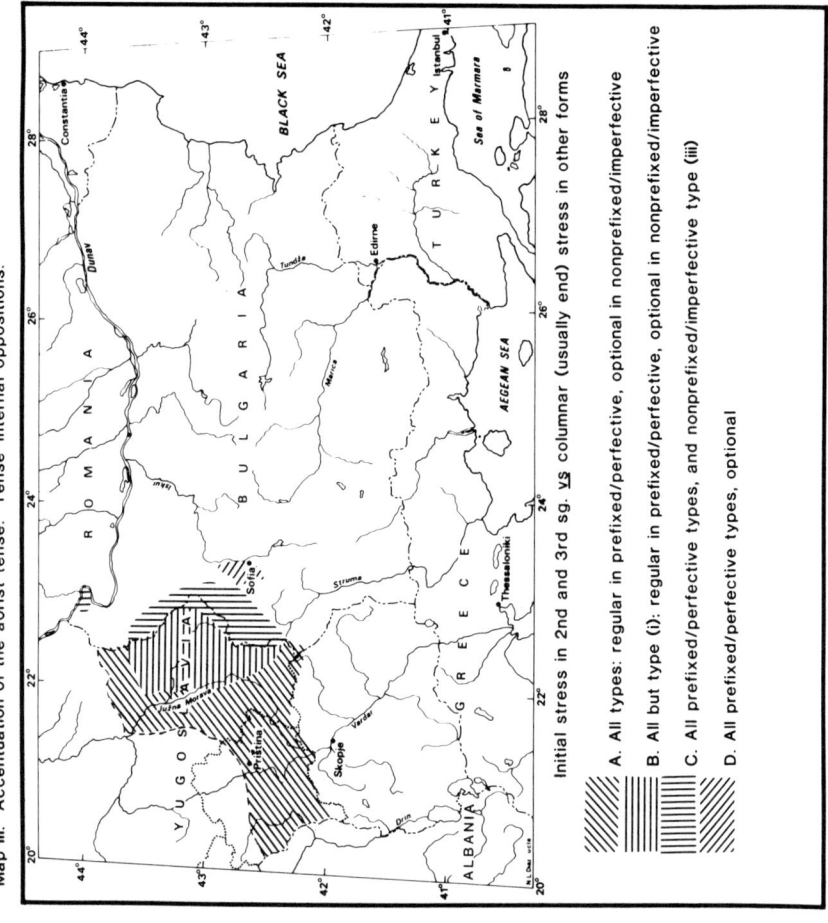

Map III: Accentuation of the aorist tense. Tense–internal oppositions.

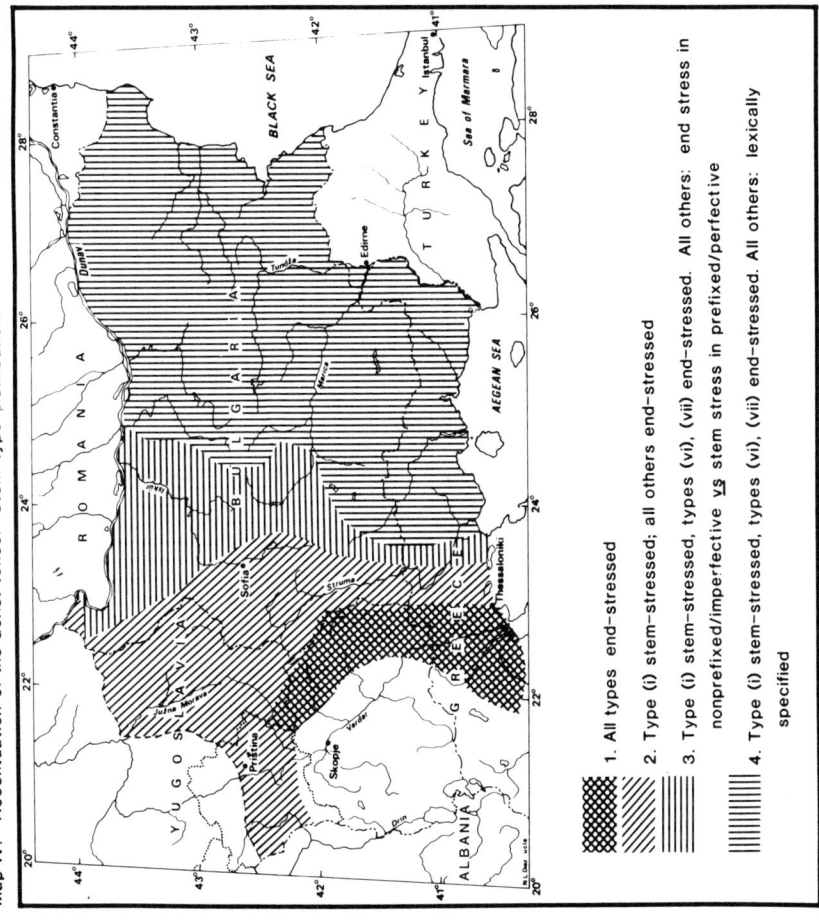

Map IV

Map IV: Accentuation of the aorist tense. Stem-type distribution.

1. All types end-stressed
2. Type (i) stem-stressed; all others end-stressed
3. Type (i) stem-stressed, types (vi), (vii) end-stressed. All others: end stress in nonprefixed/imperfective vs stem stress in prefixed/perfective
4. Type (i) stem-stressed, types (vi), (vii) end-stressed. All others: lexically specified

Map V

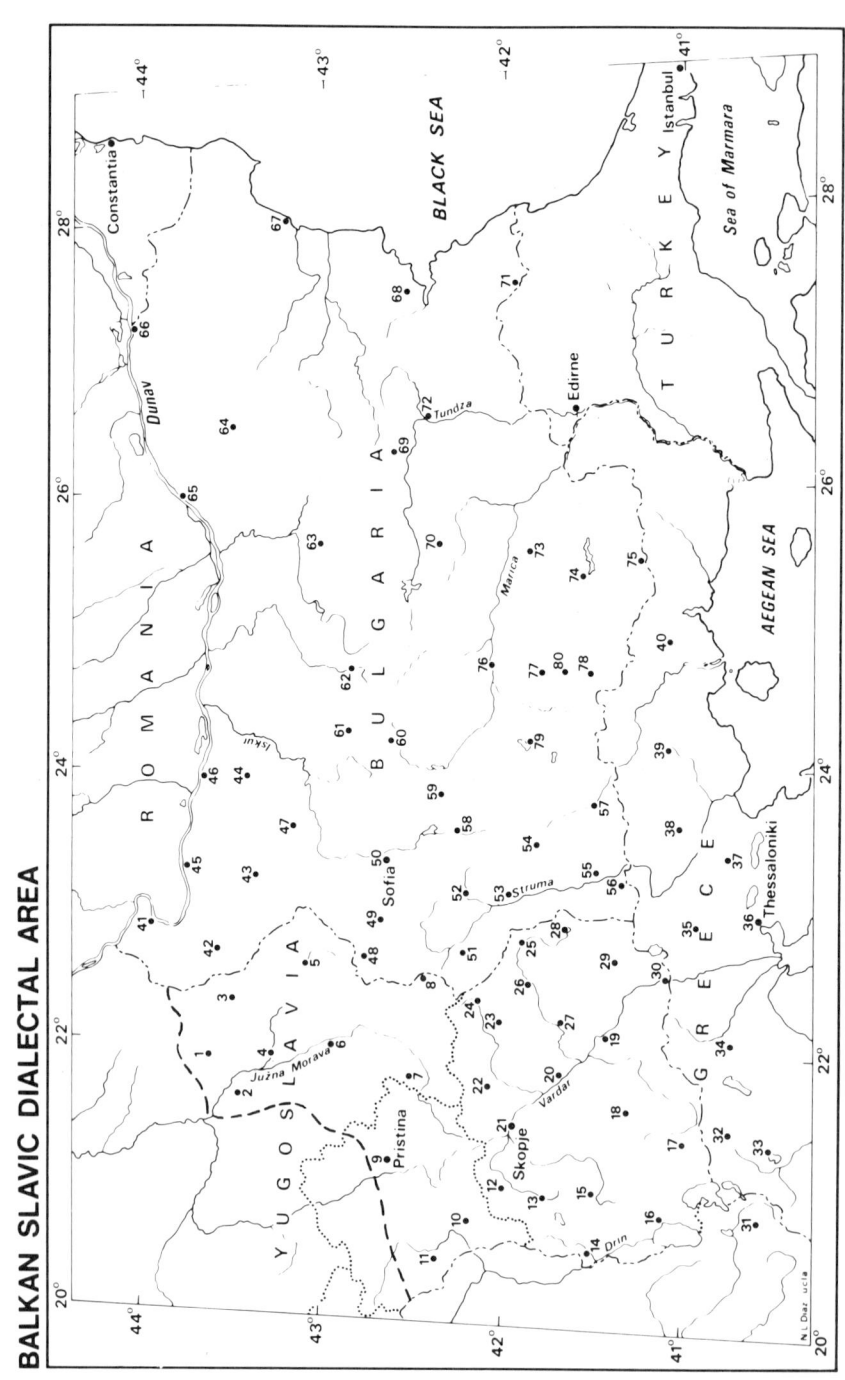

MAP V: Balkan Slavic dialectal area. Key to place names.

Serbia
1. Soko Banja
2. Aleksinac
3. Knjaževac
4. Niš
5. Pirot
6. Leskovac
7. Vranje
8. Bosilegrad
9. Priština
10. Djakovica

Macedonia
12. Tetovo
13. Gostivar
14. Debar
15. Kičevo
16. Ohrid
17. Bitola
18. Prilep
19. Negotino
20. Veles
21. Skopje
22. Kumanovo
23. Kratovo
24. Kriva Palanka
25. Delčevo
26. Kočani
27. Štip
28. Berovo
29. Strumica
30. Gevgelija

Albania
31. Korča (Korçë)

Greece
32. Lerin (Florina)
33. Kostur (Kastoria)
34. Voden (Edhessa)
35. Kukuš (Kilkis)
36. Solun (Thessaloniki)
37. Suho (Sokhos)
38. Serez (Serrai)
39. Drama
40. Ksanti (Xanthi)

Bulgaria
41. Vidin
42. Belogradčik
43. Mihajlovgrad
44. Bela Slatina
45. Lom
46. Orjaxovo
47. Vraca
48. Trăn
49. Breznik
50. Sofija
51. Kjustendil
52. Stanke Dimitrov
53. Blagoevgrad
54. Razlog
55. Sandanski
56. Petrič
57. Goce Delčev
58. Samokov
59. Ixtiman
60. Pirdop
61. Teteven
62. Trojan
63. Veliko Tărnovo
64. Razgrad
65. Ruse
66. Silistra
67. Varna
68. Burgas
69. Sliven
70. Stara Zagora
71. Malko Tărnovo
72. Jambol
73. Xaskovo
74. Kărdžali
75. Tixhomir
76. Plovdiv
77. Xvojna
78. Smoljan
79. Batak
80. Čepelare

A Comparative Sketch of Certain Anaphoric Processes in Russian and English

Robert Channon

Pronouns are commonly grouped into categories according to various criteria, one of which is anaphora. The term *anaphora* in this study will be defined as "the use of a grammatical substitute to refer to a preceding or previously introduced word or group of words" (adapted from Webster's dictionary); an *anaphoric pronoun* is thus an element which substitutes for and refers to a previously introduced noun or noun phrase (NP), while a pronoun which stands for a noun or NP not previously introduced is *non-anaphoric*. Examples of anaphoric pronouns include, among others, Rus. *он/она/оно/они, это, то* (at least in some of their uses), Eng. *he/she/it/they, that, this*, etc.; indefinite, interrogative and negative pronouns are typically non-anaphoric, e.g., Rus. *кто-то/кто-нибудь, что-то/что-нибудь, кто?, что?, никто, ничто,* Eng. *someone, something, who?, what?, no one, nothing*, etc.

Languages generally have a number of different anaphoric pronouns among which the functions of anaphora are divided. Following the practice of assigning features to lexical items (cf. Katz and Fodor 1963, and Fillmore 1969), we will regard pronouns here as being sets of features which are summed up in lexical items. Various distinctions may play a role in the system of anaphora of a given language, and the different anaphoric pronouns reflect the mapping of these distinctions in differing combinations onto lexical realizations. Languages may differ according to which features are relevant to the anaphoric system (or to the pronominal system as a whole), thereby causing them to have different mappings of features onto pronouns (in both Russian and English, for example, gender is relevant to at least a subpart of the anaphoric system [Rus. *он/она/оно*, Eng. *he/she/it*], while in Hungarian [*ő*] or Mandarin [*t'a*] it is not). They may use the same feature(s) but apply it/them differently, thereby also producing different mappings of features onto pronouns (in both Russian and English, for example, gender is a relevant feature in the anaphoric system, but in English, gender is subordinated to animacy and applies only among the anaphors of animate nouns,[1] while in Russian, gender is not dependent on animacy; the result of this difference is that while Eng. *he* [*she, it*] and Rus. *он* [*она, оно*], respectively, sometimes correspond to each other, they often do not, since they represent different mappings of features). Features which are not used elsewhere in the language may be part of the anaphoric system (in English, for example, gender is expressed in [a subpart of] the anaphoric system [*he/she*], while it is in general not expressed in the language as a whole[2]). And, finally, features which are relevant elsewhere in the language may be absent from the anaphoric system (in Russian, for example, animacy is a relevant category in the nominal system—at least in the masculine singular and in the plural—and is expressed through the morphology; it does not find expression, though, among the personal anaphoric pronouns, and the accusative forms *ego, ux* refer to nouns without regard to animacy).

It should be noted also that the present investigation is not in any way intended to address the much debated question of how and where in the grammar pronominal elements arise; it deals, rather, with the lexical selection of pronouns in the encoding of a message (or the consequences of that selection in the decoding of the message) in a slot which is, by whatever means, already known to be reserved for a pronoun. There are many different views on the provenance of pronouns. In transformational/generative grammar alone the question of the origin of pronouns has been quite controversial, and at least three major proposals have been advanced: that there is a rule of pronominalization which turns underlying full NPs into pronouns in the derived structure (cf. Lees and Klima 1963, Langacker 1969, among others); that pronouns originate in the base and are thus part of deep structure, and that they must receive semantic interpretations which associate them with their antecedents (cf. Dougherty 1969, Jackendoff 1972, among others); and that NPs in underlying structure contain only referential indices, the argument nouns being supplied from outside the clause, with pronouns serving to fill an NP identified by a second or subsequent occurrence of the same index (cf., McCawley 1970, Wasow 1975, among others). However this question is resolved, all three models will at some point—presumably in shallow structure or in surface structure—be faced with the necessity of selecting the appropriate pronominal element from among the available pronouns of the language. In other, less abstract views of syntax as well, it is still necessary at some point to choose the pronoun which will be used in a given context or to interpret the pronoun which appears in a given sentence. Thus, although one may disagree with the analysis presented here—on theoretical, factual or any other grounds—selection and interpretation of pronouns is a matter which must be dealt with regardless of linguistic orientation.

This study will concentrate on examining parts of the Russian and English anaphoric systems, identifying some of the features which play a role in defining them, finding the mapping of these features onto the available anaphoric pronouns, and comparing and contrasting the systems of the two languages. The attempt will be made, based on this analysis, to explain the distribution of the various anaphoric pronouns in given instances and to explain why the distribution in Russian and English may differ. In what follows we will be concerned only with anaphoric pronouns (to the exclusion both of other kinds of anaphoric elements and of non-anaphoric pronouns), and we will be concerned with them only in their anaphoric function (disregarding any non-anaphoric functions which they may have in other uses, and ignoring any additional functions which they may simultaneously have in their anaphoric use; cf. English *his,* which is simultaneously both anaphoric and possessive).

An initial sketch of some of the ideas presented here and of their application was given in an earlier study (Channon 1980). The present paper expands on that illustration and extends the investigation to Russian. Some simple examples of the use of anaphoric pronouns in Russian and English are given in 1-9.

1R. Маша видела вашего брата, и я тоже видел его (*ее, *их, *∅).[3]
1E. Masha saw your brother, and I saw him (*her, *it, *them, *one, *ones, *some), too.
2R. Маша видела ваш карандаш, и я тоже видел его (*ее, *их, *∅).
2E. Masha saw your pencil, and I saw it (*him, *her, *them, *one, *ones, *some), too.
3R. Маша видела вашу сестру, и я тоже видел ее (*его, *их, *∅).
3E. Masha saw your sister, and I saw her (*him, *it, *them, *one, *ones, *some), too.
4R. Маша видела вашу статью, и я тоже видел ее (*его, *их, *∅).
4E. Masha saw your article, and I saw it (*him, *her, *them, *one, *ones, *some), too.
5R. Маша видела ваше письмо, и я тоже видел его (*ее, *их, *∅).
5E. Masha saw your letter, and I saw it (*him, *her, *them, *one, *ones, *some), too.
6R. Маша видела { ваших братьев/сестер / ваши карандаши/статьи/письма }, и я тоже видел их (*его, *ее, *∅).
6E. Masha saw your brothers/sisters/pencils/articles/letters, and I saw them (*him, *her, *it, *one, *ones, *some), too.
7R. Маша купила синюю рубашку, а я купил красную ∅ (*его, *ее, *их).
7E. Masha bought a blue shirt, and I bought a red one (*him, *her, *it, *them, *ones, *some).
8R. Маша купила коричневые сапоги, а я купил черные ∅ (*его, *ее, *их).
8E. Masha bought brown boots, and I bought black ones (*him, *her, *it, *them, *one, *some).

9R. Маша купила сахару, и я тоже купил ∅ (*его, *ее, *их).
9E. Masha bought some sugar, and I bought some (*him, *her, *it, *them, *one, *ones), too.

From these examples we can draw some tentative general correspondences between items in the Russian and English anaphoric systems:[4]

Russian	corresponds to	English
он		he/it
она		she/it
оно		it
они		they
∅		one/ones
∅		some

In the case of both languages the choice of anaphoric pronoun in a given context is determined by a variety of features which the pronouns represent; in all the examples, the pronoun which appears cannot be replaced by any other anaphoric pronoun without affecting the sentence in a significant way: either the resulting sentence will be ungrammatical or it will have a different meaning. The features represented by an individual pronoun must agree with the corresponding features of the NP whose place the pronoun occupies, i.e., with those of the absent NP which the pronoun replaces,[5] rather than with those of the audible or visible antecedent. Borrowing a term from logic, this absent NP which stands behind the lexical pronoun will be called here the *referent,* to distinguish it from the *antecedent.* In the view presented here, a relation of *replacement* will be taken to obtain between an anaphor and its referent, and a relation of *coreference* will be taken to obtain between the referent and the antecedent, but no direct relation is presumed to exist between the anaphor and the antecedent; their connection is only an indirect one, through the mediation of the absent referent. The importance of making this distinction can be shown, among other ways, by an example of the following type. English alone is used here to illustrate the point, since it readily shows a distinction of definiteness, which is observable only indirectly and in restricted instances in Russian. Sentences of this type in Russian will, however, be discussed later.

	ANTECEDENT	ANAPHOR	REFERENT
10E.	Susan saw a rhinoceros, and Scott saw	it	(= *the rhinoceros*), too.
11E.	Susan saw a rhinoceros, and Scott saw	one	(= *a rhinoceros*), too.

While the antecedent and the referent agree in definiteness in 11E, they do not agree in 10E; this fact is conveyed by the difference between the anaphoric pronouns (*it/one*) which appear in the two sentences. If we take the anaphoric pronouns as reflecting the features of their referents, the differing pronoun choices can be explained and can be related to the difference in meaning between the two sentences; but if we try to relate the pronouns to the antecedents directly, there is no basis for explaining either the lexical or the semantic difference between 10E and 11E. Pronoun selection in the course of producing a sentence can thus be modeled as a process of finding the pronoun which matches the features of the referent; pronoun interpretation in the course of deciphering a sentence, correspondingly, can be modeled as the projection of the set of features conveyed by the pronoun onto the phantom referent. To the extent that the correspondence between the feature bundles and the pronouns which convey them is unique, there will be a unique referent constructed by their projection, and any ambiguities which arise in the interpretation of a sentence will be due to alternative possibilities of coreference between the referent (or as much of it as can be recaptured from the pronoun) and different antecedents. To the extent that there is syncretism among the pronouns expressing various differing bundles of features, on the other hand, alternative referents will be constructed, and these then may give rise to ambiguity with regard to the referent. These alternative referents, further, may or may not be associated with differing antecedents, thus potentially compounding the ambiguity.

Among the features which will be found to be necessary for a description of the Russian and English anaphoric systems are *person, gender, number, animacy, discreteness,* and *definiteness.*[6] As was suggested above, these features do not all function independently of each other, but are arranged in a hierarchy of applicability within subparts of the system. Thus, in both the Russian and the English pronoun systems, *gender* is subordinated to both person and number, applying in both languages only in the third person and only in the singular; in other languages, though, it could apply more widely, e.g., in Czech gender applies in the plural as well as in the singular among third-person pronouns. Further, as mentioned earlier, there is a dependency between *animacy* and person/number/gender, though here the two languages under analysis differ. In English animacy is a feature of the anaphoric system:[7] it is subordinated to person and number, but has precedence over gender. Thus, while animacy is distinguished only among third-person singular pronouns, gender is distinguished only among the animates,[8] which places animacy between person and number on the one hand, and gender on the other, in the hierarchy of features within the English system; gender also, of course, would then derivatively be subordinate to person and number. In Russian, however, as was noted above, animacy, although it is an important feature in the noun system, does not seem to play a role in the anaphoric system, at least not among the personal pronouns. Russian, though, does seem to make use of the feature *human* (not *animate*) among the (non-anaphoric) interrogative pronouns (*кто / что*) and also in certain environments for (anaphoric) relative pronouns (*тот, кто / то, что*).[9] *Discreteness* is independent of gender; animates seem always to be discrete, though this may be a fact about the real world, rather than a language-specific fact about the feature hierarchy in Russian or English; discreteness likewise does not appear to be relevant to the first and second persons, probably for extra-linguistic reasons, but it is a distinctive feature in the third person. It is important to note, however, that discreteness and number are interdependent, with discreteness taking precedence over number; number is defined only among discrete items, and not among the non-discretes. This is true in both languages under discussion here, and is no doubt a universal, rooted as it is in the meaning of "discrete" and the meaning of "number." *Definiteness* is independent of gender, number, animacy and discreteness, but it too is distinguished only in the third person, with first and second persons functioning as definite. It is not surprising that definiteness is a feature of the English anaphoric system, since it is a prominent feature of the nominal system; but it is also a feature of the Russian anaphoric system, as will be seen below, even though the category of definiteness is often thought to be lacking or is ignored in Russian. *Number* is rather high in the hierarchy, applying to all persons, and is clearly dominant over animacy and gender. Only third-person forms are treated in this investigation, and so there will be no further occasion to discuss the feature *person* in the present context.

We are now in a position to characterize the pronouns listed earlier in terms of the features discussed above (with person being omitted, with the assumption that only anaphoric uses of the pronouns are being referred to, and with the proviso that other features not mentioned here may also be relevant).[10]

    он : [definite], [discrete], [singular], [masculine]
    она : [definite], [discrete], [singular], [feminine]
    оно : [definite], [discrete], [singular], [neuter]
    они : [definite], [discrete], [plural]

    he : [definite], [discrete], [singular], [animate], [masculine]
    she : [definite], [discrete], [singular], [animate], [feminine]
    it : [definite], [discrete], [singular], [inanimate]
    they : [definite], [discrete], [plural]
    one : [nondefinite], [discrete], [singular]
    ones : [nondefinite], [discrete], [plural]
    some : [nondefinite], [nondiscrete][11]

The descriptions given above cover all the overt Russian and English pronouns in examples 1-9, but there is still one more anaphoric element found in the Russian sentences (7R-9R): ∅. A review of the correspondences shows that this zero element always corresponds to an English nondefinite pronoun, and an examination of the other Russian pronouns cited shows that they are all definite. It thus would appear that Russian has no nondefinite anaphoric pronoun, or, alternatively, that Russian makes use of a zero pronoun to express nondefinite anaphora. Comparing the Russian ∅ in 7R-9R with the explicit English pronouns found in 7E-9E, we can see that the only characteristic feature which ∅ has (from among those being considered here) is [nondefinite], since it can stand for both discrete and nondiscrete, and also for both singular and plural.[12] More will be said about the pronoun ∅ and its status below.

By a similar process of comparison of the features of the non-zero Russian pronouns with their English counterparts, it can be seen that the above characterizations allow for and even imply the non-one-to-one correspondence of Russian and English anaphoric pronouns found in most of the items under consideration here (only *они* and *they* are in a one-to-one relationship): to the extent that the feature descriptions are compatible there will be overlap, but to the extent that they are contradictory the pronouns will be unique. Thus, Russian *он* carries the features [definite], [discrete], [singular], and [masculine], which makes it compatible with English *he* ([definite], [discrete], [singular], [*animate*], [masculine]); the two pronouns differ only in that English *he* has the feature [animate], but since Russian *он* is not specified with regard to animacy, there is no conflict; if, however, the Russian pronoun were marked [inanimate], or if the English pronoun were marked [feminine], as *she* is, they would be incompatible and could not correspond to each other. While Russian *он* is compatible with English *he,* it is at the same time compatible with another English pronoun, namely, *it. It* has the features [definite], [discrete], [singular], and [inanimate], none of which is contradictory to any of the features which mark *он* (recall that *он* is not specified for animacy, while *it* is not specified for gender); *он* and *it* are thus compatible too, and this dual compatibility produces the many-to-one correspondence observed in 1-2. In similar fashion, it can be seen that *она* is compatible with both *she* and *it,* giving rise to the correspondences in 3-4. Russian *оно,* however, is compatible only with English *it,* since it has the feature [neuter], which is incompatible with both *he* ([masculine]) and *she* ([feminine]), cf. 5. Viewed from the other direction, English *it,* although specified as [inanimate], is not incompatible with any of the Russian singular definite pronouns (*он, она, оно*), since none of them is specified for animacy; *he,* however, being specified as [masculine], is compatible only with *он,* and *she,* being [feminine], can correspond only to *она*. Russian *они* and English *they* correspond uniquely to each other, cf. 6. Anaphoric Ø in Russian, as indicated earlier, must be specified only as [nondefinite]; it cannot be specified for number, since it must be compatible with both *one* ([singular]) and *ones* ([plural]), and it cannot be specified for discreteness, since it must be compatible with both of these ([discrete]) and with *some* ([nondiscrete]), cf. 7-9.

We have been treating Ø as an anaphoric pronoun (or, at least, "element") in Russian, and, in particular, as one characterized by the feature [nondefinite]. There are, however, abundant examples which appear to have Ø used as a definite anaphoric pronoun, cf. 12-13. It will be argued here that those instances are always distinct from the use of Ø as a nondefinite anaphoric pronoun, that the Ø has a very different kind of origin in those examples, and that in those uses it should not be regarded as a basic pronoun with the feature [definite].

12R. Маша смотрела этот фильм, и я тоже смотрел.
12E. Masha saw that film, and I saw it, too.

13R. Вы не видели мою ручку? Да, видел.
13E. Did you see my pen? Yes, I saw it.

Such sentences as these have English definite pronouns in correspondence with a zero element in Russian, and are unquestionably interpreted as having definite referents in both languages. Russian sentences of this type, however, always have alternate realizations in which the expected non-zero definite pronouns appear, i.e., pronouns can always be supplied to produce a "full" form of the sentence, cf. 14R-15R; in sentences where Ø is a nondefinite anaphoric pronoun, though, no pronoun can be supplied to "fill out" the sentence, cf. 7R-9R, repeated here from above.

14R. Маша смотрела этот фильм, и я тоже смотрел *его*.
15R. Вы не видели мою ручку? Да, *я видел ее*.
7R. Маша купила синюю рубашку, а я купил красную (*ее*).
8R. Маша купила коричневые сапоги, а я купил черные (*их*).
9R. Маша купила сахару, и я тоже купил (*его*).

This simple syntactic test divides sentences with Ø-anaphora into two groups on grounds which are totally independent of the feature definiteness; but the division on these grounds coincides with the distinction between the definite and nondefinite interpretations, and it can, if needed, be used as a test for definiteness in Ø-anaphors. The difference between the "full" and the "elliptical" forms of sentences like 12R-15R is stylistic, with the full forms considered more "formal" and the elliptical forms more "colloquial"; it is also true that there are several possible elliptical forms, differing according to which parts of the sentence are left out, cf. 13aR-13dR.[13]

13aR. Вы не видели мою ручку? Да.
13bR. Вы не видели мою ручку? Видел.
13cR. Вы не видели мою ручку? Да, видел.
13dR. Вы не видели мою ручку? Да, видел ее.
etc.

Because of this, the *full* form of such sentences as 13R will be taken to be the basic form, and the elliptical forms such as 13aR-13dR will be viewed as sentences with missing pronouns (and/or other parts) derived from the full forms, i.e., as full sentences which have had pronouns (or other material) deleted from them under various discourse conditions. Sentences like 7R-9R, on the other hand, will be regarded as examples with true Ø-pronouns. In a model of grammar which distinguishes differing levels of structure of a sentence we may say that sentences like 12R-15R have, in their underlying or in an intermediate form, non-zero pronouns (or, in another view, pronouns which are destined to be non-zero) which at a later stage of derivation are optionally deleted by a discourse rule, while sentences like 7R-9R have pronouns which are (or are destined to be) lexically and phonologically null. This null item called forth by the feature [nondefinite] will be regarded here as the *pronoun Ø*, i.e., as an underlying lexical item in the inventory of Russian pronouns, while the result of deletion of a non-zero definite pronoun will not be regarded as an item in the lexicon.[14] Given this distinction, it then becomes clear that the *Ø* listed in the correspondences and as a potential anaphor among the other possible lexical realizations in 1R-9R is the lexical pronoun *Ø*, and this pronoun *Ø*, since it is specified as [nondefinite], cannot be a valid choice in 1R-6R, which call for a pronoun specified [definite], but is the only choice in 7R-9R, which call for a [nondefinite] pronoun. Thus, in both the Russian and the English examples in 1-9, a pronoun with features which match those of the referent is selected to fill the slot.

In both languages, however, instances arise in which the referent, because of its complexity or its structure, either may have conflicting or contradictory features, or may not be conducive to defining the necessary features. Such cases in English have been discussed in Channon (1980), where it was proposed that the English pronoun *that* (in its anaphoric use) is unspecified for such crucial features as definiteness, discreteness, and number, and thus is able to serve as a pronoun of last resort, representing referents with conflicting or undefinable features and standing in for other pronouns which could not be used because they were too highly specified to be compatible with the referent. Such a use is also found with the Russian *это,* which, in its use as a non-deictic anaphoric pronoun, is unspecified for definiteness, discreteness, number, and gender, cf. 16-21.[15]

16R. Сережа заказал шпроты, борщ, свиную отбивную, и чай, и я тоже это (*его, *ее, *их, *∅) заказал.
16E. Serezha ordered sprats, borshch, a pork chop, and tea, and I ordered that (*it, *them, *one, *ones, *some), too.
17R. Сережа любит плавание, и я тоже ?его/это люблю.
17E. Serezha likes swimming, and I like it/that, too.
18R. Сережа любит плавать, и я тоже это (*его) люблю. / ... и я тоже люблю.[16]
18E. Serezha likes to swim, and I like ?it/?that, too.
19R. Сережа любит слушать музыку, и я тоже это (*его) люблю.
19E. Serezha likes to listen to music, and I like ?it/?that, too.
20R. Сережа любит слушать музыку в парке вечером после ужина, и я тоже это (*его) люблю.
20E. Serezha likes to listen to music in the park in the evening after supper, and I like that (*it), too.
21R. Сережа не хочет напрасно тревожить жену, и я это (*его) понимаю.[17]
21E. Serezha doesn't want to alarm his wife unnecessarily, and I understand that (*it).

In 16 the referent is an unmanageable mixture of conflicting feature specifications: it contains both [discrete] and [nondiscrete] items, [singular] and [plural] (and, in addition, the referent as a whole, being a concatenation of several items, should have the feature [plural]), [masculine] and [feminine] in the Russian form, etc. The result is that the pronouns *это/that* appear; in order for these pronouns to be compatible with the referent, they must be neutral with regard to the features which have conflicting specifications. Note that, despite the fact that several parts of the referent in the Russian sentence are masculine and feminine, singular and plural, the form of the Russian pronoun can be only neuter singular; this is, as was mentioned earlier, the default specification of the pronoun made at an intermediate stage of the derivation, and not an underlying specification as in the homonymous neuter singular form of *этот.* In 17-20 we find a series of sentences with referents which grow progressively more complex. In the case of the simplest referent (17), *это* and *that* are possible, though they are not the only possibilities, and they are, perhaps, not even the preferred variants; they grow better as the referent becomes more complex, and the other possibilities simultaneously grow worse, to the point where, with very complex referents, they may be the only or the preferred possibility. This is explained in the present analysis by the fact that, as the referent grows more and more complex, it becomes harder and harder to evaluate the necessary features over its domain, and it also becomes more and more probable that there will be conflicting feature values; there thus comes a point when the determination of the features of the referent in the customary way becomes too clumsy, and the all-purpose pronouns *это* and *that* take over. While English *it* is possible in 17-20, Russian *он/она/оно* are not, and this fact brings out another difference between these pronoun correspondences in the two languages which has not yet been seen here: Russian *он/она/оно* cannot refer to structures other than nouns or NPs (e.g., V, VP, S, etc.), whereas English *it* can, and Russian *он/она/оно* is often not felicitous in referring to an abstract referent, whereas English *it* is.[18] In 21 *это* and *that* stand for a clause, and clauses cannot readily be characterized in terms of the features which are being discussed here; thus, in such instances, too, the maximally unspecified pronouns (*это/that*) are found.

Having seen some of the ways in which the Russian and English anaphoric systems correspond to each other, let us look at some ways in which they do not correspond and try to examine the differences in terms of the analysis outlined here. One such example is given in 22-23.

22R. Алик хочет быть первым человеком в космосе, но им не будет.
22E. Alex wants to be the first man in space, but he won't be ?that/??it/*him.

23R. Нина хочет быть дирижером Московской филармонии, но им не будет.
23E. Nina wants to be the conductor of the Moscow Philharmonic, but she won't be ?that/??it/*him/*her.

22R and 23R are ordinary, acceptable sentences of Russian, but their counterparts in 22E and 23E do not enjoy the same status in English. The difficulty is, of course, the pronoun in the second clause. In the Russian sentences a form of *он* appears without problem. In the English sentences, however, no pronoun is especially felicitous here: forms of *he* and *she* are completely impossible, *it* is rather marginal, and even *that* is not very good; in fact, the best variant of the sentences is the one with no pronoun at all, i.e., with deletion of whatever pronoun might have appeared. This distinction between English and Russian follows from our analysis above. In each of the Russian sentences the referent has the features [definite], [discrete], [singular], and [masculine]; *он* matches these features exactly and appears unproblematically in the sentences in the appropriate (instrumental) form *им*. The feature [masculine] would not, in any case, cause a problem in 22R, but it might be thought that there would be incompatibility in 23R, where a woman is being spoken about. 23R illustrates, however, that it is grammatical gender rather than semantic gender which is relevant in the anaphoric system; the referent in 23R, *дирижер*, is always grammatically masculine, regardless of who happens to fill that position at any given time, and therefore *eй* is not possible, since the referent requires a masculine anaphor. As a result, there is no conflict in the features which are relevant in the given instance, and there is no difficulty in providing an appropriate pronoun. In the English examples, on the other hand, the matter is more complicated. As was seen earlier, animacy is an important feature in the English anaphoric system; *man* and *conductor* are normally taken to be animate nouns, but yet the animate pronoun *he,* which fits the features of the referents in every other respect as well ([definite], [discrete], [singular], and [masculine], to the extent that gender is specified in these referents), is entirely unacceptable in this context (the same is true of *she,* to the extent that gender is unspecified in these referents). The explanation of this peculiar situation is that we must distinguish two different senses of phrases like those which are the referents of 22 and 23: on the one hand, they designate titles, offices, or functions, and on the other they designate the *holders* of those offices, etc.[19] The holders of the offices will, of course, be specified with the feature [animate]; the offices themselves, however, are not animate, and thus they will be specified as [inanimate], cf. 24E-25E, where this difference is brought out more clearly.

24E. The Institute has a new director. He is an outstanding specialist in the field.

25E. The Institute needs a new director. It's/That's a difficult job to fill.

In 24E the sense of the referent is the holder of the office, and so the animate pronoun *he* appears; in 25E, however, the sense is the office itself, and so the inanimate *it* is found. The particular problem in 22E and 23E is that the referents are, in a way, used here in both senses simultaneously; they represent both *a* token and *the* token *par excellence* of the type. It would thus appear that they require an anaphor which can express both the feature [animate] and the feature [inanimate] at the same time, or one which is not specified for this feature. The English pronouns *he* and *it,* of course, do not satisfy this description, and thus are not suitable. Under these conditions, we might expect *that* to step in and fill the slot; while *that* can appear, and seems to be the best of the alternatives, there is still something odd about it in this context, and the matter requires further investigation. Perhaps the strangeness of *that* here is connected with the fact that it is a highly unspecified pronoun, but is being used to stand for what is in most respects a simple and narrowly specified referent. Pragmatically we expect to find with *that* a longer referent which is structurally and/or semantically more complicated than a simple noun or NP, something which would better justify the use of so powerful a pronoun. Note that this entire problem is sidestepped in Russian by virtue of the simple fact that *он/она/оно* are not specified for animacy, and therefore there is nothing to prevent *он* from being used in this context.

Let us return now to sentences of the type seen in 10 and 11. Those examples were given only in their English forms, partly because the distinction which was then being drawn was more directly observable in the English forms, and partly because the paradigm of the examples in Russian is not complete. Some further examples are given in 26-28, with both languages represented.

26R. Алеша смотрел эту пьесу, и я тоже смотрел ее.
26aR. Алеша смотрел эту пьесу, и я тоже смотрел.
26E. Alesha saw that play, and I saw it, too.
27R. Алеша смотрел интересную новую пьесу, и я тоже смотрел ее.[20]
27aR. Алеша смотрел интересную новую пьесу, и я тоже смотрел.
27E. Alesha saw an interesting new play, and I saw it, too.
28R. *Алеша смотрел интересную новую пьесу, и я тоже смотрел $\emptyset$.[21]
28aR. Алеша смотрел интересную новую пьесу, и я тоже смотрел (такую) пьесу.
28bR. Алеша смотрел интересную новую пьесу, и я тоже смотрел интересную новую пьесу.
28E. Alesha saw an interesting new play, and I saw one, too.

The sentences in 26 have a definite antecedent and a definite referent; the pronouns *ее/it* appear, occasioned by the definiteness of the referent and the other features relevant to the example given. It is possible in Russian to omit the pronoun, as seen in 26aR, but in that case the interpretation is the same as that of 26R, and the pronoun *ее* can easily be supplied: i.e., 26aR can be taken only as an elliptical form (with deleted pronoun) of the full form 26R, and 26aR does not contain the pronoun $\emptyset$. In 27 the antecedent is nondefinite, but the referent is still definite, and the same pronouns *ее/it* are found, again called forth by the definiteness of the referent. Once again there is a variant 27aR with deleted pronoun, but this variant is still interpreted as having a definite referent (i.e., as representing 27R with deletion of *ее*), and, therefore, in our terms does not contain the pronoun $\emptyset$. In 28 the intention is to convey a nondefinite antecedent and a nondefinite referent, as can be seen from the

English version 28E. The attempt, however, fails in Russian, and 28R is not an acceptable sentence of Russian *in the meaning intended*. It is, of course, a perfectly good sentence in the meaning of 27, and coincides in surface form with 27aR. Thus, if we wish to express the meaning of 28 in Russian, we cannot do it with a pronominalized form, at least not with a form from the correspondences identified earlier, since the only available form for expressing [nondefinite] among those correspondences is ∅, but ∅ is interpreted as the result of deletion of a definite pronoun, not as the occurrence of the nondefinite pronoun ∅. One way in which the meaning of 28 can be expressed is by repetition of the noun (i.e., by not attempting to pronominalize the referent), as in 28aR or 28bR.

Comparing 7R-9R and 26R-28R we come upon an apparent anomaly. On the one hand, in 7R-9R, ∅ (i.e., the pronoun ∅) serves without difficulty as a nondefinite pronoun (and only in that function), while in 26R-27R, on the other hand, ∅ is interpreted as the absence of a definite pronoun, rather than as the nondefinite pronoun ∅, and in 28R it is also not interpreted as a nondefinite pronoun: if a meaning is assigned to 28R it will be the meaning of 27R, and not the meaning of 28aR or 28bR. It might be thought that it is the presence of the contrastive adjectives in 7R-8R (or of the contrastive conjunction *a* in those same examples) which facilitates the nondefinite interpretation (since if the referent differs from the antecedent by some property or quality it must represent a token different from the one represented by the antecedent, and therefore cannot be definite), and that the absence of such cues in 28R is what disallows the nondefinite interpretation. But this would be incorrect, as can be seen from 29R, in which the adjectives do not contrast and the conjunction is the non-contrastive *u,* as well as from 9R, in which no adjective at all is present.

29R. Сережа держит красную ручку, и я тоже держу красную.
29E. Serezha is holding a red pen, and I am holding a red one, too.

In addition, 9R disconfirms the hypothesis that the pronoun ∅ can replace only a noun, not an NP, and must leave behind an adjective, determiner, or other explicit element of the NP: the entire object NP in the second part of 9R is replaced by ∅, and the nondefinite interpretation is not blocked. To explain this situation we must look further to the features which are under general consideration here and to the feature specifications of the referents in question. The referents of 7R, 8R, 9R, 28R, and 29R all have the feature [nondefinite], and the pronoun ∅ matches this, thus conveying that part of the feature specifications of the several referents. But the referents have, in addition, other features which must be expressed, and notable among these is number. It would seem, from the evidence at hand, that Russian pronominalization strategies, and those of many other languages as well, require the explicit expression of number wherever that category is distinguished (for further discussion of this question, see Channon 1982).[22] However, ∅ is not capable of expressing number, or of distinguishing between the two numbers, and thus, while it can satisfy the need to express the feature [nondefinite] of the referent, in a sense "absorbing" that part of the feature specification of the referent, it cannot "absorb" the number specification, and this remains unattached, waiting to be "absorbed" by something else. In those sentences like 7R, 8R, and 29R, in which only the noun is replaced by a pronoun and an adjective (contrastive or not) or determiner remains, the adjective or determiner can and does "absorb" and convey the number specification (i.e., the modifier left behind must still agree with what the noun would have been, and expresses the appropriate feature through its morphology). It may thus be significant, in light of this, that in English, where modifiers in general do not express the number of the head, zero-pronominalization is impossible in these cases, and the nondefinite pronoun *one/ones* is found instead; it should be noted, also, that this is just the context in which the somewhat curious plural form *ones* occurs. Examples 7R, 8R, and 29R, then, are well-formed sentences because all the necessary features of the referents have been taken up and expressed in some manner. In 28R, however, there is the need to express the number of the referent, but there is nothing available to express it; the sentence is thus not well-formed, because a feature (number) has been left hanging. Observe that, when a means of absorbing and expressing number is provided, sentences of the type of 28R (nondefinite antecedent, nondefinite referent) become perfectly acceptable, cf. 30R-33R.

30R. *Эрик видел оленя, и я тоже видел ∅.
30E. Erik saw a deer, and I saw one, too.

31R. Эрик видел двух оленей, и я тоже видел двух ∅.
31E. Erik saw two deer, and I saw two, too.

32R. Эрик видел пять оленей, а/и я видел шесть ∅.
32E. Erik saw five deer, and I saw six.

33R. Эрик видел мало оленей, а я видел много ∅.
33E. Erik saw few deer, but I saw many.

In 30R we again see the problem which was noticed earlier in 28R; 30R does not have the desired meaning (nondefinite referent) and, to the extent that it is accepted as a Russian sentence, it is construed as having a definite referent. Examples 31R-33R, however, are grammatical Russian sentences and are interpreted precisely as intended here, namely with a nondefinite referent in each case; they cannot be interpreted to have definite referents, especially in 32R and 33R, in which the quantity specified in the referent differs from that in the antecedent. In 31E-33E, in contrast to what was said above in the general case about the expression of number through modifiers in English, we have a special case in which modifiers (numerals) do express number, and it is just here that we find the possibility of zero-pronominalization for nondefinites, since number is otherwise accounted for. It remains to explain why 9R, with ∅ used for nondefinite anaphora and with no part of the referent NP present, is well-formed and can have the intended nondefinite interpretation. For this we must look back to the discussion at the beginning of this study of the interaction of the various features with each other and their positions in the hierarchy of features. As was stated there, the feature number is not defined for nondiscrete items, and *сахар*, being a mass noun, will be specified as [nondiscrete]; the referent of 9R being nondiscrete, it thus will not have any specification for number and will not require any in its anaphor, and so therefore ∅ can be used without any accompanying element expressing number. The same situation obtains in the case of collective nouns, which are also undefined for number, cf. 34R.

34R. Алик купил клубнику, и я тоже купил ∅.
34E. Alex bought some strawberries, and I bought some, too.

As has been seen above, ∅, which is commonly used to express nondefinite anaphora in Russian, cannot be used for this purpose in sentences like 28, although the meaning of 28 can be expressed through repetition of the noun or NP (i.e., by abandoning the attempt at pronominalization), as in 28aR and 28bR. Russian has, however, other strategies for expressing distinctions such as those between 27 and 28, including, e.g., the adverbs *тоже* and *также*, and the pronouns *тот/та/то же* and *то же*. In the case of the latter, the forms with full number/gender agreement represent definite referents (like those in 27), while the invariant (for number/gender) form *то же* stands for indefinite referents (like those in 28). Limitations of space prevent a discussion of sentences of these types here, but some examples are given below in 35-38; more about this will be found in Channon, forthcoming.

35R. Алик прочитал интересную пьесу, и я прочитал ту же.
35E. Alex read an interesting play, and I read it (the same one), too.
36R. Алик прочитал интересную пьесу, и я прочитал то же.
36E. Alex read an interesting play, and I read one (the same thing), too.
37R. Алик видел человека с ребенком в руках, и я видел того же.
37E. Alex saw a man with a child in his arms, and I saw him (the same one), too.

38R. Алик видел человека с ребенком в руках, и я видел то же.
38E. Alex saw a man with a child in his arms, and I saw one (the same thing), too.

In this sketch we have looked at some of the features which define the Russian and English anaphoric systems, and at how these features combine to specify individual anaphoric pronouns. We have seen that there is a means for dealing with situations in which the feature specifications of the referents are unclear or contradictory, and we have seen how the interaction of the features which define the systems may cause certain forms of pronominalization to be possible in one language, but not in the other. We have been able, within the limits of this study, to present only a few of the considerations and situations which are relevant to this topic, and the subject calls for further investigation.

University of Chicago

NOTES

[1] Except, of course, for instances of personification, especially the frequent use of *she* in referring to countries and to ships.

[2] A limited number of items must be marked in the lexicon as having the feature [masculine] or [feminine] (e.g., *man/woman, king/queen, bull/cow*), and an additional limited group must either be so marked in the lexicon or marked for taking an unproductive suffix (e.g., *lion/lioness, poet/poetess, aviator/aviatrix*); but gender is not systematically expressed through the syntax or the grammar in English, as it is, for example, in Russian, or as it is among the English anaphoric pronouns *he/she*. Note, also, that the *he/she* distinction applies not only to words of the type above which are marked as [masculine] or [feminine], but also to such words as *person, parent, child, worker, lawyer*, etc., which have only one form and are inherently unmarked for gender.

[3] In colloquial Russian subject and/or object pronouns can optionally be dropped under certain conditions. The Ø forms in these sentences are intended to represent full, underlying forms, and in those senses the Ø forms are ungrammatical, though not in the colloquial senses with dropped object pronouns. This distinction is discussed below.

[4] The pronouns here and subsequently are cited in their nominative forms, but these should be taken as referring to the entire paradigm; thus, *he* stands for *he/him/his*, *он* stands for *он/его/ему/...*, etc.

[5] This is in no way intended to suggest a choice among the competing claims about the origin of pronouns mentioned earlier. In any of the models proposed a pronoun ultimately must be aassociated with an NP whose occurrence it is taken to stand for, regardless of whether that NP consists of a deleted full NP, a base-generated element marked [+PRO], a referential index, or anything else.

[6] The term "definiteness" as used here is the familiar syntactic designation which is expressed in many NPs in a language like English through the choice of definite or indefinite article. The reader should bear in mind, though, the following effects that the specification of definiteness has *on a referent*: [definite] *in a referent* means that the tokens designated by the referent are the same as those designated by the antecedent, while [indefinite] *in a referent* means that the tokens designated are not necessarily the same as those designated by the antecedent.

[7] It may be argued that the relevant feature in English is humanness, rather than animacy, but animacy will be used here, since pronouns such as *he/she* can and frequently do refer to animals. A counterposition to this is, of course, that in just those instances where these pronouns are used for animals we are dealing with personification or "humanization" of the animal. A third possibility is that both features may have to be specified for the English system. The resolution of this matter is not important for our purposes.

[8] Except for personification; cf. note 1.

[9] Even if the English feature were also taken as "human," the basic point here would remain the same, namely, that the feature does not function in the same way in the two languages.

[10] Here and throughout this study, the feature names are used somewhat loosely, without reference to markedness values, and the designations "+" and "–" will not be used. Precisely which value of the feature is marked in which language is not the issue here, and potential problems of nomenclature can be avoided (e.g., [+singular] vs. [-plural]). The features will be labeled here with opposing designations as follows: *definite/nondefinite, discrete/nondiscrete, singular/plural, animate/inanimate, masculine/feminine/neuter*. The term "nondefinite" is used to avoid confusion with "indefinite" as in "indefinite pronoun."

[11] There is also another use of *some* in English, which is [nondefinite], [discrete], and [plural], as in i.

i. Irene saw three rabbits, and I saw some, too.

Examples of this type and their Russian counterparts will be discussed further below.

[12] Since gender is subordinated to number in the Russian system, the fact that ∅ is unmarked for number means that it necessarily will also be unmarked for gender.

[13] Since this investigation deals with pronouns and not ellipsis, no attempt is made here to discuss the differences among such examples or the constraints on which elements are not freely omissible in which contexts. It suffices for our purpose that such elliptical forms exist.

[14] The ∅ which arises from deletion of a non-zero pronoun could, in a sense, be regarded as a second-order pronoun or "pro-pronoun"; whether or not this would have any useful consequences is open to investigation.

[15] It is morphologically "neuter" *это* only, not the masculine, feminine or true neuter form, which is used in this way. This form is unspecified for gender, number, and person in the underlying structure, and a later rule marks it as [neuter], [singular], and [3rd person], as with other such unspecified elements in Russian. This use is also not to be confused with the deictic uses as an anaphoric pronoun (*тот/этот*: 'the former'/'the latter', or 'this one' as opposed to 'that one') or with adjectival uses (*этот карандаш/эта книга/это зеркало*, etc.). Cf. also the use with unspecified features (gender, number) in i.

i. Что *это*? Это карандаш/книга/зеркало/карандаши/книги/зеркала.

[16] The variant without the pronoun is probably more usual, but it represents deletion of an object pronoun, not an occurrence of the pronoun ∅.

[17] There is a reading of this sentence on which *его* is grammatical, but in that case *его* would refer to *Сережа*, not to the clause *Сережа не хочет напрасно тревожить жену*. In the reading with the clause as referent *его* is ungrammatical. Also, in this use, *это* apparently must appear; the variant with object pronoun deletion (... *и я понимаю*.) seems strange.

[18] The precise nature of the constraint(s) on the occurrence of *он/она/оно* is a matter for further investigation and will not be treated here.

[19] Or, in other terms, they designate both types and tokens of those types.

[20] There is no overt indication in Russian of the definiteness or nondefiniteness of the antecedent here. It can be taken as being definite, too, but the nondefinite interpretation is the one under discussion here and in 28, as seen in the English versions; the supporting context with the adjectives *интересную* and *новую* helps to promote the nondefinite interpretation.

[21] The sentence is ungrammatical on the reading in which the referent is taken as nondefinite; if the referent is taken as definite, of course, the sentence has a grammatical reading, as in 27aR. As in 27, the antecedent is to be taken as nondefinite.

[22] The morphological expression of number in Russian is interrelated with the expression of gender, but it is number alone, rather than gender or number/gender, which is required, as will be seen below.

REFERENCES

Channon, Robert
1980 "Anaphoric *that*: A Friend in Need" in J. Kreiman and A. Ojeda, eds., *Chicago Linguistic Society: Papers from the Parasession on Pronouns and Anaphora*. Chicago, 98-109.
1982 "On the English Pronoun *∅*" in Kevin Tuite, Robinson Schneider, and Robert Chametzky, eds., *Chicago Linguistic Society: Papers from the Eighteenth Regional Meeting*. Chicago, 61-71c.
Forthcoming "On the Expression of Nondefinite Anaphora in Russian."
Dougherty, Ray C.
1969 "An Interpretive Theory of Pronominal Reference," *Foundations of Langage* 5, 488-519.
Fillmore, Charles J.
1969 "Types of Lexical Information" in Ferenc Kiefer, ed., *Studies in Syntax and Semantics*. Dordrecht, 109-137.
Hankamer, Jorge and Ivan Sag
1976 "Deep and Surface Anaphora," *Linguistic Inquiry* 7, 391-428.
Jackendoff, Ray S.
1972 *Semantic Interpretation in Generative Grammar*. Cambridge, Mass.
Katz, Jerrold J. and Jerry A. Fodor
1963 "The Structure of a Semantic Theory," *Language* 39, 170-210.
Langacker, Ronald W.
1969 "On Pronominalization and the Chain of Command" in David A. Reibel and Sanford A. Schane, eds., *Modern Studies in English: Readings in Transformational Grammar*. Englewood Cliffs, N.J., 160-186.
Lees, Robert B. and Edward S. Klima
1963 "Rules for English Pronominalization," *Language* 39, 17-28.
McCawley, James D.
1970 "Where Do Noun Phrases Come From?" in Roderick Jacobs and Peter Rosenbaum, eds., *Readings in English Transformational Grammar*. Waltham, Mass., 166-183.
Wasow, Thomas
1975 "Anaphoric Pronouns as Bound Variables," *Language* 51, 368-384.

On 'Definiteness' in Bulgarian, English and Russian

Catherine V. Chvany

1. 'Definiteness' as a multivalent, global concept.
  Like other terms of traditional metalanguage, "definiteness" and "indefiniteness" have been used in linguistics as undefined primitives. As informal, scalar parameters, or as formal, discrete features (e.g., *[±definite]*, or *[±indefinite]*, or both pairs), they are mentioned as conditions on rules in many languages; the doubling of South Slavic objects, English *THERE*-insertion, Russian genitive/accusative case choice are familiar examples. The view that the definite article is the grammaticalized morphological expression of a concept called "definiteness" is widespread, and the term *definite* serves as convenient shorthand for disparate meanings associated with the definite noun phrase (noun phrase with definite article): *thematic, identified, given, unique, total,* as well as *referential, specified, specific* — though indefinite noun phrases can also be referential and specific. The range of "definiteness" extends far beyond the article even in those languages that possess it (Galton 1973, 5), and the distribution of the articles over lexico-semantic groups varies from language to language.[1] "Indefiniteness," moreover, is not simply the absence, or the contradictory, of "definiteness," corresponding to a zero-morph or to an indefinite article. The two articles, in those language that have both, relate to different semantic spheres: the definite article — to communicative context, the indefinite article — to linguistically encoded quantifiers.[2] Typological linguistic studies of "definiteness/indefiniteness" or "determinacy/indeterminacy" (henceforth D/I) have concentrated on the contexts of the article and its correlates in translations into languages without articles. It is well-known that D/I interacts with word order and phrasal stress (*Na stole stojala lámpa.* 'There was a lamp on the table.' *Lampa stojala na stolé.* 'The lamp stood on the/a table.' — the latter requiring contextual or situational identification of the lamp for a successful communication); that is, D/I is closely bound with the information-bearing structure of discourse. Another well-known correlation in Russian is that of definite direct objects with perfective aspect, accusative case and holistic interpretation, while imperfective aspect, genitive case and partitive interpretations associate with indefiniteness. Besides these and other well-known syntactic and morphological correlates of D/I, Revzin (1978, II) has shown that definite noun phrases are preferred triggers of agreement and reflexivization.[3] Summing up the correlates of D/I as they appear in contrastive studies, Revzin concludes (1978, 237):

(1) ... "the category of D/I is arranged in Russian as a *field*, i.e., as *a group of lexical and grammatical means having* as a rule *other functions as well*. [...] It is worth noting that in [...] typological comparison one finds an *isomorphism* between the manifestations of the category in languages with a fully grammaticalized article and systems like Russian, where the meaning of 'definiteness/ indefiniteness' has mainly a 'covert' (in Whorf's sense) expression." *(My emphasis, CVC.)*

For Revzin, as for the scholars represented in the 1979 volume edited by Nikolaeva, the definite article is the cardinal expression of definiteness; other systems of D/I are viewed in opposition to the article as less fully realized, less fully grammaticalized.

For the purposes of this paper I adopt Revzin's concept of field or global property, which is as applicable to languages with articles as it is to Russian; otherwise there would not be the isomorphism noted in (1).

2. D/I as a ubiquitous ordinary-language category.

At the same time, for the reasons outlined above, I do not equate the ideal expression of D/I with the articles. To say, as Revzina does (1979, 82), that "the opposition ... is limited to the noun" is to prejudge the issue. While it is true that only nouns (or noun phrases) have articles, one cannot assume, *a priori*, either a congruence of "definiteness" with the inherent meaning of the definite article, or the exclusion of D/I from other parts of speech. Instead of using D/I as a primitive from which to derive disparate morphosyntactic phenomena, I turn this tradition upside down. My working assumption is that D/I is not a linguistic primitive. The article is only one of several morphosyntactic contexts from which the cluster of meanings grouped together as D/I may be derivable in whole or in part. It is therefore essential to separate the manifestations of D/I from the semiotic value of the article. (As will be seen below, such an approach to D/I meanings in the Bulgarian verb system is already well established.)

Some grammars of languages possessing the article also categorize verb forms as "definite" or "indefinite," though not systematically. An earlier opposition in terms of definite and indefinite tenses (for temporal pinpointing vs. emphasis on result) is still reflected in French terminology, though today *le passé défini* is limited to third person narrative, *temps d'histoire, temps de récit*, while *le passé indéfini* has become colloquial narrative tense as well as *temps de discours, temps de commentaire* (Benveniste 1966, I; Fontaine 1978). In Bulgarian, the so-called "direct" or "witnessed" tenses, the aorist and imperfect, are often called "definite" because they relate events to specific time frames — at least in declarative main clauses. The aorist, according to Stankov 1965, "cannot be used without bringing to mind the event as it occurred in time." The perfect lacks this property and is traditionally called *minalo neopredeleno vreme* "past indefinite tense." Since no morpheme or set of paradigms can be consistently related to a D/I contrast, the classification into definite and indefinite tenses found in earlier grammars (e.g., Mladenov and Vasilev 1939) is abandoned in recent descriptions, which treat the unstable and elusive D/I meanings in terms of more basic temporal, aspectual and modal categories from which connotations of definiteness or indefiniteness are said to be predictable in context (Andrejčin 1957; Stankov 1965 and 1969; Andrejčin *et al.* 1977, representing a number of pedagogical and reference grammars). Mention of D/I in connection with English verb forms is more sporadic (e.g., Atanasova *et al.* 1963, contrasting Bulgarian and English; Diver 1963, who points out that "definite" *be ...-ing* is more compatible with definite noun phrases than indefinite ones, while "indefinite" *have ...-en* has the opposite collocational restrictions). Revzin (1978, 261) relates indefiniteness in German *es* to impersonality in Russian verbs; his observations are as applicable to English impersonal sentences with *it*. Axmanova's dictionary of linguistic terms (1966, 262 and 292) applies *neopredelennyj* and *opredelennyj* to articles, pronouns, persons, numerals, and endings, as well as to the determinate/indeterminate verbs of motion (*xodit', idti* would be respectively in the *neopredelenno-nesoveršennyj* and *opredelenno-nesoveršennyj vid*); the traditional name of the infinitive is *neopredelennaja forma* or *neopredelennoe naklonenie* "indefinite mode." Sentences may be *neopredelenno-ličnye,* those whose unspecified human subject is expressed only in plural verb endings (*Govorjat, čto ... 'They say that .../It is said that ...'; Mne skazali, čto ... 'They told me that/I was told that ...'*), while sentences whose definite recoverable pronoun subject is elliptical are *opredelenno-ličnye.* A similar range is found in Rozental' and Telenkova 1972. Axmanova's fuller listing includes *neopredelennyj glasnyj,* for a schwa-like vowel; *opredelennyj vid,* another term for the perfective aspect; and *opredelennoe vremja* defined as "*to že, čto perfekt.*" (Though no language-specific perfect tense is mentioned, Axmanova must be referring, not to the traditionally indefinite English or Bulgarian perfects, but rather to the Latin perfect, which corresponds to the Bulgarian aorist: *Veni, vidi, vici = Dojdoh, vidjah, pobedih.*) The unsystematic use of the terms in a wide range of meanings confirms the view of Bulgarian linguists, that D/I as such is not encoded in verbal systems. Still, the frequent appearance of the terms in descriptions of linguistic entities cannot be completely disregarded in a discussion of D/I.

Let us now consider the technical-terminological uses listed above in terms of ordinary-language meanings listed in dictionaries:[4] *Opredelennyj: (1) participle of opredelit' 'define' (=defined); (2) tverdo/točno ustanovlennyj; naznačennyj (=firmly/precisely established; determined); (3) točnyj, jasnyj (=precise, clear); (4) javnyj, očevidnyj; nesomnennyj, bezuslovnyj (=manifest, obvious; unquestionable, unconditional); (5) predpolagaemyj izvestnym (=assumed or presupposed to be known); (6) tot ili inoj, nekotoryj, izvestnyj (=one or another, a certain, 'izvestnyj' in the 'uncertain' sense)*. Meaning *(6)* could be called "indefinite"; it is almost antonymous with meaning *(3)*. Space does not permit reproducing definitions from Bulgarian and English dictionaries, but the meanings of Russian *opredelennyj* seem to cover the range of Bulgarian *opredelen* and English *definite*, though meaning *(3)* is less prominently featured in Bulgarian, while meaning *(6)* is less accessible in English. *Neopredelennyj, neopredelen, indefinite* have the opposite meanings, plus additional grammatical and mathematical uses.

It should be clear that different meanings of these terms are applied in different contexts, including linguistic terminology. Definiteness in nouns is associated, among other things, with identifiability of a referent. Krámský says: "It is well-known that the definite article expresses a sufficient determination of the noun which presupposes the hearer's familiarity with that which the noun designates" (1972, 39). But the referent is not necessarily an individual, for the definite article always has a generic use as well; Krámský (1972, 63) says that generic use is criterial for articlehood; it is the culmination of the development of an article from a demonstrative, cf. also Ivančev (1957/1978). Definiteness in nouns is associated with given information, whether in theme or rheme, foregrounded or backgrounded sentences. Both the definite noun and verbal tense involve deixis, some kind of pointing. In tenses, definiteness is associated with precision, with temporal pinpointing from which an identifiable occurrence may be inferred; or else with pointing to a specific occurrence for which a location in time or space could be supplied.[5] In the non-deictic aspectual D/I oppositions listed in Axmanova, definiteness is associated with greater informativeness or specificity in one cateogry, indefiniteness with lack of specification; some of Axmanova's definites — perfective aspect, determinate motion verbs — correspond to the marked members of oppositions (Jakobson 1957), i.e., to those members which are not only semantically more informative but syntactically more constrained than their indefinite, imperfective or indeterminate counterparts. In narratives, D/I distributes differently in verbs and nouns; while definite noun phrases are the normal carriers of *given* information, the marked verb forms associated with definiteness tend to carry *new* information, in the non-thematic part of the sentence.

Nikolaeva (1979, 9) points out that scholars who maintain a binary opposition (as manifested in the article or articles of a particular language), generally agree that definiteness is the unmarked, less informative member. It may seem paradoxical that definiteness in nouns should be unmarked, while definiteness in verbs is associated with marked members of grammatical oppositions. This apparent contradiction is due to different conceptions of markedness, which should be kept distinct in grammatical and stylistic descriptions. I will return to various aspects of markedness in the conclusion, where I summarize the properties of the article, independently of D/I. For the moment, I merely point out that D/I has not been (and probably cannot be) related to a pair of features with a constant, invariant meaning. Nor can D/I be uniquely associated with any particular form, including the article, for D/I pervades all areas of language. Krámský (1972, 199) relates it to a psychological universal:

(2) ... "we can suppose that human speakers, irrespective of the language they speak, have in mind certain, definite, already known objects, or uncertain, indefinite, unknown objects. This kind of differentiation ... is reflected in their languages."

Krámský's study, like other linguistic studies of D/I focuses on the noun or noun phrase as the locus of the putatively ideal manifestation of D/I in the article. But we have seen that D/I is not limited to nouns. The generalization in (2) can be trivially extended from objects to events and situations. To cover such an extension, I rephrase Krámský's generalization as follows:

(3) Human speakers have in mind not only *objects,* but *events* and *situations,* some real, certain, pinpointed in time, located in space (properties which I will call *Salient*); others irreal, uncertain, without a specified temporal or spatial frame (or *Non-Salient*). These fundamental distinctions are reflected in languages via lexical and grammatical properties that tend to cluster together (hence Revzin's term "field") and are often associated in ordinary language use with the terms *definite* and *indefinite.*

D/I seems to be nothing more than a category of ordinary language, which human speakers use to assign structure to the world, to organize experience, without concern for tidy matchings of *definiteness* with some of the Salient properties, *indefiniteness* with Non-Salient ones.

"There is no other linguistic category that is expressed by such diverse means as the category of determinedness vs. indeterminedness," says Krámský, in concluding his typological survey of over 40 Indo-European and non-Indo-European languages (1972, 199). It is this very diversity that casts the strongest suspicion on the status of D/I as an autonomous linguistic sign. A category that means so many things and turns up everywhere is a poor candidate for a linguistic prime. If D/I were a sign, or a pair of signs, its potential *signantia* would include, besides lexical D/I features and the definite and indefinite articles, elusive manifestations at all levels of language. As candidates for *signata,* "definiteness" and "indefiniteness" are equally ubiquitous and elusive. D/I, viewed apart from the article, cannot be a prime. It can only be understood as a pair of rather loose cover terms for a variety of connotations due to the interplay of more basic grammatical and lexical properties.

The approach to D/I through its ordinary-language meanings, whether or not these meanings are reflected in technical terms as well, suggests a functional explanation for the Saliency/Non-Saliency poles, which subsume D/I, in the organization of discourse. It should not be surprising that the fundamental Saliency distinctions mentioned in (3), which are expressed in the major grammatical categories, play a role in foregrounding and backgrounding in connected narratives.[6] Real events involving certain, known, individual persons or objects are more likely to be viewed as important — and to be foregrounded in narratives — than are vague or hypothetical situations. Conversely, important events involving important objects (especially people) are more likely than unimportant ones to be attributed to specific participants at specific times and places. Thus, whether as cause or effect, various manifestations of Saliency, including D/I, interact not only with the given/new and theme/rheme distinctions, but also with foregrounding/backgrounding.

These observations receive empirical support from the typological work of Hopper and Thompson (1980). They find, in language after language, a systematic correlation between the grammatical properties of subjects and objects and other features of what they call "cardinal Transitive" sentences (equivalent to our "prototypical action sentence," see above, note 3); conscious, definite, referential agents and affected, definite, highly individuated objects tend to co-occur with active, punctual, telic verbs, indicative *(realis)* mode, and affirmative rather than negative status. Statistical analyses of narratives from typologically different languages of the world show that foregrounded sentences tend to approach this prototype, while backgrounded sentences are more likely to have missing participants, or else indefinite, abstract, unindividuated ones; these properties of participants co-vary with verbal categories from the opposite pole: stative, durative, atelic, irreal or negative. Hopper and Thompson's data from many languages (including Russian genitive/accusative marking, based on Timberlake 1975) show that properties from each pole are grammaticized together. Except for the fact that the focus of their attention is on the roles of subject and object, the overlap of their clustering properties with those associated with Saliency and D/I in (3) approaches congruence. Their convincing (to my mind) functional explanation is that since the clustering properties grade actions according to their effectiveness (the "cardinal Transitive" sentence most effectively transfers an action from an agentive subject to an affected object), it is not surprising that effective actions are featured more prominently in narratives than ineffective, negated or irreal ones. Their paper, with examples of the grammaticalization of the same co-varying properties across many languages (including several associated with D/I) provides an empirical basis for the notion foregrounding/backgrounding.[7]

Let us consider now the definite article, which we have separated from D/I. Under the assumption shared by the Prague School "that the natural condition of a language is to preserve one form for one meaning and one meaning for one form" (Bolinger 1977, x), there can be no doubt that the article is the *signans* of a linguistic sign whose *signatum* must be included in the reference of "definiteness," though it cannot be all of definiteness, since the latter is expressed in many other ways in addition to the article. The semiotic value of the article must be clearly distinguished from the semantics of D/I and Saliency/Non-Saliency.[8]

3. The articles and some other correlates of D/I.

Instead of the usual approach to D/I via the articles, I will examine a Russian text with no articles and its translations into Bulgarian and English. The following selections are from Marina Cvetaeva's *Moj Puškin*.[9] The semantics of some of the referential noun phrases, their role in textual cohesion, and the uses of certain verb forms, will be examined selectively, since space does not permit exhaustive analysis. But first, a few preliminaries. Reference requires a frame, and so does discussion of reference. Cvetaeva's text presupposes a basis of common knowledge, but much of that knowledge can be inferred from the text itself. She had no way of predicting her future readers' knowledge, and there are times when communication slows down and translators feel compelled to add footnotes. It is important to know at the outset that Cvetaeva (1892-1941), a Russian poet, is writing of her childhood in Moscow. Though she tells us that Puškin was a poet who was killed in a duel, prior knowledge of Puškin's life and of his importance in Russian literature is helpful background.

The first passage, from the opening page of Cvetaeva's essay, introduces the topic of the painting through which the three year old Marina first learned about Puškin:

(4)   Cvetaeva A
(a)   Но до тайного шкафа было другое, была картина в спальне матери —«Дуэль».
(b)   Снег, черные прутья деревец, двое черных людей проводят третьего, под мышки, к саням — а еще один, другой, спиной отходит. Уводимый —
(c)   Пушкин, отходящий — Дантес. Дантес вызвал Пушкина на дуэль, то есть заманил его на снег и там, между черных безлистых деревец, убил.

In sentence *(a)*, the post-verbal position signals the introduction of new information, normally a cue for an indefinite noun phrase. Yet both translations use definite articles, even as they keep the presentational word order of the Russian, ... *beše kartina**ta** v stajata na majka mi, there was **the** picture in mother's bedroom, "The Duel"* — not *there was **a** picture in mother's bedroom, "The Duel"* — which is also grammatical. The definite article is anaphoric, referring to the translations of *drugoe — something else, nešto drugo*, which are themselves presentational indefinites; they are also cataphoric, identified by the following apposition, the name of the painting. The use of the definite article makes the links explicit. In a presentational context where indefinites are normal, the definite form is the more expressive option.

The description of the picture in *(b)* takes the form of a list of nouns, translated without articles. Though situationally established, included in the reference of the picture, the details are presented as new information, in spite of the knowledge of the picture shared by the adult Cvetaeva and her probable readers; the indefinite nouns *(Snow, black sapling branches; snjag, černi prăti na drăvčeta)* thus take us back to the three-year-old's first memory of the picture and its story, when it *was* new information. The omitted articles in the translations make this explicit, but the mere volunteering of the information in Russian has a similar effect.

In *(c)* the Bulgarian text shifts, like the original, from present to past, but uses the indirect mode for Cvetaeva's account of her first version of the story: *Dantes **izvikal** Puškin na duel, to est **podmamil** go na snega i tam, meždu černite goli drăvčeta, go **ubil**.* This version, one for which Cvetaeva no longer takes personal responsibility, summarizes a number of early tellings.[10] (One of these is reproduced later in her mother's direct speech, not shown here.) This indirect version will be in sharp contrast with the forms in (6) and (7). The second mention of snow and saplings is clearly coreferential with that in *(b)*; the articles in the translations *(**the** snow, sneg**a**; **the** ... saplings, černi**te** ... drăvčeta)* explicitly but redundantly mark the identifiability of these nouns. If the articles were missing, however, there would be a break in cohesion.

Four paragraphs separate this introduction from the next passage, Cvetaeva B, shown below in four segments (5)(6)(7)(8), each juxtaposed with its translations.

(5)   Cvetaeva B

(a)   Черная с белым, без единого цветного пятна, материнская   (Ru) спальня, черное с белым окно: снег и прутья тех деревец, черная и белая картина — «Дуэль», где на белизне снега совершается черное

(b)   дело: вечное черное дело убийства поэта — чернью.

(a)   Черната с бяло, без нито едно цветно петно мамина спалня,   (Bu) черният с бяло прозорец: снегът и прътите на ония дръвчета, чернобялата картина — «Дуел», където върху белотата на снега се

(b)   извършва черно дело: вечно черното дело — убийството на поета — от сганта.

(a) Mother's bedroom, black and white without a single spot of color; the window, black and white: snow and the branches of the saplings, the picture, black and white: *The Duel*, where a black deed is accomplished on the snow's whiteness, the eternal black deed of the murder of a poet — by the dark mass.

Here Cvetaeva continues her account of childhood experiences connected with the picture. The first noun phrase is inherently definite, identifiable even without co-reference with the mention of mother's bedroom in (4): "child" presupposes a mother, a house with a room where the mother sleeps ... *okno, the window, černijat ... prozorec* seems to be inferable, included in the reference of *spal'nja*, for bedrooms normally have windows, windows normally look out on outdoor views, hence the snow, the trees ... A reader who does not heed the colon after *okno (:)*, or who hears the text read aloud, will be led on unsuspecting until the chain of inferences is suddenly interrupted, not by an indefinite, but by a definite demonstrative, *TEX derevec, na ONIJA drăvčeta*; an extra article in English *the branches of THE saplings*; and by *derevec, saplings,* not the more general *derev'ev, trees* one would expect if the author were describing an actual window and its view. *Okno, the window,* with its equational colon, is not merely the window of the bedroom. It is the picture itself which is a window onto that eternally black and white snow scene, the duel in which Puškin was killed. This "window" has blended in dreamlike memory with the actual window of the bedroom, just as the picture's color scheme has extended over the memory of the actual room (which must have had at least some brown wood in it, and a window whose view changed with the seasons). This passage illustrates the difference between a demonstrative, which points to a specific item, and a definite noun phrase, which says no more than "search the context, a referent is identifiable."

The final clause *(b)* shifts from the specific to the generic. Consider the first instance of *černoe delo, černo delo, a black deed.* Here an indefinite interpretation is prompted, but not forced, by the post-verbal presentational word order, which is preserved in Bulgarian, rendered by a passive in English. The Russian is grammatically open to interpretation as *černoto delo,* **the** *black deed,* but that would suggest an appeal to common knowledge that a duel is a black (bad) deed,[11] and an expectation that the following context would be limiting (to Puškin), rather than generalizing. The indefinite forms in the translations explicitly present the equation *duel=black deed* as Cvetaeva's own — as a new one, not the usual stereotyped association of bad with black, and this is borne out by her play on *černoe/ čern'ju,* as well as in her original and ambivalent use of *černyj* throughout the essay. Black is bad when associated with *čern'ju,* the dark undifferentiated mass of others; but in several other passages, not reproduced here, black is good when associated with the individual, Puškin, e.g., in references to his heritage (*Puškin byl negr*), or to the blackness of the Puškin monument. The classification of the duel as a black deed does not draw on presuppositions about duels or blackness. The explicit or implicit classifier (*a* in English, the zero article in Bulgarian by virtue of opposition), makes up in part for the lost pairing of *černoe/čern'ju*. The last part of the equation is interpreted generically, without help from articles in Russian, for *večnoe* cues this interpretation. These last noun phrases illustrate the lack of clear demarcation between individual and generic usage. *Večnoe černoe delo, večno černoto delo, the eternal black deed* is cataphoric, pointing forward to the metonymic representation of the duel as one of a class of events. Though the phrase recapitulates the earlier *černoe delo* and is thus deictic in some sense, it is not referential but attributive: it modifies *ubijstva poèta, the murder of a poet, ubijstvoto na poeta,* in spite of the fact that the modified poet is subordinated to its attribute. *Večnoe černoe delo* is metonymically related both to the preceding and the following context; but the latter, *ubijstvo poèta čern'ju,* is also a metaphor for the plight of the lone poet, including Cvetaeva herself (cf. the line *Odna iz vsex — za vsex — protivu vsex!* — from her *Rolandov rog*). The English and Bulgarian differ in one element: English uses an indefinite generic *a (any) poet,* unavailable in Bulgarian, where only definite generics occur and *ubijstvoto na poeta (... of the poet)* is ambiguous. The article on *the murder* is almost obligatory (*?a murder of a poet* is barely acceptable), conditioned by the following prepositional phrase; it is hard to say what is semantically definite about it — *the murder of a poet* is equivalent to *a poet's murder* (except that a preposed poet becomes ambiguous between agent and patient readings). *Čern', sganta, **the** dark mass,* an undifferentiated mass noun, does not distinguish individual from generic — it is a one-member genus, and it refers not only to that genus, the eternal killer of the generic poet, but also to the dark mass we know, the dark threat to Cvetaeva the poet, the sum of all the others opposed to the individual. The reader is left free to identify with either one.

All the noun phrases in the next segment (6) are definite, the proper name, and the possessive ones; but only Bulgarian allows an article to co-occur with a possessive.

(6)   Cvetaeva B

    (a)   Пушкин был мой первый поэт,
    (b)   и моего первого поэта — убили.

    (a)   Пушкин беше моят първи поет
    (b)   и моя първи поет го убиха.

    (a)   Puškin was my first poet
    (b)   and my first poet was killed.

The contrast *(a) mojat, (b) moja* is said to distinguish subject from object, the *-t* of the article preserved on subjects, lost in other positions. Strangely, the attributive rather than referential Bulgarian subject in *(a)* corresponds both positionally and semantically to the Russian predicate, for in Russian only *moj pervyj poèt* could appear in the instrumental case *(moim pervym poètom)*, while *Puškinym* would be impossible in *(a)* regardless of word order. In Russian, the subject-predicate relation is determined semantically: the predicate is the including class, the subject is the individual or the included class. In Bulgarian, grammatical subjecthood — as reflected in the form of the article — is apparently less dependent on semantics than it is in Russian, and less dependent on word order than it is in English.

In *(b)* Russian marks the initial noun phrase as object, with the animate accusative case. English passivizes, in keeping with the tendency of its themes to become subjects as well. Bulgarian keeps the original word order and active voice, marking the topicalized noun phrase as object, not only with the form of the article,[12] but with the reduplicated object: *Moja părvi poet GO ubiha*. Since the article in Bulgarian developed concurrently with the loss of case inflections, it is not surprising that the article and other deictic morphemes have taken on some of the functional load of the cases. The article and the clitic pronoun, both associated with D/I, thus have other functions besides that of marking definiteness. The article helps distinguish subject from nonsubject where position offers no cue. Otherwise, the definite articles in the translations of this text *add nothing* to its meaning or cohesion, though the *omission* of the article from *(b)* would disturb this cohesion, causing a break in communication.

The doubled object marks the prominence of a non-subject theme only if that theme is identified, with a preference for human referents; reduplication is available only for individuated, referential, specific noun phrases — those Salient ones traditionally called definite. Here grammatical rules interact with the anthropocentric features of individuation. The doubled object also interacts with discourse structure, for Ivančev 1968 has shown that the Bulgarian pronoun forms potentially partition the information-bearing structure of a sentence into "exposition," "transit," "culmination." He points out that the doubled pronouns *(mene me, nego go)* occur only in the exposition; clitics alone *(me, go)* only in the transit; full forms alone *(men, nego)* only in the culmination. As Ivančev points out, this supports Firbas' tripartition into "theme proper," "transition," and "rheme proper" (cf. Firbas 1966, 278 n. 18 and references therein).

Russian has only one past tense to choose from: *ubil* in (4), *ubili* here in (6); English is forced to use a passive to preserve the preverbal position of the patient. But Bulgarian offers an opportunity not available in the original, a striking contrast to the indirect *ubil* in the translation of (4). That first account of the duel was only a report; now with *ubiha* Cvetaeva speaks as an eyewitness. The pinpointing aorist shows the effect on the child Cvetaeva of the punctual event permanently frozen in the picture. Of all clauses in the cited passages (5)–(8), this clause, with its definite, thematic, affected object and punctual definite action verb, scores highest on the Hopper and Thompson scale of effectiveness. It is also the most foregrounded sentence. The next paragraph continues the use of the aorist and imperfect, their connotation of witnessing supported by *na moix glazax, pred očite mi, before my very eyes* in (7a) below:

(7)   Cvetaeva B

(a) С тех пор, да, с тех пор, как Пушкина на моих глазах на картине Наумова — убили, ежедневно, ежечасно, непрерывно убивали все мое
(b) младенчество, детство, юность — я поделила мир на поэта — и всех, и выбрала — поэта, в подзащитные выбрала поэта: защищать поэта
(c) — от всех, как бы' эти все ни одевались и ни назывались.

(a) Оттогава, да, оттогава, откак пред очите ми убиха Пушкин в картината на Наумов, ежедневно, ежечасно, непрестанно убиваха цялото
(b) ми детство, ученичество, младост — аз разделих света на поета — и всички, и избрах поета, взех поета под своя закрила: да браня поета от
(c) всички, както и да се обличаха, както и да се наричаха.

(a) From then on, yes, from then on, since the time in Naumov's picture, when, before my very eyes, they killed Puškin, and every day, every hour,
(b) unceasingly they kept killing my whole infancy, childhood, and youth, I have divided the world into the poet — and all of *them*, and I have chosen —
(c) the poet, have chosen the poet to be among those I defend: to defend the poet — from all of *them*, however they all are garbed, however they all are named.

The entire passage is in the direct, 'witnessed' mode, even though only the first line's *ubiha* refers to a specific, if metaphoric, witnessing. The generalized *ubivaha* and the following verbs refer to personally experienced feelings, changes and decisions set in motion by that first witnessed event. But the last clauses in *(c)* have nothing to do with witnessing or with definite time; the *H*-tense in these suspended assertions points only to the temporal context of the main clauses, with no reference to the moment of speech (see note 5).

Cvetaeva's *poèt* in *(b)* continues the metonymic association first made in (5b), between the poet in the picture and the poet in general. By using a singular generic (rather than a plural *poètov*), she refers not only to the class of poets but to each member of the class standing alone against the mass of non-poets. The inclusion of Cvetaeva herself in the reference of that noun is inescapable, in the immediate context as well as in echoes of her poetry — *Moj Puškin* is autobiography.

The play on *poèt* again illustrates the non-discreteness of the specific and generic within the singular noun phrase in Russian and its counterparts with the definite article in Bulgarian and English. If one looks only at a language with articles, one may be led to assign some role to the article, to claim that its connotations of individuality and uniqueness turn the noun into a metonymic pronoun. But we can see from the Russian, as well as from the translations where specific and generic nouns have the same article, that the article itself contributes nothing: the potential for denoting type or token is inherent in the noun, not the article.

The final section of the passage, shown in (8) below, provides the context for the two noun phrases *"Kreščenie", "Krăštenieto",* the Baptism at *(b)*, and *rebenka, deteto, a child,* at *(c)*.

(8)   *(Italics mine, CVC.)* Cvetaeva B

Три таких картины были в нашем трехпрудном доме: в столовой —
(a) «Явление Христа народу», с никогда не разрешенной загадкой совсем маленького и непонятно-близкого, совсем близкого и непонятно-маленького Христа; вторая, над нотной этажеркой в зале — «Татары» — татары в белых балахонах, в каменном доме без окон, между белых столбов убивающие главного татарина («Убийство Цезаря») и — в спальне матери — «Дуэль». Два убийства и одно явление. И все
(b) три были страшные, непонятные, угрожающие, и *«Крещение»* с никогда не виденными черными кудрявыми орлоносыми голыми людьми и детьми, так заполнившими реку, что капли воды не осталось, было не менее страшное тех двух, — и все они отлично готовили
(c) *ребенка* к предназначенному ему страшному веку.

Три такива картини имаше в нашия дом на улица «Тръохпрудная»: в
(a) столовата «Явлението на Христа пред народа», с така и останалия си загадка съвсем малък и непонятно-близък, съвсем близък и непонятно-малък Христос; втората над нотната етажерка в приемната — «Татари» — татари с бели наметала, в каменна къща без прозорци, между бели колони, убиват главатаря си («Убийството на Цезар») и в спалнята на майка ми — «Дуэл». Две убийства и едно явление. И
(b) всичките три бяха страшни, непонятни, плашещи, и *«Кръщението»* с тези никога невиждани дотогава черни, къдроглави, орлоноси голи хора и деца, така запълнили реката, че капка вода не бе останала, беше не по-малко страшно от другите две — и всички те великолепно
(c) подготвяха *детето* за предопределения му страшен житейски път.

There were three pictures like that in our house on Three Ponds Lane: in
(a) the dining room — *Christ Revealed to the People* with the ever-unsolved

riddle of the utterly tiny and incomprehensibly-near, utterly near and incomprehensibly-tiny Christ; the second picture, above the music shelf in the ballroom — *"Tartars,"* Tartars in white robes, in a stone house without windows, killing the chief Tartar among the white columns *(The Killing of Caesar)*; and — in mother's bedroom — *The Duel.* Two killings and one
(b) revelation. And all three were frightening, incomprehensible, threatening, even the Baptism with people and children the like of which I had never seen, black, curly-haired, aquiline-nosed, naked, filling up the river so full that not a drop of water remained; *The Baptism* was no less frightening than
(c) those other two — and all of them prepared *a child* very thoroughly for the frightening era preordained for it.

    The capitalized proper name *"Kreščenie"* in the Russian forces a search for a referent. The articles in the translations say nothing that isn't already said by the proper name: the Bulgarian text could have had a proper name without an article, *Krăštenie Xristovo,* sending the reader on the same quest. These nouns say only that there is an identifiable referent, but they do not locate it. Linguistically they could be anaphors of something in the text, or they could be exophoric, referring to something in the situation or in the frame of reference. Our expectation of coherence leads us to search the text: cohesion is the norm, unmarked. (Indefinite forms, on the other hand, would signal a break, a new thread, and would cause some confusion: *Krăštenie, Baptism* — has a fourth painting been introduced out of nowhere?) Three pictures are mentioned at the beginning of (8). *"The Duel"* we already know — no possible relation to baptism there; *"The Killing of Caesar",* with Romans already identified by the child as Tartars, is also an unlikely co-referent for *the Baptism,* though its renaming alerts the reader to the possibility of other renamings. That leaves (a) *"Christ Revealed to the People."* Since *vse tri, all three* is repeated just before *"Kreščenie,"* the latter can't be a fourth picture mentioned as an afterthought or by mistake. From textual evidence, we can infer that there was a painting, popular enough in the 19th century to have been reproduced in black and white (if *takix* refers to *černaja s belym*), entitled *"Christ Revealed to the People,"* which depicts a baptism, an activity we can associate with Christ from extra-textual knowledge, even if the word *Kreščenie, Krăštenieto, the Baptism* (unlike *Kreščenie Xristovo*) does not tell us who is being baptized. If the picture had been called by another of its names, *Bogojavlenie,* the reader's detective work would have readily identified the same painting, but the description of people in water might not have made sense unless one knew that the reproduction of the canvas by A. A. Ivanov (1806-1858) *Javlenie messii narodu* depicts the meeting between Christ and John the Baptist at the river Jordan, where John baptizes Christ, and the heavens open and declare Christ to be the Son of God, an event commemorated in the Orthodox Church as the feast called *Bogojavlenie.*

On a first cursory reading, the Bulgarian translation caused some confusion. One native speaker stopped and wondered if *"Krăštenieto"* — which is preceded by the conjunction-particle *i* — could be a fourth picture, perhaps part of a triptych. Another source of temporary confusion was *(c) deteto*, which seemed to associate with *deca,* the children in the picture, leading one to wonder if the reference could be to a baptized child, or to Christ — an impression reinforced by the cliche *strašen žitejski păt,* suggesting Calvary. A second reading cleared this up, bringing a suggestion that *deteto* should have been *men, deteto,* 'me, the child', (or possible *edno dete,* for which generic interpretation is, however, not available), to avoid possible co-reference with *deca.* An expectation of coherence can lead one to assign co-reference incorrectly, leading to temporary incoherence. The definite article does not prevent confusion of sense and reference; it can in fact lead to it. A definite *the child* would have caused similar confusion in English: the context, with the past tense verb *gotovili, prepared, podgotvjaha,* suggests a non-generic object, while the imperfective cues an indefinite interpretation. Extra-textual knowledge of the painting, or of Christ's age at baptism, would have prevented misunderstanding; but other elements interfered with correct interpretation, if only momentarily, as in the chain, *Christ — strašen žitejski păt — Calvary.* A more literal translation of *vek* would have maintained the association of the original with the historical events of Cvetaeva's lifetime. The Russian *rebenka,* without a misleading article, does not invite co-reference with *det'mi,* partly because of the dissimilar roots, partly because there is no obvious collocation of this particular word with baptism, as there might have been with *mladenec,* or with *novoroždennyj.* It is clear that Cvetaeva is including herself in the reference of the generically used *rebenka*; she is presenting — classifying — her past self as a child being prepared for the terrible era ahead. Shared knowledge of the historical events of Cvetaeva's later life contributes to the pleasure of interpretation but is not necessary. The text informs the reader that the era ahead of the child was terrible, or would be terrible; either a real or a hypothetical intepretation is possible. But it is not possible to separate textual from extra-textual information. In using lexical items like *Xristos,* or *Kreščenie,* whose dictionary definitions include varying amounts of encyclopedic information, it is impossible to predict to what degree a hearer's definition will match the speaker's intended or unintended reference. Ušakov's dictionary mentions that *kreščenie* is a rite involving the new-born (or adults), and that a capitalized *Kreščenie* refers to a church holiday, but the full range of associations available to Cvetaeva will not necessarily be available to readers of another generation and another culture. Nevertheless, *"Kreščenie", "Krăštenieto", the Baptism* in this text is identifiable; in Bulgarian the potential ambiguity of *i* and of *deteto* caused only temporary confusion, which was righted on a second, more careful, reading.

It is sometimes said that definite articles refer to the speaker's intention, to a compact between speaker and hearer, but there is no evidence that such a meaning is linguistically encoded. The definite noun, by announcing that it has an identifiable referent, invites inferences about the speaker's expectations of the hearer's knowledge, but it does not say what the speaker's expectations or presuppositions actually were, nor can the speaker control with certainty how the noun will be interpreted (cf. Dimitrova 1978).

4. Summary and conclusions.

This paper has been concerned with the semantics of D/I as distinct from the semiotic value of the definite article. Adopting Revzin's concept of D/I as a field, not only for Russian, but for languages with articles as well, I have argued that the term *definite* and *indefinite* (and their glosses) are not labels for linguistic primes but ordinary-language items, part of the metalinguistic lexicon. These words reflect a set of universal distinctions; Krámský's generalization (2) about the human propensity to classify objects into "certain, definite, already known" vs. "uncertain, indefinite, unknown" was extended in (3) to events and situations. These are characterized as Salient and Non-Salient by clustering semantic properties which include respectively those called "definite" and "indefinite." These basic cognitive distinctions are reflected in linguistic structure, not only in the determiners and cases of nouns, but also in other categories (aspect, tense, mood) where D/I meanings appear as contextual, non-primary functions. The co-variance of grammatical categories polarized along D/I lines (or along the more inclusive Saliency hierarchy) has been documented by Diver (1963), Revzin (1978), Nikolaeva (1979), among others. The clustering properties involved in D/I and Saliency play a role in the discourse notion of foregrounding/backgrounding (Hopper and Thompson 1980; Chvany ms.). Since D/I is not congruent with the meaning of the article vs. its absence, I approach the article in the way already established in current Bulgarian analyses of verbs, where D/I is found to be predictable from more basic grammatical meanings. The ubiquitous and polysemantic D/I could not represent an autonomous linguistic sign.

The article, on the other hand, must represent a linguistic sign. Under the assumption that it is natural for a language to preserve a one-to-one correspondence between forms and meanings, there must be a meaning associated with the morpheme *T* in Bulgarian[13] and *TH* in English, and this meaning must be shared by the other members of the demonstrative-pronominal series with the same morpheme in the respective languages. The article is, in each language, semantically the most empty (least marked) of the deictic demonstrative series.[14] As shown in the examples, the articled noun points to the context or situation, saying there is an identifiable referent, but it does not say whether that referent is an individual or a class, whether it is given in the situation or context, or whether it is new information or identified by a following context. In the Russian original, the nouns had the same deictic function without help from articles; in the translations, the definite article added nothing to the meaning of the noun but functioned as a redundant marker of the noun's deixis.

Historians of the article stress the desemantization of a demonstrative as it develops toward articlehood, the loss of spatial specification: while a demonstrative may be replaced in some situations by a pointing gesture, an article cannot (Krámský 1972, 63; Revzin 1978, 224). It is the loss of spatial meaning that allows the article to be used generically, to refer to a class rather than single out an individual. Ivančev (1957/1978) shows that generic use in Bulgarian has been the final step in the history of the definite article, spreading first to subjects, then to other positions, part of an inertial tendency to mark subjects. This is found in language after language, in the same chronological order. Tracing the history of articles in German and French, Žirmunskij describes the generic use as the final step: "In those cases where a singular noun is used as a symbol for a collective or a group, the article lacks any defining function: that is the highest point of its development." (1939, 254; cited by Ivančev 1957/1978, 148 n.) As we saw in (5) and (7), it is not possible to separate nouns referring to individuals from nouns referring to classes (referentially or attributively). The ability to designate type or token is built into the noun, whether or not the language has an article. The tendency to mark subjects, noted by Ivančev and illustrated in (5), confirms Revzin's observation in (1), that the correlates of D/I have other functions as well.

It may seem paradoxical that the definite article, whose most common function is believed to be one of identifying or singling out, cannot be called an article unless it can be used generically as well. But if we look at the Russian examples, we see that individual and generic reference are contextually no less distinguishable without any contribution from articles. The deictic article is "definite," but it is much more weakly "definite" than the demonstratives, which are specified for additional spatial features. In the examples (4)–(8), the article on a referring noun phrase added nothing to the meaning that was not present in the original Russian; but omitting the article from *snega, the snow* in (4c), or from *"Krăštenieto", the Baptism* in (8b) would have signaled a lack of anaphoric link, creating a break in communication. The lack of a definite article, then, marks a new classification, or a new topic, by virtue of opposition with an overt definite article.

In closing, I would like to return to the question of *markedness,* a term used in the literature in at least two different, if overlapping, senses. The sense of *markedness* as *linguistically specified* is that of Jakobson (1957): the marked member of an opposition is the one with an inherent linguistic specification lacking in the unmarked member. In this sense, the article is "marked": there is a morpheme, in Bulgarian *T,* in English *TH,* which spells out a feature I have called *[+deictic]* in similar but not identical contexts of the respective languages. The meaning of this feature is roughly translatable as "watch the context, a referent is identifiable." If a hearer fails to identify the intended referent, there may be misunderstanding; if the hearer cannot locate a referent, a definite form may elicit a *WH*-question. (Similarly, the "definite" verb tenses elicit *WHEN*-questions if used infelicitously; this consequence of the deictic feature unites "definite" tenses with the definite article.) The feature *[+deictic]*, realized as *T/TH*, is opposed to a minus-valued feature corresponding to the absence of the article. (The indefinite article, where it exists, is the marker of another opposition, see §1 above; also Jespersen MEG VII (1954/1958, 469), on conflict between articles.). The feature *[-deictic]* says nothing about pointing, but may connote non-pointing, that is, signal a new, not yet contextually established topic. In context this connotation may be removed; in (8c) *a child,* translating *rebenka,* did refer to the contextually established Marina but presented her in a new classification.

The other sense of *marked* is synonymous with *informative;* *unmarked* with *normal, expected (in a particular context).*[15] This is the sense in which Nikolaeva summarizes the conventional wisdom on D/I as manifested in the article: "Practically all the authors who took part in [the collective 1979 volume] have come to the following conclusions: 1) definiteness is unmarked, indefiniteness is marked; its introduction carries greater semantic information; 2) the functional loads of definiteness and indefiniteness are on different levels; viz.: definiteness equates, identifies, contributes to textual cohesion *(otoždestvljaet, identificiruet, skrepljaet tekst)*; indefiniteness is a marker of new information, a communicative interruption, it classifies" (1979, 9). This use of *unmarked* reflects the fact that definite noun phrases refer to given information, hence are less informative than indefinite noun phrases which introduce new topics or classifications; this aspect of indefinites is supported by the examples in §3, but definiteness, while it reflects links within a text, does not *contribute* to textual cohesion: it is normal for a noun to refer to some identifiable object, person, or class; it is also normal for texts to be cohesive, and normal for their cohesiveness to be manifested partly through nouns with perspicuous reference. Our expectations of coherence lead us to search for referents. The definite article is but an overt marker of this normal, expected phenomenon.

Massachusetts Institute of Technology

NOTES

[1] Nikolaeva (1979, 3-10) stresses the close relation of "definiteness" to the semantics of nouns. Contrastive studies — and mistakes by foreigners — show that languages segment the continuum from proper to common noun at different points, allowing articles with proper names, kinship terms, names of body parts, or not; co-occurrence with determiners and possessives also varies (Stojanov 1968; Aleksova 1979; Kufnerova 1980). The indefinite article is sensitive to morphosyntactic classes (e.g., in English, to the count/mass distinction), to subject vs. predicate position, as well as to a scale of quantification (Revzin 1978, 198-215; see also Penčev 1979). Typological studies stress the scalar nature of articlehood and of "definiteness"; the most extensive one is Krámský 1972.

[2] Revzin 1978, II; Nikolaeva 1979, 3-10. Revzina's article in the Nikolaeva collection summarizes Revzin's model, which systematically distinguishes the communicative and cognitive (including quantificational) aspects of language. Translations from these works are my own. See also Jespersen (1954/1958, 420) on the infelicity of the term 'indefinite article', "which actually refers to a definite item, even if it is not made known which class member is mentioned."

[3] Revzin's syntactic correlates of definite noun phrases are, as it happens, almost exactly those of the "subject par excellence" — the thematic subject of the prototypical action (or "ergative") sentence. The important paper by Hopper and Thompson (1980) sheds light on this coincidence, as will be seen below.

On the notions "subject par excellence" and "object par excellence," i.e., of subject and object as multivalent, scalar categories, and on the lexically predictable, scalar nature of "agent," see Chvany (1975, 15-28). A scalar approach to "subjects" is justified on a cross-linguistic basis in Keenan 1976 and other papers in Li, ed. 1976.

[4] The definitions in Russian are blended and slightly rearranged from those in the Academy four-volume dictionary and the four volume dictionary edited by Ušakov. The Bulgarian-English dictionary consulted is Čakalov, ed. 1961. The translations of the Russian definitions are my own but correspond to definitions in several editions of Webster; the overlapping variety is such that there is not room (or need) to copy them here.

[5] Scholars differ on which meaning should be considered primary. Stankov's view is that temporal pinpointing is derived from an inherent meaning of "witnessing." In a different approach to the meanings of the Bulgarian tense morphemes (rather than full forms), I have argued that the H-morpheme of the aorist and imperfect cannot be the carrier of the meaning "witnessed," for it is found in irreal contexts, such as the conditional, and the imperfect and pluperfect in contrary-to-fact conditions. The deictic H-morpheme denotes only a distancing in time or reality from the speech event. The connotation of witnessing, or closeness, is due to opposition with doubly distanced indirect forms in the system (Chvany 1978). In embedded clauses, reference to the speech event may be replaced by reference to other elements in the context; on this phenomenon see Brecht 1974, and example (7c) below.

[6] Sentences may be characterized along a continuum as more or less Salient, in proportion to the distribution of Salient and Non-Salient properties in them. I call this continuum the Saliency Hierarchy.

[7] A comparison of their scale with a Saliency hierarchy that makes no reference to D/I as such is found in Chvany (ms.), a study which quantifies the isomorphism mentioned by Revzin in (1).

[8] I adopt the distinction formulated by Benveniste 1966, II, 20-21.

[9] Space permits only a small sample of the texts analyzed for this study. Foregrounding/backgrounding in Cvetaeva's prose and in Vazov's novel *Pod igoto* is discussed in Chvany ms. and further work in preparation.

[10] When used in brief reports of recent speech, the indirect forms suggest a verbatim account (this is probably due to opposition with the direct present or perfect, which are used for material asserted in the speaker's own words). That connotation is not found in fairy tales (one of the more common contexts of the indirect forms), or in distantly remembered stories like this one.

[11] One Bulgarian speaker queried about a version with *černoto delo* (without the following context), said it would be all right if it were followed by something narrowing it to Puškin's murder, but she had difficulty assigning co-reference to the duel, since her associations with the word had more to do with honor than with murder.
[12] The *-t* on subjects is optional, especially in spoken usage, hence the lack of *-t* alone does not unambiguously signal non-subject. The distinction is possible only in the masculine.
[13] The rest of the Bulgarian article carries gender or number features (Scatton 1980).
[14] I cannot agree with Krámský (1972, 63), who claims that the article acquires some additional element of the noun's meaning that is absent in the demonstrative; I believe his conclusion is due to the fact that the article is often the carrier of the noun's gender markings, and overtly marks its referentiality. Demonstratives also have these properties.
[15] The first kind of markedness is invariant; the second contextual. Together they measure the economy of grammatical descriptions. But that is a topic for another paper.

REFERENCES

The transliteration system distinguishes Russian and Bulgarian as follows: Russian х is *x*; Bulgarian х is *h*; Russian ъ is "; Bulgarian ъ is ă.

Cited texts

Marina Cvetaeva, *Rolandov rog,* in *Izbrannye proizvedenija.* (*Biblioteka poèta. Bol'šaja serija*), 2nd ed. Moscow-Leningrad, 1965, 168.
Marina Cvetaeva, *Moj Puškin.* Moscow, 1967, 33-36.
Marina Cvetaeva, Anna Ahmatova. *Mojat Puškin. Eseta,* transl. by Cveta Lenkova. Varna, 1979, 15-16.
Marina Tsvetaeva, *A Captive Spirit: Selected Prose,* transl. and ed. by J. Marin King. Ann Arbor, 1980, 319-20.

Bibliography

Aleksova, Vasilka
  1979 Nabljudenija vărhu upotrebata na opredelitelnija člen v bălgarskija i rumănskija ezik. *Săpostavitelno ezikoznanie* IV/8, 12-17.
Andrejčin, L.
  1957 Kăm harakteristikata na perfekta (minalo neopredeleno vreme) v bălgarski ezik. *Ezikovedski izsledvanija v čest na akademik Stefan Mladenov.* Sofia, 57-64.
Andrejčin, L., K. Popov, St. Stojanov
  1977 *Gramatika na bălgarskija ezik.* Sofia.
Atanasova, T., N. Radulova, M. Rankova, R. Rusev
  1963 *Anglijska gramatika v sravnenie s bălgarski ezik.* Sofia.
Axmanova, O. S.
  1966 *Slovar' lingvističeskix terminov.* Moscow.
Benveniste, Emile
  1966 *Problèmes de linguistique générale.* I-II. Paris.
Bolinger, Dwight L.
  1977 *Meaning and form.* London-New York.
Brecht, Richard D.
  1974 "Tense and infinitive complements in Russian, Latin, and English" in Brecht and Chvany, eds., 193-218.

Brecht, Richard D. and Catherine V. Chvany, eds.
1974 [1977] *Slavic Transformational Syntax.* (= *Michigan Slavic Materials* 10). Ann Arbor.
Chvany, Catherine V.
1975 *On the syntax of BE-sentences in Russian.* Cambridge.
1978 "Denotative and connotative-meaning of the 'preterite' and 'perfect' in Bulgarian and English," *BLS* IV, Berkeley, 30-42.
ms. "Foregrounding and transitivity."
Chvany, Catherine V. and Richard D. Brecht, eds.
1980 *Morphosyntax in Slavic.* Columbus, Ohio.
Dimitrova, Stefana
1978 "Aktualizacija predloženija i ee zavisimosť ot predstavlenija govorjaščego o stepeni osvedomlennosti adresata (na materiale russkogo jazyka)," *Bolgarskaja rusistika* V, 47-57.
Diver, William
1963 "The chronological system of the English verb," *Word* 19. 141-81.
Firbas, Jan
1966 "On defining the theme in functional sentence analysis," *TLP* 1, Prague, 267-280.
Fontaine, Jacqueline
1978 "Sur les rapports syntaxiques de l'aspect verbal et des pronoms indéfinis. *Revue des études slaves,* LI/1-2, 97-105. (Paper read at VIII International Congress of Slavists, Zagreb.)
Galton, Herbert
1973 "The function of the definite article in some Indo-European languages: The grammatical category of determinacy," *Linguistics* 107, 5-13.
Hopper, Paul J. and Sandra A. Thompson
1980 "Transitivity in grammar and discourse," *Language* 56, 251-99.
Ivančev, Svetomir T.
1957 "Nabljudenija vărhu upotrebata na člena v bălgarskija ezik," *Bălgarski ezik* XII. Reprinted in Ivančev 1978, 128-152.
1967 "Kăm văprosa za členuvane na generično upotrebenija podlog," *Ezik i Literatura* XXII. Reprinted in Ivančev 1978, 152-57.
1968 "Problemi na aktualnoto členenie na izrečenieto," *Slavjanska filologija,* X. *Ezikoznanie.* Reprinted in Ivančev 1978, 158-72.
1978 *Prinosi v bălgarskoto i slavjanskoto ezikoznanie.* Sofia.
Jakobson, Roman
1957 "Shifters, verbal categories and the Russian verb," Harvard University. Reprinted in *Selected Writings* II. The Hague, 1971, 130-47. Translation in Revzina, ed. 1972, 95-113. ("Šiftery, glagoľnye kategorii i russkij glagol").
Jespersen, Otto
1954 (1958) *A modern English grammar* VII. Completed & ed. by Niels Haislund. London.
Keenan, Edward L.
1976 "Toward a universal definition of 'subject of'" in Li, ed., 303-33.
Krámský, Jiří
1972 *The article and the concept of definiteness in language.* The Hague–Paris.
Kufnerova, Zlata
1980 "Za kategorijata 'opredelenost' v bălgarskija i češkija ezik," *Săpostavitelno ezikoznanie* V/4, 16-23.
Li, Charles N., ed.
1976 *Subject and Topic.* New York.
Mladenov, Stefan and St. Vasilev
1939 *Gramatika na bălgarskija ezik.* Sofia.

Nikolaeva, T. M., ed.
　1979　*Kategorija opredelennosti-neopredelennosti v slavjanskix i balkanskix jazykax.* Moscow. (Editor's introduction, 3-10).
Penčev, Jordan.
　1967　"Kăm văprosa za vremenata v săvremennija bălgarski ezik," *Bălgarski ezik* XVII/2, 131-43.
　1979　"Nepravilno izpuskane na členni formi," *Bălgarski ezik* XXIX, 554-55.
Revzin, I. I.
　1978　*Struktura jazyka kak modelirujuščej sistemy.* Moscow.
Revzina, O. G.
　1972　*Principy tipologičeskogo analiza jazykov različnogo stroja.* Moscow. Revzina, ed.
　1979　"Funkcional'nyj podxod k jazyku i kategorija opredelennosti-neopredelennosti" in Nikolaeva, ed., 64-89.
Rozental', D. È. and M. A. Telenkova
　1972　*Spravočnik lingvističeskix terminov. Posobie dlja učitelja.* Moscow.
Scatton, Ernest A.
　1980　"On the shape of the Bulgarian definite article" in Chvany and Brecht, eds., 204-211.
Stankov, Valentin
　1965　"Za značenieto na aorista v săvremennija bălgarski ezik," *Bălgarski ezik* XV, 488-503.
　1969　*Bălgarskite glagolni vremena.* Sofia.
Stojanov, St.
　1968　"Gramatičeskata kategorija 'opredelenost' v bălgarski ezik i nejnite săotvetstija v drugi slavjanski ezici," *Slavjanska filologija,* X. Sofia.
　1965　*Členuvane na imenata v bălgarskija ezik.* Sofia.
Timberlake, Alan
　1975　"Hierarchies in the Genitive of Negation," *Slavic and East European Journal* XIX, 123-38. (Reprinted 1977 in *Soviet-American Russian Language Contributions,* ed. by Richard D. Brecht and Dan E. Davidson. Urbana, 123-38.)
Whorf, Benjamin Lee
　1965　*Language, thought and reality: Selected writings of Benjamin Lee Whorf,* ed. by John B. Carroll. Cambridge, Mass.
Žirmunskij, V. M.
　1939　*Istorija nemeckogo jazyka.* Leningrad. (Cited in Ivančev 1957 [1978])

Names with Stems ending in {l-} in Old Russian

James Ferrell

This is an examination of names with a stem ending in {l-} and with the nominative singular desinence {-o} in Old Russian. There are two valuable compilations of Old Russian names that provide the data used: Tadeusz Skulina, *Staroruskie imiennictwo osobowe* (Wroclaw-Warsaw-Cracow, 1973-4) and S. B. Veselovskij, *Onomastikon* (Moscow, 1974). The two works are compiled from documents of different periods. Skulina based his work on documents from the beginning to the fourteenth century, while Veselovskij based his on documents from the fifteenth through the seventeenth centuries.

Names with stems ending in {l-} form a relatively small portion of each work and, as will become plain, allow of various derivations in individual instances. Yet the names in Skulina's work differ sharply from those in Veselovskij's in that where a vowel precedes in Skulina's work this vowel is normally {i} and never {a}. The dominance of the sequence {il} seems to imply the presence of a diminutive suffix {-il-} as the most frequent formant in Skulina's collection, while the absence of the sequence {al-} makes it doubtful that deverbative agent nouns in {-l-} occur as names in the older period.

Veselovskij's list, on the other hand, shows several examples of names with stems ending in the sequence {al-}, which implies the presence of agent nouns in {-l-}, though, of course, this does not argue against the presence of diminutive stems as well in the latter group. In other words, a change in name formation exists between the two lists as will become apparent from a detailed examination of the data from the two works. Incidentally, the inclusion of nouns of the second as well as the first declension from Skulina's list reflects his practice and that of his sources. I am uncertain whether the absence of second-declension forms in Veselovskij's work reflects the reality of his sources or his editorial policies.

The material from Skulina follows:

Čurilo can be derived from *čurit'* 'squint' or from *čura* 'gravel' or 'grain of snow.' Etymologically it is a variant of *Kirill.*

Dobrilo can be a diminutive of *dobro* 'treasure' or an agent noun from *dobrit'* 'treat lovingly.'

Dročilo or *Dročila* can be derived from *drok* or *droča* 'period when cattle behave insanely' or from *dročit'* 'pet, spoil.'

Dušila can be a diminutive of *duša* 'soul,' cf. *dušen'ka* 'darling' or can be an agent noun from *dušit'* 'smother.'

Gostila can be a diminutive of *gost'* 'guest' or 'merchant' or can be an agent noun from Old Russian *gostiti* 'entertain' or 'be a guest' or 'trade.'

Javilo might be a diminutive of *java*, which Dal' attributes to the dialect of Pskov in the sense of 'exhibit, wonder.' It would be atypical as a derivative of *javit'* 'reveal,' since normally only imperfective stems form agent nouns in East Slavic.

Kirilo or *Kirila* is the saint's name *Kirill*, which was borrowed from Greek and has no Slavic derivation.

Kolotilo can be a diminutive of *kolot* 'churning pestle' or an agent noun from *kolotit'* 'hit.'

Mestilo can be a diminutive of *mest'* 'vengeance' or a diminutive of *Mstislav* or an agent noun from *mstitit'* 'avenge.'

Petrilo or *Petrila* is a diminutive of the name *Petr* 'Peter.'

Radilo can be a diminutive of *Radoslav* or *Radogost* or *Radolud*, or it can be a diminutive of *rada* 'my joy,' a term found in the Olonec and Tver' regions according to Dal', or it can be an agent noun from *radit'* 'strive.'

Sdila is probably a diminutive of Old Russian *zъdъ* 'wall' or of some compound name, cf. Polish *Zdzisław*.

Selilo or *Selila* could be a diminutive of *selo* 'settlement' or a diminutive of the name *Sil'vestr*.

Stanilo or *Stanila* could be a diminutive of *stan* 'encampment, house' or of a name of the type *Stanislav*.

Stroilo could be a diminutive of *stroj* 'structure' or an agent noun from *stroit'* 'build.' It could also be a diminutive of a name paralleling Serbo-Croatian *Strojislav* or *Strojimir*.

Sudilo or *Sudila* could be a diminutive of *sud* 'vessel' or an agent noun from *sudit'* 'judge.' It could also be a diminutive of *Sudislav* or *Sudimir*.

Šilo, if the reconstruction is correct, is homonymous with a word meaning 'awl.' It could also be an agent noun from *šit'* 'sew.'

Terpilo, if correct, can be a diminutive of *terp'* 'patience' or an agent noun from *terpet'* 'be patient.' It could be a diminutive of a name such as Polish *Cirzpisław* or Serbo-Croatian *Trpimir*.

Tešila can be an agent derivative of *tešit'* 'satisfy, please' or a diminutive of a name of the type of Polish *Ciechosław* or Serbo-Croatian *Tjehorad*.

Tverdilo or *Tverdila* can be a diminutive of *tverd* 'fort' or agent noun of *tverdit'* 'strengthen' or a diminutive of a name such as *Tverdislav*.

Voilo or *Voila* is homonymous with a word meaning 'dewlap' in the neuter form. It can also be a diminutive of *voin* 'soldier.'

Židilo or *Židila* can be a diminutive of *žid* 'Jew' or of a name of the type *Židimir* or *Židislav*.

From the foregoing material it is plain that though there are instances in which a deverbative derivation is possible, there are a number of instances in which such a derivation is precluded. The dominant type is denominative, specifically desubstantival. We shall find the materials from Veselovskij noticeably different.

Veselovskij's data can, in many instances, be denominative, but in many, only deverbative. In some instances the deverbative solution may offer semantic difficulties, e.g., *Toršilo,* but no denominative alternative appears to exist. Stems ending in {al-} generally resist denominative solutions since there is no suffix that could account for the stem termination. It is of considerable interest that the material from Skulina is more or less paralleled by material gathered from old Serbo-Croatian documents by T. Maretić in his "O narodnima imenima i prezimenima u Hrvata i Srba," *Rad Jugoslovanske Akademije Znanosti i Umjetnosti,* 82 (1886), 114-15, which also shows an absence of stems ending in {al-} while showing the presence of ones in {-il-}.

The following materials are from Veselovskij:

Cydilo is possibly derived from *cedit'* 'strain' and is an agent formation.

Čurilo has already been analyzed in the preceding list.

Dulo is homonymous with a noun meaning 'muzzle.' It can also be an agent formation from *dut'* 'blow, light (a lamp), drink a lot, whip.'

Dunilo can be derived from the verb *dunit'* 'repeat something continuously.' It could also be a diminutive from the name *Dunja,* but such a formation would be atypical for a male name.

Durilo can be a diminutive of *durak* or *dura* or can be derived from *durit'* 'frolic, make a fool of oneself.'

Durlo is without satisfactory derivation.

Gadalo is derived from *gadat'* 'tell fortunes'; cf. *gadala* in Dal'.

Gruzilo can be derived from *gruz* 'burden' or *gruzit'* 'load.'

Guslo can be derived from *gusnut'* 'thicken.'

Jakšilo can be derived from *jakšit'sja* 'be friends.'

Jarilo is homonymous with a word meaning 'a strawman burned on the eve of St. John the Baptist.' It can also be a diminutive derived from *jar* 'heat, fire.'

Kačalo can be derived from the verb *kačat'sja* 'rock back and forth'; cf. *kačala* in *SRNG.*

Komšit' can be derived from *komšit'* 'crumble, beat, squeeze'; cf. *SRNG.*

Kormilo is homonymous with a word meaning 'stern of a boat.' It can also be derived from *korma* 'nourishment' or from *kormit'* 'nourish, rear.'

Kurilo is etymologically a variant of the name *Kirill.* Derivationally it could be from *kurit'* 'fumigate, distil.' Dal' enters *kurila* in the sense of 'drunkard' and *SRNG* in the sense of 'farter.'

Kutilo can be derived from *kutit'* 'go on a binge' and mean 'desperate drunkard'; cf. Dal' under *kutila*. It is unlikely that it could be derived from *kut* 'angle.'

Lepilo is derived from *lepit'* 'stick' and means a 'bad smith, bad moulder, maker of cardboard shoes'; cf. *lepila* in Dal' and *SRNG*.

Lyzlo is, according to Vasmer's *Russisches etymologisches Wörterbuch*, derived possibly from *lyzgat'*. Synchronically its derivation is unclear.

L'jalo is an agent formation from an Old Russian verb *lijati* 'pour' or possibly from *lijat'* 'be sleepy.'

Mazilo is an irregular derivative of *mazat'* 'smear' (one would expect *mazalo*); cf. *mazila* 'smearer, axle-greaser' in *SRNG* and 'bad painter, soiler' in Ušakov. It could also be a diminutive of *maz* 'grease.'

Maslo is homonymous with the word for 'butter.' I am uncertain whether it is analyzable in Russian synchronically. Historically, it is an instrument derivative of *mazat'*.

Močalo is homonymous with a noun meaning 'bast.' It could also be an agent derivative of *močat'*, a frequentative of *močit'* 'wet,' cf. *pomogat'*.

Morsalo is homonymous with a word meaning 'bilberry juice' or 'cranberry juice,' according to Veselovskij.

Mužilo can be a diminutive of *muž* 'man.' If from *mužat'*, 'reach manhood,' the derivational process is irregular.

Obeščalo is derived from *obeščat'* 'promise'; cf. *obeščala* 'unreliable promiser' in Dal'.

Opaxalo is synonymous with a word meaning 'fan,' but could be an agent derivative of *opaxat'* 'fan' from the time when the form functioned as an imperfective.

Petrilo is a diminutive of *Petr* 'Peter.'

Podšivalo is derived from *podšivat'* 'hem, line,' though Dal' defines *podšivala* as 'tease.'

Pogonjalo is from *pogonjat'* 'urge on, hasten.'

Pomogalo is derived from *pomogat'* 'help.'

Povirala is derived from *povirat'* 'lie from time to time.'

Pustilo is derivable from *pustit'* 'lay waste.' Dal' lists the verb as imperfective, while Sreznevskij opts for perfective.

Putilo is derivable as a diminutive from *puto* 'fetter.' It could be an irregular derivative of *putovat'* 'tangle.'

Rykalo is derived from *rykat'* 'yell'; cf. *rykala* 'yeller' or 'howler' in Dal'.

Rylo is homonymous with a noun 'snout,' but can also be an agent derivative from *ryt'* 'dig.'

Skubilo is a dialect form *skubit'*, which is synonymous with *skoblit'* 'scrape, pluck (a bird),' see Vasmer.

Skurlo has no satisfactory derivation.

Spešilo is derived from *spešit'* 'hasten' or from *spex* 'haste.'

Strekalo is derived from *strekat'* 'stick, sting'; cf. *strekala* in Dal'.

Stromilo can be a diminutive of *strom* 'tree' or an agent noun from *stromit'* 'shame.'

Stropilo can be a diminutive of *strop* 'roof' or an agent derivative of *stropit'* 'roof.' Dal' also gives the meaning 'hasten.'

Sviblo has no satisfactory derivation.

Šatalo is derivable from *šatat'sja* 'wander about without employment,' cf. *šatala* in Dal'.

Šatilo is derivable from *šatit'sja* 'wander about without employment'; cf. *šatila* in Dal'. It can also be a diminutive of *šata* 'cloak.'

Šilo is homonymous with the word for 'awl.' It can also be an agent noun from the verb *šit'* 'sew.'

Šumilo can be derived from *šumet'* 'be noisy.' It can also be a diminutive of *šum* 'noise.'

Tjablo is homonymous with a word meaning 'cornice of an iconostasis.'

Tjurilo can be a diminutive of *tjurja* 'a simple bread and saltwater soup' or it can be an agent of *tjurit'* 'crumble bread into such a soup.'

Tomilo can be an agent noun from *tomit'* 'weary, torment' or can be a diminutive of *toma* 'weariness.'

Torčila can be derived, somewhat irregularly, from *torčat'* 'stick up, stick out'; cf. *torčilo* 'anything that sticks out' in Dal'.

Toršilo may, perhaps, be derived from *toršit'* 'break up ice with shot,' a verb found in Dal'.

Tryzlo has no satisfactory derivation.

Verzilo is homonymous with a noun denoting a 'tall, lanky fellow.'

Vodilo is derived from *vodit'* 'lead'; cf. *vodilo* 'the seeker' (in a type of hide-and-seek game) in SRNG. It can be a diminutive of *voda*.

Vorošilo is derived from *vorošit'* 'touch, turn over'; cf. *vorošila* 'a person who touches something he has no business to.'

Xapalo is derived from *xapat'* 'seize.'

Zažigalo is derived from *zažigat'* 'set afire, temper, begin a quarrel, strike a ball solidly.'

Z'jalo is an agent formation from Old Russian *zijati* 'yawn' or Russian *zijat'* or *z'jat'* 'shine.'

Zvonilo is derived from *zvonit'* 'ring' or from *zvon* 'tinkle.'

Želybalo is derived from *želybat'* 'eat, bite, rock stongly, beat.' Dal' defines the word as 'eat greedily with a spoon.'

Žerebilo is a diminutive formed from the stem found in *žerebec* or *žerebenok* 'colt.' It can also be derived, though with semantic difficulties, from *žerebit'* 'foal.'

Žerlo is derived from *žrat'* 'devour.' *SRNG* defines *žorlo* as 'glutton.'

While in the Skulina list the dominant type was the denominative diminutive, in the Veselovskij list the dominant type is the deverbative agent, a type that Russian shares with Polish as a source of names. These agent nouns are generally, though not always, colored by contempt or humor. They seem to have established themselves as an important source of names around the fourteenth century in Russian. The beginning of attestations of similar names in Polish is about the same period; see Zofia Kurzowa, *Polskie rzeczowniki męskie na -o na tle słowiańskim* (Wroclaw-Warsaw-Cracow, 1970), 43 ff. This new style is characterized by the presence of names with stems ending in {al-}, a type absent in the earlier list.

The social factors lying behind this shift would be well worth an investigation.

University of Michigan,
University of California, Los Angeles

DICTIONARIES CONSULTED

Dal'	V. Dal'. *Tolkovyj slovar' živogo velikorusskogo jazyka,* 3rd ed., rev. and exp. by J. Baudouin de Courtenay, I-IV. St. Petersburg-Moscow, 1903-09.
Sreznevskij	I. I. Sreznevskij. *Materialy dlja Slovarja drevne-russkogo jazyka,* I-III + Suppl. St. Petersburg, 1893-1912.
SRNG	*Slovar' russkix narodnyx govorov,* ed. by F. P. Filin, I- . Moscow-Leningrad, 1965- .
Ušakov	*Tolkovyj slovar' russkogo jazyka,* ed. by D. N. Ušakov, I-IV. Moscow, 1935-40.
Vasmer	M. Vasmer. *Russisches etymologisches Wörterbuch,* I-III. Heidelberg, 1953-58.

The Alternation *l* ~ *v* in East Slavic

Michael S. Flier

In standard Ukrainian (U) and Belorussian (BR) the past tense suffix for vocalic and quasi-vocalic[1] verb stems is distinguished from its Russian (R) counterpart by the presence of an alternation *l* ~ *v*, which sets the masculine singular apart from the other forms of the singular and from the plural. The Old Russian (OR) perfect participle, the source of the modern past tense forms in East Slavic, shows no such alternation in the suffix.

Table 1
COMPARISON OF EAST SLAVIC PAST TENSE (PERFECT) FORMS

Form	Old Russian[2]	Russian	Ukrainian	Belorussian
masc.sg.	далъ	да́л	да́в	да́ў
fem.sg.	дала	дала́	дала́	дала́
neut.sg.	дало	да́ло	дало́	дало́
pl.	дали	да́ли	дали́	далі́

Two theories—one phonetic, the other morphological—have been proposed to explain the Ukrainian-Belorussian development.

The phonetic theory, first espoused by Potebnja in 1865, views the *v* of the Ukrainian-Belorussian past/masc.sg. as the product of the same phonological development responsible for *v* in Ukrainian and Belorussian reflexes of old *tьlt/*tъlt forms (hereafter simply *tьlt).

Table 2
COMPARISON OF *tьlt FORMS AND PAST/MASC.SG. IN EAST SLAVIC

Form	Old Russian	Russian	Ukrainian	Belorussian
**tъlst-*	тълстъи	то́лстый	то́встий	то́ўсты
**vьlk-*	вълкъ	во́лк	во́вк	во́ўк
*dalъ	далъ	да́л	да́в	да́ў

According to the phonetic theory, tautosyllabic (weak) *l* in the western dialects of Old Russian came to be pronounced as a bilabial glide [w], thus pre-U/BR *vьlkъ* [wŭlkŭ] > [wŭwkŭ]. The pronunciation *l*[w] remained in effect for a time even after the fall of the jers, since it was valid for *l* in the new weak word-final environment, thus OR *dalъ* > Early U *dal* [daw]. In the post-jer period, *v* itself was introduced into weak environments as [w] (Shevelov 1979:294), e.g., OR *děvъka, xlěvъ* > Early U *děvka* [d'ȋewka], *xlěv* [xl'ȋew]. The development of *l*[w] and *v*[w] established weak environments as positions of neutralization for *l* and *v*, thus permitting the possible rephonologization of *l*[w] as *v*[w], e.g., Early U *volk* [wowk] > *vovk* [wowk], *dal* [daw] > *dav* [daw]. The major weakness of the phonetic theory is that it does not explain satisfactorily why all instances of new weak *l* that arose after the fall of the jers were not rephonologized as *v*, e.g., OR *palъka, stolъ* > U *palka, st'il*, not **pavka, *st'iv*.

The morphological theory, advanced by Mixaľčuk in 1893, maintains that the alternation *l* ~ *v* in the Ukrainian-Belorussian past tense suffix has nothing to do with the patently phonological change *l* > *v* in **tъlt* forms, despite the fact that all dialects with the former development have the latter as well. Instead, the new past/masc.sg in *v* is viewed as nothing more than the nom.sg.masc. short form of the old past active participle (PAP), which simply replaced the inherited past tense form in *l*. By contrast the remaining nonmasculine past tense forms in *l* were preserved, apparently because they differed too radically in form from the corresponding participles, thus Early U past/masc.sg. *dal* is replaced by *dav* (PAP), but *dalá, daló, dalý* resist replacement by *davšy, dav, davše* (Shevelov 1979:419).

To this date the few scholars who have supported the morphological theory (see Meľničuk 1958, Bezpaľko et al. 1962, Filin 1972, Wexler 1977, Shevelov 1979) have not been able to make a convincing case for the proposed morphological substitution. The numerous citations documented by Meľničuk from Old Russian texts, in which the past active participle is used in an "absolute predicate function," invariably turn out to be examples in which the participle is subordinated to, or coordinated with, an independent predicate in the larger discourse. There are no cases in which the participle renders a simple, independent past tense construction like Russian *Иван приехал в Москву*.[3] And apart from the lack of functional motivation, the morphological theory is suspect because it fails to account for the limitation of this particular case of morphological substitution to the western dialects of East Slavic when it had pan-Slavic potential.

The purpose of the present study is to reexamine the traditional phonetic theory in order to clarify aspects of the phonological change *l* > *v* that have been viewed with skepticism in the context of the Ukrainian-Belorussian past tense alternation. We will propose instead a phonetic-morphophonemic hypothesis to account for the morphological limitation on the alternation *l* ~ *v* in the western dialects of East Slavic. In our view, the course of the phonetic change [l] > [v] was affected by phonetic environment, just as the rephonologization of *l* as *v* was affected by categorial restrictions on morphophonemic alternation.

Following a brief discussion of the historical and dialectological evidence pertaining to the *l* ~ *v* alternation in East Slavic, we will review the traditional phonetic theory, including later modifications and accretions, and will attempt to put the residual problems into historical perspective. The latter will entail an examination of phonetic change itself and the role that morphology plays in the course of a change. Typological parallels involving the morphophonemic exploitation of phonetic variation in East Slavic will be adduced as well.

Historical Evidence

The most comprehensive survey of historical evidence relevant to the change *l* > *v* is provided by Shevelov in his 1979 historical phonology of Ukrainian. Documentation of the change is represented in texts from the 15th century on in one of four ways: 1) replacement of the letter л with в, 2) replacement of the letter л with оу, 3) omission of the letter л and 4) replacement of the letter в with л. Such "misspellings" are rare throughout the Middle Ukrainian period (15th–late 18th centuries), testimony to the strength of orthographic tradition (Shevelov 1979:412).

The earliest examples cited by Shevelov from northern Ukrainian-Belorussian texts are from the second half of the 15th century, e.g., **Єлхимъ** for the Greek name Εὐθύμιος (1469), **невдовже** 'soon' (1489), **вовноу** 'wool' acc.sg. (1496). Acording to Shevelov (418) the first example of the past/masc.sg in *v* from this area occurs in the Peretc Gospel from ca. 1510, which Shevelov (402) believes to be a Ukrainian copy of a Belorussian original: **никтоже смивь ... въпросити** 'no one dared ask.' The same text shows hypercorrect spellings of the PAP with the letter л: **оставилше** 'having left,' **пристѫпилше** 'having approached.'

Shevelov (414) emphasizes the chronological posteriority of similar attestations in southwestern texts.[4] The earliest examples of southwestern *tъlt* misspellings date to the mid-17th century, e.g., *Pustinka* (= *Povsten'*), *Puczkiufce* [sic] (= *Vovčkivci*), *Taustaigne* (= *Tovstyn*), all from 1653; **човно** 'boat' (1667). The first examples of the southwestern past/masc.sg in *v* are from Ivan Vyšens'kyj's *Knyžka* of 1600, although Shevelov (418) admits the possibility of a Northern Ukrainian copyist: **половил или прелстив** 'caught or seduced,' **оулакомил и прелстив** 'enticed and seduced,' **щез и пропав** 'disappeared and vanished,' **еси ... раздѣливсга** 'you divided yourself.' A hypercorrect spelling with л in the Didactic Gospel from Jazlovec' (late-16th c.) is seen in **и пристоупилъ воздвиже ю** 'and having come near, he lifted her.'

Relevant Ukrainian words in foreign texts from before the 17th century are rendered with the letter *l*: Hungarian (13th–15th cc.), Polish (14th–15th cc.). Early borrowings into Yiddish and Moldavian dialects of Romanian indicate Ukrainian weak *l* rather than *v* in the 13th–14th centuries (Shevelov, 413). One must not lose sight of the fact, however, that nearly all of these foreign accounts record Ukrainian toponyms, whose pronunciation with [l] may have been known to foreigners long before these particular attestations, which simply continue to reflect an older pronunciation. Furthermore, in the midst of a phonetic change which allows considerable variation, toponyms might reflect a more conservative pronunciation.

On the basis of his survey of extant texts, Shevelov (414, 418) establishes the following chronology for the *l* > *v* changes he views as phonological (*t_b/l* forms) and morphological (past/masc.sg.) in the western dialects of East Slavic:

Table 3

SHEVELOV'S RELATIVE CHRONOLOGY OF *l* ~ *v*

northern Ukrainian-Belorussian	southwestern Ukrainian
a. phon. *l* > *v*: mid-15th c. b. morph. *l* > *v*: early 16th c.	a. morph. *l* > *v*: early 17th c. b. phon. *l* > *v*: mid-17th c.

Shevelov concludes that since the phonological change *l* > *v* precedes the morphological change *l* > *v* in the north by approximately half a century, but follows it in the south by approximately half a century, there can be no doubt that the two changes have nothing whatsoever to do with one another; otherwise one would expect the phonological change to precede the morphological change in both areas. It is beyond the scope of the present paper to respond to Shevelov's lengthy analysis point by point, but a few general observations are in order.

First, existing texts are invaluable in providing rough approximations of the chronology of a given change, but must not be viewed as precise indicators of absolute chronology. If no written evidence for the change *l* > *v* is to be found before the 15th century, this does not mean that the change, or certain phonetic phases of the change, did not take place earlier (Šaxmatov 1915:308). A scholar investigating phonological changes linked to the fall of the jers in the pre-Ukrainian dialects (mid-12th century on) must reckon with the fact that great numbers of texts were destroyed during and after the Tatar invasions of the 13th century. Second, Shevelov is quite arbitrary in deciding when scant evidence is to be taken seriously. Thus, the existence of past/masc.sg. in *v* in the southwest some 50 years before the phonological change *l* > *v* is assumed on the basis of *one* hypercorrected PAP from a late-16th century text and four past/masc.sg. forms in *v* from a text dated 1600 that may actually have been copied by a scribe from the north. On the contrary, evidence of southwestern *tъlt forms in *v* earlier than the mid-17th century is rejected by Shevelov as inconsequential, e.g., исмовившисд 'having come to agreement' (1422 charter, Sambir),[5] Hungarian record *Wewche* (= Vovče, 1425), довгъıи 'long' (Adelphotis, 1591),[6] товчет 'pounds, crushes' (*Knyžka* by Ivan Vyšens'kyj, 1600). One might also note that Shevelov inexplicably omits mention of the form тоуку 'interpreter' dat.sg. from a Polotsk gramota of 1418-20 cited by Šaxmatov (1915:308), and putative Belorussian past/masc.sg. forms in *v* from the late 15th century (Bulyka et al. 1979:237). Third, the margin of delay between the time of the emergence of an actual innovation in the spoken language and its first appearance as a textual error can easily exceed 50 or even 100 years. Shevelov would appear to be uncharacteristically incautious in proclaiming a 50-year gap between two linguistic innovations on the basis of very spotty documentary evidence.

If Shevelov's analysis of the written sources is questionable, there is little doubt that his interpretation of the geographical direction of the change *l* > *v* is correct. It appears to have originated in the northern Ukrainian-Belorussian area and spread outwards, reaching the southern and southwestern Ukrainian dialects later. Of the two changes involved in this development—the phonetic [l] > [w] and the phonemic (rephonologization) *l* > *v*—it would appear that the misspellings surveyed reflect the second, phonemic change. As long as speakers continue to assign [w] from etymological *l* to *l*, there is less likelihood of orthographic slips. Textual misspellings involving л and в are reflections of a later period when *l*[w] in different environments is occasionally or consistently subject to reinterpretation as *v*[w]. The written evidence indicates that the phonemic change *l* > *v* occurred earlier in the north than in the south, but provides no direct information about the absolute chronology of the phonetic change [l] > [w]. We know only that the *terminus a quo* of [l] > [w] occurs before the early 15th century.

Dialectological Evidence

There are two basic types of East Slavic dialects relevant to the development of weak *l*: 1) *l*[w] dialects, in which weak *l* is productively realized as [w] but unverified (not prevocalic, consistently weak) cases of *l*[w] may be rephonologized as *v*[w], e.g., *tъlt forms, and 2) *l*[l] dialects with historical *l*[w], in which weak *l* is productively realized as [l] but unverified cases of older *l*[w] and *l* of the past/masc.sg. have been rephonologized as *v*. We will call dialects of the first type—with phonetic *l*[w]—"unrestricted" and dialects of the second type—with lexical *v* < *l* or morphophonemic *l* ~ *v*—"restricted."

The unrestricted, phonetic system is characteristic of the Sjan, Dniester, Bojkian and Bukovyna-Pokuts'k dialects of southwestern Ukrainian,[7] some southwestern Russian dialects contiguous with Belorussian and Ukrainian, and a large number of northeastern Russian dialects. The restricted, morpholexical system is characteristic of Belorussian, the rest of Ukrainian except for certain Lemkian and western Ukrainian dialects,[8] and some dialects in the contiguous southwestern Russian zone. Based on Ukrainian examples, table 4 juxtaposes the relevant phonemic and phonetic forms.

Table 4
UNRESTRICTED AND RESTRICTED DIALECT FORMS

Old Russian Form	Unrestricted System		Restricted System	
вълкъ	*vovk* or *volk*	[w]	*vovk*	[w]
столъ	*stil*	[w]	*st'il*	[l]
стола	*stola*	[l]	*stola*	[l]
палъка	*palka*	[w]	*palka*	[l]
палъкъ	*palok*	[l]	*palok*	[l]
далъ	*dal*[9]	[w]	*dav*	[w]
дала	*dala*	[l]	*dala*	[l]

The dialect geography of the alternation *l* ~ *v* in the western part of East Slavic territory confirms the conclusions reached on the basis of written evidence above. Unrestricted systems with *l*/[w] appear to have arisen first in the Belorussian-northern Ukrainian area and spread later to contiguous dialects. Subsequently *l*/[w] became unproductive in the original northern zone and was replaced by the restricted system, as indirectly reflected by misspellings in the texts. Southwestern Ukrainian dialects preserved, and in some cases continue to preserve, the unrestricted system longer than the northern dialects, and for that reason the texts from the southwest reflect the change *l* > *v* later. It should be noted, however, that the misspellings in southwestern texts occur almost exclusively in *tъlt forms and the past/masc.sg. (covert morphophonemic change), a fact that sustains our contention that these orthographical errors reflect the phonemic change *l* > *v*, not the phonetic change [l] > [w].

The unrestricted *l*/[w] dialects of North Russian can be understood as products of the same historical development that produced the change [l] > [w] in Belorussian, Ukrainian and contiguous southwestern Russian dialects. One of the major conclusions of Orlova et al. (1970) is that most of the modern northeastern Russian dialects, which share many phonological and morphological traits with Belorussian and Ukrainian, are descendants of the Old

Novgorod dialect area, whose speakers were cut off from the southwest following the Tatar invasions and the expansion of the Grand Duchy of Lithuania in the first half of the 14th century. With the rise of Muscovite Rus' many were forcibly resettled to the east. From this perspective the unrestricted phonetic change [l] > [w] was a general development for most of the western dialects of East Slavic. The replacement of the unrestricted system by the restricted *l* ~ *v* originated in the "central" Belorussian–northern Ukrainian region, but has yet to encompass all of the original "periphery," southwest Ukrainian, with which it was politically joined as a result of the Union of Lublin in 1569, and Novgorodian Russian, from which it was politically and later geographically severed; cf. Orlova et al. 1970:54, 282ff.

The Phonetic Theory Reconsidered

In the traditional phonetic theory the change *l* > *v* is ascribed to the distant past because, with one major exception, it is relevant only for instances of weak *l* that existed before the fall of the jers (*tъlt forms), thus U *вовк, повний*, but *палка, стіл*. Secondary forms like U *човен* and BR *човен* (cf. R *чёлн*) are often cited as evidence that *l* > *v* did indeed take place before the fall of the jers, since the later epenthesis of a vowel between the etymological liquid and the stem-final consonant reveals *v* and not *l*. Actually this evidence is inconclusive, since the *v* in such forms could have been extended from the other forms in the paradigm lacking an anaptyctic vowel, e.g., U *човна*, BR *чоўна* (Žovtobrjux et al. 1979:224).

If the phonemic change *l* > *v* did take place before the fall of the jers, the phonetic realization of weak *l* as [w] had to continue for a while in the post-jer period, since the new weak *l* in the past/masc.sg. is affected as well and ultimately rephonologized as *v*: *dalъ* > *dal*[w] > *dav*[w]. It remains to explain why the rephonologization was limited to this verb form alone.

Linguists have accounted for the limitation on *l* > *v* on the basis of relative phonetic chronology or morphological analogy. Ogonowski (1880:67-8) advances the unlikely proposal that weak jers fell earlier in verbs than in other word classes, resulting in *l*[w] > *v*[w] in the past/masc.sg., but delaying the emergence of weak *l* elsewhere. By the time the weak jers were lost in nonverbal forms, the pronunciation of weak *l* as [w] had ceased to be productive, thus introducing in effect a categorial limitation on the distribution of the change *l* > *v* . Ogonowski's theory has never found support. Brandt (see Miklosich 1886:372-3) suggests that *l*[w] did arise in new weak environments in the post-jer period, but that [l] was reintroduced in all forms except the past/masc.sg. by analogy to other paradigmatic forms with *l*[l] before a vowel, thus Early U *stôl*[w] > *stôl*[l] by analogy to *stola*[l], *stolu*[l],*palka*[w] > *palka* [l] by analogy to *palok* [l]. In the past/masc.sg. *l*[w] was maintained, however, and reidentified as v[w], thanks to support from the PAP. Thus Early U *bral* [w] > *brav* [w] by analogy to PAP *brav* [w], *bravšy* [w]. Brandt does not explain why the other past tense forms with *l* before a vowel did not have a similar leveling effect on the past/masc.sg., e.g., *bral* [w] > *bral* [l] by analogy to *brala* [l], *bralo* [l], or why these other past tense forms would have exerted less influence than the PAP on the past/masc.sg. Šaxmatov (1915:308) simply assumes that instances of new weak *l*[w] were identifed as *l* or *v* according to grammatical category, *v* assigned to the past/masc.sg., and *l* assigned to all other forms. Simovyč (1937) proposes a structural explanation of the past/ masc.sg. in *v*, linking it to the past/masc.sg. innovations from unsuffixed stems that arose as a result of final cluster simplification, e.g., *paslъ* > *pasl* > *pas*. He establishes an analogical ratio between the forms of the past/masc.sg. and the short-form PAP/nom.sg.masc.—*pas* (< *paslъ*) : *pas* (< *pasъ*) = X : *znav* (< *znavъ*). The analogical X past/masc.sg. is *znav*. Unfortunately, Simovyč fails to provide functional justification for the juxtaposed forms becoming homonymous; cf. the opposite tendency in Russian with PAP *n'os* (identical to past/masc.sg. *n'os*) ultimately avoided in favor of *n'osši* (short-form PAP/ nom.sg.fem.). A number of scholars, including Mixaľčuk (1893), Meľničuk (1958) and Shevelov (1979), actually maintain that the Russian past tense forms like *пас, нёс, грёб* are old past active participles, but this position is untenable. Since the majority of these past tense forms became homonymous with the corresponding past active participles in Middle Russian, we must look to the diagnostic cases which would not have become homonymous unless morphological substitution were involved. In fact the opposite is true: vocalic stems and quasi-vocalic stems in *d* and *t* all maintain the inherited past tense forms, thus R *писал/писала, вёл/вела, мёл/мела* and not **писав/писава, *вёд/вела, *мёт/мела* or **вёд/*ведла, *мёт/*метла*. Also left unexplained is why such analogy was limited to East Slavic when it was capable of operating in any Slavic language.

Our brief survey of the traditional phonetic theory of *l* > *v* in the past/ masc.sg. in its basic variants leads us to the conclusion that although there is ample evidence against the morphological theory, existing explanations based on phonetic change are unsatisfactory (see Bulaxovs'kyj 1956/1977:154-57). We will restrict our comments below to three major issues relevant to the alternation *l* ~ *v* in East Slavic: 1) the relative chronology of [l] > [w] and *l* > *v*, 2) the limitation of *l* > *v* to the past/masc.sg., and 3) the functional motivation for the alternation *l* ~ *v* in the past tense.

The Relative Chronology of [l] > [w], *l* > *v*

On the basis of Late Common Slavic developments and the presence of [w] < CSl **v* in contemporary East Slavic dialects, we assume that Old Russian *v* was a bilabial glide, at least in the dialects of concern here. As for Old Russian *l*, we break with received opinion by considering it to be a "middle" (European) [l̇] as opposed to the velarized variety [ł] currently found in the standard languages of East Slavic. In point of fact there are massive dialect areas of East Slavic in which varieties of [l̇] predominate, including most of northeast Russian, scattered pockets and islands on the rest of Russian-speaking territory, and large portions of the central Ukraine with the so-called Poltava *l*; see Prokopova 1960, Teplova 1967, Bilodid 1969:167-71, Orlova et al. 1970:50-54. Given the East Slavic tendency to velarize *l* in the historic period and the present geographic spread of middle [l̇], the standard explanation of late substratum (presumably Finnic) influence on the "original" [ł] is highly dubious (see Avanesov 1949:171).[10]

The phonemes *v* and *l* did not have identical environmental distribution in Old Russian. Both occurred in prevocalic (strong) environments, but only *l* could appear in syllable-coda position (weak), namely, in *tъlt* forms.[11] If we assume that strong *v* and *l* were realized phonetically as [w] and [l̇], respectively, then what was the phonetic value of weak *l*? A synchronic analysis of East Slavic *telt* and *tъlt* forms makes it clear that before the appearance of the earliest texts weak *l* had, at the very least, become acoustically flat (velarized) in syllable-coda position, since the tonality of the preceding acute vowels was lowered as well: [el̇] > [oł], [ьl̇] > [ъł], thus CSl *melko*, *mьlčati* > OR *moloko*, *mъlčati*.[12] What we are unable to discern is the degree to which the flatting and concomitant reduction in consonantality had proceeded before the fall of the jers, i.e., what point on the gradient phonetic scale [l̇] ... [ł] ... [w] had weak *l* reached before the emergence of new instances of weak *l*? If weak *l* in *tъlt* forms was pronounced [w] in the relevant dialects of Old Russian, for example, does it imply that weak *l* was rephonologized as *v* before the fall of the jers? There are three basic correlations that might be posited (strong and weak pronunciations are juxtaposed in brackets):

1. Weak *l* was pronounced [ł] and identified as *l*

   l [l̇/ł]   vs.   *v* [w/—]

2. Weak *l* was pronounced [w] and identified as *l* (there is no contrast of weak *l* and *v*)

   l [l̇/w]   vs.   *v* [w/—]

3. Weak *l* was pronounced [w] and identified as *v* (there is no contrast of *l* and now weak *v*)

   l [l̇/—]   vs.   *v* [w/w]

Although most proponents of the phonetic theory assume the third correlation with early *l* > *v*, the fact that *l* and *v* did not contrast in weak position before the fall of the jers suggests that the first and second correlations are equally plausible and that weak *l* could have been pronounced [ł], [ł] ~ [w], or [w] and not be reidentified as *v*. As we shall see below, the actual phonetic realization of weak *l* as [ł], [w] or something in between turns out to be less crucial to the ultimate development of weak *l* than the simple fact that it was phonetically distinct from strong *l*.

After the fall of the jers, weak environments arose for both *v* and *l* that had not existed before (see table 5).

Table 5
WEAK ENVIRONMENTS FOR *v* AND *l* AFTER THE FALL OF THE JERS
(Early Ukrainian examples)

	Original weak environment	New weak environments		
	V__C > V__C	#__ьC > #__C	V__ьC > V__C	__ь# > __#
v	—	*vpysaty* [w] ~ [u̯] ~ [u]	*dêvka* [w]	*xlêv* [w]
l	*volk* [ł] ~ [w] ?	*lba* [i̇] ~ [i̯]	*bêlka* [i̇]	*stôl* [i̇]

\# = word boundary   V = vowel   C = consonant

In initial position before a consonant, *v* was apparently realized with greater sonority, resulting in variation between [w], [u̯][13] and the vowel [u]. Since weak jers in word-initial syllables were among the first to be lost, we find traces of this variation in manuscripts from the 11th century on, e.g., **оупи-сати, въчинити** for **въписати, оучинити** (Shevelov 1979:294-95). Similar orthographic slips are found in some of the Novgorod birchbark letters (Dean S. Worth, personal communication, and *contra* Filin 1972:292) and other manuscripts from the Novgorod region. Weak *l* in initial position seems to have been realized with greater sonority as well, resulting in variation between [i̇] and syllabic [i̯]. In some cases the vocalized jer from other forms of the paradigm was generalized, e.g., Early U лоб/лба > лоб/лоба, but in other instances the syllabic *l* was diphthongized and ultimately reidentified as a sequence of two phonemes, e.g., Early BR лоб/лба > лоб/лба ~ ілба. In some southwestern Ukrainian dialects the reflexes of OR **лъжица** 'spoon' are *óžyc'a, ožýc'a* or *žýc'a* (*AUM* II, map 65). There was apparently no confusion of initial weak *v* and *l* because of their distinct phonetic realization.

In medial position before a consonant and finally before a word boundary, new instances of weak *v* and *l* contrasted with one another, e.g., Early U *děvka, bělka, xlěv, stôl*. It is important to note that new weak *v* and *l* are distinct from old weak *l* (in *tъlt forms) not only before the fall of the jers (inasmuch as they are in strong position before a jer), but in the post-jer period as well. With few exceptions (see below) they alternate with instances of strong *v* and *l* before a vocalized jer or vowel in other paradigmatic forms and are thus verified; cf. *děvok, bělok, xlěva, stola*. The old weak *l*, on the contrary, is unverified both *before* and *after* the fall of the jers, e.g., OR *vъlkъ, vъlka* > Early U *volk, volka*. This fact leads us to consider the role of environment in phonetic change.

It has been suggested (Timberlake 1978) that the progress of a phonetic change can be affected by the presence or absence of the conditioning environment in morphologically related forms. In essence the presence of the conditioning environment in all related forms—a UNIFORM ENVIRONMENT—tends to favor the change, while the absence of the conditioning enviroment in some of the related forms—an ALTERNATING ENVIRONMENT—tends to retard the change. The phonetic flatting of weak *l* (velarization and labialization) that began before the fall of the jers and continued, at least for a while, after the fall of the jers, would, in this view, have occurred earlier and with greater consistency in the uniform environment presented by *tъlt forms, than in the alternating environments found in non-*tъlt forms. At any given point in time, a phonetic gradience of flatting in weak *l* might influence its perception and consequent phonemic identification.

In Table 6 the forms listed provide a range of environments more or less favorable to the flatting of *l*: unverified *l* in *tъlt forms (*volk*), verified *l* before word boundary (*stôl*), verified *l* before consonant (*bělka*) and verified *l* before vowel (*luk*). Once the flatting process begins, the environment theory predicts a range of phonetic variation with the most advanced variant occurring in the most favorable environment and the least advanced variant occurring in the least favorable environment. At time period I, prior to the introduction of flatting, all instances of *l* are pronounced as middle [l]. At II, still prior to the fall of the jers, flatting occurs solely in *tъlt forms, the only forms with weak environments. As noted above, the degree of flatting cannot be discerned from available evidence. At III, in the post-jer period, flatting advances unhindered in uniform environments (*volk*), but is retarded in alternating environments (*stôl, bělka*) and blocked completely in strong, prevocalic environments (*luk*). At IV, flatting is complete in uniform environments, but lags behind in alternating environments. Furthermore, we allow for the introduction of velarized [ł] into strong environments as well, the progressive variant that eventually predominates in most East Slavic dialects and in the standard languages.

Table 6

EFFECT OF VARIATION IN FLATTING ON PHONEMIC INTERPRETATION

Time	Before the fall of jers		After the fall of jers			
	I	II	III	IV	V (a)	V (b)
volk	l [l̩]	l [ɫ]	l [ɫ] ~ [w]	l [w]	v [w]	v or l [w]
stól	l [l̩]	l [l̩]	l [l̩] ~ [ɫ]	l [ɫ] ~ [w]	l [ɫ]	l [w]
bêlka	l [l̩]	l [l̩]	l [l̩] ~ [ɫ]	l [ɫ] ~ [w]	l [ɫ]	l [w]
luk	l [l̩]	l [ɫ]	l [l̩]	l [l̩] ~ [ɫ]	l [ɫ]	l [ɫ]

Every generation of speakers must infer the phonemic constituency of morphemes from phonetically realized morphs. Despite the difference between the phonetic representation at time periods I and IV, the phonemic identification in both is identical. But a single phoneme like *l* with a range of variation in different forms admits of the possibility that distinct variants may be identified as manifestations of different phonemes (abductive innovation), in our examples *l* and *v*, rather than the same phoneme (abductive preservation), in this case *l*. Should the phonetic change lose momentum for whatever reason, the community of speakers is left with two analyses, the innovating analysis with *l* in some forms and *v* in others, and the conservative analysis with *l* in all forms. If the innovating analysis perseveres, it will tend to replace the conservative analysis over time. Remedial changes like [ł] ~ [w] > [ł] instantiate the systemic correlation of phoneme and allophone. At time period V, we allow for alternative developments in the phonetic flatting of *l*. For speakers at V-a, phonetic flatting is no longer productive: they have reidentified unverified weak *l*[w] in uniform environments as *v* (*volk* > *vovk*), but have continued to identify weak *l* in alternating environments as *l* and have lost earlier instances of [w] in these cases. The variant [ł] has been generalized in prevocalic environments (except for dialects that maintain variants of middle [l] in strong position). Excluding the past/masc.sg. suffix in *v*, the analysis at V-a corresponds to the restricted systems found in most of Belorussian and Ukrainian. For speakers at V-b, however, phonetic flatting of *l* remains productive: they continue to identify all variants as *l*, although unverified, uniform weak *l*[w] may at any time be reidentified as *v*[w]. The pattern at V-b corresponds to the unrestricted systems found in southwestern Ukrainian and northeastern Russian dialects. Of crucial importance is that the unverified, uniform instances of *l*[w] in *both* systems, restricted and unrestricted, are susceptible to reinterpretation as *v*[w].[14]

Limitation of *l* > *v* in New Weak Environments

According to the environment theory presented above, the development of past/masc.sg. forms in final *l* should be identical to that of other paradigmatic forms ending in *l*, thus unrestricted *dal* [w]/*dala* [l], *stôl* [w]/*stola* [l] and restricted *dal* [l]/*dala* [l], *stôl* [l]/*stola* [l]. Instead the restricted dialects have *l* in reflexes of *stôl* (*st'il* [l]), but *v* in reflexes of *dal* (*dav* [w]). This discrepancy can be explained by considering a corollary of the theory represented by Timberlake. While alternating environments can retard the progress of a phonetic change, it is also possible for a change to be promoted by specific grammatical morphemes in order to give expression to grammatical distinctions hitherto subject to syncretism. In the case of the past tense, continuation of phonetic flatting in the post-jer period produced variants of *l* capable of reinterpretation as *v*, variation that raised the possibility of formally distinguishing the suffix of the masculine singular from that of the other forms of the past tense. The diacritic potential of the phonetic change in the past tense suffix tended to promote the change and thus negated the retarding effect of the nonmasculine suffix allomorphs with verified *l*. To understand why a verb form favored the reidentification of *l*[w] as *v*[w] while other forms did not,[15] we must turn out attention to the relationship between grammatical categories and morphophonemic alternation in East Slavic.

Functional Motivation for *l* > *v* in the Past Tense

Prior to the fall of the jers, gender distinction in the perfect participle (new past tense) is expressed by a synthetic gender-number suffix, e.g., -ъ (masc.sg.), -*a* (fem.sg.), -*o* (neut.sg.). In the post-jer period the singular pattern remains the same; only the expression of masc.sg. changes -ъ > -∅. Thus OR *pisalъ/pisala/pisalo* > Early BR *p'isal∅/p'isala/p'isalo*. But two phonetic developments—compensatory lengthening and cluster simplification—had consequences for morphophonemic alternation in East Slavic.

In Ukrainian the loss of the final weak jer in the past/masc.sg. of unsuffixed verbs with neoacute intonation resulted in the lengthening of root vowels *e* and *o* to *ē* and *ō*, later *ê* and *ô*, respectively. These tense vowels, ultimately realized as diphthongs or *i*, distinguished the root vocalism of the past/masc.sg. from that of the other forms; cf. U *ніс/несла, пік/пекла, міг/могла*.

In all of East Slavic the loss of the final weak jer resulted in sonorant-final clusters that tended to be simplified. In the case of the lateral, a syllabic pronunciation of *l* elicited the development of an anaptyctic vowel adjacent to the sonorant, a segmental diphthong that was eventually analyzed as an independent vowel + *l*, i.e. *l* > V + *l*. The variant V + *l* was exploited in the morphophonemic system of substantives, resulting in nonetymological alternations characteristic of monosyllabic stems in specific grammatical environments, e.g., OR *uglъ/ugla* > Middle R *ugl/ugla* > *ugol/ugla*; cf. OR *sъnъ/sъna* > Middle R *son/sna*. A nonsyllabic, alternative pronunciation of the lateral, however, saw the weakening and frequently the complete loss of *l*, i.e., *l* > ∅. This zero variant was utilized by the verbal morphophonemic system in the expression of the past/masc.sg. of unsuffixed, nonvocalic stems, e.g., OR *strìglъ/strìgla* > Middle R *strìgl/strìgla* > *strìg/strìgla*.

The fall of the jers thus gave rise to phonetic change with morphophonemic consequences for the expression of the past/masc.sg. Of particular concern here is the emergence of a new East Slavic past tense allomorph {∅} which serves simultaneously as a direct symbol of the past tense and as an index of the grammatical categories masculine-singular. The indexical function of the past tense allomorph {∅} in nonvocalic stems had no analogue in vocalic stems, that is, not until the western dialects yielded /[w] in word-final position. The possibility of extending the indexical reference of masc.sg. to *all* stems would have favored the early and consistent flatting of weak *l* in vocalic stems and its subsequent reidentification as *v*, thus, Early BR *p'isal* [w] > *p'isav* [w], but *p'isala* [l], *p'isalo* [l]. The past tense suffix allomorphs in the western dialects, at least in the restricted dialects, are functionally analogous:

nonvocalic stems: {∅} masc.sg. vs. {l} fem.,neut.sg.
vocalic stems: {v} masc.sg. vs. {l} fem.,neut.sg.

Since the change /[w] > v[w] in the past tense was limited to a single suffix, it could be used for suffixal allomorphy, a common phenomenon in verbal inflection, e.g., Early U infinitive suffix {ty} ~ {sty} ~ {čy}, non-past person-number suffix {š} ~ {mo} ~ {te} ~ {t'}. In nonverbal forms, however, /[w] simply served as a root-final consonant. It was not reidentified as *v*[w] because the alternation of root-final consonants in inflection was severely limited both by consonant typology and grammatical environment. In addition to alternations involving velars and dentals (cf. U *нога/нозі*), the morphophonemic relationships of nonverbal forms in the post-jer period linked nonpalatals and palatals (cf. BR *нізкі/ніжэйшы*), nongeminates and geminates (cf. BR *ноч/ноччу*), and nonpalatalized and palatalized consonants (cf. BR *сусед/суседзі*). In all these cases the derived alternant appears before a vowel, in strong position. If stem differentiation is found with a {∅} desinence, it is accomplished through vowel alternation, e.g., U *стіл/стола, ніч/ночі, палка/палок, день/дня*. An alternation {l} ~ {v} in the environment before the desinence {∅} (nom.sg.masc., gen.pl.fem-neut.) thus found no support in the inherited system of nonverbal morphophonemic alternation and was not developed.

From the above we see that the presence (most Ukrainian, Belorussian dialects) vs. absence (most Russian dialects) of the alternation *l* ~ *v* in the past tense is directly tied to the continuation vs. cessation of the phonetic flatting of weak *l* in the post-jer period. In the dialects that preserved phonetic flatting (cf. U *товстий*, BR *тоўсты*), past/masc.sg. /[w] > v[w], thus U *дав/дала* and BR *даў/дала* in line with U *ніс/несла* and BR *нёс/нясла*. In dialects that did not develop the phonetic flatting of weak *l* in the post-jer period, weak *l* continued to be identified as *l*, thus R *дал/дала*, in spite of *нёс/несла*.

The development of the unrestricted North Russian dialects with /[ɨ̇/w] or /[ɫ/w] confirms the role of phonetic environment (verified vs. unverified) and grammatical categories (verbal vs. nonverbal forms) in determining the course of weak *l*. Weak /[w] in many fringe areas of these dialects is being replaced by /[ɫ] or /[ɨ̇], apparently under the influence of the literary language with /[ɫ/ɨ̇]. Despite disclaimers by Teplova (1967:169ff) that grammatical categories and phonetic environment play no role in the course of the change *l*[w] > *l*[ł] or *l*[l], the data show clearly that the forms most resistant to this change are unverified *tъlt forms and the past/masc.sg. Furthermore, the data presented by and large manifest a hierarchy of resistance to the loss of *l*[w], one that reflects both phonetic verification and grammatical category: *tъlt forms ⩾ past/masc.sg. ⩾ nouns of the *igolka* type ⩾ nouns of the *stol* type. In *tъlt forms the [w] is unverified and probably identified as *v*[w]. In the past/masc.sg. the [w] is verified but probably identified as *v*[w], which, together with {∅}, serves to distinguish the masc.sg. from the other past tense forms in *l*. In nouns of the *igolka* type, [w] is verified as *l*, but only in one form, gen.pl. *igolok*. The opposite is true for nouns of the *stol* type, in which [w] is verified as *l* in all forms except the nom-acc.sg. There is no accounting for the discrepancy in behavior between verbs and nouns under otherwise identical circumstances unless the roles of verifiability and grammatical function are recognized. Teplova's invocation of word frequency (1967:171)—past/masc.sg. forms occur more frequently than nouns with word-final *l*—is unconvincing and cannot explain the distinct behavior of nouns like *igolka* on the one hand, and *stol* on the other. Moreover, the greater frequency of past/masc.sg. forms might be expected to have the opposite effect, that is, the earlier and more consistent spread of the progressive variant *l*[ł] or *l*[l] in verbs rather than nouns. This is clearly not the case. The development towards a uniform manifestation of *l* in weak and strong environments in North Russian is accomplished by means of a transitional "restricted" stage reminiscent of the restricted systems found in the western dialects. Whatever differences arise can be ascribed to the considerable influence of the literary language, a factor absent in the case of the original developments in Ukrainian and Belorussian.

Historical Parallels

The most obvious historical parallel to the skewed development of weak *l* in Ukrainian and Belorussian is the functionally analogous development of the alternation *l* ~ ∅ in the past tense of nonvocalic unsuffixed verb stems, e.g., R *нёс/несла, грёб/гребла, пёк/пекла*. It was the distinct morphophonemic patterns of verbal and nonverbal categories that favored the change *l* > V + *l* in nouns (Middle R *ugl* > *ugol*), but *l* > ∅ in verbs (Middle R *n'osl* > *n'os*); cf. similar morphophonemic exploitation of phonetic variation even in dialects that eventually tolerated syllabic *l*, e.g., Czech dial. *ved/vedla* 'lead,' *vedel/vedla* (Bělič 1972:81-2 and map 13), Slovak dial. *védel/védla, vjédol/vjédla*, West and Central Slovak dial. *vjédov/vjédla, vídov/vídla* (with grammatically limited reidentification of weak *l* as V + *v*, Krajčovič 1975:93).

Another parallel is provided by the history of the adjectival-pronominal desinence *-ovo* (gen.sg.masc.-neut.) in North and Central Russian. The waning stages of phonetic lenition of *g* produced a number of variants, the most advanced of which (completely lenited) were found in intervocalic uniform environments. The partially or fully lenited *g* [γ] in the original desinence *-ogo* was particularly susceptible to reinterpretation as *v* because the functional relationship of the categories signaled by the paradigm of desinential consonants was better served by *v* than by *g*. Instances of uniform and alternating intervocalic *g*, however, continued to be identified as *g* for the most part because of categorial constraints on morphophonemic alternation (see Flier 1983 for details).

Conclusions

The determination of a more precise chronology of the phonetic and phonemic changes that underlie the alternation *l* ~ *v* in East Slavic depends on the discovery of additional textual evidence from the period between the fall of the jers and the 15th century. The lack of such documentation, however, need not discourage us from drawing general conclusions concerning the nature and timing of these changes.

1. The basis of the alternation *l* ~ *v* in the past/masc.sg. suffix in East Slavic is the historical phonetic alternation [l] ~ [w] and not morphological contamination or substitution of the old perfect participle with the past active participle. The best evidence for the phonetic explanation is the consistent correlation between the alternation *l* ~ *v* and the presence of *v* < *l* in original *tъlt forms. It is hardly coincidental that the alternation *l* ~ *v* in East Slavic presupposes *tovt < *tъlt.

2. The most plausible source of the phonetic alternation [l] ~ [w] in East Slavic is the prehistoric increase in secondary low tonality (flatting) of *l* in tautosyllabic environments, a gradual phonetic change that encompassed nearly all *tolt/*telt and *tъlt/*tьlt forms in East Slavic, as shown in the modern reflexes of Ukrainian, Belorussian and Russian.

3. There is no reason to assume that the flatting of weak *l* along the continuum [l] ... [ł] ... [w] was achieved in full measure before the fall of the jers. The skewed distribution of *l* and *v* from weak *l* and the relatively late attestations of the rephonologization of *l* and *v* suggest that the flatting process gained or lost momentum in the century or two following the loss of the jers, with consequent phonetic and phonemic ramifications.

4. The apparent center of the flatting process was the western dialects of East Slavic, particularly the territory occupied by modern Belorussia, the northern Ukraine and contiguous Russian dialects. Subsequent migrations or displacement have obscured the geographical unity of this process.

5. East Slavic dialects with the alternation *l* ~ *v* in the past tense typically reflect the historic loss of the phonetic alternation [l] ~ [w] and the subsequent

reinterpretation of certain instances of *l*[w] as *v*[w], the reinterpretation itself affected both by the impact of phonetic environment on the rate of the phonetic change and categorial constraints on potential morphophonemic alternation.

6. The emergence of the alternation *l* ~ *v* in the past tense suffix of vocalic and quasi-vocalic verb stems was supported by the development of an analogous alternation *l* ~ Ø in unsuffixed nonvocalic stems.

The history of the alternation *l* ~ *v* in East Slavic provides ample illustration of the diverse ways in which phonetic, phonemic and morphological factors can influence the course of a linguistic change. Moreover, it serves as a reminder of the functional coherence of language and of the correlations between sound and meaning which cannot be ignored.

University of California, Los Angeles

NOTES

[1] The term "quasi-vocalic" refers to those consonantal stems rendered vocalic by morphophonemic readjustment rules, e.g., truncation (*znaj-* ⇒ *zna-, klad-* ⇒ *kla-*) and substitution (*žn-* ⇒ *ža-*) in the formation of the Russian past tense.

[2] We omit reference to grammatical distinctions in Old Russian that have no consequence for the later development, i.e., dual number, gender distinction in the plural.

[3] Of course, once the new past tense lost its association with the perfect, it became possible for an indeclinable form of the short-form past active participle to take on a different function, as witnessed by the independent perfects found in certain Central and North Russian dialects, e.g., *собака вышедши из будки прочь и лает* 'the dog has left ...,' *недавно один [заяц] был прибегши в деревню* 'recently one had run into the village.' But this phenomenon is almost exclusively confined to perfective intransitive verbs denoting change of state or position (Meščerskij 1972:224-27), less than 25% of the verb lexicon, and is not to be confused with the alternation *l* ~ *v* in the Ukrainian and Belorussian past tense, which is not restricted lexically.

[4] In this instance "southwest" is more narrowly defined as dialects lying west of the line between the Sjan—Rava Ruśka—Kamjaneć-Podiľśkyj.

[5] Shevelov is quick to cite Polish influence in the loss of *l* from the root {molv}, but this explanation is anachronistic if the general Polish change *ł* > *w* is dated to the 16th century (Stieber 1973:110-11).

[6] This example is rejected (414, n. 5) because the text is a collective work of students from various parts of the Ukraine.

[7] Shevelov (1979:411) notes that in some of these dialects there are restrictions on the appearance of word-final *l*[w], that is, *l*[w] is losing productivity.

[8] The exceptional dialects have experienced the change *l* > *w* in all positions, including prevocalic; cf. Polish. Shevelov (411) views this change as a late development (19th century), but does not rule out a change in common with Polish.

[9] It is quite possible that the past/masc.sg. suffix in the unrestricted system has been rephonologized from *l* to *v*, since weak *v* is also realized as [w]. If so, this reinterpretation would serve as an example of covert morphophonemic change, i.e., the replacement in morphological environments of a phonetic alternation [l] ~ [w] with a morphophonemic alternation *l* ~ *v* (see Flier 1982).

[10] Avanesov views [ł] as secondary because of the existence of northeastern Russian dialects in which strong prevocalic [ł] alternates with weak [w]. Since *l*[w] must develop from *l*[ł], and not

directly from /[l̩], he assumes that the original allophone in strong position must have been [ł] as well. Thus original /[ł] developed to [l] in strong position (loss of flatting), and to [w] in weak position (increase in flatting). But this is a theoretical conception of strong-weak environmental relationships unsubstantiated in fact. There are no theoretical strictures on stability of phonetic realization in strong environments and instability in weak environments. In fact, this kind of distribution is quite common.

[11] We ignore as irrelevant to the present discussion the allophonic variation of *v* and *l* before grave (back) and acute (front) vowels. We also disregard instances of "weak" *v* in foreign names and terms that were undoubtedly not characteristic of colloquial speech, e.g., *Euthymios, august*. Such forms become relevant after the fall of the jers when *v*[w] appears in weak position in native words as well.

[12] The exceptional development of certain *telt forms (cf. R *селезень* 'drake,' U *велетень* 'giant,' R dial. *пелед* 'shed,' *мелен* 'mill') shows that the flatting of weak *l* and preceding acute vowel was more consistent in *tъlt forms.

[13] Although one assumes a gradience in sonority among [w], [u̯] and [u], further study is required before a more precise distinction can be made between [w] and [u̯] (see Teplova 1967:155, n. 7; Bilodid 1969:137; Padlužny and Čèkman 1973:46-8, 226-32). For this reason we have avoided making any claim that might differentiate weak *v* and weak *l* solely on the basis of the phonetic distinction [u̯] vs. [w], respectively, even though this distinction may have been valid prior to the reidentification of weak *l* as *v*.

[14] Theoretically, unverified /[w] from any source, *tъlt forms or forms with medial unverified *l* that arose after the fall of the jers, should show one and the same pattern of development. Unfortunately, there are too few cases of unverified new /[w] to permit confirmation. Thus OR **олътарь** 'altar' > U *вівтар*, but BR *алтар*. It is possible that the unexpected *l* in the Belorussian form is due to Russian *алтарь* or even Lithuanian *altõrius*; the form [awtará] is attested in the northwestern Belorussian dialect of Vawkavysk (Karskij 1908/1955:319).

[15] A notable exception is the unchanging form of the originally declinable Old Russian prefix **полъ-/полоу-**. Once the form of the prefix became fixed in Ukrainian and Belorussian, the analysis with reidentification of /[w] as *v*[w] predominated, the *v* now serving to distinguish the prefix (U *пів-*, BR *паў-*) from the correlated adverb (U *навпіл*, BR *напалам*) and the noun (U *половина*, BR *палавіна*).

REFERENCES

AUM = Atlas ukrajins'koji movy, II. Kiev, Unpublished.
Avanesov, R. I.
    1949   *Očerki russkoj dialektologii*, pt. 1. Moscow.
Bezpal'ko, O. P. et al.
    1962   *Istoryčna hramatyka ukrajins'koji movy*. 2nd rev. ed. Kiev.
Bělič, Jaromír
    1972   *Nástin české dialektologie*. Prague.
Bilodid, I. K., ed.
    1969   *Sučasna ukrajins'ka literaturna mova: Vstup. Fonetyka*. Kiev.
Bulaxovs'kyj, L. A.
    1956/1977   *Pytannja poxodžennja ukrajins'koji movy* reprinted in *Vybrani praci v pjaty tomax*, II: *Ukrajins'ka mova*. Kiev, 9-216.
Bulyka, A. M., A. I. Žurawski, I. I. Kramko
    1979   *Histaryčnaja marfalohija belaruskaj movy*. Minsk.
Filin, F. P.
    1972   *Proisxoždenie russkogo, ukrainskogo i belorusskogo jazykov*. Leningrad.
Flier, Michael S.
    1982   "Morphophonemic change as evidence of phonemic change: The status of the sharped velars in Russian" in *Slavic linguistics and poetics: Studies for Edward Stankiewicz on his*

60th birthday, 17 November 1980, ed. by Kenneth E. Naylor, Howard Aronson, Bill J. Darden and Alexander M. Schenker. Columbus, Ohio, 137-148 (= *IJSLP* 25/26).
1983 "The origin of the desinence *-ovo* in Russian" in *From Los Angeles to Kiev*, ed. by Dean S. Worth and Vladimir Markov. Columbus, Ohio.

Karskij, E. F.
1908/1955 *Belorusy: Jazyk belorusskogo naroda*, no. 1: *Istoričeskij očerk zvukov belorusskogo jazyka*. Moscow.

Krajčovič, Rudolf
1975 *A Historical phonology of the Slovak language*. Heidelberg.

Mel'ničuk, A. S.
1958 "Razvitie predikativnogo upotreblenija pričastij na -(v)ъ, -(v)ъš- v vostočnoslavjanskix jazykax," *Slovjanske movoznavstvo: Zbirnyk statej*, I. Kiev, 91-159.

Meščerskij, N. A., ed.
1972 *Russkaja dialektologija*. Moscow.

Miklosich, F.
1886 *Sravnitel'naja morfologija slavjanskix jazykov*, III. Moscow.

Mixal'čuk, K.
1893 "K južnorusskoj dialektologii," *Kievskaja starina*, XLII, 478-80.

Ogonowski, E.
1880 *Studien auf dem Gebiete der ruthenischen Sprache*. Lvov.

Orlova, V. G., et al.
1970 *Obrazovanie severnorusskogo narečija i srednerusskix govorov po materialam lingvističeskoj geografii*. Moscow.

Padlužny, A. I. and V. M. Čèkman
1973 *Huki belaruskaj movy*. Minsk.

Potebnja, A. A.
1865 "O zvukovyx osobennostjax russkix narečij," *Filologičeskie zapiski*, Voronež.

Prokopova, L. I.
1960 "Do artykuljacijnoji xarakterystyky tak zvanoho poltavs'koho l," *Seredn'onaddniprjans'ki hovory*, ed. by F. T. Žylko et al. Kiev, 100-07.

Shevelov, George Y.
1979 *A historical phonology of the Ukrainian language*. Heidelberg.

Simovyč, V.
1937 "Pro poholosnene ukrajins'ke 'l'," *Zapysky Naukovoho tovarystva im. Ševčenka*, CLV. Lvov, 139-52.

Stieber, Zdzisław
1973 *A historical phonology of the Polish language*. Heidelberg.

Šaxmatov, A. A.
1915 *Očerk drevnejšego perioda istorii russkogo jazyka*. Petrograd.

Teplova, V. N.
1967 "Zvuki [ł], [l], [u̯] na meste ètimologičeskogo *l* tverdogo i ix mesto v fonologičeskix sistemax severnorusskix govorov," *Očerki po fonetike severnorusskix govorov*, ed. by L. L. Kasatkin et al. Moscow.

Timberlake, Alan
1978 "Uniform and alternating environments in phonological change," *Folia Slavica* 2, nos. 1-3, 312-28.

Wexler, Paul
1977 *A historical phonology of the Belorussian language*. Heidelberg.

Žovtobrjux, M. A., V. M. Rusanivs'kyj, V. H. Skljarenko
1979 *Istorija ukrajins'koji movy: Fonetyka*. Kiev.

Did Slavic Develop Declension Classes?

Frank Y. Gladney

The nominal declension classes which we posit for the Slavic languages resulted from the fusion of the thematic vowel with the case-number marker. Whereas reconstructed *vĭlkom and *genām show a common accusative singular marker preceded by different thematic vowels, attested vlĭkŭ and ženǫ are said to show the accusative singular endings of different declension classes. This fusion of thematic vowel with case-number marker was variously affected by the stem consonant. Thus gen. sg. ženy and dat. sg. ženě differ in their final vowels from gen. sg. dušę and dat. sg. duši. The differences could be ascribed to a further development of declension classes, say, hard second declension vs. soft second declension. Meillet, however, writes: "Ces différences entre thèmes en -a- et thèmes en -ja-, réglées par des règles strictes d'alternance, ne constituaient pas des différences de flexion en slave commun."[1] Indeed, if there are rules which account for the differences, there is no need for declension classes.

The alternations in question are treated in §19 of Diels' *Altkirchenslavische Grammatik*, where it is noted, "eine und dieselbe Flexionsklasse kann ... ganz verschiedene Endungen aufweisen, je nachdem ob der letzte Konsonant des Stammes ein unpalataler (harter) oder ein 'palataler' (weicher) ist."[2] This is referred to as a *Lautgesetz*, which, Diels notes, is valid generally, not merely in noun declension. But the formulation of it is not rigorous enough to account for the two most problematic alternations. Consider its ambivalence on the key points: "Nach den palatalen Konsonanten erscheint in Aksl. allgemein o als e, ŭ als ĭ, y als i (manchmal auch als ę), ě nicht selten als i, z.B...." (70). Moreover, although Diels' grammar is on the whole synchronic the passages quoted are part of a chapter entitled "Vorgeschichte der altkirchenslavischen Vocale." The latter issue is addressed by Vaillant in the preface to his *Manuel du vieux slave*. He writes: "Ce manuel est une grammaire descriptive.... Les explications historiques par le préslave, ses traitements phonétiques et son système morphologique, sont remplacées par l'observation des alternances et des variantes de formes qui existent dans la langue."[3] Regarding descriptive adequacy, when we turn to the chapter on "Les Alternances," we find "les alternances des voyelles dures et molles," comprising six of the alternations found in the paradigms of žena and duša—ŭ/ĭ, o/e, a/ä, y/i, u/ü, and ǫ/ǭ— but not the problematic y/ę and ě/i (76-77). Trubetzkoy's posthumous grammar also grapples with this problem.[4] At the close of the chapter "Das

Lautsystem" he speaks of the twofold (*zweigestaltige*) declension, which takes endings in two shapes: after a sharp (*hocheigentoniger*) stem consonant, endings appear in their "front-vowel shape," while after a flat or neutral stem consonant, endings have their "back-vowel shape." He is aware of course that the "hintervokalische Gestalt" of the dat. sg. ending of *žena* is not a back vowel and that the "vordervokalische Gestalt" corresponding to the gen. sg. ending in *ženy* is different from that corresponding to the instr. pl. ending in *grady*. Perhaps for this reason in the chapter on inflection he speaks, somewhat more abstractly, of "die hocheigentonige Gestalt" vs. "die nichthocheigentonige Gestalt" of the endings (118-19).

More rigorously synchronic grammars of Old Church Slavonic, such as Vaillant's, Trubetzkoy's, and Lunt's, include a morphophonemic component sandwiched in between phonology and morphology, while Diels' grammar comprises only a phonology and a morphology. Even so, these grammars fail to reconcile *y/ę* with *y/i* and *ě/i* with *ě/a*. Trubetzkoy's morphophonemics addresses the question, "Welche lautlichen Alternationen innerhalb eines und desselben Morphems sind möglich, ohne daß das Gefühl der Einheitlichkeit der Morphems in Sprachbewußtsein zerstört wird" (101). This way of viewing the matter may be apposite in the case of longer, root morphemes, where, to cite Vaillant's examples, alternations like *čistŭ/očestiti* and *počiti/pokoi* merely "modifient gravement la forme des thèmes," while in *načĭnǫ/iskoni* "la lien entre les formes alternantes cesse d'être senti" (83). It seems less so in the case of shorter, ending morphemes, where, to the extent that the alternation *grady/mǫži* preserves the unity of the instr. pl. ending, the alternation *ženy/dušę* destroys the unity of the gen. sg. ending, and to the extent that the alternation *siděti/ležati* preserves the unity of the thematic vowel, the alternation *ženě/duši* destroys the unity of the dat. sg. ending.

Generative phonology invests psychological judgments of morpheme identity with operational content. Two allomorphs either represent a single lexical entry, their surface differences accounted for by phonological rules, or else they represent two lexical entries, possibly suppletive. Regarding gen. sg. -*y* and -*ę*, there seem to be two ways to express their identity. They could have the lexical representation -*y* and it could be stipulated that after a palatal stem consonant it is fronted, opened, and nasalized in a genitive singular environment (but in an instrumental plural environment only fronted). The advantage of this proposal is that the lexical representation would be identical with one of the allomorphs. But it is unsatisfactory because it shows helplessness vis-à-vis the traditional goals of research in this area, which have been to find phonetic environments for alternations which on the surface have only grammatical environments. The other way to unify the two allomorphs is more purely phonological but involves a degree of abstraction. Gen. sg. -*y*, but not instr. pl. -*y*, is represented as containing in itself the potential for nasality and openness. This potential is realized in the environment of a palatal stem consonant, independently of syntactic environment. This is the solution proposed by Lunt in the Epilogue to the sixth edition of his *Old Church Slavonic Grammar*.[5] Lunt sets up a gen. sg. ending -*ons*. In *ženy* it is nonnasal because it is high; it is high because of the underlying final nasal plus consonant, and it is tense because of the nasal. In *dušę* the ending is realized on the surface as nasal and nonhigh because, as Lunt proposes, it is a front vowel (fronted by the palatal stem consonant), otherwise it would have remained high and lost its nasality, as in *ženy*. For the dat. sg. ending Lunt posits underlying -*oi*, which monophthongizes to -*ě* after a hard consonant but which fronts to -*ei* after a palatal consonant (as do other high or lax vowels) before monophthongizing to -*i*. In this way, "the two-fold substantival and pronominal declension collapse into one," Lunt concludes (153).

Lunt's solution works: it accounts for all the facts which are taken to constitute the synchrony of Old Church Slavonic.[6] It is liable to some of the criticism that has been leveled against generative phonology descriptions, viz. that the lexical representations that it posits are too abstract. If Lunt's -*ons* and -*oi* can be shown to transgress admissible limits of abstractness, they will need to be rejected and in their place we will need to recognize pairs of endings representing different declension classes. The purpose of this paper is to examine the treatment of Slavic nominal ending alternations in terms of declension class as opposed to phonology. Discussion of this question has tended to be one-sided, solely from the standpoint of phonology. It is generally assumed that sound change in Slavic has resulted in a more highly ramified inflectional morphology. But as long as the mechanisms of the latter remain unexplored, it is not possible to weigh the cost of phonological complexity, such as Lunt's abstract lexical representations and ordered rules, against that of morphological complexity. We should not expel an alternation from the domain of phonology until we see how it is handled in the adjacent domain of morphology.

Declension class is a mechanism for matching endings and stems with the help of lexical features. For example, *žen-* is marked in the lexicon as a DC2 (declension class 2) noun, and -*ǫ* is entered in the lexicon as the DC2 acc. sg. noun ending. How an explicit grammar accounts for the appearance of -*ǫ* to the right of *žen-* in the appropriate syntactic environment is far from simple, and as far as I am aware there exists no coherent, generally accepted account.

For a useful perspective compare the somewhat simpler case of **genām*. In both *ženǫ* and **genām* the form of the word is determined by a combination of factors: the relationship of the word to other words in the sentence, chiefly the main verb; the way in which the word presents the number of the referent; and the form class of the particular noun. Stated in familiar terms, the form of a noun reflects its case, number, and declension class. Since case shows the word's relationship to other words in the sentence, it may be described by means of a transformational rule which assigns one or another case marking to it in one or another sentence environment. Number is more or less independent of other sentence members, being simply a feature of the noun phrase in which the given noun occurs; therefore it is best described by the rules of the base component (phrase-structure rules). Case and number are thus syntactic features of nouns in Slavic. Declension class, on the other hand, is a purely lexical feature, correlated to some extent with meaning, but lexical in any case. In the case of *genām the syntactic features of case and number receive a segmentally discrete expression, -m. For this reason we could envisage a description of Proto-Slavic in which the phrase-structure rules analyzed (rewrote) the symbol Noun as $Stem_n$ plus $Ending_n$. The ending constituent would bear the features of case and number, and for accusative singular it would be lexicalized as $[_{E_n} m]$, independently of the lexicalization of $Stem_n$.[7]

For ženǫ, assuming that it must be analyzed as žen- plus -ǫ, a phrase-structure rule Noun → $Stem_n$ $Ending_n$ is less feasible. Since -ǫ is the exponent of lexical features of the stem in addition to syntactic features, the presence of an $Ending_n$ node in the preterminal string would, following the lexicalization of $Stem_n$, necessitate some sort of agreement rule to make the ending agree with the stem for declension class. To obviate this (clearly undesirable) necessity, several writers have proposed dealing with declension class in the phrase-structure component via subcategorization.[8] Phrase-structure rules rewrite Noun as $Noun_{DC1}$, $Noun_{DC2}$, $Noun_{DC3}$, and so on, and this subcategorization is continued by the rule which rewrites Noun as $Stem_n$ plus $Ending_n$. The result is a preterminal string with noun-stem nodes at which only stems having the same declension class as the following ending nodes can be introduced. Now subcategorization is commonly employed to handle facts of co-occurrence in the sentence, for example, to limit the occurrence of transitive verbs to sentence slots which have object NPs and the occurrence of intransitive verbs to sentence slots which do not. But nouns in Slavic can differ in declension class and yet belong to the same syntactic and semantic classes—even be synonymous. There could thus be no syntactic grounds which would justify limiting the choice of a noun stem being inserted at a noun-stem node to a noun stem of a particular declension class. Declension class is a purely morphological, i.e., lexical, problem and should not be dealt with syntactically via subcategorization.

The fusion of case-number marker with thematic vowel is said to have increased the inflectional nature of Slavic.[9] As a result the word acquired a greater importance as a term in the description of Slavic sentences.

Accordingly we assume that the preterminal symbols of the base component of the grammar are categorial symbols representing words—Noun, Verb, Adjective, and so on—rather than stems and endings. It is these symbols that undergo lexicalization and then acquire government and agreement features in the transformational component of the grammar. At the same time we assume that inflected words in Slavic comprise stems and endings and that it is stems and endings that are stored in the lexicons of Slavic languages.[10] The recognition of endings in the lexicon in turn commits us to special transformational rules called segmentation rules. Segmentation rules follow the feature-assigning transformations which complete the feature specifications of the word constituents; operating on those constituents they create nodes immediately to the right of them, associating with those nodes the features needed by the later lexical insertion rules which introduce the appropriate endings.[11]

The complexity of segmentation rules encourages the search for alternatives. For example, the fusion of thematic vowel with case-number marker could be assigned to synchronic Slavic phonology so that the ending would not need to reflect declension class. This would not be far-fetched in cases like *ženǫ*, but less clear in *ženě* and *ženy*, while for some of the plural noun forms which are clearly analyzable into thematic vowel plus case-number marker it may be an attractive option.[12] Or we could deny endings lexical status and assume what are sometimes referred to as spell-out rules, transformations which actually create endings to the right of stems a segment at a time. This approach, like an approach which operated with stored paradigms of word-forms rather than stems and endings, would simply eliminate the set of problems being discussed in this paper.[13] Let us proceed on the assumption that word-forms like *ženǫ* comprise two lexical items, a stem and an ending.

The question before us is how the differences in inflection between *žena* and *duša* are accounted for with the mechanisms of declension class. Surely some of the differences are purely phonological. Thus for the relevant noun classes there would be a single gen. pl. ending in the lexicon, -*ŭ*, and it would be shifted to -*ĭ* by phonological rule after a palatal consonant. But there would be two gen. sg. endings and two dat. sg. endings for these nouns. The lexical rule which introduces -*ę* at the ending node to the right of *duš*- must have at its disposal the features Genitive, Singular, DC2, and some feature which distinguishes it from -*y*, which is also Genitive, Singular, and DC2. Let that feature be Soft (or, to make it a binary feature, +Soft). DC2 and +Soft, which are segmented out of the noun constituent together with the syntactic features Genitive and Singular, are both lexical features, but they differ. Whereas DC2 is arbitrary and unpredictable, +Soft is predictable and hence redundant. All noun stems in Old Church Slavonic with a palatal stem consonant are +Soft, which feature is assigned to them by a lexical redundancy rule. In the lexical entry for -ę the feature +Soft is matched up with the phonetic features –High, –Back, and +Nasal; compare the lexical entry for -y, in which the feature –Soft is matched up with the features +High, +Back, –Round, and –Nasal. There is thus a match-up of phonetic and nonphonetic (grammatical) features at two points in the description, in the lexical redundancy rules applicable to noun stems and in the lexical entries of the endings. The more these matchings duplicate each other, the more they invite elimination in favor of a phonological rule. The more arbitrary and random they are, the more necessary. Thus the correlation between phonetic +High in the stem consonant of *duš-* and its lexical feature +Soft is asymmetrical with that between +Soft and –High, –Back, and +Nasal in -ę.

In the case of the dat. sg. ending, on the contrary, the lexical feature +Soft mediates between +High (also –Back) in the stem consonant and +High in the feature specifications of the ending -*i*. We might then consider dispensing with +Soft in this case in favor of an assimilation rule which stated that the dat. sg. ending is +High following a +High –Back stem consonant, otherwise –High. A phonological rule such as this, it should be noted, would be applicable only in the specific grammatical environment of the dat. sg. DC2 ending. With this severely limited generality it is not a particularly attractive addition to the phonology of Old Church Slavonic. If it deserves consideration at all, it is only relative to an abstract underlying -*oi* on the one hand, and the cumbersome apparatus of declension class on the other. It is also worth noting that the phonological regularity under discussion is different from the historically supported rule proposed by Lunt, that underlying -*oi* is fronted to -*ei* after a palatal stem consonant. It is a secondary regularity lacking an historical counterpart and as such it encourages us to look for other secondary, ahistorical phonological regularities among nominal endings in Slavic.

For an ending alternation to be phonological rather than a matter of declension class, it must be phonologically conditioned at both ends. In the lexical entry for an ending the declension-class feature always has phonetic correlates, endings often being monophonemic and implementing a limited number of feature oppositions. The crucial question then is whether there are phonetic correlates for the declension-class feature in the stem. Where there are none, as in the case of the feature DC2, there is no phonological alternative to declension class.

Consider the case of "soft" stems in Old Church Slavonic which were no longer phonetically soft. Diels writes: "Im Aksl. scheinen manche der 'palatalen' Konsonanten ihre Palatalität (wenigstens mundartlich) eingebüßt zu haben, doch hindert uns das nicht, auch sie zu den palatalen zu rechnen, da die von ihnen ausgeübten Wirkungen dem Verlust der Palatalität meist vorausliegen" (69-70). This diachronic statement is readily transposable into synchrony by means of slightly abstract representations of the stems. For the stems of *ovĭca* and *polīʒa/polīza* with their presumably −High consonants, we might posit the lexical representations /ović-/ and /polīʒ́-/. The relationship between /ć/ and [c], /ʒ́/ and [ʒ] is biunique.[14] The problem remains how to describe noun declension in a late Common Slavic dialect which has lost the ʒ/z opposition, so that the relationship between /ʒ́/ and [z] is no longer biunique. In such a dialect the fact that *polīza* and *stīza* select +Soft endings while *groza* and *slīza* select −Soft endings is not predictable from the surface shape of the stem. There may be alternations that would justify giving the *z* in *polīza* and *stīza* a different lexical representation from the *z* in *groza* and *slīza*, such as a diminutive form of *stīza* with *ž*. But in the absence of such justification a phonologically differentiated representation of these stems would amount to merely recoding a declension-class lexical specification as a phonological one.

The problem raised by OCS *stīza/slīza* appears full-blown in Czech. Modern Czech has a number of ending alternations in its nominal declensions, some, e.g., gen. sg. and nom. pl. *ženy/duše* and dat. sg. *ženě/duši*, inherited from Common Slavic and others, e.g., nom. sg. *žena/duše*, acc. sg. *ženu/duši*, and instr. sg. *ženou/duší*, resulting from the fronting of back vowels after palatal consonants in Czech (*přehláska*). Czech grammars order these facts under "hard" and "soft" declension types. A possible alternative treatment via phonology would need to account for both ending alternations and stem differentiation. The ending alternations might be amenable to phonological description, especially the *přehláska* alternations, which historically lie closer to the surface. But differentiating the stems is a problem, owing to the limited implementation of softness in consonants in modern Czech. For the three palatals *ť, ď,* and *ň* the ending distribution is motivated on the surface, e.g., *ženu/bani*. For *c, č, š,* and *ž* a somewhat abstract representation could be used which did not violate biuniqueness (cf. OCS *ovĭca*). But for labial consonants, e.g. acc. sg. *zimu/zemi*, it is not clear what facts in Modern Czech—other than the inflectional alternations under consideration—would justify their differentiation. DC2 stems in *s* and *z* seem to offer counter-evidence to a phonological solution. Native Slavic nouns such as those for 'threat' and 'soot' take "hard" endings (*hrůza, hrůzy, hrůzu*) or "soft" endings (*saze, saze, sazi*) according to whether they derive from plain stems (**groz-*) or palatal stems (**sadj-*) in Common Slavic.[15] But there are numerous borrowings into Czech with stem-final *s* and *z*, and some of them (e.g., *devisa, masa*) take hard endings while others (e.g., *komise, faze*) take soft. Since the opposition *s/ś* and *z/ź* was lost at least four centuries before these nouns entered the language,[16] their different declension-class assignments could not have been determined by the perceived quality of the stem consonant. This being the case historically, one hesitates synchronically to describe the declensional differences as dependent on a phonological stem differentiation.

Let us turn again to the question of endings. As the result of a Proto-Slavic innovation, masc. DC1 nouns in Old Church Slavonic with stems in a palatal consonant came to select the vocative ending -u, e.g., mǫžu, vraču, zmiü. Compare grade and otiče, with -e after stem consonants which are not underlying palatals. Diels notes (159) that the difference in endings goes back to an earlier difference in declension class, and for his historically oriented description there can be no doubt of their being lexically distinct. But their lexical distinctness in a strictly synchronic description of Old Church Slavonic is less obvious. If -ě, a front vowel, can represent for Trubetzkoy the "hintervokalische Gestalt" of the -ě/-i endings, why can't -u, even though a back vowel, represent the "vordervokalische Gestalt" of an -e/-u ending? Why for Trubetzkoy does ženo/duše show a single ending, while for masculine nouns -e is "die normale Endung" but nouns with sharp stem consonants show "eine andere Endung" (p. 125)?

There are of course reasons for not relating voc. -e to -u by means of a single lexical representation. Assuming the lexical representation would be (closer to) -e, the rule which gave -u would need to be a dissimilation rule. Using the older, Jakobsonian phonological features, one could state that stem consonants with high tonality induce maximally low tonality in the masc. voc. ending. But in the Chomsky-Halle features a −High −Back vocative ending would become +High +Back (and +Round) in the environment of a +High −Back stem consonant, a curious assimilation for one feature with simultaneous dissimilation for another. In a generative treatment -u would be represented as a diphthong, perhaps -ou, but -e could only be an underlying simple vowel. The fact that otĭci and kŭnęži with their surface palatals do not select -u poses no problem, according to Lunt (192), since the choice between -e and -u is made on the basis of underlying otĭk- and kŭning-. But for the analysis of -e and -u as a single underlying ending, the younger form knęzu (Diels, 159) poses a problem, because it would necessitate marking underlying kŭning-e as an exception to palatalization so that g could undergo progressive palatalization and condition the shift of -e to -u. A phonological solution to the alternation grade/mǫžu is therefore not necessarily preferable to a declension-class solution. It is nevertheless odd that in the case of grammars of Old Church Slavonic which include morphophonemics such alternations were not even judged to lie within the scope of that component of the grammar.[17]

In modern standard Russian the gen. pl. ending -ov is found after hard stem consonants (and j) and gen. pl. -ej is found after palatalized and palatal stem consonants (except j). This distribution represents a change from Common

Slavic: -ej was once limited to stems of the third declension class (*kostej, putej*), but it spread to DC1 noun stems with palatal consonants (except *j*); compare Old Russian gen. pl. *koní, muží, monastyrí*.[18] Michael Shapiro has proposed the alternation is phonological: a single underlying ending consisting of a mid vowel plus a homorganic glide takes on the tonality of the stem consonant.[19] The traditional analysis which Shapiro's challenges is a declension-class analysis. The term may not seem appropriate with reference to alternating classes of endings each comprising a single member, but consider: *-ov* and *-ej* are distinct lexical entries which are distinguished by what may be called the lexical feature ±Soft. This feature, although a redundant feature of noun stems in Russian, is nevertheless a lexical feature which must be segmented out of the stem together with the other features which determine the occurrence now of *-ov*, now of *-ej*. But the fact that ±Soft is a redundant feature of noun stems in Russian creates the possibility of collapsing *-ov* and *-ej* into a single phonologically differentiated ending.

Of the modern Slavic literary languages perhaps Polish offers the greatest variety of alternations in its nominal inflection and hence is of greatest interest in the matter of declension class. The ending alternations in question are characterized as hard/soft, and Polish, like Russian, developed the hard/soft correlation in consonants (and unlike Czech retained it). Even in the case of labial consonants, which neutralize the hard/soft opposition before a zero ending and (for many speakers) realize it with a glide before a vocalic ending, contrasting paradigms justify differentiating stem consonants in the lexicon; for example, *sierp, sierpa, sierpowi, sierpem, sierpie* vs. *karp, karpia, karpiowi, karpiem, karpiu*. The ending alternations include several which were inherited from Common Slavic and/or which are parallel to alternations already touched on. Thus we have nom. sg. *lustro/morze*, voc. *Stanisławie/Stasiu*, dat. sg. *żonie/duszy*, gen. pl. *stołów/kluczy* (≅ R *stolov/ključej*). These will not be discussed further.

A distinctively Polish development is seen in the nom. pl. ending. The +High/−High alternation conditioned by the stem consonant, which in *żony/dusze* was inherited from Common Slavic, was productive: *lampy/ tramwaje, wazy/montaże*. The ending in *żony* was originally and continues to be distinct from the nom. pl. masc. DC1 ending, which is now limited in its distribution to nouns denoting male persons, e.g., *sąsiedzi, Polacy* (underlying -i) but *ptaki* (underlying -y).[20] The difference in ending between *sąsiedzi* on the one hand and *goście* and *przyjaciele* on the other was a matter of declension class in Common Slavic, but in modern Polish it is determined phonetically. This is because *-e* is productive for soft stem consonants also in nouns denoting male persons, e.g., *bibliofile, złodzieje*. Perhaps this was conditioned by the fact that the endings of *goście* and *przyjaciele* fell together with that of *dusze* as the result of sound changes, the three having been distinct in Common Slavic. As a result of these developments we now have parallel alternations in male-personal nouns and in the other (non-neuter) nouns: *-i/-e* and *-y/-e*. They invite unification by means of a phonological rule: the +High endings *-i* and *-y* dissimilate to −High following +High −Back stem consonants.

Another distinctively Polish development is seen in the locative singular. Next to the inherited hard/soft alternation seen in DC2 *żonie/duszy*, Polish has developed a hard/soft alternation in DC1 (*na*) *stole/polu*. There persist in Polish alternations supporting the analysis of *u* as underlying *ou*, e.g., *kupować/kupuję*. An underlying *-ou* for the soft loc. sg. ending in *polu* would differ by only a single feature from the *-oi* which, following Lunt, we could posit as the underlying representation of the ending in *żonie/duszy*. The soft loc. sg. DC1 ending would present a dissimilation of underlying *-oi*: the glide of this diphthong would assume low tonality in environment after a stem consonant with high tonality. Since DC1 velar stems no longer take *-e* in the locative singular, but *-u*, it may be possible to state that the shift of *-oi* to *-ou* takes place following DC1 stems in a +High consonant.[21]

In this paper I have posed the question, When is an inflectional alternation in Slavic accountable by phonological rules and when does it represent distinct lexical entries, a matter of declension class. I have suggested that the phonology of nominal endings should not be considered solely on general phonological grounds but also against the background of explicit mechanisms for matching stems with endings. The question in the title of the paper should not be answered affirmatively without some consideration of those mechanisms.

University of Illinois, Urbana-Champaign

NOTES

[1] A. Meillet, *Le Slave commun*, 2nd ed. revised with A. Vaillant (Paris, 1934), 399.
[2] Paul Diels, *Altkirchenslavische Grammatik*, pt. 1 (Heidelberg, 1932), 70.
[3] André Vaillant, *Manuel du vieux slave* I (Paris, 1948), 9.
[4] Nicholas S. Trubetzkoy, *Altkirchenslavische Grammatik: Schrift-, Laut- und Formensystem* (Vienna, 1954).
[5] Horace G. Lunt, *Old Church Slavonic Grammar*, 6th ed., revised and extended with an epilogue "Toward a Generative Phonology of Old Church Slavonic" (The Hague, 1974).
[6] The alternation *byti/bǫdǫtŭ*, which for him is underlying *bůj-/bond-*, Lunt calls suppletion (p. 184), putting it outside the domain of phonology. Had he chosen to recognize here a suffixal *-d-* (cf. *iti/idǫtŭ, čxati/čdǫtŭ*) and an infixed *-n-* (of possible use in explaining some of the aspectual properties of this verb), arriving at underlying *by-n-d-* with a high vowel, he would find it harder to

claim that in intermediate *žen-yns* the ending remains high and loses nasality because it is a back vowel (rule YN, 203).

[7] After high thematic vowels -*m* would be lost with no effect on the preceding vowel, via the synchronic counterpart of the known historical processes. Whether the stem is *gena-* or *gen-* which is lexically specified to undergo thematicization for -*a-* in noun environments is immaterial to the point being made.

[8] For example, Paul Postal, *Constituent Structure: A Study of Contemporary Models of Syntactic Description* (= *IJAL*, 30, no. 1; Bloomington: Indiana Univ. Research Center in Anthropology, Folklore, and Linguistics, 1964), 45; Andreas Koutsoudas, "The Handling of Morphophonemic Processes in Transformational Grammars," *Papers in Memory of George C. Pappageotes*, ed. Robert Austerlitz (Publ. of the Linguistic Circle of New York, 5, 1964), 38; Dean S. Worth, "'Surface Structure' and 'Deep Structure' in Slavic Morphology," *American Contributions to the Sixth International Congress of Slavists*, vol. 1, ed. Henry Kučera. (The Hague, 1968), 401.

[9] "The PS and even the Early Slavic declension of nouns was organized on the basis of stems.... In historical evolution this organization was replaced by the paradigm (type) system, based essentially on grammatical gender ...". F. V. Mareš, "The Historical Development of the Slavic Noun Declension, I (The System of Categories)," *Slavia* 36 (1967), 485-506, on 503.

[10] This means that a categorial symbol such as N, representing a word, is lexicalized with lexical items like *žen-, duš-*, etc.—noun stems. I do not at the present see any alternative.

[11] Segmentation (segmentational) rules were first proposed in Paul M. Postal, "On So-Called 'Pronouns' in English," in David A. Reibel and Sanford A. Shane, eds., *Modern Studies in English: Readings in Transformational Grammar* (Englewood Cliffs, N.J., 1969), 201-24 (originally published in 1966), but as far as I am aware their suitability for handling inflectional morphology has not been explored. A textbook, Roderick A. Jacobs and Peter S. Rosenbaum, *English Transformational Grammar* (Waltham, Mass., 1968), uses "segment transformations" to account for inflection and also the articles in English (81-91).

[12] For the Slavic verb the need for inflectional classes, e.g., 1st conj. /-ot/, /-ut/ vs. 2nd conj. /-it/, /-at/ in Russian, is easily obviated through a more abstract representation of these endings. An analysis into thematic vowel plus personal-number marker is supported by the fact that the person-number marker is independent of aspect but the thematic vowel is not. See my "Item and Process in Russian Verbal Inflection," *American Contributions to the Eighth International Congress of Slavists*, vol. 1, ed. Henrik Birnbaum (Columbus, 1978), 317-36.

[13] Joan B. Hooper "assume[s] that a verb form [in Spanish] consists of a stem and at most three suffixes: [stem + theme vowel (ThV) + tense/mood (TM) + person/number (PN)]." *An Introduction to Natural Generative Phonology* (New York, 1976), 141. I take this to be the claim that the phrase-structure rules of Spanish include the rule V → Stem ThV TM PN (although this is slightly weakened by "at most"). ThV, however, does not undergo lexicalization but rather a series of transformations. The first of them rewrites ThV as Ø in certain phonetic and grammatical environments and as an unspecified V elsewhere. Subsequent rules rewrite this V as *a* if it is specified +1st conj.—we are not told how or when a ThV to the right of a stem constituent lexicalized as a 1st-conj. verbal stem acquires this feature—and in the case of a −1st-conj specification as *e, ye,* or *i* in three different grammatical environments. Hooper's main thrust is the superiority of Natural Generative Phonology over other theories, but her intense focus on phonology blurs her treatment of contiguous matters in morphology. If noun endings in Slavic received "phonological interpretation" in the manner of Hooper's ThVs, the problem of declension class would disappear.

[14] The lexical redundancy rule which specifies certain stems +Soft would of course work best when the stem consonants in question form a natural class. But we should not dismiss the possibility of disjunctions in the class of selecting consonants; e.g., a noun stem is +Soft if its rightmost segment is +High −Back *OR* if it is a strident noncontinuant. Compare the class of stem consonants selecting gen. pl. -*ov* in Russian (below).

¹⁵ The archaic and dialectal *slze* (soft declension) next to standard *slza* warns us against assuming a rectilinear development from Common Slavic to modern Czech.

¹⁶ *Historická mluvnice česká* I: *Hláskosloví*, by Miroslav Komárek (Prague, 1958), 159.

¹⁷ The voc. *-u* is discussed by James Ferrell in "Some Observations on the Form of the Nominative and Vocative Singular of the *O-* and *Ĭo-*stems in Common Slavic," *Scando-Slavica* 11 (1965), 93-109. He comments: "A rule that *-e* in the base type be replaced by *-u* (*-ou*) in the derived type was phonologically peculiar but unambivalent" (105).

¹⁸ A. A. Šaxmatov, *Istoričeskaja morfologija russkogo jazyka* (Moscow, 1957), 57.

¹⁹ "The Genitive Plural Desinences of the Russian Substantive," *SEEJ* 15 (1971), 190-98.

²⁰ In a grammar which included a morphophonemic component, this could be handled differently. *Polacy* and *ptaki* could be analyzed as both having the ending /-i/ and the stem alternations could be described under morphophonemics.

²¹ A development parallel to loc. sg. *mężu* in Polish may be seen in dat. sg. *mǫžu* in Common Slavic. F. V. Mareš reconstructs *mangiuei, which because of the "difficult and rare group" giu underwent metathesis to *mangieu (> *mǫžu*). "Słowiański Celownik Liczby Pojedynczej," *Studia Linguistica in Honorem Thaddai Lehr-Spławiński* (Cracow, 1963), 121-25. A dissimilation, i ... i → i ... u, seems to be as likely as metathesis.

The Ethnogenesis of the Slavs in the Light of Linguistics

Zbigniew Gołąb

I. At the very outset of this paper it should be stated clearly that the idea of the Slavic peoples as a whole is first of all a linguistic concept based upon the undeniable linguistic kinship between the historical Slavic languages. In other words, there was a period of one common Slavic language, Proto-Slavic, from which the individual historically attested Slavic languages developed. But since no language exists in a vacuum, realistic historical thinking must assign to such a posited Proto-Slavic language a concrete society, an ethnos: the Proto-Slavs. Now, the main problem of the present paper is *when, where, and eventually under what socio-cultural conditions* such a prehistorical Slavic ethnos, the bearer and user of Proto-Slavic, was formed, existed, developed, and ultimately dissolved into the historical Slavic peoples.

Since as stated above, the very concept of the Proto-Slavs is first of all linguistic and I am myself a linguist, the method applied is, understandably, a linguistic one, strictly speaking, the method of historical-comparative linguistics. Of course, where possible, historical, extralinguistic evidence is used to support suggestions and hypotheses arrived at by a purely linguistic analysis. However, it should be emphasized that I have deliberately neglected highly controversial archaeological theories because I am convinced that archaeological "cultures" have no direct relation to prehistorical ethno-linguistic groups (which is, of course, supported by ethnographic evidence). Similarly, I have also neglected theories of physical anthropology, since a simple observation of historical peoples instructs us about their internal racial diversity. These fundamental facts observed by ethnologists and physical anthropologists seem to corroborate the thesis that the boundaries of material culture and anthropological boundaries (in the sense of the range and distribution of racial types) do not overlap with the linguistic boundaries, and it is the latter that are decisive for the establishment of separate ethnic entities.

II. *The genetic position of Proto-Slavic within the Indo-European (IE) linguistic family.*
From among the schemes representing the late Proto-Indo-European (PIE) distribution of dialects, that proposed by Jerzy Kuryłowicz (1956) has been adopted as best fitting the early historical distribution of old IE languages. Within this scheme (see Figure 1) Slavic (or rather Pre-Slavic) occupies the easternmost position in the North European group of prehistorical IE dialects

(Pre-Germanic, Pre-Baltic, Pre-Slavic), showing an impressive number of common prehistorical innovations with Baltic. The latter fact is a sufficient basis for the hypothesis of the prehistorical Balto-Slavic linguistic unity, which is discussed more extensively below. Here it should be emphasized that one of the causes of the diversification of IE languages was probably a foreign ethno-linguistic substratum. In this connection a hypothesis is suggested that for Baltic one can accept some influence of a Proto-Finnic substratum, whereas for Slavic the influence of an earlier IE substratum. The latter possibility seems to be connected with a thicker stratification of IE population in those regions where Proto-Slavic ultimately crystallized. This point can be illustrated with some interesting morphological correspondences between the Slavic and Armenian verbal tenses which are lacking in Baltic. These are an innovative Slavic and Armenian periphrastic perfect with the participle in -*lo*- and the auxiliary '*be*' in its second component; an old asigmatic-thematic aorist as a common archaism. All these features are unknown to Baltic, which suggests that Pre-Slavic developed its verbal system in contact with prehistorical IE dialects quite remote from Baltic. This possibility would also explain the rather heterogeneous character of the Proto-Slavic verbal system. Another point which is worth mentioning is the relative phonological similarity between Early Proto-Slavic and Iranian. This last fact allows us to assign to Early Proto-Slavic an intermediary position between Baltic and Iranian.

III. *The stratification of Proto-Slavic vocabulary.*

The inherited IE vocabulary in Slavic can be analyzed and presented from the standpoint of the following layers: 1) "kentum", 2) Eastern, 3) North-Western, 4) Northern, 5) Balto-Slavic, and 6) Innovative Proto-Slavic. These layers (or strata) are established on the basis of prehistorical correspondences between 1) Slavic and the "kentum" IE dialects (the treatment of *k', *g', *$g'h$ as k, $g(h)$, etc. in Slavic is decisive here!); 2) Balto-Slavic and Indo-Iranian; 3) Balto-Slavic, Germanic, and Italo-Celtic; 4) Balto-Slavic and Germanic; 5) Baltic and Slavic; and on the basis of 6) Proto-Slavic innovations.

The order of the lexical strata essentially reflects their relative chronology, although in many cases we should assume older and younger elements which represent different periods of contacts and exchange between prehistorical IE dialects within the same stratum. This is characteristic of the "kentum" elements, among which we undoubtedly have very old ones (e.g., B-S *$kăru̯ā$ from *$korHu̯ā$'cow', etc.), usually occurring in Slavic and Baltic, and younger ones (e.g., PSl. *gǫsь* : Lith. *žąsìs* 'goose', etc.), often occurring only in Slavic. A similar double relative chronology can be assumed for Slavic-Iranian correspondences: the older elements come from the period of dialectal contacts within Proto-Indo-European (still about 3000–2500 B.C.), the younger elements represent lexical-semantic readjustments between Proto-Slavic and Northern Iranian (Scythian and Sarmatian) in the first millenium B.C. An example to the former is *kъrnъ 'with truncated ears or nose, etc.'; to the latter belongs bogъ. Statistically the older strata (i.e., "kentum", Eastern, North-Western) are more or less equal (50–60 words), and the younger ones are much more numerous, e.g., Slavic-Germanic—164 words, Slavic-Baltic (i.e., Balto-Slavic innovations) within nouns only—289 words. But semantically there are significant differences between individual strata: the two older strata contain a high percentage of social, religious, and moral terms (the two latter groups of terms are especially characteristic of Slavic-(Indo)-Iranian correspondences) whereas the younger strata, starting already with North-Western IE terminology, represent chiefly technical terms (e.g., referring to agriculture and handicraft). Here it is worth mentioning that the basic terms referring to cattle breeding seem to belong to the old "kentum" layer, e.g., *čerda 'herd', kopyto 'hoof', *korva 'cow', kotiti sę 'litter' (about small animals), krotiti 'tame', *kъrdo 'flock', *kъrmъ 'fodder', *kъrvъ 'ox'. On the basis of Slavic, Germanic, and especially Italic (Latin) correspondences in handicraft terminology (e.g., pottery)—with a characteristic exclusion of Baltic—Trubačev (1963) suggests the existence of a prehistorical Central-European cultural zone, in which at least a part of the Proto-Slavic tribes was included, and which was a focus of lexical radiation. This hypothesis seems to be strongly supported by new data presented in a 1978 essay by V. V. Martynov about special Slavic-Latin correspondences.

I have treated the problem of Balto-Slavic lexical innovations extensively, trying to show that they do not produce uniformly corresponding lexicons in the two groups of languages (i.e., Baltic and Slavic).[1] Besides numerous old correspondences which represent obvious innovations, we also find in these languages strikingly deep lexical differences belonging to very basic strata of vocabulary (cf. J. Rozwadowski's views). I have analyzed comparatively Baltic (i.e., Lithuanian) and Slavic agricultural terminologies, proceeding from the assumption that in such an old and fundamental domain of traditional peasant life there should be more prehistorical common Balto-Slavic innovations than in other areas. The results of this analysis are surprising: from among twenty-three agricultural concepts in the two groups of languages compared, eleven are expressed by common IE archaisms. The rest are expressed in most cases by unrelated words which represent independent innovations; there is only one probably common Balto-Slavic innovation here, namely the 'plowshare' *lemesja- (PSl. lemešъ). This situation is significant. It seems to prove that the socio-cultural split between the prehistorical Balts and Slavs (or rather their ancestors) took place in quite a remote epoch of primitive agriculture. The semantic specialization of PIE ("European") *g'r̥Hno*-'grain' in the meaning 'pea' in East Baltic—in Slavic it has preserved its primary meaning (Lith. žìrnis, Sl. *zьrno*)—is symptomatic. As is well known, the cultivation of peas belongs to the most archaic achievements of agriculture.

From the lexical stratification of Proto-Slavic presented above, some conclusions about the changing geographical distribution of late PIE dialects can be drawn. The basic assumption with which this stratification must be combined in order to produce a convincing picture of the prehistorical process of Slavic ethnogeny is the hypothesis about the location of the oldest retrievable habitat (*Urheimat*) of the Indo-Europeans in the East Ukrainian and South Russian steppes and parklands. On the map of that region of Eastern Europe the scheme of late PIE dialects suggested by Kuryłowicz can be projected, which gives us as a result the convincing location of the North IE dialectal group (Germanic-Baltic-Slavic, or rather Pre-Germanic and Pre-Balto-Slavic) in the Upper Dniepr and Upper Don basins, reaching the Oka river in the north; the south-eastern boundary of that North IE dialectal zone is represented by the line separating the steppes from the forests, i.e., the strip of transitional parklands. The linguistic ancestors of the prehistorical Slavs (the Pre-Slavs) most probably dwelt along that line in the Upper Don basin, having to the northwest the Pre-Balts as their immediate neighbors, to the southeast the Pre-Aryans; the ancestors of the Teutons at that time (about 3000 B.C.) dwelt west of the Pre-Balts in the Upper Dniepr (and Oka?) basin. If we agree that the main prehistorical movement of the Indo-Europeans in that part of Europe was from the east to the west (except for the ancestors of the Aryans?), then the very net of waterways indicates the direction and routes of the prehistorical migration of the Pre-Teutons to the Baltic Sea, which they crossed in its more northern section (frozen in winter!) to Scandinavia, etc.; their route towards the Baltic was then followed by the Balts, but the Pre-Slavs, located along the forest-steppe line (parklands favorable to primitive agriculture) moved along this line in a southwesterly direction. This route had to bring them along to the vicinity of later Kiev and across the Middle Dniepr to Volynia, where they ultimately lost close contact with the Balts.

During those gradual movements (which were taking place in the third and second millennia B.C.), the linguistic ancestors of the Balts and of the Slavs maintained close socio-linguistic contacts, which accounts for the Balto-Slavic innovations, especially in the lexicon. Of course, the dialectal ties with the Pre-Teutons, who had emigrated toward the Baltic Sea and further, were broken earlier. The southwesterly direction of the prehistorical migration (or rather gradual demographic spread and shift) of the Pre-Slavs, moving in the parkland zone, in opposition to the straight western route of the Pre-Balts, moving within the northern forest zone, brought the former into close contact with the West IE "kentum" dialects (Pre-Italo-Celtic and Pre-Illyrian), whose oldest habitat (about 3000 B.C.) should be located somewhere in the Western Ukraine. This fact may account for some characteristic Slavic-Italic lexical correspondences. A parallel between these prehistorical movements of PIE dialectal groups (or may we say simply tribes?) and the later early historical movements of the Slavs suggests itself, since the geographical landscape with its natural routes and the basic means of transportation (foot, horse, ox-wagon) did not change for millennia. The westward movement of the Slavs north of the Carpathians toward Silesia and then south to Moravia and Bohemia could be compared with the hypothetical prehistorical route of the Italo-Celtic group, and the southward movement of the Slavs across the Eastern Carpathians to Pannonia and Dacia and then to the Balkans can be compared with the hypothetical prehistorical route of the Pre-Greeks, etc. This obvious parallel has not been taken into consideration by previous scholars involved in the study of Indo-European antiquities.

IV. *The primary habitat of the Slavs.*
By "primary habitat" I mean that region in Europe where the linguistic ancestors of the Slavs ultimately crystallized as a separate IE ethno-linguistic group, i.e., distinct from the Balts, and from where they began already in prehistorical times their expansion towards the regions occupied at the beginning of history. The method used in answering these questions is a combination of linguistic and historical data. First, in connection with the suggestions of the preceding section, which indicate the region of the Central Dniepr basin as the crystallization zone of the Proto-Slavs, and particularly the province of Volynia, I will attempt the etymology of this toponym.

Volynь//Velynь (these variants occur in Old Russian) is from the PSl. **Velyn'i//*Volyn'i*, an abstract deverbal noun from *velěti* 'command' with the basic meaning 'dominion' (→ 'country', parallel to **volstь*, cf. OCS *vlastь*, Russ. *volost'*, etc., from **voldǫ*, **volstvi*, cf. OCS *vladǫ, vlasti*, etc., 'rule'). This etymology seems to prove that for the Proto-Slavs *Volynia* was their dominion, their country par excellence.

Next I will discuss the etymological analysis of hydronyms in the Middle Dniepr and Vistula-Odra basins. This analysis in a broader framework of hydronymic studies reveals the following facts: the Upper Dniepr basin was primarily Baltic (more than 50% of the hydronyms here have an obvious Baltic etymology), and only relatively late was it colonized by the Eastern Slavs (starting about 500 A.D.); the Slavic hydronyms, among them very archaic ones, are concentrated between *Prypeć*—Middle Dniepr and Upper Dniestr (according to Trubačev, 1968), with some characteristic Illyrian[2] (and South Slavic[2]) hydronyms in the Upper Dniestr basin. This latter fact points towards the old migration route through the Central Carpathians southward. Consider also the Iranian etymology of the hydronyms *Dъněprъ and *Dъněstrъ. I interpret *Dъněprъ as stemming, through early Ossetic, from Iranian *Dān(u)-aip(i)ra-, literally "river-upper", i.e., 'upper river' (where *aipira- represents PIE *epiro- 'oben befindlich', cf. Pokorny 323-324), and Dъněstrъ—through the same intermediary from Iranian *Dān(u)-aēšra-, literally "river-swift", i.e., 'swift river' (where *aēšra- ⩽ PIE *eisro-, an adjective in -ro- from the verbal root *eis- 'sich in eilige Bewegung zetzen' [cf. Bartholomae 31 s.v. aēš- and Pokorny 299], known in hydronymy, e.g., Lith. Eisra, Gr. Ἴστρος 'Lower Danube', etc.).

As the primary original Slavic name of the Dniepr I accept the hydronym Dunaj, a hypothesis justified by, among other things, the oral tradition of the White Ruthenians and Ukrainians (of course, the Slavic name of the Danube, Lat. Danuvius//Danubius, which sounds Dunaj//Dunav, represents only the transfer of the original Slavic hydronym to a river whose foreign name was similar to the native Slavic Dunaj).

I would like to emphasize the etymological connections (in many cases obvious identities) between the Vistula (Visla) basin hydronyms and the Middle Dniepr basin hydronyms as an indication of the westward prehistorical movement of the Slavs.[3] There is also a layer of "Old European" hydronyms (according to a more traditional interpretation, Illyrian and Venetic) concentrated on the Polish territory in sub-Baltic and sub-Carpathian regions, in both the Vistula and Odra basins, which can be connected with an earlier (pre-Slavic "kentum" substratum, later absorbed by the expanding Proto-Slavs. Some "kentum" and North-West IE lexical elements in the PSl. vocabulary are undoubtedly linked with this substratum. In this connection, I regard the ethnicon Veneti, used by the ancient Roman and Greek authors with reference to the Slavs and treated by some scholars as the trace of a pre-Slavic kentum people in the Vistula basin, as most probably of Slavic origin, with the primary social meaning 'warrior class': *u̯en(H)ét-// *un̥Htó- 'winner, warrior', an agent noun or a stative adjective from the root *u̯en(H)-, which is explained by Pokorny (1146) as "ursprünglich 'streben', woraus 'wünschen, lieben, befriedigt sein' und 'arbeiten, Mühe haben', perfektiv 'erreichen, gewinnen, siegen'. It was only secondarily identified by the western neighbors of the Slavs with the etymologically cognate (in IE terms) Italic Veneti. So this ethnicon seems to be irrelevant as alleged evidence of a kentum people preceding the Slavs in the Vistula basin.

The names of trees from the next linguistic argument on behalf of the westward prehistorical movement of the Proto-Slavs from the Middle Dniepr basin to the Vistula basin and further on. The situation looks quite clear: the names of the western trees, i.e., those which do not grow in the Dniepr basin, are of foreign, non-Slavic origin: *bukъ* 'beech' from German, *(j)avorъ* 'plane-tree' from Germanic, **modro-dervъ*, cf. Pol. *modrzew* 'larch', a loan-translation from Germanic, *tisъ* 'yes', probably from a West IE dialect cognate to Celtic. Their phonetic treatment in Slavic betrays their relatively late borrowing (fourth century A.D.?). A more precise delineation of their range should, however, exclude the Central Vistula and Warta basins, which seems to indicate that these regions were settled by the Slavs earlier than the sub-Baltic and sub-Carpathian zones (cf. K. Moszyński, 1957).

A very important topic is the oldest (ancient) historical i.e., written) information about the Slavs and their ethnica in the Greek and Roman sources. First, the ethnicity of the Herodotian Νευροί and Βουδῖνοι (sixth century B.C.) can be analyzed on the basis of the geographical location of these tribes and the etymology of their names. The Νευροί dwelt virtually in Volynia, the Βουδῖνοι in the Upper Don basin. I reconstruct the former ethnicon as PSl. **Nervi* and interpret it as the Slavic continuation of PIE **neru-* 'vital force, strength', hence **nerųos* 'mature man' (cf. PSl. **norvъ* 'nature', OI *nara-* 'man', Gr. ἀ-νήρ 'man'). The latter ethnicon can be reconstructed as **Bydin-* and interpreted as a singulative from the collective **Bydь*, etc., meaning 'tribe', hence **Bydinъ* 'tribesman' (the basic noun represents a derivative in *-dhi-*, etc., from the PIE verbal root **bheų̯ə-*, PSl. *by-ti*, 'grow', etc., cf. Gr. φυλή 'tribe' from the same root!). The slavicity of the Βουδῖνοι is, however, controversial, since it is also possible to etymologize their name as Finno-Ugric (*Votyak*), although their location according to Herodotus would rather suggest the Slavic origin (notice that the Upper Don was posited above as the primary region of the Pre-Slavs within the PIE dialectal zone!). Second, the ethnicon *Veneti*, as presented above, does not need to be a vestige of a "kentum" IE people preceding the Slavs in the Vistula basin; an explicit identification by Jordanes (sixth century A.D.) of the *Veneti* with the *Sclaveni* (as far as their origin is concerned) is the decisive argument on behalf of the slavicity of the former.[4]

The next ethnicon which I would like to mention is *Slověne,* the oldest endogenous name of the Slavs as a separate *ethnos.* Its oldest forms Σουοβηνοί//Σταυανοί[5] = **Svoběne//*Slověne* are attested by Ptolemy as the names of two different tribes, the former east of the Volga (sic!) but close to the location of the Herodotian Βουδῖνοι, the latter in the Middle Dniepr basin, roughly coinciding with the location of the Herodotian Νευροί. It seems obvious that we are dealing here with one and the same *ethnos,* whose name is quoted by Ptolemy in two chronologically different forms, the older, **Svoběne*, being decisive for the etymology of the ethnicon in question. I derive **Svoběne* from the adjective **svobъ* (PIE **sųobho-*), cf. PSl. *svobodá,* etc., whose primary meaning against the IE comparative background was 'affine'; hence *Svob-ěn-e 'the affines'. The younger form, *Slověne, which proved historically successful, is the result of folk etymology associating the dissimilated *Slobĕne (cf. the PSl. variant slobodá) with slovo 'word' and sloviti 'speak', as if in opposition to Němьci 'the mute' = 'the Teutons, the Germans'.

The geographic distribution of the Slavic hydronyms, of the trees with the original Slavic names on the one hand, and the ethnographic and geographic information of the ancient authors on the other is synthesized in a map on which the respective lines are drawn (see Figure 2). Where they overlap, forming a thick bundle, we obtain a sharp boundary of the primary habitat of the Slavs, but where they do not form such a thick bundle the boundary is vague; the latter may prove a relatively later expansion. From the map obtained in this way the prehistorical habitat of the Slavs presents itself as a quite extended belt of parklands running from the Upper Don basin (notice the location of the Herodotian Βουδῖνοι and the Ptolemian Σουβηνοί) westward to the Central Vistula-Warta basins (notice the location of the ancient *Veneti*), with the Middle Dniepr basin, particularly Volynia, as its center (notice the location of the Herodotian Νευροί and the Ptolemian Σταυανοί). The extension of that primary habitat of the Slavs undoubtedly proceeded from the east to the west, the Upper Don basin being the starting point at the Pre-Slavic, i.e., IE dialectal stage (about 3000–2500 B.C.). It should however be noted that the Upper Don basin was most probably never abandoned (at least until early historical Turkic invasions) by the easternmost Proto-Slavic tribes. In this connection I have analyzed etymologically the main hydronyms in the Upper Don basin and obtained results corroborating the hypothesis about the old Slavic character of that region (only one big river, *Xopër* ⩽ **Xoprъ* has an Iranian etymology). Against this the Middle Dniepr basin (the region south of Kiev, and Volynia) appears as the crystallization zone of the Proto-Slavic ethnos, where the main bulk of the Slavic population was concentrated between the sixth century B.C. and the first century A.D. The Central Vistula and Warta basins represents an early zone of westward expansion undertaken by the *Veneti* already before the birth of Christ (notice that according to my etymology *Veneti* means 'warriors' and primarily, in Proto-Slavic, denoted the warrior-class, not the whole West PSl. group; the transfer of the social term to the whole ethnos was an act of the western neighbors of the Slavs, the Teutons). It should also be emphasized that the *Veneti* reached the South Baltic coast (between the Vistula and Odra rivers) and the Upper Odra basin quite early: in this way the old "amber route" crossed the Slavic territory about the birth of Christ. There are two toponyms which should be mentioned in this connection: Ptolemy's Καλισία (from Latin **Caliscia*) in the Warta basin, which most probably renders PSl.

*Kališča 'muddy, swampy place', and Pol. Śląsk (*Sьlęžьsko), 'Silesia', derived from the hydronym Śleża (*Sьlęža), an obvious Slavic (indirect) continuation of the Germc. ethnonym Silingi (latinized from PGermc. *Silingōz). We know that the latter dwelt for some time (before the great migration of peoples) in lower Silesia. This last fact seems to point toward Silesia, i.e., the Upper Odra basin, as an old and important contact zone between the prehistorical Slavs and the Teutons, already before the birth of Christ.

V. *Conclusions.*
Now let us attempt to formulate concisely the essential conclusions which will answer the questions raised at the beginning of this article: when, where, and how the Slavs came into existence as a separate ethno-linguistic entity.

The first question can be answered only approximately in connection with the position of Slavic within the gradually disintegrating IE linguistic community. In this respect everything seems to indicate that after the final dissolution of the PIE linguistic community, which took place most probably between 3000–2500 B.C., and after a transitional period of Balto-Slavic "community," the linguistic ancestors of the Slavs got separated from the Balts and became an autonomous ethno-linguistic entity somewhere about or rather just after the year 1000 B.C. Therefore after that time we are entitled to speak of Proto-Slavs. The linguistic ancestors of these Proto-Slavs should be referred to as "Pre-Slavs", either as a subgroup within the Balto-Slavic community or earlier as a subgroup within the North European dialectal zone of late Proto-Indo-European. The oldest historical references about the Proto-Slavs thus defined are undoubtedly found in the work by Herodotus (fifth century B.C.) under the ethnica Νευροί (*Nervi) and Βουδῖνοι (*Bydь). These two tribes, the northern neighbors and allies of the Pontic Scythians, must have been well established in their respective regions in the sixth century B.C., which means that their sojourn there was not of a recent date.

The second question has been answered by combining linguistics and geography. As the starting point from which the Pre-Slavs began to move gradually southwest (along the parkland belt), the Upper Don basin is posited. This movement, which must have started about 2500 B.C., brought the Pre-Slavs (all that time in close relations with their more northern neighbors, the Pre-Balts) across the Middle Dnieper (the primary Slavic name of this river is *Dunaj*!) to the Kiev and Volynia regions, where they ultimately loosened their contacts with the Pre-Balts, becoming in this way a separate Proto-Slavic ethno-linguistic community. So the Middle Dniepr basin and the regions south of Kiev and west of Kiev (Volynia) appear to be the crystallization center of the Proto-Slavs. It is significant that the first two Proto-Slavic tribes attested historically, Νευροί and Βουδῖνοι, are, roughly speaking, located by Herodotus in the regions which seem to represent the prehistorical migratory zone of the Pre-Slavs, namely: the Βουδῖνοι in the Upper Don basin, the Νευροί in Volynia and the region south of Kiev on the west bank of the Dniepr. This location of the two tribes seems to indicate that in spite of the basic shift of the main bulk of the Pre-Slavs, represented by the Νευροί, from the Upper Don basin southwest to the Middle Dniepr basin and particularly to Volynia, a significant portion of the Pre-Slavic population remained in the Upper Don basin and, maintaining close contacts with their western relatives, was involved in the process of the Proto-Slavic ethnogenesis.

But the Proto-Slavs began quite early to expand further westward. The close etymological ties between the Middle Dniepr basin and the Vistula basin hydronyms and the fact that the hydronym *Vistua* (*Vistla*), undoubtedly of Slavic origin, is well established by about the birth of Christ prove quite convincingly that the expansion of the Proto-Slavs westward started much earlier, at least about two centuries B.C., if not sooner. It is probable that its beginning could be related with the invasion of the Pontic area by the Scythians (approx. 700 B.C.), who simply blocked the southeastern direction for the Proto-Slavic expansion.

The western expansion of the Proto-Slavs from Volynia across the Bug river to the Vistula basin and further on, as the geography of the trees with original Slavic and borrowed (Chiefly Germanic) names indicates, spread first in the central part of this basin (the sub-Carpathian and sub-Baltic zones were primarily omitted). It was carried by the *Veneti*, originally a social term in Proto-Slavic meaning 'warrior-class', then secondarily extended by the Teutons to all the Slavs expanding westward. In this way the social term became an ethnicon, but as such it has a clear exogenous character, i.e., it is used about the Slavs only by foreigners. So ultimately by the birth of Christ the Proto-Slavs seems to have occupied quite a long belt of parklands running from the Upper Don basin (?) through the Middle Dniepr basin to the Vistula and Upper and Middle Odra basins, reaching the Baltic coast along the Vistula river in the north. That extended belt of the gradual prehistorical Slavic expansion can be segmented into three chronologically successive parts: the Upper Don basin as the base from which the Pre-Slavs began to spread, the Middle Dniepr basin (Kiev-Volynia) as the nucleus where the Proto-Slavic *ethnos* crystallized, and the Vistula-Odra basins representing the zone of prehistorical expansion and colonization by the Proto-Slavs. Whether all these regions belonged to the Proto-Slavic habitat simultaneously about the birth of Christ, especially the eastern base, is questionable. However, the ethnica Βουδῖνοι (Psl. *Bydъ), Νευροί (PSl. *Nervi), and *Veneti* (PSl. *Venete?) and their location seem to reflect quite clearly the prehistorical process of the Pre-Slavic and Proto-Slavic expansion presented above. In this connection the reader should be reminded that the oldest Proto-Slavic endogenous ethnicon used from time immemorial for the self-identification of the Slavs, *Slověne* (≤ *Slobĕne // *Svobĕne) is attested by Ptolemy (second century A.D.) in two places: east of the Volga (sic!), but on the latitude of the Upper Don (cf. the location of the Βουδῖνοι), and south of the Prypeć, i.e., roughly speaking, where the Νευροί dwelt. This fact cannot be neglected.

Let us now pass to the last question, concerning the causes, particularly the socio-linguistic processes, which brought about the formation of the Slavs. In this respect one can suggest the following conditions that seem to have determined a gradual separation of the Pre-Slavs from other IE groups and their final transformation into a separate *ethnos* with a separate language, social organization, culture, and, which is indispensable in such cases, a separate self-identity (the latter usually expressed in a general endogenous ethnicon, in our case in the ethnicon *Svobĕne // *Slobĕne ≥ *Slověne*). These conditions are as follows:

First, the gradual territorial spread of the Pre-Slavs along the parkland belt in a southwestern direction, which enabled them to develop a basically agricultural way of life, in contradistinction to their more northern neighbors and relatives, the Pre-Balts, who were expanding westward in a forest zone: among the latter cattle-breeding seems to have played a more important role. The difference in economy is quite obviously reflected in the respective vocabularies, characterized by the virtual lack of common Balto-Slavic innovations in agricultural terminology.

Second, contacts and cultural-linguistic exchange with other IE groups, which had started in the late PIE period and developed successively. Here one should make some important distinctions: on the one hand, the early contacts with the speakers of various late PIE dialects (3000–2500 B.C.) are to be taken into account; on the other, the later contacts with separate IE peoples speaking already separate languages. It is also important to distinguish the contacts taking place between the neighbors (i.e., between coterminous groups) and those between the older conquered and the younger conquering groups, i.e., between the ethnic substratum and the ethnic superstratum. As far as the first type of contacts is concerned, those within the late PIE dialectal zone, there is no question about some ties of the Pre-Slavs and the Pre-Aryans, which tended to orient the linguistic ancestors of the Slavs more toward their southeastern neighbors than toward the northwestern neighbors, the Pre-Balts and the Pre-Teutons. This orientation is reflected in the old lexical ties between Proto-Slavic and Aryan, especially Iranian, that cannot be treated as later loan words. The ties with the Pre-Aryans were then loosened and the ties with the Pre-Balts strengthened (the period of Balto-Slavic lexical innovations), but the geographical orientation of the linguistic ancestors of the Slavs towards the forest-steppe boundary brought them again into closer relations with the Iranian branch of the Aryans roaming the Pontic steppes. this happened, however, at the time when the Pre-Slavs were already linguistically crystallized into the Proto-Slavs, speaking a separate language; the same can be said about the Northern Iranians (the Scythians). It is highly probable, and this is my hypothesis, that the decisive factor in the transformation of the Pre-Slavs into the Proto-Slavs and in their ultimate split from the Pre-Balts (the termination of the so-called Balto-Slavic ethno-linguistic unity) was an additional IE substratum which the linguistic ancestors of the Slavs had encountered and absorbed in the Middle Dniepr area, the center of their crystallization as Proto-Slavs. In this way the basic difference between the Slavs and the Balts in terms of the historical differentiation of the IE languages would lie in that the former had absorbed an additional IE substratum (or substrata), which on the one hand complicated the IE elements in their grammar and lexicon and on the other hand contributed to a relatively more innovative character of Proto-Slavic; the latter (the Balts), on the contrary, free from any additional IE substratum, have preserved a relatively more conservative character of their language. These distinctions can be observed first of all in the conjugations of the respective languages. In this connection some interesting correspondences between Slavic and Armenian should be emphasized, which suggest a possible IE substratum absorbed by the Pre-Slavs in the Ukraine and perhaps representing Pre-Armenian. But the most probable IE substratum absorbed by the linguistic ancestors of the Slavs and then by the Proto-Slavs themselves is a "kentum" substratum. The analysis of the "kentum" elements in Balto-Slavic reveals that many of them (e.g., cattle-breeding terms) go back to a remote epoch of late PIE dialects. But others are undoubtedly younger. In this context, by "kentum" elements I understand not only the PIE words with the "kentum" treatment in Slavic (i.e., $*k'$, $*g'(h) \geqslant *k, *g$, etc.), but also the old IE lexical elements common to Proto-Slavc and North-West Indo-European, especially Italo-Celtic. A characteristic phenomenon in this respect is the exclusion of Baltic from these correspondences. As Trubačev has convincingly pointed out, we are dealing here with the linguistic (lexical) reflection of a kind of prehistorical Central European cultural-linguistic area, which at least partly encompassed some PSl. tribes (undoubtedly the western ones, the *Veneti*). This area covered today's Poland, and its IE (kentum) population (maybe identical with the tribes of the so-called Lusatian culture, 1300–600 B.C.) was gradually ousted or absorbed by the Proto-Slavs (the *Veneti*) expanding from the east. Thus the lexical elements with obvious West IE correspondences and with "kentum" treatment penetrated Proto-Slavic, strengthening its distinction from Baltic. It is characteristic that these western elements belong mainly to technical terminology (pottery, primitive metallurgy, etc.).

So in the gradual formation of the Proto-Slavs as a separate ethno-linguistic entity, i.e., detached from the Balts, the decisive role should be assigned on the one hand to the contacts with the Pre-Aryans and the Iranians and on the other to the absorption of additional IE substrata, the Pre-Armenian (?) substratum and a West IE (kentum) substratum, the former undoubtedly older (somewhere in the Ukraine), the latter younger (somewhere in today's Poland). Of course, later contacts and lexical exchange between the prehistorical Slavs on the one side, and the Pontic Iranians, the Teutons, and even some Altaic peoples on the other, affected an already clearly individuated Slavic community speaking the separate Proto-Slavic language and representing a separate socio-cultural entity.

The above synthesis is based first of all upon linguistic, then upon geographic and some historical evidence. Archaeology has deliberately been omitted in this presentation. It is the task of the representatives of this latter discipline to compare the above synthesis with the achievements of their own investigations and to accept or reject the results of the synthesis, depending on whether they harmonize or not with the archaeological synthesis about the origins of the Slavs. I am, however, deeply convinced that the decisive vote here belongs to linguistics.

The University of Chicago

NOTES

[1] For a more detailed discussion of this and other points in this paper, see my forthcoming book, *The Origins of the Slavs: A Linguist's View*.

[2] I.e., hydronyms with correspondences in West Balkan and South Slavic regions. But a recent work by J. Udolph (1979, pp. 600-618) has proven that most of the alleged Illyrian and Thracian hydronyms can be explained as originally Slavic, and others as "Old-European."

[3] In this connection, the Slavic etymologies of *$Vistla \geqslant Wisła$, *$V_ъrta \geqslant Warta$, *$Odъra \geqslant Odra$, and of *Bug*, all of which have correspondences in the Dniepr basin, are discussed and substantiated in Gołąb: forthcoming.

[4] The ethnicity of the *Veneti* in the Vistula basin and at its estuary (Pliny, Tacitus, Mela, Ptolemy, first-second centuries A.D.) is discussed and their location delineated in Gołąb: forthcoming.

[5] Corrupted from Στλαυανοί?; recently V. V. Trubačev in *Voprosy jazykoznanija* 1979, 4, p. 41, advanced an attractive hypothesis that the form represents an Aryan *calque linguistique* (loan-translation) of Sl. *Slověne* (according to him, connected with *slovo, sluti* 'be called, be famous'), namely *Stávāna-*, cf. OI *stávāna-*, Av. *stavana-* 'praised' from OI *stáuti*, Av. *staoiti* 'he praises'.

REFERENCES

Abaev, V. I.
  1965 *Skifo-evropejskie izoglosy: na styke vostoka i zapada.* Moscow.
Brandenstein, W.
  1936 "Die erste 'indogermanische' Wanderung". *Klotho* 2.
Czarnecki, J.
  1975 *The Goths in Ancient Poland.* Coral Gables, Florida.
Friedrich, P.
  1970 *Proto-Indo-European Trees.* Chicago.
Gołąb, Z.
  1972 "'Kentum' Elements in Slavic". *Lingua Posnaniensis* 16:53-82.
  1974 "The Oldest Ethnica Referring to the Slavs: Νευροί and Βουδῖνοι in Herodotus's Description of Scythia". *Onomastica* 19:125-139.
  1975 "*Veneti//Venedi*—the Oldest Name of the Slavs". *The Journal of Indo-European Studies* 3(4):321-336, Winter.
  1976 "Stratyfikacja słownictwa prasłowiańskiego a zagadnienie etnogenezy Słowian". *Rocznik Slawistyczny* 38(1):15-30.
  forthcoming *The Origins of the Slavs: A Linguist's View.*
Hajdu, P.
  1975 *Finno-Ugrian Languages and Peoples.* London, 39-40.
Hančar, F.
  1955 *Das Pferd in prähistorischer und früh historischer Zeit.* Vienna.
Joki, A.
  1973 *Uralier und Indogermanen: die älteren Berührungen zwischen den uralischen und indogermanischen Sprachen.* Helsinki.
Kiparsky, V.
  1934 *Die gemeinslavischen Lehnwörter aus dem Germanischen.* Helsinki.
Krahe, H.
  1964 *Unsere ältesten Flussnamen.* Wiesbaden.
  1970 *Einleitung in das vergleichende Sprachstudium.* Innsbruck.
Kuryłowicz, J.
  1956 *L'apophonie en indo-européen.* Wrocław. (especially chapters V, VIII, and Appendix)
Lehr-Spławinski, T.
  1946 *O pochodzeniu i praojczyźnie Słowian.* Poznań.
Łowmiański, H.
  1963 *Początki Polski. Z dziejów Słowian w I tysiącleciu n.e.*, v. I-II. Warsaw.
Martynov, V.V.
  1963 *Slavjano-germanskoe leksičeskoe vzaimodejstvie drevnejšej pory.* Minsk.
  1978 *Balto-slavjano-italijskie izoglosy: leksičeskaja sinonimija.* Minsk.
Meillet, A.
  1937 *Introduction à l'étude comparative des langues indo-européennes,* 8th ed., Paris.
Moszyński, K.
  1925 "Badania nad pochodzeniem i pierwotną kulturą Słowian I". *Polska Akademia Umiejętności, Wydział Filologiczny—Rozprawy* 62(2).
  1957 *Pierwotny zasiąg języka prasłowiańskiego.* Wrocław.
Pokorny, J.
  1959, 1969 *Indogermanisches etymologisches Wörterbuch.* v. I, v. II, Bern-Munich.

Rozwadowski, J.
1912 "O pierwotnym stostunku wzajemnym języków bałtyckich i słowiańskich". *Rocznik Slawistyczny* 5:1-36.
1948 *Studia nad nazwami wód słowiańskich.* Cracow.
Schmid, W. P.
1972 "Baltische Gewässernamen und das vorgeschichtliche Europa". *Indogermanische Forschungen* 77(1):1-18.
1968 "Alteuropäisch und Indogermanisch". *Akademie der Wissenschaften und der Literatur in Mainz, Abhandlungen der Geistes- und Sozialwissenschaftlichen Klasse*, Nr. 6: 244-258.
Toporov, N. V. and O. N. Trubačev
1962 *Lingvističeskij analiz gidronimov Verxnego Podneprov'ja,* Moscow.
Trubačev, O. N.
1966 *Remeslennaja terminologija v slavjanskix jazykax.* Moscow.
1968 *Nazvanija rek pravoberežnoj Ukrainy.* Moscow.
Udolph, J.
1979 "Studien zu slavischen Gewässernamen und Gewässerbezeichnungen". *Beiträge zur Namenforschung, Neue Folge, Beiheft* 17, Heidelberg.

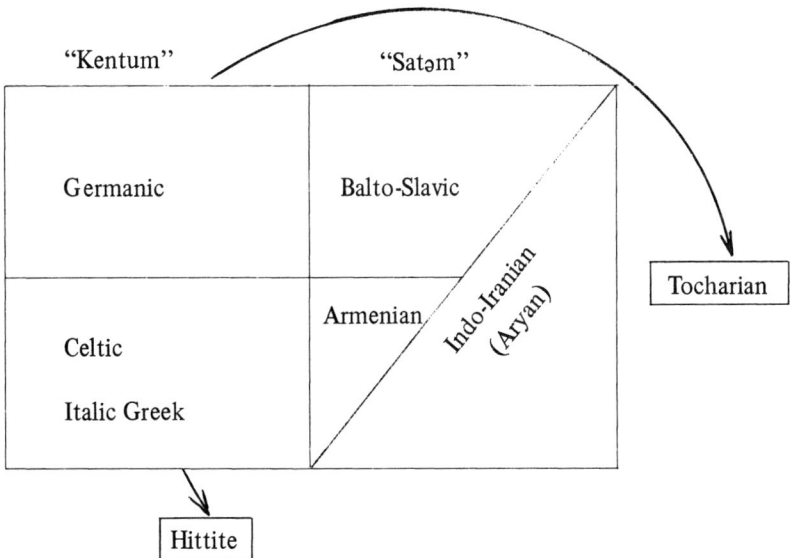

Figure 1

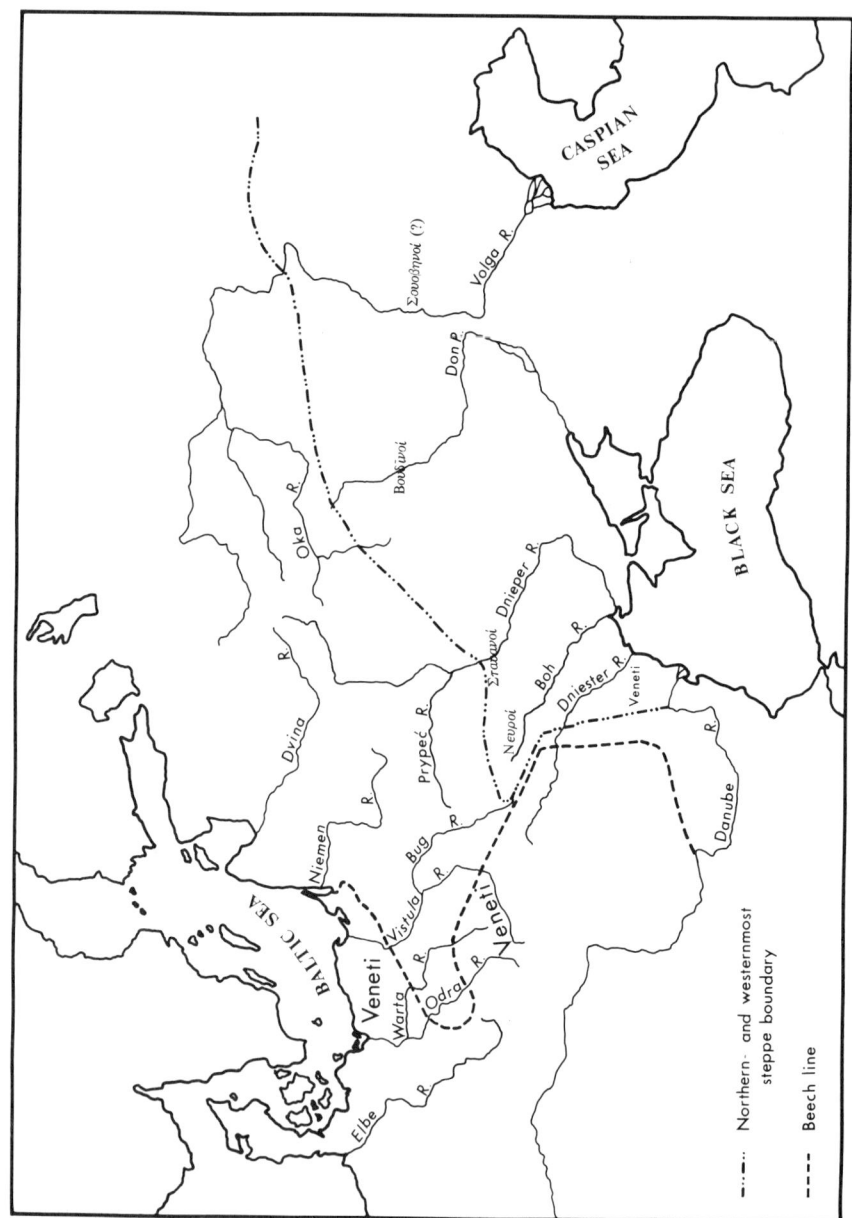

The Second Old Slavonic Legend of St. Wenceslas: Problems of Translation and Dating

Marvin Kantor

There is hardly any doubt that the Latin *Vita* of St. Wenceslas by Gumpold, the bishop of Mantua, provided the model for a considerable portion of the autograph of the so-called *Second Old Slavonic Legend of St. Wenceslas*. Around the year 980, Gumpold, one of the leading hagiographers of his time, was commissioned by Emperor Otto II (967-983) to write a *Vita* of St. Wenceslas. Since the Italian author was not familiar with the local tradition regarding the saint, he drew much of his material from an earlier Latin work about him known as *Crescente fide*. As concerns the Old Church Slavonic (henceforth OCS) work, it has been generally assumed that it was composed in Glagolitic by an anonymous Slavic author in Bohemia not long after Gumpold's work came into being, and has been dated between the years 994-1000. Unfortunately, it did not survive in the country of its origin. But in one form or another, the text found its way into Russia during the eleventh century where it was copied and survived in two Church Slavonic redactions: the *Kazan' Manuscript (early sixteenth century) and the Petersburg Manuscript* (second half of the sixteenth century).[1] The present analysis is based on the *Kazan' Manuscript*, but the *Petersburg Manuscript* was consulted for clarification as well as Vašica's commentaries.[2]

In producing the Slavic version the translator-author had to face a number of obstacles in dealing with the complexities of the Latin text, the most intricate of which was the problem of rendering Latin sentence structure with its sophisticated means of syntactic dependency. In the final analysis, the "obstacles" were not always overcome with equal deftness. More concerned in places with a lexical approximation on the word level than with the coordination of word units in higher syntactic structures, the Slavic version at times adhered so closely to the Latin in word order that on the sentence level of OCS it produced a rather scrambled conglomeration of words. And compounding these difficulties were the errors and/or corruptions that found their way into the text during the various transcribing processes. Because of this, parts of the Church Slavonic text are felt either to be decipherable only with the aid of the Latin text or simply enigmatic. It is apparently this unclarity that is responsible for the two approaches taken in translating certain portions of the Church Slavonic text. While the contemporary Czech translation[3] shows complete reliance on the Latin text, the contemporary Russian translation[4] exhibits considerable literary license. Both approaches do indeed have one thing in common—they basically ignore the Church Slavonic text. And nowhere is this more apparent than in the Prologue to the *Second Old Slavonic Legend*, a section justifiably considered the most recondite of all.

Thus, the purpose of this paper is twofold: to compare the Prologue in the Church Slavonic *Second Old Slavonic Legend* with the Latin source and the contemporary Czech and Russian translations; and, to reopen the question of dating the original Slavic work on the basis of information that I believe is contained only in the Church Slavonic text.

Before examining the Church Slavonic version of the *Vita*, let us take a brief look at Gumpold's Prologue. It is quite an unusual introduction to a saint's life. It does, to be sure, contain some of the commonplaces typical for this genre. For example, the entire Prologue, which concludes with successive statements of self-abasement and vindication and notes the prominence of the saint, can be viewed as an extended apology for writing the *Vita*. However, it also contains a critique. For much to the chagrin of the hagiographer, the current interest in and enthusiasm for mathematics, science, "pagan literature" (i.e., classical Latin literature) and philosophy were leading "the wise men of this era" to ignore the glory of God and His holy men, thereby relegating the writing of saints' lives to second place after these new pursuits. This critique apparently represented the view of the Church hierarchy. But what is especially curious about it is that it makes oblique reference to the leading intellectual of the Ottonian Renaissance, Gerbert of Aurillac, the future Pope Sylvester II (999-1004), a passionate lover of learning who rallied against the intellectual tyranny of the Church and the ignorance and corruption of its bishops, and about whom the monks purportedly whispered after his death "Homaqium diabolo fecit, et male finivit."[5]

Under the patronage of the Ottos, who regarded the clergy as the great civilizing force and strove to appoint worthy men to positions of importance, learning flourished again in some of the monasteries and cathedral schools of the Empire. In addition to this some cultural contacts were opened with the Muslims, whose science remained generally unknown to tenth-century Europe. Although the tenth century has been considered a "Dark Age," there was nevertheless a considerable amount of intellectual activity and progress owing to the efforts of the Ottos and, in no small measure, to their protégé Gerbert, the greatest scholar and humanist of that era. He was, in the words of Henry Osborn Taylor, "the redeeming intellect of the tenth century and the cravings of his mind compassed the intellectual predilections of his contemporaries."[6] Surprisingly, he was not dominated by religious motives, despite the fact that he was reared among monks, became abbot of Bobbio, archbishop of Rheims and then of Ravenna, and finally Pope. Gerbert's chief interests were literary studies and mathematics; he was also accomplished in music, philosophy and science. He taught his pupils to identify musical tones by means of a vibrating string (the monochord); he constructed an astrolabe and armillary sphere and taught how to represent the universe, find the stars, and make celestial and terrestial measurements. Furthermore, he inspired an enthusiasm for dialectical arguments and created a desire for Greek and Arabic scientific knowledge as well as for ancient Greek philosophy; he urged his students to read the Latin classics and imitate the style of Horace and Cicero.[7]

Many of Gerbert's interests make up the bulk of the subject matter of Gumpold's Prologue. This material, according to Nikoľskij, was translated into OCS "almost verbatim."[8] And as already mentioned, Vašica has apparently assumed the same, judging by his rendition of the Prologue into Czech.[9] After examining the Prologue, making a translation of it from Church Slavonic into English[10] and comparing it with Gumpold, I found that this section, which was said to be the most dependent on the Latin, deviated from it significantly. This is not to say that some word-for-word translation does not occur here; rather, that significant portions of the Prologue cannot be considered verbatim translation. On the contrary, the Church Slavonic differs considerably from the Latin in a number of places. Apart from supplementing a portion of Gumpold's work, it also departs from the Latin by now abridging and/or expanding the text, now altering expressions.

There are many examples of this, and we can begin by looking at the opening words of the Prologue:

Studiorum⁴ igitur¹ genera³ multiforma² varias⁷ ciuque¹⁰ mortalium¹¹ ingerere⁶ solent⁵ ingeniorum⁹ curas⁸ ...
(Therefore, various types of studies usually arouse the diverse interests of the mind in each mortal)[11]

Although the Church Slavonic version approximates the "grammatical" word order of the Latin, the meaning is altered and the sentence makes a much more generalized statement, cf.:

Snagъ⁴ po¹ istinně³ rody² mnogoobraznya¹⁰ komuždo v rodě¹¹ smertnyx i⁵ obyčai⁶ iměju̯tь⁹ xitrosti i⁸ pečali ...
(Verily, various types of endowments have the traits of reason and solicitude in each among the genus of mortals)

In view of the fact that Vašica based his translation on the Latin text, the Czech version fails to capture the difference that is found in the Church Slavonic manuscript, and remains a distinct echo of the Latin:

Přerozmanité obory věd budivají zajisté v každém ze smrtelníků zájem o jinou duševní práci ...
(The most diverse branches of learning indeed arouse in each mortal an interest in various intellectual work)

As concerns the Russian translation, it is difficult to say what motivated its solution. Part of it is a gloss of the Church Slavonic text, and part is pure fabrication:

Každomu iz smertnyx dany poistine raznoobraznye vidy dejateľnosti i oni probuždajut neobyčnuju tosku ...
(Verily, each among mortals is given various types of occupations and they arouse an unusual yearning)

Since the primary concern in this paper is with the Church Slavonic text, all further comparisons will begin with it. In the next example the Russian translation follows the Church Slavonic text quite closely but is, nevertheless, inaccurate. By mistranslating the Church Slavonic demonstrative pronoun *onъže* (that, i.e., "that one" as opposed to "this one" (*sei*), or one ... another) it distorts the sentence and loses the contrast between the two types being compared:

Church Slavonic

sei poistinně umomъ smyslenyi, popravъ mirъskaę igrišta, vyšnix želaet; onъže iskovanъ na vysotu čъstii, gorę duxomъ, uběgaę mirъskix, vyšnix želaet ...
(One, who is truly rational of mind, having scorned worldly amusements, desires the supernal; yet another, who is molded for the pinnacle of honors, being ardent of soul and evasive of the worldly, desires the supernal)

Russian

Takoj čelovek, poistine odarennyi umom, popiraja mirskie radosti, stremitsja k vysšemu. I on vykovan byl na vysote česti, gorit duxom, izbegaet mirskogo, želaet vysšego
(Verily, such a man, who is gifted in mind, scorning worldly joys, strives for the supreme. And he was molded for the pinnacle of honor, is ardent of soul, evades the wordly, desires the supreme)

By contrast, the Church Slavonic text differs from the Latin and Czech in several ways. It in turn lost—for whatever reason—the contrast between the "aims" of the two types being compared, and altered the attributes of "that one." Besides, it did not record the metaphor found in the Latin text, which was preserved in the Czech translation.

Latin

Hic namque mente moderatus, spreto caducorum ludicro, superna intendit, ille extructos in altum honores ardenti rerum fugacium siti exaestuans desiderat
(For one with a well-ordered mind, having spurned the folly of fleeting things, seeks the supernal, another, with a raging thirst for fleeting things, desires high honors)

Czech

Neb ten, jsa rozvážné mysli, oprovrhl světskými hřičkami a zatoužil po metách vyšších, onen zase si žádá nejvznešenejších poct, prahna žizní po věcech prchavých
(For one, being of serious disposition, spurned worldly amusements and yearned for higher goals, another again, parched with thirst for fleeting things, desires for himself the highest honors)

Continuing by contasting "this one" and "that one," the Church Slavonic text focuses on "this," the bold, and the indolence of "that" (or the indolent) as generalized, active character features and the results thereof:

semu remestvu xraborьstii drьzaę mudrostь xotęštu poxvaly slavu priati, a drugomu dělъ različnyx trud xitrostьnyi lěnostь izvlačitь, umy roditelnyę tonostiju izmučaetъ
(the bold dare to engage in the arts, wishing to gain wisdom and the glory of praise, but indolence draws the other away from the skillful execution of various tasks, (and) jades natural intelligence by refinement)

The Russian translation once again loses the specific contrast by turning, inexplicably, from "the bold" to "other people." It also glosses the activity of the former:

V ètom dele derzaja podvizať sja, xrabrye xotjat prijať slavu poxvaly. A drugix ljudej lenosť otvraščaet ot različnyx iskusnyx trudov i ix vroždennyj razum iznurjaet utončennosťju
(Daring to act in this manner, the bold wish to gain the glory of praise. But indolence turns other people away from various skillful tasks and exhausts their natural intelligence by refinement)

However, the Latin text does not have these character types at all and speaks abstractly of a type of boldness (*audax prudentia*) and passively of indolence. As a result the Church Slavonic version departs significantly from its source:

huic artis bellicae audax prudentia appetibilem laudis gloriam promeretur, illi operum diversorum labor artificiosus desidiam eximit, mentisque naturalem subtilitatem extorquet
(bold prudence in the art of war wins for one the desired glory of praise, the skillful execution of various tasks drives away another's indolence and wrenches the natural subtlety of his mind)

Of course, the Czech translation faithfully follows the Latin:

> tomy smělý důmysl v umění válečném zjednává žádoucí slávu a čest, a onoho umělecká výroba rozličnych děl vytrhuje z netečnosti a napíná vrozenou bystrost jeho ducha
> (bold sagacity in the military art secures for one the desired honor and glory, but the skillful execution of various tasks draws another away from indolence and strains the natural acumen of his mind)

The Prologue now turns to the interests of the "wise men of this era," who, among other things, "try to explain with very special calculations" questions relating to the physical sciences. For example:

> podvizanie zvězdъ toli tečeniemъ nepodvižnym rastojatъ ... kiimъ li ustavom vse po činu vyšnee količestvie uravnano tverdostiju
> (and which immutable course fixes the motion of the stars ... by which principle is all supernal quantity regularly equalized by mass)

In rendering this passage, the Russian translation takes liberties with the Church Slavonic text, now by inversions, now by additions to and/or deletions from sections of the original:

> dviženie zvezd, podčinennoe neizmennym zakonam ... kakim obrazom vse vyššee po ustanovlennomu porjadku uravnovešeno tverdosťju
> (the motion of the stars that are subject to immutable laws ... in which way is all the supernal counterbalanced by mass according to an established order)

The Church Slavonic text, on the contrary, can hardly be described as a verbatim translation of its source. For, as the following translation shows, it had on its own taken considerable liberties with the Latin text:

> quo ordine siderum motus ac fixione non mutabili disponantur ... quove dictu tota per numerum decurrat summa quantitatis soliditatisque
> (in what order and immutable stability are the motions of the stars arranged ... how is it possible in terms of numbers to reduce the entirety of quantity and mass)

As concerns the Czech translation, it is interesting to note that Vašica's original version of the latter sentence treats it rather freely, cf.:

> ... aneb na čí rozkaz hýbe se v rytmu vše, co má kolikost a hustotu
> (by whose authority does everything that has quantity and mass go into motion)

However in a later version this entire passage was brought into agreement with the Latin:

> jaky řad a jaké neměnne zákony určují pohyb hvězd ... aneb jak se dá vyjádřiti číslem pohyb všeho toho, co se vyznačuje kolikostí a hustotou
> (what order and what immutable laws determine the motion of the stars ... or how is it possible to express in terms of numbers the motion of all those things that are designated by quantity and mass)[12]

It is well known that at Christmas in 980 or, at the latest, at the beginning of the following year, there was a public disputation in Ravenna at the request of Emperor Otto II, who acted as arbiter. The dispute concerned the divisions of philosophy—which Gerbert had laid out as the "science of things divine and human"—and the principal opponents were Gerbert and Otric, the learned rector of the episcopal school at Magdeburg. Hence, it is not surprising that the Prologue also makes mention of the peroccupation with dialectical argumentation:

> li kotorym věstii obrazom podъ istinnym i ložnym predi položenymъ ustavom i ix neudobnym směšeniemъ tako glubokoe glagoljuštix podpolzaetsję rasčitanie, imъže vyšnyx i nebesnyx razmyšleniimi ispytati potęstesję tružajutsję
> (or by what manner of communication can a most profound reckoning of those who speak of the supernal and heavenly, which they labor arudously to investigate in their meditations, progress when set forth under the notion of truth and falsehood and the equivocal confusion of them)

This passage is reworked in a most flagrant manner in the Russian translation. Its editorializing can hardly be justified:

> ili kakim obrazom raspoznaetsja istinnoe i ložnoe, suščestvovavšee prežde vsex opredelennyx zakonov, i skrytoe ix smešeniem, kak govorjat gluboko rassuždajuščie, i ètim postiženiem oni stremjatsja poznať vysščij nebesnyj smysl
> (or in which way is discerned truth and falsehood which existed before all defined laws and was concealed by their confusion, as those who reason profoundly say, and by understanding this they strive to learn the supreme, celestial purport)

Although the Church Slavonic version of this passage is not by any means a verbatim translation of the underlying Latin, it does attempt to include the various syntactic elements of the latter. However, it is curious that in this instance the Czech version fails to do so. For some reason the final clause is totally omitted:

Latin

> vel qua opinionum imagine sub veri falsique proposito eorumque difficilli commixtione tam profunda eloquentium subrepat disputacio, per artium scrupulositates investigare desudant
> (or by what semblance of opinions, under the notion of truth and falsehood and the troublesome confusion of them, can move along such profound disputation of eloquent men who investigate arduously through the integrity of the arts)

Czech

> neb jaké je schema úsudků, kterými se própetá hluboká disputace řečníků, jejímž předmětem jest pravda (later version: majicí za předmět pravdu ...) a klam a obtížne změtení jich

(or what is the scheme of opinions by which is entangled the profound disputation of orators, who have as their subject truth and error and the troublesome confusion of them)

There are many more of these types of differences among the texts under discussion which any close reading would reveal. But there is as yet another noteworthy discrepancy, which will serve as my final example. Indeed the most important difference between the Prologue in Church Slavonic and its Latin source was completely overlooked in the existing translations. There is a passage in the Church Slavonic text—one hitherto considered a corruption of the Latin and/or enigmatic—which, according to my reading, has no counterpart in the Latin text. Let us return to the "interests" of the "wise men" where we read:

Church Slavonic

kaa ili kakova měra zemskago veličestvia počatok eterym aki tainym stroimъ po obrazъcemъ geometrьskim na istinuju žatvu obyjati istęgnet
(which or what sort of measure expands, either through some mystical providence or according to geometric formulas, to include the genesis of the earth's magnitude (and) the actual end of the world)

Latin

quae aut qualis mensura terrenae magnitudnis ambitum, quadam quasi latenti racione, per formulas geometricales ad certam metiendi comprehensionem asstringat
(what measure can determine the earth's magnitude, as if by a certain hidden calculation, by geometrical formulas according to a certain notion of measuring).

It is obvious from the English translations that the Church Slavonic text does not simply translate the Latin passage but expands on it in a significant way by adding the notion of the "actual end of the world," expressed metaphorically in the image of the harvest (*žatva*). That the image of the harvest can indicate the end of the world is indisputable. Take, for example, the parable of the seed and of the tares in Mt 13:24-30:

> The kingdom of heaven is likened unto a man which sowed good seed in his field: But while men slept, his enemy came and sowed tares among the wheat, and went his way. But when the blade was sprung up, and brought forth fruit, then appeared the tares also. So the servants of the householder came and said unto him, Sir, didst not thou sow good seed in thy field? from whence then hath it tares? He said unto them, An enemy hath done this. The servants said unto him, Wilt thou then that we go and gather them up? But he said, Nay, lest while ye gather up the tares, ye root up also the wheat with them. Let both grow together

until the harvest: and in the time of harvest I will say to the reapers, Gather ye together first the tares, and bind them in bundles to burn them: but gather the wheat into my barn.

Explaining this parable, Jesus says:

He that soweth the good seed is the Son of Man; The field is the world; the good seed are the children of the kingdom; but the tares are the children of the wicked one; The enemy that sowed them is the devil; *the harvest is the end of the world* (italics mine, MK); and the reapers are the angels. (Mt 13:37-39)

This same image appears again in Rev 14:14-16, where we read:

And I looked, and behold a white cloud, and upon the cloud one sat like unto the Son of Man, having on his head a golden crown, and in his hand a sharp sickle. And another angel came out of the temple, crying with a loud voice to him that sat on the cloud, Thrust in thy sickle, and reap: for the time is come for thee to reap; for the harvest of the earth is ripe. And he that sat on the cloud thrust in his sickle on the earth; and the earth was reaped.

The *Second Old Slavonic Legend of St. Wenceslas* was not the only Slavic work with the image of the harvest signifying the end, the death of man. There is, for example, the eleventh-century OCS translation of the *Life of St. Nicholas,* the alleged fourth-century archbishop of Myra in Lycia (*Žitie i čudesa sv. Nikolaja Mirlikijskogo i poxvala emu*). He was the most popular of the non-martyr saints in both the Eastern and Western Churches and became the patron saint of Russia whose feast day (December 6) was celebrated simultaneously with Christmas (cf. the American Santa Claus). In this *Life* there is the following line: *žatva bo estъ člvčju rodu smrtъ* (for the harvest is the death of mankind).[13]

In commenting on this section, Vašica states that the difference in the texts resulted from a misreading of the Latin, i.e., the gerund *metiendi* (measuring) was read as *metendi* (harvesting) by the translator.[14] Although this explanation is possible, I find it unconvincing. It is not that translators and/or copyists did not make mistakes, rather that they did not ordinarily translate or copy nonsense, in which a *metendi* reading would have resulted. I am assuming here, as I do whenever working on problems of translation, that the text did indeed communicate some sense. Had it failed to do so, it probably would not have been preserved. With the exception of the phrase in question, the Church Slavonic text in this passage followed the Latin quite carefully both grammatically and syntactically, and offered no problem in translation. Thus, if the translator had indeed read *metendi,* the Slavic counterpart would have been *žatьe* (harvesting) which, as stated above, would not have made sense. Instead he utilized a different noun, *žatva* (Latin: *messis*), to which he added an adjectival modifier *istinaja* (actual). Neither this modifier nor the resulting new thought could possibly have been motivated by the Latin text, given the date of its composition (c. 980), and the context of the phrase in question. Rather, I believe, this addition was made to inject consciously a new thought, one which was on the minds of many at the time this work came into being. I shall return to this thought below.

Hence, it is not surprising that Vašica's translation into Modern Czech omits all mention of the "actual harvest," and that he renders it in complete accordance with the Latin text, cf.:

> ktera a jaká míra zmenšuje s pomocí geometrických vzorců objem velikosti zemské jakoby nějakým tajemným kouzlem až tak, že jej možno změříti
> (to what degree, as if by some secret progress, with the aid of geometric formulas is it possible to measure the extent of the earth's magnitude)

Not only is the reference to the "actual harvest" omitted but the verbal phrase *obyjati istęgnet* (expands to include) is glossed away as is the noun *počatok* (genesis). The Russian translation once again exhibits considerable literary license. It makes no attempt to cope with the Church Slavonic original, nor is any explanation offered for the solution it attained. It simply glosses away the problem, cf.:

> i [postič'] nekim tainstvennym obrazom, kakova mera veličiny zemli po obrazcam geometričeskogo izmerenija
> (and [to perceive] in some mysterious way, according to a geometric formula, what the magnitude of the earth is)

It seems to me that the difference between the Latin and Church Slavonic passage was occasioned by the specific time the original OCS version was transcribed. For if my reading concerning the reference to the end of the world is correct, then it refers to a phenomenon which was awaited in Europe at the approach of the year 1000, the final year of the sixth and last millennium—the "harvest of the world." And this notion would help to date the original Slavic work and to explain the significance the Prologue had in Russia approximately 500 years later (the date of the *Kazan' Manuscript*) during a period when almost all of the subject matter of the Prologue was outmoded and undoubtedly totally irrelevant. Consequently, the original OCS manuscript should be dated *after* the year 1000, i.e., after the anticipated "harvest of the world." I would suggest a very early date in the eleventh century, when questions about when the "actual" end of the world would occur were once again of great and immediate concern. Thus, this passage in the OCS manusript is in place and quite appropriate for the time.

As concerns the notion of the "end of the world," classical apocalyptic traditions displayed a pronounced interest in the number and duration of the ages of the world. There were a number of schemes which varied considerably.

However, by the second century A.D. there arose in patristic writings an apparently preferred scheme, one which was based on seven periods of one thousand years each or the "cosmic week." And this doctrine was joined with yet another element in patristic apocalyptic writings, viz., that of the thousand-year kingdom of Christ (cf. Rev 20:4-6). The messianic reign was related to the calculations of the astrologers on the cosmic week consisting of seven millennia, which in turn had its roots in speculations concerning the first chapter of Genesis. The creation of the world was over in six days; the seventh day was sanctified by God. Thus, the cosmic seventh day coincided with the year 1000, the year of the anticipated advent of the Lord.[15]

There were many ominous portents in the prevailing disorders and conflicts in Europe of the late tenth century which were interpreted by students of prophesy to be an exact fulfillment of the signs of the end of the world as foretold by Jesus: war, apostasy, famine and pestilence. But perhaps the most foreboding of all the signs was the death of Pope Gregory V in 999. Morbid terror gripped European Christendom as the thousandth year neared. There was a prevailing feeling of misery and hopelessness. "In many places a general social disorganization set in: many left off attending to the ordinary affairs of life; some gave themselves up to licentious living, and many others left their countries to be near Jerusalem, where it was expected that the Son of Man would set up the Great White Throne of judgment."[16] Therefore, it is not unreasonable to assume that this mood also affected the Christianized Slavs; and that a Slavic author of that time might also be preoccupied with thoughts of the end; and that he could suggest that the "actual end of the world" ought to be recalculated, since it was painfully obvious to him that the previous calculations were in error: The world, after all, had not ended in the year 1000.

The question that arises now is, of what relevance was the aforementioned apocalyptic traditions to Russia of the early sixteenth century? It should be recalled that upon its Christianization, Russia adopted the Byzantine calendar—a system of chronology which was based on the number of years from the Creation. According to this system, the Nativity took place in the year 5508. The first month of the year was September. The Russians also borrowed from Byzantium the notion that the world would end in the year 7000. Hence, in Russia the end of the world was anticipated on September 1, 1492, i.e., on the dawn of the seventh millennium which would bring the second advent of Christ and the Last Judgment.[17] Indeed, expectations of the end were as widepsread in Russia at the end of the fifteenth century as they had been in Europe some five centuries earlier. There were also similar, foreboding signs: uninterrupted war, famine and heresy. And this was especially keenly felt in Northern Russia, particularly in Novgorod whose food supplies were being controlled by Moscow as a way of suppressing independence, and where a new heresy (of the so-called Judaizers) had surfaced. And the atmosphere of doom which pervaded life in Novgorod was even further aggravated by the anticipated end of the world in the year 7000 (1492). In fact one of the Novgorodian paschal tables—which was brought up to the year 7000 only—ends with the following words: "*zde strax, zde skorbь ... v sie leto čaem i vsemirnoe tvoe prišestvie*" (there is fear here, there is sorrow here ... this year we indeed await Thy universal advent).[18] The notion that the world would end at the start of the seventh millennium was the view of the official Church and it further fueled the arguments of the heretics—who long since had rejected this date—when the world failed to end in the year 7000. Thus the issue of the end of the world was destined to be disputed for a long time.

Finally, it is interesting to note that the older of the two surviving Russified manuscripts, the *Kazan' Manuscript*, originated in Northern Russia in the Soloveckij Monastery, which was founded sometime after 1435. This monastery was located in the province of Arkhangel'sk on an island in the White Sea, and from its very inception fell under the jurisdiction of the archbishopric of Novgorod, from where it received its hegumen. It is quite unlikely that the monks at this monastery would not have been aware of the apocalyptic controversy which was raging in Novgorod, and the apocalyptic content of the work they had transcribed which—despite the already-mentioned fact that this manuscript had been dated from the early sixteenth century—the compilers of a work known as *A Description of the Manuscripts of the Soloveckij Monastery that are Located in the Library of the Kazan' Theological Academy* (Kazan', 1885) had dated 1494, i.e., a time when the apocalyptic issue was still of exceptional concern.[19] And what is especially curious about the *Second Old Slavonic Legend of St. Wenceslas* is that it was included in the Menology as the reading for September 1st. Is it possible that this manuscript owes its very survival to that curious apocalyptic reference?

Given the fact that the original OCS manusript of the work in question has been lost and the surviving manuscripts are of a relatively late date, it is hardly likely that one can reconstruct a text which with any degree of certainty can be said to reflect the "original" OCS version. And this is by no means an unusual or atypical situation with regard to medieval Slavic manuscripts in general (cf. the *Vita of Constantine,* the *Vita of Methodius* or Xrabr's treatise *On Letters*, et al.) or the Slavic textual tradition connected with St. Wenceslas in particular (cf. also the *First Old Slavonic Legend of St. Wenceslas*). Furthermore, as concerns the textual tradition in Slavic as a whole, there evolved a system of transcribing works in the Slavic Middle Ages in which the copyist often performed yet another function, viz., that of editor-rewriter. It was not uncommon for him to adapt his text not only to a new stylistic usage (witness the fifteenth-century adaptations of *Russkaja Pravda* vis-à-vis the Second

South Slavic Influence), but also to a new conceptual framework (e.g., the treatment of Bořivoj in *Crescente fide* and in the Czech translation thereof). Thus, a given work might continue to be "recreated," in a manner of speaking, even after its inception, the extent of which depended on the individual copyist, his time and milieu.

Northwestern University

NOTES

[1] The *Second Old Slavonic Legend of St. Wenceslas* or *Nikoľskij Legend* was discovered in Russia by Professor N. K. Nikoľskij in 1904 in two manuscripts. The *Kazan' Manuscript* originally belonged to the Soloveckij Monastery, but was transferred to the Kazan' Theological Academy. The *Petersburg Manuscript* originally belonged to the Pafnuťev-Borovskij Monastery, but was transferred to the Library Archives of the Holy Synod in St. Petersburg. Both manuscripts—which differ little in their essence—were published by Nikoľskij in 1909 in *Pamjatniki drevnej pis'mennosti i iskusstva*, CLXXIV as *Legenda Mantuanskogo Episkopa Gumpoľda o Sv. Vjačeslavě Češskom v Slavjano-Russkom Pereloženii*.

[2] Josef Vajs, ed., *Sborník staroslovanských literárních památek o Sv. Václavu a Sv. Lidmile* (Prague, 1929), p. 84-87.

[3] *Ibid.*, p. 84-124. Translation by J. Vašica.

[4] *Skazanija o načale češskogo gosudarstva v drevnejrusskoj pis'mennosti* (Moscow, 1970), p. 86-102. Translation by A. I. Rogova.

[5] W. J. Townsend, *The Great Schoolmen of the Middle Ages* (London, 1881), p. 73.

[6] Henry Osborn Taylor, *The Medieval Mind,* I (Cambridge, 1959), p. 283.

[7] Frederick B. Artz, *The Mind of the Middle Ages* (New York, 1966), p. 199-200.

[8] N. Nikoľskij, *Legenda Mantuanskogo Episkopa Gumpoľda o Sv. Vjačeslavě Češskom v Slavjano-Russkom Pereloženii* (Russia, 1909), p. xviii.

[9] In his introduction to the revised translation of the *Second Old Slavonic Legend of St. Wenceslas,* Vašica writes: "About two-thirds of the Slavic text is a verbatim translation of Gumpold ..." See Vaclav Chaloupecký, *Na úsvitu křesťanství* (Prague, 1942), p. 134.

[10] See Marvin Kantor, *Monumenta Bohemica, Michigan Slavic Publications* (forthcoming).

[11] I should like to acknowledge the help that I was given with the Latin text. I am indebted to Professor Mario Trovato of the Department of French and Italian and Professors Stuart Small and John Wright of the Classics Department here at Northwestern University.

[12] Cf. translation of passage in question in *Sborník,* p. 85 and *Na úsvitu,* p. 136.

[13] *Slovar' russkogo jazyka XI-XVII vv.,* 5 (Moscow, 1978), p. 77.

[14] Vajs, p. 85.

[15] Bernard McGinn, *Visions of the End. Apocalyptic Traditions in the Middle Ages* (New York, 1979), p. 14-18.

[16] Townsend, p. 70-71. I am aware of the fact that the tradition connected with the year 1000 has been considered a myth.

[17] I realize that one might argue that the reference to the "actual end of the world" was never a part of the original OCS manuscript but was added to the Russified versions of it sometime after 1492. This is possible, however I tend to doubt it, given the overall state of the *Kazan' Manuscript.*

[18] *Istorija russkoj literatury,* II: *Literatura 1220-1580 vv.* (Moscow-Leningrad, 1946), p. 377.

[19] Nikoľskij, p. ii.

The Genitive-Accusative as a Slavonicism in the Laurentian Manuscript of 1377:
The Problem of Text Segmentation

Emily Klenin

The language of the Primary Chronicle is often described in terms of distributional contrasts that can be found in its extant texts: the distribution of pleophonic forms as contrasted with nonpleophonic ones, the word order characteristic of religious passages as contrasted with secular ones, and so on. In the following discussion, I present an analysis of one more pair of competing forms: the accusatives *ego* and *i* of the masculine singular anaphoric pronoun. As is well known, *ego* and *i* compete in East Slavic writing from its earliest period, until *ego* replaces *i* completely. The generalization of *ego* was apparently over by the end of the 14th century, although *i* continued to appear in some kinds of archaizing writing much later. The Primary Chronicle in the Laurentian Manuscript of 1377 is unusually conservative for a text of its time,[1] since it still uses *i* instead of *ego* over 90% of the time in direct object position; in prepositional phrases *i* (in the form *nь*) always appears instead of *nego*. In contrast, not only East Slavic treaties and legal texts but also religious writing even in the 13th century use *ego* instead of *i* as much as half the time. Somewhat unexpectedly, the use of *ego* in the Primary Chronicle (Laurentian MS.) does not represent a colloquial innovation of the 14th century, but is associated mainly with fairly complex syntactic constructions, some degree of literariness, and religious contexts, especially quotations from liturgical sources. It is my contention that *ego* in the Primary Chronicle (Laurentian MS.) is not an innovative but a conservative element, reflecting the influence of sources underlying the chronicle's 12th-century compilation; moreover, it is extremely dubious that *ego* functioned as an element of conscious style at any stage of the transmission of the Primary Chronicle down to 1377. Although mainly a Slavonicism in the Primary Chronicle, *ego* is nevertheless in principle an East Slavic form as well, and it was becoming more widespread in Russian Slavonic texts at the same time as it was beginning to occur in non-Slavonic East Slavic ones; thus, an apparently archaic Slavonic text preserved in the chronicle may use *ego* rarely, if at all, whereas *ego* occurs freely in all kinds of texts in the later-12th-century parts of the Suzdal Chronicle that follows the Primary Chronicle in the Laurentian Manuscript. In short, as we will see below, *ego* in the Primary Chronicle (Laurentian MS.) is an historical Slavonicism that does not function stylistically as a Slavonicism; moreover, the fact that *ego* and *i* occur as competing forms in this 14th-century text is absolutely unrelated to the fact that *ego* and *i* must have been competing in contemporary (14th-century) East Slavic dialects.

The Primary Chronicle (Laurentian MS.) contains about 220 anaphoric accusative masculine singular forms in direct-object position, and about 17 of these accusatives are the genitive-accusative *ego*—around 8%. These occurrences of *ego* were not apparently introduced by the two 14th-century scribes. This can be shown on the basis of the distribution of *ego* both in the Primary Chronicle and in the Suzdal Continuation of the same manuscript. Within the Primary Chronicle, the usage of the two scribes differs very little. On the whole, the second scribe (who copied three-fourths of the relevant forms) used *ego* very slightly more often than the first scribe (8½% of all occurrences, as opposed to 6%), and he twice uses the plural genitive-accusative *ix*, which is lacking in the work of the first scribe. In addition to the purely statistical similarity of the work of the two scribes, their use of *ego* is also subject to the same general syntactic tendencies, most strikingly the tendency for *ego* to occur as the object of verb forms other than the personal ones (see Klenin 1980). Thus, there are 5 occurrences of *ego* as direct object of a present active participle, and no such occurrences of *i*; in addition, *ego* is chosen disproportionately often as the object of past active participles and imperatives. Altogether, occurrences as the object of participles and imperatives account for 70% of all occurrences of accusative *ego*, but only about 18% of occurrences of *i*; only 3 of the 17 occurrences of *ego* are objects of personal verb forms, all of them in the work of the second scribe. Altogether, the pattern in the Primary Chronicle is essentially uniform over the work of both scribes, with an insignificant, or nearly insignificant, tendency for the second scribe to use *ego* (and *ix*) both more often and, apparently, more freely.

However, this same second scribe (that is, Lavrentij) also copied the Suzdal Continuation, where his usage is completely different. The use of *ego* and *ix* in the Suzdal Chronicle is discussed in detail in my forthcoming book, and for that reason will not be dealt with fully here. However, in summary it can be noted that Lavrentij continues to use *ego* with very slightly increasing frequency through the first part of the Suzdal Chronicle, up to about the 1160s (the boundary is not clear), after which he uses both *ego* and (for the first time) *ix* about as frequently as their nongenitive-accusative counterparts. He continues this type of usage (where, of course, neither *ego* nor *ix* is restricted either syntactically or with respect to textual content) until the beginning of the 13th century, and then, from roughly 1205 to the end of the chronicle, the frequency of *ego* declines to the level of the 1160s and then continues the slow upward curve characteristic of its distribution in the Primary Chronicle and the early part of the Suzdal Chronicle. These shifts in the use of *ego* and *ix* in the Suzdal Chronicle correspond to putative changes in the compiler's sources: roughly, a southern text used decreasingly beginning in 1157 until it ended in the 1170s, a northern source taking over from the southern one but also ending about 1205, and a Rostov source used from 1205 on. Without even considering the specifics of source texts, it is at least clear that the shift in frequency of *ego* and *ix* corresponds to shifts in the geographic focus of the narrative—and the geographic factor is obviously unlikely to have influenced Lavrentij directly. Mostly for this reason, I conclude in my book that the Suzdal Chronicle's use of *ego* is mainly a reflection of usage found in the chronicle's sources, and was not imposed by Lavrentij in 1377.

Having established that Lavrentij was a rather conservative copyist, following his source texts' use of *i* and *ego* regardless of his own linguistic habits, we may wonder whether Lavrentij's conservatism with respect to the genitive-accusative is reflected in the Primary Chronicle as well. We have already noted the existence of syntactic conditions favoring the use of *ego*; however, these conditions are not entirely precise, since, for example, both imperatives and past active participles, as well as infinitives, take both *i* and *ego*. By combining our syntactic description with a study of other factors in the choice of *ego* or *i*, a much fuller characterization of the use of *ego* in the chronicle is indeed made possible.

Can the Primary Chronicle, like the Suzdal Chronicle, be divided up into those parts of the text where *ego* appears frequently and those where it does not? Of the 17 occurrences in the Primary Chronicle, 2 are in the life of Antonij (s.a. 1051/6559), 2 are in the narrative on the death of Feodosij (s.a. 1074/6582) and the translation of his relics (s.a. 1091/6599), 3 are in the Instruction of Vladimir Monomax (s.a. 1096/6604), 2 are in the story of the blinding of Vasilko (s.a. 1097/6605) and its aftermath (s.a. 1100/6608), 2 are in the chronicler's comments on a prayer attributed to Vseslav Izjaslavovič s.a. 1068/6576, a third is in the report of his birth in 1044/6552, and 1 occurrence is found in each of the following passages: the story of the boy fording the Dnieper to the Pečenegs at Kiev (s.a. 968/6476), the speech of the philosopher s.a. 986/6494, Volodimer's conversion and casting out of Perun (s.a. 988/6496), Jan's speech to the wizards s.a. 1071/6579, and the chronicler's brief comment on the murder of Jaropolk in 1086/6594. (Three of these examples are not clearly genitive-accusatives, but could be argued to represent genitive case forms; the examples will be discussed below, but the problem does not substantially affect my results.) Of the 17 examples listed, at least 12 are in religious passages—about 70% of the total, as compared with about 60 out of 203 occurrences of *i*, or only about 30%. Thus, *ego* apparently is favored by religious narrative content, a clue to possible status as an element of Slavonic language or style. It is particularly useful that this narrative-content influence on the choice of *ego* accounts for several examples that are syntactically unmotivated. There are, however, two limitations on this generalization. One, perhaps unexpected, is that it is not always clear when the environment in which *ego* occurs should be considered religious. In my count here, I have included as religious all passages with known liturgical sources—these examples are discussed below—as well as all occurrences of *i* and *ego* that have as their antecedents either the Christian God, Christ, the Cross, or the Antichrist. I have also counted as religious the narratives of events taking place in monasteries or churches, or events (such as the martyrdom of Boris and Gleb) narrated from a Christian point of view. I have not counted as religious, for example, the story of the conversion of Volodimer and his casting out of Perun to float down the Dnieper; obviously, a conversion is a religious event, but there is actually little reference in the story in question to a specifically Christian world view. On the other hand, the murder of Jaropolk in 1086 is not inherently an obviously religious event, but the chronicler's commentary includes specifically Christian pieties, and the commentary must be counted as religious, even if the narrative of the event itself is not. Since the Primary Chronicle was compiled and transmitted by monks, any event had at least to be interpretable in a Christian context in order for it to be included in the chronicle; however, the narrative is not in all places equally informed by Christian piety, and the religious status of individual portions of the text is very much a matter of degree.

The second limitation on the characterization of *ego* as typically an element of religious language is that *ego* is not distributed at all evenly across the religious passages of the chronicle. On the contrary, it is possible (and even necessary) to be much more specific about the kinds of context that favor the appearance of *ego*. Thus, for example, the two religious passages with the most occurrences of *i/ego* are the stories of the monks of the Cave Monastery, narrated s.a. 1074/6582 (24 examples), and the speech of the philosopher, with 21 examples; each of these passages uses *ego* only once, a somewhat lower proportion than in the chronicle as a whole. On the other hand, 3 out of the 4 examples in the religious introduction to the Instruction of Monomax show the genitive-accusative; in contrast, the narrative and epistle of Monomax (5 examples) have only *i*. (The so-called Prayer of Monomax has no examples of either *i* or *ego*.) Consequently, religious passages may use *ego* much less or much more than is typical for the chronicle as a whole. Moreover, the religious passages that use *ego* the least are not particularly restrictive syntactically, so that the content restrictions on the use of the genitive-accusative cannot simply be combined with the syntactic restrictions to produce the correct results.

One obvious basis of the heterogeneity of the religious passages is their reliance on source texts that do or do not themselves use the genitive-accusative.

For example, 2 of the 3 examples of *ego* in Monomax's Instruction are from the 36th (37th) Psalm (verse 22-23):[2]

(1) *bl(a)goslovęščii jego naslědę/ t/ zemlju klenuščii že jego potrebęt sę ö/ t/ g(ospod)a*
   (leaf 78 c, 25-27)
   'they that bless him shall inherit the earth, and those that curse him shall be destroyed by the Lord.'

This same passage occurs, with *ego* in both instances, as early as the Sinai Psalter, so that *ego* in the chronicles here quite likely represents quotation from traditional sources. Similarly, the only example of *ego* in the speech of the philosopher is from Psalm 116 (117):1:

(2) *d(a)v(y)dъ xvalite g(ospod)a vsi jazyci i poxvalite jego vsi lju/ d//(ь)e* (leaf 33 b, 27)
   'David (says): "Praise the Lord, all nations and praise him, all people."'

Here, the Sinai Psalter (and the Old Church Slavonic tradition in general) has *i*, but *ego* occurs in the Russian Slavonic tradition as early as the 11th-century Byčkov/Sinai Psalter (see Altbauer 1978:113).[3] However, other kinds of Slavonic sources, like non-Slavonic ones, show a general increase in the use of accusative *ego* through the 14th century. It is therefore unremarkable that a highly conservative Slavonic passage such as the speech of the philosopher (see L'vov 1968) should in general prefer *i* but use *ego* in a psalm quotation.

In addition to psalm quotations, there are other passages apparently modeled on liturgical sources, some of which, however, cannot be precisely fixed. An example of this is the chronicler's commentary attached to Vseslav's prayer in 1068/6576 (leaf 58 b, 21 ff.):

(3) *kr(e)st(o)mъ* (sic) *bo knęze/ m/ v brane/ x/ posobitь vъ brane/ x/ kr(e)st(o)mъ sogražajemi věrnii ljudьe. poběžajutь supostaty protivnyja. kr(e)stь bo vskore izbavlęe/ t/ ö/ t/ napastii prizyvajušči/ m/ jego s věroju.*[4]
   'For the Cross aids the princes in battles. In battles the faithful are made safe by the Cross, with it they conquer the Enemy, for the Cross quickly saves from the traps that are laid for them that call on it with faith.'

Altogether, about 7 of the occurrences of *ego* in the 1377 copy of the chronicle are in known or putative quotations from liturgical texts, sermons, or similar traditional religious literature. This includes all the occurrences of *ego* in Monomax's Instruction (see Tschižewskij 1969: 315 and sources quoted therein), the other 2 examples cited above, the chronicler's comment on Jaropolk's death s.a. 1086/6594, Jan's admonition to the wizards s.a. 1071/6579, and excludes the narratives about the Cave Monastery. The sizeable proportion of occurrences of *ego* that seem to be or are known to be part of quotations underlines the importance of establishing source texts in evaluating even low-level grammatical phenomena, and tends further to limit the usefulness of comparing all the religious passages as a whole with all passages that are not religious. We can conclude that the relative frequency of *ego* in religious passages is a consequence of its occurrence or nonoccurrence in specific sources. On the whole, religious sources, often of non-Russian Slavonic origin, tended to use *ego* relatively more often than other kinds of sources; we now turn to a discussion of the examples of accusative *ego* in secular narrative.

The 5 examples from apparently nonreligious passages include 3 from widely separated places in the chronicle, and 2 from the story of the blinding of Vasilko and its aftermath. Of these 5 occurrences of *ego*, 1 is the object of a form *strělejušče*, a verb whose case government in Old Russian is unclear. Judging from the rection of *streljat'* in modern Russian, it is quite likely that *strěljati* in Old Russian need not have governed the accusative, and that *ego* at leaf 19 b, 24, in the chronicle is really a genitive-case object, and not a genitive-accusative. Three of the other four constructions with *ego* in secular passages are also odd, but the accusative status of *ego* probably has to be accepted. Thus, at leaf 52 c, 22, we read:

(4) *m(a)t(e)ri bo rodivši jego by/s/(tь) jemu jazveno na glavě jego* (s.a. 1044/6552)
'for when his mother bore him, there was a caul on his head'.

The verb *roditi* is attested unusually often with the genitive-accusative, including the neuter *slova*, referring to Christ, in the Prayer of Monomax:

(5) *o prepětaja m(a)ti rožьšija vsě/x/ s(vę)t(y)xъ prěs(vę)t(a)go slova* (leaf 84 d, 18-19)
'O most praised Mother, who bore the most holy Word of all the saints!'

(On the neuter genitive-accusative, cf. Suprasliensis 448.23-26.) *Roditi* triggers unusual genitive-accusatives in Old Church Slavonic as well, for example, at Suprasliensis 396.4, but I have been able to discover no evidence that it ever governed the genitive instead of the accusative. In example (4) above, the use of the genitive-accusative is encouraged not only by the choice of the lexical item itself, but also by its participial form, and, in particular, its syntactic status as a dative absolute.

Similar considerations lead to accepting as genitive-accusatives the occurrences of *ego* after *ötrěvaite* (leaf 40 b, 15) and in a clause with a negated subject (leaf 88 d, 5). Both environments might seem intuitively to permit genitive objects, but there is no clear evidence that they do. It may be pointed out in passing that distinguishing genitive-accusatives of all types from genitive objects of verbs is a persistent problem, especially since the genitive-accusative arose by means of reanalysis of genitive objects, where genitive rection was being lost. In the chronicle texts in particular, the prevalence of genitive-accusative *ego* in Slavonic quotations is a special problem since certain verbs that had genitive rection in at least some Old Church Slavonic texts (see Xodova 1963:63) seem to have been strictly transitive in Old Russian (outside of Old Church Slavonic quotations); thus, forms that can be interpreted as having been genitive-accusatives for our chronicle scribes may well have been genitives for the authors of the older Slavonic texts that they are quoting. In the present study, I have treated these forms as genitive-accusatives, with additional commentary as needed.

The 3 secular examples of accusative *ego* that have been discussed above are all well motivated syntactically, since they are governed by participles or imperatives. The present active participle, in particular, and the dative absolute construction are characteristic of Slavonic writing, and the occurrence of *ego* as the object of such forms fits the general pattern of *ego* as characteristically Slavonic. However, the remaining two examples of accusative *ego* are both direct objects of personal verb forms in secular narrative, and, as such, they are not well motivated in terms of this working hypothesis. In fact, these two examples are of particular interest, because they show the limited practical utility of unqualified characterization of forms as Slavonic or non-Slavonic in a text, such as the chronicles, whose composition and editing took place over a prolonged period of time.

The two examples at issue are both from the story of Vasilko. One example has been mentioned above as problematical, because the subject of the governing verb is negated; it reads as follows:

(6) *i ne jazъ jego slěpilъ* (leaf 88 d, 15)
 'And it wasn't I that blinded him'.

Although it may be tempting to discount the example altogether by calling it a genitive case form conditioned by negation, this is not possible, because, although confusion with the genitive of negation may have influenced the appearance of *jego,* nevertheless, subject negation does not in general trigger the appearance of a genitive direct object (cf. *bratъju* at leaf 24 a, 17). Even if example (6) above could somehow be discounted, the other example still would have to be explained:

(7) *da jego kormi/m/ sdě* (leaf 92 c, 17)
 'that we may feed him here'.

This example, like (6), is problematic, although for different reasons. Most notably, the other chronicle texts with which the Laurentian Manuscript is to be compared differ not only with respect to the choice of *ego* over *i*, but also in making the whole construction quite different in other ways as well. As it is, *ego* in the Laurentian Manuscript is preposed in its clause for no apparent reason, and this, in combination with the textual variation in other manuscripts, suggests that the whole passage is slightly garbled. On the other hand, in the context of the Laurentian Manuscript, example (7) cannot be interpreted other than as a genitive-accusative, and as one lacking either syntactic motivation or any other motivation that might justify calling it Slavonic.

There is no reason why, of course, Lavrentij cannot be permitted the introduction of any occurrences of *ego*; even if example (7) represents Lavrentij's choice of forms, this does not affect the overall status of *ego* as predominantly a conservative element. Moreover, regardless of who introduced *ego* in (7), the lack of an apparent Slavonic motivation for the use of the form does not mean that the form was *not* Slavonic. Slavonicisms are common nearly everywhere in the chronicle, and in the story of Vasilko, one of the chronicle's most literary parts, Slavonicisms are perfectly normal. The author of the story, Vasilij, was most likely a priest or monk, who can be expected to have written in Slavonic. All in all, example (7) can equally well have been introduced in the 12th century or in the 14th, and its status as either Slavonic or colloquial is not clear. Thus, this example does not speak to the question at hand.

The two occurrences of accuative *ego* in the story of Vasilko do, however, fit a pattern of a different sort—namely, the appearance in the last part of the Primary Chronicle, from about 1093 onward, of accusative forms that are otherwise lacking or rare in the Primary Chronicle, but which are common in the Suzdal Chronicle. Two such anomalous accusatives are the masculine noun plurals in the conjoined objects of the following example (s.a. 1097/6605):

(8) *sozva bolęrъ i kyjanъ* (leaf 87 d, 14)
'called together the boyars and the Kievans'

Even if introduced by Lavrentij in 1377, these genitive-accusative nouns are still quite early; but *bolęrъ*, in particular, occurs regularly as a plural genitive-accusative in the Suzdal Chronicle, although only the non-genitive accusative plural of this word is found elsewhere in the Primary Chronicle. Thus, the genitive-accusatives in (8) may represent a much earlier use of the noun plural genitive-accusative than has been generally believed.

Also in this later part of the Primary Chronicle (s.a. 1093 and 1095, at leaf 72 d, 20, and leaf 76 a, 26, respectively) are 2 occurrences of *i* as an anaphoric accusative **plural**; this very peculiar form is common in the Suzdal Chronicle, but occurs only once earlier in the Primary Chronicle—in the story of the founding of Perejaslavl' Russkij (s.a. 992/6500, leaf 42 b, 26), a story that must have been composed, like the narrative of the 1090s, by the author or editor of the Primary Chronicle, and was not originally part of the chronicle text in which it was embedded (see, e.g., Šaxmatov 1916, Lixačev 1950:347). The chronicle's usual anaphoric accusative plural is the originally Slavonic *ja*; the specifically East Slavic form *ě* occurs only twice, s.a. 1096 and 1103. Thus, *ě*, like *i*, is an anomaly in the Primary Chronicle text of 1377, and is found only in its last entries. (Another form, *e*, spelled with the "e poluležačee," occurs 16 times, mainly in the early part of the chronicle.) Finally, the genitive-accusative plural *ix* also occurs only twice in this chronicle text, s.a. 1096 and 1110. All of these forms recur in the 12th-century part of the Suzdal Chronicle, and thus unite the last, approximately, twenty-five years of the Primary Chronicle with the Suzdal Chronicle and separate it from the earlier parts of the Primary Chronicle. Thus, just as the frequency of accusative *ego* increases gradually across the Primary Chronicle and the first part of the Suzdal Chronicle, with no clear boundary between them, similarly, other types of accusative morphology are also shared by the end of the Primary Chronicle and the Suzdal Chronicle. Such a distribution is unlikely to have been imposed by the scribe of 1377.

The problems of the authorship and editing of the final entries of the Primary Chronicle are well known; they are also, certainly, too complex to be even reviewed here. It is at least of some interest, however, that the difficulties and disjunctures of the conclusion of the Primary Chronicle are reflected in the distribution of genitive-accusative and other accusative-case forms.

I believe that what has been said here provides strong evidence of extreme scribal conservatism with respect to the use of *ego* and *i* in the Laurentian Manuscript. A negative result of this analysis is to discount the value of the manuscript as a source of information about innovations in 14th-century East Slavic, and to reinforce the view that its linguistic usage is very heavily Slavonic in origin, even in the use of forms shared by Slavonic and East Slavic. At the same time, my results suggest the possible value of low-level linguistic patterns as an aid to locating textual seams in the Primary Chronicle. In summary, the distribution of *ego* in the Primary Chronicle is mainly a phenomenon not of the 14th-century text, but of earlier textual components, and is indicative not of colloquial innovation by the 14th-century scribes, but rather of the highly conservative nature of their labors. The word "conservative" here should be understood in its most literal meaning, as a judgment about textual transmission, and not about stylistic choice; with respect to accusative *ego*, the word "Slavonic" should be used the same way.

University of California, Los Angeles

NOTES

[1] The term "Primary Chronicle (Laurentian Manuscript)" is used to mean everything in the manuscript up to and including Sylvester's codicil of 1116, which appears after the entry for 1110/6618 (leaf 96). This text naturally includes work not part of the first edition of the chronicle (e.g., the Instruction of Monomax) and excludes whatever of the chronicle was not copied into the 1377 manuscript, but is included in Karskij's and other editions on the basis of the evidence of other manuscripts, such as the Radziwill.

[2] This example, like all the others, is quoted from a photocopy of the Laurentian Manuscript. In my transliteration, "ö" is used for omega, "ę" for the "jus malyj"; "poluležačee e" and "e" are both transliterated "e", and the titlo of abbreviations is omitted. Superscripts are between slashes, and letters omitted from the manuscript are in parentheses.

[3] I wish to thank Horace G. Lunt for bringing to my attention the evidence of the Byčkov/Sinai Psalter, and for other helpful comments on an earlier version of this paper.

[4] Karskij has "izbavlęe" for "izbavlęe/t/", but the superscript "t" is clear in the photocopy.

REFERENCES

Altbauer, Moshé, ed.
    1978 with the collaboration of Horace G. Lunt, *Saint Catherine's Monastery, Mount Sinai. An Early Slavonic Psalter from Rus', I: Photoreproduction.* Cambridge.

Karskij, E., ed.
    1926-1928 *Polnoe sobranie russkix letopisej, I: Povest' vremennyx let.* Leningrad. (Reprinted 1962 in Moscow and 1977 as *Handbuch zur Nestorchronik,* I, ed. Ludolf Müller, Munich.

Klenin, E.
    1980 "On the Genitive-Accusative of Anaphoric Pronouns in the Laurentian Manuscript of 1377," *Slavic and East European Journal* 24, 52-62.
    in press *Animacy in Russian: a New Interpretation.*

Laurentian Manuscript
    1377 (Photocopy made available through the courtesy of the Harvard Ukrainian Research Institute.)

Lixačev, D. S.
    1950 'Kommentarii' in *Povest' vremennyx let, č. 2: Priloženija,* ed. V. P. Adrianova-Peretc. Moscow, 203-484.

L'vov, A. S.
    1968 "Issledovanie Reči filosofa" in *Pamjatniki drevnerusskoj pis'mennosti. Jazyk i tekstologija,* ed. V. V. Vinogradov. Moscow, 333-396.

Severʼjanov, Sergej, ed.
    1904 *Codex Suprasliensis. (Editiones Monumentorum Slavicorum veteris dialecti.)* St. Petersburg. (Reprinted 1956, Graz).
    1922 *Sinajskij psaltyr'. (Editiones Monumentorum Slavicorum veteris dialecti.)* Petrograd. (Reprinted 1954, Graz).

Šaxmatov, A. A.
    1916 *Povest' vremennyx let,* I. Petrograd. (Reprinted 1969, The Hague).

Tschiževskij, Dmitrij
    1969 "Anmerkungen" in *Die Nestor-Chronik (Slavistische Studienbücher,* VI). Wiesbaden, 298-321.

Xodova, K. I.
    1963 *Sistema padežej staroslavjanskogo jazyka.* Moscow.

A Semantic Model of Verbal Aspect

Henry Kučera

INTRODUCTION

Linguistic inquiry into the problem of Slavic aspect dates back, albeit in tentative form, to the early 19th century. In spite of the length of time and the large number of scholars who have been interested in Slavic aspectology, a definitive solution still eludes us, and Slavic aspect remains a matter of continuing interest. This, perhaps, should already suggest that the approaches of the past may deserve a critical reappraisal and that new methods of inquiry into this highly complex issue may well be warranted.

Paradoxically, the same phenomenon which makes Slavic aspect an area of special interest has also predetermined the methods of inquiry and—quite possibly—impeded the unravelling of the aspectual mystery: the existence of a well-established formal opposition of imperfective and perfective aspectual pairs has biased the inquiry of Slavic aspectologists in an essentially interpretivist direction, one which proceeds from form to the definition of meaning and thus, in the final analysis, views its task as a description of the mapping of the binary formal opposition into the appropriate semantic concepts. This approach, which focuses on linguistic expression and thus may seem to have the virtue of theoretical realism, is of course not the only possible one. The converse method, which would attempt to define the appropriate semantic domains first and then specify their mapping into linguistic form, can be expected to offer a different set of insights. It is this essentially deductive approach that the present paper attempts to justify. Before doing so, however, a brief discussion of the traditional analysis is needed.

The interpretivist approach in the analysis of aspect has, almost unavoidably, two major consequences. The first is the impetus to find an all-encompassing definition of the meaning of one or of both aspects, an impetus that—in its ultimate form—leads to attempts to present the formal and semantic systems as isomorphic; as is the case with other grammatical categories, the discovery of recurring semantic relations among the morphemes of a language is then considered as the principal task of the analysis (cf. for example, van Schooneveld 1978). Semantic invariance, albeit stated in highly abstract terms, needs then to be imputed to a grammatical form.

The other consequence of the interpretivist method is that it makes it difficult to compare languages that express meanings of an aspectual character by different formal means. In German, for example, where aspect is not an overt category (because it is not systematically grammaticalized), distinctions comparable in both morphology and syntactic behavior to the Slavic imperfective-perfective oppositions nevertheless occur. The examples are well known: so the German verbs *jagen* and *erjagen* exhibit not only a parallel morphology to that of the Slavic aspect formation (zero prefix vs. prefix) but also the same syntactic constraints. The verb *erjagen*, like the corresponding Slavic perfective, cannot cooccur with a duration adverbial; compare the following sentences:

(1) Sie jagten den Hirsch den ganzen Tag 'They chased the deer the whole day'
(2) *Sie erjagten den Hirsch den ganzen Tag 'They caught the deer the whole day'

If a systematic grammaticalization of a putative semantic distinction is a requirement for recognizing that a particular language "has aspect", then one clearly must argue that German has none, in spite of these similarities. It is this line of reasoning, combined with a narrow view of what qualifies as aspect, that has led to such drastic claims that not even English possesses the category of aspect (cf. Zandvoort 1962).

A comparison between the Slavic languages and English is particularly instructive in this respect because English presents an interestingly mixed system. Some semantic distinctions similar to the Slavic aspectual contrasts are lexicalized, while other semantic relations of an apparently aspectual kind, such as the progressive vs. non-progressive relation, are systematically grammaticalized. If aspects have to do—not with localization of some situation in time—but rather with a "temporal distribution or contour" (Hockett 1958:237) or 'internal temporal constituency of a situation" (Comrie 1976:3), then the so-called progressive vs. non-progressive opposition in English is surely an excellent candidate for aspectual status, with the perfect vs. non-perfect contrast a possible one. (For a detailed discussion of these Slavic-English issues, cf. Ridjanović 1976).

The English system is a useful illustration of the fact that we cannot expèct a given language to have "pure" aspectual oppositions only. As a matter of fact, mixed situations can be found even within the Slavic family: The Czech contrast *chytat* vs. *chytit* 'chase' vs. 'catch' is an indisputable example of an aspectual pair; the same semantic relation in Russian and, interestingly enough, in English, is lexicalized in the same manner: Russian has *lovit'* vs. *pojmat'*, and English *chase* vs. *catch*. One might object, of course, that this illustration represents a trivial case of a marginal lexical gap, as far as Russian is concerned. Let me therefore put forth a more interesting example, the case of the English "simple present"—as it is often, and mistakenly, called. Consider three simple sentences:

(3) John loves Mary
(4) Peter writes books
(5) Jack builds a house

The first observation that needs to be made is that none of the three sentences describes what is commonly considered to be the essence of the "present tense": an activity taking place at the moment of speech. Sentence (3) describes a state and the truth value of the assertion, stated in it, can be determined only with reference to the stative (non-dynamic) meaning of the verb *to love*. The interesting thing about (4) is that it, too, denotes a state, the assertion that Peter is a book writer; this time, however, the state is expressed as an unbounded series of accomplishments. Once again, the truth value of (4) can be determined only in this sense, having nothing whatsoever to do with the fact that Peter may or may not be engaged in the writing of a book at the moment of speech.

The most interesting case, however, is that of sentence (5): *Jack builds a house* can be a headline, a chapter heading, or a reported event—a so-called "historical present"—in each case denoting an event viewed as accomplished, but under no circumstances can (5) refer to an activity taking place at the moment of speech. To put it more sweepingly still: the English "simple" present can never denote an activity at the moment of speech, not even if the verb is intransitive or has no object: *The child walks* or *Her husband smokes and drinks* are statements about attributes, not about ongoing activities.

In Czech and in Russian, of course, the present tense of an imperfective verb is often ambiguous as to the state/activity reading: *Jan pracuje v knihově, Ivan rabotaet v biblioteke* can denote an ongoing activity, or state the fact that John is a library worker. Notice that this contrast also determines the choice of Slavic translations of the English sentences (3) through (5): while the first two can be rendered only by a present tense of an imperfective verb, the third can be expressed by a past tense of a perfective or, in highly stylistically marked manner, by the present of an imperfective.

Let us now consider the implications of the English situation: is the simple present tense in English, which never signals the present activity but can designate either a state, a habit or a reported past event—all categories of an aspectual nature—, to be viewed as a grammaticalization of the category of aspect? My answer will hardly satisfy absolutist minds: the English simple present—like Russian aspectual forms—has its meaning determined by a *cognitive computation* of the lexico-semantic properties of the verb and the "tense" form; the result is then variably the denotation of a non-dynamic stativity, of a dynamic habit, or of a reported event. The grammatical form (i.e., the simple present) is a necessary but not a sufficient factor in this computation. Being a part of the computation, however, the English tense form contributes to the correct aspectual reading of the sentence.

THE MEANING OF ASPECT

The major problem with the emphasis on some unified formal system as a prerequisite to the analysis of aspect is the conclusion that the grammaticalization of aspect, when it exists, makes the role of lexical and syntactic parameters in the aspectual analysis redundant. This then results in attempts to give a semantic definition of both aspects or of at least the "marked" perfective forms (in such theories as the Praguian markedness analysis) that would hold for all the verbs of the system regardless of their lexico-semantic class.

There have been a number of efforts to define the meaning of the perfective in Slavic. All these definitions, which—by necessity—need to be highly abstract in order to accommodate the variability of different verbs—have turned out to be vulnerable because of the existence of verbal subsets that refuse to behave as required. So, for example, the definition which attempts to equate perfectivity with instantaneousness or temporal "punctuality" is contradicted not only by the entire class of atelic perfectives formed by the prefix *po-* or *pro-*, as in Czech and Russian *postát, postojat'* 'to stand for a while', or *prostát, prostojat'* 'to stand through (some period)', but also by the telic perfectives which assume some duration of the event. Such sentences (with Czech examples followed by Russian ones) as *Napsal knihu včera večer, On napisal knigu včera večerom,* as well as their English equivalent, *He wrote a book last night,* owe their pragmatic incongruity to the fact that constructions with the class of verbs which includes *write* plus direct object assume a process of some duration to reach the goal.

Similarly, the common definition of the perfective as denoting the completion of an action, popular in textbooks but having a respectable scholarly status as well (cf., for example, Jakobson 1971), faces not only such awkward cases as *uvidět, uvidet'* 'to catch sight of, to see' which, within this analysis, would presumaby have to be interpreted as designating 'the completion of the initial phase of seeing,' but also the class of verbs such as the Czech and Russian *zůstat, ostat'sja* 'to remain,' *vydržet, vyderžat'* 'to last,' and others, which, if anything, denote the obverse of completion. Space limitations do not allow me to deal with these problems in detail in this paper, nor can I discuss the special form of the semantic invariance approach, the Praguian theory of marked and unmarked categories. The interested reader can find a more detailed discussion of these topics in some of my previous papers (primarily in Kučera 1980 and 1981).

THE SEMANTIC MODEL

The difficulties encountered by the interpretivist model of aspect lead to the consideration of the other approach: the examination of how the principal semantic entities are mapped into surface linguistic forms, without necessarily assuming any isomorphy in this process, i.e., without advocacy of a one-to-one relation between the meaning and form systems. The comparative aspectual model, proposed for the two Slavic languages (Czech as well as Russian) and English, is given in Figure 1 (a-b-c).

As Figure 1 points out, the proposed aspect model is based on a ternary semantic taxonomy of processes, events and states. Since there are only two major aspectual forms in the Slavic languages, this implies that the relation between the binary formal contrast and the ternary semantic model cannot be accommodated within a theory which assumes an isomorphic relation between form and meaning.

While some of the terms and examples in Figure 1 are self-explanatory, others require comment. This is true, first of all, of the contrast between processes and events. It is difficult, in fact, to give a logical definition of this contrast, but easier to offer a reasonable characterization. As the term suggests, processes are durative situations viewed by an observer-participant as continuous. Events, on the other hand, are closed occurrences, conceptually viewed as entities, that are generally considered to result in a new state of affairs, a new history. Events are observable only from the outside, i.e., their reference point cannot be an instance or an interval within the occurrence. Events are specific (although not necessarily involving definite arguments) and anchored in time. Time is measured in events, not in processes. As an explanatory metaphor consider the following example: Imagine a disk with no markings on it, rotating at constant speed. This is a process; since there are no discernible orientation points chopping up the process into events, this disk cannot be a clock. If we put markings around the disk which give it orientation points, the rotation can now be divided into a series of events, and a time measure is possible.

ACCOMPLISHMENTS AND ACHIEVEMENTS

The concepts *telic* and *atelic* are crucial to the model but caution is important here since these terms are not always uniformly used by linguists; I follow here the more exact usage (e.g., that of Comrie 1976). There are situations that have a terminal point built into them, and others that do not. Either can be represented as a process but the first will be telic, and—if continued—would eventually result in a necessary termination; the other atelic, with no necessary

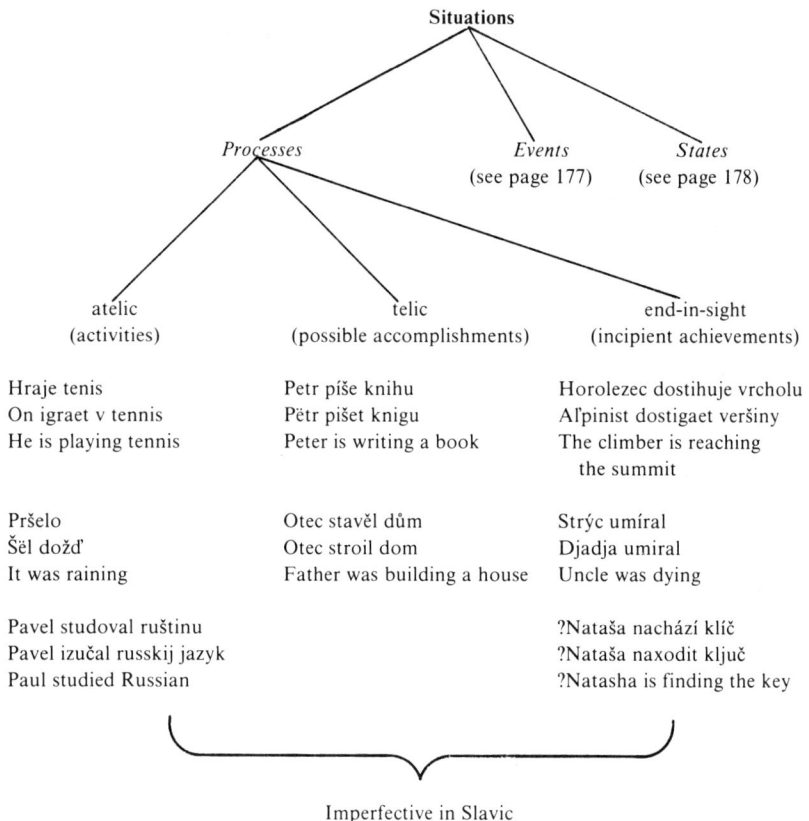

Note: In Czech and Russian, atelic events and accomplishments may be expressed by their process equivalents in positive sentences. This is not the case with achievements, however. In negative sentences, process equivalents are possible in both categories in Russian but only for accomplishments in Czech.

FIGURE 1a.

A SEMANTIC MODEL OF VERBAL ASPECT

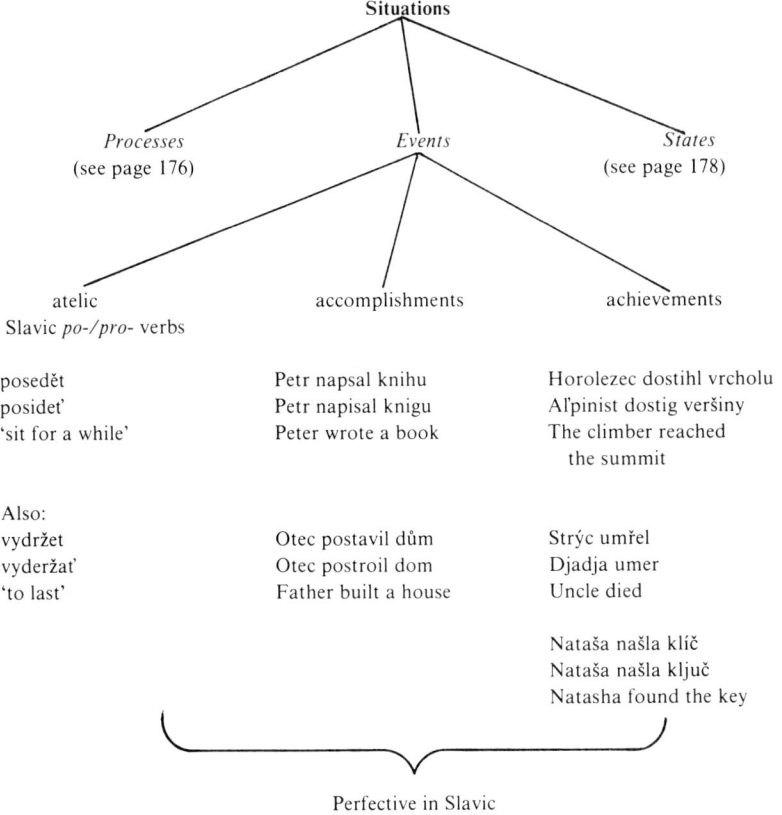

FIGURE 1b.

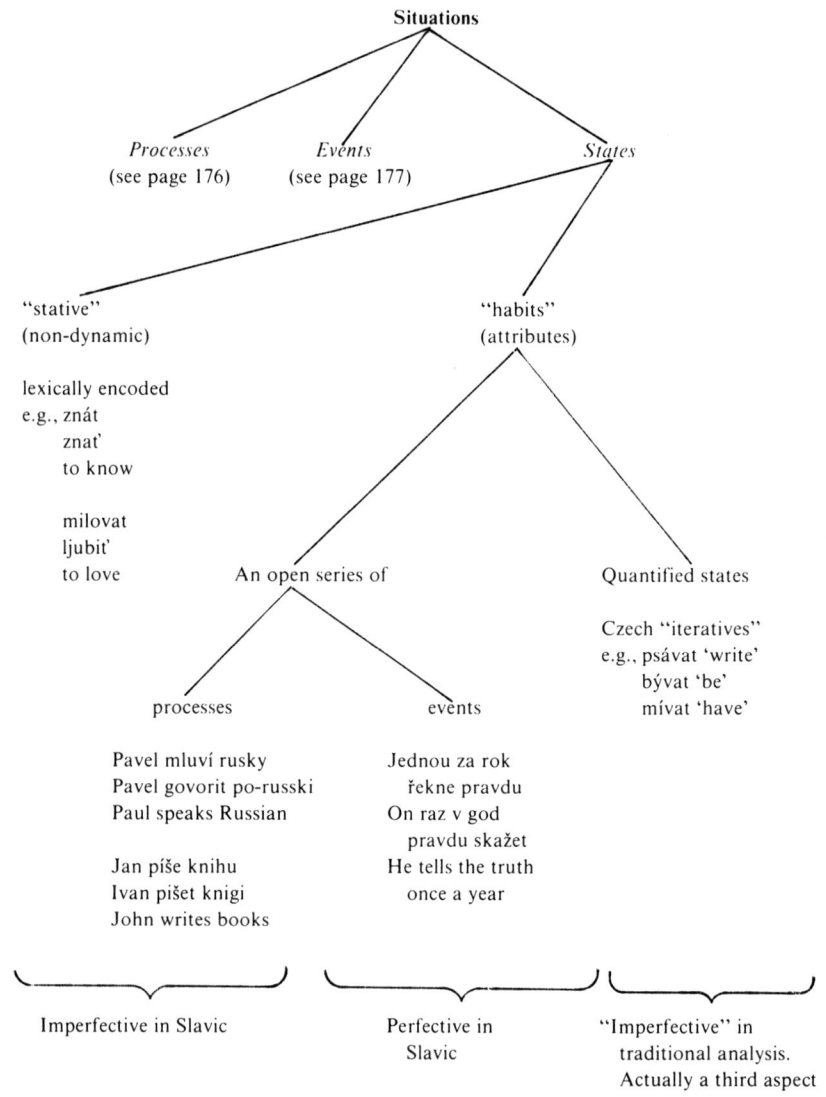

FIGURE 1c.

termination point. Examples from English are more illuminating than Slavic ones because the tense structure of English makes it possible to demonstrate the different entailment relations for telic and atelic constructions. Consider such expressions as *Jack was singing* vs. *Jack was building a house.* The first has no terminal point—Jack can stop singing at any time and it will still be true that Jack has sung. But the same is not true of "building a house." *Jack was building a house* does not entail that Jack has built a house. Notice, incidentally, the important fact that building a house involves a telic process and that, consequently, the complete event corresponding to it, i.e., *Jack (has) built a house,* has a durative element. Consequently, as pointed out above, we have pragmatic difficulty with *Jack built a house last night.* Adding a specific time point to this sentence then reduces its grammaticality to the point where most speakers will find it unacceptable, as in **Petr napsal knihu včera v 5:15, *Petr napisal knigu včera v 5:15, *Peter wrote a book yesterday at 5:15.*

Telic verbal expressions, which represent the second branch in both processes and events in Figure 1, are commonly referred to in linguistic philosophy as *accomplishments,* following the terminology proposed by Vendler (1967). This distinguishes them from the third branch in Figure 1, which Vendler labeled *achievements.* Although this terminology is not ideal, I shall use it in further discussion because of its familiarity.

The third verbal category, which again appears in both processes and events in Figure 1, was labelled *achievements* by Vendler, when denoting events. Vendler mistakenly thought that achievement verbs do not have progressive forms in English, having this negative property in common with stative verbs. This is, of course, not the case: while some verbs, such as *find,* resist the progressive, other members of the achievement class take it readily. When they do not denote events, however, achievements imply a process that has almost reached its goal; I am thus using the descriptive designation of an "end-in-sight" process for such constructions. This category contains such verbs as *najít 50 centů, najti 50 centov, to find 50 cents; poznat někoho, uznat' kogo-nibuď, to recognize someone; dostihnout vrcholu, dostignut' veršiny, to reach the top; zastavit se, ostanovit'sja, to stop; spatřit letadlo, uvidet' samolët, to spot a plane;* as well as intransitive constructions, e.g., *umřít, umeret', to die; utonout, utonut', to drown;* etc. The difference between accomplishments and achievements lies in the fact that achievements have an extremely limited durational process capability. That is also the reason that some members of this class resist a process function: *nachází klíč, on naxodit ključ, he is finding a key,* are, as process descriptions, quite unnatural in all three languages. An important property of all achievement verbs is that, in a process description, they can indeed by employed only if the goal or end is in sight. *Horolezec dostihuje vrcholu, Aľpinist dostigaet veršiny, The climber is reaching the summit* cannot be properly said if the climber is still at the bottom of the mountain. In contrast to this, accomplishment verbs are not subject to such constraints: *Jan píše knihu, Ivan pišet knigu, John is writing a book* is felicitous even if John has written only one page of the work.

As a consequence of these semantic differences, other constraints on achievements exist to which accomplishment verbs are not subject. As a good example, consider the set of Czech and Russian verbs with the prefix *do-*, which, in most cases, have also derived secondary imperfectives; their function is to denote end-phase events: *dopsat, dopisat'* 'to finish writing,' *dojíst, doest'* 'to finish eating,' *dohořet, dogoret'* 'to finish burning,' etc. Since only accomplishments can comfortably have an end phase in the first place, the model, presented here, will correctly predict that this class of perfectives will be found with accomplishments but not with achievements: such forms as **domírat,* **domirat'* or **doumírat,* **doumirat',* 'to finish dying,' **donacházet,* **donaxodit'* 'to finish finding,' **dotonout,* **dotonut',* 'to finish drowning,' **dovracet se,* **dovozvraščat'sja,* 'to finish returning' do not exist. As the English translations of these nonexistent verbs indicate, English demonstrates the same facts by different formal means. The "phasal verbs" *stop* and *finish* can freely occur with processes that denote potential accomplishments: *He stopped writing his dissertation, reading the book, learning Russian; He finished writing his dissertation, reading the book, learning Russian.* Neither of these phasal expressions, however, combines with achievement verbs. All of the following expressions with *finish* plus achievement verb are ill-formed: **He finished drowning, dying, spotting the plane, finding the mushroom, returning,* etc.

Equally worthy of attention is a comparison between the phasal verbs *přestat, perestat'* and the English *stop.* We can say *Přestal psát disertaci, číst knihu, učit se rusky, On perestal pisat' dissertaciju, čitat' knigu, izučat' russkij jazyk,* just as we can say in English *He stopped writing his dissertation, reading a book, learning Russian.* But we cannot have **Přestal umírat, tonout, nacházet klíč, dostihovat vrcholu, vycházet,* **On perestal umirat', tonut', naxodit' ključ, dostigat' veršiny, vyxodit',* just as we cannot have in English **He stopped dying, drowning, finding the key, reaching the top, returning.* These constraints, too, are consistent with the model in Figure 1; achievement verbs assume that the goal or end is "in sight," is imminent, and thus will be reached. "Stopping" it results in semantic incongruity. Naturally, a decision as to the exact status of the starred sentences will vary with the relative assignment of linguistic facts to the domains of syntax and semantics and thus be given different treatment in different linguistic theories.

The contrast between accomplishments and achievements makes some interesting predictions about the natural state of Slavic aspectual oppositions. Recall that accomplishments always involve a process, regardless of whether the verbal construction itself denotes a process (i.e., is imperfective), e.g., *Jan psal dopis, Ivan pisal pis'mo*, 'Jack was writing a letter,' or an event (i.e., is perfective), e.g., *Jan napsal dopis, Ivan napisal pis'mo*, 'Jack wrote a letter.' Consequently, perfective accomplishment verbs in Slavic are generally derived from imperfective activity verbs: *napsat, napisat'* from *psát, pisat'* 'to write,' *vypít, vypit'* from *pít, pit'* 'to drink,' *přečíst, pročitat'* from *číst, čitat'* 'to read,' etc. The converse is true of achievements; since the natural state of achievements is the denotation of a "leap" into a new state, the basic form of these verbs is the perfective, with the imperfective derived: *dostihnout, dostignut'* is the source for the imperfective *dostihovat, dostigat'* 'to reach,' the perfective *vstát, vstat'* for the imperfective *vstávat, vstavat'* 'to get up,' the perfective *přestat, perestat'* gives rise to the imperfective *přestávat, perestavat'*, etc.

Another interesting consequence of the accomplishment-achievement distinction can be seen in the usage of the imperfective past in Czech and, even more often, in Russian, for situations that refer to specific events, and where a perfective might thus be expected. In most such cases, the imperfective is optional and could be replaced, albeit with a different nuance, by a perfective. The classical examples of this usage are such sentences as *Četl jste Annu Kareninu? Vy čitali Annu Kareninu? Už jste obědvali? Vy uže obedali?*, etc. Again, we find here a correlation between usage and our verbal categories: while process forms commonly substitute for events in accomplishment verbs, this is not the case with achievements. **Už jste nacházel klíč? Ano, nacházel*; **Vy uže naxodili ključ? Da, naxodil*; **Její strýc už umíral? Ano, umíral*; **Eë djadja už umiral? Da, umiral*; etc. are not well-formed expressions. Surely, *Did he fall?* cannot be translated into Czech as *Padal?* or into Russian as *On padal?*. The ability of the imperfective to substitute for the perfective in the signaling of specific events is thus not a general property of the imperfective aspect but again depends on the semantic characteristics of the verb.

STATES AND ACTIVITIES

Although this distinction has often been made by both philosophers and linguists, it needs to be interpreted carefully. It is crucial to realize that, besides inherently stative verbs, there are other means to express states, namely as an unbounded series of activities or events. We thus want to make a careful distinction between inherently stative verbs (such as *love, like, know*) which express non-dynamic states, and such verbal constructions as *Rosalyn speaks with a southern accent*, which are expressions of states via a non-stative verb. In this latter case, we have a series of activities which then constitute a characterizing "habit," an attribute. The tests that can be applied to differentiate between activities and states are applicable to both subsets of states.

Neither non-dynamic states nor habits can properly answer an activity question, such as *Co dělá?, Čto ona delaet?, What is she doing?* Just as the answer cannot be **Má ráda poesii, *Ona ljubit poeziju, *She likes poetry,* so one cannot use—at least in English, where the formal distinction between activities and states exists—such an answer as **She speaks German.* In Slavic, where the reading of the present tense is ambiguous between states and activities, the same answer, i.e., *Mluví německy, Ona govorit po nemecki,* limits the possible interpretation to the activity reading, blocking the attribute one.

It is equally important to realize that this kind of state (i.e., a habit) does not need to be expressed only as an unbounded set of activities but can be presented as an unbounded set of events. So, in addition to *She speaks German,* we can also have *She writes books,* (i.e., she is a book writer, she is an author) or *He catches dogs* (he is a dog catcher). Notice that this is precisely the situation where a perfective in Slavic is needed to express a state. Thus we have *Ten člověk řekne pravdu jednou za rok, Ètot čelovek raz v god pravdu skažet,* 'That man tells the truth once a year'; *Kdo hledá, najde, Kto iščet, vsegda najdët,* 'He who seeks will always find,' etc.

QUANTIFIED STATES

The last branch in the diagram of states in Figure 1 of my aspectual model pertains primarily to situations in Czech. Formally, the verbs in question are the so-called iteratives, a set of verbs commonly referred to in Czech linguistic literature as *násobená slovesa.* Although Russian also has a small number of iterative verbs, this aspectual class is unproductive in Russian and quite marginal in standard use. In Czech, however, the iteratives, derived from imperfectives by the infix *-va-,* are common in all styles of speech: *psávat* is derived from *psát* 'to write,' *mívat* from *mít* 'to have,' etc. The productivity of this class is evidenced by the fact that even loans, such as the verb *telefonovat* 'to telephone,' have iterative forms, e.g., *telefonovávat.*

Although Czech iteratives have present tense forms, they cannot denote an action overlapping with the moment of speech. This fact, already observed by Kopečný (1948, 1962), explains the ungrammaticality of sentences such as (6):

(6) *Zrovna teď mi psává dopis 'Right now he writes me a letter'

The fact that Czech iteratives have a morphological present tense thus requires an explanation. To clarify it, consider the following sentence:

(7) Maminka sedává na pavlači 'Mother sits (habitually) on the porch'

Obviously, the proposition asserted in (7) does have a truth value at the moment of speech but not as an activity but rather as a "habit," i.e., a state.

Whether mother is actually sitting on the porch at the moment of speech is of no relevance to the truth value of this assertion. The essential functions of Czech iteratives to denote states can be easily demonstrated also for the past and future tenses.

While iterativeness and states tend to coincide, this is not always the case. Consider the following examples:

(8) Pavel mi psával 'Paul used to write to me'
(9) Pavel v sobotu sedává v hospodě 'Saturdays Paul tends to sit in the pub' (i.e., usually on Saturday, but not necessarily every Saturday)
(10) Němci mluvívají špatně česky 'Germans tend to speak Czech badly' (i.e., most but not all Germans)
(11) Švédové bývají světlovlasí 'Swedes tend to be blond' (i.e., many Swedes, but not "iteratively")
(12) Generálové umírávají v mladém věku 'Generals tend to die young' (i.e., most but not all generals)

While sentence (8) could be fitted into a conventional analysis of iteratives as denoting repetition, the rest of the sentences, (9) through (12), cannot. In none of these cases is repetition being asserted. Instead, (9) through (12) denote what might best be called *quantified states* (for details of this analysis, cf. Kučera 1980). The quantification can extend over the adverbial of a sentence, as in (9), or the plural subject, as in (10) through (12). Sentence (12) presents a particularly clear case of any lack of repetition since the semantic character of the verb *umírávat,* 'to die,' clearly prevents any iterative reading.

CONCLUSION

The outline of a semantic model of aspect, given in this article, has been shown to be applicable to Czech, Russian and English, although different mappings of the basic semantic domains into surface forms exist in these languages. While space limitations have not made it possible to demonstrate the entire set of detailed arguments for this analysis in this paper, I hope that even this brief exposition of the model has succeeded in showing that the approach which takes as a point of departure semantic domains rather than formal grammatical categories is capable of providing a more useful insight into the properties of Slavic aspect than the conventional analysis and can also facilitate a comparative study of aspectual phenomena in languages where the formal means of expression are quite different.

Brown University

REFERENCES

Comrie, B.
   1976   *Aspect*. London.
Hockett, C. F.
   1958   *A Course in Modern Linguistics*. New York.
Jakobson, R.
   1971   "Shifters, Verbal Categories and the Russian Verb," in *Selected Writings, 2: Word and Language*, The Hague, 130-47.
Kopečný, F.
   1948   "Dva příspěvky k vidu a času v češtině," *Slovo a slovesnost* 10, 151-158.
   1962   *Slovesný vid v češtině*. Prague.
Kučera, H.
   1980   "Markedness in Motion" in *Morphosyntax in Slavic*, C. V. Chvany and R. D. Brecht, eds. Columbus, Ohio, 15-42.
   1981   "Aspect, Markedness and t_o," in *Syntax and Semantics* 14, P. Tedeschi and A. Zaenen, eds. New York, 177-89.
Ridjanović, M.
   1976   *A Synchronic Study of Verbal Aspect in English and Serbo-Croatian*. Cambridge, Mass.
van Schooneveld, C. H.
   1978   *Semantic Transmutations: Prolegomena to a Calculus of Meaning, I: The Cardinal Semantic Structure of Prepositions, Cases, and Paratactic Conjunctions in Contemporary Standard Russian*. Bloomington.
Vendler, Z.
   1967   *Linguistics in Philosophy*. Ithaca.
Zandvoort, R. W.
   1962   "Is Aspect in English a Verbal Category?," *Gothenburg Studies in English*, 15, 1-20.

From Language Interference to the Influence of Area in Dialect-Geography

Rado L. Lencek

1.0 One of the most curious facts about languages in contact is the occurrence of striking parallels in sound structure in totally unrelated or very remotely related languages of restricted geographic areas. Among the dialects of the Germanic languages which as a rule have not developed nasalized vowels, certain Upper German (Swabian) dialects have nasalized vowels in lieu of the older $V + N$ combinations.* It is not accidental that these dialects are spoken in proximity to French (Sapir 1921), and that one of the dialects of the same language family (South Bavarian), touches upon Slavic dialects in Austria which "retained" the old Common Slavic nasal vowels till today (Trubetzkoy in Jakobson 1975: 403).

A number of areas of linguistic affinities, as strucutral parallels of this kind are known in areal linguistics, — e.g., the occurrence of so-called "Balkanisms" in South Slavic languages (Sandfeld 1930), or of phonemic vowel quantity and of phonemic polytony in languages across Europe (Jakobson 1936) — have been identified in Slavic linguistics; they have helped us to understand better some aspects of the evolution of Slavic languages.

Nonetheless, it has been shown that linguistic areal investigations, based on observations of the effects of languages upon one another, can never be entirely non-arbitrary. Speaking of the influence of sound systems in more restricted geographic areas this means that there is no general sound change externally caused which would not potentially result from a common heritage, viz. from internal development of one of the languages in contact (Greenberg 1957). If, therefore, one admits the possibility of convergence through internal development, or even the possibility of chance convergence in contiguous unrelated languages in a given area, the *prima facie* conclusions of the areal method may be in conflict with the conclusions drawn by historical and structural evidence of the internal evolution of languages in contact. Such a conflict, which apparently does not represent any problem for areal linguistics, searching to discover the action of the "l'esprit de communauté" of larger

---

* The abbreviations used in this paper are *instr.* = instrumental (case), N = any nasal consonant, *pres.* = present (tense), *sg.* = singular (number), V = any vowel; *Čak.* = Čakavian, *Friul.* = Friulian, *It.* = Italian, *La.* = Latin, *Rez.* = Rezian (dialect), *Rom.* = Romance dialect derived from Low Latin, *Sle.* = Slovene, *Ven.* = Venezian.

linguistic areas (Jakobson 1936), may, however, be crucial to the "l'esprit particulariste" of the languages in the narrower contact situation which ultimately concerns the historical axis of either one of the languages in contact.

A close examination of a few isoglosses in a narrow mini-area of Slavic dialects in contact with unrelated languages would help to bring home this point.

2.0 Our close-up view will be directed at a short strip of Slovene speech area northeast of Udine (Sle. Viden) where the dialects of Venetian Slovenia and Rezia meet with Friulian, a language of the Rhaeto-Romance family. It is in reference to this mini-area that a few contact features, formulated by Pellegrini (1969), will be sifted to illustrate four types of interlinguistic contact phenomena in conflict with the historical development of the dialects in question, as well as with the evolution of their narrower hinterland of western Slovene and northwestern Čakavian as spoken around the Gulfs of Kvarner and Trieste in the Adriatic. This broader area is known as a unique meeting point of at least three genetically unrelated language families — Slavic, Romance, Rhaeto-Romance, Germanic — and is usually considered to represent a classic relic area with a network of contradicting, parallel, and confluent evolutions.

The territorial distribution of the contact phenomena which can be observed in the area beyond the immediate contact is, of course, neither uniform nor congruent. As everywhere in long settled areas, every linguistic feature has its own isogloss, and each isogloss individually crosses the linguistic border from one dialect to the other and continues in their broader hinterlands. We will not make any attempt to trace these isoglosses in individual languages, nor to discuss them in their dialectal distribution. Our discussion is aimed at a classification of linguistic parallels, actual and seeming, caused by evolutionary possibilities rather than interlinguistic influences.

3.0 Theoretically, any number of interlinguistic phenomena can be reduced to at least four possibilities of relations and interference situations between dialects in contact.

3.1 **Two languages in contact, A and B, share an element in the structure of their dialects in contact, which is borrowed from the structure of one of the languages in contact** (e.g., B from A, or A from B). **This is a clear case of language interference.**

Example One. The passage of the palatal l' to j ($l' > j$), observed in Friulian, e.g., *pàje,* It. *paglia* 'straw,' *famèje,* It. *famiglia* 'family'; In Venezian in Istria, e.g., *síja,* It. *ciglio* 'eyelash,' *j:ájo,* It. *aglio* 'garlic,' *famíja* 'family'; in peripheral western Slovene dialects, e.g., Ter-Rezia *kráj,* Sle. *kralj* 'king,' *wója,* Sle. *volja* 'will'; however in Kras: *krâl', wôl'a.* The same phenomenon is known to a few Čakavian dialects, e.g., *póje* from *polje* 'field,' *zémja* from *zemlja* 'land.'

The change is characteristic of the Friulian and Venezian dialects (Ascoli 1873). The Friulian dialects do not know the palatal l' among their consonants, and the same situation extends to the Venetian Slovenia and Rezia dialects, whereas the neighboring Slovene dialects to the east, the dialects of Upper Soča, Western Kras, southern regions of Notranjsko, and Istria, preserved the palatal /l'/. The *l'* > *j* isogloss of the western Slovene dialects is therefore limited to the areas of intense contact with Friulian. The same is to be said about the *l'* > *j* isogloss in the Čakavian dialects across the Liburnia and Kvarner islands. Completely separated from this Slovene dialectal isogloss, the *l'* > *j* change here is again peripheral and conditioned by contact with Romance dialects.

3.2 Two languages in contact, A and B, share an element in the structure of their dialects in contact; the same element appears also independently in one of these two languages outside the contact area. Viewed impressionistically such a situation might not warrant being termed interference at all.

Example Two. The passage of the word-final *-m* to *-n* (*-m* > *-n*), observed in Friulian, e.g., *ùltin*, It. *ultimo* 'last,' *disìn*, It. *diciamo* 'we say'; and in Ter-Rez. dialects: *ósan*, Sle. *osem* 'eight,' *ja znán* (1 sg.pres.), Sle. *znam* 'I know,' *z móžan* (instr. sg.), Sle. *z možem* 'with a man.'

In Friulian dialects, the *-m* > *-n* change is, as a rule, attested everywhere except in some regions of the Central Friuli (Francescato 1966). Further, it is known to the Venezian dialect, to old Tuscan, and to a number of northern Italian dialects. In the Slovene speech area, it is recorded in a broad strip of dialects contiguous with Friulian and Venezian, including the dialects of Zilja, Rezia, Venetian Slovenia, Brda, Upper Soča, Kras, Istria, and part of the Notranjsko. From this point the isogloss continues southward into the area of Kajkavian, Čakavian, and Štokavian dialects along the Adriatic.

On the other hand, the *-m* > *-n* change is also known to the Slovene dialects of the Pannonian dialectal base, viz. Prlekija, Središče, Prekmurje, to the adjoining Croatian Kajkavian dialects, linked at an earlier point in their evolution with the Pannonian Slavic dialectal base. Such a geographic distribution suggests a linguistic contact of a different kind and calls for a more complex explanation.

3.3 Two languages in contact, A and B, have independent evolutions of some equivalent elements in their systems without interference in the dialects of the contact. Such developments follow latent internal tendencies of individual languages. They are parallel and exclude the notion of interference.

Example Three. It has been claimed that the Slovene dialects of our contact area share with the adjoining Friulian dialects a propensity for diphthongization of strong mid-vowels. Thus, the diphthongization of the Slovene dialectal long *e* and *o* is assumed to be "patterned on the Friulian model" which consists of a diphthongization of the Friulian "vocali forti" *ê* and *ô* (Pellegrini 1969).

In the Friulian of Eastern Carnia one indeed finds *fréit* for standard Friul.

frêt, It. *freddo* 'cold,' *nóųf* for *nûf*, It. *nuovo* 'new'; and in Slovene Ter dialect: *lięto*, Sle. *leto* 'summer,' *nùǫjć*, Sle. *noč* 'night,' *γaspùǫt*, Sle. *gospod* 'reverend'; Kras *lięto*, *nûć*, *γaspût*; and in one part of the Central dialects *léįtu*, *nôuč*, *gaspût* (Lower Carniola).

It is recognized that the propensity for diphthongization of long vowels is shared by most languages with quantitative opposition in their vowel system. This phenomenon is today known to the conservative Friulian dialects (Francescato 1966), certainly to most Slovene dialects (Ramovš 1936), to the area of the northwestern Čakavian, and Kajkavian dialects (Ribarić 1940, Belič 1927). The phonetic process of diphthongization here went through stages: long *e* and *o* became narrow, tense, and changed in two directions: either to /ei/ and /ou/ or to /ie/ and /uo/. Thus, indeed, the Friulian and Slovene-Čakavian-Kajkavian diphthongization of long vowels does not differ phonetically; the differences are to be sought in internal factors of Friulian and Slavic and the possibilities of their evolution, in the origin of phonological quantity in each language and in its phonological relevance (Francescato 1966). What this means is that the diphthongization of long vowels in Friulian and Slovene is part of their individual evolutions.

3.4 Two languages in contact, A and B, have separate and independent evolutions of equivalent elements of their systems and a peripheral interference in their dialects in contact. Such parallel evolutions, which need not be contemporaneous, may interact in the development of either of the systems in a contact situation.

Example Four. An example of interference of this kind — often creating the impression of areal convergence in process — can be seen in the parallel occurrence of the palatal plosives *k'* and *t'* in Friulian and Slovene-Čakavian dialects in contact, respectively, e.g., in Friulian in general: *vink'*, It. *venti* 'twenty,' *k'àze*, It. *casa* 'house,' *vèk'o*, It. *vecchio* 'old'; in western Slovene in general, e.g., in the Ter dialect: *svít'a* ~ *svíća* and *svęt'a* ~ *svęća*, Sle. *sveča* 'candle,' *nuǫ́t'* ~ *nuǫ́jć* and *nút'* ~ *núć*, Sle. *noč* 'night'; in Čak., e.g., *kȕt'a* ~ *kȕća* 'house,' *nôt'* ~ *nôć* 'night.'

By origin, the Friulian *k'* represents Latin **ka* (La. *casa* 'house'), or **ti* (La. *viginti* 'twenty'), and **tie* of Romance origin (Rom. *martello* > *mark'iel* 'hammer'); the Slovene and Čakavian dialectal *t'* represents Common Slavic **tj* (**svetja* 'candle'), **kt'* (e.g., **nokti-* 'night'), and an early Sle. *tьj (tVj)* group (e.g., *vénći* < **vętьjьjь* 'larger').

In Friulian dialects which have the palatal plosive *k'*, the unification of *ki* and *ti* is complete; the resulting sound is classified as a palatal stop of the *k'* type, though acoustically it differs very little, if at all, from *t'* (Francescato 1966). The latter is found in Slavic dialects throughout the entire Rhaeto-Romance—Romance contact area, in Čakavian (Belić 1909, Milčetić 1895), in some

Štokavian dialects of Istria (Ribarić 1940, Ivić 1958), and in western Slovene dialects (Baudouin de Courtenay 1904, Škrabec 1921, Rigler 1963).

In the total system of sound relations of South Slavic dialects, however, the palatal stop *t'* represents merely a combinatory variant of the phoneme /ć/. The perception of *t'* and *ć* in individual dialects as two phonemes is contrary to the system of sound relations peculiar to these dialects and to their phonemic and etymological unity with the broader area to which these dialects phonologically and genetically belong.

The phonetic overlapping of the Friulian *k'* and the Slavic *t'* in peripheral dialects, however, should be treated as a case of a phonic interference, a simple substitution of sounds whose phonetic character changes to phonemic at a linguistic boundary. One may see in this substitution a potential interference "sous l'angle des intérêts du système phonologique" (Jakobson 1929), governed by the structure of either one of the two languages in contact.

Example Five. The same type of two separate and independent evolutions with a peripheral interference has been observed in morphology and syntax. We are referring to the parallel usage of present gerund forms and their syntactic patterns in the dialects on both sides of the Friulian-Slovene linguistic boundary. Friulian has its present gerund forms in *-ant, -int,* Slovene dialects in *-oć, -eć*. Their syntactic structures are parallel. Thus, one finds in the Friulian: *Al va pes ostariis, ciantant strofetis* ('He goes round the taverns singing songs'), and in the Ter-Rez. dialects: *An je šal jočajoć* ('He left crying'); or in the Friul.: *La vin cialade a jevâsi* ('We saw her get up'), and in the Ter. Rez. dialects: *San jo vidu plešoć* ('I saw her dance').

Both syntactic patterns — one with a gerund linked to the subject and the other with a gerund functioning as the main object of the sentence — are quite frequent in the dialects on both sides of the contact area, but not in Contemporary Standard Slovene; nonetheless the usage of both patterns in contact dialects mirrors the usage of earlier gerundial patterns known from sixteenth-century written Slovene texts (Lencek 1976).

Since in Rhaeto-Romance and Romance dialects the frequency of gerundial forms seems to be higher, and the variety of their syntactic patterns greater and more typical than in Slavic, the existence of a "gerundial grammatical habit" in Slovene dialects in contact may be easily understood only as a result of direct grammatical interference, a case of the "mixing of the morphologies" of the contact languages, which may be qualified as follows:

At one point of their evolution, two languages, A and B, in contact, may possess some identical phonetic or grammatical features. In their subsequent development, one of these two languages, e.g., language B, may lose some of these features, whereas some of its dialects which are in contact with language A may retain them. Thus, this kind of grammatical interference does not consist simply in a transfer of phonemes, morphemes, syntactic patterns *per se* from language A to the dialects of language B; it involves the maintenance or even the extension of linguistic features and their functions in either one of the two languages in contact.

4.0 To summarize: The existence of common linguistic peculiarities in adjacent, yet unrelated languages and dialects, is easily susceptible to generalizing interpretations. Many times such parallelisms have been rationalized on the basis of substratum theory, more recently on the basis of posited convergence tendencies which in concrete linguistic areas presuppose an interaction of languages in contact. It must be recognized, however, that every contact situation ultimately concerns the historical axis of each of the two adjoining languages, and that latent internal tendencies of development of each of the languages in contact exist even without the intervention of foreign influence. Thus, language contact and resulting interference can very often be considered to have, at best, no more than a trigger effect, releasing or accelerating developments which may mature quite independently in the internal diachronic evolution of the individual languages in contact.

Columbia University

REFERENCES

Ascoli, G. I.
    1873   *Saggi ladini*, I (= *Archivio glottologico italiano*, 1). Rome, Turin, Florence.
Baudouin de Courtenay, J.
    1904   *Materialien zur südslavischen Dialektologie und Ethnographie, II. Sprachproben in den Mundarten der Slaven von Torre in Nordost-Italien* (= *Sbornik ORJaS Imp. AN*, 78, 2. St. Petersburg.
Belić, A.
    1909   "Zametki po čakavskim govoram," *Izvestija ORJaS Imp. AN 1909 g.*, 14, no. 1, 181-266. St. Petersburg.
    1927   Kajkavski dijalekat. *Narodna enciklopedija srpskohrvatsko-slovenačka*, 2 (Zagreb), 222-228.
Francescato, G.
    1966   *Dialettologia Friulana*. Udine.
Greenberg, J. H.
    1957   *Essays in Linguistics*. Chicago.
Ivić, P.
    1958   *Die serbokroatischen Dialekte, Ihre Struktur und Entwicklung. I: Allgemeines und die Štokavische Dialektgruppe*. The Hague.
Jakobson, R.
    1929   *Remarques sur l'évolution phonologique du russe comparée à celle des autres languages slaves* (= *Travaux du Cercle Linguistique de Prague*, 2). Prague.
    1936   "Sur la théorie des affinités phonologiques entre les langues," *Principes de Phonologie par N. S. Trubetzkoy*, trans. J. Cantineau. Paris, 1947, 351-365.
    1975   (ed.). *N. S. Trubetzkoy's Letters and Notes*. The Hague.

Lencek, R. L.
  1976 "On the Use of the Gerund in -č in the Slovene Dialects Contiguous with Friulian," *Linguistica,* 16 (Ljubljana), 65-79.
Milčetić, I.
  1895 "Čakavština Kvarnerskih otoka," *Rad JAZU,* 121 (Zagreb), 92-131.
Pellegrini, G.
  1969 "Contatti linguistici Slavo-Friulani," *Studi linguistici in onore di Vittore Pisani,* 2 (Brescia), 761-776.
Ramovš, F.
  1936 *Kratka zgodovina slovenskega jezika,* I. Ljubljana.
Ribarić, J.
  1940 "Razmještaj južnoslovenskih dijalekata na poluotoku Istri," *Srpski dijalektološki zbornik,* 9 (Belgrade), 1-207.
Rigler, J.
  1963 *Južnonotranjski govori. Akcent in glasoslovje govorov med Snežnikom in Slavnikom* (= *SAZU, Razred za filološke in literarne vede, 13; Institut za slovenski jezik, 7*). Ljubljana.
Sandfeld, K.
  1930 *Linguistique balkanique, problèmes et résultats.* Paris.
Sapir, E.
  1921 *Language. An Introduction to the Study of Speech.* New York.
Škrabec, S.
  1921 "Nekoliko slovenske slovnice za poskušnjo," *Jezikoslovni spisi,* II, 1. Ljubljana.
Trubetzkoy, N. S.
  1931 "Phonologie und Sprachgeographie," *Travaux du Cercle Linguistique de Prague, 4,* 228-234.
Weinreich, U.
  1953 *Languages in Contact. Findings and Problems. (Publications of the Linguistic Cirle of New York,* 1) New York.

The Typology of Cyrillic Manuscripts
(East Slavic vs. South Slavic Old Testament Manuscripts)

Robert Mathiesen

Paleographers, codicologists, textual critics, historical linguists, and scholars in many other fields who work professionally with ancient and medieval manuscripts and with early printed books, all seem at present to be searching energetically for new and more productive tools and methods of work. There is a feeling in the air that the old tools and methods, as useful as they have been and continue to be, cannot always yield sufficiently precise and reliable answers to many of the questions which one would now like to ask about these treasures of our common past. Some of our colleagues have begun to draw on the resources of space-age technology: electron radiography, radiocarbon analysis, Fourier transform holograms, digital image processing, and of course the electronic computer have all been applied in recent years to paleographical and codicological problems of considerable intractability.[1] Others have tried to refine older methods by using them with greater logical or mathematical sophistication than formerly.[2] As one eminent paleographer recently noted, "Mit technischen Mitteln ist die Paläographie, die eine Kunst des Sehens und der Einfühlung ist, auf dem Wege, eine Kunst des Messens zu werden."[3] Clearly, it is a time of opportunity and exhilaration for those of us who study manuscripts and early imprints, whatever our more narrow interests in them may be.

Among the older methods which are now being refined is the typological study of manuscripts, i.e., the investigation of many manuscripts for the purpose of sorting them into a few significant types according to relevant criteria. Such investigations have been carried out more or less informally for a long time, most frequently by textual critics who have had to edit texts found in large numbers of manuscripts, e.g. Biblical and liturgical texts in various languages. By far the most impressive of the earlier typological studies are those on the manuscripts of the Greek Septuagint, the Catenae on the Greek Bible, and the Syriac Pešiṭta; and a similar treatment of the ca. 350 Greek manuscripts containing ancient works on the theory of music is to appear shortly.[4] What is essentially a typological survey of the entire body of surviving Greek manuscripts up to 1600 was provided by R. Devreesse in the second part of his *Introduction à l'étude des manuscrits grecs* (1954), and within the last decade a collective work of similar scope and importance for cyrillic manuscripts has been published in the U.S.S.R. under the editorship of L. P. Žukovskaja and her colleagues.[5]

In most of these studies, manuscripts have been sorted into types solely on the basis of the texts which they contain, without any reference to the arrangement of these texts in the manuscripts. Yet manuscripts differ from one another and resemble one another in both these respects, both of which must be taken into account in specifying the textological structure of every manuscript. Two manuscripts containing the same texts, but in different orders, have different textological structures, just as do two manuscripts containing different texts. Moreover, texts may be arranged in manuscripts in ways more complicated than simple linear orders, or sequences. Divisions between successive parts of a manuscript may vary in importance or rank (as often can be seen from variations in the size, shape and place of headpieces and tailpieces, the layout of titles and rubrics, etc.), indicating groups and subgroups of more or less closely linked texts within the manuscript; and if a manuscript has a sufficiently complex layout (e.g., with interlinear glosses, parallel texts or marginal commentaries), its textological structure may not be linear at all.[6] Some of these latter possibilities have been very instructively analyzed by L. Holtz.[7]

Some Russian and Soviet textologists have been aware of these complexities, e.g., V. I. Istrin and A. A. Šaxmatov; and recently the attention which Soviet scholars have begun to pay, as they edit a particular text, to its "convoy," i.e., to the other texts which regularly coöccur with it in its manuscripts, has proven its value many times over.[8] Perhaps the most painstaking, sophisticated and valuable of all the Soviet studies have been those by L. P. Žukovskaja on the typology of Church Slavonic Gospel manuscripts.[9] It was through her early work that I first became interested in the typology of manuscripts, and her subsequent publications have continued to nourish my interest.

Cyrillic manuscripts which contain Church Slavonic translations of the various books of the Old Testament lend themselves to typological study in particularly interesting ways. If we set aside the several kinds of Psalters and the several liturgical books which contain Old Testament lections, there remain at least 141 Church Slavonic manuscripts of the XII-XVI centuries which contain one or more books of the Old Testament, with or without a commentary or catena.[10] The great majority of these manuscripts were written in an East Slavic variety of Church Slavonic in the fifteenth or sixteenth century; but 11 manuscripts are earlier, and 24 were written in a South Slavic variety of Church Slavonic.

These manuscripts, as well as the Psalters and the liturgical books with lections from the Old and New Testaments, contain various parts of the slowly

TABLE 1.

DISTRIBUTION OF MANUSCRIPTS BY CENTURY
AND BY VARIETY OF CHURCH SLAVONIC

	South Slavic	East Slavic	Total
XII century	0	3	3
XIII century	0	1	1
XIV century	1	6	7
XV century	7	41	48
XVI century	16	64	80
uncertain age	0	2	2
Total	24	117	141

growing corpus of texts which eventually, at the end of the fifteenth century, became a complete Church Slavonic Bible. For our purposes here it will suffice to distinguish four stages in the growth of this corpus, or four historical layers of texts which that corpus contains.

The first layer consists of translations which were made in Great Moravia and Pannonia by Constantine-Cyril and Methodius (with the aid, surely, of some of their disciples) during the second half of the ninth century. To this layer belong most or all of the New Testament translations, the translations of the Old Testament lections (in a variety of liturgical books), and the translation of the Psalter. The first layer, therefore, is only of marginal interest for the purposes of this study.

The second layer contains translations of about two-thirds of the books of the Old Testament. Most or all of these translations were made in Bulgaria during the late ninth or the tenth century. All translations in these first two layers were made from the Greek.[11]

The third layer contains only a single translation, the Book of Esther, which was made from the Hebrew by an East Slav sometime in the eleventh or twelfth century. The fourth layer contains translations of the remaining books of the Old Testament, which were made during the 1490s at the behest of **Archbishop Gennadij of Novgorod, in order to have a complete Church Slavonic Bible available for his own use and for the use of the Russian Orthodox Church.**[12] The Gennadian translations occur in thirteen manuscripts only, all of which are East Slavic. Four of these manuscripts are complete Church Slavonic Bibles (mss. 107, 108, 119, 120); and there is one incomplete Old Testament (ms. 17), which now lacks the Octateuch and the Tetrabasileion at the beginning as well as the Psalter and the Song of Songs in the middle.[13] There are three complete copies of the whole corpus of

Gennadian translations and Esther by themselves (mss. 7, 41, 85+87), and four other manuscripts containing Tobit (mss. 15, 66, 123) or Tobit and Judith (ms. 43).

The Gennadian translations are all from the Latin, and in fact Archbishop Gennadij's complete Church Slavonic Bible conforms to the model of the Latin Vulgate Bible — more precisely, to the model of one of the most common fifteenth-century forms of the Vulgate Bible — not only in the choice and arrangement of its books, but in its very concept. During the Middle Ages it was principally Latin scribes who would write manuscripts of the complete Bible. Many thousand such manuscripts survive, greatly outnumbering the very few Latin manuscripts which contain only isolated parts of the Old Testament (other than the Psalter). Elsewhere in medieval Christendom the reverse was generally true. There still exist about 650 Greek Old Testament manuscripts (excluding Psalters), but no more than 12 of them contain the entire Old Testament, and of these 12, only 8 have the New Testament as well. Much the same observation can be made about Georgian or Syriac or Coptic or Ethiopic Old Testament manuscripts from the Middle Ages. Only in the case of Armenian manuscripts do complete Bibles outnumber parts of the Old Testament, but this feature of Armenian scribal tradition seems to have taken shape in Cilicia during the late twelfth and the thirteenth centuries under Catholic influence.[14]

TABLE 2.
THE COMPOSITION OF ARCHBISHOP GENNADIJ'S BIBLE,
SHOWING THE HISTORICAL LAYERS IN ITS TEXT

Old Testament:

Octateuch 2	Job 2
Tetrabasileion 2	Psalms 1
I–II Chronicles 4	Proverbs 2
Prayer of Manasseh 4	Ecclesiastes 2
I Esdras 4	Song of Songs 2
Nehemiah 4	Wisdom of Solomon 4
II Esdras 4	Wisdom of ben Sirach 2
III Esdras 4	**Sixteen Prophets** .... (1?+)2+4
Tobit 4	I–II Maccabees 4
Judith 4	*New Testament* 1
Esther .... 3+4	

The remaining manuscripts contain various selections and arrangements of books of the Church Slavonic Old Testament belonging to the second and third historical layers of translation. The twelve books of the Octateuch and Tetrabasileion (Genesis — IV Kings), four of the Sapiential books (Job, Proverbs, Song of Songs, Wisdom of ben Sirach), and the Sixteen Prophets are extant in South Slavic manuscripts as well as East Slavic ones, but Ecclesiastes and Esther occur only in East Slavic manuscripts.

As already noted, each manuscript has its own textological structure, and it happens that some of these structures occur often enough in the manuscripts under examination so that we may speak of certain well-defined types of Church Slavonic Old Testament manuscripts. Interestingly enough, the types obtained on the basis of South Slavic manuscripts differ from the types obtained on the basis of East Slavic manuscripts.

In South Slavic manuscripts the first twelve books of the Old Testament are characteristically found either as a single volume (mss. 3, 6, 50, 62, 138), or as two volumes with the division after Ruth, yielding Octateuchs (mss. 1, 65, 135) and Tetrabasileia (mss. 2, 10, 125, 136). In East Slavic manuscripts these same twelve books are characteristically found as two volumes with the division after Deuteronomy, yielding Pentateuchs (mss. 19, 24, 30, 31, 39, 44, 49, 60, 68, 70, 71, 83, 84, 131, 140) and volumes beginning with Joshua and ending with IV Kings, to which Esther is usually appended (mss. 14, 28, 32, 33, 42, 45, 88, 98, 116, 132, 134 with Esther, ms. 76 without Esther). With one problematic exception (ms. 13), already discussed, no East Slavic manuscript is now extant which contains all twelve or thirteen of these books by themselves; but there are a number of manuscripts which begin with this sequence of twelve or thirteen books and then continue with other texts, most or all of which are non-Biblical. Manuscripts of this kind do not constitute a type in the strict sense, for the added — and, in some cases, interpolated — texts can vary greatly, but in the loose sense one might describe them as manuscripts of a chronographic "type" (mss. 18, 29, 36, 51, 79, 93?, 105+15, 121 with Esther, mss. 34, 48, 123, 133 without Esther).

TABLE 3.
SOUTH SLAVIC AND EAST SLAVIC TYPES OF MANUSCRIPTS
OF THE FIRST TWELVE OR THIRTEEN BOOKS OF THE OLD TESTAMENT

	Gn Ex Lv Nu Dt	Jsh Jdg Rth	IK IIK IIIK IVK	Esth
South Slavic	Octateuch + Tetrabasileion (5)			xxxxxx
	Octateuch (3)		Tetrabasileion (4)	xxxxxx
East Slavic	Chronographic volume without Esther (4)			xxxxxx
	Chronographic volume with Esther (8?)			
	Pentateuch (15)	Joshua — IV Kings (1)		xxxxxx
		Joshua — Esther (11)		

As might be expected, the textological structures of the 12 South Slavic manuscripts are replicas of those common among Greek manuscripts of the Old Testament. What is more surprising is that the textological structures of the East Slavic manuscripts described above are virtually unique in medieval Christendom. Neither Greek nor Latin nor Georgian nor Armenian scribes commonly wrote manuscripts of the Pentateuch; such manuscripts are characteristic, however, for Syriac Christian scribes, and the Jews and Samaritans are well known for the special care which their scribes take in copying the Pentateuch by itself. Moreover, the position of Esther after IV Kings is without parallel anywhere else in the scribal practices of Christianity and Judaism.[15] This position of Esther is surely nothing more than the result of a casual innovation by some East Slavic scribe, who appended that translation from the Hebrew at the end of the body of available earlier translations from the Greek, for its presence is optional, and there is even one manuscript in which it occurs after Ruth (ms. 69).[16] The East Slavic preference for Pentateuchs, however, cannot be so simply explained, but probably follows a Semitic model, and most likely a Jewish one. A certain number of East Slavic Pentateuchs in fact contain certain textual features, including glosses and corrections, which can only have been derived from a Hebrew Pentateuch, and which seem not to be found in any South Slavic manuscript of the same books.

This difference in textological structure between South and East Slavic manuscripts of the books in question can be correlated with textual differences so extensive that one must speak of South and East Slavic redactions of one and the same translation into Church Slavonic. Clearly these two branches of the tradition diverged at a very early date.

The Church Slavonic translation of the Sixteen Prophets is found in a very large number of manuscripts, about 50 in all. These books were originally translated from the Greek together with a catena drawn largely from the commentaries by Theodoretus of Cyrrhus. It is still extant in this form, i.e., as a single volume with the catena present, in 23 East Slavic manuscripts (mss. 12, 21, 25, 26, 35, 40, 46, 47, 53, 73, 74, 82, 94, 100, 101, 102, 103, 110, 113, 114, 115, 122, 129; ms. 57, a small fragment, may belong here too); and it occurs together with other texts in six larger compilations, none of which constitutes a type (mss. 52, 55, 61, 75, 117, 130). It appears that all of these copies descend from a common archetype with several great defects, and several of them preserve a colophon written by the priest Upirь Lixyi at Novgorod in 1047. This same translation, but with the catena unskillfully removed, occurs in 14 other East Slavic manuscripts, containing the same defects and — in a few copies — the same colophon by Upirь Lixyi. In 5 of these 14 manuscripts it constitutes a volume by itself (mss. 63, 72, 109, 118, 139), and in 5 others it is part of the Bible of Archbishop Gennadij (mss. 17, 107, 108, 119, 120); in the remaining 4 manuscripts it occurs together with various other texts (mss. 16, 23, 67, 123).

There are also five South Slavic manuscripts containing these texts. Three of them lack the catena, and are clearly South Slavic copies of some East Slavic manuscript of the fifteenth or sixteenth century from which the catena had already been removed (mss. 4, 5, 124). There seem to be neither typological nor textual differences of any great interest between the South and East Slavic manuscripts of the Sixteen Prophets without the catena. The other two manuscripts (mss. 27, 106) have been little studied, but it is clear that the catena is present and that the text may represent a South Slavic redaction different to some extent from the redaction of the East Slavic manuscripts. The most reasonable conjecture, on the basis of what little is known about them, is that they too descend from the same defective archetype as the East Slavic manuscripts, but that the two branches of the tradition diverged at a much later date than in the case of the Octateuch and Tetrabasileion.[17]

These last two South Slavic manuscripts are closely related not only in their text of the Sixteen Prophets with a catena, but also by the presence in each of them of the same collection of four Sapiential books directly following the Prophets. This collection contains Proverbs, Song of Songs, Wisdom of ben Sirach and Job, in that order, and it is also found in a third manuscript, where it follows the Tetrabasileion (ms. 9). This manuscript, too, has been little studied, so that any conjecture as to the origin of the Sapiential Collection would be premature.[18] Nevertheless, one may remark that South Slavic manuscripts seem on the whole to order their contents more strictly than East Slavic manuscripts: the scribal traditions seem to be more uniform. The preferred South Slavic order seems to be the Octateuch in first place, the Tetrabasileion in second, the Prophets in third, and the Sapiential Collection last.

TABLE 4. SOUTH SLAVIC BIBLICAL COLLECTIONS

Octateuch + Tetrabasileion .... mss. 3, 6, 50, 62, 138
Tetrabasileion + XVI Prophets + Sapiential Collection 27
Tetrabasileion + Sapiential Collection 9
XVI Prophets + Sapiential Collection 106

Types of a more trivial character are constituted by volumes which contain only one work — usually a commentary — by itself. One might cite the East Slavic manuscripts of Job with an abridgement of the commentary by Olympiodorus (mss. 54, 95, 99) and those of the Song of Songs with the commentary by Philo of Carpasia (mss. 58, 96), or the South Slavic manuscripts of Job with the complete commentary by Olympiodorus (mss. 8, 111, 127) and those of the Song of Songs with the commentary by Theodoretus of Cyrrhus (mss. 126, 128). Perhaps other manuscripts could be classified into "types" in a looser sense, e.g. the manuscripts containing various parts of Daniel with the commentary by Hippolytus (mss. 22, 38, 56, 78, 91, 97, 137, 141) in a variety of contexts. In any event, there will generally be a residue, as there is here, of manuscripts which are unique in their textological structure, and thus escape classification.

* * *

Typological investigations of the sort presented here and in the author's handlist (cited in footnote 10) do not so much solve textological problems as suggest new lines of approach to their solution. In the case of the Church Slavonic Old Testament, the present investigation strengthens some of the conclusions reached already by A. X. Vostokov, A. V. Gorskij, K. I. Nevostruev, S. M. Kul'bakin, I. E. Evseev, A. V. Mixajlov, P. S. Kuznecov, N. A. Meščerskij, and other textologists.[19] It also raises new problems, such as those connected with the manuscripts of Ecclesiastes and the two South Slavic manuscripts of the Sixteen Prophets with the catena, which should engage the attention of textologists in the future, and more humbly it serves as an aid in the examination of newly discovered manuscripts, or the reexamination of well-known ones. Finally, it can shed a modicum of light on the cultural history of Slavia Orthodoxa during the Middle Ages, as for example on the poorly understood matter of non-Slavic cultures within Kievan Rus' and their relation to the dominant Orthodox Slavic culture.

More generally, the contrastive and comparative typological study of manuscripts from all the cultures of medieval Christendom, Judaism and even Islam will undoubtedly enable us to map more accurately the many currents of development and influence, borrowing and transplantation, as well as the many barriers to these currents, which arose, persisted, changed, and vanished at various times and in various places within the chronological and geographical boundaries of the Medieval World.

Brown University

NOTES

[1] J. F. Benton, A. R. Gillespie, J. M. Soha, "Digital Image-Processing Applied to the Photography of Manuscripts," *Scriptorium* 33 (1979), 40-55; A. Velkov, "Fotografskijat metod za vъzproizveždane na filigrani ot arxivni dokumenti i rъkopisi," *Slavjanska paleografija i diplomatika: Dokladi i sъobštenija ot seminara po slavjanska paleografija i diplomatika, Sofija,*

septemvri 1979 (Sofija, 1980), 148-152; E. Ziesche, D. Schnitger, "Elektronenradiographische Untersuchungen der Wasserzeichen des Mainzer Catholicon von 1460," *Archiv für Geschichte des Buchwesens* 21 (1981), coll. 1303-1360.

2 J. P. Gumbert, "A Proposal for a Cartesian Nomenclature," *Essays Presented to G. I. Lieftinck* IV (Leiden, 1976), 45-52; J. M. Kitzman, "The Three-Dimensional Graphing of Scripts," *Viator* 10 (1979), 433-439; R. Mathiesen, "The Determination of Norms (A Problem in the Diachronic Study of Church Slavonic)," *American Contributions to the VIII International Congress of Slavists* I (Columbus, 1978), 483-494.

3 B. Bischoff, *Paläographie des römischen Altertums und des abendländischen Mittelalters* (Berlin, 1979), 17.

4 A. Rahlfs, *Verzeichnis der griechischen Handschriften des Alten Testaments* (Berlin, 1914); R. Devreesse, "Chaines exégétiques grecques," *Supplément au Dictionnaire de la Bible,* ed. L. Pirot, I (Paris, 1928), coll. 1084-1233; *List of Old Testament Peshitta Manuscripts (Preliminary Issue),* ed. the Peshitta Institute, Leiden University (Leiden, 1961), T. J. Mathiesen, "Towards a Corpus of Ancient Greek Music Theory: A New Catalogue Raisonné Planned for RISM," *Fontes Artis Musicae* 25 (1978), 119-134.

5 *Metodičeskoe posobie* (or: *Metodičeskie rekomendacii*) *po opisaniju slavjano-russkix rukopisej dlja Svodnogo kataloga rukopisej, xranjaščixsja v SSSR,* ed. L. P. Žukovskaja *et al.,* I-II (Moscow, 1973, 1976).

6 On the concept of a manuscript's textological structure see R. Mathiesen, "Some Methodological Problems in Describing Old East Slavic Cyrillic Manuscripts and Printed Books," to appear in *Polata Knigopisnaja* 8.

7 L. Holtz, "La typologie des manuscrits grammaticaux latins," *Revue d'histoire des textes* 7 (1977), 247-269. Cf. also E. G. Turner, *The Typology of the Early Codex* (Philadelphia, 1977).

8 Cf. D. S. Lixačev, *Tekstologija na materiale russkoj literatury X-XVII vv.* (Moscow-Leningrad, 1962), 44-51, 232-267; R. Pope, "Hilandar No. 485 as a Sbornik and the Principles According to which it was Compiled," *Cyrillomethodianum* 5 (1981), 146-160, breaks new ground along these lines.

9 L. P. Žukovskaja, "Tipologija rukopisej drevnerusskogo polnogo aprakosa XI-XIV vv. v svjazi s lingvističeskim izučeniem ix," *Pamjatniki drevnerusskoj pis'mennosti: jazyk i tekstologija* (Moscow, 1968), 199-332; *id., Tekstologija i jazyk drevnejšix slavjanskix pamjatnikov* (Moscow, 1976).

10 R. Mathiesen, "Handlist of Manuscripts Containing Church Slavonic Translations from the Old Testament," to appear in *Polata Knigopisnaja* 7. The manuscripts in this handlist are numbered serially, and will be cited by their serial numbers in this paper. The handlist provides the full bibliography for each of the 141 manuscripts and the Old Testament texts contained therein, so there is no need to repeat these references in the present study.

11 It is possible that the translation of the last four Minor Prophets (Zephaniah, Haggai, Zechariah, Malachi) belongs to the first layer, as may perhaps also be true of a peculiar translation of Daniel (with a few passages from other Prophets) found in just two Chronographs (mss. 48, 133). It is also possible that the translation of Ecclesiastes was the work of an East Slav, for it alone of all the texts in the second layer is not extant in any South Slavic manuscript.

12 The Gennadian translations include twelve full books of the Old Testament (counting the Prayer of Manasseh, of which an earlier translation exists as well), the parts of Esther not in the Hebrew text (and therefore not in the earlier Church Slavonic version either), and certain passages from Jeremiah and Ezekiel translated to fill textual gaps present in all manuscripts of the earlier **translation of the Sixteen Prophets. See table 2.**

13 Ms. 13, the only extant East Slavic manuscript containing just the Octateuch and Tetrabasileion, may be either the missing first half of ms. 17, or a later replacement for it.

14 S. Berger, *Histoire de la Vulgate pendant les premiers siècles du Moyen Âge* (Paris, 1893), R. P. Blake, "The Athos Codex of the Georgian Old Testament," *Harvard Theological Review* 22 (1929), 33-56; M. Ter-Movsesjan, *Istorija perevoda Biblii na armjanskij jazyk* (St. Petersburg, 1902). For

Greek and Syriac manuscripts see the lists cited by footnote 4 above. There seem to be no ancient or medieval manuscripts of the complete Bible or Old Testament in Coptic or Ethiopic.

[15] Berger, *op. cit.*, p. 337 (nos. 157-158), cites two manuscripts of the Latin Vulgate in which Esther now follows IV Kings, apparently for special reasons. It is not likely that either of these manuscripts had any influence on East Slavic scribal traditions.

[16] This manuscript contains Joshua, Judges, Ruth and Esther. There are a number of Greek manuscripts in which Esther follows Ruth, but only as part of a larger collection than what is contained in the East Slavic manuscript.

[17] Greek manuscripts of the Sixteen Prophets with a catena similar to the one found in the Church Slavonic manuscripts are still extant, but none of the few known copies seems to correspond very closely to the Church Slavonic translation. Further investigation is clearly needed. (Cf. Rahlfs. *op. cit.*, pp. 428-430.)

[18] The Sapiential Collection is not paralleled in any Greek or East Slavic manuscript, nor — to judge by the limited information available to me — in any other medieval Christian or Jewish manuscripts.

[19] See their textological studies listed in the bibliography of my "Handlist."

On Expressing "Definiteness" in the Slavic Languages and English

Kenneth E. Naylor

INTRODUCTION

The category of "definiteness" is a linguistic universal. We must, however, note that while the category is fundamental, the means for its expression will differ from language to language. This must not be taken to mean that the importance of the category in a given language depends on the presence or absence of a particular type of surface marker, i.e., an article.[1] Definiteness is often associated with the definite article and in the same way indefiniteness is associated with an indefinite article, but an examination of the Slavic languages shows that a variety of other means exists for the expression of these categories even in those languages which have not yet developed a formal definite or indefinite article.

It is clear that the existence of the category of "definite" implies in binary terms that there is also a category of "indefinite"; thus the first question which can be raised is whether "nondefinite" (which would be the normal binary opposition of "definite") is the same as "indefinite." Despite my natural impulse to say that it is the same, consideration of evidence from the Slavic languages make it clear the opposite is more likely true. As Krámský (1972:19) notes, the basic notion here is one of "determinedness" vs "nondeterminedness." Nondeterminedness can further be subdivided into "specific" and "nonspecific" as Kazazis and Pentheroudakis (1976) have suggested for Albanian and Modern Greek, which means that we are not simply dealing with the difference between definite and nondefinite.

A meaning which is frequently given for "definite" is "known," which would then imply that the opposite of "definite" would be "unknown." Although this is clearly *one* meaning of the category it is certainly not the basic meaning. Examination of data from a number of contexts indicates that "known" is applicable only in a limited number of cases whereas definite can also be used to indicate various other things, including "uniqueness," e.g., English "the sun," or "the moon," while in other instances the definiteness of a particular notion may be explained within the context itself, e.g., "the week *after they moved* was the most hectic of their marriage." Here again, an examination of the indefinite direct object examples from Albanian and

Modern Greek cited by Kazazis and Pentheroudakis suggest that "nondefinite" is not equal to "unknown." It has been the attempt to follow this line of reasoning which has led so many astray in discussing the concept of definiteness.[2]

In this paper, I shall work within the following framework: **definite** will mean "determined," usually by some characteristic which may, or may not, be easily identified from the immediate context in which the person or thing is mentioned. **Nondefinite** will mean that the person or thing described is not determined but is simply a member of the class. Here, however, we must make the further division of "nondefinites" into "specific" vs. "nonspecific."[3] Schematically, the oppositions would look like this:

(+) Definite	Nondefinite	(−)
	Particular/ Specific (+)	General/ Nonspecific (−)

This diagram also suggests something about the formal marking of these categories in the Slavic languages. Definite concepts tend to be more clearly marked than nondefinite concepts and at the same time specific concepts are formally more clearly marked than those which are nonspecific.[4]

There are certain problems in considering the expression of definiteness in the Slavic languages. The first is that two of these languages, Macedonian and Bulgarian, have a clearly established formal marker—the definite article <-t->.[5] The other languages have not yet regularly introduced articles into their structures but this should not imply that they are unable to express the category and it is revealing to see what means are available to them and used for this purpose.

All of the Slavic languages have free word order, and this is a complication at the same time that it is a syntactic convenience. In Slavic, the definite element of the sentence or phrase (the theme) must be placed ahead of that which comments on it (i.e., the rheme which follows). In those Slavic languages which have not developed a formal article, there is therefore the need to indicate themes by placing them at the head of the sentence or phrase. In Macedonian, and to some extent Bulgarian, which have developed a definite article and which have, incidently, lost the declension as the formal marker of grammatical function, it is the function of the reduplicated pronominal object (definite or indefinite) which is placed at the head of the phrase in which the object occurs, where it acts as the surrogate theme for the object coming later in the phrase, which it mirrors.[6]

The fact that two languages have definite articles does not, however, mean that their structures are alike or that they will use the article in the same way and that the article will have the same meaning or distribution in the languages. English and Macedonian provide us with an interesting instance of this.[7] In English we can distinguish three articles: *the* the definite article, *a/an* the indefinite article and a "zero-article," which I shall note as Ø. Macedonian, on the contrary, has a definite article <-t->, an indefinite article <ed#n-> (*in statu nascendi*) and a "zero-article." The unclear status of the indefinite article means that the zero-article has a different meaning and function in Macedonian than in English, which in turn affects the function and distribution of the definite article. These differences can be seen clearly in the following charts which give the distribution of the articles in the two languages.

ENGLISH

	GENERIC		NONGENERIC[10]	
	Abstract[8]	Concrete	Definite	Nondefinite
Sing	Ø	the/a[9]	the	a/an
Plur	DNA	DNA	the	Ø

MACEDONIAN

	GENERIC		NONGENERIC[10]	
	Abstract[8]	Concrete	Definite	Nondefinite
Sing	-t-	-t-	-t-	Ø
Plur	DNA	DNA	-t-	Ø

As can be seen, the distribution of the zero-article in Macedonian is such that it always means "nondefinite" (nongeneric), which makes it unsuitable for use when an abstract generic is meant. This is in clear contrast to English where the zero-article means abstract generic with a singular and nondefinite with a plural. This difference alone accounts for much of the difference in distribution which we find in the two languages.

One other question should be raised at this point, viz., "Is it possible for a language to have an indefinite article without a definite article?" Krámský (1972:110-19) discusses a number of languages which appear to, but on closer examination it can be seen that in many cases what is involved is the use of the word for "one" with a particularizing meaning.[11] Ivić (1971) presents a convincing case for this in Serbocroatian. (The Serbocroatian situation is further complicated by a partially still extant opposition definite/indefinite in adjectives.) We should therefore consider that rather than viewing these uses of "one" as "indefinite article" we should view them as the means of expressing a particularized indefinite.

In this paper, first I shall consider definite expressions in Slavic, then the expression of nondefiniteness, including the cases where *edьnъ* is used as an indefinite article.[12] In addition, I shall make a brief comparison of article use in English and Macedonian. The emphasis will be on the South Slavic languages with additional material being drawn from other Slavic languages.[13]

THE EXPRESSION OF DEFINITENESS

There are a number of ways in which definite is expressed in the Slavic languages which have not yet introduced a formal definite article morpheme. In spoken language, this can be done by the use of intonation (see Nikolaeva 1979a for a discussion of this point). In written language, however, other ways must be found to convey this category. For this reason, we must consider the category of definiteness as syntactic as well as grammatical. The primary syntactic means for marking definiteness is by word order with the concept (or action in which it is involved) which is viewed as definite placed at the head of the phrase as the *theme* and the other members of the phrase following as the *rheme,* which comments on it. Clearly this requires that the language have a morphological mechanism, i.e., the marking of grammatical function formally with case, which tells us which member of the sentence is the subject and which is the object (direct and/or indirect). If the language lacks these morphological mechanisms, then word order must provide this information.[14]

Another means which can be employed syntactically to convey the category of definiteness is the use of a demonstrative adjective under certain conditions. There are a number of problems with such constructions, since it is often difficult to determine when the demonstrative has the original deictic meaning and when it is being used metaphorically to designate a definite member of the group without the physical act of pointing—or even without the designee being physically present.

We should not assume, however, that these two means—word order and the use of a demonstrative—are independent. In fact, it would appear that the reverse is true. In some instances, a peculiarity of word order may prevent the theme, which will be definite if it is a substantive, from occupying its proper place to indicate that it is definite. In such cases, we often find that another means, most often the use of a demonstrative to call attention to the theme, is necessary. In fact, it is hard to consider one of these topics without making reference to the other. For practical purposes here, I shall first consider the expression of definiteness by word order alone, i.e. theme/rheme construction, and then the use of demonstratives for this purpose.

The Theme/Rheme Marking of Definiteness

Because the Slavic languages have free word order, they commonly make use of theme/rheme constructions to indicate that a concept is definite. We can find two types of examples, viz., (a) those without a relative clause which serves as the rheme to specify the concept and (b) those with relative clauses. I shall consider first those where word order itself is the marker. It is easy to find many examples of type (a).

(1) a. Kníha je na stole. (CZH)
    b. Knjiga je na stolu. (SBC)
    c. Kniga na stole. (RUS)
       The book is on the table.

(2) a. Mladá dívka rozbila vázu. (CZH)
    b. Devojka je slomila čašu. (SBC)
    c. Devuška razbila stakan. (RUS)
       The (young) girl broke a vase/cup/glass.

(3) a. Devuška vošla v komnatu (RUS)
    b. Mladá dívka vešla. (CZH)
    c. Devojka je došla. (SBC)
       The (young) girl came/entered (the room).

In each of these sentences the placement of the concept, i.e., 'book' in (1) and 'girl' in (2) and (3) at the head of the setnence marks it as being of primary importance (the theme), and hence definite, while the remainder of the sentence is rheme, which makes a comment on it. When, however, the order is reversed, the concept which was the theme (and definite) now becomes the rheme (and indefinite) while the object, if any, is definitized, as in (4-6).[15]

(4) a. Na stole je kníha.
    b. Na stolu je knjiga.
    c. Na stole kniga.
       A book is on the table.

(5) a. Vázu rozbila mladá dívka.
    b. Čašu je slomila devojka.
    c. Stakan razbila devuška.
       The vase/cup/glass was broken by a/the (young) girl.

(6) a. V komnatu vošla devuška.
    b. Vešla mladá dívka.
    c. Došla je devojka.
       A (young) girl came/entered (the room)

There are also examples where the theme is echoed by a "WH-word," or relative pronoun, i.e., *who, which,* which heads a relative clause. Here the relative pronoun occupies the theme position in its clause and effectively makes the original noun definite. These examples are more explicitly definite because the relative clause also tells us what characteristic or fact sets the original noun apart from other members of the class.

(7) Video sam čoveka koji je juče došao. (SBC)
I saw the man who came yesterday.

(8) Čovek što znae da rabotuva ḱe bide bogat. (MAC)
The man who knows how to work will be rich.

(9) Lakej i kučer, kotorye videli ètix ljudej, ne obratili
na nix vnimanija (RUS)
The footman and the coachman, who saw the people, paid
no attention to them.

(10) Nam nužen student, kotoryj znaet kitajskij jazyk. (RUS)
We need a student who knows Chinese.

(11) Wiesz, auto, które parkuje przed naszymi drzwiami,
wydaje mi się znajome. (POL)
You know, the car, which is parked in front of our gate,
seems familiar (known) to me.

In some cases where there is a WH-word, the definiteness of the theme can be further underscored by the addition of a demonstrative which emphasizes to the hearer precisely which person/thing we have in mind, as in (7a) and (10a):

(7a) Video sam onog čoveka koji je juče došao.
(10a) Nam nužen tot student, kotoryj znaet kitajskij jazyk.

Definitizing by the use of word order is not limited to subjects, or subjects vs. objects, but may also be found between the direct and indirect object as in (12-13).

(12) a. Muščina podaril devuške cvety. (RUS)
The man gave the girl flowers.
b. Muščina podaril cvety devuške. (RUS)
The man gave the flowers to a girl.

(13) a. Dao sam devojci knjigu. (SBC)
I gave the girl a book.
b. Dao sam knjigu prijatelju. (SBC)
I gave the book to a friend.

The fact is that the use of the first position in the phrase, or, as we have seen in (12) and (13) in regard to two objects, relative position in the phrase, to mark a concept as definite is not restricted to those Slavic languages which lack a formal definite article. Macedonian requires, and Bulgarian permits, the fronting of a reduplicated pronominal object when the direct object is definite. Functionally this is the same kind of echo theme which we find with the WH-word in a relative clause, but here the pronoun serves to tell us that the object which follows will be definite even though it does not occupy the theme position (which is expected), as in (14-15).

(14) Ja krena glavata i zagleda vo svojot sin. (MAC)
He turned his (lit. 'the') head and looked at his son.

(15) Toj ḱe mi gi topli kostite na stari denovi. (MAC)
He will warm my (lit. 'the') bones in my old days.

Thus we can see that the formal marking of definiteness by the article is not always sufficient; syntactic means may be necessary as well.

The Use of Demonstratives to Express Definiteness

There is a further relationship between the demonstratives and the expression of definiteness in Slavic. As is well known, the definite article in Macedonian and Bulgarian—as well as number of other Indo-European languages—developed from demonstrative adjectives.[16] It is therefore not surprising to find examples in the other Slavic languages, which have not developed a formal definite article, in which the demonstrative serves to convey the notion of definiteness.[17] In most of the examples I have found of this type, the demonstrative seems to function as a definiteness-marker (I am reluctant to use the term "definite article") where there is a hindrance to marking definiteness by regular syntactic means, e.g., by the use of a theme/rheme construction.[18]

I have found two syntactic environments where definiteness is expressed by the use of a demonstrative in a nondeictic sense (see Topolińska 1981:45-47 for a discussion of instances where deictics, which she refers to as *deixis in absentia,* have this function.).

I. Constructions where imperatives stand in the first place (theme position) in the sentence.

(16) Daj mi tu knjigu. (SBC)
Give me the book!

(17) Čitaj tu knjigu i reci mi šta misliš. (SBC)
Read the book and tell me what you think.

(18) Pročitajte ètu knigu! (RUS)
Read the book!

(19) Dej mi tu knihu! (CZH)
Give me the book!

The placement of the object before the imperative would lead to the hearer to expect further comment, e.g.,

    (20)   Knigu pročitajte, ne žurnaly! (RUS)
             Read the book, not magazines.

II. In sentences where the definite concept is the object and the construction is such that the theme position is already occupied and there is no rheme for the object,

    (21)   Ja ne našel èto pis'mo. (RUS)
             I didn't find the letter.
    (22)   Video sam ovoga čoveka. (SBC)
             I saw the man.

In sentences such as these, there could also be a relative clause with a "WH-word" which would make clear why the concept is definite, e.g.,

    (21a)   Ja ne našel to pis'mo, kotoroe bylo u menja na stole. (RUS)
              I didn't find the book which was on my table.
    (22b)   Video sam ovoga čoveka koji stanuje kod tebe. (RUS)
              I saw the man who lives in your building.

Reversal of the expected word order may give an emphatic meaning or imply surprise but not necessarily be definite so that we expect further information to be supplied.

    (23)   Čoveka sam video ... (SBC)
             I saw a man ... *or* A man I saw ...

Some examples have been a rheme or relative clause which seems to explain why the demonstrative was used, but many of these can be analyzable as the conjunction of two independent sentences, e.g.,

    (24)   Daj me tu knjigu tamo na stolu! (SBC)
             Give me the book which is there on the table!

This sentence can be analyzed as *Knjiga je na stolu* and *Daj mi knjigu*.

The major function of the demonstrative in such sentences is to remove all ambiguity as to exactly which member of the class we want by providing additional information or complete specification which might otherwise not be understood.

(But compare a similar sentence without the demonstrative where word order also conveys definiteness in a particular context.)

    (25)   Pis'mo ja našel. (RUS)
             I found the letter.
    (26)   Čoveka sam video. (SBC)
             I saw the man.

Both sentences convey the notion of definiteness but at the same time there is also a connotation of surprise or emphasis. At the same time, both still seem somewhat incomplete and the hearer may want more information. This information would be supplied by a relative clause which explains "what" or "which" letter or man is being discussed.

(27) Pis'mo ja našel, to kotoroe ja iskal. (RUS)
    The letter I found, that which I was looking for.

(28) Čoveka sam video, je taj koga ti dobro znaš. (SBC)
    The man I saw is the one (that) whom you know well.

These compare to more conventional, and less emphatic, sentences like (29 and 30):

(29) Ja našel to pis'mo, kotoroe ja iskal. (RUS)
    I found *the* letter which I was looking for.

(30) Video sam ovog čoveka koji te mnogo hvali. (SBC)
    I saw *the* man who praises you a lot.

Some examples, like (31), are interesting in that the use of the demonstrative seems to go along with the relative clause which follows,

(31) Nam nužen tot student, kotoryj znaet kitajskij jazyk.[19] (RUS)
    We need *the* student who knows Chinese.

There is also a construction in Serbocroatian which optionally uses a demonstrative with a possessive adjective. Although examples of this construction are not sanctioned in the grammars, it is fairly widespread in both spoken and written languages.[20]

(32) Ovaj tvoj sin je tako radio.
    Your son did this.

(33) Cilj je ovoga moga rada ...
    The goal of my work is ...

THE EXPRESSION OF NONDEFINITENESS

There are two ways to express nondefiniteness in Slavic, depending upon whether the further category of "specific" is implied. This point is also tied to the question of whether there is an indefinite article in Slavic. As already mentioned, the status of the indefinite article in Slavic is still in a state of flux. In part this is due to the fact that in many instances the use of *edьnъ*[21] in the various languages is still to a certain degree optional, or would appear to be so, especially in the South Slavic languages where there is still a partial maintenance of the opposition of definite/indefinite in the adjectives. But there is still sufficient evidence to support the contention that *edьnъ* is acquiring the function of an indefinite article as shown by the studies by Friedman (1976) for the Bulgarian, Ivić (1971) for Serbocroatian and Topolińska (1981) for Macedonian. As both Ivić and Topolińska suggest, the use of *edьnъ* is, however, tied to whether the person or thing is viewed as a particular (= specified) member of the class or just one of the class without any particularities (= unspecified). This explains, I believe, the large number of examples which exist without the use of *edьnъ* where only an indefinite adjective, or no adjective at all, is found.

Before looking at the examples, we should examine some of the statements about the status of *edьnъ* as an indefinite article in the various languages. Stevanović (cited by Ivić 1971:103) states "Broj *jedan* se vrlo često u našem jeziku upotrebljava ne da se označi broj, nego je to onda više kao neka vrsta neodredjenog člana...." Koneski (1954:91, 102), writing about *eden* in Macedonian, indicates that the numeral can have the same function as *nekoj* 'a certain,' so that we may safely assume that *eden* has certain of the characteristics of an indefinite article in Macedonian. This is stated more explicitly by Topolińska (1981:63): "In my opinion at least in Macedonian *eden* in some uses should be treated as an article." Further, Friedman (1976:339) says unequivocally "[*e*]*din* is used as an indefinite in Bulgarian, in a semantic or syntactic context which demands a referential indefinite article."

But, as already noted, there is the further complication that *edьnъ* is not used everywhere that we would expect an indefinite article to be found. Ivić (1971:112) clarifies this by pointing out that *jedan* in Serbocroatian carries the added meaning of particularity: "Dok se *jedan* javlja uvek samo gde je važno notirati *pojedinačnost* [my italics—KEN], *neki* je specijalizovan za situacije neodredjenosti u širokom smislu reči." At the same time, we should note that there are still indefinite adjectives in the language and they can be used to convey the category of indefiniteness without *jedan* when nonspecificity is intended. The following examples show the relation between *edьnъ* to mark specificity, and its omission to indicate nonspecificity.

(34) Dečak je držao neobičan predmet u rukama. (SBC)
The boy held an unusual object in his hands.

(35) Kupio sam nov čamac. (SBC)
I bought a new boat.

(36) To nije velik problem. (SBC)
It's not a great problem.

(37) Zamislite, videli smo najzad pravu, živu žirafu. (SBC)
Imagine, at the last we saw a real live giraffe.

(38) Slabi studenti prave probleme i više se svi bave njima
na štetu dobrih studenata. (SBC)
Poor students make problems and everyone is more occupied
with them at the expense of good students.

(39) Ima dobar pes. (MAC)
He has a good dog.

(40) Toa beše dobar predznak. (MAC)
That was a good omen.

(41) Beše studeno utro, prvoto grizenje na zimskiot stud....
It was a cold mroning, the first nipping of the winter's chill....

In each of these examples, we can see that there is an unspecified thing indicated. Hendriks (1976:218) has referred to sentences of this type, i.e., without a clear article as having a "zero-article" which "generally signifies indefiniteness." However, I would suggest that they indicate nonspecificity as well and in this way they differ from those sentences which contain *edьnъ* to express specificity. The following examples, all of which contain a form of *edьnъ*, are noteworthy because of that additional meaning.

(42) Pred kapijom sam ugledala i jednog dečka. (SBC)
In front of the gate I also noticed a [specific] young boy.

(43) Pričao mi jedan njegov zemljak. (SBC)
A [specific] fellow countryman of his told me.

(44) Reče mi jedan čoek / na jedome mestu / kod jednoga čoeka /
jednu stvar / ne mogu ti reći dje / odma bi se sjetio koji je. (SBC)
A [specific] fellow told me / in a [specific] place / at a [specific]
fellow's place / a [specific] thing / I can't tell you where / if I could I'd
immediately remember who he is.
(This example is particularly interesting because of the multiple
instances of *jedan*.)

(45) ... lep je doživljaj upoznati se s filozofijom jednog Dekarta. (SBC)
... it is a pleasant experience to get acquainted with the philosophy of a
Descartes.

(46) Ex zašto, zašto u nas njama edin Lenin. (BUL)
Oh why, why don't we have a Lenin.
(Examples 45-46, it should be noted, are interesting because by
definition *Descartes* and *Lenin* are specific, and the omission of *jedan* or
edin would in effect be definite, i.e., refer to the individuals named.)

(47) Došao je jedan nov sveštenik u selo. (SBC)
A [specific] new priest came to the village.

(48) Bio jedan bogat čovek imao tri sina. (SBC)
A [specific] rich man had three sons.

(49) Ќe ispratam jedno momče ... na lov. (MAC)
I'm going to take a [specific] young boy ... hunting.

(50) Sega ima dovolna voda duri i za edna žetva da dade rod. (MAC)
Now there is water enough to bring a harvest to fruit.

(51) Mi dadoa edno pismo za tebe. (MAC)
They gave me a [specific] letter for you.

(52) Edna takva kuḱa ušte neman videno. (MAC)
I've still not seen such a house.

(53) Otvori eden mazan sad što stoeše na policata nad pečkata. (MAC)
He opened a glazed jar which stood on the shelf above the stove.

I have also found an example of *edьnъ* in Russian which clearly shows that such constructions also occur in that language.

(54) Saraj byl podaren emu za odnu uslugu, kotoryx on mnogo okazyval raznym ljudjam.
The shed was given to him for a [specific] service, many of which he did for various people.

In this context, we should mention the relationship between *edьnъ* and *neki/nekoj*. I should note that in none of these sentences could *neki/nekoj* (or Russian *nekotoryj*) be substituted without a serious change in meaning; most notably, it would change the meaning from "a specific" to "one or another." Topolińska (1981:62), writing about Polish and Macedonian, states that *nekoj* (*jakiś/któryś z*) function "as a marked member signalling the speaker's inability to identify the referent of the noun phrase," i.e., to attribute a particular quality to it. Ivić (1971:112) states, as already mentioned, that in Serbocroatian *neki* tends to be indefinite in the broadest sense of the term. Both suggest that *edьnъ* is more specific than *neki/nekoj*, etc.

Although this topic needs further investigation, I believe that the following observation is correct:

Edьnъ is acquiring, if it has not already done so, the status of an indefinite article in Slavic. However, it has a special status in that it marks particularity rather than being a general indefinite article and in this way it differs from the indefinite article found in English, French and German, which simply indicates that the concept is not definite.[21]

The following example found in Koneski's grammar (1954:21) offers an excellent instance of this, and is also interesting, given the fact that it is one of the few I have found which contain a reduplicated pronominal direct object.[22]

(55) Razvieno prvobitno vrz takvo vospriemanje toa vo jazikot može i da se oddel sosem od nego, pa da imame prostranstveno opredel kvanje ne po toa kak vistinski *ja* [my italics—KEN] doživavame *edna* [my italics—KEN] situacija ami kao ja zamisluvane kako si ja pretstatuvame subjektivno.

COMPARISON OF ARTICLE USAGE IN ENGLISH AND MACEDONIAN

The fact that two languages both have a formal definite article should not lead us to believe that its function and distribution is the same; cf. English and Macedonian. Examples like the following make this clear:

(56) Man is mortal.
Čovekot e smrten.

(57) Love is sweet.
Ljubavta e slatka.

(58) Smoking is prohibited.
Pušenjeto e zabraneto.

They are striking at first glance because in each of the cases Macedonian is articulated while English has the "zero-article" which is the marker of a generic abstract. However, as we have suggested, this and other differences in the distribution of the definite article between the two languages can be explained by the difference in meaning of the zero-article in the languages.[23]

A similar difference can be seen in the obligatory use of the definite article with possessive adjectives in Macedonian, an environment where the use of an article is forbidden in English.

(59) Ja krena glavata i zagleda vo *svojot* sin.
He turned his head and stared at his son.

(60) Vo *svojata* vistinska služba članot ja označuva opredelenostta.
In its true function the article signifies definiteness.

(61) "Posni ja *negovata* puška, Džo," reče toj.
"Bring his gun, Joe," he said.

(62) Ajde vo *mojata* kuḱa.
Let's go to my house.

In each of these examples, the formal articulation of the possessive serves to mark the definiteness of the construction. Example (59) also offers another difference between use of article in the two languages, i.e., the indication of possession with only an article and without the use of a possessive adjective, for inalienable body parts

(59) Ja krena glavata i zagleda vo svojot sin.

Examples of this type of construction abound.

(63) Toj ḱe mi gi topli kostite na stari denovi.
He [the grandson] will warm my bones in my old days.

(64) ... dodeka čovekot stoeše nabljuduvaḱi go bez nikavo izraz na liceto.
... while the man was standing looking at/watching him without any expression on his face.

Nevertheless, it is interesting to note that both languages use an article when the possessive is a derived adjective (or in English involves a possessivized noun), e.g.,

(65) Edmondzovoto momče i Alek Sender veḱe bea jale....
The Edmondses' boy and Alec Sander had already eaten....

(66) ... drvenata vrata na tatkovata soba....
... the wooden door of the father's room....

(67) ... na majčinoto koleno....
... on the mother's knee....

We have already suggested that the major reason for the discrepancy between the two patterns of article usage is due to the quite different meaning of the zero-article in the two systems. In English, it conveys the meaning of abstract-generic (in singular) and nondefinite unspecified (in plural), whereas in Macedonian the zero-article is always a marker of nondefinite. This fact, combined with the absence of an established indefinite article which does not connote specific in Macedonian means that generic expressions of the English type (68-69) are not possible, i.e.,

(68) A whale is a mammal.
(69) A horse is a four-footed animal.

The lack of a formal indefinite article can also be seen in examples like (70) where English requires an indefinite article in the rhemic part of the equation when a concrete generic is involved,[24] i.e.,

(70) The horse is an animal.
Konjot e životinje.

We can account for the most striking differences in the use of the definite article in two languages by the fact that Macedonian requires marking of definiteness in all environments because the omission of a formal marker is taken to mean that the concept is nondefinite, since that is the meaning of the zero-article in the language. One wonders if, and how, the development of *eden* into an indefinite article will change this system.

The Ohio State University

NOTES

[1] Here I must disagree with Mathesius that the category of definiteness seems to be a more "substantial part of the system of grammar" in the Germanic and Romance languages than in the Slavic languages, where it is "something occasional" (quoted from Krámský 1972:16-17). It is clear that the category is a fundamental part of language and affects parts of speech other than just nouns and that it is not just to be equated with the presence or absence of a (definite) article. The fact that an article has not developed in a number of Slavic languages can be explained by various factors, including the existence of a definite/indefinite opposition in the adjectival system, word order, possible expression by the use of cases. Thus, it seems unfortunate to assume, as many people have, that the development of an article in Macedonian and Bulgarian is due to the influence of the other languages of the Balkan *Sprachbund* or that the development of an article in North Russian dialects is the result of linguistic contact with Finnic languages; these are clearly, I believe, the result of normal internal tendencies and have only been accelerated by language contact.

[2] Some of the same problems exist when we try to equate definite with concretization (= known). There is no reason to assume that a definite article automatically means that the concept modified is known to the speaker who uses it. In fact, as I shall try to show later, it may be dictated by the set of formal conditions in the particular language. Many of the same objections can be offered to the other theories which are summarized by Krámský (1972:18-29). The major problem has been the tendency to analyze the *definite* article without trying to see how it relates to the zero-article and indefinite article—if there is one in the language—as well as the other ways which exist in a particular language to express the concept of definiteness, even where there is no article.

[3] I shall view the terms "specified/nonspecified" and "particular/general" as equivalent and use them interchangeably. The former may be more appropriate for examples like those cited from Modern Greek and Albanian while the latter seems better for those examples cited from Serbocroatian (34-38) and (42-48).

I disagree with Nikolaeva (1979b:8-9), who states that definite is unmarked in relation to indefinite, which is marked. There are two reasons for this. First, from a semantic point of view, specific is more marked than general, and if we assume that "definite" is more specific than "indefinite," this should apply. Second, the fact that we find the further opposition of "specific"/ "nonspecific" under indefinite suggests that this is the less marked member of the opposition, since marked members usually do not undergo further subdivision in a binary system. In addition, we find that in the Slavic languages definites tend to be more marked, formally, than indefinites.

[4] This distinction can be seen in the following examples from Serbocroatian, which I have overheard in conversation, viz.

(A) Jedan nov sveštenik je došao u selo.
One new (indef.) priest came to the village.
A new priest came to the village.

(B) Moraš da kupuješ svaki sedam osam godina nov frižider.
You have to (sg) that you buy (sg) every 7-8 years new (indef.) refrigerator.
You have to buy a new refrigerator every 7 or 8 years.

In (A) the priest is viewed as being a specific member of the class and is set apart for some reason, hence the need to doubly mark the specificity by the use of *jedan* as well as the use of the indefinite adjective, whereas in (B) the idea is general with any member of the class being acceptable thus *jedan* is omitted. In fact, *jedan* cannot be used in (B) as it would convey the numeral meaning. In (A) the omission of *jedan* would also change the meaning, just as the use of the deifnite *novi*, which, I believe, would imply that such an event takes place on a regular basis or that the priest has been somehow identified to us previously.

⁵ Examples of partially developed articles based on the demonstrative adjectives can be found in a number of other languages and in many instances they seem to be *in statu nascendi*; the discussion of demonstratives to express definiteness offers some examples from Russian, Czech, and Serbocroatian which suggest this. Since definite articles have developed historically from demonstratives it is not surprising to see them used in this way. (Fritz Abel's statement that the definite article in the Romance languages almost always has a deictic value [quoted by Birkenmaier 1979:90] is interesting in this connection, even though I believe he overstates his case.)

⁶ I wonder if the development of fixed word order in those Slavic languages which have the article would lead to the elimination of the reduplicated pronominal object. I also wonder if English or French would have developed fixed word order had such a surrogate theme been available to mark definite objects.

⁷ Even two neighboring and closely related languages like Bulgariani and Macedonian show different uses of the definite article. A striking difference in the use of zero-article between British and American English, can also be seen, e.g.,

"to go to Ø hospital" (British)
"to go to *the* hospital" (American).

⁸ Included with abstract generics are mass—or uncountable—nouns like *water, milk, rice, bread* which can exist as concretes (in a definite context) with a definite article but may not take an indefinite article when used as abstracts (= mass nouns).

⁹ See Burton-Roberts (1976) for a discussion of the use of indefinite article in concrete generic statements in English. It should be noted that it normally occurs in the rheme of such statements as well, e.g., "the/a horse is a four-footed animal."

¹⁰ The opposition "specified/nonspecified" has been omitted from this chart because of the unclear status of <ed#n-> in Macedonian and the fact that English tends to use a demonstrative or another means, e.g., "a given, a specific, a particular" to express this.

¹¹ Givón (1981:35) is less cautious about this point stating that use of "one" as an indefinite article is universal. However, it seems to me that he overstates the case in absolute terms, although the tendency is certainly universal.

¹² I shall beg the question of the relation of "some" (SBC *neki*, MAC *nekoj*, RUS *nekotoryj*, POL *niektóry*, etc.) to the status and question of the indefinite article use of *edьnъ*. This point cannot be discussed properly until we have more data about the status of an indefinite article in the various languages.

I have followed Topolińska (1981) in referring to this form in its Common Slavic shape, which will be realized in each of the modern Slavic languages according to the regular phonological developments. I have referred to the forms in the modern languages using only the masculine singular although it should be understood that there can be forms which agree in case, number and gender with the head which *edьnъ* modifies.

¹³ Examples have been drawn from a number of primary and secondary sources; these include Birkenmaier (1979) and Zaliznjak and Padučeva (1979) for Russian, Ivić (1971) for Serbocroatian, Koneski (1954) for Macedonian, Krámský (1972) for Czech, Naylor (in press) for Macedonian, Topolińska (1981) for Macedonian and Polish. Additional Macedonian and Serbocroatian examples come from conversations.

The following abbreviations will be used to identify examples in the text: BUL = Bulgarian, CZH = Czech, MAC = Maacedonian, POL = Polish, RUS = Russian and SBC = Serbocroatian.

¹⁴ Sometimes, the case system itself can be used to express definiteness as well. In Russian, sentence pairs of the type *Ja ždal poezd* vs. *Ja ždal poezda* 'I waited for the/a train' the traditional explanation has been that the accusative is specific, i.e., definite, while the genitive is indefinite. The same kind of explanation has been given for the alternative useof genitive vs. accuative after negation, e.g., *Ja ne našel pis'mo* vs. *Ja ne našel pis'ma* 'I didn't find the/a letter.' There seems to be

evidence that this distinction is breaking down in colloquial Russian with speakers tending to consistently use either accusative or genitive for both meanings (see Graudina, Ickovič and Katlinskaja 1976:33-42 for a discussion of this point).

[15] It is interesting to note that sentences of this type with nonstative verbs and inanimate objects seem to have a passive meaning when the animate subject is indefinitized as part of the rheme and the object is the theme.

[16] In Bulgarian and Macedonian the articles are distinguished from the demonstraitve adjectives by their syntactic placement—articles are postposed while clitics and demonstratives are preposed and retain, within the limits of the phonological system, their own stress. On the other hand, Macedonian, at least in principle, maintains the three-way opposition of "here," "there," and "over yon" in the article which is also found in the demonstratives.

[17] It should be understood that the basic function of the demonstratives is deictic and metaphorically they remain so when they become definite articles—or quasi-articles. I have already noted that Abel (note 5) contends that the definite article still has this deictic function in the modern Romance languages. This may be due to the fact that in French in any case, the article may also serve as the subject of verbs with a pronominal function; *Les sont arrivés* 'They have come.' This is not the case in Slavic as noted above.

[18] In these and other examples, I assume a context has already been established which makes clear why this person or thing is set apart from the other members of the class and hence is definitized. For this reason, I shall not provide a complete context with the examples.

[19] It is possible that this sentence can be interpreted as a regular demonstrative sentence, i.e., 'We need *that* student who knows Chinese,' however, it is unlikely that there are several students who know Chinese in a group and (b) the speaker is pointing to just one of those. In fact, the very existence of the relative clause "who knows Chinese" implies that this is the distinguishing characteristic of a particular student who is being sought.

[20] On the face of it, it is difficult to explain the redundant use of a demonstrative in this construction unless it is connected with sentences like "ovaj, njegov prvi dan...." 'This, his first day....' However, we should note that in Macedonian, possessive pronouns and adjectives require a definite article in all occurrences to formally mark them as definite since zero-article in Macedonian is indefinite.

[21] In examples which contain other adjectives, *едьнъ* functions to indicate the fact that a particular member of the class is intended but at the same time, that no definite individual is meant, i.e., the sentence is not definite. In certain instances, the specificity is also marked by the context and here it seems that *едьнъ* underscores this specificity.

[22] Kazazis and Penthoroudakis (1976) provide a number of examples from Albanian and Modern Greek, in which the specificity of an indefinite indirect object is shown by the reduplicated pronominal. I have found only two examples of this in Macedonian (both incidentally in Koneski 1954) and Friedman (1976:338) provides one for Bulgarian, i.e., *Edna žena ja risuva edin xudožnik* 'An artist is drawing a woman.' It is possible that this reduplication is not as well developed in the Slavic languages as in Albanian and Greek. (Certainly, in Bulgarian it is facultative and nonstandard in Bulgarian with definite direct objects.) At any rate, this does not mean that specificity is not present as a category but rather that its expression is different.

[23] There is a further difference here which may also influence the system, viz., the fact that Macedonian still has the opposition definite vs. indefinite in adjectives means at least potentially that the opposition can be expressed in those instances when the adjective carries the opposition. Given the fact that this distinction is highly restricted in its frequency of occurrence and distribution, it can hardly be said to be functional.

[24] It should also be noted that the English distinction between abstract and concrete generics is not found in Macedonian; compare (70) with examples (56-58).

BIBLIOGRAPHY

Birkenmaier, Willy
    1979 *Artikelfunktionen in einer artikellosen Sprache: Studien zur nominalen Determination im Russischen.* Munich.
Burton-Roberts, Noel
    1979 "On the Generic Indefinite Article." *Language* 52:427-448.
Elson, Mark J.
    1979 "The Definite Article in Bulgarian and Macedonian." *Slavic and East European Journal* 20:275-279.
Friedman, Victor A.
    1976 "The Question of a Bulgarian Indefinite Article." *Bulgaria, Past and Present,* ed. by Thomas Butler, Columbus, 334-340.
Givón, Talmy
    1981 "On the Development of the Numeral 'One' as an Indefinite Marker." *Folia Linguistica Historica* 2, i:25-54.
Graudina, A. K.; V. A. Ickovič; and A. P. Katlinskaja
    1976 *Grammatičeskaja praviľnosť russkoj reči: Opyt častotno-stilističeskogo slovarja variantov.* Moscow.
Hamm, Josip
    1967 *Grammatik der serbokroatischen Schriftsprache.* Wiesbaden.
Hendriks, Peter
    1976 *The Radožda-Vevčani Dialect of Macedonian.* Lisse.
Ivić, Milka
    1971 "Leksema *jedan* i problema neodredjenog člena." *Zbornik za filologiju i lingvistiku* 14/1:103-120.
Kazazis, Kostas and Joseph Pentheroudakis
    1976 "Reduplication of Indefinite Direct Objects in Albanian and Modern Greek." *Language* 52:398-403.
Koneski, Blaže
    1954 *Gramatika na makedonskiot literaturen jazik. II,* Skopje.
Krámský, Jiří
    1972 *The Article and the Concept of Definiteness in Language.* The Hague–Paris.
Naylor, Kenneth E.
    In press. "The Use of the Articles in English and Macedonian." *Festschrift for Blaže Koneski.* Skopje.
Nikolaeva, T. M.
    1979a "Akcentno-prosodičeskie sredstva vyraženija kategorii opredelennosti-neopredelennosti" in *Kategorija opredelennosti-neopredelennosti v slavjanskix i balkanskix jazykax,* Moscow, 119-175.
    1979b "Vvedenie" in *Kategorija opredelennosti-neopredelennosti v slavjanskix i balkanskix jazykax,* Moscow, 3-10.
Stojanov, Stojan
    1980 *Gramatičeskata kategorija opredelenost v bălgarskija ezik.* Sofia.
Topolińska, Zuzanna
    1981 *Remarks on the Slavic Noun Phrase.* Wrocław.
Zaliznjak, A. A. and N. V. Padučeva
    1979 "Sintaksičeskie svojstva mestoimenija 'kotoryj'," in *Kategorija opredelennosti-neopredelennosti v slavjanskix i balkanskix jazykax,* Moscow, 289-329.

The Pragmatics of Raising in Old Russian and Common Slavic*

Johanna Nichols & Joe Schallert

This paper deals with accusative-plus-participle constructions as shown in the Old Russian (OR) examples below.[1] This construction is analogous to the accusative-plus-infinitive construction of Greek and Latin. The construction is derived by raising: the understood, or underlying, subject of the participle has been moved into the main clause, where it functions as object. (A zero form of 'be' rather than a participle can be used, as in (5)–(8).)

(1) Pečenězi že mněša knjazja prišedša   (L 968)
    'The Pechenegs thought it was the Prince who had come', lit. 'thought the Prince having arrived'

(2) mnjašče u/ž/ končinu suščču   (L 1230)
    'thinking the end had already come', lit. 'thinking the end being (present)'

(3) v to že vremja vojevaša Litva Ljaxy mnjašče mirni sušče   (Ip 1229)
    'at that time the Lithuanians were waging war against Poland. [The Lithuanians] thought that they were at peace' [with a third party] (Perfecky 1973:34), lit. 'thinking (themselves and the third party) being at peace'[2]

(4) i mnozi mnjaxu m/esja/cь idušče čresъ n/e/bo   (L 1230)
    'and many thought that the moon was going across the sky', lit. 'thought the moon going aross the sky'[3]

(5) bě bo uměja pečenežьski. i mnjaxutь i svoego   (L 968)
    'for he knew the Pecheneg language and they thought him one of their own' (van Schooneveld 1959:146)

(6) uzrěša naši storoževe polkъ v poli. i mnjaxu bolgarьskyi polkъ   (L 1184)
    'our guards saw the army in the field and thought it was the Bulgarian army'

(7) prišedše vzjaša i mertva mnjašče   (L 1074)
    'they came and took him, thinking him dead'

(8) "O/t/če, jeda jedinъ mnišisja xodja?"
    Volodimer že re/če/, "A xto tja mnělъ sdě?"   (L 1128)
    (Izjaslav to Vladimir) "Father, do you really think you're walking alone? (lit. 'do you think yourself going alone?')
    Vladimir answered, "So who thought you were here?" (lit. 'and who thought you here?')

This construction is described for the OR verb *mьněti (sja)* 'think,' etc. in Nichols 1980. The present study pursues two observations made there. First, the verb *mьněti* in this construction has counterfactual implicature and means 'think (mistakenly),' 'pretend,' etc. For example, in (1) the Pechenegs mistakenly think an approaching retinue is that of the prince, when in fact it is that of his lieutenant. In (2), the end of the world did not come in 1230. In (7), Isaac has not died. In (8), Vladimir is not alone. Counterfactual implicature with participles is standard for the verb *mьněti (sja)* in OR of the Chronicles and early period. Second, the raising construction displays a consistent, distinctive pragmatic property: the complement of the participle (or of the zero, as in (5)–(8)) is the focus of the construction, which can often be rendered with English clefting:

(1) 'The Pechenegs thought it was the prince who had come'
(cf. emphatic *himself* in Cross's translation (1953:85): 'the Pechenegs thought the prince himself had come'

(4) 'and many thought it was the moon crossing the sky'

or emphatic intonation (here shown by underlining):[4]

(5) 'and they thought he was theirs'

(7) 'thinking him dead'

(8) 'So who thought you were here?'

Although the counterfactual component of the meaning of *mьněti* is clearly presuppositional, we will use the looser term *implicature* since for many of our verbs it is not clear whether we are dealing with presupposition or implication. We will use the terms *counterfactual, neutral,* and *factual* to describe implicature. We use *focus* in the technical sense first proposed by Chomsky (1971), although he used it to refer to the focus of contrast or question, while for us it refers to the focus of other pragmatic operators. We use *topic* and *comment* in a more or less standard sense to refer to the informational structure of a clause.

We will be talking about three aspects of syntactic constructions: their form, their function, and their derivational history. *Form* refers to morphology, e.g., the choice of infinitive vs. participle. *Function* refers, roughly, to meaning (minus lexical content) or to the role a given formal unit plays in grammatical structure or discourse organization. *Derivational history* is the (synchronic) generation of surface from underyling structure. (Below we will use *derive, derivation,* etc. to refer only to synchronic generation; when tracing etymology we will use *evolve, reconstruct,* etc.) Form and function apply to surface grammar. We use *syntactic relation* and *construction (type)* to refer to formal-functional units, and standard labels for transformations (*raising, deletion*) to refer to derivational units. This paper explores the relation between a formal-functional unit and some derivational units, a relation whose statement is necessarily colored by linguistic theory.

We surveyed OR and Old Church Slavic (OCS) texts to determine whether raising can be reconstructed for Common Slavic, whether it is usually correlated with focus, whether it is usually correlated with counterfactual implicature, and whether the raising-focus association can be reconstructed for Common Slavic.

The raising-focus association is of typological importance because, if systematic, it will indicate that Common Slavic was the type of language that restricts the domain of operators such as focus to main clauses: raising conflates main and subordinate clauses, thus making what would otherwise have been a subordinate clause accessible to focus. Since it has been suggested (Van Valin and Foley 1980) that the question of whether pragmatic operators like focus affect all clauses or only main clauses has implications for the presence and type of voice operations and switch-reference devices, a demonstration that focus in Common Slavic affected only main clauses would bear on our understanding of passivization, inverse verbs, the dative absolute, and the conjunct participle. It would also align Common Slavic typologically with the Uralic, Altaic, and North Caucasian languages, which cover most of northern Eurasia, since these are languages which for the most part restrict pragmatic operators to main clauses. Any such findings, of course, would be of obvious relevance to the reconstruction of Proto-Indo-European.

The reconstructability of raising for Common Slavic is in doubt because the construction is virtually unattested in the modern languages.[5] Also, it is not particularly frequent in OR or OCS. The morphological form is not consistent within Indo-European: **Greek and Latin use primarily infinitives; Slavic, primarily participles.**

Nonetheless there is evidence in favor of reconstructing raising. The rule exists elsewhere in older Indo-European: it is well established in Latin and Greek. Its contemporary distribution in Balto-Slavic — it is productive only in Baltic and in Slovenian (Musteikis 1972:221; we have not looked at Slovenian) — is peripheral, thus indicative of conservative status. The history of complementation with *mьněti (sja)* in OR is one of gradual attrition of raising; extrapolating backward, it must once have been productive. Furthermore, we will show that in the translation of Greek raising constructions, OCS uses participles under the same conditions as OR does, sometimes departing from the Greek infinitives. If OCS scribes had their own, consistent, opinions about the proper choice of nonfinites in the construction, and if those opinions coincided with OR usage, then the construction must have existed in their native Slavic. We therefore reconstruct raising for Common Slavic.

We will refer to three other construction types. One is constructions derived by deletion (Equi-NP deletion, in standard terminology):

(9) i viděduxъ božii sxodęštъ jako i golǫbь (OCS: Mt. 3:16, Mr.)
 'and he saw the Spirit of God descending like a dove'

(10) vidě jedinogo sědjašča na svinьi (L 1074)
 'he saw one of them sitting on a pig'

Deletion differs from raising in that in deletion constructions the direct object of the main verb was not raised to that position but is an original direct object of the verb; it is modified by a complement clause whose (understood, deleted) subject is coreferential to the direct object.

For all verbs surveyed, raising and/or deletion contrast with finite subordinate clauses having a conjunction such as *jako*. We refer to these as *jako* constructions.

(11) i uvidě Olegъ. jako Oskoldъ i Kirъ knjažita (L 882)
 'and Oleg saw that Ascold and Dir were reigning'

We will refer to participial clauses and *jako* clauses as embedded clauses.

Finally, there are inverse constructions with reflexive verbs, which have predicate nominals rather than participial clauses:

(12) ašče li komu ne věrno mnitь/sja napisanoe se (PKP 114-5)
 'if what is written here seems untrue to anyone'

(13) sadъ že onъ na/m vidit sja (F Stud 8)
 'it (heaven) looks like a garden to us'

(14) vamъ že vъ očьju lošadь li vidit sja ili žena (Sb Sof 12)
 'does that look like a horse or a woman to you?', 'what do you see there — a horse or a woman?'

The inverse construction is widespread and shows a high degree of lexicalization: for example, *viděti sja* means 'seem, look like,' not 'be seen.' In it the element *sja* simply marks derived intransitivity, and is not coreferential to any nominal in the sentence. The inverse construction rarely contains participles, using a zero form of 'be' instead. For these reasons we regard the predicate nominal in inverse constructions as a simple NP complement rather than as a reduced embedded clause, although we suggest below that a rule of raising figures in the etymology of the inverse construction.[6]

We use the term *participial construction* to cover raising-derived and deletion-derived constructions (even though, strictly speaking, some instances of embedded 'be' surface as zero rather than in participial form). We use the following criteria to establish whether a construction is derived by raising or by deletion. It reflects deletion if: the verb can take its direct object as a simple

NP complement, without loss of grammaticality, meaning, or truth value (e.g., for (9), *i vidě duxъ božii* 'and he saw the Spirit of God' is grammatical, meaningful, and as true as (9)); if the main verb and the participle are time-coreferential;[7] or if the construction does not permit a translation with English *that* or a paraphrase with *jako*. It reflects raising if: V + NP is ungrammatical, meaningless, or of different truth value than V + NP + participle (e.g., for (1): *Pečenězi že mněša knjazja* is meaningless, presumably ungrammatical, and without ascertainable truth value); if there is no time coreference (both types of derivation may have time coreference; deletion-derived constructions must have it, while raising-derived ones need not); or if a translation with *that* or paraphrase with *jako* is possible. As a rule of thumb, process complements are derived by deletion, fact complements by raising; therefore, if the participial verb is stative, raising is likely. These criteria entail that, at least as surface constructions, the two types are in complementary distribution and do not contrast in either form or function. We are dealing with a single syntactic relation.

In asserting this absence of formal-functional contrast we do not claim to have proven that there is no distinction in derivational histories for this construction. Rather, we maintain that arguments about derivational history and arguments about surface contrast are at cross purposes. If derivational history is the object of description and OR facts are the means by which derivational history is argued for, then evidence for distinct derivational histories can be found (and we find it below in the evolution of OR constructions: raising gradually ceases to be a source of participles, which are now derived only by deletion). If, on the contrary, OR surface syntax is the object of description and derivational history is just one possible means of describing it, then the formal-functional unity of the construction is clear (as we show it to be below). Both approaches must be admitted if OR and OCS history are to be adequately described. On the one hand, the reality of a contrast in derivational history is revealed in the change just mentioned: raising-derived constructions are gradually replaced while deletion-derived ones are retained. On the other hand, absence of surface contrast is revealed in the frequent ambiguity and indeterminacy of individual examples, the clear lack of derivational unity underlying the clear surface unity of one formulaic expression type, and the fact that (under foreign influence) the inherited construction type was expanded on the basis of its surface unity and without regard to derivational history.

OCS — at least when viewed as a corpus of texts, as we must view it — is a language of translation and calque whose syntax for the most part gives us direct evidence about New Testament Greek syntax and indirect evidence about Slavic syntax. The indirect evidence can be arrived at only by interpretation. In interpreting OCS we assume that calques doubtless distorted normal text frequency and the contextual distribution of construction types, but they were not ungrammatical in OCS. For instance, we claim below that in translating Greek raising-derived constructions OCS reordered the Slavic conditioning features for infinitives and participles, and dispensed with one pragmatic constraint on a construction type. But the resultant construction was grammatical even the first time it was used — although, as we argue in our conclusions, grammaticality is determined by the linguist's syntactic theory and not by refrence to OCS norms, real or imputed. It is gratifying that OCS follows Slavic rather than Greek rules for choice of nonfinite forms, thus strengthening our faith in the value of OCS texts for comparative Slavic syntax. We also note that the differences between earliest OR and OCS are not profound, and for the most part involve relative frequency.

We assume that in OR or OCS the choice of construction types or morphological forms was based on weighing a number of conditions, each of which favors one or the other output but none of which requires one or the other. (This approach goes back to Timberlake 1975.) Since we see focus as one such condition, our goal is to establish the existence of conditions determining type of complementation. (A complete list of the conditions which appear relevant is given as the Appendix.) We have little to say about what might be called the contextualization of those conditions: whether all of them are equally applicable for all verbs, in all documents, in all chronological stages and styles, etc. are questions we do not answer here. Therefore we have not systematically covered the entire OR or OCS corpus, or even any historical segment, in our survey. Rather, we have examined a number of synchronic slices of the corpus, assuming that this would reveal the existence of conditions and give us enough examples to make valid generalization possible, and enough variety in sources to guarantee general applicability of our conclusions. The result is a panchronic grammar of sorts, based on extrapolation from the slices, with some attention to temporal stratification of the corpus and Greek influence. We have made three kinds of surveys:

(1) Individual verbs. We surveyed all examples in the lexical files of the Old Russian Dictionary Project of the Russian Language Institute of the Academy of Sciences, Moscow, for the following verbs:

mьněti	sъkazati sja
mьněti sja	pokazati sja
čuti sja	javiti sja
slyšati sja	viděti sja

This means that in principle we have looked at every relevant occurrence of each of these verbs throughout the history of OR until the 14th century. (Below we refer to this technique as *lexical file survey*.)

(2) Individual texts. We surveyed the following texts for possible instances of raising:

> Russkaja Pravda
> Laurentian Chronicle, first half
> Novgorod Chronicle (Synod copy), first half

We call this tchnique *text survey*. Since our text surveys looked mostly for raising, the resultant corpus is skewed against deletion.

(3) Individual texts for particular verbs. Using word indices in published editions, we checked all occurrences of *viděti (sja)* and *slyšati (sja)* in the following documents:

> Laurentian Chronicle, first half
> Izbornik of 1076
> Marianus

We also surveyed Marianus for *mьněti (sę)* and cross-checked all examples of raising with this verb with Zographensis, Savvina kniga, and Assemanianus. (We call this technique *word-index survey*.)

We have also culled an occasional example from secondary sources. The resultant corpus is ample and representative, but unbalanced and therefore of no value for statistical generalizations. Below we use numbers to give the reader some idea of the size of the corpus and the amount of support for our claims, not with the intention of making comparisons of text frequency.

Survey. OR *mьněti (sja)* was investigated by lexical file survey for all of OR (Nichols 1980). The use of raising and the association of raising with focus are well attested for this verb in earliest OR. The verb is used frequently with participles: our corpus includes 22 examples with raising from the OR chronicles alone. Almost all of these examples show focus as illustrated in (1)–(8) above. And almost all of them have counterfactual implicature.

OCS *mьněti (sę)* (word-index survey for all of Marianus) is like OR *mьněti (sja)* in being used frequently with raising. It differs from the OR cognate in allowing infinitives and participles with equal frequency: of the nine examples of raising with this verb in the Gospel texts, four have participles ((15)–(18) below) and five have infinitives ((19)–(23) below). (Only Marianus has all nine examples; five examples are attested in all four of our sources, four of them in three, and one in two.) The four texts are always uniform, with one exception: Zographensis uses *jako* plus finite verb while the others use an infinitive in (19) below.

The Greek text uses the infinitive in eight of the examples and *hoti* 'that' plus finite verb in one (our (19); Zographensis is thus the only OCS text to calque the Greek construction). (We checked variants in the Greek text in Nestle and Aland 1965 and in Vajs 1927, 1935a, b, 1936. There are no variations in the use of infinitives and *hoti* among the Greek texts. Some texts omit *dokei ekhein* 'thinks he has' (OCS mьnitъ sę imy) in (15).)

The examples (cited from Marianus) where OCS uses participles:

(15) i eže ašte mьnitъ sę imy vъzęto budetъ otъ nego   (Mt 25:29)
 kai ho ekhei/dokei ekhein arthēsetai ap' autou
 'even that which he thinks he has will be taken away'

(16) mьnevъša že i v družinĕ sǫstь   (Lk 2:44)
 nomisantes de auton einai en tēi sunodiai
 'but supposing him to be in the company'

(17) i eže mьnitъsę imejǫ otymetъ sę otъ nego   (Lk 8:18)
 kai ho dokei ekhein arthēsetai ap' autou
 'even what he thinks that he has will be taken away'

(18) mьnĕaxǫ d/xъ vidǫšte   (Lk 24:37)
 edokoun pneuma theōrein
 'they supposed that they saw a spirit', 'they thought it was a spirit they saw'

(19) i prišedъše prъvii mьnĕaxę sę vęšte prijęti   (Mt 20:10)
 kai elthontes hoi prōtoi enomisan hoti pleion lēmpsontai
 'those who had come first thought they would receive more'

(20) vĕste ĕko mьnęštei sę vlasti jęz/ky ustojętъ imъ   (Mk 10:42)
 oidate hoti hoi dokountes arkhein tōn ethnōn katakurieuousin autōn
 'you know that those who are supposed to rule over the Gentiles lord it over them'

(21) bystъ že i pьrĕ vъ ixъ kyi mъnitъ sę (ixъ) byti volei   (Lk 22:24)
 egeneto de kai philoneikia en autois, to tis autōn dokei einai meizōn
 'a dispute also arose among them, which of them was to be regarded as the greatest'

(22) ĕko vy mъnite vъ nixъ imĕti životъ vĕčьny   (J 5:39)
 hoti humeis dokeite en autais zōēn aiōnion ekhein
 'because you think that in them you have eternal life'

(23) da vъsĕkъ iže ubietъ vy. mьnitъ sę služьbǫ prinositi B/u   (J 16:2)
 hina pas ho apokteinas humas doxēi latreian prospherein tōi theōi
 'when whoever kills you will think he is offering service to God'

The choice of infinitive vs. participle in OCS is based on tense-modal meaning: with the possible exception of (20), the infinitive is used when the embedded clause has future force or has to do with prediction or intent; the participle is used elsewhere. In (19), (21), and (22) the time reference of the infinitive clause is future relative to preceding context. In (23) it is also future relative to the preceding context, although it is simultaneous to the relative clause *iže ubietъ vy* 'who kills you' on its subject. In addition, (23) is a prediction and (19) and (22) is a thwarted prediction. In (20), the possible exception, the clause could perhaps have been construed as having to do with intent; more likely the infinitive was substituted for a more grammatical participle to avoid ambiguity, since *mьněštei sę vladǫšte would presumably have meant 'thinking themselves to rule.'

All participles are present active. The preference for the present active participle in these constructions, and the future-modal force of the infinitive, are shared by OR. OCS differs from OR only in the relative ranking of its conditioning factors: for OCS a statement about future-modal force suffices to predict infinitives, raising-derived as well as those in clauses of purpose and intent; for OR the construction type is the primary conditioning factor, and tense-modal meaning is, in the oldest texts, either a minor factor or a metagrammatical observation about infinitives.

Of the nine examples, six are clearly counterfactual and the others (15), (17), (22:24) arguably so. There is no evidence for regular focus-raising correlation: only (18) seems to have focus.

The fact that OCS uses participles in contexts of the kind favoring participles in OR, departing from the Greek original, is powerful evidence for the reconstructability not only of raising but also of the tense-modal conditioning of infinitives vs. participles.

Focus-raising association is equally clear for OR, OCS *tvoriti (sja/sę)* 'accuse (falsely),' 'pretend,' although the frequency of this verb with raising is lower and our survey of its occurrences was not systematic (text survey only). We have one OR example of raising:

(24) jako tvorjaxutь e perevetъ drьžašče kъ Svjatoslavu   (Nov 34v)
    'as they charged them (falsely) with conspiring against Svjatoslav', 'as they
      made them out to be conspiring ...'

and two OCS examples, both reflexive:

(25) tvorěašę sę dale iti   (Lk 24:28)
    'he pretended to be going farther'

(26) posъlašę zasědьniky tvoręščę sę pravedьnici sǫšte   (Lk 20:20)
    'they sent spies who pretended to be sincere'

In the OCS examples, the choice of infinitive vs. participle is again conditioned by tense-modal meaning; it also coincides with Greek usage.

All three examples are clearly counterfactual. All three plausibly involve focus (although the clefting diagnostic does not work because, for irrelevant reasons, these constructions cannot cleft in English).

A first conclusion from our survey is that all other verbs turn out to differ from *mьněti (sja)* and *tvoriti (sja)* in all respects: their text frequency with raising is low; correlation with focus is not demonstrable; and there is no demonstrable counterfactual implicature. Nonetheless text frequency of deletion-derived participial constructions is fairly high for a number of these verbs (and recall that part of our survey is skewed against deletion). We now survey the individual verbs, then propose an explanation for the unique behavior of *mьněti (sja)* and *tvoriti (sja)*.

Other verbs of cognition. Verbs with the root *zna-* 'know' (Ger. *kennen,* Fr. *connaître*) provide no clear examples of the raising construction (text survey only). For the most part they take simple NP objects. We do have two examples of complementation from Russkaja Pravda. One is ambiguously an asyndetic finite clause and a raising-derived finite construction:

(27) zane ne znaetь u kogo kupivъ   (RP 320-21)
    'since he does not know who he bought it from'

On the asyndetic reading, the clause *u kogo kupivъ* is finite (with past participle functioning as finite perfect) and has an anaphoric zero subject. This reading is supported by parallel instances with finite *kupilъ* elsewhere in the text. On the raising-derived reading, it has a zero reflexive pronoun, the object of *znaetь*, as its original subject, and the participle is not a finite perfect but a nonfinite. (The zero form of the reflexive pronoun, and the nominative agreement with the main-clause subject rather than with the accuative *sja*, are normal for OR: cf. (3) and fn. 2.)

The second example probably represents deletion:

(28) aže kto poznaetь če/lja/dinъ svoi ukradenъ   (RP 329-331)
    lit. 'if someone recognizes his own laborer stolen'

It is evidently the laborer himself, rather than the fact of his disappearance, that the master recognizes; this means that the construction is derived by deletion rather than raising.

These verbs have neutral to factive implicature. They give no evidence of focus in the participial clause.

Verbs with the root *věd-* 'know' (Ger. *wissen,* Fr. *savoir*) (text survey) regularly take clausal complements rather than simple NP objects. They provide examples of raising. We have no participial constructions with *vědati*, which take finite subordinates in our examples. The verb *věsti* provides two examples of raising, in the formulaic construction discussed immediately below ((34), (35)). The verbs *uvědati* and *povědati* give one example of raising each, both from the chronicles:

(29) Frjazi že uvedavъše jata Isakovica, voevaša volost okolo goroda
                                                             (Nov 1204)
    'when the Franks learned that Isakovich had been taken prisoner, they sacked the area around the city'

(30) i povedaša emu Volodimera v Černigove a Izjaslava vъ Starodubě
(Mosc 47)
'and they informed him that Vladimir was in Chernigov and Izjaslav in Starodub'

These verbs are consistently factual in implicature. They give no evidence for association of focus with raising.

A formulaic construction (text survey). The participial construction figures in a fixed expression type used to introduce biblical quotes:

(31) slyšimъ že paky x/sa kъ iudeomъ gl/jušča   (Izb 1076 189.13)
    'for we know (lit. hear) the words of Christ to the Jews'

(32) poneže slyšimъ b/a glagoljuštja   (ibid. 219.7)
    'since we hear the words of God'

(33) slyšimъ pavъla gl/jušča   (ibid. 257.3)
    'we hear the words of Paul'

(34) ne vědyj proroka glagoljušča   (L 983)
    'not knowing that the prophet says'

(35) onъ že se slyšavъ vъznesesja serdce ego bolma, ne vědyj Davida glagoljušča
(L 1015)
    'when he heard this he became proud, since he did not know that David says'

Clearly a formula represents a unity construction type, and clearly at the surface level there is a single construction type here. But when we ask whether this construction involves raising or deletion, we reach an impasse. The verb *slyšati*, as will be shown below, takes both raising and deletion in non-formulaic examples. Examples (31)–(33) do not have a meaning like 'we hear that Christ speaks to the Jews,' etc., and therefore cannot be raising-derived. But neither do they meet the criteria for deletion: they do not mean 'we hear Christ speaking to the Jews,' etc. (unless they were meant rhetorically); the combination of verb and direct object (*slyšimъ x/sa* 'we hear Christ,' etc.) is not true; the time when Christ, God, or Paul spoke is not coreferential to the time of the main verb.[8] Thus the first three examples do not unambiguously represent either of the two participial construction types. The last two are more clearly raising-derived: the verbs with *věd-* do not take deletion and do not take simple NP objects, and the translations 'not knowing that the prophet says,' etc. make sense. In short, the derivational history of the formula as used with *slyšati* is indeterminate; and the derivational history of the formula taken as a whole, with both verbs, is non-unique. Yet the construction has a single surface form and a single text function. The formal and functional unity at the surface and the indeterminate derivational history indicate that the distinction of raising vs. deletion is not required for proper description of the OR participial construction *qua* construction, but is an artifice imposed by English bias and/or emphasis on derivational history. On the surface, raising-derived and deletion-derived participial constructions are not in contrast in OR, but are part of the range of contextual variants subsumed by a formal-functional unit.

This particular formula belongs to the learned, Greek-influenced written tradition of OR, although not all examples originate in calques: (31)–(33) come from a translated document, and, while (31) is exactly parallel to the available Greek text, (29) is missing from the Greek text and (33) corresponds to a finite subordinate in Greek. (34)–(35) are from the chronicles, and thus not translated. That the formula does not always calque Greek points to its independent existence as an element of OR syntax (of a particular stylistic level).

The verbs attested in this construction are factual in implicature, and clearly the formula itself is factual in implicature. It gives no evidence for a focus-raising correlation: although the name of the speaker or writer (Christ, God, Paul, etc.) receives obvious salience, this is not focus. The constructions do not mean 'since we know it was the prophet (and not someone else) who has said,' etc.

Verbs of perception. Viděti 'see' (word index survey) in OR yields a total of 34 participial constructions, of which 12 seem to represent raising (most of these are from the Laurentian Chronicle):

(36) i vidě tu ljudi suščaja   (L Intro, 3)
      'and he saw that there were people there'

(37) i viděvъ ju dobru suščju zělo licemъ   (L 955)
      'and having seen that she was very pretty of face'

(38) Volodimerъ viděvъ cr/kvь sveršenu   (L 996)
      'Vladimir, having seen that the church was completed,'

(39) zautra že viděsa ljudьe kn/jazja bežavša   (L 1069)
      'the next day the people saw that the prince had fled'

(40) vidja plъtь svoju žilište b/žie sušte   (Izb 1076 120.1)
      'seeing that his flesh was the dwelling place of God'

and the rest represent deletion:

(41) vidě otroča plačjušče   (L 986)
      'saw the child crying'

(42) i viděxomъ vъ xramě/x. mnogi služby tvorjašča   (L 987)
      'and we saw (them) in their temples performing many services'

(43) ježe mja viděsta tvorjaštja. i vy tvorita da sp/seta sja   (Izb 1076 111.9)
      'what you saw me do(ing), you do too in order to save yourselves'

Again, raising and deletion are not in contrast. Those examples classifiable as raising-derived have "be" or another stative as their participial verb (as in (36)–(38), (40)) or have a time-reference discrepancy between the main verb and the participle ((38), (39)). Those classifiable as deletion have action verbs as their participles, and time coreference between main verb and participle. This complementary distribution — together with the difficulty we experienced in classifying a number of examples — indicates that again a distinction between the two surface construction types is artificial. We are again dealing with a single surface construction.

The verb *viděti* is of neutral-to-factual implicature. There is no clear association of focus with raising, nor with participial constructions in general.

Reflexive *viděti sja* is also lexicalized as an inverse copula which takes a simple predicate nominal rather than a participial clause. See (13), (14).

The verb *viděti* in OCS (word-index survey) yields 49 participial constructions, of which some half dozen are possibly classifiable as raising and the rest are good examples of deletion. Possible raising examples (with alternate deletion readings):

(44) dondeže vidętъ cs/rtvi b/žie prišedъše(dъše)e vъ silě (Mk 9:1)
 'until they see that the kingdom of God has come with power' (raising),
 'until they see the kingdom of God in power' (lit. 'having come in power'; deletion)

(45) viděvъ že I/sъ priskrъbenъ byvъšъ reče (Lk 18:24)
 'when Jesus saw that he was very sorrowful he said' (raising),
 'when Jesus saw him (having become) sorrowful he said' (deletion)

Deletion examples:

(46) viděxomъ etera. o imeni tvoemь izgonęšta běsy (Lk 9:49)
 'we saw a man casting out demons in your name'

(47) viditъ vlъka grędǫšta (J 10:12)
 '(he) sees the wolf coming'

(All examples are cited from Marianus.)

OCS differs from OR not in its syntax but in the text frequency with which stative verbs and discrepant time reference are used in participial constructions. Again there is no contrast of raising with deletion. From the surface perspective there is a single construction, one whose contextual distribution and, consequently, semantics, have — if the text frequency difference is significant (which we cannot guarantee) — begun to drift away from the OR mean: fewer instances of the OCS construction than of the OR construction are used in contexts where western Indo-European would employ raising. As in OR, the OCS verb is neutral to factual in implicature; and there is no evidence for association of focus with raising or with participial clauses in general.

slyšati 'hear' (word-index surveys) yields a total of eight OR and four OCS examples of relevant participial constructions. The OR examples include the three formulaic ones given above ((31)–(33)), which cannot be unambiguously classified as representing either raising or deletion. The same source yields one non-formulaic example, probably involving raising:

(48) i paky slyšimь (inog)/o vъ vasъ beština xod/jašča. i ničьto že dělajušta. nъ
   licemĕrьstvujuštjaja   (Izb 1076 68v.5)
   'and in addition we hear that one of you goes around idly and does nothing,
   but is hypocritical'

Reflexive *slyšati sja* appears in one example of raising (where *sja* is the direct object):

(49) slyša sja i svoego c/srtvьja izgnanъ   (Hamart. 239a)
   'he heard that he had been chased out of his own kingdom'

It also appears in two examples involving deletion (where *sja* marks the verb as passive), e.g.:

(50) i sedmiceju peščь ražženu vverženi. i v nei b/a pojušče slyšaxu sja
                                     (Gr Bog 164)
   'they were put into an oven made seven times hotter than usual, and in it
   they could be heard singing (the praises of) God'

Slyšati sja is also frequent as a lexicalized inverse copula 'be known as,' 'have the reputation of,' in which function it takes simple predicate nominals rather than participial clauses.

(51) xoščete li agnьci gs/ni slyšati/s. i ovcě imenovati sja   (F. Stud. 223d)
   'do you want to be known as lambs of God (lit. 'the Lord') and called sheep?'

The raising and deletion constructions are not in contrast. We found ourselves calling an example deletion-derived if the participle was present, raising-derived if it was past, with no assurance that the distinction was relevant to OR. Again we assume there is a single construction type. The verb is neutral to factual in implicature. There is no evidence of focus in the participial construction.

Although the participial construction with *viděti* is evidently native Slavic, that with *slyšati* occurs in translated or Greek-influenced texts and presumably represents foreign influence.

The verb *slyšati* patterns similarly in OCS. There we found a total of four examples, all clearly involving deletion (all examples are cited from Marianus):

(52) i pristǫpь edinъ otъ kъnižьnikъ. slyšavъ ję sъtęʒajǫštę sę   (Mk 12:28)
   'and one of the scribes came up and heard them disputing with one another'

(53) slyšavъ že narodъ mimo xodęštь (Lk 18:36)
 'and hearing a multitude going by'

(54) slyšašę že farisěi narodъ rъpьštǫštь o nemь se (J 7:32)
 'the Pharisees heard the crowd thus muttering about him'

(55) my slyšaxomъ i gl/jǫštь (Mk 14:58)
 'we heard him say'

The verb is neutral to factual in implicature when used in participial constructions, and there is no evidence that the participial construction is associated with focus.

Since OCS usage calques Greek in all four instances and OR usage reflects Greek influence or translations, *slyšati* gives no direct evidence bearing on reconstruction. It does, however, fit into the inherited surface pattern and thus give evidence of the general construction type into which the reconstructed pattern evolved. That a derivationally indeterminate construction could be fitted into an inherited construction independently in OR and OCS indicates that the native construction was itself indeterminate, and it virtually proves that the construction was derivationally indeterminate after assimilation of the loan.

Verbs of speech. There is only one clear example of raising in the OR corpus, with reflexive *skazati sja* (ancestral to modern *skazat'sja,* used now with simple predicate nominals) (lexical file survey):

(56) skazasta sja šedša vъ s/tyi gradъ. i poklonьša sja č/stьnomu drevu
 'they said they had gone to the holy city and bowed down to the cross'

The following example is three ways ambiguous, depending on the interpretation of *pravověrnaja* as 'orthodox' or 'Orthodox,' and on whether the reflexive verb is considered lexicalized:

(57) roditelja že ego sъ slavoju žitьja ot/idosta. patrikija bo běsta pravověrnaja
 skazasta sja (Prol 1383, 131)
 'His parents passed away with honor. They were patricians and had adopted
  the Orthodox faith' (lit. 'had said themselves Orthodox')
 or '... and had been called right-believing'
 or '... and had been known as right-believing'

On the first reading, *sja* is direct object of *skazasta*. On the second reading the verb is passive, still raising-derived, and *sja* is a marker of the passive. On the third reading the verb is simply a copula 'known as,' and there is no raising; *sja* marks derived intransitivity.

The verb is of neutral implicature. There is no evidence for focus in the raising-derived construction. (We surveyed only reflexive *skazati sja* in lexical files; we found no examples of non-reflexive *skazati* with raising in our text survey.)

The remaining verbs — reflexives *čuti sja, pokazati sja, javiti sja* — give no evidence for raising and in fact no evidence of any productive participial constructions. All function as inverse copulas which take simple predicate nominals and can be glossed roughly 'seem.' All have other senses as well: *javiti sja* is a tense-aspect auxiliary, *pokazati sja* is 'reveal oneself (as),' *čuti sja* is often identical in meaning to modern *očutit'sja*. The survey of verbs permits the following generalizations.

Raising and deletion produce a single surface construction, a formal-functional unit with a non-unique derivational history. Since derivational history is in fact ambiguous or indeterminate for many individual examples, for the construction as a whole, for the construction with some individual verbs, and for the formulaic construction, we conclude that the conditions for employing the construction in texts and the grounds for its expansion to include the Greek-influenced use with *slyšati* referred to the formal-functional configuration and not to the derivational history. Synchronically, for OR and for OCS, derivational history was irrelevant. Below we suggest an invariant text function for the construction; and we claim that derivational history gradually becomes relevant and determinate in the history of Russian.

The great majority of OR and OCS verbs taking clausal complements have neutral-to-factual implicature. The verbs *mьněti* and *tvoriti* are the only ones in our corpus regularly having counterfactual implicature with nonfinite clauses. We call them *counterfactual verbs,* leaving open the question of whether the entire lexeme or only its use in this construction carried the counterfactual meaning.

Focus is regularly associated with participial constructions — for counterfactual verbs only. This means that only for *mьněti* and *tvoriti* is the focus-participial correlation clear. Since for these verbs the participial construction represents only raising and not deletion, it is impossible to say whether focus is associated with raising or with participial constructions in general.

The restriction to counterfactual verbs is not accidental. The focus, in examples like (1)–(8), is focus not of contrast or interrogation (the two usual referents of the term, at least for English), but precisely of the counterfactual implicature. Thus in (1), *knjazja* 'prince' is focus, and the example means 'the Pechenegs thought it was the prince who had arrived (when in reality it was his lieutenant)'. That someone had arrived was correct; *prišedša* is thus the presupposition component of the focus-presupposition construction. But the Pechenegs erred in assuming it was the prince; *knjazja* is thus the focus of counterfactual implicature. In (4), it is clear that something is in the sky; the mistaken assumption is that it is the moon. In (8), it is true that Vladimir is walking; his mistake is in thinking he is alone. The restriction of focus to counterfactuals, in other words, is due to the fact that the particular type of focus relevant to participial constructions is focus specifically of counterfactual implicature.

Participial constructions contrast formally with *jako* constructions, as we have said. We surveyed representative examples of *jako* constructions to determine what properties of participial clauses are shared with *jako* clauses and what properties are unique to participials. There are a number of conditions which appear to favor use of participial constructions over *jako* constructions (a complete listing is given in the Appendix). One is the topic-comment structure of the embedded clause: if the entire clause is old information, or if its principal participants are mentioned in immediately preceding narrative, the raising construction is favored; more new information, and especially reintroduction of participants not mentioned in the given year entry, favors use of *jako* constructions. For example, in (11) above, Askold and Dir have been mentioned previously in the Chronicle, but have not figured in events of the last few years.

Another condition is the archaic vs. productive nature of the construction. Formulas and fixed phrases favor participial constructions. More precisely, participial constructions include formulas and fixed phrases (as well as open, productive constructions), while *jako* constructions appear not to include any formulas.

Jako constructions tend to contain more participants; specifically, they are likely to contain adverbials (which are often comment). Participial constructions, in contrast, tend to be pared down to the subject (which is often zero), the participle, and occasionally its direct object or other strongly governed participant.

The lexical content of participial constructions is distinctive. Lexical classes of participles in our corpus are shown in table 1.

TABLE 1. LEXICAL CLASSES OF PARTICIPLES
(OR, OCS; NON-REFLEXIVE MAIN VERBS ONLY)

states, including 'be,' 'have'	30
motion	28
position	18
transitives*	13
speech**	11
intransitive actives	8
miscellaneous	4

*Non-referential or empty direct object.
**No overt direct object in clause.

The transitives are invariably part of fixed constructions, lexical functions (Mel'čuk 1982), or other close lexical units in which the direct object is non-referential or otherwise semantically predictable from the verb. The complex of verb and direct object contributes only one single lexical notion to the content of the message; it is thus a functional equivalent to an intransitive verb. Examples:

(58) perevetъ drъžašče (in (56) above)
 lit. 'holding a conspiracy,' i.e., simply 'conspiring'

(59) služby tvorjašča (in (38) above)
 'performing services,' i.e., roughly 'worshiping'

(60) prosjašča xlěba (L 1096)
 'begging bread,' i.e., simply 'begging'

The verbs of speech are also transitive; but in the participial construction they lack direct objects in their own clauses (they typically function as parentheticals to the following quotes which they introduce). Both types of transitives, then, lack real direct objects and can be functionally likened to intransitives. *Jako* clauses have no such lexical restrictions, and this is another respect in which participial clauses are pared down in comparison to *jako* constructions.

Jako constructions often have a clear topic-comment structure, or at least an identifiable comment. Participial constructions may have a focus, and the entire construction may have what we will call *plot salience* below; but they often lack classic topic-comment organization.

There are some fairly mechanical conditions as well. There appears to be a stylistic constraint against uncoordinated strings of participles, so that an adjacent relative or conjunct participle favors use of *jako*. The tense-modal force of the independent infinitive cannot be rendered with any participle; thus we have *jako* as in:

(61) i povedaše Noj jako byti potopu (L 986)
 'and Noah foretold that there was to be a flood'

Jako constructions can be transformed into raising constructions, not into deletion constructions; we have already noted that paraphrase or translation with *jako, that,* etc. is criterial for derivation by raising. *Jako* constructions, predictably, share semantic properties with raising-derived participial constructions, notably time-reference discrepancy between main and embedded verb and frequent absence of direct perception. Put differently, *jako* constructions and raising-derived participial constructions show some functional overlap.

Let us review briefly the history of raising in early post-Common Slavic. We have given evidence that a rule of raising was inherited from Proto-Indo-

European. In Slavic, both raising and deletion created participles, and we have proposed for OR and OCS a surface-oriented analysis which views the two types of participles as a single formal-functional unit. But we can still continue to talk about the history of raising in OR and OCS, since raising is one source of participles and thus the raising-derived construction is a variant of the participial construction. Raising-derived participles are in the minority in the earliest OR documents and become extremely rare by the fourteenth century; they appear to be fewer in OCS than in earliest OR, but more frequent there than in later OR. Both languages, then, manifest the same evolutionary tendency (although we see actual evolution only in OR): raising dies out as a component of the participial construction, to be supplanted by *jako*, etc. Consequently, the participial construction gradually changes its character, so that in later OR it is mostly deletion-derived and in modern Russian can be described as exclusively deletion-derived.

We have presented evidence above for the archaic and restricted nature of the raising-derived construction even in earliest OR. Further evidence is the association of the construction with written narrative style, and the lexical restrictions mentioned above. Overall, raising was a moribund construction even in earliest OR.

We have already mentioned that participial clauses contain few optional actants such as adverbials and modifiers. The lexical restrictions shown in Table 1, together with the loss of embedded actants produced by raising and deletion, guarantee that there will be few governed actants. The pared-down character of participial clauses has implications for pragmatic structure. Focus, as we have defined it above, is applicable only to *mьněti* and *tvoriti* constructions. But we have informally observed a kind of salience associated with participial clauses regardless of main verbs:

(26) Frjazi ze uvědavъše jata Isakovica ... (Nov 1204)
'but when the Franks found out that Isakovich was imprisoned ...'

The clause *jata Isakovica* is salient or highlighted in a sense that must remain partly impressionistic for now. Both *jata* and *Isakovica* are old information to chronicler and reader, but to the Franks the entire clause is new information. The information is of sufficient importance to cause a revolt by the Franks. This clause, then, is important to the plot. Consider also the formulaic expressions used to introduce biblical quotes:

(32) ... ne vědyj Davida glagoljušča (L 1015)
'... not knowing that David says'

To chronicler and reader, David's words are old information. They are not known to the participant, however, and (in the chronicler's interpretation of history) this ignorance causes his downfall. Although it is commentary on plot rather than on plot itself, this clause contains information important to the development of the plot. Finally, the examples where raising is clearly associated with focus are also crucial to the plot, in that the mistaken judgment or assumption is usually the reason for a critical turn of events. We will use the term *plot salience* to capture this discourse function. It is our impression that plot salience is typical of participial constructions regardless of main verb or derivational history. *Jako* clauses are not pared down, are not part of the main clause, and for the most part lack plot salience.

We suggest that participial clauses are able to have plot salience because their pared-down character allows each clause constituent a measure of prominence that would not be available in a more elaborate clause. We cannot either characterize the semantics of plot salience precisely, or explain its association with participial constructions, without a better general-linguistic understanding of pragmatics and discourse structure. We tentatively reconstruct plot salience as a feature of Common Slavic participial constructions. This reconstruction is supported by our observation that the dative absolute — another participial construction — also has plot salience, at least in the Laurentian and Hypatian chronicles. (Participial relative clauses appear not to have plot salience, probably because they are not main-clause constituents but modifiers to clause constituents.)

Conclusions. This study has shown that raising and counterfactual implicature are not strongly correlated: although counterfactual verbs do take raising and not deletion, several other verbs also take raising. We have also failed to find a general correlation of raising with focus. There is partial correlation, which we have accounted for. The question of whether raising in Common Slavic or Indo-European existed in order to make embedded clauses accessible to pragmatic parameters remains open; but it can now be posed with more refinement. We now know that the relevant pragmatic parameter for Slavic is not focus in general, but precisely focus of counterfactual implicature. We also know that plot salience must be investigated more thoroughly in this connection.

We did find other, less direct, evidence supporting a correlation of some pragmatic factor — not necessarily focus — with participial constructions in general. For many of the verbs we investigated, the construction type involving inversion, lexicalized reflexive verb, and predicate nominal is extremely frequent (examples are (12)–(14) above). The predicate nominal construction can be traced back to a raising- or deletion-derived participial construction, affected by two restrictions: the verb is 'be' (used as copula, i.e., with a predicate nominal), and the surface form of that verb is zero rather than participial.[9] The surface result was a simple NP complement — the predicate nominal — rather than an embedded clause. The appearance of the simple NP complement, and the use of inversion, were both made possible by the use of raising or deletion. The considerable text and lexical frequency of inverse constructions with fossilized raising or deletion suggests that making inversion possible may have been an important function of the ancestral rules for participial formation. Much of the motivation for participle formation may have lain in its ability to get the relevant nominal out of the embedded clause and into the main clause. This is entirely consistent with the assumption that there was some pragmatic parameter available only to main clauses, and it thus supports our reconstruction, although of course it neither identifies the pragmatic parameter nor actually demands the reconstruction. We know far too little about the history of inversion in Slavic to make more specific claims.

Finally, there is typological precedent. Preliminary field work has shown us that raising is associated with focus in Finnish:

(62) Huomasin *Kallen*   tulleen   kotiin
     I noticed K.-GEN   come-INFINITIVE   home   (raising)
     'I noticed that *Kalle* had come home'   (focus on Kalle)

(63) Huomasin että   Kalle   oli   tullut   kotiin
                that   K.-NOM   Aux   come   (no raising)
     'I noticed that Kalle had come home'   (no focus)

and with both focus and scope of operators in Swedish. English provides a parallel to our reconstructed OR use of raising to make possible the application of a subject-creating rule: raising is far more natural in examples like (64), which are passivized, than in examples like (65), which are not.

(64) He is known (thought, considered, said, believed) to be a fool.

(65) ?We know (think, consider, say, believe) him to be a fool.

And the verb *repute* lacks an active entirely.

Our surface-oriented approach allows us to describe the OCS raising-derived infinitive as motivated linguistic change rather than as isolated calquing. Recall that in raising-derived constructions OR *mьněti* takes participles (or zero), while OCS *mьněti* takes infinitives and participles with equal frequency. OCS usage is influenced by Greek usage. Since OCS is a language of translation and calque, we may safely reconstruct the OR system as conservative. But the OCS pattern is a motivated development of the OR pattern. OR *mьněti* did take infinitive complements, but not in the sense 'think,' with raising; infinitives were used in clauses of intent, purpose, and future-modal meaning, where the verb means 'intend.' An approach stressing derivational history must regard the OCS use of the infinitive with raising as originally ungrammatical, since the proper output of one rule appears as the output of another. But a surface view points out that both infinitive and participle were possible with OR *mьněti*, and therefore extension of the infinitive amounted to using an established construction in a new semantic context rather than producing an ungrammatical construction. (Recall that the extension was accomplished by reordering conditions for nonfinite choice.) That the OCS system can be diachronically motivated when the OR system is taken as input, is itself evidence supporting our reconstruction of raising.

We have reconstructed a participial construction whose derivational history is ambiguous-to-indeterminate while its discourse and pragmatic function of plot salience is unitary and lends itself to description in terms of invariance. It is not unusual for syntactic reconstructions to display grammatical indeterminacy but discourse-functional unity: cf., for example, Ickler 1977, 1981 on the topicalizing and relativizing functions of OR *že*. To some extent this may be an inherent hazard of the comparative method. But in the case of Slavic it also suggests a generalization about syntactic evolution: The descendants of the Common Slavic participial construction have lost the ancestral discourse-functional unity, but gained derivational determinacy. The change from discourse-based to syntax-based functions of participles may have been part of an overall typological change in Slavic.

Our results car be summarized as one claim:

> Raising is reconstructable for Common Slavic. Its loss, now virtually complete, is underway in the first historical records, and may wel. ave begun in late Common Slavic.

three hypotheses:

> Participial constructions, regardless of derivational history, had plot salience in Common Slavic, or at least in OR.

> Raising and deletion made embedded clauses accessible to pragmatic operators available only to main clauses. We cannot identify the operators.

> The written history of Slavic attests development from discourse-based to clause- or sentence-based syntax.

and one observation:

> OCS, despite its artificial nature, has provided crucial data bearing on the comparative reconstruction of Common Slavic syntax.

University of California, Berkeley

APPENDIX

CONDITIONS DETERMINING CHOICE OF PARTICIPLE VS. *JAKO*

favors participle:	favors *jako*:	
focus-presupposition	topic-comment	pragmatics of embedded clause
plot salience	no plot salience	discourse function
all old	some new	information structure of embedded clause
older	later	date of document[10]
fixed, formulaic	open, productive	lexical stability of construction
finite	participial	form of main verb
minimal	more elaborate	array of actants in embedded clause
immediately preceding	more distant	previous mention of actants
zero	overt	anaphora of embedded-clause actants
imperfective, nonpast	other	tense-aspect of embedded verb
zero	overt	form of embedded 'be'
mьněti, viděti, slyšati, ...	skazati, čuti, pokazati, ...	hierarchy of main-verb government
lesser	greater	degree of Russian Church Slavic admixture (for OR)
lesser	greater	degree of Greek admixture
OR	OCS	language
narrative	other	type of discourse
deletion-producing	raising-producing	deep structure

NOTES

* Research for this project was supported by grants from IREX and the Office of Education (to JN in 1975-76) and by the Center for Slavic and East European Studies and the Committee on Research of the University of California, Berkeley. We are grateful to G. A. Xaburgaev of Moscow State University and to the staff of the Russian Language Institute, Academy of Sciences, Moscow, for facilitating JN's work in the card files of the Old Russian Dictionary Project. We also wish to thank Francis J. Whitfield for comments on this project and for arousing our interest in older Slavic in the first place. And thanks to Jan-Ola Östman for the Finnish and Swedish data.

[1] We use the slash to mark abbreviations and to enclose linearized letters. Parentheses mark our additions, clarifications, etc. to translations, except that within quoted published translations square brackets mark our additions, etc. to the author's translation. We have occasionally supplied quotation marks and question marks, but otherwise we follow the punctuation in the text, Word divisions and emendations in the text are the editors', not ours. We normalize OR nasal vowel letters to *ja/a, ju/u*.

[2] The embedded clause contains an anaphoric zero instead of a reflexive pronoun. The participial clause shows nominative agreement with the main subject rather than accusative agreement with the reflexive pronoun, as is typical even with overt reflexive pronouns. (Cf. also (27).)

[3] The participle *idušče* does not agree with *m/esja/c'*; this reflects the loss of inflection in these participles.

[4] Our claim pertains to English emphatic intonation only. But if OR focus was manifested in accent, then our reading of (8) requires contrastive accent on a clitic pronoun. Our corpus includes three other examples suggesting contrastive accent on clitics; one of them is (43) below.

[5] Raising could be posited to account for Russian *sčitaju ego durakom* beside *sčitaju, čto on durak*. But this is clearly an isolated lexical pattern rather than a manifestation of a syntactic rule or an instance of a well-established construction type: it is limited to this verb; the verb of the lower clause must be 'be' and it must surface as zero. In contrast, OR raising is attested with several verbs and permits a much wider range of lower verbs. In addition, the OR construction gives overt evidence of complementation in the form of the participle, whereas the modern construction lacks an overt verbal form. Raising might also be posited for the verb *kauzirovat'*; this, too, is an isolated lexical pattern, and if it involves raising then it calques the western European implementation of raising with infinitives.

[6] Raising to subject can be used to derive inverse constructions: e.g., Russian *on kažetsja molodym* can be derived from a structure like that of *kažetsja, čto on molodoj*. It is difficult to posit such a derivation for the OCS and OR constructions, however, since for most verbs we lack examples of impersonals analogous to *kažetsja, čto*.... In terming these constructions inverse, we assume they differ from the direct constructions in a more fundamental way than would be accomplished by simple clause-to-clause transportation of one actant.

[7] Since, as is well known, "present" inflection in nonfinite forms is semantically simultaneous to the main verb rather than absolute present, this implies that the majority of deletion-derived participles will be present. This is true: the great majority are present active participles.

[8] These participles are evidently present because they refer to timeless truths, thus our translations 'the prophet says,' etc. To the best of our knowledge, deletion-derived participial constructions are cross-linguistically rare where the verb which would be nonfinite has this timeless meaning. This is due to the (cross-linguistically typical) time-coreference constraint on deletion: a predicate which is timeless cannot be coreferential to a time-bounded main verb. The fact that these OR participles refer to timeless truths is in itself an argument against derivation by deletion.

[9] Given the great frequency of present active participles in our participial constructions, this is another way of saying that the present active participle of *byti* began to disappear only in OR. As with the other forms of *byti* that are replaced by zero, this one was lost in an ordered progression of contexts, of which we have just named one.

[10] In one telling example (29) is replaced in the Commission copy of some 150 years later with a *jako* construction.

REFERENCES

Avanesov, R. I., ed.
    1966 *Slovar' drevnerusskogo jazyka XI-XIV vv: Vvedenie, instrukcija, spisok istočnikov, probnye stat'i.* Moscow.
Borkovskij, V. I., ed.
    1979 *Istoričeskaja grammatika russkogo jazyka. Sintaksis: Složnoe predloženie.* Moscow.
Chomsky, N.
    1971 "Deep structure, surface structure, and semantic interpretation" in D. Steinberg and L. Jacobovits, eds., *Semantics.* Cambridge, England, 183-216.
Cross, S. H., and O. P. Sherbowitz-Wetzor
    1953 *The Russian primary chronicle: Laurentian text.* Cambridge, Mass.
Ickler, N.
    1977 "Topicalization and relativization in Old Russian," *BLS* 3.656-669.
    1981 The particle *že* in Old Russian: The discourse origins of conditionals and relatives. Ph.D. dissertation, University of California, Berkeley.
Mel'čuk, I. A.
    1982 "Lexical functions in a lexicographic description," *BLS* 8, to appear.
Musteikis, K.
    Sopostavitel'naja morfologija russkogo i litovskogo jazykov. Vilnius.
Nestle, E., and K. Aland
    1898, 1927/1965 *Novum testamentum Graece cum apparatu critico.* Stuttgart.
Nichols, J.
    1980 "The syntax of Old Russian *mīněti (sja)*" in K. Klar et al., eds., *American Indian and Indoeuropean studies.* The Hague, 421-39.
Perfecky, G. A.
    1973 *The Hypatian Codex II. The Galician-Volynian chronicle: An annotated translation. (Harvard series in Ukrainian studies* 16.2.) Munich.
Timberlake, A.
    1975 "Hierarchies in the genitive of negation. *SEEJ* 19:2.123-38.
Vajs, J.
    1972 *Evangelium sv. Marka a jeho poměr k řecké předloze.* Prague.
    1935a *Evangelium sv. Marka: Text rekonstruovaný.* Prague.
    1935b *Evangelium sv. Matouše: Text rekonstruovaný.* Prague.
    1936 *Evangelium sv. Jana: Text rekonstruovaný.* Prague.
van Schooneveld, C. H.
    1959 *A semantic analysis of the Old Russian finite preterite system.* (*Slavistic printings and reprintings,* 7.) The Hague.
Van Valin, R., and W. Foley
    1980 "Role and reference grammar" in E. Moravcsik and J. Wirth, eds., *Current approaches to syntax.* (*Syntax and semantics,* 13.) New York, 329-52.

SOURCES

(Published editions are cited only when they were used for text and word-index surveys. For locations of unpublished manuscripts see Avanesov ed. 1966. We use the abbreviations there unless otherwise indicated.)

F St	Feodor Studit, Catechism sermons. (Avanesov ed. 1966: 168.)
Gr Bog	16 sermons of Grigorij Bogoslov, with commentary. (Avanesov ed. 1966: 100, GB XI.)
Hamart	OR translation of the Chronicle of Georgios Hamartolos. (Avanesov ed. 1966: 99, GA XIII-XIV.)
Ip	Hypatian Chronicle. (Published: *Polnoe sobranie russkix letopisej*, 2. Moscow, 1962.) (Original ed. St. Petersburg, 1908.)
Izb 1076	1076 Miscellany. (Published: V. S. Golyšenko et al., eds., *Izbornik 1076 g.* Moscow, 1965.)
L	Russian Primary Chronicle, Laurentian copy. (Published: *Polnoe sobranie russkix letopisej*, 1. Moscow, 1962.) (Original ed. Leningrad, 1926.)
Mar.	Codex Marianus. (Published: V. Jagić, *Quattuor evangeliorum Codex glagoliticus....* Graz, 1954.) (Original ed. St. Petersburg, 1903.)
Mosc	Moscow Chronicle, cited in Borkovskij ed. 1979: 113.
Nov	Novgorod Primary Chronicle, Synod copy. (Published: A. N. Nasonov, *Novgorodskaja pervaja letopis' staršego i mladšego izvodov.* Moscow, 1950.)
PKP	Kievan Crypt Patericon (letters of Simon and Polycarp). (Avanesov ed. 1966: 156.)
Prol 1383	Calendar for mid-March. (Avanesov ed. 1966: 158, Pr 1383.)
RP	Russkaja Pravda. (Published: E. Karskij, *Russkaja pravda po drevnejšemu spisku.* Leningrad, 1930.)
Sb Sof	Late 14th-century miscellany. (Avanesov 1966: 162, Sb Sof k. XIV.)

On Loanwords between Baltic and Slavic

David F. Robinson

The idea of a period of Balto-Slavic unity, after some decades of debate (see in particular Meillet 1908, Senn 1941 and 1953, and Szemerényi 1957), now seems to be largely, if not universally, accepted. The early work of Trautmann (1923) is now seen to be naive in proposing, according to the reckoning of Sławski (1970), 289 substantives which are Balto-Slavic lexical innovations, 195 basic words and 94 derivatives. Whether this number is too high, as it would seem to most linguists, or whether, as Salys concedes (1955:4), there are "only" 100 or so such Balto-Slavic innovations, the number is certainly high enough to be impressive. The common lexicon of Baltic and Slavic, and the remarkable parallelisms in nominal accentual systems, taken together, provide convincing evidence of a Proto-Balto-Slavic period.

This paper concentrates on the purely lexical part of the Balto-Slavic inheritance; in Section I, 37 words proposed by other specialists as being of a clear Balto-Slavic nature are given, to which this writer has added 12 more. The usual criteria used in identifying Balto-Slavic lexical innovations are semantic and formal identity or close similarity in the Baltic and Slavic words; in addition, cognates in other Indo-European languages seem either to be absent, or differ significantly from the Baltic and Slavic words semantically.

To avoid certain particularly uncertain etymologies, onomatopoeia and interjections are omitted.

In each section, words are referenced by the surname of the scholar(s) who have identified the item as a Balto-Slavic innovation. The scholars and the relevant publications are Eckert 1973:60-64, Fraenkel 1950:106, Karaliūnas 1968:259-267, Leumann 1955:160-162, Meillet 1908:46-47, Otrębski 1970:361-364, Salys 1955:4, Senn 1941:255-257, Szemerényi 1957:120-122.

The notation DR in Section I means that the present writer is here proposing that the word indicated is a Balto-Slavic innovation.

Note that English, not Lithuanian, alphabetic order is used here. All items are listed first by Lithuanian word, then Old Church Slavonic (unless another Slavic language is indicated).

I. Balto-Slavic Innovations

1. *abù* 'both': *oba*. Leumann.
2. *aitrùs* 'bitter,' dialectally also *átrus*: *jadъ* 'poison,' perhaps also *jarъ* 'sharp.' DR.

3. *álkti* 'to hunger': *alъkati*. Fraenkel, Meillet.
4. *álvas* 'tin,' OPr. *alwis* 'lead': Russ. *olovo* (< **olvo*). Lith. *ālavas* is a later loan from East Slavic. DR.
5. *anglìs* (f.) 'coal': *ǫglь* (m.). Leumann; he argues that the difference of gender speaks against a recent borrowing.
6. *árklas* 'plow': *ralo* (< **ordlo*). Szemerényi; he considers the "innovative refashioning" of the suffix particularly convincing as a Balto-Slavic innovation.
7. *asẽtras* 'sturgeon,' also OLith. *erškẽtas* <*eškėtras* (cf. OPr. *esketres*): Russ. *osëtr*. DR.
8. *biaurùs* 'ugly': *burja* 'storm' (< **baurja*). Otrębski has this etymology; Vasmer's dictionary (1953-58, I:151) has instead Lith. *paburmjai* [sic] 'stormily'; Fraenkel (1962-65:520) has *paburmey* (modern *paburmiai*) 'in heaps,' which he relates to *būrỹs* 'troop, detachment'. In our opinion, *būrỹs* is not related to *biaurùs*. DR.
9. *blãgnas* 'unfit': Russ. *blagoj* 'hateful.' Lith. *blõgas* 'weak, bad' is a loan from East Slavic *blagoj*. DR.
10. *blùkti* 'to fade': Russ. *blëknut'* (< **blьk-*). DR.
11. *blusà* 'flea': *blъxa*. Meillet.
12. *dienà* 'day': *dьnь*. Szemerényi; he considers the problem of the root vocalism soluble in a complicated way; Senn argues that the vocalism speaks against a Balto-Slavic innovation.
13. *draũgas* 'friend': *drugъ*. Leumann.
14. *eldijà*, also *aldijà* 'boat': *alьdija, ladii* (< **oldьjь*). Fraenkel, Meillet.
15. *ė́sti* 'to eat (of animals)': *ěsti, jasti*. See also *sėdėti*. Leumann.
16. *galvà* 'head': *glava* (< **golva*). In spite of contrasting stem intonation, Lith. acc. sg. *gálvą* (with acute) but Slavic circumflex, as in Russ. acc. sg. *golovu* and Serbo-Cr. *glavu*, this word is universally regarded as a Balto-Slavic lexical and accentual innovation. Leumann, Meillet, Szemerényi.
17. *geležìs* 'iron': *želėzo*. Fraenkel, Meillet.
18. *giñti* 'to hunt, drive out,' *ganýti* (iterative of preceding), *gãnas* 'herdsman': *gъnati, goniti* 'to drive.' Leumann.
19. *grim̃sti* 'to sink,' *gramzdýti* 'to dip in water': Russ. *gruz* 'burden' (< **grǫzъ*), Russ. *grjaz'* 'dirt' (< **gręzь*). Because of ablaut in both Baltic and Slavic, we cannot determine whether this item is a loanword. DR.
20. *gul̃ti* (< **lugtei*?) 'to lie down': *lešti* (< **legtī*). Also *gulėti* (< **lugētei*?) 'to be lying down': *ležati* (< **ležātī* < **legētī*). We propose metathesis, as in Lith. *kèpti* (< **pekti*) 'to bake.' Related Lithuanian words without metathesis are *lagamìnas* 'suitcase, trunk,' and *palėgti* 'to lie down,' cf. OCS *lešti* (< **legtī*). DR.

21. *gurgulas* 'lump, bundle, knot': *gъrstъ* 'handful.' Eckert, who proposes this as a loanword from Slavic to Baltic; we do not feel that Eckert's own criteria outlined under *piršys,* Section III below, including demonstrated greater productivity in the lending language than in the borrowing language, have been met; we therefore regard this as a Balto-Slavic innovation.

22. *jáunas* 'young': *junъ.* Szemerényi, who points to new root vocalism and new suffix here.

23. *káina* 'price': *cěna.* Leumann.

24. *kárvė* 'cow': *krava* (< *korva). Salys, who mentions the semantic closeness of the two forms. Vasmer 1953-58 and Fraenkel 1962-65 show other Indo-European cognates, but only Baltic and Slavic share both semantic identity and morphological similarity.

25. *ketverì* 'four (collective)': *četveri, četvero.* Leumann.

26. *kiáunė* 'marten': Russ. *kuna* 'marten pelt.' Salys.

27. *klė́tis* 'store room, granary': *klětъ.* Eckert, Fraenkel. Eckert states that this is a possible loan from Baltic to Slavic or from Slavic to Baltic; not enough facts are at hand to make a final determination. Fraenkel claims this must be a Balto-Slavic word and not a loan from Slavic to Baltic, because Lithuanian would have had **klietis.*

28. *líepa* 'linden': *lipa.* Meillet.

29. *mãžas* 'small': Russ. *mizinec* 'small finger.' DR.

30. *mègzti (mezg-)* 'to knot, knit': Russ. *mozg* 'brain.' DR.

31. *mė́klinti* 'to think, mean': *mekati.* DR.

32. *nýtis* 'thread': *nitъ.* Eckert, who lists this as a loan from Slavic to Baltic. Not so Fraenkel (1962-65:505), who dismisses this claim and argues for its Balto-Slavic nature.

33. *pãslauga* 'service': *posluga, sluga.* Also *slaugýti* 'to care for.' Lith. *slūgà* and OLith. *slūžyti* are late loans from Slavic. Fraenkel.

34. *péntis* 'butt of axe': *pęta* 'heel.' Also related are *pìnti* 'to weave, twist,' *péndėti* and *péntėti* 'to wither, rot' and Russ. *pnut'* 'to kick.' This writer feels there are many problems with the semantics of the Baltic forms. Salys.

35. *pir̃štas* 'finger': *prъstъ.* Leumann, Senn.

36. *pósūnis* 'stepson': Russ. *pasynok.* DR.

37. *prė́skas* 'fresh': Russ. *presnyi.* Fraenkel doubts the connection of the Balto-Slavic with Germanic *frisc* because of the Lithuanian root vowel. DR.

38. *rãgas* 'horn': *rogъ.* Fraenkel, Leumann, Meillet.

39. *rasà* 'dew': *rosa.* Leumann.

40. *šakà* 'branch': *soxa* 'kind of plow,' Otrębski.

41. *šalnà* 'hoarfrost': Russ. Ch. Slav. *slana* (< *solna). Leumann.

42. *sėdėti* 'to sit': *sěděti.* Leumann, who remarks that Baltic and Slavic

alone among the Indo-European languages have this ablaut grade in both *sėdėti* and *ėsti*, q.v.

43. *siuvėjas* 'tailor': ORuss. *švějь*. Leumann.
44. *stragùs* 'strict': *strogъ*. Karaliūnas. This connection is not made by either Fraenkel (1962-65) or Vasmer (1953-58).
45. *talkà* 'collective assistance': Bulg. *tlaka*. Leumann.
46. *táuka* 'lard': *tukъ* (< *tauku*). Leumann.
47. *vartai* 'gate': *vrata*. Both are pluralia tantum. Leumann.
48. *větra* (f.) 'storm': *větrъ* (m.). Leumann, who argues that the gender difference speaks against a recent borrowing.
49. *ýnis* 'hoarfrost': Ch. Slav. *inьjь*, Russ. *inej*. Vasmer (1953-58, II:483) states that the intonation in the Lithuanian makes the possibility of a loan from Slavic remote. Because of this, and because of a lack of clear cognates in other Indo-European languages, we propose this as a Balto-Slavic lexical innovation. DR.
50. *žẽmė* 'earth': *zemlja*. Leumann.
51. *žiemà* 'winter': *zima*. Leumann.
52. *žvaigždẽ* 'star,' cf. OPr. *svaigstan*: *zvězda*. Meillet.

II. Loanwords from Proto-Baltic into Proto-Slavic

The following words are being proposed as very early loans from Proto-Baltic into Proto-Slavic, soon after the Balto-Slavic period. Except for the word *rankà*, whose status as a loan from Baltic into Slavic has been argued by R. Eckert, all other suggested loans are proposed by this writer.

It must be emphasized that the authorities cited in this section are of the belief that the words concerned are Balto-Slavic innovations, and *not* loans dating after the Balto-Slavic period.

The writer considers the following words to be loans from Proto-Baltic into Proto-Slavic on the basis of the apparently greater productivity of the Baltic root (usually by ablaut).

There are undoubtedly other such loanwords; this is not meant to be an exhaustive list.

1. *áiža* 'crack,' *iẽžti*, *eĩžti*, *ìžti* 'to hull, shell': *jazva* 'wound.' DR.
2. *aumuõ* 'understanding,' *omenìs* 'mind,' *omẽ* 'instinct': *umъ*. Fraenkel shows as Balto-Slavic. DR.
3. *brilà*, *bylà* 'margin, crust,' *ãtbraila* 'ledge, brim': *bryla*, *brila* 'lip.' DR.
4. *degùtas* 'tar,' *dègti* 'to burn,' *dagà* 'intense heat': Russ. *dëgot'* 'tar.' K. Būga, cited in Fraenkel 1962-65 (86), claims this as a loan from Baltic into Slavic, but apparently later than the point in time we have in mind in this section. We propose this as a loan from Proto-Baltic into Proto-Slavic in view of the ablaut grades shown in the Lithuanian. DR.

5. *mèsti* 'to throw,' *mė́tyti* (intensive of preceding), *ātmata* 'descent,' *išmata* 'feces': *mė́tati, mesti* 'to throw.' Meillet; DR as loan.

6. *pirtìs* 'kiln,' *peřti* 'to beat': ORuss. *pьrtъ* 'bathhouse.' Salys; DR as loan.

7. *rankà* 'hand, arm,' *riñkti* 'to gather': *rǫka.* Eckert (specifically suggests this is an early loan from Proto-Baltic "ins Urslawische"); Fraenkel, Leumann, Meillet, Salys.

8. *šelmuõ,* gen. sg. *šelmeñs* 'beam, roof ridge,' *šalmà* 'long beam': Russ. Ch. Slav. *slěmja* (< **selmę*). Other cognates uncertain. Leumann; DR as loan.

III. Loanwords from Proto-Slavic into Proto-Baltic

The following words are proposed as very early loanwords from Proto-Slavic into Proto-Baltic, soon after the Balto-Slavic period.

Except for the word *piřšys,* whose status as a loan from Slavic into Baltic is the contribution of Eckert (1973) in his convincing and ground-breaking article in *Baltistica,* all other suggested loans are proposed by this writer.

As mentioned above under Section II, the authorities cited are of the belief that the words concerned are Balto-Slavic innovations, and *not* loans.

The writer considers the following words to be loans from Proto-Slavic into Proto-Baltic on the grounds of the apparently greater productivity of the Slavic root (usually by ablaut).

More such loanwords will undoubtedly be proposed in due course; this is not claimed as an exhaustive list.

1. *áiškus* 'clear': *jasьnъ* 'clear,' *iskra* 'spark.' DR.

2. *ą́žuolas* 'oak,' OPr. *ansonis*: Russ. *uzel* (if from **vǫzlъ,* then ablaut shown in *vęzati* 'to tie'). DR.

3. *braũkti* 'to hit, wipe': Russ. *brokat', brukat'*; also Russ. *brus* 'whetstone.' DR.

4. *kèpti* (< **pèkti*) 'to bake': *pešti* (< **pektī*), *potъ* (< **pokťъ*) sweat.' DR.

5. *piřšys, pìlšys* 'horse's chest': *prъsi* 'breast,' and many other Slavic derivatives. Eckert, in proposing this as a loan, argues that the Slavic is rich in derivatives, Lithuanian having none; the Slavic is rich in semantic range, Lithuanian having only one narrow meaning; the Lithuanian variant *pìlšys* shows that *piřšys,* as a loan, was less familiar to Baltic speakers; and Slavic loans from Lithuanian in East Slavic and Polish border areas are noted, but other Slavic areas do not have such forms.

6. *vařnas* 'raven': Russ. *v'oron;* also *várna* 'crow': Russian *vor'ona.* Szemerényi claims these words are definitely related to Slavic *variti* 'to boil'; a Proto-Indo-European adjective **wornos* means 'burned, black.' The Balto-Slavic developments are called innovative and striking. DR as loan.

It should be restated that the writer is a believer in a period of Balto-Slavic linguistic unity. In Sections II and III above, then, we do not intend to attack the notion of a Proto-Balto-Slavic period but rather to show that at least a few of the words commonly taken to be Balto-Slavic innovations may in fact be loanwords between Proto-Baltic and Proto-Slavic in either direction, after the period of Balto-Slavic linguistic unity. If this is the case, it does not contradict the evidence for the Balto-Slavic hypothesis provided by words of the type in Section I above.

It is hoped that other Balticists, Slavists and Indo-Europeanists will continue and improve on the work begun here, either to expand these lists or to show why they must be shortened. If it can be established, for example, that some of the proposed loanwords in Sections II and III ought not to be considered loanwords at all because the evidence for such a status is too weak, then those words should be added to those in Section I as additional evidence in favor of the Balto-Slavic hypothesis.

Ohio State University

REFERENCES

Eckert, R.
   1973   "Zur Frage der frühen Lehnbeziehungen zwischen Slawisch und Baltisch." *Baltistica* 9:59-65.
Fraenkel, E.
   1950   *Die baltische Sprachen.* Heidelberg.
   1962-65   *Litauisches etymologisches Wörterbuch,* I-II, Heidelberg-Göttingen.
Karaliūnas, S.
   1968   "Lie. stragùs = sl. *strogъ". *Baltistica* 4:259-267.
Leumann, M.
   1955   "Baltisch und Slawisch." *Corolla Linguistica* (Sommer Festschrift), Wiesbaden, 154-162.
Meillet, A.
   1908   *Les dialectes indo-européens.* Paris.
Otkupščikov, Ju.
   1971   "Iz istorii balto-slavjanskix leksičeskix otnošenij." *Baltistica* 7:119-128.
Otrębski, J.
   1970   "Lit. *šakà* und Verwandtes." *Donum Balticum* (Stang Festschrift), Stockholm, 361-364.
Salys, A.
   1955   "Baltic languages." *Encyclopedia Britannica* 3:3-5.
Senn, A.
   1941   "On the degree of kinship between Slavic and Baltic." *American Slavic and East European Review* (*The Slavonic Year Book, American Series* I) (= *Slavic Review* 20), 251-265.
   1953   "Die Beziehungen des Baltischen zum Slawischen und Germanischen." *KZ* 72:162-188.

Sławski, F.
 1970 "Lexikalische Neuerungen im Baltisch-Slawischen." *Donum Balticum* (Stang Festschrift), Stockholm, 501-06.
Szemerényi, O.
 1957 "The problem of Balto-Slav unity: A critical survey." *Kratylos* 2:97-123.
Trautmann, R.
 1923 *Baltisch-Slavisches Wörterbuch*. Göttingen.
Vasmer, M.
 1953-58 *Russisches etymologisches Wörterbuch*, I-III, Heidelberg.

Главные пути лексических заимствований в славянских языках
(на материалах чешского, польского и восточнославянских языков X-XVI вв.)

А. Шенкер

1. Больше тридцати лет тому назад выдающийся украинский ученый Леонид Арсеньевич Булаховский высказал мнение, что «вопрос о взаимоотношениях славянских литературных языков до сих пор не был в науке предметом особо интенсивной разработки» (1951: 37). Не отрицая, что этот вопрос «не мог, конечно, совсем остаться вне поля зрения славистов», Л. А. Булаховский поражается, что он не привлек большего внимания: «... при всей ценности уже добытого усилиями отдельных ученых ... бросается в глаза самое количество исследований, слишком небольшое сравнительно с тем, что мы имеем на поле штудий сравнительно-исторических, более или менее случайный, попутный характер едва ли не большинства их, отсутствие большого интереса к углублению подобной проблематики на путях славяноведения вообще» (1951: 38).

Каковы же причины этого невнимания к одной из самых важных и интересных областей славяноведения? Л. А. Булаховский считает, что всестороннему изучению взаимоотношений славянских литературных языков препятствовали с одной стороны «опасение неблагоприятной общественной реакции на обнаружение чужого славянского 'влияния' на родной язык», а с другой «малая выразительность признаков заимствования из одного языка в близко родственный же язык», ограничивающая поле действия исследователя и не обещающая больших результатов (1951: 37).

Факторы упомянутые Л. А. Булаховским не потеряли своей актуальности и в наши дни. Первый из них, несмотря на частые уверения в обратном, все еще бытует в сознании некоторых ученых, лишая их полной объективности суждений[1]. Второй же всегда был и всегда остается главной помехой в работе над взаимоотношениями славянских литературных языков, особенно в пределах одной и той же языковой группы (например, в западнославянских языках). Поэтому неудивительно, что характеристика, данная Л. А. Булаховским, применима в своих главных чертах и к сегодняшней славистике, даже если ограничиться вопросами словарных заимствований, которые, по словам Л. А. Булаховского, гораздо лучше исследованы, чем проблемы фразеологии и синтаксиса[2].

2. Однако ни узкий национализм, ни большое сходство сравниваемых языков не несут полной ответстсвенности за неудовлетворительное состояние изучения взаимоотношений славянских литературных языков. К этим двум факторам следует добавить недостатки лексикографического и прежде всего методологического порядка.

Что касается лексикографии, то сегодняшнее положение вещей, конечно, намного лучше условий, в которых приходилось работать Л. А. Булаховскому и современным ему ученым. Как бы то ни было, у нас сейчас имеются многие материалы по истории славянской лексики, которых не было в сороковые годы. Достаточно упомянуть исторические словари тех языков, о которых здесь идет речь, чтобы понять, сколько ценной работы уже проделано[3]. Тем не менее, это только начало. Для того чтобы полностью удовлетворить нужды исторической лексикологии, потребуются еще многие десятилетия кропотливой лексикографической деятельности. Нужно согласиться с замечанием С. Кохмана, что славянская историческая лексикология еще не вышла из пеленок и что виной этому: «duża pracochłonność oraz wielkie braki w zakresie pełnych słowników historycznych poszczególnych języków słowiańskich» (Kochman 1975: 138).

Еще серьезнее представляется положение в области методологии изучения истории славянской лексики. Огромное большинство исследований довольствуется рассмотрением влияния одного языка на другой, не вдаваясь в прослеживание более общих, комплексных тенденций во взаимоотношениях целого ряда славянских литературных языков и в их отношении к неславянским языкам. Между тем эти тенденции, возникшие на фоне общеевропейских исторических и культурных процессов, предоставляют нередко весьма ценные сведения, позволяющие определить, чтó в лексике данного языка унаследовано из общеславянского языка, чтó является местным неологизмом, а чтó заимствовано из других языков. Рассмотрим, например, польское существительное *duchowieństwo* 'духовность, духовенство'. Можем ли мы с полной уверенностью утверждать, что оно является заимствованием из чешского языка? Имеются, конечно, соображения хронологического, семантического и текстуального порядка, указывающие на чешское происхождение этого слова, но как справедливо отмечают М. Басай и Я. Сятковский, «rodzimość tej formacji w języku polskim pod względem formalnym nie budzi zastrzeżeń» (Basaj, Siatkowski 1966: 74). Однако когда мы учтем, что древнечешское *duchovenstvie* является калькой средневерхненемецкого *geistlîchkeit* и что польское *duchowieństwo* было заимствовано восточнославянскими языками как *духовенство,* с польским ударением на предпоследнем слоге, тогда предположение заимствования из чешского языка в польский окажется тем необходимым звеном, которое свяжет остальные звенья в одну логически последовательную цепь[4].

Цепная передача лексики из одного языка в другой — явление обычное в истории языков. Рассмотрим, к примеру, дальнейшую участь польских богемизмов на *D,* прочно осевших в польском литературном языке (т.е. не так называемых эфемерных заимствований, а тех, которые продержались в языке до нынешнего времени): *diabeł* 'дьявол', *doba* 'время', *dowcip* 'остроумие', *dowód* 'довод', *drab* 'пеший солдат', *duchowieństwo* 'духовенство', *dufać* 'надеяться', *dynia* 'дыня', *działo* 'орудие', *dzieciństwo* 'детство', *dziekan* 'декан', *dziesięcioro przykazań* 'десять заповедей', *dziękować* 'благодарить', *dziwny* 'чудесный'. Некоторые из этих слов возникли в чешском языке (*dowcip, dufać*), другие были заимствованы чешским языком из латинского (*diabeł, dziekan*), немецкого (*duchowieństwo, dziękować*) или древнецерковнославянского (*dziwny*). Все они проникли из польского языка в восточнославянские языки, главным образом в украинский и белорусский.

Существование таких лексических цепей легко объяснимо. Потребности литературных языков намного превышают словарный запас, унаследованный из общеславянского языка. Удовлетворение этих потребностей требует пополнения словаря новообразованиями и заимствованиями. Такой процесс лексического обогащения повторяется в разных славянских языках в разное время, по мере приобщения этих языков к общеевропейской культуре, по мере распространения культурных и цивилизационных ценностей. Как сказал А. Брюкнер: «W wiekach średnich chętnie z gotowego korzystano, nie podejmowano się dwukrotnie, niezawiśle, tych samych trudów» (Brückner 1906: 42).

Цепи лексических заимствований не являются, конечно, специфической чертой славянских языков. Диффузия предметов, понятий и институтов из страны в страну неизбежно влечет за собой диффузию соответствующих терминов. Для иллюстрации достаточно вспомнить встречные течения, несущие франкские и арабские элементы в романские языки. Франкские заимствования в древнефранцузском передаются дальше на юго-запад, арабские же слова попадают сперва в испанский язык и распространяются оттуда в северо-восточном направлении; ср. франкский *busk* 'лесок', перешедший во французском языке в *bois* и переданный дальше из провансальского *bosc* в итальянский *bosco* и испанский *bosque*; или же арабский *faras* 'конь', прошедший цепью через испанский *alfaraz*, провансальский *alferan* и французский *auferrant*.

3. Каковы же главные пути диффузии славянской лексики до XVIII в.? Наглядным ответом на этот вопрос может послужить история глагола *vitati* 'жить, пребывать'. Вопреки тому, что пишется в этимологических словарях,[5] этот глагол не праславянский. Он возник в древнецерковнославянском языке и был заимствован оттуда восточнославянскими языками в своем первоначальном значении (ср. русское *витать, обитать*) и чешским языком в новом значении 'приветствовать', возникшем на базе императива *vitaj* 'пребывай > живи > будь здоров > здравствуй'. Из чешского языка глагол *vitati* был заимствован другими западнославянскими языками и, наконец, был передан польским языком в восточнославянские языки и в литовский. Таким образом, оба значения глагола *витать,* отмеченные словарем Даля: (1) 'пребывать, проживать, жить' (с производными 'двигаться в облаках, носиться')[6] и (2) 'привечать, приветствовать' импортированы в русский язык, первое с юга, второе с запада.

Эти два пути и являются основными магистралями, вдоль которых лексический материал передавался из одного славянского языка в другой в эпоху Средневековья и Ренессанса. Один путь вел из болгарского центра церковнославянской письменности в восточнославянские литературные языки, второй из древнецерковнославянского языка моравской редакции в чешский язык, из чешского в польский, а из польского дальше на восток в украинский, белорусский, русский, литовский, а иногда и румынский[7]. В то время как первый, восточный, путь довольно хорошо изучен, значение второго, западного, пути недооценивается в лексикологической литературе. Между тем оба пути сыграли чрезвычайно важную роль в истории славянской лексики и оба они заслуживают равной трактовки и равного внимания.

4. На первый взгляд, сходство между восточным и западным путем невелико. Недолговечная традиция моравско-чешской разновидности церковнославянского языка, казалось бы, не может соперничать с живучестью и творческой силой традиции, исходящей из Болгарии и оставившей столь глубокие следы в языках православного славянства, прежде всего в русском языке. Однако тщательный разбор культурной жизни Чехии X-XI вв. не подтверждает такого впечатления. Кирилло-мефодиевская традиция, перенесенная на чешскую почву после изгнания из Моравии славянских монахов и разрушения моравского государства мадьярами, не только сохраняется в литургии (Сазавский монастырь),

но и обогащается многими новыми сочинениями, из которых достаточно упомянуть жития св. Вацлава и св. Людмилы. Более того, чешский очаг церковнославянской традиции оказался достаточно мощным, чтобы распространить свое влияние на окружающие Чехию страны. В своем ценном обзоре чешского участия в церковнославянской культуре Р. О. Якобсон доказывает, что в радиусе чешского культурного влияния находились не только самые близкие соседи чехов: поляки, лужичане, хорваты и венгры, но и жители более отдаленных земель, как Киевская и даже Новгородская Русь (Jakobson 1940: 12-19). К выводам Р. О. Якобсона мы можем добавить весьма правдоподобную догадку Ф. Мареша, что чешская церковнославянская религиозная терминология проникла и в язык полабских славян (Mareš 1962: 513-523).

Экспансия чешской церковнославянской терминологии является первым этапом на западном пути распространения славянской лексики[8]. Второй этап начинается в XII в., когда славянское богослужение в Чехии было полностью вытеснено латинским обрядом и когда чешский язык начал постепенно перенимать все большее количество функций культурного языка. Уже в XII и XIII вв. появляются чешские церковные песни, самая ранняя Святовацлавская и более поздние Островская и Кунгутина, а также переводы псалтыри[9]. С конца XIII в. и первых десятилетий XIV в. начинается расцвет чешского народного языка, обслуживающего все новые области словесного искусства, включая эпос (Alexandreida), летопись (Dalimilova kronika) и драму (Mastičkář), а со второй половины XIV в. чешский язык, достигший высокого художественного и экспрессивного уровня, становится моделью для окружающих Чехию славянских литературных языков, прежде всего для польского языка. В этой связи следует подчеркнуть особое значение гуситского движения и сопряженной с ним литературной и идеологической деятельности. Чешское культурное и языковое влияние продолжается вплоть до конца XVI в. и прекращается, когда Чехия теряет свою независимость после поражения у Белой Горы в 1620 г.[10]

Типологически чешские заимствования в польском языке относятся к тем же семантическим полям, что и заимствования в других языках, где, аналогично с чешско-польской обстановкой, зрелая культура служит моделью для младшей культуры (ср., например, французско-латинское влияние на английский язык). К чехизмам причисляются слова из таких областей жизни, как наука, техника, городская администрация, религия, образование, военное дело и, прежде всего, литературная, отвлеченная лексика.

Ко времени политического упадка Чехии, завершившегося тридцатилетней войной и белогорской катастрофой, Польша достигла полного расцвета своих творческих сил как на культурном, так и на политическом поприще. Польская литература XVI в. может уже гордиться достижениями западноевропейского уровня. Недаром такие польские писатели как Миколай Рей, Ян Кохановский, Лукаш Гурницкий стяжали этому периоду название «золотого века» польской литературы. В политическом отношении Польша, распространившая свое влияние на Литву, Белоруссию, Украину, стала одним из крупнейших государств Европы. В этот период начинается шествие польской лексики в восточнославянские языки, начинается следующий, третий этап диффузии славянской лексики по западному пути.

В своих главных чертах культурные условия, определяющие польское влияние на восточнославянские языки, не отличаются от условий, характеризующих чешское влияние на польский язык. Поэтому и семантические категории, представленные украинскими и белорусскими полонизмами, совпадают, как правило, с семантикой польских богемизмов[11]. Совпадает также количество заимствованных слов. Согласно М. Л. Худашу, в украинских деловых документах XVI и XVII вв. имеется приблизительно 17% полонизмов[12], т.е. столько же сколько, по моим подсчетам, имеется богемизмов в польском языке (Schenker 1978: 583).

5. Исследования посвященные чешскому воздействию на польский язык, достаточно многочисленны[13]. Все они в большей или меньшей мере признают значение чешского влияния, но и все наталкиваются на одно и то же препятствие в определении степени зависимости польского языка от чешской модели: внешнее сходство чешских и польских слов славянского происхождения. Перед всеми исследователями встает одинаковый вопрос: как проследить историю слов, лишенных формальных признаков иноязычного происхождения.

Это недоумение частично разрешимо, если признать свидетельство процессов лексической диффузии, с их почти закономерным характером. Сведения о распространении слов могут быть использованы как один из критериев в изучении межъязыковых лексических связей, прежде всего в решении спорных вопросов по истории славянских слов с небольшой формальной выразительностью, или же полностью лишенных ее[14]. Иначе говоря, заимствование польского слова одним из восточнославянских языков может свидетельствовать о том, что данное слово не является исконно польским, а заимствовано из иноязычного источника (в случае слов славянского происхождения — скорее всего из чешского языка). Подчеркиваю: *может* свидетельствовать, так как сам факт наличия полонизма в восточнославянских языках не является, конечно, обязательным признаком его иноязычного происхождения в польском языке. Этот принцип может служить лишь как вспомогательный довод, сопровождающий другие соображения, которые дают право подозревать, что данное слово действительно является заимствованием в польском языке. Приведенная выше история польского существительного *duchowieństwo* — яркий пример такого косвенного доказательства. Вот несколько других польских слов, которые по всем признакам, кроме формального, могли бы быть богемизмами: *daremny* 'напрасный', *dbać* 'заботиться', *duchowny* 'священник', *dworny* 'придворный, изысканный', *dworski* 'куртуазный, изящный', *dziedzic* 'наследник'. Все эти слова были заимствованы из польского в восточнославянские языки, и этот факт, совместно с другими семантическими, историческими, диалектными показаниями, мы вправе считать подтверждением догадки об их иноязычном (в данном случае, чешском) происхождении[15].

С другой стороны, такие польские слова как *darowizna* 'дар', *dwoisty* 'двоякий', *dzieje* 'история', хотя они и проникли в восточнославянские языки (Shevelov 1975: 456-458), не могут считаться чешскими заимствованиями, так как для такого предположения нет других объективных данных.

6. Пренебрежительное отношение к историзму ведет к злоупотреблению этимологическим методом в исследовании славянской лексики. Во многих лексикологических работах слова со славянскими корнями, наличествующие в большинстве славянских языков, зачисляются почти автоматически к праславянскому лексическому фонду. При этом не учитываются культурно-социальные факторы,, хронология, диалектология и, что важнее всего, процессы лексической диффузии. Отдавая предпочтение этимологии, исследователи забывают о том, что процессы диффузии слов играют не менее важную роль в истории языков, чем процессы преемственности слов из праязыка, и не уделяют достаточно внимания фундаментальной разнице между этими процессами. Смешение понятий «общеславянский» и «праславянский» приводит к методологической путанице и затрудняет объективный подход к истории славянской лексики[16].

Ярким примером такого «этимологического заблуждения» может послужить история русского существительного *награда* и родственных ему образований, присутствующих во многих славянских языках (чешское *náhrada,* польское *nagroda,* украинское *нагорода,* и т.д.). Еще недавно считалось, что это слова праславянского происхождения, и что отсутствие полногласия в русском языке является результатом церковнославянского влияния[17]. Несостоятельность этого предположения вскрыл С. Кохман в своей поучительной работе о полонизмах в русском языке (Kochman 1975: 93-95). С. Кохман доказал, что перед нами слово возникшее, в древнечешском языке и заимствованное оттуда в XVI в. в польский язык, который в свою очередь передал его восточнославянским языкам и литовскому языку. С соответствующей адаптацией это слово появляется в полногласной форме *нагорода* в староураинском и старобелорусском языках и в русском деловом языке XVI-XVII вв. Начиная с XVII в. входит в обращение русская форма *награда*, адаптированная согласно А. Брюкнеру (Brückner 1927: 353) и С. Кохману, с польского *nagroda*. Праславянский характер *награды* казался этимологам чем-то столь очевидным, что, кроме А. Брюкнера, ни один из них не заметил полного отсутствия этого слова в церковнославянской лексике.

Случаев неправильного толкования истории славянских слов можно привести больше. Так, например, на основании форм, наличествующих во многих, особенно северных, славянских языках, праславянские словари реконструируют праформы *dĕditi* 'наследовать' и *dĕditjь* 'наследник' (Трубачев 1977: 226, Sławski 1979: 111-113). Однако детальный разбор истории этих слов показывает, что в праславянском языке не существовало общих всем славянам терминов 'наследовать' и 'наследник,' и что мы имеем дело с чешскими неологизмами XIII в., которые проникли из Чехии в большинство севернославянских языков и в самые северные из южнославянских языков[18].

Подобные соображения заставляют сомневаться в правильности предположения, что в праславянском языке существовал глагол *dъbati* 'заботиться, стараться' (Трубачев 1964: 486). Хронология появления этого глвавола в центральной полосе севернославянских языков наводит на мысль, что перед нами чешский неологизм, распространившийся в другие языки. Самой ранней формой этого глагола является древнечешское *tbáti* (Alexandreida), перешедшее в *dbáti* с ассимиляцией по звонкости начального согласного. Древнепольский глагол *dbać* (изредка и *tbać*) был заимствован из чешского языка и передан дальше на восток; ср. украинское *дбати* (Leeming 1968: 294), белорусское *дбаць* (Булыка 1972: 88), западнорусское *дбать* (Даль 1903: 1030-1031), литовское *bóti* и *dabóti* (Skardžius 1931: 45 и 60)[19].

7. Полвека тому назад Р. О. Якобсон приравнял роль чешского языка в развитии польского литературного языка к той положительной роли, какую церковнославянский язык сыграл в истории русского литературного языка (Jakobson 1934-1935: 72). Хотя мысль Р. О. Якобсона осталась неиспользованной и неразработанной в последующих исследо-

ваниях о польском литературном языке, соображения, высказанные в настоящей статье, полностью ее поддерживают. Правда, на первых порах истории польской культуры значительную часть тех функций, которые имел церковнославянский язык среди православного славянства (Slavia Orthodoxa)[20], выполняла латынь. Однако уже во время гуситского движения и особенно протестантизма значение латыни уменьшается и соответственно возрастает роль чешского языка. Он становится образцом народного литературного языка, идущего на смену отступающей латыни. Читая высказывания таких писателей польского Ренессанса как Лукаш Гурницкий и Ян Малецкий, трудно не поддаться впечатлению, что чешский язык, сопрягающий *dignitas* языка самого развитого и зрелого государства римского славянства (Slavia Romana) с преимуществами народного, удобопонимаемого языка, употреблялся образованными поляками (и другими западными славянами) как своего рода *lingua franca* культурного общения. Чешское лексическое наследие, прочно осевшее в польском литературном языке, стало частью того культурного достояния, которое передавалось дальше на восток, в украинский и белорусский языки, откуда отдельные слова проникали и в русский язык[21].

Значение диффузии чешского словарного материала, обогащающего языки, находящиеся в сфере чешского культурного влияния, должно быть в полной мере признано и оценено, прежде чем изучение взаимоотношений между чешским, польским и восточнославянскими языками сможет продвинуться вперед. Пока процессы лексической диффузии не будут надлежащим образом вскрыты, сожаления Л. А. Булаховского о том, что большинство исследований о взаимоотношениях славянских литературных языков носит «случайный, попутный характер» останутся в силе.

ПРИМЕЧАНИЯ

[1] Отдельные случаи тенденциозности в оценке, например, польско-украинских языковых отношений отмечены М. Л. Худашом (1960: 121-122, прим. 1) и Ю. Шевелевым (Shevelov 1975: прим. 9).

[2] Здесь мы не можем детально разбирать работы по лексическим взаимоотношениям славянских языков. С библиографией чешско-польских связей легче всего познакомиться по работам М. Басая и Я. Сятковского, прежде всего по их превосходному обзору польских чехизмов (Basaj, Siatkowski 1964-1980); состояние польско-украинских лексических связей обсуждается Ю. Шевелевым (Shevelov 1975: 449-451); польско-белорусским лексическим связям уделяет много внимания А. М. Булыка, особенно в своем ценном труде о

лексических заимствованиях в белорусском языке (1980); исчерпывающий обзор научной литературы по польско-русским языковым контактам дается С. Кохманом в его двух монографиях о полонизмах в русском языке (Kochman 1967: 5-18, Kochman 1975: 5-27).

[3] Например, такие словари, как *Staročeský slovník* (Havránek 1968-), *Słownik staropolski* (Urbańczyk 1953-), *Słownik polszczyzny XVI wieku* (Mayenowa 1966-), *Словник староукраїнської мови XIV-XV* ст. (Гумецька 1977-1978), *Гістарычны слоўнік беларускай мовы* (Жураўскі (в печати)), *Словарь русского языка XI-XVII вв.* (Бархударов 1975-).

[4] Ср. Е. И. Мельников (1967: 100-101). В заимствованиях типа *духовенство* Е. И. Мельников видит «чешский элемент» в русском языке, тогда как, на наш взгляд, это полонизмы чешского происхождения. Хотя статья Е. И. Мельникова является одной из немногих, известных мне, попыток показать чешско-польско-русские лексические связи в их комплексном аспекте, она упускает из виду роль украинского и белорусского языков, чрезвычайно важного промежуточного звена между польским и русским языками (см. Hüttl-Worth 1963: 11-13).

[5] См., например, Holub, Kopečný 1952: 417 или Шанский 1968: 109.

[6] Значение 'парить (в облаках, в эмпиреях)' развилось из 'жить (в облаках, в эмпиреях)'. История глагола *vitati* в славянских языках обсуждается в моей статье "Common Slavic vs. Generalized Slavic: The Case of *vitati*" в журнале *Rocznik Slawistyczny* (в печати).

[7] В XIX в. движение заимствований по этим путям пошло в обратном направлении: русский язык стал моделью для еще неокрепших южнославянских литературных языков, а польский язык оказал влияние на возрождающийся чешский литературный язык.

[8] Неславянская лексика, которая проникала в польский язык через посредство чешского языка, здесь не обсуждается.

[9] О древнечешских переводах псалтыри см. Flajšhans 1903: 75-79.

[10] Чтобы показать, в какой степени польский литературный язык зависел от чешских образцов, А. Брюкнер цитирует следующее заявление Яна Малецкого, известного польского протестантского писателя XVI в. (1547 г.): "neminem unquam litteras sacras in linguam polonicam vere ac proprie vertere posse sine adminiculo linguae bohemicae et sacrarum litterarum lingua bohemica editarum" (Brückner 1915: 120).

[11] Религиозная терминология занимала особое положение, так как употребление ее зависело от церковной принадлежности верующих. Соотношение церковнославянской и чешско-польской религиозной лексики (включая, конечно, исконно латинские и немецкие термины) на территории великого княжества Литовского до сих пор детально не изучено; ср. Булыка 1980: 168.

[12] Материал, использованный М. Л. Худашом почерпнут из староукраинских документов Львовского Ставропигийского Братства (Худаш 1960: 138, прим. 9). Ю. Шевелев, основываясь на данных нескольких словарей украинского языка XV-XX вв., считает, что полонизмов в украинском языке приблизительно 14% (Shevelov 1975: 452-453, прим. 12).

[13] Краткий обзор работ по польским богемизмам дается М. Басаем (Basaj 1966: 7-8). Из новейших работ следует назвать чрезвычайно ценный критический разбор польских чехизмов М. Басая и Я. Сятковского, упомянутый выше в примечании 2; монографию о ранних лексических богемизмах Ю. Речека (Reczek 1968) и две сжатые, но содержательные статьи С. Урбанчика (Urbańczyk 1970, 1972).

[14] Значение лексической диффузии в истории славянских языков обсуждается более детально С. Кохманом (Kochman 1975: 14-16) и мною (Schenker 1978: 579-580).

[15] Подробный разбор этих слов дается в моем докладе "Czech Lexical Borrowings in Polish Re-examined," прочитанном на конференции об образовании славянских литературных языков, состоявшейся в Оксфорде 6-11 июля 1981 г.

[16] Думается, что привычка употреблять термины «общеславянский» и «праславянский» с одним и тем же значением слишком сильно внедрилась в научный язык, чтобы ее можно было искоренить. Поэтому кажется целесообразным ввести термин «распространенный»

("diffused") для обозначения тех слов, которые проникли во многие языки путем лексической диффузии.

[17] См. Фасмер (Vasmer) 1971: 37 и Шанский и др. 1975: 281.

[18] См. примечание 15.

[19] Глагол *dbáti* не получил убедительной этимологии. Как это ни странно, древнечешские формы с *tb* игнорируются всеми этимологами, кроме А. Брюкнера: Миклошич связывает *dbáti* с **dybati* 'подстерегать, метить' (Miklosich 1886: 53), Голуб и Копечный с **doba* 'время' (Holub, Kopečný 1952: 97), Махэк с латинским *dubitāre* 'сомневаться' (Machek 1957: 81-82), Славский с **bъděti* 'бодрствовать', с перестановкой согласных (Sławski 1952-1956: 142-143). Один Брюкнер постулирует связь с корнем **teb-*, намекая на родство с польским *wścibiać* 'втыкать, всовывать' (Brückner 1927: 86). Однако предложенная Брюкнером этимология вызывает не меньше сомнений, чем остальные этимологии, так как в древнечешском языке нет производных от корня **teb-*. Тем не менее, попытка объяснить формы с *tb* кажется единственно правильной. Кстати, этимология Брюкнера предполагает заимствование из чешского языка в польский, потому что исконная польская форма ожидалась бы с *dźb* вместо *db* (ср. польское *swadźba* < **svatьba*). Глагол *dbáti* будет предметом более подробного обследования в отдельной статье.

[20] Весьма удобные термины Slavia Orthodoxa и Slavia Romana были введены Р. Пиккио (Picchio 1972: 7-13). По аналогии с ними, употребленные выше термины «восточный путь» и «западный путь» распространения славянской лексики могли бы быть заменены терминами «via Orthodoxa» и «via Romana».

[21] Вопросом прямого чешского влияния на украинский язык, доказанного Й. Мацуреком в области языка ранних украинских грамот, мы здесь не занимаемся. Критический разбор работ Й. Мацурека по этой проблеме дается Л. Л. Гумецькой (1967: 92-95); ср. тоже Й. Ф. Андерш 1976: 59-66.

ЛИТЕРАТУРА

Андерш, Й. Ф.
1976 «До питання про чесько-українські мовні зв'язки найдавнішої доби» в кн. *Слово і труд*. Київ, стр. 59-66.

Бархударов, С. Г., ред.
1975- *Словарь русского языка XI-XVII вв.* Москва.

Булаховский, Л. А.
1951 «К истории взаимоотношений славянских языков», *Известия Академии Наук СССР, Отделение литературы и языка*, т. X, стр. 37-49.

Булыка, А. М.
1972 *Даўнія запазычанні беларускай мовы*. Мінск.
1980 *Лексічныя запазычанні ў беларускай мове XIV-XVIII стст.* Мінск.

Гумецька, Л. Л.
1967 «Чи впливала старочеська мова на мову українських грамот XIV-XV ст.?», *Мовознавство* 4, стр. 92-95.
1977-1978 (ред.) *Словник староукраїнської мови XIV-XV ст.* Київ.

Даль, В.
1903-1909 *Толковый словарь живого великорусского языка*, тт. I-III, 3-е изд. под ред. И. А. Бодуэна де Куртенэ. С.-Петербург.

Жураўскі, А. І., ред.
(в печати) *Гістарычны слоўнік беларускай мовы*. Мінск.

Мельников, Е. И.
 1967 «О чешских лексических элементах в русском языке заимствованных через посредство польского и других языков (в XIV-XIX вв.)», *Slavia*, т. XXXVI, стр. 98-114.
Трубачев, О. Н.
 1964 Дополнения к Фасмер, М. (Vasmer, M.), *Этимологический словарь русского языка*, т. 1. Москва.
 1977 (ред.) *Этимологический словарь славянских языков*, вып. 4. Москва.
Фасмер, М. (Vasmer, M.)
 1964-1973 *Этимологический словарь русского языка*, тт. I—IV. Москва.
Худаш, М. Л.
 1960 «Спостереження над лексичними полонізмами в українській актовій мові кінця XVI-початку XVII ст.», *Дослідження і матеріали з української мови*, т. III. Київ, стр. 121-139.
Шанский, Н. М.
 1968 *Этимологический словарь русского языка*, т. I, вып. 3. Москва.
Шанский, Н. М. и др.
 1975 *Краткий этимологический словарь русского языка*, 3-е изд. Москва.
Basaj, M.
 1966 *Bohemizmy w języku pism Marcina Krowickiego*. Wrocław.
Basaj, M.; J. Siatkowski
 1964-1980 «Przegląd wyrazów uważanych w literaturze naukowej za bohemizmy», *Rozprawy Komisji Językowej, Łódzkie Towarzystwo Naukowe*, t. X-XII; *Studia z filologii polskiej i słowiańskiej*, t. VI-XIX.
Brückner, A.
 1906 *Dzieje języka polskiego*. Lwów.
 1915 «Wpływy języków obcych na język polski» в кн. *Język polski i jego historia*, cz. 1, *Encyklopedia Polska*, t. II, dział III, Kraków, str. 100-153.
 1927 *Słownik etymologiczny języka polskiego*. Kraków.
Flajšhans, V.
 1903 *Nejstarší památky jazyka i písemnictví českého*, t. I. Praha.
Havránek, B., red.
 1968– *Staročeský slovník*, Praha.
Holub, J.; F. Kopečný
 1952 *Etymologický slovník jazyka českého*, Praha.
Hüttl-Worth, G.
 1963 *Foreign Words in Russian, 1550-1800*, Berkeley.
Jakobson, R.
 1934-1935 «Slezsko-polská cantilena inhonesta ze začátku XV. století», *Narodopisný Věstník Českoslovanský*, t. XXVII-XXVIII, Praha. str. 56-84.
 1940 «Český podíl na církevněslovanské kultuře» в кн. Mathesius, V., red. *Co daly naše země Evropě a lidstvu*. Praha, str. 9-20.
Kochman, S.
 1967 *Polsko-rosyjskie kontakty językowe w zakresie słownictwa w XVII wieku*. Wrocław.
 1975 *Polsko-rosyjskie stosunki językowe*. Opole.
Leeming, H.
 1968 «Polonisms in a 17th-Century Ruthenian Text», *The Slavonic and East European Review*, v. XLVI, pp. 282-314.
Machek, V.
 1957 *Etymologický slovník jazyka českého a slovenského*. Praha.
Mareš, F. V.
 1962 «České prvky v polabské slovní zásobě», *Slavia*, t. XXXI, pp. 513-523.

Mayenowa, M. R., red.
1966– *Słownik polszczyzny XVI wieku.* Wrocław.

Miklosich, F.
1886 *Etymologisches Wörterbuch der slavischen Sprachen.* Wien.

Picchio, R.
1972 «Questione della lingua e Slavia cirillometodiana» в кн. Picchio, R., red. *Studi sulla questione della lingua presso gli Slavi. Roma,* pp. 7-120.

Reczek, J.
1968 *Bohemizmy leksykalne w języku polskim do końca XV wieku.* Wrocław.

Schenker, A. M.
1978 «The Role of Czech in the Formation of the Polish Literary Language», в кн. Birnbaum, H., ed., *American Contributions to the Eighth International Congress of Slavists,* v. I. Columbus, Ohio, pp. 574-596.

Shevelov, G. Y.
1975 «On Lexical Polonisms in Literary Ukrainian», в кн. Erlich, V. et al., eds. *For Wiktor Weintraub.* The Hague, pp. 449-463.

Skardžius, P.
1931 *Die slavischen Lehnwörter im Altlitauischen.* Kaunas.

Sławski, F.
1952-1956 *Słownik etymologiczny języka polskiego,* t. I. Kraków.
1979 (red.) *Słownik prasłowiański,* t. III. Wrocław.

Urbańczyk, S.
1953– (red.) *Słownik staropolski,* Wrocław.
1970 «Rola Wielkich Moraw i Czech w kulturze Polski średniowiecznej» в кн. *Kraków i Małopolska przez dzieje.* Kraków.
1972 «Der altpolnische Wortschatz und die höhere Kultur», *Anzeiger für slavische Philologie,* B. VI. Wiesbaden, s. 124-137.

Morphological Considerations on the Balto-Slavic Problem

William R. Schmalstieg

1. In papers delivered at the 2nd and 4th All-Union Conferences on Baltic Linguistics I have discussed phonological changes which may have been common to the Baltic and Slavic languages. Following this plan I shall attempt here to explain certain morphological features consistent with the hypothesis that there was a period of Balto-Slavic unity. I say at the outset and I will repeat in my conclusion that this is only one way of interpreting the material and that I do not believe that it 'proves' Balto-Slavic unity. I am merely demonstrating that the morphological features which I have chosen to discuss do not 'disprove' the hypothesis of Balto-Slavic unity. I will discuss first several features of nominal morphology and then pass to a few features of verb morphology.

2. A number of explanations have been suggested for the Old Prussian gen. sg. ending *(deiw-)as* '(of) God.' Stang, 1966, 10, writes that the **o*-stem genitive singular ending derives from **-s(i̯)o*. Schmitt-Brandt, 1971, 226, writes that Old Prussian *deiwas* derives from **dei̯u̯oso* and maintains that we encounter a cognate ending in Proto-Norse *godagas* where the final *-as* derives from **-oso*. Mažiulis, 1970, 94-97, proposed that the **o*-stem genitive singular ending was *-as* < Indo-European **-os* and that the nominative singular and genitive singular, being originally identical, were only later differentiated by means of stress. Etymologically then Old Prussian *deiws* derives from **déiw-as* and *deiwas* derives from **deiw-ás*.

Already in 1876 Leskien, 32-33, suggested that the OP **o*-stem genitive singular ending **-as* had been borrowed from the etymological **ā*-stem endings. Leskien defends his view by pointing out the various parallels between the **o*- and **ā*-stem endings, e.g., nom pl. **o*-stem **deiv-ai*, **ā*-stem *gen-ai*, gen. pl. **o*-stem **deiv-an*, **ā*-stem **gen-an*, acc. pl. **o*-stem *deiv-ans*, **ā*-stem *gen-ans*, etc. Vaillant, 1958, 30, has proposed that the original Old Prussian **o*-stem genitive singular was **-ā* to which the ending *-s* from other stems was added.

Possible support for Leskien's or Vaillant's view would come from several recently publicized Old Prussian fragments. In 1969, 275-276, Sjöberg reported on the existence of an Old Prussian fragment in the 1583 Onomasticum published in Berlin by the alchemist Leonhard Thurneysser. Under the heading *Deves* one finds the proverb: *Deves does dantes, Deves does geitka* which is explained as meaning that since God gives bread he also gives teeth so that one can bite the bread. Actually the meaning would seem to correspond better to the Lithuanian *Diẽvas dãvė dantis, Diẽvas duõs ir dúonos* 'God gave teeth, so he will give bread also.' The form *geitka* is perhaps difficult to understand, but Sjöberg suggests a genitive singular corresponding syntactically with the genitive singular of Lith. *dúonos*.

The recently discovered Basel epigram reads:

<table>
<tr><td>Kayle</td><td>rekyse .</td><td>thoneaw</td><td>labonache</td><td>thewelyse</td></tr>
<tr><td>Health</td><td>sir</td><td>you not</td><td>good</td><td>fellow</td></tr>
<tr><td>Eg.</td><td>koyte.</td><td>poyte</td><td>nykoyte</td><td>pēnega doyte</td></tr>
<tr><td>If</td><td>you want</td><td>to drink</td><td>you don't want</td><td>money to give.</td></tr>
</table>

Although there are still problems with the translation it seems to mean something like 'To your health, sir! You are not a good fellow, if you want to drink and do not want to pay any money.' (McCluskey, 1975, 161.) It seems to me that one could certainly interpret *peneg-a* '(any) money' as representing an *$*o$-stem genitive singular ending also.

In sum then the Old Prussian *$*o$-stem genitive singular ending *-as* is either borrowed from the *ā*-stem nouns or is derived from a contamination of the older etymological ending *-ā* plus *-s*. The ending then does not offer evidence against a proposed Balto-Slavic unity.

3. In Slavic the *$*o$-stem accusative singular ending is *(grad-)ъ* and the *$*ā$-stem accusative singular ending is *(rǫk-)ǫ*. This difference is usually ascribed to the fact that the ending *-ъ* derives from Indo-European *$*-oN$ ($N = n$ or m), cf. Latin *(serv-)um* 'slave,' Sanskrit *(dev-)am* 'god,' Greek *(lóg-)on* 'word,' etc., whereas the ending *-ǫ* derives from *$*-ām$, cf. Latin *(ros-)am* 'rose' Sanskrit *(bāl-)ām* 'maiden,' Greek *(arkh-)ḗn* 'rule,' etc. Baltic, on the other hand, shows exactly the same ending for both the *$*o$- and the *$*ā$-stem accusative singular, cf. Lithuanian *$*o$-stem *(gar̃d-)ą* 'pen, enclosure,' *$*ā$-stem *(rañk-)ą* 'hand,' Latvian *$*o$-stem *(tev-)u* 'father,' *$*ā$-stem *(rok-)u* 'hand,' Old Prussian *$*o$-stem *(tāw-)an* 'father,' *$*ā$-stem *(rānk-)an* 'hand.'

It would be possible, however, to assume that the *$*o$- and the *$*ā$-stem accusative singular endings had merged as *$*-aN$ in Slavic in common with Baltic. I propose that the common ending *$*aN$ passed to proto-Slavic *$*-uN$ in word final position. At a later period the generalized ending *$*-uN$ began to appear in position before words beginning with either a consonant or a vowel.

Thus, proto-Slavic *$*gord-uN$ and *$*ronk-uN$ appeared both in preconsonantal and prevocalic sandhi positions. In prevocalic position *$*uN$ passed to *$*-u$ (loss of final *$*-N$) whereas in preconsonantal position *$*-uN$ passed to *$*-ǫ$.

At the earliest period the endings *-*u* and *-ǫ* were distributed automatically for both the **o-* and the **ā-*stem categories and later they were separated out on a morphological rather than a phonological principle. This is somewhat similar to the way in which the English pronominal adjectives *my* and *mine* were originally automatic variants, but later the etymological automatic difference came to be realized as a semantic or morphological distinction.

A Slavic phonological parallel to the above development is the fate of the morpheme **sun* which developed into *sъn-* when the following morpheme began with a vowel (cf. OCS *sъn-ьmъ* 'gathering, synagogue') but into *sǫ-* when the following morpheme began with a consonant (cf. OCS *sǫ-sědъ* 'neighbor'). The later development into the preposition *sъ* is well known and needs no further comment.

4. It is sometimes averred that the differing outcomes of the definite adjective in Baltic and Slavic can be used as an argument against Balto-Slavic unity (Senn, 1966, 148). Thus proto-Slavic **bosŭ-jĭ* 'the barefooted one' does not correspond exactly with Lithuanian *basàs-is* < *basas + jis*. According to Senn: "If this feature were old, one would expect in Slavic **bososĭ*, or at least **bosŭšĭ* (< **bosos + jis*)." I would object, however, that the constant renewal of the definite adjective formation is a characteristic of the Baltic and Slavic languages. An etymological definite adjective form equivalent to the Lith. nom. sg. masc. *miel-às-is* 'dear, beloved' (< **meil-as-is*) would have developed into Slavic **mīl-os-ī*, which, renewed again with the personal pronoun **jī*, would have been **mīl-os-jī*. This latter form would have become Slavic **mil-oš-ь* and may be the origin of the Serbian name *Miloš*. The Slavic suffix -*oš*- could well owe its origin to a petrified form of the definite adjective, cf., e.g., Polish *dług-osz* 'joking name for an excessively tall person,' *biał-osz* 'white horse' derived from *długi* 'long, tall' and *biały* 'white' respectively (See Torbiörnsson, 1924, 278-279).

The very productivity of the procedure for the formation of the definite adjective is indicated by the fact that within Lithuanian in addition to the definite form of the standard language *(balt-)às-is* 'the white one' we also encounter dialectal *baltàjis* and *baltùjis*. I would quote also the Latvian *(pirm-)a-is* 'the first' and Old Prussian *pirmoys* which I would phonemicize as /pirmais/ thereby bringing the form into alignment with the Latvian form sound for sound. (The orthographic -*o*- is merely the German rendering of /a/ in position after a labial consonant, in this case /m/).

In fact, then, Old Prussian and Latvian go together in forming the *o*-stem definite adjective from the stem vowel -*a*- plus the personal pronoun **is*; in addition Lithuanian dialects show the addition of the personal pronoun *jis* 'he' to the stem vowel of the adjective.

It appears then, that the standard Lithuanian definite form *(balt-)às-is* is the exception and could be viewed as an innovation. In fact, of course, the dialect ending *(balt-)ù-jis* would correspond sound for sound with Slavic *(bĕl-)ъ-jь*.

Thus, the argument that the details of the method of formation of the definite adjective do not agree in Baltic and Slavic is without substance in the determination of Balto-Slavic unity.

5. Beginning with the third person present which is, of course, not distinguished for number in Baltic, the major difference between the Baltic and Slavic etymological thematic verbs is that Baltic has generalized the vocalism -*a* (< Indo-European **o*) and Slavic has generalized the vocalism -*e*-. Thus we encounter Lith. 3rd pres. *nēš-a* = Slavic 3rd sg. pres. *nes-e-t-*. The absence of a Baltic 3rd sg. primary ending *-ti* is surprising, particularly in view of its retention in such athematic forms as Lith. *ĕs-ti* 'there is, there are.' The unification of the thematic vowel in both Baltic and Slavic is due to the influence of the etymological **je/o*-stem verbs, although the details of the development differ in the two language families.

In Slavic, of course, the phonemic sequences */je/ and */jo/ merged completely so that a 3rd sg. **pis-je-t-* would pass to *piš-et-* 'writes', whereas a 1st pl. **pis-jo-m-* would pass to *piš-em-*. The unification of the thematic vowel in the **je/o*-stem verbs led to the unification in the **e/o*-stem verbs.

In Baltic, on the other hand, the etymological sequence */Cje/ (C = any consonant) merged with */Ce/ erasing the possibility of a phonological distinction between the **je/o*- and the **e/o*-verbs in the 3rd person. Thus **peiš-je* would have passed to **peiš-e* allowing no morphological distinction from **neš-e*. The distinction could have been maintained in, e.g., the first person plural where **peiš-ja-m-* is clearly distinct from **neš-am-*. In order to maintain the distinction between the **je/o*- and **e/o*-stem verbs the thematic vowel -*a(-)* was introduced in the Baltic third person and second person plural.

Thus the same phonological phenomenon, i.e., the existence of the **je/o*-stem verbs led to the unification of the thematic vowel in Baltic and in Slavic, although in a different way in each language family.

6. The Baltic and Slavic 2nd singular endings do not correspond. In fact, of course, there is even a discrepancy between East and West Baltic and there exist many possible explanations of its origin. At first glance one would think that the full form of the ending is retained in such a Lithuanian reflexive present as *neš-íe-si* 'you (sg.) bring for yourself.' Most probably the apparent full form of the ending -*íe-*, which only exists in 'protected' position (i.e., before some enclitic such as the reflexive particle) had its origin in such athematic verbs as *es-i* 'you (sg.) are' which derives from an earlier **es-si*. In a

paradigm such as *es-mi, es-i, es-ti* the element *-i* came to be felt as the 2nd singular ending, and was transferred to the thematic class. The relationship between the 1st sg. ending *-u* to the reflexive counterpart *-uo-si* influenced the 2nd sg. ending *-i* and led to the creation of the reflexive *-ie-si*. In other words *-u:uo-si :: -i:-ie-si*.

Most probably the original Baltic thematic 2nd (singular) present is represented by Old Prussian *giwassi*, also written as *gīwasi* 'you (sg.) live' undoubtedly to be phonemicized /gīvasi/. The morphological cuts are as follows: root *gīv-*, thematic vowel *-a-* and 2nd (singular) ending *-si*. One notes here the Slavic thematic type, e.g., Old Church Slavic 2nd sg. present *živ-e-ši* 'you (sg.) live.' The difference between the Baltic and Slavic thematic vowels has been explained above. The contrast between Slavic *-š-* and Baltic *-s-* is clearly the result of the Slavic generalization of the *-š-* which developed naturally in the etymological *ī-stem verbs, viz. *pros-ī-s- > *pros-ī-x > *pros-ī-š- (i, ī, ei?). Although all of the modern Slavic languages seem to show the reflex of 2nd singular present ending *-šь, Old Church Slavic has *-ši*, which is difficult to explain. This OCS ending could possibly be explained as deriving from a contamination of *-š-* plus *-ei*, but there is some question, as mentioned above, as to whether there ever was a Baltic ending *-ei*.

Brugmann, 1904, 590, has suggested that the endings of Slavic 2nd sg. pres. *je-si* 'you (sg.) are,' *da-si* 'you give' derived from the 2nd singular middle ending *-sai* and that this final *-i* was transferred to the ending *-šь* giving *-ši*. Aitzetmüller, 1978, 176, objects that Slavic could not originally have had an ending *-sai* because this would have passed to *sī* rather than *-šī*. If one assumes with Brugmann that the 2nd singular middle ending is indeed *-sī*, and that it is from forms like *je-si* and *da-si* that the ending *-i* is transferred to the *-šь* ending, Aitzetmüller's objection is no longer valid. Suffice it to say, however, that the Slavic ending *-ši* does indeed offer a problem and that there is no exact cognate in any other Indo-European language.

7. It is commonly assumed that Greek and Sanskrit maintain the etymological Indo-European distribution of the first singular primary ending *-ō (Sanskrit present *bhár-ā-mi*, Greek *phér-ō* 'I carry'), secondary ending *-om (Sanskrit imperfect *ábhar-am*, Greek *épher-on* 'I carried'). Baltic seems to show only the result of the Indo-European primary ending *-ō, cf. Lith. 1st sg. pres. reflexive *neš-úo-si* 'I bring for myself.' The ending *-u* is also encountered in the preterit, cf. Lith. 1st sg. *nešia-ū* 'I carried' where it is said to have been transferred from the present tense.

The accepted view is that the Slavic 1st sg. pres. ending *-ǫ* derives from *-ām, whereas the 1st sg. secondary ending *-ъ* derives from *-om. I propose, however, that the Slavic endings *-ǫ* and *-ъ* both derive from the secondary ending *-om, the phonological development being similar to that of the *ā- and *o-stem accusative singular endings -ǫ and -ъ as described above. The very archaic paradigm of Latin sum (< *e-sóm) provides support for the etymological existence of an *-om in the present tense.

Following Szemerényi (1970: 308) I see the ending *-ō arising in Indo-European from an earlier *-om. Although the existence of the present tense ending *-om could be a Slavic archaism (cf. Latin sum), there exists the possibility that it could have been an analogical substitution from non-present forms. Thus both Baltic and Slavic may originally have had the same distribution of the first person singular endings, viz. *-ō in the present and *-om in the non-present.

8. One might suggest that the lack in Baltic of a thematic aorist form such as that encountered in the Slavic 3rd sg. ved-e 'led,' nes-e 'carried,' vez-e 'transported' should be considered an important difference militating against the assumption of Balto-Slavic unity.

I propose that the preterit of such verbs as Lithuanian vèsti 'to lead' reflects an old (1st sg.) *vedam < *vedom, (2nd sg.) vedes, (3rd) vede(t). With the unification of the thematic vowel the *vedam was replaced by *vedem. There existed beside the conjugation *vedem, *vedes, *vede(t) a conjugation *pirkam (standing for underlying *pirkām, since long diphthongs were phonologically impossible), *pirkās, *pirkā(t). In Common East Baltic the primary endings (1st sg.) -u, (2nd sg.) -i, replaced the secondary endings, giving *vedau (for underlying *vedeu), vedeĩ and pirkaũ, pirkaĩ. The lengthening of the final vowel of *vede(t) follows the proportion: pirkaũ, pirkaĩ are to *pirkā as *vedeu, vedeĩ are to x and x = *vedē.

Thus the cognate Lithuanian 3rd person preterit forms vẽd-ė, nẽš-ė and vẽž-ė may indeed reflect the Indo-European thematic aorist.

For Old Prussian the question concerns the length of the preterit formant *-ē, i.e. is it long as in Lith. (vẽd-)ė? Old Prussian forms with their apparent Lithuanian cognates are given below:

Old Prussian			Lithuanian	
/per-traukē/	pertraūki	'closed up'	tráukė	'dragged, drew'
/dŕáudē/	driāudai	'forbade'	draũdė	'forbade'
/is-migē/	ismigē	'fell asleep'	užmìgo	'fell asleep'
/kūrē/	kūra	'created'	kũrė	'established'
/vedē-din/	weddēdin	'brought her'	vẽdė	'led'
/ēmēt{a}s/	jmmitz, ymmeyts, ymmeits, ymmits		ẽmė	'took'

Although I have phonemicized all of the Old Prussian words as though the preterit ended in -$\bar{e}$, I consider it quite reasonable to question this assumption. A short vowel -*e* would be just as possible, in which case the third person would reflect an old thematic aorist form here. Certain comparisons could be made with Slavic if this is the case. For example, Old Prussian *is-mig-ē* 'fell asleep' is undoubtedly cognate with Old Russian *mьgnuti* 'to blink,' a verb which belongs etymologically to the Slavic -*nǫti* class. In Slavic, verbs of this class usually have the thematic aorist. On the basis of a comparison with the Slavic example a case could be made for assuming that Old Prussian *ismigē* should be phonemicized as /is-mig-e/ with a short final vowel, namely the thematic vowel of the old thematic aorist.

Similarly, as mentioned previously, the Old Church Slavic aorist *vede* 'led' could be considered exactly cognate with an assumed Old Prussian /vede/, another etymological thematic aorist. Whether the -$\bar{e}$ of *weddēdin* denotes a long vowel or not is particularly questionable in view of the fact that the cognate third person present *perweddā* 'lead' should probably be phonemicized as /per-veda/ with a short final vowel, cf. Lith. *vēda* 'leads.'

Whether Old Prussian had a preterit in -$\bar{e}$ or not remains an open question. If it did, then this -$\bar{e}$ reflects a Common Baltic -$\bar{e}$, a preterit formation which is some kind of transformation of the thematic aorist in -*e*.

Of the seven morphological features discussed here none can be considered to disprove the hypothesis of Balto-Slavic unity. The discussion merely shows the possible direction in which various morphological changes may have gone.

The Pennsylvania State University

REFERENCES

Aitzetmüller, R.
   1978 *Altbulgarische Grammatik als Einführung in die slavische Sprachwissenschaft.* Freiburg i. Br.
Brugmann, Karl
   1904 *Kurze vergleichende Grammatik der indogermanischen Sprachen.* Strassburg.
Leskien, A.
   1876 *Die Declination im Slavisch-litauischen und Germanischen.* Leipzig.
Mažiulis, Vytautas
   1970 *Baltų ir kitų indoeuropiečių kalbų santykiai: Deklinacija.* Vilnius.
McCluskey, Stephen C., William R. Schmalstieg and Valdis Zeps
   1975 "The Basel epigram: a new minor text in Old Prussian," *General Linguistics* 15, 159-165.
Schmitt-Brandt, Robert
   1971 "Die Herausbildung der slavischen Sprachgemeinschaft," *Donum Indogermanicum,* ed. by Robert Schmitt-Brandt. Heidelberg, 224-243.

Senn, A.
1966 "The relationships of Baltic and Slavic," *Ancient Indo-European dialects*, ed. by Henrik Birnbaum and Jaan Puhvel. Berkeley and Los Angeles, 139-151.
Sjöberg, A.
1969 "Ob odnoj drevneprusskoj poslovice," *Scando-Slavica* 15, 275-276.
Stang, Christian S.
1966 *Vergleichende Grammatik der baltischen Sprachen.* Oslo-Bergen-Tromsö.
Szemerényi, Oswald
1970 *Einführung in die vergleichende Sprachwissenschaft.* Darmstadt.
Torbiörnsson, T.
1924 "Die bestimmten Adjektivformen der slavischen Sprachen," *Zeitschrift für slavische Philologie* 1, 267-279.
Vaillant, André
1958 *Grammaire comparée des langues slaves.* II, Part 1. Lyon and Paris.

The Collective and Counted Plurals of the Slavic Nouns

Edward Stankiewicz

1. The singular/plural opposition, which is shared by all Slavic languages, offers a clear case of the asymmetry which marks the relation of the marked and unmarked members of grammatical oppositions. The singular, which is semantically unmarked in that it does not specify the meaning of quantity, exhibits the maximal distinctions of case and gender, which are in one way or another neutralized in the plural. The imbalance between the singular and plural is only partially offset by grammatical, lexical or emotive distinctions which find their expression in the plural, but cannot be formally conveyed by the singular. Thus, for example, the Russian acc. plural carries a distinction between the animate and inanimate nouns of any gender, whereas the acc. singular limits this distinction to nouns of masculine gender; the Polish nom. plural discriminates between the neutral and pejorative meaning of masculine personal (virile) nouns (e.g., *rzeźnicy, bandyci, Żydzi* vs. *rzeźniki, bandyty, Żydy*) which the singular is able to convey only by means of derivational devices or by circumlocution.[1]

The grammatical asymmetry between the singular and plural cuts much deeper, however, complicating the nature of the stated imbalance. A closer analysis of the Slavic noun shows that the plural is not a simple, monolithic type, but one which breaks down into several quantitative categories. The relation between the singular and the plural is thus not merely one of a complete vs. underdifferentiated, "defective" set, but one of complementarity in which the singular allows maximal scope for the categories of gender and case, while the plural provides maximal range for distinctions of quantity. The capacity of the plural to split into several subcategories is implicit in the very nature of linguistic plurality which, unlike the idealized, mathematical concept of number, presents a variety of specific aspects which are largely connected with qualitative meanings.

The diverse categories of the plural appear in the Slavic languages in a great variety of forms whose occurrence is delimited by the meaning of the given plurality and the grammatical categories with which they occur. All these forms can be viewed, however, as the variant manifestations of two quantitative oppositions which are utilized to a greater or lesser extent in all Slavic languages. These oppositions involve:

(1) an indefinite quantity (to be called the *simple plural*) which is opposed to a finite or definite quantity whose number is specified by a numerical or

adverbial quantifier (the so-called *counted plural*), and

(2) an indefinite quantity which implies a *sum* of constituents and which is opposed to quantity viewed as an undifferentiated or cohesive *whole*, or, in Cassierer's terms a quantity whose "parts are equivalents of the whole," (the so-called *collective plural*).[2]

It should be clear that the first term of the two oppositions constitutes the semantically unspecified, unmarked category of quantity inasmuch as the simple plural can contextually refer to a finite quantity (such as "the planets," "the Gospels" or "the cardinal sins"), or to an integral whole (such as "the scissors," "the breeches," "the tongs").

The use of a quantifier converts any indefinite plurality into a counted plural. But what is peculiar about the Slavic languages is that they express the counted plurality not only by means of a numerical quantifier but also by a distinctive form of the noun and, less frequently, by a special form of its syntactic modifiers, and it is by virtue of its distinctive form that we treat the counted plural as a separate grammatical category.

The collective plural, which marks a whole, is not commonly subject to numerical quantification, and the infrequent use of this form with a numeral has given rise to the view that this is one of its outstanding characteristics.[3] This view is not accurate. Although the collective plural does not combine with cardinal numerals, it can be easily quantified by any one of the collective numerals, which are themselves derivatives from the cardinal numerals. The collective numerals perform a double function in the Slavic languages: they quantify nouns with an inherent collective meaning (e.g., Polish *oboje państwo (przyszli)*; Russ. *tróe detéj, četvero rebját*; S-Cr. *tròje dècē, četvero čèljadi*), and they serve to establish an opposition between the non-collective meaning of a noun (expressed through the simple or counted plural) and collective plurality (expressed through a collective numeral and the gen. plural of the noun); e.g., Russ. *tri soldáta, četýre sýna, pjat' synovéj* vs. *tróe soldát, četvero, pjátero synovéj*; S-Cr. *dvâ jàgānjca, trî Sȑbina* vs. *dvòje jàganjācā, tròjica Sȑbā*). The collective plural has a limited range: it is mostly used with lower numbers and carries a pronounced popular nuance. It is distinctively used with personal or animate masc. noun (cf. the foregoing examples), and its persistent presence in the Slavic languages derives primarily from the fact that it quantifies nouns with an inherent collective meaning.

The collective counted plural rounds out the picture of the Slavic plurals which yields a four-fold scheme in which the counted and collective (marked) plurals are opposed to the simple (unmarked) plural by a single semantic feature, whereas the counted collective plural is doubly marked, for it combines the concept of counted plurality with that of plurality as a cohesive whole.

The following table should make more transparent the use of the four types of plurals in various contemporary Slavic languages. (The forms separated by a virgule represent variants.)

		Plural	Counted Plural
	Russ.	studénty, sëstry; loskutý, klokí, (dial.) telënki	(tri) studénta, sestrý
	Bulg.	vojníci, drúmovi, túrci, žení	(pet) vojníci/vojníka, drúma
	Maced.	vojnici, snopovi, patovi, planini	(pet) vojnika, snopa
	S-Cr.	sȉnovi, pòlja, jȁgānjci, pȉlići	(dvȃ) sȋna, pȍlja, jȁgānjca/jȁgnjeta, pȉlića/pȉleta
	Polish	chłopcy, wujowie, panowie	—
COLLECTIVE PLURAL	Russ.	loskút'ja, klóč'ja; (dial.) teljáta	pjátero studéntov, professoróv
	Bulg.	drúmišta, turčá, ženurjá	dváma, petína vojníci, túrci
	Maced.	patišta, snopje, planinje	dvajca, petimata vojnici, trgovci
	S-Cr.	pȉlād, jȁgnjād	dvȍje jȁgnjādi, pȉlādi; dvòjica stùdenātā
	Polish	(kochani) wujostwo, państwo	trzech chłopców (poszło); oboje wujostwo

It will be apparent from the above table that the simple plural is the most productive category of the noun, whereas the marked plurals are in all Slavic languages subject to various formal and semantic restrictions. Thus some Slavic languages utilize only one or the other of the marked categories (e.g., the counted or the collective plural), while other Slavic languages reduce to a minimum the use of all the marked categories (e.g., Polish lacks a counted plural and makes limited use of the collective and counted collective plural). The East Slavic languages and Slovene (at least their literary varieties) have few collective plurals, whereas the Southeast Slavic languages have a full complement of the marked forms. It is noteworthy that these forms are optimally represented in those languages (i.e., Macedonian and Bulgarian) which have lost in the plural the categories of gender and case.

2. The fact that the above listed categories of the plural are unevenly distributed in the Slavic world accounts, no doubt, for some misconceptions concerning their usage and function. Thus it has been argued by some Russian scholars that "the category of collectivity excludes the notion of plurality," while some Macedonian scholars are inclined to believe that where Macedonian has recourse to the collective plural other Slavic languages resort to the collective singular.[4]

The collective singular and the collective plural do, indeed, share a number of traits. The collective plurals of Serbo-Croatian are inflected as singular nouns (e.g., S-Cr. *jägnjād, vlastèla, gospòda*), while some of the Russian collective plurals exhibit the same derivational features as the collective singulars (e.g., *pén'ja, úgol'ja, korén'ja, kamén'ja, zúb'ja* and (coll. sing.) *pén'e/ pen'ë, úgol'e;* (dial. Russ.) *korén'e, kamén'e, zub'ë*). The two types of collectives are, nevertheless, distinct: the collective plural designates wholes which imply discrete and countable components, whereas the collective singular is non-committal as to the make-up of the wholes; in its most common, primary function it emphasizes rather the non-discrete, continuous nature of its elements. The collective singular is consequently most commonly used with nouns which lack or suppress the difference between the whole and the parts (plants, bushes, masses of objects; such as Russ. *dubnják, bereznják, dub'ë, komar'ë*), whereas the collective plural is eminently suited for the expression of personal and animate nouns which designate kinship, ethnic origin, social status and the progeny of animals and man. It is within such nouns that the simple and collective plurals find their clearest and widest utilization, e.g., Bulg. *dáskali, cígani, gráždani, Sə́rbi, Túrci, magáreta* vs. *daskaljá, ciganjá, graždanjá, Sərboljá, magarjá;* S-Cr. *jägānjci, tȅoci, jȁrići, Tûrci;* (dial.) *brȁti, svȁti* vs. *jägnjād, tȅlād, jȁrād, Tȗrād, brȁća,* (dial.) *svȁća;* dial. Slov. *teleta, ščeneta, pišceta* vs. *teliči, ščenci, piščenci;* dial. Russ. *rebënki, žerebënki, volčónki, telënki* vs. *rebjáta, žerebjáta, volčenjáta, teljáta.*[5]

A comparison of the Serbo-Croatian phrases (coll. singular) *gospoda se nije mešala s narodom* 'the gentry did not mingle with the people' and (collective plural) *gospoda se jesu zavadila* 'the lords had a falling out' shows that the distinction between the collective singular and the collective plural is also relevant for the last group of personal nouns.

It is interesting to note that for many personal and animate nouns it is the collective rather than the simple plural that constitutes their primary, basic form. The complex (plural and totalizing) meaning which adheres to the collective plural makes it possible for such nouns to dispense with the use of the simple plural, or to derive it from a semantically marked *singulative* form. Thus some Serbo-Croatian dialects employ only the collective plural (e.g., *djèca, brȁća, vlastèla (su išla), tȅlād, pȉlād, jȁrād (su pȁsla)*), whereas other Serbo-Croatian dialects match it with a corresponding plural which betrays its singulative (mostly diminutive) origin (e.g., *tȅoci, pȉlići, jȁrići*). A similar relation obtained in Old Russian in masc. nouns which designated social or territorial entitites: their primary plurals were collective forms marked by the suffixes *-ane, -are, -iči,* whereas their simple and "countable" plurals were based on singulatives formed with the suffix *-in* (e.g., *krestjanin, bojarin, tatarin, volxovitin:* pl. *krestjaniny, bojariny, tatariny, volxovitiny.*[6])

The grammatical opposition between the simple and collective plurals is, like many such oppositions, accompanied by secondary semantic and stylistic connotations. Thus, the Bulgarian collective plurals *gərčoljá, ženurjá, ciganjá, drúmišta, kə́tišta* carry pronounced pejorative overtones, while the Serbo-Croatian and Russian simple plurals *jägānjci, p̀ilići*; *volčónki, porosënki* convey a marked diminutive nuance. Of greater importance, however, is the tendency of the two plural forms to acquire secondary lexical meanings which may in the course of time supersede the grammatical opposition. Such a transformation of the semantic functions affected to a large extent the East Slavic literary languages where the collective plurals formed with the suffix -#j- became lexically or stylistically distinct from the simple plurals, or yielded formally differentiated variants of one single category of the plural (cf. the modern lexical difference between Russian *zúby, kóly, vólosy, listý* and *zúbja, kól'ja, volós'ja,* and the simple plurals *krýl'ja, kolós'ja, derév'ja, muž'já, druz'já*).

As a result of such historical change the modern Slavic literary languages present two more or less distinct typological areas: a South Slavic area (S-Cr., Maced. and Bulg.) which has largely preserved the opposition between a simple and collective plural, and an East and West Slavic area which has eliminated the opposition, or confined it to a small group of nominal stems. It is interesting to note that a similar bifurcation has taken place in the Romance languages. Thus, some of them make wide use of the simple/collective plural opposition (e.g., Rhaeto-Romance *ogns/ogna, pums/puma, meils/meila*; Ital. *muri/mura, frutti/frutta, ossi/ossa, mobili/mobilia*), whereas other Romance languages (e.g., modern French) have lost it, or converted it into a single plural with lexically or stylistically differentiated forms.[7]

3. Unlike the collective plurals, which are unevenly distributed in the Slavic world, the counted plurals are well represented in most Slavic languages, and it is to them that I shall devote the rest of this paper. In contrast to the collective plurals, the counted plurals can be traced back to a single source, the Common Slavic dual. In spite of their common origin the contemporary Slavic counted plurals present three distinct and largely incompatible types:

1. A *dual* which is used with or without the numeral "two";
2. a *paucal* which occurs with the numerals "two," "three" and "four" and
3. A *general counted plural* which is used with any numeral but "one." The last type is best known from Bulgarian and Macedonian, and I shall occasionally use the Bulgarian term *brojna forma* to set it apart from the other types.

The distribution of the three types is as follows: type (1) occurs in Upper and Lower Lusatian, Kashubian (especially Slovincian) and Slovene; type (2) in East Slavic and in Serbo-Croatian; type (3) in Macedonian, Bulgarian and in the Southeastern Serbian dialects. Literary Ukrainian combines types (2) and

(3) and renders their distinction by means of different morphological forms (see below). The Čakavian dialect of Novi combines the use of the dual with a special form of the paucal after the numerals "three" and "four."

Transitional forms of the three types appear in a number of Slavic areas. Thus, some Eastern Serbian dialects employ alternatively the paucal and the *brojna forma*, whereas some Slovenian and Croatian dialects relinquish the dual and the paucal forms in favor of the simple plural. The last form tends to replace the paucal also in colloquial Ukrainian and eliminates it in a number of East Slavic dialects.[8]

The counted plural is a poorly understood grammatical form. In spite of its wide occurrence and vitality it has been described as an irregular, residual or superfluous phenomenon. A historical bias has often identified it with the dual, while in East Slavic grammars it is generally treated as a genitive singular even though the use of this "genitive" with the gen. plural of adjectives (as in *dva xoróšix studénta, četýre málen'kix selá, tri vysókix gorý*) produces a striking syntactic discrepancy. The lack of syntactic agreement between the counted substantive and the adjective has prompted some Russian linguists to characterize it as an "anomaly" which finds "no justification in the system of cases, nor in the meaning of the nouns."[9] The paucal forms of Ukrainian and Byelorussian are usually accorded a similar treatment by being described as a "nom. plural with a singular stress," or as forms which have historically overlapped with the plural.[10] An outstanding exception to this common practice are the perspicacious remarks of the Russian linguist Roman Brandt, who years ago recognized the autonomous status of the Russian paucals (which he called *malinnye formy*).[11]

One must also treat with some skepticism the view that the counted plurals constitute a "superfluous" category inasmuch as their meaning could presumably equally well be expressed by the simple plural.[12] This view, which would press language into a logical mold, underestimates the role of linguistic redundancy and the specific, marked meanings of the counted plurals; moreover, it ignores the fact that the use of one or another grammatical category entails concomitant reference to other, oftentimes complementary grammatical meanings. Thus, for example, the duals of Lusatian and Slovincian distinguish between the masc. and non-masc. gender whereas their plurals differentiate a virile and a non-virile gender; the Bulgarian *brojna forma*, which is used with non-personal masc. nouns, introduces indirectly a gender distinction which does not arise in the Bulgarian plural; the Slovenian plural renders the difference between a masc., fem. and neut., while the dual lumps together the fem. and the neut. The various constraints which limit the expression of concomitant grammatical meanings follow a systematic and hierarchical order and define the structure of a language no less than the presence or absence of a given grammatical category. The order of these constraints finds a cogent illustration in the forms and development of the Slavic counted plurals.

The counted plurals suppress most of the case distinctions which figure in the singular and in the simple plural. In this they resemble most closely the numerals, which tend to reduce to a minimum the number of cases. Among the counted plurals it is only the dual which admits as many as three cases in Lower Lusatian and Slovincian (the nom.-acc., gen. and dat.-instr.-loc.) and two cases in Upper Lusatian (nom.-acc. and dat.-instr.-loc.) and Slovene (nom.-acc. and dat.-instr.). The paucal is incompatible with the oblique cases, while the *brojna forma* lacks, of course, any distinction of case. The East Slavic languages reduce the use of the paucal also in the acc. of personal or animate nouns, where it may vary with or be replaced by the simple plural; e.g., Ukr. *dvox bratív, žinók* or *dva bráty, dvi žinký*; BR. *dvux asób, sjascër* or *dzve asóby*, Russ. *dvux studéntov, dévušek, koróv* but colloquial Russ. *dve kózy, koróvy*).

Similar constraints govern the combination of the counted plurals with particular genders. These involve either the neutralization and rearrangement of the gender distinctions carried by the simple plural or the elimination of the counted plural from the marked fem. and neut. genders.

Slovene, which differentiates three genders in the nom. pl. and two in the acc. pl., presents a masculine/non-masculine distinction in the nom-acc. dual (e.g., *dvâ mláda otróka, možâ* vs. *dvệ mládi žéni, detẹ́ti*). The masc./non-masc. distinction is found in the nom. dual of Upper and Lower Lusatian, both of which carry a virile/non-virile opposition in the acc. dual and plural. Serbo-Croatian distinguishes in the nom. plural three genders, but relinquishes these distinctions in the paucal.

The counted plurals, which are preserved in stems of any gender in the East Slavic languages, narrow their distribution in the South Slavic languages.

Serbo-Croatian maintains the paucal in nouns of masc. and neut. gender, but replaces it with the plural in nouns of fem. gender (e.g., *svà trî dòbra brȁta, tèleta, mjȅsta* vs. [nom. pl.] *svȅ trî dòbre žène, sèstre, glâve*). The overt distinction between the masc.-neut. and fem. genders is here merely a corollary of the paucal/plural opposition. A similar tendency to restrict the use of the dual or paucal is observed in the fem. stems of Slovene and Russian: the former tends to use the plural in fem. nouns with a mobile stress (*dvệ lepệ žẹnệ, sestrệ, rokệ, gubệ*) and the latter in prepositional phrases with a quantifier (e.g., *na vse četýre stórony, za óbe ščëki*).

The Southeast Slavic languages confine the use of the *brojna forma* mostly to nouns of masc. gender. Isolated examples of feminine counted forms are found in the Bulgarian dialects (*šest nédeli/nédel, gódin, stótin, dúši/dúš, séstri* vs. pl. *nedéli, godíni, stotíni, duší, sestrí*),[13] while the spoken literary language and some dialects employ the counted plural with masc. nouns of personal and non-personal gender (e.g., *pet stóla, léva, oréla, studénta, vojníka*); the Bulg. literary norm limits it further to masc. non-personal nouns, and Macedonian excludes it from masc. polysyllabic nouns and from nouns preceded by an adjective (e.g., *tri mladi junaci, dva stari konji*).

The ability of nouns to express the counted plural varies, in addition, according to declension. The principal carriers of the counted forms are nouns belonging to the productive *-a* and *-o* declensions, whereas nouns of the *-i* and the consonantal declensions display them in isolated cases (e.g., Ukr. *dvi máteri, skáterti* vs. pl. *materí, skaterí*; BR. *try načý* vs. pl. *nóčy*; Slov. (Kras) *dvệ nôči, rêči, vêsi* (<*nočʹi, rečʹi, vəsʹi*). The modern "dual" endings of the *-a* and *-o* stems differ, however, from those of the original dual as a result of the pressure exerted upon them by the endings of the plural.

This pressure has, in most Slavic languages, led to a loss of the original dual endings in the *-a* stems and in the neuters. The old dual endings *-ě/-i* are best preserved in the languages which have inherited the dual and in the paucals of some East Slavic dialects (including the older norm of literary Ukrainian); e.g., Slov. *dvệ vretẹ́ni, ókni, pọ̑li; žẹ́ni, gọ́ri*; L. Lusat. *rybʹe, dušy, slowe, mori*; Ukr. *try rucí, nozí, jábluci, vidrí*; dial. BR. *dzve halavé, starané, pisʹmé, duplé*; dial. Russ. *brylé, skulé, šulé, brudé, mudé/múdi*. The dual endings of the *-a* stems have in the East Slavic languages and Serbo-Croatian ceded place to the nom.-acc. endings of the plural (notice that the paucals of the Serbo-Croatian *-a* stems have, as a consequence, become identified with the plural). A similar process took place in the neuters, which have adopted the endings of the plural and have, as a consequence, become identified with the plural). A similar process took place in the neuters, which have adopted the endings of the plural and have, as a result, fallen together with the masc. "dual" (as in Serbo-Croatian and East Slavic), or which lost completely the counted plural (as in Southeast Slavic).

The ending which remained most immune to the influence of the plural was the dual ending *-a* of the masculine stems, which was replaced by the nom.-acc. plural ending in Ukranian and Byelorussian, but which is hitherto extant in South Slavic and in Russian. The presence of a homophonous ending *-a* in the nom.(-acc.) plural of Russian nouns has, nevertheless, reduced its distinctive force. This loss was in Russian, as well as in the other East Slavic languages, amply compensated by alternations of stress, which are here the principal carriers of the paucal/plural opposition. These alternations are also productive in the East Slavic neuter stems, whereas they are of peripheral importance for the South Slavic neuters (but cf. S-Cr. *trî põlja, sèla, plëmena, dùgmeta* vs. nom.-acc. pl. *pòlja, sèla, plemèna, dugmèta*).

As a result of these changes, the modern Slavic languages differ not only in the types and use of the counted/non-counted plural opposition, but also in the means by which they express it: the East Slavic languages express it primarily or solely by means of stress, whereas the South Slavic languages which have preserved the original endings of the masc. dual and the nom. plural (-*a* vs. -*i*, -*ovi*/-*ove*) render it by means of different endings.

4. The paucal/plural opposition was in the East Slavic languages greatly enhanced by the formation of a new type of stress alternation which plays but a marginal role in South Slavic, i.e., the alternation of stress from the endings of the singular and counted plural to the last syllable of the stem in the plural. Consequently, all three East Slavic languages exhibit a two-fold stress alternation: one from the singular and paucal to the endings of the plural (the $\alpha \sim \beta$ alternation) and another from the endings of the singular and paucal to the stem of the plural (the $\beta \sim \alpha_1$ alternation).

It is generally maintained that the two types of alternations serve to sharpen the opposition between the singular and the plural. What is less frequently emphasized is the distinctive function which they fulfill in opposing the otherwise homonymous (or nearly homonymous) forms of the counted and simple plurals. The role of the stress in opposing these forms can be seen from the following examples: Russ. *(tri) dóma, bérega, kólokola; okná, selá, veretená; kozý, storoný, sestrý* vs. (pl.) *domá, beregá, kolokolá; ókna, sëla, veretëna; kózy, stórony, sëstry*; Ukr. *(try) sýny, čolovíky, hóluby; bolóta, sidlá, pys'má; sosný, ruký, dočký* vs. (pl.) *syný, čoloviký, holubý; bolóta, sídla, pýs'ma*; BR. *(dva) zubý, razý; krylý, akný, vjaslý; baradý, sjastrý, harý* vs. (pl.) *zúby, rázy; krýly, vókny, vësly; baródy, sëstry, hóry*.

The historical origin of the above alternations is far less transparent than their synchronic function and has been the source of diverse and hitherto inconclusive interpretations. Specifically they concern the origin of the unaccented nom.(-acc.) ending -*a* of the dual and the accented nom.(-acc.) plural ending -*á* of Russian masc. stems with an initial (historically circumflex) stress in their base form. According to a well-established view, the stress of the modern "dual" is an innovation, whereas the original stress of the dual is to be seen in such traces of the dual as Russ. *(dva) rjadá, razá, časá, šagá* and in the Bulgarian and Russian plurals such as *kraká, rogá; beregá, boká, rogá*. It is the latter forms in -*á* which were presumably responsible for the generalization of this ending in the nom.(-acc.) plural of a large number of Russian masc. stems with an underlying initial stress, such as *cvetá, snegá, glazá, pojasá, gorodá, večerá, kolokolá*. The above view has never fully explained why the marked form of the dual should have influenced the plural, nor why the stress had shifted from the ending to the stem in the dual.

Both problems have invited alternative solutions. The nom.(-acc.) plural ending -*á* could have arisen (as argued originally by Jagić)[14] by analogy with the nom.-acc. of the neuters (after the loss of gender distinctions in the plural), as well as with the oblique endings of the plural (-*am*, -*ami*, -*ax*). This assumption is confirmed by the fact that the ending -*á* of the nom.(-acc.) plural of masc. stems is a fairly recent development begun in the eighteenth and nineteenth centuries, whereas the unstressed dual ending -*a* of masc. circumflex stems is found in all Slavic languages which have preserved this ending and a mobile stress; e.g., Slov. *(dva) možȃ, svetȃ, gradǫ̑va*; S-Cr. *(trȋ) zûba, nȍsa, bȍga*; Russ. *(dva) róga, bóga, véčera*; Bulg. *(pet) mɔ́ža, zɔ́ba, nósa*. In literary Bulgarian the unstressed ending is generalized even in stems with an underlying oxytonic stress; e.g. *(pet kónja, vóla, pópa, oréla*. Moreover, an initial (or circumflex) stress also appears in the most representative forms of the dual, the numerals *dva* and *oba*; e.g. S-Cr. *dvȃ, ȍba*; Slov. *dvȃ, obȃ*; Russ. and Bulg. *dvá, óba*. Consequently, it has been argued (notably by N. van Wijk, L. Bulaxovskij and most recently by V. A. Dybo)[15] that the initial accent presents the original, Common Slavic position of the stress.

The proposed reconstruction of the dual stress stumbles, however, against serious difficulties. In the first place one will have to explain why the original initial stress shifted to the endings in the various remnants of the dual. Bulaxovskij attempted to explain this shift by positing a secondary stress in the word group *dvá rjadà > *dva rjadá*, but failed to indicate why a similar transposition of stress did not take place in other such word groups (e.g. in the phrases *íz nosu, ná ruku, pó polju*).[16] In his effort to project the contemporary stress into a Common Slavic period, he assumed the existence of an initial stress in all circumflex masc. and fem. -*a* stems (e.g., *'*zǫba*, *'*goda*; *'*rǫ̑čě*, *'*nožě*), but posited a desinence stress in the dual of -*i* stems simply because he encountered such a stress in some residual dialectal forms (e.g. Russ. *dva gostí*, Slov. *dvȋ kukušì*). A closer analysis of the pertinent facts would, however, show that traces of a desinential stress in the nom.-acc. can be found in all types of circumflex stems; e.g. Fem.: Slov. *(dvę̄) góri, nógi* (< *gor'i, nog'i*); dial. Slov. *vȍdè, nòhé*; *nôči, rêči* (<*noč'i, reč'i*) vs. pl. *vȍde, nȍhe*; *nočȋ*; Ukr. *(dvi) rucí, nozí, holovi̇́*; dial. BR. *(dzve) halavé, starané*; Neut.: dial. Russ. *brylé, skulé, šulé, mudé*; dial. BR. *az'arý, pal'í* vs. pl. *az'óry, pal'á*; Masc.: Russ. *(dva) razá, šagá, rjadá*; dial. Russ. *glazá, besá, domá, gusjá*; BR. *(dva) zubý, vusý, razý* vs. pl. *zúby, vúsy, rázy*. The conservative character of the cited forms leaves little doubt about the final position of the Common Slavic dual stress. A comparison with the Lithuanian numerals *dù, abù* prompts us to posit such a stress also for the Common Slavic *dъvá, *oba (which is probably preserved in the Ukr. *obá* and the BR. *abádva/abódva*). The conclusion imposes itself that the initial stress of the nom.-acc. dual which prevails in the modern Slavic languages is an innovation due to analogy with the initially stressed forms of the nom.-acc. plural which was used with the "neighboring" numerals "three" and "four." A parallel change also took place in the numerals *dъva, *oba, mostly likely in step with the new initial stress of the dual forms, and thanks to the influence of the numerals 'trьje, 'pętь, 'šestь. This influence of the nom.-acc. plural on the stress of the dual was, of course, amply reciprocated when forms of the dual spread, in turn, to the plurals used with the numerals "three," "four" in East Slavic, and with any numeral in Southeast Slavic.

5. The category of the paucal is in Ukrainian and some neighboring Byelorussian dialects matched by a *counted gen. plural* which is used after numerals above "four" and which carries the same accent as the singular and the paucal.

The Ukrainian paucal and counted gen. plural are variant realizations of one "general" counted plural and the closest equivalents of the *brojna forma* which is found in Southeast Slavic where the lack of a case system prevented the split of this form into contextual variants.

Unlike the paucal, which occurs with stressed and unstressed stems of any gender, the counted gen. plural is limited to masc. and fem. stems with a thematic (mostly initial) stress in their base form. The counted gen. plural is less stable than the paucal, especially in colloquial speech where it overlaps with the simple gen. plural in the oblique cases (e.g. *vid pjat'óx bokív, rokív, knyžók, doščók*), and sometimes even in the direct cases. The precarious status of the counted gen. plural is most likely responsible for the fact that it is passed over in silence by standard Ukrainian grammars and incompletely recorded by the most recent and fairly complete Ukrainian dictionaries.[17] The large number of forms which implement this category leaves, nevertheless, no doubt as to its significance. The linguistic interest of this category lies, further, in the fact that it throws light on a Ukrainian accentual development which is not encountered in the other Slavic languages.

As indicated above, the opposition between the counted and simple gen. plural is in the masc. and fem. nouns rendered by means of a distinctive stress: the counted gen. plural carries, like the paucal (and the singular), the stress on the stem, whereas the nom.(-acc.) and gen. of the simple plural carry the stress on the ending. The distinction between the counted and simple plurals can be illustrated by the following examples:

Masc.: *(dva) bóky, róky, týžni, zájci, mísjaci, párubky, učýteli; (pjat') bókiv, rókiv, týžniv, zájciv, mísjaciv, párubkiv, učýteliv*

vs. (nom. pl.) *boký, roký, tyžní, zajcí, misjací, parubký, učyteli; (gen. pl.) bokív, rokív, tyžnív, zajcív, misjacív, parubkív, učytelív;*

Fem.: *(dvi báby, xáty, cérkvy, písni, knýžky, žínky, molýtvy, jáhidky, učýteľky; (pjat') báb, xát, cérkov, písen', knýžok, žínok, molýtov, jáhidok,*

učýteľok
vs. (nom. pl.) *babý, xatý, cerkvý, pisní, knyžký, žinký, molytvý, jahidký, učyteľký*; (gen. pl.) *bab(ív), xat(ív), cerkóv, pisén', knyžók, žinók, molytóv, jahidók, učyteľók*.

In contrast to the masculine stems, which display the alternation in monosyllabic and polysyllabic stems, the feminine stems exhibit it mostly in polysyllabic stems (including vowel plus zero stems) and only in a few (four or five) monosyllabic stems which form their gen. plural with the ending *-iv*. This restriction of the alternation to polysyllabic fem. stems, and especially to stems containing a final zero (i.e., a "mobile" vowel) accounts for the frequent occurrence of the alternation with derivatives, in the first place with diminutive derivatives formed with the suffix *-#k(a)*.

The above-stated stress alternation between the counted and simple gen. plural of feminine *-a* stems is clearly connected with the corresponding stem ~ desinence ($\alpha \sim \beta$) alternation between their singular and plural and helps us gain insight into his historical development. Although this alternation might have been influenced by the stem ~ desinence alternation in masc. and neuter nouns (such as *sád, véčir, hólub; místo, póle, čúdo*: (pl.) *sadý, večerý, holubý; mistá, poljá, čudesá*), analogy with these forms cannot account for its emergence, for it does not explain why the alternation did not occur in fem. monosyllabic stems, nor why it did not similarly affect the other Slavic languages. A more cogent explanation of the $\alpha \sim \beta$ alternation in the fem. *-a* stems was suggested by V. Skljarenko, who observed on the basis of old Ukrainian texts that the alternation had first made its appearance in the gen. plural of stems containing a "mobile vowel."[18] But the modern facts show that the alternation also occurs in polysyllabic stems without such a vowel (e.g., *týsjača, stárosta, máty*: (pl.) *tysjačý, starostý, materí*). What Skljarenko's study does imply, however, is that in its earliest phase the stress alternation arose first in the oblique cases of the fem. plurals; in this it followed the pattern of masc. and fem. circumflex stems which carraied a stem stress (α) in the sing. and nom.(-acc.) plural and a desinence stress (β) in the oblique cases of the plural; that is, the accentuation of the nouns *písni: pisén', knýžky: knyžók, máteri: materéj, stárosty: starost(ív)* was based on such masc. and fem. alternations as *bóky: bokív, zúby: zubív, zémli: zeméľ, hólovy: holív, vívci: ovéc', svýni: svynéj, nóči: nočéj*. Such an alternation is still common in a number of stems regardless of their original accentual type (e.g. *dóčky: dočók, séstry: sestér, kósti: kostéj, díty: ditéj*). The generalization of the desinential stress in the oblique cases of the plural did not, however, affect the counted forms of the gen. plural which have hitherto preserved their original thematic stress (*šist' knýžok, písen, máterej*, etc.) in opposition to the end stress of the simple gen. plural.

The role of stress in carrying this opposition should also explain why the new stem ~ desinence alternation affected only the polysyllabic fem. stems (including the stems with a final zero), for these were the only stems in which the stress could perform a contrastive function.[19] The same opposition was, in turn, extended to the masculine nouns when their counted gen. plural adopted the thematic stress of the nom.-acc. dual, i.e., when *p'ját' bókiv, rókiv, dúbiv* acquired by analogy the stress of *try bóky, róky, dúby* (from the older and dial. Ukr. *tri bóka, róka, dúba*). In their subsequent development the masc. and fem. stems generalized the desinential stress of the oblique plural cases in the nom.(-acc.) plural, establishing thereby a clear-cut distinction between the forms of the paucal and the nom.(-acc.) plural. It goes without saying that the accentual distinction which serves to oppose the counted and simple forms of the plural is also of functional value in differentiating the forms of the singular from those of the plural.

The last development should indicate that the relation between the simple and the marked plural has not been one of unilateral dependence: although the unmarked category has repeatedly impinged upon the forms of the marked category, the latter has, in turn, helped define the shape of the former. This influence is otherwise quite apparent in the structure of the modern Slavic plurals which have to one or another extent inherited the endings of the original dual.

6. We may now summarize our findings and draw some conclusions of a general linguistic and diachronic import.

(1) The relation of the singular and plural is like that of other grammatical categories characterized by an asymmetry which involves the suppression of certain semantic distinctions in the marked member of the opposition. However, this asymmetry represents a statistical constant rather than a general linguistic law. As demonstrated by the Slavic categories of the plural, the marked term may introduce secondary, compensatory distinctions which balance the relation between the marked and unmarked members of an opposition.

(2) The unmarked categories of number (i.e., the singular or the simple plural) are less restricted in meaning and range than their marked counterparts (the collective and/or counted plurals) and constitute the basic or primary term of the quantitative opposition(s). However, under certain conditions (i.e., within specific semantic groups) the relationship is reversed and the marked categories (such as the collective plural) make up the basic or primary terms within the set.

(3) The unmarked categories are diachronically more stable than their marked counterparts and exert upon them a continuous influence which may

lead in time to their complete loss. The marked categories (e.g., the Slavic dual) influence in turn, however, their opposite numbers and may produce profound changes in their meanings and forms (e.g., the formation of the *brojna forma* and paucal in the contemporary Slavic languages and the modern accentuation of the "dual").

(4) The marked categories represent in most cases the historically older forms, whereas the unmarked categories are subject to more rapid change and innovations in form. The changes in the latter are not, however, independent of the changes in the former which may influence the development of the less marked categories (cf. the accentual changes in the plural of Ukr. *-a* stems).

(5) The loss of acquisition of a grammatical category does not depend on the loss or preservation of its external form. Language may constantly resort to new means for the accomplishment of certain semantic ends (cf. the loss of the distinctive endings of the dual in East Slavic and the utilization of stress in the same or expanded function).

The above caveats do not invalidate the significance of general, predictive linguistic laws, but lend to these laws a more supple and probabilistic character.

Yale University

NOTES

[1] Stankiewicz, E. (24).
[2] In Cassirer's German formulation: "Jeder Teil eines Ganzen erscheint dem Ganzen selbst ... als solcher äquivalent (9:71).
[3] Unbegaun, B. (30:298).
[4] Koneski, B. (13:15); Vinogradov, V. (33:157). In the Russian: "Kategorija sobiratel'nosti naxodit svoe grammatičeskoe vyraženie v otsutstvii form množestvennogo čisla" (157). See also in this connectino Markov's critical remarks (16:72).
[5] Šuman, J. (28:100); Rozanova, E. J. (19:157); Meščerskij, N. A. (17:126).
[6] Unbegaun, B. (30:64).
[7] Tekavčić, P. (29:93ff.).
[8] Avanesov, R. (3:132); Karksij, E. F. (12:108); Žylko, F. T. (35:125).
[9] Vinogradov, V. (33:295).
[10] Šerex, Ju. (26:249); Karskij, E. F. (12:19).
[11] Brandt, R. (5:35ff.). The role of these forms in Byelorussian is treated in detail in connection with the stress by Smułkowa (23).
[12] Koneski, B. (13:30). Vaillant (31:315) speaks in the same vein about the loss of the dual: "Une simplification plus radicale était de le laisser se perdre, puis qu'il n'était que traditionel et ne servait a rien de précis."
[13] Kočev, I. (14).
[14] Jagič, V. (11).
[15] van Wijk, N. (32); Bulaxovskij, L. (8); Dybo, V. A. (10:127).
[16] Bulaxovskij, L. (7:113).

[17] This is true even of the thorough and most recent orthoepic dictionary edited by Žovtobrjux (34).
[18] Skljarenko, V. (21; 22).
[19] In his *Historical Phonology* (20:122) Shevelov embraces Skljarenko's view that the shift of stress from the stem originated in -*a* stems containing a final zero and attempts to account for this fact as follows: "In the pl. of fem. and neut. substantives which originally had a *jer* in the penultimate syllable, the source of the stress shift was the gen. form. The final stressed *jer*, in losing its stressability, moved its stress onto the preceding *jer*." The proferred explanation misses the point, for what is to be explained is not the retraction of stress from the final *jer* (which at that time must have anyway been lost) but the progressive shift of the stress from the stem to the ending which did not depend on the state of the final *jers*.

REFERENCES

1. Andrejčin, L.
   1944 *Osnovna bəlgarska gramatika,* Sofia.
2. Atraxovič, K. K. (ed.)
   1962 *Hramatyka belaruskaj movy,* I, Minsk.
3. Avanesov, R.
   1959 *Russkaja dialektologija,* Moscow.
4. Bevzenko, S. P.
   1960 *Istoryčna morfolohija ukrajins'koji movy,* Užhorod.
5. Brandt, R.
   1905 "O dvoinnyx formax i ob ograničennom čisle," *Novyj sbornik statej sostavlennyj i izdannyj učenikami V. I. Lamanskogo,* St. Peterburg, 35-44.
6. Budmani, P.
   1867 *Grammatica della lingua serbo-croata (illirica),* Vienna.
7. Bulaxovskij, L.
   1980 "Intonacija i količestvo form *dualis*," *Izbrannye trudy v pjati tomax,* ed. I. K. Beloded, 4, Kiev, 112-127.
8. 1927/28 "Zametki po russkoj morfologii," *Slavia,* 6, 641-647.
9. Cassirer, E.
   1925 *Sprache und Mythos,* Leipzig-Berlin.
10. Dybo, V. A.
    1980 "Balto-slavjanskaja akcentnaja sistema s tipologičeskoj točki zrenija i problema rekonstrukcii indo-evropejskogo akcenta, *Balto-slavjanskie ètnojazykovye kontaky,* Moscow, 91-150.
11. Jagić, V.
    1889 *Kritičeskie zametki po istroii russkogo jazyka,* St. Petersburg.
12. Karskij, E. F.
    1956 *Belorusy: Jazyk belorusskogo naroda,* 2-3, Moscow.
13. Koneski, B.
    1952 *Gramatika na makedonskiot literaturen jazik,* 2, Skopje.
14. Kočev, I.
    1966 "Brojni formi pri səštestvitelni ot ženski rod v njakoi iztočni bəlgarski govori," *Izvestija IBÈ,* 11, 411-415.
15. Kuznecov, P. S.
    1959 *Očerki istoričeksoj morfologii russkogo jazyka,* Moscow.
16. Markov, V. M.
    1974 *Istoričeskaja grammatika russkogo jazyka: Imennoe sklonenie,* Moscow.

17. Meščerskij, N. A., ed.
    1972 *Russkaja dialektologija*, Moscow.
18. Obnorskij, S.
    1925 "Dualspuren in der nominalen Deklination des Russischen," *Zeitschrift für slavische Philologie*, 2, 1925, 61-77.
19. Rozanova, E. J.
    1914 "Nabljudenija nad govorom kresťjan derevni Maslovki i Xitrovki Sudž. uezda Kurskoj oblasti,"*Izvestija Otdelenija russkogo jazyka*, 157.
20. Shevelov, G.
    1979 *A Historical Phonology of the Ukrainian Language*, Heidelberg.
21. Skljarenko, V.
    1968 "Poxodžennja ruxomosti naholosu v imennykax typu *knýžka*," *Movoznavstvo*, 4, 34-40.
22. 1956 "Akcentolohična problematyka formy rodovoho vidminka množyny imennykiv," *Movoznavstvo*, 6, 33-41.
23. **Smułkowa, E.**
    1978 *Studia nad akcentem języka białoruskiego*, Warsaw.
24. Stankiewicz, E.
    1962 "The Singular-Plural Opposition in the Slavic Languages," *International Journal of Slavic Linguistics and Poetics*, 5, 1-15.
25. Stevanović, M.
    1966 *Gramatika srpskohrvatskog jezika*, Cetinje.
26. Šerex, Ju.
    1951 *Narys sučasnoji ukrajins'koji literaturnoji movy*, Munich.
27. Štrekelj, K.
    1886 *Morphologie des Görzer Mittelkarstdialektes mit besonderer Berücksichtigung der Betonungsverhältnisse* (= Kais. Akademie der Wissenschaften, Philologisch-historische Klasse, 113), Vienna.
28. Šuman, J.
    1882 *Slovenska slovnica*, Ljubljana.
29. Tekavčić, P.
    1972 Grammatica storica dell'italiano, 2.
30. Unbegaun, B.
    1935 *La langue russe au XVI siècle (1500-1550)*, 1: *La flexion des noms*, Paris.
31. Vaillant, A.
    1958 *Grammaire comparée des langues slaves*, 2, Lyon.
32. van Wijk, N.
    1920 "Zur Betonung des slavischen Duals," *Neophilologus*, 5, 113-115.
33. Vinogradov, V.
    1947 *Russkij jazyk: Grammatičeskoe učenie o slove*, Moscow-Leningrad.
34. Žovtobrjux, M. A., ed.
    1973 *Ukrajins'ka literaturna vymova i naholos*, Kiev.
35. Žylko, F. T.
    1951 *Ukrajins'ka dialektolohija*, Kiev-Lvov.

Compensatory Lengthening in Slavic, 2: Phonetic Reconstruction

Alan Timberlake

1. Introduction. A number of Slavic languages show distinctively long (or tense) reflexes of vowels in syllables before a Late Common Slavic weak jer, but a short (or lax) reflex in syllables before other vowels, as in Upper Sorbian *měd/mjedu, bór/boru, kóń/konja,* Polish *miód/miodu, bór/boru, sól/soli,* Serbo-Croatian *mêd/měda, bôr/bòra, rôg/ròga,* Ukrainian *pič/peči, bir/boru, rih/roha*. Although there is evidently some similarity in the development of this change, there are also considerable differences in the specific phonological conditions under which individual Slavic dialects have developed long (or tense) reflexes.

Traditionally it has been assumed that the long reflex is in some way a result of the phonetic weakening and the eventual phonemic loss of the following jer vowel, and the phenomenon is appropriately termed "compensatory lengthening" (hereafter, CL). Perhaps because of the divergences among Slavic dialects, however, there is to date no discussion of the phenomenon that is both general enough to account for the evident similarity in the reflexes of CL across Slavic languages and flexible enough to account for the significant dialect differences.

This paper advances a hypothesis about CL as a phonetic process, and attempts to account for the divergent reflexes in different dialects by giving an explicit reconstruction of CL and the factors that governed its development as a phonetic process. It is suggested that Late Common Slavic was subject to a constraint on the preservation of word timing, such that phonetic reduction in one syllable (containing the "weak" jer) was compensated for by increased phonetic duration in the preceding, "strong" syllable. In addition, various factors — accent, position in the word, and the intervening consonant — could affect the phonetic duration of a vowel in strong position. Distinctively long (or tense) reflexes resulted when the phonetic lengthening was sufficient to permit the strong vowel to be evaluated as phonemically long (tense) at the time when jers were eliminated phonemically. Although the basic mechanism for CL proposed here is by no means novel — if anything, this interpretation represents the majority view — what is perhaps new is the attempt to deal systematically with the factors that are responsible for dialect divergences.

The present paper is the second of a two-part study of compensatory lengthening. The first part (Timberlake 1983) gives an extended survey of the reflexes of CL in Slavic languages, along with discussion of some controversial questions of interpretation. In this paper I will rely on that survey, and give here only a compact summary of its results.[1]

2. Background and Survey. This survey is organized according to the three major dialect zones of Late Common Slavic (= LCSl), with additional divisions into subzones. In West Slavic (= WSl) it is convenient to distinguish the southern subzone of Slovak, Czech, and Upper Sorbian (= S-WSl) from the northern or Lekhitic subzone of Polish and Kashubian-Slovincian (= N-WSl). In Lower Sorbian, presumably a transitional dialect between S-WSl and N-WSl, the evidence for CL is obscure (Schuster–Šewc 1958), and in Polabian, on the far periphery of N-WSl, there is no evidence of CL, so both languages are omitted from the survey. South Slavic (= SSl) can be divided into the southeastern subzone of Bulgarian and Macedonian (= SE-SSl), in which there are no reflexes of CL, and the northwestern subzone of Slovenian and Serbo-Croatian (= NW-SSl) (as in Ivić 1958a). Under Serbo-Croatian only Štokavian and Čakavian dialects are discussed, on the assumption that Kajkavian belongs prosodically with Slovenian (Ivić 1965:130). East Slavic can be divided roughly into a southwestern subzone of Ukrainian and southern Belorussian (= SW-ESl) and a northeastern subzone without reflexes of CL of central and northern Belorussian and Russian (= NE-ESl) (as suggested by Trubetzkoy 1925). In effect, there are four zones to be discussed: S-WSl, N-WSl, NW-SSl, and SW-ESl.

The survey documents the effect of three distinct factors on CL: the consonant following the strong vowel; the position of the strong vowel and the weak jer, taken as a disyllabic unit (which can then be "final" or "internal"); and the accent of the strong vowel. For accent, I assume a standard reconstruction of LCSl with a distinction of acute accent (= Act, notationally ˝ on long vowels and, in the final syllable only, ` on short vowels) vs. circumflex (= Cmflx, notationally ˆ on long vowels and ˵ on short vowels) (Stang 1957, Jakobson 1963). In addition, it is convenient, and I think ultimately necessary, to recognize the neoacute accent as a distinct accent contour (= NAct, notationally ´ on long vowels and ` on short vowels). This accent contour, which arose by retraction of the accent from originally accented jers and in certain other contexts, had unique effects on CL in some dialect zones, and it is therefore reasonable to assume that it had been phonemicized by the fall of the jers. In fact, the effect of accent on CL suggests a hypothesis about the history of accent and quantity in LCSl, the presentation of which is a major goal of this paper. Accent was of course distributed according to morphological category, but here that distribution is presupposed (for discussion, see Timberlake 1983).

Within the subzone of S-WSl, Slovak has CL of *e, o only under the NAct, and then across any consonant and in any word position: nom. sg. *kosjь > kôš, gen. pl. *ženъ > žien, l-participle *vedlъ > viedol, internal *nožьka > nôžka. CL does not occur under other accents: nom. sg. *mŏstъ > most, *mĕdъ > med, *dĕdъ > ded, internal *mătъka > matka. In Czech, if one adopts the principle that current attestations of length are relics and then reconstructs the maximal domain for CL, it appears that Czech also has length of *e, o under the NAct across any consonant in any word position: nom. sg. *postъ > půst, *kosjь > OCz kóš, internal *slovъko > slůvko, *jezerъko > jezírko. In addition, CL occurs not under the NAct before sonorants and voiced fricatives but not before voiced stops and voiceless obstruents: nom. sg. *dŏmъ > dům, *bŏgъ > bůh vs. *rŏdъ > rod, *nŏsъ > nos. In Upper Sorbian, on the periphery of the S-WSl subzone, CL occurs for *e, o without restriction, except that the lengthened reflexes (ě, ó) are restricted to the initial syllable: nom. sg. měd, *kŏstь > kósć, *kŏlsъ > kłós, *konjь > kóń, gen. pl. *gorь > hór, internal nóžka, *kotъlà > kótła. To summarize the development in S-WSl, CL affects *e, o under the NAct without restriction by consonant or word position throughout the subzone. Not under the NAct, CL increases from the center in Slovak (no CL outside of the NAct) to Czech (CL restricted to sonorants and voiced fricatives) to the periphery in Upper Sorbian (unrestricted).

In N-WSl (Polish and Kashubian), it is clear that CL developed regularly before sonorants and voiced obstruents in final position, for all vowels: nom. sg. *dőbъ > dąb, *bêrgъ > dial. bžèg, OPol dóm, Kash *sỹnъ > sin vs. *pętъ > pięć, *sŏkъ > sok, *măkъ > Kash mak, *nítь > Kash nic. It is often assumed that this is the maximal distribution of reflexes of length in N-WSl, but in addition there is evidence for CL under two further conditions. First, under the NAct, regardless of the intervening consonant: Pol dial. kósz, póst, l-participle niósł < *neslъ. Second, in internal position before sonorants and voiced obstruents (usually de facto under the NAct), with a geographical distribution such that length increases from south to north within the zone: southern Pol dial. nožka, *kołdъka > kłodka vs. northern dial. nóžka, kłódka, Kash nóžka, *jăgodъka > jagᵘódka. To summarize, CL applies under the NAct in final position regardless of the intervening consonant. Not under the NAct in final position, CL applies before sonorants and voiced obstruents but not before voiceless obstruents. In internal position, CL is restricted geographically and structurally. It increases in application from the relative center (South Polish) to the periphery (Kashubian). Internal CL occurs only before sonorants and voiced obstruents.

In NW-SSl the most important constraint is accent. In Slovenian final short Cmflx are lengthened but final NAct and Act are not: *bộg, kộst* vs. *kònj, pòst*, **rȁkъ > ràk, dèd*. Internally, however, NAct and Act are lengthened: **dvorъ̀skъjь > dvợrski, *solmъka > slâmka*. In Serbo-Croatian, CL of short final Cmflx likewise occurs throughout the dialects regardless of the intervening consonant: *bôg, mêd, môst*. CL of NAct and Act depends on the consonant and on word position, and the reflexes vary by dialect. In Štokavian CL of Act and NAct occurs only before *j* in final position (**krȁjь > krâj* vs. **prȁvъ > prȁv, kònj, djȅd, mȁk*) but before all sonorants internally (*prȃvda, stȃrca*). The most liberal conditions on CL of Act and NAct are found in South Čakavian (Hvar), where CL occurs before sonorants and voiced obstruents finally and internally: **rȁjь > rôj, kûoń, dîd, *moȑzъ > mrôz, *bobъ̀ > bûob* vs. *mȁk*; internally, *zdrȏvje, sȇlski, *susȅdъstvo > susȋstvo*. These are the two extreme cases of conditions on CL of Act and NAct in Serbo-Croatian dialects; other dialects generally have CL of NAct and Act both finally and internally before sonorants (Posavian, North Čakavian Vrgada, North Čakavian Novi — except no CL in final position before *v*). The facts of CL in NW-SSl can be reduced to three hierarchical statements of conditions: (1) Cmflx ≥ NAct, Act; (2) internal ≥ final position; and (3) *j* ≥ other sonorants ≥ *v* ≥ voiced obstruents ≥ voiceless obstruents.

In SW-ESl lengthened reflexes of CL are found for **e, o (ê/ô, ı̂e/u͡o*, or — in most dialects of Ukrainian — *i/i*). Throughout this subzone, **o* lengthens under all conditions: *dim, *sòlь > sil', kin', *nočьka > nı́čka*. In the southern part, **e* lengthens before **ь* under all conditions but before **ъ* only under the NAct: **pečь̀ > pič, *veselьje > vesíllja* vs. **mȅdъ > med*, gen. pl. **selъ̀ > sil*. Similarly, pleophonic sequences show CL consistently only under the NAct: gen. pl. **solmъ > solóm*, internal **solmъka > solómka* vs. **bordъ̀ > boríd, *bordъka > borídka*; *l*-participle **kollъ > kolóv* vs. **volklъ̀ > volík*. These constraints on CL eventually disappear in the northern part of the SW-ESl zone (Polissian dialects of Ukrainian, southern Belorussian), at least in pockets: *mid/mêd/m'u͡od, lid/lêd/l'u͡od* (the latter extending south well into the Ukrainian language area), *korı́vka/korôwka/koru͡ȏwka*. In summary, the major constraint in SW-ESl is accent — NAct ≥ Cmflx, Act — and this constraint loses its effect going from the center to the periphery of the zone. Two minor constraints that will not concern us are that CL occurs more regularly before **ь* than before **ъ*, and **o* lengthens more regularly than **e*. There is apparently no effect of word position or the intervening consonant.

3. Phonetic Reconstruction. In this section I will give a model for the reconstruction of CL as a phonetic process, and in subsequent sections refine the model to describe the effect of three factors — consonant, word position, and accent — on the development of CL. Before actually presenting this model, however, I would first like to address three questions concerning the rationale for this model: Why do reconstruction at all? Why do phonetic reconstruction? And why do the particular form of phonetic reconstruction adopted here?

In a general sense, the reason for doing reconstruction is to force us to be explicit in the description of historical phonology. If the reconstruction is explicit, then it is possible to check it for internal consistency, and, as a derivative result, to formulate further questions to be investigated about the process of CL and the phonological system of LCSl.

To justify the notion of phonetic reconstruction, I should state that the model below is understood to be embedded in a structuralist view of historical phonology. On this view, phonemic representations are implemented by concrete rules of allophonic variation and neutralization. These rules may to some extent be motivated by universal phonetic principles, but it is clear that particular rules must be sanctioned by the phonological structure of a given language at a given time. Throughout the history of a language phonetic implementations are analyzed by new speakers, who may or may not arrive at the same set of phonemic relationships and phonetic implementations as prior speakers (see Jakobson 1929, Andersen 1973).

Given this view of phonology, one can in principle appeal to at least two basic descriptive devices to account for dialect divergences: a difference in phonetic implementation between dialects, or a difference in phonemic analysis, given comparable phonetic implementation. In addition, morphological and lexical considerations may affect either the development of the phonetic process or the eventual distribution of phonemic reflexes.

In proposing specifically a phonetic reconstruction of CL, I am in effect adopting the assumption that dialect divergences in the reflexes of CL are produced first and foremost by differences in phonetic implementation (which must, however, be sanctioned by differences in phonological structure). This assumption is not necessarily correct, and at least one of the factors discussed below cannot be described in this way. But it seems to me the best operating procedure, for three reasons. First, given that phonemic differences arise in the analysis of phonetic implementations, it is a priori natural to look first for differences in phonetic implementation. Second, it is easier to be explicit about phonetic differences than about phonemic differences. And third, it turns out to be easier to describe the actual dialect differences in reflexes of CL in phonetic rather than phonemic terms.

Finally, there is the question of the particular form of phonetic reconstruction adopted here. Below I will assume an additive model, in which the duration of vowels is adjusted by adding or subtracting increments of duration depending on various factors. Alternatively, one could imagine other models, notably one in which duration is affected multiplicatively (for example, under the presence of a certain factor, a vowel's duration would be some percentage of the vowel's duration in another context). I have chosen to use the additive model because it is easier to express the effect of multiple factors, but it should be emphasized that the choice of model is arbitrary. All that is important is that the model be able to express the simultaneous effect of various factors on the duration of the vowel in strong position. It is also true that the actual numerical values for duration used below are intended to be highly approximate.

In this model, the basic phonetic mechanism is compensatory: reduction of a jer in one syllable conditions an increase in duration in the vowel of the preceding strong syllable. Adopting the mora as an arbitrary unit of duration, let us assume that short vowels have a base duration of 1.0 morae. As a jer is reduced by a variable amount α, that amount is added to the base duration of the strong vowel. This is shown in the formula in (1). The directional symbol $>$ is to be read as "is realized phonetically as." Here and in the following, we use a single symbol ə for both jers.

(1) CL as a Phonetic Process
   /CVCə/ $>$ [CV$^{1.0+\alpha}$Cə$^{-\alpha}$]

This is the basic formula we will use for CL throughout the following discussion, although it will be necessary to complicate it by the addition of other variables to describe the effect of different factors.

The formula in (1) takes no position on the inherent duration of jers. Jers are often termed "reduced" vowels, as if they were inherently shorter than other short vowels. I see no reason for assuming this. On the contrary, it is more reasonable to assume that jers historically began as short vowels of full duration (nearly or exactly 1.0 morae) that, over time, were gradually reduced in duration by increasing amounts, say by 0.2 morae, then 0.4, 0.6, and eventually even 0.8 morae. In terms of the formula in (1), this implies the phonetic implementations in (2), which can be understood as sequential stages of development:

(2) Jer Reduction and CL
   a. /CVCə/ $>$ [CV$^{1.2}$Cə$^{-.2}$] {α = 0.2}
   b. /CVCə/ $>$ [CV$^{1.4}$Cə$^{-.4}$] {α = 0.4}
   c. /CVCə/ $>$ [CV$^{1.6}$Cə$^{-.6}$] {α = 0.6}
   d. /CVCə/ $>$ [CV$^{1.8}$Cə$^{-.8}$] {α = 0.8}

On this view, jers were "reduced" vowels in the sense that they were subject to increasing reduction of duration over time.

Historically jers were eliminated phonemically, either by identification with another vowel or by identification with null. It is generally agreed that jers were eliminated phonemically earlier in central dialects than in peripheral dialects of Slavic (Šaxmatov 1915:203-216). This observation implies some difference in the rate of development in different dialect zones, but it is not specific as to whether the difference lies in the rate of phonetic development or in the rate of phonemic development. Accordingly, this observation is open to two more specific interpretations.

One interpretation is based on the assumption that jers were eliminated phonemically only at an extreme degree of reduction, on the order of 0.8 morae. If jers were eliminated earlier in the center than on the periphery, the central zones would be areas that underwent accelerated phonetic development. On this view, all dialects of Slavic would have to go through the same phonetic stages of development before eliminating jers, and differences in the rate of development would not predict any dialectal differences in the development of CL.

An alternative view is that the jers could be eliminated phonemically at different degrees of reduction. If the center developed faster than the periphery, the phonemic decision to eliminate jers would arrive earlier in the center than on the periphery. Given the further assumption that CL is proportional to jer reduction, this view predicts that CL will develop less in the center than on the periphery. Since this alternative view predicts differences in the development of CL, I will adopt it in the following.

When reduced jers were eliminated phonemically, the phonetic phase of CL was necessarily interrupted, and the lengthened variant of a vowel in strong position had to be identified as phonemically long (tense) or short (lax). It can be assumed that a phonetic duration of approximately 1.5 morae was the minimum required for a vowel to be analyzed as phonemically long (tense). At a stage of weak reduction, as in (2a, 2b) above, the strong vowel would be shorter than the critical duration, and would be analyzed as short (lax), as diagrammed in (3a, 3b). In (3) the symbol $\Rightarrow$ is to be read as "is analyzed phonemically as."

(3) Phonemic Analysis

    a. $[CV^{1.2}C\mathrm{ə}^{-.2}] \Rightarrow /CVC/ \quad \{\alpha = 0.2\}$
    b. $[CV^{1.4}C\mathrm{ə}^{-.4}] \Rightarrow /CVC/ \quad \{\alpha = 0.4\}$
    c. $[CV^{1.6}C\mathrm{ə}^{-.6}] \Rightarrow /C\bar{V}C/ \quad \{\alpha = 0.6\}$
    d. $[CV^{1.8}C\mathrm{ə}^{-.8}] \Rightarrow /C\bar{V}C/ \quad \{\alpha = 0.8\}$

At a stage of strong reduction, as in (2c, 2d) above, the strong vowel would surpass the critical duration of 1.5, and would be analyzed phonemically as long (tense) at the loss of the jers, as in (3c, 3d). Thus, different phonemic reflexes result, depending on the degree of reduction of jers when they were eliminated phonemically. Given further the assumption, outlined above, that the phonemic loss of jers occurred at an earlier phonetic stage of development in the center than on the periphery, the sequence of (3a) to (3d) can be read as a geographical progression from center to periphery.

4. Consonant. We turn now to consider the effect of three factors on CL, starting with that of the consonant following the strong vowel.

As noted in the survey above, there is in one sense considerable variation among Slavic languages in the effect of the consonant on CL. In another sense, however, the effect is uniform across all languages; it is consistent with a single hierarchy: sonorants (= R) ⩾ voiced fricative (= Z) ⩾ voiced stop (= D) ⩾ voiceless fricative (= S) or voiceless stop (= T), ranked in order of greater to fewer reflexes of length in CL. Different languages draw the line in different places along the hierarchy (or, a given language may draw the line in different places for different prosodic contexts). Posavian and North Čakavian dialects of Serbo-Croatian lengthen Act/NAct shorts before sonorants. Czech apparently developed length under the Cmflx before sonorants and voiced fricatives. Likewise, it appears that Kashubian lengthened before the suffix *-ьstvo before the same set of consonants, although the available evidence is restricted (see Timberlake 1983). Length developed in Polish under the Act/Cmflx and in South Čakavian before sonorants and all voiced obstruents. There are no consonant restrictions at all in Ukrainian and Upper Sorbian, and none under the NAct in Slovak, Polish, and (possibly) Czech, and none under the Cmflx in Serbó-Croatian.

One noteworthy observation emerges from this summary. In each of the languages in which the consonant affects the phonemic reflexes of CL, it does so only in one accent context; in each case there is also another accent under which CL develops without consonant restriction. This fact places some constraints on the reconstruction of the effect of the consonant.

Most importantly, it suggests that the effect of the consonant was in fact an effect on the phonetic development of CL. Evidently, the duration of the strong vowel was adjusted depending on the following consonant, but the duration of the strong vowel differed under different accents. I will return to the duration of vowels under different accents later. As for the effect of the consonant, the adjustment in duration of the strong vowel could be represented in any of three ways: lengthening before consonants favorable to CL, shortening before consonants unfavorable to CL, or complementary distribution of duration depending on the consonant. As far as I can tell, there is no strong reason to prefer one of these options over the others, but I will adopt the mechanism of shortening (consistent with notion of "vowel abridgement" in Andersen 1969).

In the reconstruction here, the effect of the consonant can be represented by subtracting an amount β of duration from the strong vowel, where the value of β depends on the particular consonant involved. For sonorants, β can be assumed to be 0.0, which is less than the value for voiced obstruents, which in turn will be less than the value for voiceless obstruents. The effect of the consonant is stated in general terms in (4):

(4) Effect of Consonants on CL
$$/CVC\partial/ > [CV^{1.0+\alpha-\beta}C\partial^{-\alpha}]$$
$$\beta_{C=R} \geqslant \beta_{C=Z, D} \geqslant \beta_{C=S, T}$$

Given that some languages show no effect of the consonant on the phonemic reflexes of CL, it seems likely that the total range of variation in β from sonorants to voiceless obstruents could vary significantly depending on the dialect zone. In SW-ESl (Ukrainian), where the consonant leaves no phonemic traces on CL, the total range can be assumed to be minimal, perhaps less than 0.1 morae: $\beta_{C=R} = 0.0$, $\beta_{C=Z, D} = 0.033$, and $\beta_{C=S, T} = 0.067$. Given such minimal variation in the value of β, the consonant is not likely to have phonemic effects.

In zones such as N-WSl and NW-SSl, where the consonant clearly does leave phonemic traces, the range of β can be assumed to be larger, at least on the order of 0.2 morae: for example, $\beta_{C=R} = 0.0$, $\beta_{C=Z, D} = 0.1$, and $\beta_{C=S, T} = 0.2$. Given significant variation in the value of β, the consonant could easily produce phonemic differences. To describe, for example, CL in Polish (in final position, under the Act/Cmflx), a value of $\alpha = 0.6$ would produce the correct phonemic results, as shown in (5):

(5) Effect of Consonants on CL (Polish)
  a. $/CVR\partial/ > [CV^{1.6}R\partial^{-.6}] \Rightarrow /C\bar{V}R/$ $\{\alpha = 0.6, \beta = 0.0\}$
  b. $/CVZ\partial/ > [CV^{1.5}Z\partial^{-.6}] \Rightarrow /C\bar{V}Z/$ $\{\alpha = 0.6, \beta = 0.1\}$
  c. $/CVS\partial/ > [CV^{1.4}S\partial^{-.6}] \Rightarrow /CVS/$ $\{\alpha = 0.6, \beta = 0.2\}$

Given these values of α and β, the net duration would equal or surpass the critical duration of 1.5 morae before sonorants and voiced obstruents, but fall below it before voiceless obstruents.

In two areas of Slavic the effect of consonants leads to an isogloss internal to a major dialect subzone, where the consonant restrictions on lengthening decrease from center to periphery. The gradation is clear in Čakavian, from the Novi dialect (length before sonorants except *v*) to Vrgada (length before all sonorants) to Hvar (length before sonorants and voiced obstruents). A complete gradation occurs in the S-WSl subzone under the Cmflx: no length before any consonant in the center (Slovak), length before sonorants and voiced fricatives in a transitional area (Czech), and length before any consonant on the periphery (Upper Sorbian).

These two gradations can be explicated by appealing to the consonant hierarchy and to the two general assumptions sketched above: first, CL is proportional to the degree of reduction of jers, and second, jers were eliminated at an earlier stage of reduction in the center than on the periphery of LCSl. For example, in North Čakavian — relatively central in the dialect geography of LCSl — jers following Act and NAct vowels were only slightly reduced when jers were eliminated phonemically, so that the phonetic development of CL was sufficient to yield phonemically long reflexes only in the optimal environment. The development is sketched in (6), where α is assumed to be 0.5.

(6) Effect of Consonants on CL (North Čakavian)
  a. /CVRə/ > [CV$^{1.5}$Rə$^{-0.5}$] ⇒ /CV̄R/ $\{\alpha = 0.5, \beta = 0.0\}$
  b. /CVZə/ > [CV$^{1.4}$Zə$^{-0.5}$] ⇒ /CVZ/ $\{\alpha = 0.5, \beta = 0.1\}$
  c. /CVSə/ > [CV$^{1.3}$Sə$^{-0.5}$] ⇒ /CVS/ $\{\alpha = 0.5, \beta = 0.2\}$

In South Čakavian, relatively peripheral in LCSl, jers had reduced more (hypothetically, $\alpha = 0.6$), so that phonemic length developed across voiced obstruents as well. The development for South Čakavian is given in (7):

(7) Effect of Consonants on CL (South Čakavian)
  a. /CVRə/ > [CV$^{1.6}$Rə$^{-0.6}$] ⇒ /CV̄R/ $\{\alpha = 0.6, \beta = 0.0\}$
  b. /CVZə/ > [CV$^{1.5}$Zə$^{-0.6}$] ⇒ /CV̄Z/ $\{\alpha = 0.6, \beta = 0.1\}$
  c. /CVSə/ > [CV$^{1.4}$Sə$^{-0.6}$] ⇒ /CVS/ $\{\alpha = 0.6, \beta = 0.2\}$

The gradation in S-WSl can be analyzed in the same way, if a small difference is introduced in the value of β for voiced fricatives (let $\beta = 0.067$) and voiced stops (let $\beta = 0.133$). In central Slovak, the degree of reduction may have been only $\alpha = 0.4$ under the Cmflx, so that the strong vowel would fall short of the critical duration before any consonant. In transitional Czech, if the degree of reduction were $\alpha = 0.6$, the strong vowel would surpass the critical duration before sonorants (1.0 + 0.6 - 0.0 = 1.6) and voiced fricatives (1.0 + 0.6 - 0.067 = 1.533), but not before voiced stops (1.0 + 0.6 - 0.133 = 1.467) or voiceless obstruents (1.0 + 0.6 - 0.2 = 1.4). Finally, in peripheral Upper Sorbian, if the degree of reduction were $\alpha = 0.8$, the strong vowel would be longer than the critical duration before any consonant, including voiceless obstruent (1.0 + 0.8 - 0.2 = 1.6).

Thus, the local divergences in the reflexes of CL within major dialect subzones of LCSl can be described using a uniform effect of the consonant on vowel duration and the general assumption that jer reduction increased from center to periphery.

The effect of consonants on vowel duration has been studied extensively in acoustical and perceptual terms. Some comments on this literature are in order.

First, it has been established that there is significant variation across languages in the extent to which consonants affect the duration of preceding consonants. The ratio of vowel duration before voiceless consonants is roughly 0.61 in English, but falls in the range from 0.78 to 0.87 for other languages investigated (Korean, Russian, Norwegian, Spanish, and French, in that order) (see Chen 1970). It is therefore reasonable to suppose, as we did above, that the effect of consonants on vowel duration is a parameter that can vary across languages.

Second, one concern in this literature is to find a physiological mechanism that would account for the cross-linguistically regular effect of consonants on vowel duration. None of the proposed mechanisms is obviously correct (see House 1961, Chen 1970, Lisker 1974). In particular, it is not obvious whether, in those languages where the effect is significant, the mechanism involved is shortening, lengthening, or complementary distribution of length.

Third, this literature deals primarily with the difference between voiced and voiceless obstruents. In all investigations it is clear that vowels are longer before voiced than before voiceless obstruents, and longer before fricatives than before stops (House and Fairbanks 1953, House 1961, Peterson and Lehiste 1960, Chen 1970, Umeda 1975). No information is given about the effect of liquids and glides on vowel duration, presumably because of the difficulty of segmenting vowels and these sonorants. Nasals have been discussed in some of the studies (House and Fairbanks 1953, Peterson and Lehiste 1960, Umeda 1975), and somewhat surprisingly, nasals appear to condition shorter vowels than voiced obstruents, or fall between voiced stops and voiced fricatives in their effect on vowel duration. This is problematic for the reconstruction above, which requires (at least for North Čakavian and Posavian) that all sonorants condition longer vowels than voiced obstruents. A range of explanations is possible: the fact that nasals condition shorter vowels than voiced fricatives in English could be an artefact of the segmentation procedures used; it could be a property that varies across languages; or it could be that the ranking of sonorants over voiced obstruents in Slavic does not directly reflect a difference in phonetic duration of the vowel, but a perceptual difference in the analysis of phonetic duration at the fall of the jers. Here we must leave the question open.

Concerning the effect of the consonant on CL, we note the following conclusions. There is a uniform hierarchy of consonants across Slavic, a hierarchy that is generally (although not entirely) consistent with instrumental measurements of attested languages. Dialects of LCSl can differ in the extent to which consonants affected phonemic reflexes of CL. Major differences among dialect zones — SW-ESl vs. other zones — may well represent a significant typological difference in the consonant system. There are in addition local differences within dialect zones in the effect of the consonant; these are played out geographically from the center (more restrictions) to the periphery (fewer restrictions).

5. Word Position. Unlike the consonant following the strong vowel, the position of the strong vowel–weak jer disyllable in the word does not have a uniform effect across Slavic. In N-WSl, final position (when the weak jer is absolute final, the strong vowel penultimate) is favored over internal position (when the weak jer is penultimate or antepenultimate, the strong vowel antepenultimate or preantepenultimate). In NW-SSl the reverse is true. In S-WSl and SW-ESl there is no evidence for the effect of word position on CL one way or the other.

Any interpretation of the effect of word position must be tentative. One possibility that is consistent with the general approach here is the following. Vowels vary in length depending on their position in the word. Conceivably, the difference between N-WSl and NW-SSl reflects a difference in orientation of length assignment: in N-WSl, vowels decreased in length from initial to final syllable, while in NW-SSl vowels increased in length from initial to final syllable. If so, in WSl jers in final position could have been more reduced than internal jers, and would have conditioned more CL. In SSl, final jers would have been less reduced, and contributed less than internal jers to CL. This is reflected in (8) in the hierarchical statement of reduction for final jers (α) and internal jers (α'):

(8) Word Position and CL
    a. /CVCə/ $>$ [CV$^{1.0+\alpha}$Cə$^{-\alpha}$]
    b. /CVCəCV/ $>$ [CV$^{1.0+\alpha'}$Cə$^{-\alpha'}$CV]
        N-WSl: $\alpha \geq \alpha'$
        NW-SSl: $\alpha \leq \alpha'$

The difference between α and α' is likely to have been small — on the order of 0.1, or 0.2 morae at the most — but values of α and α' in the neighborhood of 0.5 or 0.6 morae could easily lead to phonemic differences in CL between final and internal positions.

This interpretation is admittedly speculative, but there is some indirect supporting evidence in other facts involving the fall of the jers. On the basis of textual evidence it is generally agreed that in SSl jers were lost earlier from initial than from other positions, a fact which is consistent with the hypothesis of increasing length from initial to final syllable. Conversely, in Polabian, on the far periphery of WSl, jers in canonical weak position (= not before a weak jer) were sometimes preserved in the initial syllable, although weak jers in other syllables were eliminated in accordance with Havlík's Law. Note, for example, *t'ęnǫz* < **kъnęžь, t'åmə* < **tьma, kåtü* < **kъto* but *jącmin* < **jęčьmenь, jopt'ü* < **jablъko, vüce* < **ovьcě* (Lehr-Spławiński 1929: 51ff.). The preservation of weak jers in initial position is consistent with the interpretation that length decreased from initial to final syllables in WSl. Closer to the home of CL, in Kashubian jers in canonical strong position were eliminated before voiceless obstruent, as in *stòłk* < **stolъkъ, dǫmk* < **domъkъ* (Shevelov 1965:457, Andersen 1969). This is true of "strong" jers in the penultimate syllable. In the antepenultimate syllable, strong jers before voiceless obstruent were sometimes preserved, sometimes eliminated, as in *stołäčk* ~ *stòłčk* < **stolъčьkъ, domäčk* ~ *dòmčk* < **domъčьkъ*. If these variant forms are genuine, they suggest that antepenultimate jers were longer than penultimate jers, which is consistent with the hypothesis of decreasing length from initial to final syllable in WSl.

This is at least indirect evidence in support of the claim that WSl and SSl differed in orientation of length assignment. It should be noted, however, that this interpretation produces a conceptual difficulty for SSl. In general, phonological processes in SSl appear to apply from right (the end) to the left (the beginning) of the word. The neoacute retraction operates in this direction in SSl, as it does elsewhere in Slavic. And later in Serbo-Croatian, posttonic longs are eliminated more systematically than pretonic longs. The interpretation of word position and its effect on CL may well be in need of some revision for SSl.

In one subzone of LCSl, word position leaves a local isogloss such that CL applies in fewer cases on the side of the isogloss closer to the center of LCSl than on the peripheral side. This is the isogloss of South Polish *nożka, kłodka* vs. North Polish *nóżka, kłódka*. As observed above, CL applies in more and more contexts in the direction from south to north in N-WSl, but we concentrate here on this one representative isogloss.

The isogloss can be interpreted as follows. Given the hypothesis that vowels (including jers) are shorter finally than internally in WSl, there could have been a difference in degree of jer reduction, and hence a difference in phonetic CL, between internal ($\alpha' = 0.4$) and final positions ($\alpha = 0.6$). If, in a relatively central dialect such as South Polish, jers were eliminated phonemically at this stage of development, phonetic CL would have been transformed into phonemic length in final but not internal position. The development hypothesized for South Polish is given in (9):

(9) Word Position and CL in South Polish
    a. /CVCə/   > [CV$^{1.6}$Cə$^{-.6}$]   ⇒ /CV̄C/   {α = 0.6}
    b. /CVCəCV/ > [CV$^{1.4}$Cə$^{-.4}$CV] ⇒ /CVCCV/ {α' = 0.4}

Towards the periphery of N-WSl, in North Polish and Kashubian, the phonemic elimination of jers occurred later. As a result, reduction of jers in internal position could have caught up with reduction of final jers (α, α' = 0.6 or α = 0.7, α' = 0.6), with the result that phonemic length developed in both internal and final positions of CL. This is schematized in (10):

(10) Word Position and CL in North Polish and Kashubian
    a. /CVCə/   > [CV$^{1.6}$Cə$^{-.6}$]   ⇒ /CV̄C/   {α = 0.6}
    b. /CVCəCV/ > [CV$^{1.6}$Cə$^{-.6}$CV] ⇒ /CV̄CCV/ {α' = 0.6}

Thus, this isogloss (which is representative of a series of isoglosses in N-WSl) can be explicated as a consequence of two assumptions: the assumption, specific to WSl, that length decreased from initial to final syllables, and the general assumption that jers were eliminated earlier in the center of each subzone of LCSl than on the periphery.

6. Accent. Of the three conditions considered here, accent is the most intriguing. As observed above, accent divides Slavic into two large areas: in NW-SSl, CL applies more consistently under the Cmflx than under the Act or NAct, while in SW-ESl and both subzones of WSl, CL develops more consistently under the NAct than under the Cmflx or Act. This clear difference in the effect of tone on CL suggests a hypothesis about the history of accent and quantity in LCSl. To develop this hypothesis, let us review the history of accent and quantity until the fall of the jers in LCSl.

We depart from the point in the history of Common Slavic when original quantitative distinctions were transformed into qualitative distinctions. Following this process of qualitative differentiation, the vowel system for the earliest point of LCSl was as in (11); it is convenient to divide the system into two subsystems of tense and lax vowels:

(11) LCSl Vowel System

	tense			lax	
i	y	u		ь	ъ
ę		ǫ		e	o
ě [ä]	a				

This was the vowel system that a few dialects of Slavic (for example, Polish) had at the fall of the jers. The vowel system of other dialects can be derived by the application of some transparent changes (raising of *ě from a low vowel [ä] to a mid vowel [ie͡]; denasalization of *ę, ǫ).

It is reasonable to assume that the accent system that is generally reconstructed for earlier periods of Common Slavic held at this time: Act could occur on any syllable of the word, at least on tense vowels; Cmflx occurred on the initial syllable of words lacking an Act (Jakobson 1963).

It is important to emphasize that, once Slavic reinterpreted its original quantitative oppositions as qualitative ones, there was no longer a phonemic opposition in quantity, and it was possible to develop allophonic variants for quantity. In particular, tense vowels were subject to allophonic shortening depending on position in the word (shortening of all final syllables), number of syllables in the word (general shortening in polysyllabic words, depending on position with respect to accent), and most importantly, accent. The shortenings due to accent show considerable dialect variation, a point we will return to later. The allophonic variants created in these conditions were phonemicized at some later point in some but not all dialects of Slavic, leading to the development of new phonemic oppositons at least for tense vowels; long partners to the lax vowels were created (dialectally) by contraction and, eventually, CL.

It is important to note that the establishment of phonemic quantity is a late, dialectally restricted phenomenon. Given that the allophonic variants were conditioned in part by accent, this means that there was a considerable period of history in which LCSl had a distinction of accent but *no* phonemic opposition of quantity. This observation runs counter to a proposed universal of Trubetzkoy (1925:302-303), according to which "Sprachen mit musikalischem Akzent aber ohne Quantitätsunterschiede ... nirgends in der Welt vorkommen."

We come now to the question of the NAct. The NAct is not an original accent. It arose by retraction from a following accented syllable. The best known environment for retraction and creation of a NAct is of course an originally stressed jer, and because we are dealing with a phonetic change conditioned by jers, all of the NAct cases discussed here necessarily involved jers. But the NAct also arose regularly in other contexts, notably in the present tense (outside of the 1st sg.) in verbs of accentual class *b*. This class, which presumably was previously oxytonic (Stang 1957, Dybo 1962), developed an accentual paradigm that might be termed "neomobile": alternation of desinential accent, as in Russian *molotít'*, North Čakavian *mlatȉti* < *moltíti*, and predesinential NAct, as in Russian *molótiš'*, Čakavian *mlȁtiš* < *mol̃tiši*. The origin of the NAct in these and other cases not involving jers is problematic,[2] but whatever its origin, it appears to have been a Common Slavic development, and quite likely arose well before the fall of the jers.

The development of the NAct can be hypothesized to have had two significant consequences. First, it forced the restructuring of the inherited accent system of Act and Cmflx. Second, it forced the issue with respect to the status of distinctive quantity in LCSl. Both of these developments produced significant dialect divergences, which we will examine by dialect zone, starting with NW-SSl.

In NW-SSl, the original Act on tense vowels had been allophonically shortened. The NAct could develop either onto lax vowels (redundantly short) or onto tense vowels (maintained as long pretonically). When the NAct developed, the NAct on lax vowels was evidently identified with the shortened Act, to judge by the fact that they have the same behavior under CL.[3] That is, the development of the NAct created an opposition of phonemic quantity for the merged Act/NAct accent: length from the NAct onto a tense vowel, brevity from NAct onto a lax vowel or shortened Act on tense vowel. Quantity was also phonemicized for the Cmflx: length from the Cmflx on a tense vowel (allophonically maintained as long), brevity from Cmflx on a lax vowel. This is roughly the development assumed for NW-SSl by various investigators (Ivić 1958b, 1965; Pešikan 1969). The contribution here is to identify chronologically the merger of NAct onto lax with shortened Act and the establishment of phonemic quantity in the system.

In SW-ESl, the NAct behaves differently with respect to CL than either the Act or Cmflx. The development of the NAct, then, can be assumed to have triggered the identification of the original Act with the Cmflx. Unlike in NW-SSl, the development of the NAct did not lead to the establishment of phonemic quantity, and there is in general no reason to assume any opposition of phonemic quantity in ESl (contrary to Trubetzkoy 1925, Nazarova 1975).

Here one could also mention NE-ESl. Although no dialects of NE-ESl show reflexes of CL, at least some dialects show a distinction of two back mid vowels that reflects accent: /o/ represents *o under the Cmflx, as in *bŏkъ > bok, *vŏdǫ > vódu, *gôrdъ > górod, while tense /ô/ represents *o under the Act, as in *kořva > koróva, *okъnò > oknô, and, notably, under the NAct, as in *konjь > kôn, *mòžeši > môžeš'. The obvious interpretation is that NE-ESl maintained accent distinctions until the fall of the jers, but when the NAct arose it merged with the Act. Although the pattern of merger is different from that of SW-ESl, it is confirmation for the general hypothesis that the development of the NAct led to the reorganization of the inherited accent system.

The development in WSl is somewhat more complicated. In the northern subzone (and evidently Slovak as well), both the inherited Act on tense vowels and the Cmflx on tense vowels were subject to allophonic shortening. Under CL, the NAct behaves differently from either the (shortened) Act or Cmflx. On the analogy of the development in NW-SSl, this fact suggests that the Act and Cmflx merged when the NAct developed. Again, as in NW-SSl, it is reasonable to assume that the development of the NAct led to the establishment of phonemic quantity. This, however, leads to a typologically unfortunate conclusion. The NAct could occur on long (formerly tense) vowels and on short (formerly lax) vowels, but the new Act/Cmflx accent could occur only on short vowels (either original lax vowels maintained as short, or shortened tense vowels). That is, there would be a distinction of accent on short vowels but not on longs. It is conceivable that long Act/Cmflx vowels were created by contraction, which would make the system more symmetrical. Despite the problem with this reconstruction, it is nevertheless necessary to conclude that N-WSl (and Slovak) had a distinction of accent on short vowels, inasmuch as NAct shorts lengthen differently from Act or Cmflx shorts.

Finally, the development in S-WSl is apparently heterogeneous. As noted above, Slovak presumably had the same development as N-WSl. In Czech, tense Cmflx vowels were allophonically shortened, while tense Act vowels generally were not. As elsewhere in Slavic, the NAct could develop onto lax vowels (redundantly short) or onto tense vowels (maintained as long). As elsewhere, it is reasonable to assume that the development of the NAct led to the institution of phonemic quantity and the reorganization of the accent system. If the Act and Cmflx merged, there would have been an opposition of quantity both under the NAct and the new Act/Cmflx (short from Cmflx, long from Act). If the Act merged with the NAct, there would have an opposition under the Act/NAct but not under the Cmflx (short only). This latter development would have the same unfortunate consequence as the development considered for N-WSl above, namely a distinction of accent on shorts but not on longs. In Upper Sorbian, the development of the NAct evidently did not lead to the institution of phonemic quantity (as it did not in SW-ESl). As in Czech, the position of the inherited Act is unclear. Although accent did not leave any effects on CL per se, it appears to have affected the development of jers in strong position, as in the contrast of Cmflx *rŏžь > rož vs. NAct *rъtъ > rót (Dybo 1963). This shows that Upper Sorbian maintained some sort of accent contrast until the fall of the jers.

Summarizing the discussion above, we have the following course of development. Qualitative differentiation led to the creation of tense and lax vowels with no phonemic distinction of length, although vowels were subsequently adjusted allophonically for length depending on accent, position in the word, and number of syllables in the word. The development of the NAct, a retraction of accent to a preceding syllable from jers and (under unclear conditions) from other vowels, led to two major changes: 1) reorganization of the accent system, with either merger of Act and Cmflx (N-WSl, Slovak, possibly Czech and Upper Sorbian, and SW-ESl) or merger of the NAct with the Act (NW-SSl, NE-ESl); and 2) dialectally, the phonemicization of previously allophonic quantity (W-Sl except Upper Sorbian, NW-SSl, but not SW-ESl).

It remains to consider the effect of accent on CL in the major dialect zones of LCSl. To do this, two hypotheses are necessary: one concerning the tonal contour of the different accents, and a second concerning the effect of accent on quantity. Parallels from contemporary Serbo-Croatian dialects (see Ivić and Lehiste 1963, 1965; Lehiste and Ivić 1977) suggest very strongly that the implementation of an accent opposition on short vowels involves a disyllable, over which the suprasegmental phonetic parameters of tone, intensity, and duration are distributed in a complex fashion. If we adopt this constraint for the reconstruction of accent in LCSl, it is possible to hypothesize a relatively uniform tonal contour for all dialects of LCSl, with the stipulation that the origin of the two accents is different in different dialects. One accent can be assumed to have a rising tone on the first syllable (the phonemically accented syllable) and a falling tone on the second (postaccented) syllable, as diagrammed in (12). (This accent represents the merged Act/NAct of NW-SSl and NE-ESl, and the NAct of WSl and SW-ESl.) The second accent can be assumed to have a falling tone on the accented first syllable, and a neutral or perhaps rising tone on the postaccented second syllable, as diagrammed in (12b). (This accent represents the Cmflx of NW-SSl and NE-ESl, and the merged Cmflx/Act of N-WSl.)

(12) Accent Contours on LCSl
  a. rising
     /V́CV/ > [╱ . ╲]
  b. falling
     /V̂CV/ > [╲ . ╱]

Although it is possible to reconstruct a relatively uniform tonal contour for the two accents in LCSl, it is clear from the development of CL that the distribution of quantity over the two syllables was *not* uniform across Slavic. As noted earlier, in NW-SSl the "falling" accent undergoes CL more readily than the "rising" accent, while in W-Sl and SW-ESl the reverse is true. This difference in the effect of accent on CL recalls another major prosodic isogloss that distinguishes NW-SSl from WSl, namely that Cmflx long vowels were maintained as long in NW-SSl but shortened in WSl. This isogloss suggests that NW-SSl and WSl (and by extension, SW-ESl) utilized different strategies for relating quantity to accent.

If NW-SSl maintained Cmflx length, it evidently evaluated phonetically falling tonal contours as relatively long and, by complementarity, other contours as relatively short. Given the reconstruction of tonal contours for the two accents in (12), it could be expected that the initial syllable of a rising disyllable would be shorter than the corresponding initial syllable of a falling disyllable, and the second syllable of a rising accent would be longer than the corresponding syllable of a falling accent. The difference in each syllable may have been on the order of 0.1 morae. There is more than one way to schematize the relation between accent and quantity, but to simplify matters, let us assume that an amount γ (where $\gamma = 0.1$ morae) is subtracted from the initial syllable of a rising disyllable, and the same amount is subtracted from the second syllable of a falling disyllable. This is shown in (13):

(13) Accent and Quantity in NW-SSl
   a. rising
      /V́CV/ > [V$^{-\gamma}$CV]
   b. falling
      /V̂CV/ > [VCV$^{-\gamma}$]

Now if the second syllable contained a weak jer, it would be reduced by different amounts depending on the accent contour. In a rising disyllable it would be reduced relatively little (by the amount $-\alpha$), and contribute only that amount to the length of the strong vowel. In a falling disyllable the jer would be reduced more (by the amount $-\alpha-\gamma$), and it would contribute relatively more to the length of the strong vowel. This difference is given in (14):

(14) Accent and CL in NW-SSl
   a. rising
      /V́Cə/ > [V$^{(1.0-\gamma)+\alpha}$Cə$^{-\alpha}$]
   b. falling
      /V̂Cə/ > [V$^{1.0+(\alpha+\gamma)}$Cə$^{-\alpha-\gamma}$]

Given this relation between quantity and accent, it is possible to predict a phonemic difference in the development of CL by accent. If, for example, the degree of reduction is $\alpha = 0.6$ and $\gamma = 0.1$, the resulting duration of the rising disyllable would be 1.5, right around the critical duration required for phonemically long vowels. Under these conditions phonemic length in a rising disyllable would occur only before the maximally favorable consonants, namely sonorants, since before other consonants the resulting duration of the strong vowel would fall below the critical duration. The strong vowel of a falling disyllable would be 1.7, enough to guarantee phonemic length even before voiceless obstruents. This is evidently the development in North Čakavian, and the development in other dialects can be described by minor adjustments.

Thus, it is possible to predict the effect of accent on CL in NW-SSl by appealing to a general reconstruction of accent contours for LCSl and to a reconstruction of the relationship between accent and quantity that is specific to NW-SSl.[4]

WSl consistently shortened long Cmflx; in other words, it evaluated falling tones as short. Assuming the accent contours reconstructed above in (12), this would imply a relatively short first syllable in the falling tone (the merger of Act and Cmflx), and a relatively short second syllable in the rising accent (the NAct). This is schematized in (15):

(15) Accent and Quantity in WSl
    a. rising
        /V̀CV/ > [VCV$^{-\gamma}$]
    b. falling
        /V̀CV/ > [V$^{-\gamma}$CV]

Again, when the second syllable contains a jer, it will be more reduced as the second syllable of a rising disyllable, and contribute more to CL, as shown in (16):

(16) Accent and CL in WSl
    a. rising
        /V̀Cə/ > [V$^{1.0+(\alpha+\gamma)}$Cə$^{-\alpha-\gamma}$]
    b. falling
        /V̀Cə/ > [V$^{(1.0-\gamma)+\alpha}$Cə$^{-\alpha}$]

For a value of $\alpha = 0.7$ and $\gamma = 0.1$, the duration of the strong vowel would be 1.8 under the rising (NAct) accent, enough to allow the strong vowel to be analyzed as long before any consonant, including voiceless obstruent. Under the falling (Act/Cmflx) accent, the duration of the strong vowel would be 1.6. This duration would be reduced to 1.4 before voiceless obstruent, so that phonemic length would emerge only before sonorants and voiced obstruents. This set of assumptions, then, predicts the development of CL in N-WSl. The development in S-WSl is slightly problematic, but in principle the dialect chain from Slovak through Czech to Upper

Sorbian can be predicted by assuming somewhat lesser effect of the intervening consonant (β ranges from 0.0 to 0.1 or 0.15) and, crucially, increasing values of reduction from Slovak (α = 0.5) to Upper Sorbian (α = 0.8). Incidentally, although in Upper Sorbian accent does not leave any effect on CL per se, it does affect the reflex of strong jers in disyllabic words, as argued above. This latter fact shows that Upper Sorbian must have maintained a distinction of accent up to the fall of the jers. Hence the absence of any effect of accent on CL cannot be attributed to the otherwise plausible hypothesis that Upper Sorbian eliminated accent distinctions; it must rather be accounted for, as suggested immediately above, by positing an extreme degree of reduction of jers.

SW-ESl shows in principle the same effect of accent as WSl, although the effect is limited to specific contexts (*e before *ъ, pleophonic sequences). And although SW-ESl does not show direct evidence for the shortening of falling tones, it is natural to adopt the same mechanism for SW-ESl as for WSl to account for the effect of accent on CL (as suggested by Andersen 1978). In effect, the first vowel of a rising (NAct) disyllable will be longer than the corresponding vowel of a falling (Act or Cmflx) disyllable, and the weak jer in the second syllable will be correspondingly shorter, thereby contributing more to the development of CL.

The effect of accent fades out in northern Ukrainian and southern Belorussian, to judge by the fact that tense reflexes appear in *mĕdъ, *lĕdъ (earlier in the latter than in the former) and in pleophonic sequences such as *vorňъ, *korvъka. One can imagine more than one account of this geographical development. The one that is consistent with the approach here is that the effect of accent on quantity remained in effect throughout the SW-ESl zone, but the phonemic elimination of jers occurred later on the periphery of this zone than in the center. As a result, when jers were eliminated on the periphery, weak jers were more reduced, and the second vowel in pleophonic sequences was more fully developed, thereby allowing tense reflexes to develop both in the Cmflx *e before *ъ context and in pleophonic sequences. In effect, the later loss of jers on the relative periphery of the SW-ESl zone undermined the effect of accent on CL. This, then, is another case of a local isogloss within a subzone of LCSl that can be explicated by appealing to the assumption that jers were eliminated later (in the sense of a later stage of phonetic development) on the periphery than in the center, with the consequence that reflexes of CL increase from center to periphery.[5]

This concludes the reconstruction of CL and its conditions.[6]

7. **Conclusions.** We have argued that reflexes of long (tense) vowels for LCSl short (and shortened) vowels in syllables preceding weak jers should be viewed as the result of a phonetic process of compensatory lengthening. Other interpretations of the reflexes, notably the notion of length in newly closed syllables, are doubtful. On the view proposed here, a vowel acquired length in proportion to the phonetic reduction of the jer in the following syllable. The degree of reduction increased over time, the result of which was a geographical increase in reduction from the center to the periphery of major dialect zones of LCSl. In addition, reduction was affected dialectally by the position of the strong vowel-weak jer disyllable in the phonological word. The length of the strong vowel itself was adjusted dialectally for the immediately following consonant, according to the hierarchy sonorants ≥ voiced fricatives ≥ voiced stops ≥ voiceless obstruents. Accent also affected the distribution of duration over the strong vowel-weak jer disyllable, simultaneously influencing the inherent length of the strong vowel and the degree of reduction of the jer. Phonemic long (tense) reflexes resulted when the phonetic length of the strong vowel equalled or exceeded a critical duration at the time when jers were eliminated phonemically.

The interpretation of CL offered here is consistent with that of many, perhaps most, investigators, and in its general outlines is by no means novel. What is perhaps novel is the attempt to deal with the constraints on CL through the technique of phonetic reconstruction. This technique has two things to recommend it.

First, through this technique it is possible to accommodate the significant dialect divergences among dialects of LCSl within a uniform view of the process of CL. These divergences are of two kinds.

On the one hand, some divergences take the form of isoglosses dividing the major dialect zones or subzones of LCSl. Such is the case with the effect of accent on CL, which divides NW-SSl from WSl and SW-ESl, and probably with the effect of position in the word, which divides NW-SSl from at least N-WSl (S-WSl and SW-ESl are apparently neutral with respect to this factor). Such may well be the case with the effect of the intervening consonant, which shows up (at least in some context) throughout WSl and (except Slovenian) NW-SSl, but leaves no reflexes in SW-ESl. This type of divergence requires that significant differences in phonological structure be reconstructed for dialect zones of LCSl — for example, in the case of accent, a difference in the relationship between duration and accent contours.

On the other hand, some dialect divergences reflect differences in the degree of development of CL, and take the form of relatively local isoglosses within major dialect zones of LCSl. Further, these isoglosses always have the property that the reflexes of CL increase from center to periphery. A number of such cases were documented above: in S-WSl, increasing development of CL not under the NAct from Slovak (none) through Czech (restricted by consonant) to Upper Sorbian (unrestricted); in N-WSl, increasing development of CL in terms of position in the word from South Polish (none) through North Polish (some) to Kashubian (nearly complete); in NW-SSl, increasing development of CL under the Act/NAct accent both in terms of word position — from Slovenian (no final CL) to Serbo-Croatian (at least restricted final CL) — and intervening consonant — from North Čakavian (only before sonorants) to South Čakavian (before sonorants and voiced obstruents); and finally in SW-ESl, increasing development of CL not under the NAct both for *e before *ъ and in pleophonic sequences. These local differences in CL can be explicated by assuming more or less constant phonological constraints on CL for a given subzone and increasing development in the degree of reduction of jers from the center to the periphery. Increasing reduction of jers is motivated under the assumption that jers were eliminated phonemically later on the periphery than in the center.

Second, this technique requires explicitness not only in the reconstruction of the process of CL itself but also in the reconstruction of the phonological structure of dialects of LCSl. In some cases (for example, the conclusion that SW-ESl is less sensitive to the effect of consonants than other zones of LCSl) the reconstruction does not go much beyond the observed facts; in other cases (for example, the treatment of the effect of word position or the apparent restriction of CL to *e and *o in some dialects) the reconstruction leads to new, unresolved problems. But in other cases the reconstruction leads to potentially interesting results, as for example in the effect of accent on CL. This effect suggests that the accent and quantity system of LCSl was thoroughly restructured before the fall of the jers. Quite possibly, the previously allophonic neoacute accent contour was incorporated into the phonemic system of LCSl, such that either the NAct merged with the Act (NW-SSl, NE-ESl) or the NAct became a phonemic accent, distinct from the old (merged?) Act and Cmflx (WSl, SW-ESl). The phonemicization of the NAct was presumably also the point in LCSl at which quantity was reestablished phonemically, at least dialectally (NW-SSl, WSl except Upper Sorbian, but not ESl). The effect of accent on CL, which divides NW-SSl from WSl and SW-ESl, can be partially correlated with another major prosodic isogloss, the preservation of long Cmflx in NW-SSl vs. shortening in WSl. In any case, the mere fact that CL developed differently depending on the accent in *all* dialect zones that have reflexes of CL shows that these dialects had some sort of accent contrast until the fall of the jers, although they did not necessarily have a phonemic opposition in quantity. Dialect zones that do not show reflexes of CL (SE-SSl, Polabian on the extreme periphery of N-WSl, NE-ESl) may well have shifted to a permutative stress system in advance of the fall of the jers.

University of California, Los Angeles

NOTES

[1] We are interested in cases of CL defined ostensively by the examples above: a full vowel is lengthened before a weak jer. Some other changes that could be considered to be compensatory lengthening in a more general sense are 1) progressive lengthening after a weak jer of the type *kъto > Polish dial. któ, 2) lengthening in Slovenian of shortened acute to long circumflex (often termed "neocircumflex") before a syllable containing a long vowel that is shortened, as in *mýsliši > *mıslīš > mısliš, and, most notably, 3) the development of strong jers in accordance with Havlík's Law, when the vowel in strong position is itself a jer. In this study we will not be concerned with such cases.

A recent article in general linguistics (de Chene and Anderson 1979) discusses another type of change that is often termed "compensatory lengthening," in which consonants in syllable coda position are lost with eventual lengthening of the syllable nucleus. The authors argue convincingly that this type of change actually involves two changes, weakening of the consonant in coda position to a glide, and monophthongization of the glide with the syllable nucleus. Given this interpretation, one could question whether the term "compensatory lengthening" is appropriate to this type of change at all. In any case, it is clear that this type of change, which is intrasyllabic, is significantly different from the change of CL discussed here, which is intersyllabic, and there is no reason to expect that there is anything in common in the phonetic mechanisms involved in the two types of change.

[2] Stang (1957) argues that the NAct here arose by retraction just in case the accent on the theme vowel was Cmflx. That is, Act *moltjǫ̃ does not retract (Russian moločú) but Cmflx *moltīši does (Russian molótiš'). Aside from the fact that the reasoning here is circular (an internal Cmflx is posited just in case retraction occurs), this reconstruction has the unusual property of positing internal Cmflx accent at a relatively late point in Slavic. Work by Dybo (1962) and Illič-Svityč (1963) suggests that the accent on the theme vowel in these cases goes back to a much earlier barytone circumflex accent, but the conditions under which retraction from the theme vowel occurred are still obscure.

[3] In general, there is no place in NW-SSl (or in Slavic generally) where short Act, NAct, and Cmflx all behave differently one from the other. One possible exception is Kajkavian. There short Cmflx is distinguished from short NAct and short Act with respect to CL, as elsewhere in NW-SSl. Short NAct lengthens in nominal paradigms (*sèla > sēla) but shortened Act does not (*kràva > *kràva > kráva). If the lengthening here were purely phonetic, it would imply a difference between short Act and short NAct. As Ivić (1965:130, fn. 1) points out, however, short NAct does not lengthen in the neomobile verb paradigm (*nòsiši > nòsiš, not *nōsiš). This suggests that the lengthening of short NAct was not a purely phonetic process, and it is therefore not evidence that the short NAct and Act were necessarily distinct.

[4] It would be desirable to have contemporary parallels for this reconstruction. Instrumental studies on contemporary Serbo-Croatian dialects, both Štokavian (Ivić and Lehiste 1963, 1965) and Posavian (Lehiste and Ivić 1977), do show some difference in duration in the accented syllable and the postaccented syllable between rising and falling accents, but the difference is

not always that supposed in the reconstruction here; further, it is not consistent across speakers. Some examples for the comparison of accent types x̀x̄ vs. x̋x̄: subject D3 has (in centiseconds) 9.1, 6.9 for x̀x̄ vs. 8.6, 7.5 for x̋x̄ — consistent with the reconstruction here; subject D2 has x̀x̄ 9.6, 6.7 vs. x̋x̄ 10.3, 7.2 — at least the postaccented syllable of the rising disyllable is longer than that of the falling disyllable; and subject D1 has x̀x̄ 11.9, 9.3 vs. x̋x̄ 12.5, 8.3 — exactly opposite of our reconstruction (Ivić and Lehiste 1965:81-82). Another possible source for a contemporary parallel is the shortening of postaccented longs in contemporary Štokavian dialects: longs are better preserved after a new Štokavian rising tone (Ivić 1965:143), which is consistent with the claim here that the postaccented syllable of a rising tone is longer than that of a falling tone.

[5] This analysis is a slight modification of an alternative hypothesis (Andersen 1978), which runs as follows. If the difference between NAct and Act/Cmflx were viewed as a specific innovation of the central region of SW-ESl — an innovation of shortening under both Act and Cmflx — the development of tense reflexes for Cmflx *e before *ъ and in pleophonic sequences could represent the loss of this central innovation. This alternative would seem to imply that the effect of accent on CL should disappear simultaneously for both Cmflx *e before *ъ and pleophonic sequences. This does not appear to be the case in the Hajnówka dialects of Belorussian in Poland (Kondratiuk 1964). For much of this area length is attested in *mědъ but not in pleophonic sequences: in Grabowiec m'ed (with CL) but soróčka, kólos, hólos (no CL), and in Policzna m'id (with CL) but moróz, xólod, hólod, hólos (no CL). Since accent continues to affect CL in one context, there must still have been a difference in vowel duration due to accent. That is, the development of CL appears to be a change in *other* conditions for CL (degree of reduction of the jers, or inherent quantity of the second pleophonic vowel) while the accent condition is maintained.

[6] One possible condition not discussed here is the question of which vowels undergo CL. Throughout S-WSl and in SW-ESl, only *e, o show the results of lengthening, suggesting a hierarchical ranking of vowels in terms of likelihood of undergoing CL, namely $o, e \geqslant$ other vowels. It is not clear, however, what this hierarchy reflects.

In SW-ESl and in Upper Sorbian, the restriction of CL to e, o is probably a reflex of the phonological system of these languages at the fall of the jers. Unlike other languages with reflexes of CL, these two dialect zones did not have a phonemic opposition of quantity for all vowels, but rather a limited opposition of tense vs. lax for one or both mid vowels. At the fall of the jers, phonetically lengthened allophones $[e^{+a}]$, $[o^{+a}]$ of /e/, /o/ were identified as tense mid vowels /ê/, /ô/. It is conceivable that other vowels were phonetically lengthened by CL, but given that SW-ESl and Upper Sorbian lacked distinctive quantity, any differences in phonetic length did not lead to phonemic results.

Slovak and Czech had distinctive quantity at the fall of the jers. In Slovak CL occurs only under the NAct accent, and because *e, o (and jers) are the only short vowels that could occur under the NAct (a NAct onto any vowel would have preserved length), CL was naturally limited to e, o. Only Czech, then, gives direct evidence for the proposed hierarchy of $e, o \geqslant$ other vowels. Even here, however, the significance of this constraint is not clear. It seems unlikely that it reflects directly the ability of vowels to undergo phonetic lengthening, given that instrumental studies consistently show that inherent duration varies inversely with articulatory vowel height, that is, high vowels $\leqslant$ mid vowels $\leqslant$ low vowels (House and Fairbanks 1953:111, Ivić and Lehiste 1963:36-37). Given that *e, o were lax vowels, they may well have been shorter than all other vowels, including high vowels. It is conceivable that, as lax vowels, a small difference in duration would be easier to analyze as distinctively long than for tense vowels.

REFERENCES

Andersen, H.
 1969 "Kashubian *dobëtk 'dobytek'* and its Kind," *WdSl* 15, 61-76.
 1973 "Abductive and Deductive Change," *Lg* 49, 567-593.
 1978 "Perceptual Complexity and Abductive Change" in *Recent Developments in Historical Phonology*, ed. by J. Fisiak. The Hague, 1-22.
Chen, M.
 1970 "Vowel Length Variation as a Function of the Voicing of the Consonant Environment," *Phonetica* 22, 129-159.
de Chene, B. and S. R. Anderson
 1979 "Compensatory Lengthening," *Lg* 55, 505-535.
Dybo, V. A.
 1962 "O rekonstrukcii udarenija v praslavjanskom glagole," *Voprosy slavjanskogo jazykoznanija* 6, 3-27.
 1963 "Ob otraženii drevnix količestvennyx i intonacionnyx otnošenij v verxnelužickom jazyke" in *Serbo-lužickyj lingvističeskij sbornik*. Moscow, 54-83.
House, A.
 1961 "On Vowel Duration in English," *JASA* 33, 1174-1178.
House, A. and G. Fairbanks
 1953 "The Influence of Consonant Environment upon the Secondary Acoustical Characteristics of Vowels," *JASA* 25, 105-113.
Illič-Svityč, V. M.
 1963 *Imennaja akcentuacija v baltijskom i slavjanskom. Sud'ba akcentuacionnyx paradigm*. Moscow.
Ivić, P.
 1958a *Die serbokroatischen Dialekte. Ihre Struktur und Entwicklung. Allgemeines und die štokavische Dialektgruppe*, 1. The Hague.
 1958b "Osnovnye puti razvitija serboxorvatskogo vokalizma," *VJa*, 1958, no. 1, 3-20.
 1965 "Glavne linije razvoja prozodijskog sistema u srpskohrvatskom jeziku" in *Studia z filologii polskiej i słowiańskiej* 5, 129-144.
Ivić, P. and I. Lehiste
 1963 "Prilozi ispitivanju fonetske i fonološke prirode akcenata u savremenom srpskohrvatskom književnom jeziku," *Zbornik za filologiju i lingvistiku* 6, 31-71.
 1965 "Prilozi ispitivanju fonetske i fonološke prirode akcenata u savremenom srpskohrvatskom jeziku, 2," *Zbornik za filologiju i lingvistiku* 8, 75-117.
Jakobson, R.
 1929 "Remarques sur l'évolution phonologique du russe comparée à celle des autres langues slaves," *TCLP*, 2.
 1963 "Opyt fonologičeskogo podxoda k istoričeskim voprosam slavjanskoj akcentologii. Pozdnij period slavjanskoj praistorii" in *American Contributions to the Fifth International Congress of Slavists*. The Hague, 153-178.
Kondratiuk, M.
 1964 "Wokalizm białorusko-ukraińskich gwar powiatu hajnowskiego," *Slavia Orientalis* 13, 339-356.
Lehiste, I. and P. Ivić
 1977 "Fonetska analize jedne slavonske akcentuacije," *Referati i saopštenja MSC* 6, no. 1, 67-84.
Lehr-Spławiński, T.
 1929 *Gramatyka połabska*. Lvov.

Lisker, L.
1974 "On 'Explaining' Vowel Duration," *Glossa* 8, 233-246.
Nazarova, T. V.
1975 "Zaminne podovžennja v ukrajins'komu areali na tli sxidnoslovjans'kyx prosodyčnyx peretvoren'," *Movoznavstvo*, 1975, no. 6, 22-32.
Pešikan, M.
1969 "O osnovima štokavske akcentuacije," *JF* 28, 107-142.
Peterson, G. and I. Lehiste
1960 "Duration of Syllabic Nuclei in English," *JASA* 32, 693-703.
Schuster-Šewc, H.
1958 "Reflexe alter Längen im Niedersorbischen," *ZfSl* 3, 264-271.
Shevelov, G.
1965 *A Prehistory of Slavic: The Historical Phonology of Common Slavic.* New York.
Stang, C.
1957 *Slavonic Accentuation.* Oslo.
Šaxmatov, A. A.
1915 *Očerk drevnejšego perioda istorii russkogo jazyka.* (= Ènciklopedija slavjanskoj filologii, 11.) Petrograd.
Timberlake, A.
1983 "Compensatory Lengthening in Slavic, 1: Conditions and Dialect Geography" in *From Los Angeles to Kiev,* ed. by D. Worth and V. Markov. Columbus, Ohio.
Trubetzkoy, N.
1925 "Einiges über die russische Lautentwicklung und die Auflösung der gemeinrussischen Spracheinheit," *ZfSlPh* 1, 287-319.
Umeda, N.
1975 "Vowel Duration in American English," *JASA* 58, 434-445.

Contribution to the Systematic Comparison of Morphological and Lexical Semantic Structures in the Slavic Languages

C. H. van Schooneveld

Every science tries to construct predictabilities. It tries to predict, given a number of phenomena at hand, what will happen an hour from now, and tries to predict, given these phenomena, what will be the state of affairs a thousand years from now. In linguistics, the first type of prediction is done by synchronic rules, and the second type of prediction — if feasible at all — is done through the diachronic investigation of language.

If one now looks to what extent linguists consider predictability possible, then one finds essentially two views: a) language is a random collection of entities; any ordering in the material is introduced extrinsically by the describing linguist. For this approach. F. W. Householder has coined the term "hocus–pocus linguistics"; b) language constitutes a structure, that is to say, it has a number of recurrent components which make it into a system. This view holds further that in diachronic development only a limited number of alternatives are open. These alternatives are determined by the laws of structure, which in turn entail laws that determine which structures can replace other structures. Structures are physically ascertainable in the sense that phonological structure consists of contrasting sound waves, which can be measured; semantic structure is more difficult to ascertain, but is in any case based upon social values which can be ascertained, analyzed and verified by methods akin to those of sociological investigations. F. W. Householder has called this approach "God's truth linguistics."

The latter view generally reckons with the possibility that there is a residue in language which is not strictly governed by structural laws; for instance, so-called petrified forms are seen to be remnants from a diachronically preceding stratum and, in this view, do not quite follow the new synchronic rules. But where is the boundary of the structural law and where does no man's land begin? Why are certain entities preserved from an older period while others are discarded by the new synchronic state?

It seems to me that the time has come to consider a third alternative: language is a totally structured system, seeming exceptions are structurally conditioned with an iconic function — and fit into the synchronic system; in fact, language is a subconscious semantic calculus, only more elaborate than arithmetic.

If one ponders, in fact, the direction in which the methodology of the Prague School has developed in the course of a number of decades, one sees it move on several points towards a replacement of more complicated analyses by solutions in terms of privative binary oppositions. Trubetzkoy's intricate theory of oppositions of 1939 is amended in the same year by Jakobson's equation of the consonantal triangle with the vowel triangle in Ghent in 1939, and in 1952 it is replaced with an analysis of the distinctive features of the languages of the world in terms of privative binary oppositions except in the case of the compactness – diffuseness relation and the acuteness – gravity relation. Thus the principles of phonological structure given in Jakobson's definition of the phoneme *Ottův slovník naučný* in 1932[1] are vindicated by the analyses of the later years, and this is even more the case when in the second, revised edition of *Fundamentals of Language*, which was originally published in 1956, the polarity of acuteness and gravity finds its logical solution through correction by empirical acoustic data in that acuteness and gravity turn out to be two independent distinctive features in their own right.[2] Thus the last holdout against privative binarism in phonology is the ternary contrarious opposition compact – diffuse.

One sees a similar development in Jakobson's morphological work, for instance, in his analysis of the case system. In 1936, in the "Beitrag zur allgemeinen Kasuslehre," it seems to him that the Russian case system operates with four markings and that the opposition between the two genitives and the two locatives is different from the opposition between the directional cases and the cases unmarked for directionality. In 1958 he publishes in "Morfologičeskie nabljudenija nad slavjanskim skloneniem" an improved analysis, according to which the oppositions between the genitives and the locatives are also varieties of the directionality opposition. The case system turns out to constitute a totally regular privative binary system which Jakobson symbolizes by a cube. The structuralist had originally not been structuralist enough. I say "improved analysis," since the new system explains a few usages, such as *iz lesu* vs. *iz lesa* or *s času*, which are hard to interpret under the old 1936 analysis, where the *-u* genitive is marked for partitivity and the *-a* genitive is unmarked.[3]

It would be a cause for wonderment if this totally regular Russian case structure would constitute an integral part of a semantic system which, according to practically all analyses performed up to now, is far from the picture of perfect regularity displayed by the category of case in all its crystalline elegance.

Puzzled by this question, I started investigating a number of decades ago the system of Russian prepositions and preverbs, and later extended this investigation to the Russian paratactic conjunctions, to Russian word formation, to the gender system, to the Russian system of parts of speech (word categories), to the grammatical categories of the verb, to the lexicon and to the relationship between morphemes, that is, the relationship between lexical + word-formative + word categorial + grammatical morphemes as articulated within the Russian word.[4] The preliminary results are as follows:

1. All of the categories just mentioned operate with a maximum of six conceptual features, of which the case system utilizes three and the prepositional system five, the case system on one level of deixis and the prepositional system on another. These features not only oppose the units within one category, but they also differentiate, by means of several levels of deixis, the categories themselves.

2. There are four levels of deixis, which I call perceptional,[5] transmissional (this is the type of deixis that has been traditionally called "deixis" in the literature) singulative perceptional and singulative transmissional. As to informational content, transmissional deixis contains perceptional deixis; conversely, the referential range of transmissional deixis is a subset of the referential range of perceptional deixis. For a detailed explanation of the differences between the levels of deixis I refer to other work of mine,[6] and I must introduce them here simply as operational givens. As such, the four levels of deixis multiply the six conceptual features by four. Ext'''', restr'''' and obj'''' apparently signify agreement.[7] The resulting structure is of a degree of complexity no greater than that of molecules in organic chemistry.

3. I shall return to the concept of deixis later on, when I mention the notion of autopoiesis, but will now briefly discuss the conceptual features themselves. They constitute a hierarchically ordered set, as follows:

1. plurality (I formerly called this feature "transitivity")
2. dimensionality
3. distinctness (I formerly called this feature "duplication")
4. extension (corresponding to Jakobson's case feature of directionality)
5. restrictedness (corresponding to Jakobson's case feature of marginality)
6. objectiveness (corresponding to Jakobson's case feature of quantification)

I shall return to the ordering of this hierarchy shortly; in fact, the theme of this entire contribution is the structure of the hierarchy of conceptual features.

The actual occurrence of the features can be very roughly exemplified in the chart on the following page (which disregards the differentiations by deictic levels and which is not complete):

	plur	dim	dist	ext	restr	obj
preposition/preverb		+	+	+	+	+
conjunction			+	+		
case				+	+	+
number	+					
gender			+	+		
personal pronoun	+	+	+	+		
part of speech		+				+
verbal grammatical categories	+	+	+	+	+	
lexicon	+	+	+	+	+	+
word formation	+	+	+	+	+	+
comparative	+					
structure of the word,	+	+	+	+	+	+
i.e. the syntagmatic sequence of morphemes within a given word: lexical + word-formative + word-categorial + grammatical + agreement morphemes.						

If one introduces the levels of deixis into the picture, one can illustrate the sum total of possible occurrences of the conceptual features in Russian by the chart given below. I use for the four levels of deixis notations by means of primes: perceptional: ', transmissional: ", singulative perceptional: ''', singulative transmissional: ''''.

At this point it is important to underscore the difference between deixis and autopoiesis. Perceptional plurality (transitivity) and dimensionality are autopoietic, but not perceptionally deictic.[8] Nevertheless I mark these two features with single primes to distinguish them from the features on deictic levels other than the perceptional and also to distinguish their operation on the perceptional level from the features in general, without regard to their operation on one of the four levels of deixis.

Dimensionality implies (or, as I have used the term in previous publications, presupposes) plurality (transitivity) and plurality (transitivity) implies (presupposes) the effectuation of an unspecified (intransitive) perception act. Only with distinctness (duplication) does the hierarchy become deictic, that is, imply the effectuation of a specific perception act. Anyhow, implication (Husserl's *Fundierung*[9]), or presupposition, as I have termed it in several publications, has now found a better name in the notion of autopoiesis, recently proposed in biology.[10]

The chart is followed by a listing of the features actually occurring in a specific example, to wit, the instrumental singular *tolkovost'ju* (the instrumental plural would be marked additionally for $\frac{dist''''}{plur'''}$, that is, plur''' in the fourth column). The fourth prime (singulative – transmissionally deictic) features

SEMANTIC STRUCTURES IN THE SLAVIC LANGUAGES

∅'''' (lex)	tr'''' (wf)	dim'''' (p.o.s.)	dupl'''' (grammatical)	ext'''' (agreement)	restr'''' (agreement)	obj'''' (agreement)
tolk-	-ov-	-ost'-	-ju	[case] [number]	[p.o.s.] [gender]	[pers. pron.]
plur'(tr')	plur'(tr')	plur'(tr')	plur'(tr')	plur'(tr')	plur'(tr')	plur'(tr')
dim'	dim'	dim'	dim'	dim'	dim'	dim'
dist'(dupl')	dist'(dupl')	dist'(dupl')	dist'(dupl')	dist'(dupl')	dist'(dupl')	dist'(dupl')
ext'	ext'	ext'	ext'	ext'	ext'	ext'
restr'	restr'	restr'	restr'	restr'	restr'	restr'
obj'	obj'	obj'	obj'	obj'	obj'	obj'
plur''(tr'')	plur''(tr'')	plur''(tr'')	plur''(tr'')	plur''(tr'')	plur''(tr'')	plur''(tr'')
dim''	dim''	dim''	dim''	dim''	dim''	dim''
dist''(dupl'')	dist''(dupl'')	dist''(dupl'')	dist''(dupl'')	dist''(dupl'')	dist''(dupl'')	dist''(dupl'')
ext''	ext''	ext''	ext''	ext''	ext''	ext''
restr''	restr''	restr''	restr''	restr''	restr''	restr''
obj''	obj''	obj''	obj''	obj''	obj''	obj''
plur'''(tr''')	plur'''(tr''')	plur'''(tr''')	plur'''(tr''')	plur'''(tr''')	plur'''(tr''')	plur'''(tr''')
dim'''	dim'''	dim'''	dim'''	dim'''	dim'''	dim'''
dist'''(dupl''')	dist'''(dupl''')	dist'''(dupl''')	dist'''(dupl''')	dist'''(dupl''')	dist'''(dupl''')	dist'''(dupl''')
ext'''	ext'''	ext'''	ext'''	ext'''	ext'''	ext'''
restr'''	restr'''	restr'''	restr'''	restr'''	restr'''	restr'''
obj'''	obj'''	obj'''	obj'''	obj'''	obj'''	obj'''

mark various types of morphemes: $\emptyset''''$ is carried by lexical meaning, $plur''''$ marks word formation, dim'''' is the semantic marking of the category of parts of speech, while $dist''''$ is the feature carried by grammatic categories. The features ext'''', $restr''''$ and obj'''' serve to indicate various types of agreement. Thus, in the phrase *izumitel'noj tolkovost'ju* the instrumental of the head word is carried by $\dfrac{dist''''}{restr'}$, but the instrumental of the agreeing adjective *izumitel'noj* is carried by $\dfrac{ext''''}{restr''''}$ and the feminine gender of the same adjective is carried by $\dfrac{restr'}{dist'''}$.
ext'''

A form like *tolkovost'ju* carries a selection of features under each column. The following notation is tentative:

tolk-	-ov-	-ost'-	-ju			
$\emptyset''''$	$plur''''$	dim''''	$dist''''$	ext''''	$restr''''$	obj''''
plur'	dist'	dim'	restr'			
ext'		obj'				
plur''		dist'''				
dim''		ext'''				
dist''						
obj''						

$\emptyset''''$: *plur'* : the concept can be considered transitive because it involves a patient rather than an agent

        ext' : the patient is minimally affected by the action bearing upon it since the action does not create but only bears upon the patient

    plur'', *dim''*, *dist''*, and *obj''* create the semantic field of thinking of which *tolk(-ovat')* is a member

plur'''' : *dist'* : the word-formative suffix *-ov* signifies derivatives that are associated with the deriving term, but are not part of it

dim'''' : *dim'*   and *obj'* signify substantives

      dist'''   and *ext'''* signify the feminine gender

dist'''' : *restr'* : the case feature of marginality

Although I think that the above analysis is in principle correct, I also believe that we have just scratched the surface of the semantic mechanism which is at work. I shall now discuss a few aspects of this semantic mechanism and specifically autopoiesis. This concept will lead us to the semantic dominant and to interlinguistic semantic calculus. I continue my listing of the conclusions to which the investigation has led so far:

If one starts seeking ways to describe the semantic invariants carried by each feature, one finds empirically that these invariants are best formulated in terms of perception acts. No other methodology will cover all usages. The features essentially indicate how to identify a certain segment of exogenous reality, in terms of the identification process itself. For example, plurality instructs the addressee to repeat the perception act. Extension says: look for a referent that was the objective of a perception act and is still perceivable. Restrictedness says: look for a referent that, while having been the objective of a perception act, cannot be perceived again in a similar fashion. The only invariant that all perception acts have in common is (the perception of) the perception act as such.

The semantic features constitute a hierarchy, in that each succeeding feature implies the preceding one. For instance, restrictedness implies extension (see above) because it comments upon the continuity of perceptibility indicated in extension, by denying it. In order to be denied by restrictedness, this continuity has first to be posited by extension. In a comparable fashion, dimensionality implies plurality, distinctness implies dimensionality, extension implies distinctness, restrictedness implies extension, and objectiveness implies restrictedness. As a corollary, dimensionality contains plurality, distinctness contains dimensionality, extension contains distinctness, and so on. The perception act codified by the preceding feature is incorporated into the next feature. From distinctness on, the system is deictic, since it relates to the perception of one specific referent and not simply to the perception of any referent whatsoever. In Russian this automatically makes the notion modified by the referent also specific and deictic, since in that language, unlike, for instance, French, the modifier can be noncontiguous to the modified. This means that from extension on, the same referent is considered more than once, from various vantage points. These vantage points represent different moments in time. For details, I refer to my forthcoming paper "Contribution to the Quest for Meaning in Language." The following chart tries to show that each succeeding feature incorporates the preceding one. The arrows point to the relation of the referent to the perception of the initial point (modified). While the original relation of the modified to the referent (the modifier) remains in the memory, the actual position of the modified with regard to the modifier changes from feature to feature. Since the referent gives information about the modified, it can be stated in general that the modified follows the modifier in the sense that the position of the modified in space is conceived of in its relationship to the modifier. Since the position of the modifier (referent) is in turn conceived of in terms of its relation to the original modified – modifier relationship, the modified can be said to be conceived of indirectly in terms of its original relationship to the modifier (referent), that is, its original location in space as given in distinctness. In transitivity (plur.), the modified is, at the end of the verbal process, one (or more) of the peers of the referent. In dimensionality, it is contained in the space occupied by the referent. From distinctness on, the differences between comparable conceptual features as they are embedded as components in the structures of various languages become very noticeable. Russian distinctness, for instance, has a range of reference which differs considerably from the range of reference of French distinctness. In Russian, the modified of distinctness can be located anywhere in relation to the modifier, provided the space intervening between them is seen as a continuum (a topological neighborhood). In restrictedness and objectiveness the modified follows the modifier again. It is this relation between the reference and the initial point (modified) which constitutes the information given by the particular conceptual feature.

Each feature is essentially a scanning device that tells the perceiver how to zero in on the referent. The incorporation of the preceding feature(s) into the next one entails taking into account the preceding perception acts. Since each feature results in a perception act, each succeeding feature, too, gives instructions for the perception and identification of the referent in terms of the perception act itself. Meaning, then, appears to be a scanning device that calibrates exogenous reality in terms of its own scanning. In my lectures, I have used for a number of years the image of an instrument flight in which the pilot gets no instructions from the ground after take-off and executes each navigation decision on the basis of his previous decisions. The same image is used a number of times by Maturana and Varela for their characterization of the working of the perception mechanism of nervous systems in living beings.[11] In fact, if one thinks through the question of invariance in perception to its utmost consequences, then one is bound to come to the conclusion that the ultimate invariant which all perception acts have in common must be the factuality of the perception act itself.

The conceptual features form, therefore, a hierarchy about which it can be said that it is created by the fact that the features observe themselves operate. They perceive themselves perceive. To be sure, from a linguistic point of view this statement is no more than a metaphor. However, the operation and structural hierarchy of the nervous system is based precisely upon this principle:

> ... the nervous system [has the] capacity to interact with its own states; ... there is no possible distinction between internally and externally generated states of nervous activity. There are two sources of deformations ...: one is constituted by the external environment as a source of independent events; the other is constituted by the system itself as a source of states which arise from compensations of deformations, but which themselves can constitute deformations that generate

SEMANTIC STRUCTURES IN THE SLAVIC LANGUAGES 329

Plurality
  (transitivity)

Dimensionality

Distinctness
  (duplication)

Extension

Restrictedness

Objectiveness

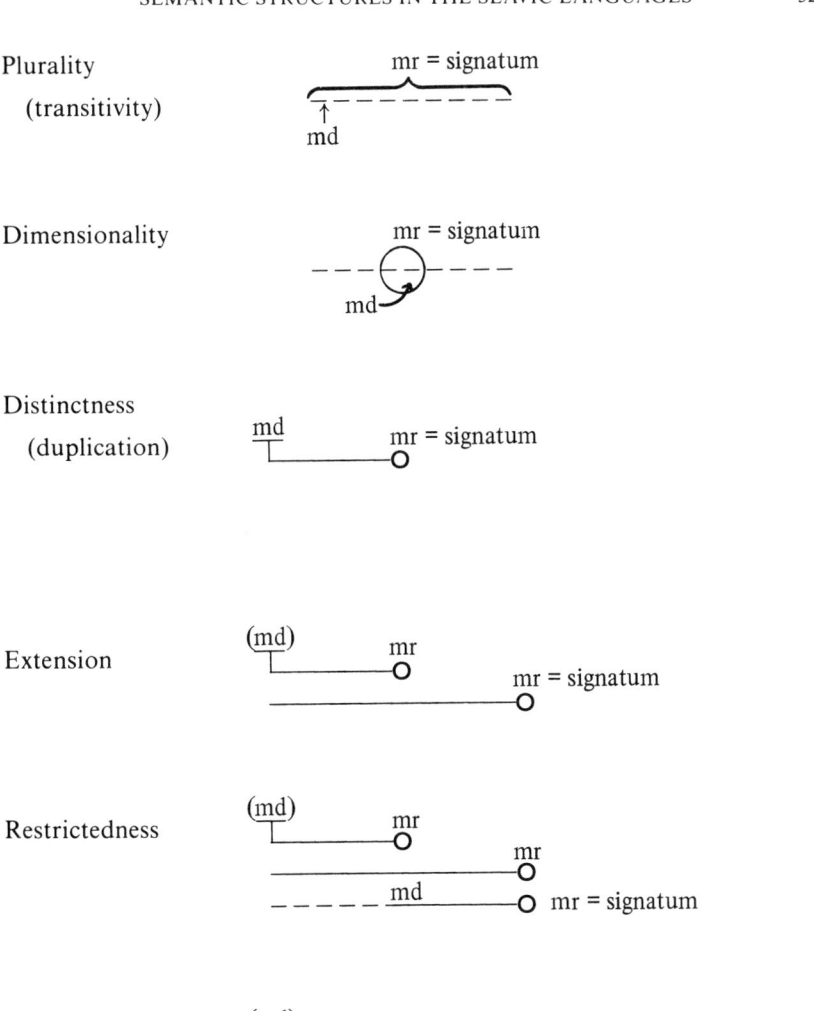

further compensatory changes. In the phenomenology of the autopoietic organization these two sources of perturbations are indistinguishable; ... the organism becomes an observer ...; ... such an observer ... can ... *describe* himself *describing* himself ... endlessly. An organism with a nervous system capable of interacting with its own states ... can *describe* its describing.[12]

It seems that in language, the possibilities of creating new features are not infinite, but are exhausted by objectiveness, after which the feature hierarchy switches over to the next level of deixis, until the levels of deixis exhaust themselves in turn with singulative transmissional deixis. What is in linguistic meaning totally parallel, however, to the autopoiesis of the nervous system as described by Maturana and Varela, is that each succeeding perceptional feature is established on the basis of the fact that the preceding perception technique is applied in an actual perception act. Moreover, the possibility of recursion of any given feature on more than one deictic level makes the present system for all practical purposes limitless. The application of the preceding feature has to be observed. The parallel with Saussure's distinction between *langue* and *parole* and the notion of deixis as the term is traditionally used is obvious: deixis in the traditional sense (I prefer to use the term *transmissional* deixis) is the codification into *langue* of (an instance of) *parole*. In my opinion, this circular principle of alternation between the code and its individual application applies to all meaning, and not only to meaning traditionally called deictic. Not only the perception of a speech act (*parole*), but any perception act is recodified so as to form a new semantic feature.

It is important to ask the question why it is the perception act itself that has actually to be observed. This is so since the features are based precisely on perceptional procedures. Thus we can conceive of the hierarchy as a game of musical chairs with two chairs: one the chair of the perception act, the other the chair of the perception code. The system is built by switching back and forth between the two positions: the actual application, say of the dimensionality feature is recodified into the distinctness feature; the actual application of the distinctness feature is recodified into the extension feature, and so on.

Obviously, in a linguistic system as it has been fully acquired by a speaker of the language the game of musical chairs between application (perception act) and code (feature) constitutes an established and enduring synchronic relationship. If this is so, then the acquisition of the hierarchy by the individual must follow an established pattern, as it is imposed by the language and the way it is used by its speakers. It follows a predetermined pattern. In the ontogeny (acquisition) of the operation of a nervous system we see the same thing.

> The notions of acquisitions of representations of the environment or of acquisition of information about the environment ... do not represent any aspect of the

operation of the nervous system.... Thus, development specifies and determines both an initial repertoire of behavior over which all new conduct is built in a historical process of transformation, and an initially structurally specified set of possible associations that changes in an integrated manner with the historical transformation of behavior. Any modification of the transfer function of a nerve cell, resulting from new concomitances of activity occurs modifying a preexisting behavior in a system that operates through maintaining invariant its definitory internal relations.... The nervous system is a strictly deterministic system whose structure specifies the possible modes of conduct that may emerge (be synthesized) from its functioning in a manner that varies according to the species ... [C]hanges during development, maturation ... or learning do not modify the deterministic character of this organization but change the capacity that the system has at any moment to synthesize behavior.[13]

If one examines the way in which the hierarchy of linguistic conceptual features is structured a little further, one comes to the same conclusion. Each feature is the containing set of the preceding one; conversely, the perceptional range of each feature is a subset of the perceptional range of the preceding feature. Hence, each feature must be produced from the preceding one by means of an addition, respectively a subtraction operation. There are two possibilities: either the addition/subtraction operation is the same from feature to feature, or it differs. If the first alternative is the case, then dimensionality plus/minus entity x = distinctness, distinctness plus/minus entity x = extension, extension plus/minus entity x = restrictedness, and so on. If the second alternative is the case, and each addition/subtraction is done in a different manner, then we not only lose a convenient working hypothesis but we cannot proceed deductively using this working hypothesis and must switch to a purely empirical approach at an earlier point in our investigation. However, if we assume that language is regularly structured, then the first alternative has a chance to be proven when tested. To be sure, it is not new; the Sapir-Whorf hypothesis makes essentially the same claims. In my book on the prepositions I opted for the first choice and I assume there a semantic dominant which governs the creation of supersets/subsets, that is to say, conceptual features in a hierarchy, in a uniform manner; in my book, I use a term which I have since then abandoned, namely, semantic coefficient.[14] Apparently, the semantic dominant corresponds to the "manner recursively selected" in which "the connectivity of the nervous system changes along the ontogeny [acquisition pattern. CHvS] of the organism"; the connectivity of the nervous system is determined in turn by "the properties of the neurons, their internal structure, shape and relative position," which constitute the nervous system "as dynamic network of neuronal interactions ..."; "[E]very nervous system has a definite architecture determined by the kinds and the number of neurons that composes it; therefore, members of the same species have nervous systems with similar architectures to the extent that they have similar kinds and numbers of neurons. Conversely, members of different species have nervous systems with different architectures according to their specific differences in neuronal composition. Therefore, the closed organization of the nervous system is realized in different species in different manners."[15] Maturana and Varela think, in fact, that the difference between species is due precisely to the difference in the organization of their nervous systems, whereas it is evident that where human languages are concerned, such differences in organization exist from language to language, that is, within the human species. These differences in organization of linguistic structures, including the semantic structures of human languages, seem to be very systematic. It seems that every time an alienation, or subtraction operation, creates a new feature in the hierarchy of conceptual features, this operation is by itself identical. The result it produces is different from feature to feature, nevertheless, since every time it operates on a different feature (the preceding feature in the hierarchy), it narrows the range of reference and thus creates a new, different range of reference for the newly resulting feature in the hierarchy. I call this uniform subtraction operation on the range of reference the semantic dominant. If the semantic units on the categorial level, such as case, preposition or lexical morphemes, are composed of semantic (conceptual) features and these features are in turn decomposable into operations of the semantic dominant of the given language, languages must differ only by the distinctions in their respective semantic dominants. It is this assumption for which I will try to adduce some evidence. My effort to test this hypothesis on Slavic languages is of long standing. If this hypothesis appears to be correct, a systematic procedure for the comparison of the semantic structures of the Slavic languages with each other and with those of non-Slavic languages would become a possibility.

By way of introduction let me give two examples, one comparing German and Russian and one comparing Serbocroatian and Russian prepositions respectively. Prepositional relations always concern a modified and a modifier. The latter consists of the preposition and its object (regimen). The relation modified – modifier is not unique, because we find it, although usually in a far more abstract form, in any linguistic meaning. Any linguistic meaning will, like the modifier, give information about something, the modified. In the final analysis, the modified is a point in space set by the speaker. In the prepositional category the relationship modified – modifier is very easy to visualize and that is why I use this category for my examples. Now, in a Russian prepositional relationship, the modifier can be contiguous with the modified, but it does not have to be. When both are seen as two separate entities, for instance, as is the case in distinctness, the modifier and the modified can still be contiguous, as in *on vzjal eë za ruku* 'he took her by the hand' and they also may not be, as in *gorod daleko za Dneprom* 'the town way beyond the Dnieper.' In German distinctness, there is contiguousness only. The German preposition marked by mere distinctness is *auf*, which implies the contiguousness of two distinct entities: the modified and the modifier (German *zu* corresponds to Russian *na*). In extension, the next feature, the same phenomenon occurs. German *um*, which is marked by extension and dimensionality, corresponds to Russian *o* (marked by the same feature in their Russian variety) only when there is contiguity between the modifier and the modified: *er geht um das Haus* will correspond to Russian *on obxodit dom*, but Russian *govorit' o knigax* cannot be rendered into German by using *um*. One has to use *über*: *über Bücher reden* 'to speak about books.' *Um Bücher reden* would mean direct involvement of the prepositional object *Bücher*: 'to talk for the sake of books.' The same spatial relationships that apparently exist in distinctness seem to recur in Russian and German, each in their own way, in more than one feature. German and Russian must each have its own semantic dominant, which regulates the spatial relationships between the modifier and the modified in the respective languages.

If we compare distinctness in Serbocroatian and in Russian, we find a difference between the Serbocroatian preposition *za* and Russian preposition *za*, both exclusively marked for distinctness as this feature *mutatis mutandis* occurs in the two languages. The feature recurs in other prepositions marked by other features than distinctness and also elsewhere in the two languages, in each language in a different but apparently consistent way. Serbocroatian *za* is used only when the prepositional relationship, as indicated, for instance, in *on stoji za stolom*, has not preceded the narrated situation. Thus, if the agent first *sat* behind the table and then *stood* behind it, one cannot use the sentence just given. One has to use a construction with *iza*. This constraint does not exist in Russian. We find the same spatial relationship, different from Russian every time in a parallel fashion, in other Serbocroatian prepositions, such as *pod, pred* and *nad* vs. *ispod, ispred* and *iznad*.

Thus we can graphically represent the relation between prepositional relationship and narrated situation in Russian and in Serbocroatian as follows:

(1) ——————— prep. rel.
    ——————————— verbal process

(2) ——————————— prep. rel.
    ——————— verbal process

In Russian, both types (1) and (2) are allowed. In Serbocroatian, only type (1) is allowed. (I am leaving out of consideration the various possibilities with respect to the moments of termination of the prepositional relationship and the verbal process, since they don't play a role in the present argumentation).

Moreover, we find the same trait in the meaning of the Serbocroatian aorist. In contradistinction to the Old Russian or Old Church Slavonic aorists, which are unmarked, the Serbocroatian aorist is marked. The Serbocroatian perfect merely indicates a fact in the past. The Serbocroatian aorist introduces into an already existing narrated situation a new past event. In other words, the past event introduced by the aorist cannot have taken place before the given narrated event. It cannot serve as a pluperfect. The aorist in Serbocroatian indicates the same relationship of its referent to the narrated situation that the referent of the Serbocroatian prepositional object indicates. Their markings are the same in that both are dominated by the same relationship to a point in (time and) space, the narrated event, that is an already-given which is set by the speaker.

These two examples are highly simplistic and sketchy. In what follows I shall try to present a somewhat more precise picture of what semantic dominants might eventually appear to be like. I shall thereby largely present material and conclusions drawn in the research of J. Levenberg,[16] D. Soudakoff and S. Soudakoff. One thing seems to be quite clear: whereas the semantic (conceptual) features specify relationships between points in space (and time) that have already been selected, semantic dominants give rules that hold, differently for each language, for the selection of these points before the features come into play.

As a first example, a few characteristic usages of Serbocroatian *za* will be discussed with special regard to their differences with the use of *za* in Russian and in Polish. Besides 'behind' and 'in exchange for,' Serbocroatian *za*[17] indicates destination in general: *voz za Beograd, krenuo je za šetnju, kamen za zidanje kuća, generalni sekretar za spoljni poslove, uči se za lekarja, prijemljiv za nešto.* In Russian and Polish, this usage does not exist. It is possible in Serbocroatian because Serbocroatian *za* has three semantic characteristics. First of all, it shares with Russian *za* and Polish *za, mutatis mutandis*, the feature of distinctness (formerly, I used the term duplication): the identification of the referent of the prepositional object marked by distinctness takes place independently of any other contextual element. Thus Serbocroatian, Russian and Polish *za* all state that the referent of the prepositional modifier (object, regimen) must be identified independently of the modified. In Russian *jaščik stoit za stolom* 'the chest stands behind the table,' the table and the chest are identified through two separate perceptions. Specific to Serbocroatian are, moreover, two other semantic properties: the relation between modifier and modified cannot take place before the rest of the narrated situation takes place; thus, as I mentioned before, a Serbocroatian *za* construction cannot refer to a relationship which antecedes a verbal process which it modifies; Serbocroatian *on stoji za stolom* cannot refer to a situation in which the process of standing (*stoji*) was preceded by a process of sitting. In that case, Serbocroatian must use *on stoji iza stola.* Thus, the prepositional relationship cannot antecede the narrated situation in general. A third semantic property, and the second one which is specifically Serbocroatian, consists of the fact that the referent of the prepositional modifier can be identified at any point within the narrated situation irrespective of the location of the modified; within the constraints imposed by the narrated situation as set forth above, the relation between any modifier and modified in Serbocroatian may be said to be dominated by the rule that the referent of any modifier is potentially maximally distant of any modified.

In this connection, it is not surprising that *za* is used as an independently given parameter in comparisons and constructions implying measuring: *za malenko rumanije, kopajte me za metar duboko, godišnje poraste za metar,* and as a retrospective or prospective parameter of time: *za ove tri godine, za celu godinu.*

The referent of the modifier of Russian *za*, while remaining separate from the modified, is in an area contiguous with the modified; Russian distinctness (duplication) operates within a topological neighborhood (that is, in a space seen as a continuum of contiguous points), whereas Serbocroatian prepositions do not do so. Polish distinctness also operates within a topological neighborhood, but it seems that the identification of the referent of the modifier of any Polish prepositional construction takes place before it applies in a prepositional relationship. Thus, while Russian *oni sideli za stolom* means either 'they were sitting at the table' or 'they were sitting behind the table,' Polish *oni siedzieli za stołem* means either 'they were sitting behind the table' or 'they were sitting at the table'; in contradistinction to Russian, however, the latter variant is possible only if the table is characterized by a particular property which applies only in the given narrated situation. The table must be being used, say, either for a specific conference, or for a special dinner. In Russian *za*, it does not matter where the modified is located with regard to an implicit observer — whether on the other side of the table or at the same side of the table as the observer. The concept of 'behind,' often conveyed by Russian *za*, is merely the consequence of the simplest possible perception operation admissible under the rules of Russian distinctness; this simplest possible perception operation is guided by a straight line which leads from the implicit observer via the referent of the prepositional modifier (prepositional object) to the referent of the prepositional modified. The meaning 'behind' is, to use Jakobson's term, the basic meaning (Grundbedeutung) of Russian *za*. In any case, in Russian distinctness, a broken line leading from the implicit observer to the modified via the modifier is possible as well. In Polish, it is possible only if the referent of the modifier has been identified before the prepositional relationship goes into effect by means of a special, conspicuous property. In Polish prepositional constructions, the referent of the modifier must always be identified beforehand by the given implicit observer, and this implies either an observer who is directy opposite the modified at the other side of the modifier, or a modifier which has unique characterisitics. Hence, the straight line of perception from the implicit observer to the modified via the modifier is practically always behind. The *za* relation thus becomes in Polish exclusive in that only one *za* relation is possible at a time. Typical of the *za* relation in Polish is a precarious, since once-occurring, balance. Only if this once-occurring relation is there can *za* be used: Polish *Janka poszła za nią* (where Russian will use *sledom za*), Polish *zawołał za nim Orłowski* (Russian: *vsled*); Polish *za czymś przykładem* (Russian: *po č'emu-libo primeru*); Polish *za pozwoleniem* (Russian: *s (č'ego-libo) razrešenija*); Polish *wynająć sie za stróża* (Russ: *v storoža*); Polish *uznać za wodza* (Russ: instrumental); Polish *przebrać się za kobietę* (Russ: instrumental). In Russian, the once-occurring relationship is rendered by a variety of constructions, among which the instrumental is prominent. The instrumental signifies a modifier whose validity is restricted to the given narrated situation (restrictedness) and case as a grammatical category denotes a property of the modified rather than a substantivity on a par with the modified, as the category of preposition is apt to do.

Proceeding from the preposition *za* to the discussion of the preposition *o*, we find *o* used in Serbocroatian when two conditions are fulfilled: the referent must engage in the modification relationship not before existence of the rest of the narrated situation, and the referent of the prepositional modifier must be potentially maximally distant from the referent of the modified. Moreover, the modifier is individualized, since *o* carries dimensionality as well as extension. I prefer to begin my discussion of the extension feature with examples of *o* rather than with examples of *po*, since the differences between the Polish, Russian and Serbocroatian *o* constructions are more easily seen than the corresponding differences with *po*. Typical examples of the use of Serbocroatian *o* are *lupiti o vrata, odupreti se o kamen, odupreti se o zid, viseti o koncu, obesiti o zid, nositi pušku o ramenu, ogrešiti o svoju iskrenost* (Russian: *protiv*), *svađati se o prihod* (Russian: *iz-za*), *sumnjavati se o* (Russian: *somnevat'sja v*), *briga o, stvaranje o, živeti o plati, o šilingu je proveo tri dana, o zalazu sunčanom, o školjskom rasputu*. In the latter two examples Russian can also use the preposition *o*, but Russian *o* in these instances implies repetitiveness, whereas Serbocroatian *o* does not.

When we look at *o-* as a preverb, then Russian *o-* will state that the agent of an intransitive verb compounded with *o-* or the patient of a transitive verb compounded with *o-* is completely affected by the verbal process as far as it is applicable to this agent or patient, respectively. However, there are no further consequences than those due directly to the verbal process. Thus, for instance, *okamenet'* 'to become petrified' vs. *poblednet'* 'to become pale' (where the subject is not necessarily affected in its totality by the verbal process; note that *po*, unlike *o*, is unmarked for dimensionality), or *okutat'* 'to wrap' vs. *pokrasit'* and *pokryt'*, 'to paint' and 'to cover,' respectively.

The Serbocroatian preverb *o-* shows in its use a shift in emphasis compared to that of the Russian preverb *o-*; cf. *ogrozditi* 'to form grapes (of a grapevine),' *olistati* 'to form leaves (of a tree),' *onovčiti se* 'to become rich (to provide oneself with money),' *okrepiti kavom* 'to sustain someone by giving him coffee' (Russian will use here the preverb *pod-*: *podkrepit'*), *oglądneti* 'to become hungry,' *oprašiti* 'to cover with dust' or 'to remove dust,' *obasijati* 'to shart shining' (Russian *zasijat'*). In all these instances, the working of the Serbocroatian verbal lexical morpheme as a cogwheel in the semantic mechanism of the Serbocroatian language is different from that of the Russian verbal lexical morpheme with respect to the functioning of Russian preverbs. In Russian, the preverb indicates the status in which the agent or patient will be *after* the operation of the verbal process. In Serbocroatian, the preverb indicates the status in which the agent or patient will be *through* the working of the verbal process. In Serbocroatian, the verbal process operates on an element which exists as a generally identifiable but otherwise unspecified element; the element is specified only in the given modification relationship, that is, *in casu*, during the verbal process. This element can, with regard to the modified, *in casu*, the verbal process, be anywhere, since in Serbocroatian any modifier is always potentially maximally distant from any modified which stands in a relation to it. It is the verbal process itself that *forms and shapes* the agent or patient (the referent), rather than that the referent is *reshaped* by it, as is the case in Russian, since the identification and the modification relationship take place at the same time. In the relation between the verbal lexical morpheme and the preverb, the lexical morpheme modifies the referent and the preverb modifies the lexical morpheme. Since in Serbocroatian the lexical morpheme modifies a referent (agent or patient) which is potentially maximally distant and at the same time not identifiable before the modification period, the semantic effect of this modification will be considerably greater than the effect of the comparable modification relationship in Russian. The modification relationship in question will, in Serbocroatian, tend to imply a creation or recreation rather than an influence with a certain effect. Hence, we find in Serbocroatian verbal composition on the one hand, a certain number of lexical morphemes, to wit, lexical morphemes signifying a creative action, that we are less apt to find in Russian; cf. examples like *ogrozditi, olistati, ogladneti, oprašiti* and *obasijati* given above. Nonetheless, since identification of the referent takes place only during the situation to which the modification of the subject/object by the verbal lexical morpheme refers, the continued existence of the referent needs affirmation. We find therefore in Serbocroatian a coupling of verbal lexical morphemes indicating creativity with preverbs carrying the marking of extension, such as *o-* and *po-*.

Polish *o* is used in several ways which provide interesting comparisons with Russian. First of all, I may mention the type in which the referent of the regiment is the objective of a mental activity, the objective of a request for information, the objective of care or concern, or the objective of a fighting to attain or to preserve. In Polish, all these types except for the last one (fighting to preserve), which takes *za* + accusative, take *o* (the first one taking the locative, the others the accusative). Apparently, Polish can use *za* only when the objective (which he is fighting to preserve) is existing and under direct control of the agent. In Russian, the first type (the objective of a mental activity) takes *o* + loc., the others *za* + acc. Russian takes *o* (+ acc.) only if the object (since it is merely the objective of a static mental activity) is physically remote and not under the direct influence of the agent; in the latter cases, Russian takes *za* + acc.

One finds a parallel in the occurrences of Russian and Polish *o* in which the relation between the agent and the referent of the regimen is one of contact between two physical bodies. In Russian, *o* is used when the referent of the prepositional object constitutes an obstacle: *spotykat'sja o kamen'*; but otherwise other prepositions are used: *uronil trostočku, prislonennuju k stolu*; *xlopnul beretom po ladoni*; *tolkal ego grud'ju v rjuksak*; *operlis' na parapet*. In Polish, in all these cases *o* is possible: *upuścił laseczkę opartą o stół, uderzając czapką o dłoń, zawadzając piersią o jego plecak, oparli się o kamienne obmurowanie*. In Polish, evidently, intention is sufficient and *o* has a greater range of usage than in Russian. What seems to be important in Polish is that while the referent of the prepositional object is identified before the prepositional relationship actually takes place the referent of the prepositional object does not constitute a natural target for the activity of the agent but is deliberately chosen by him or her as such. In that sense, modifier (i.e., the referent of the prepositional object) remains maximally independent of the process. Given the fact that this referent (modifier) is selected before the actual prepositional relationship takes place, the prepositional modifier is minimally affected by the prepositional relationship in that no enduring merger between the agent (or, in transitive verbs, the patient) and the modifier takes place. If the intention on the part of the agent is brought to the fore and the implication is that from the point of view of the agent the referent (modifier) is a willed or natural objective, Polish will have a *na* or *w* construction while Russian will have *o*: *lomaet o koleno prut'ja* vs. *łamie na kolanie patyki, ruka ob ruku* vs. *ręka w rękę*. The question is further discussed by D. Soudakoff, who gives a convincing explanation why Russian also can have a *v* construction: *plečo o plečo* vs. *plečo v plečo*. One finds a similar difference in the descriptive usage of Polish *o* and Russian *o*. Descriptive Russian *o* indicates an unusual characteristic: *stol o trex nožkax, telënok o dvux golovax*. In Polish, *o* is used, to paraphrase D. Soudakoff, in order to indicate an outstanding characterizing feature, where Russian uses *s* in the overwhelming number of cases: *chłopaczek o nieznikającym radosnym uśmiechu* vs. Russ. *mal'čik s postojannoj radostnoj ulybkoj*; Pol. *człowiek o nie ukończonych wyższych studiach* vs. Russ. *s nezakončennym vysšim obrazovaniem*. In the Polish *o* construction we have to do with an enduring characteristic, whereas a Polish *z* construction indicates a temporary relationship; D. Soudakoff states the Pol. *chodzić z kijem* means 'to walk carrying a stick,' whereas *chodzić o kiju* means 'to walk with a cane; as an enduring habit.' While the extension and dimensionality features carried by *o* give an outstanding individual characteristic, the semantic invariant or coefficient which seems to dominate the entire Polish system seems to convey a nuance of naturalness of the characteristic. The semantic dominant of Polish, which seems to indicate the identification of the referent previous to the (prepositional) modification relationship evidently lends to the extension feature a sense of the referent being predestined to serve as a characteristic.

The preposition/preverb *po* in Serbocroatian, Russian and in Polish shows parallel differences again.

Whereas *o* in Serbocroatian indicates that the modifier is an individual entity which, while identifiable independently, does not engage in the prepositional relationship before the verbal process takes place, Serbocroatian *po* signalizes the state of one or more units which, while identifiable independently, only engages in the prepositional relationship after the verbal process has begun. In Russian, the referent of the modifier is not generally identifiable. In Russian therefore, the referent of the modifier constitutes a background to the verbal process which forms a continuum that is established in the course of the process. In Serbocroatian, the referent of the modifier of *po* is an objectively given. The modifier of Serbocroatian *po* has therefore the tendency to indicate repetitiveness, whereas the modifier of Russian *po* is less biased in this respect. Thus, as S. Soudakoff astutely argues, in an expression like 'shooting at' Russian uses *po* to indicate that the target forms a continuous range, whereas Serbocroatian will use *pucati u*, or *pucati na* for a continuum. However, Serbocroatian uses the preposition *po* for a not necesarily continuous area which is objectively given: *sneg je padao po brdima* and *sneg je ležao po brdima.* For 'to go through the darkness,' in which instance the darkness is objectively given, Serbocroatian will use *ići po mraku*, whereas Russian has to indicate that the darkness is a container by the prepositional feature of dimensionality (for which *po* in both Serbocroatian and Russian is unmarked) and has in that sense a wider existence. Thus, Russian will have *vo mrake, v mrak* or *pod mrakom.* Both *v* and *pod* are marked for dimensionality. The Serbocroatian preverb *o* puts special emphasis on the fact that an existing objective is affected to the fullest possiible limit by the verbal process. Thus, in contradistinction to Russian, where *popisat'* implies an attenuative nuance conveyed by the preverb *po-*, Serbocroatian *popisati* means 'to list,' 'to copy,' or 'to describe'; and Serbocroatian *popiti* corresponds to Russian *vypit'* 'drink to exhaustion.' Non-continuous *po-* recurs in Serbocroatian *posedati* corresponding to Russian *rassest'sja, usest'sja, zanjat' mesta.* The general perceptibility of the objective (agent or patient, of the verbal process) implied by any Serbocroatian preposition or preverb is the reason that a repeated application of a verbal process to the same objective has to be specified. The sequential application of the verbal process to several objectives, as in Serbocroatian *posedati,* suggests a repetitiveness of the process which is signaled by the extension feature of the preverb *po-.* In those instances, the extension feature indicates that the objective is affected by the process to the extent that it is ready to be affected by the same process again; thus Serbocroatian *poznavati* means 'to know over a longer period of time,' 'to be acquainted with.' Moreover, the lexical meaning of the verb may emphasize the fullness of the power with which the verbal process affects the objective. Thus the lexical meaning of Serbocroatian *-noviti* combines with the preverb *po-* to yield the meaning 'to repeat.' The semantic dominant of Serbocroatian, which appears to indicate the general perceptibility of the objective (the referent of the prepositional modifier or its preverbial analog) and the preverb *po-,* which is marked by extension, both emphasize the enduring identity of the objective. Hence, the lexical meaning of the Serbocroatian verb *ponoviti* 'to repeat' indicates repetition by stating that the action, which in this case is its own objective, is renewed.

For Polish, I adduce a few major subcategories as discussed by D. Soudakoff.

One of the most important subcategories can be discussed best by starting from the Russian type *po vstuplenii v gimnaziju on pokazal bol'šuju sklonnost' k jazykam* 'upon entering the gymnasium he showed a great propensity for languages.' Here *po* gives through its modifier the first term of a time sequence, but in contradistinction with *posle vstuplenija* ... etc., there is a causal link between the terms (the modifier and the modified) and there is also contiguousness between them. In Polish, temporal *po* followed by the locative "can be used when there is a pure sequential relationship between modifier and modified, with the modified merely following the modifier in time without there necessarily being any other relationship between the two.... Polish uses *po* to indicate almost any type of sequence in time, whether it be of objects or of activities, regardless of the length of separation between the times in question and whether or not they have any additional relationship to one another." In Russian, the terms "are closely related to one another, with the modified usually following upon the heels of the modifier." Therefore, in Russian "*po* used to indicate sequence stipulates that the preposition joins two actions, not objects."[17]

As a consequence, the range of usage of Polish *po* is far wider than that of Russian *po*. In Polish, the temporal relation between the modifier and the modified is both unlimited in duration and accidental. It is merely by willed assignment by the speaker of the modifier to the modified that the relation is established. The identity of the modifier is predetermined by the speaker. Thus we find Pol. *dobrze po północy wrócił Jacek*, Russ. *uže za polnoč' vernulsja Jacek*; Pol. *po jakichś dwustu krokach uspokaja się*, Russ. *šagov čerez dvesti on uspakaivaetsja*; Pol. *w klatce po kanarku*, Russ. *v kletke gde prežde žila kanarejka*; Pol. *puszka po sardynkach*, Russ. *banka iz-pod sardin.* The relation between modifier and modified makes an impression of randomness. In this connection it is interesting to quote a comparison made by D. Soudakoff between three types of propositional qualification, in which Polish *po* has a narrower range of usage than Russian *po*: Polish *koledzy po piórze*, Russian *tovarišči po peru*; Polish *mistrz w boksie,* Russian *čempion po boksu*; Polish ... *ja jestem z zawodu kamieniarz, ale z urodzenia polityk* ..., Russian ... *po professii ja kamenotës, no po prirode politik.* Only the first example fulfills the condition of arbitrariness of the relationship between modifier and modified, required in Polish, but not required in Russian for the use of the preposition *po*. The referent of the modifier of Polish *po* cannot be an inherent property of the referent of the modified. As D. Soudakoff remarks, "whereas in Russian *po* is used freely to provide a regulatory background against which an action can take place, in Polish it cannot be used as soon as any type of order is introduced into the modification relationship." Hence, Russian *govorit' po telefonu* has to be translated by Polish *mówić przez telefon* and as "a capstone to this argumentation note Polish *płynąć z prądem* vs. Russian *plyt' po tečeniju.*" The "basic difference [between the two languages is that] of unordered [Polish] vs. ordered [Russian] relationship." The Polish relationship has to be ad hoc.

It seems to me that we can make an educated guess as to the differences between the Serbocroatian and Polish semantic dominants as compared to the semantic dominant of Russian. In Serbocroatian, the modification relationship cannot take place before the narrated situation in general (unless specifically stated, for instance, by *iza, ispod, ispred* and *iznad*); within the area of the narrated situation the modifier (any modifier) is potentially maximally distant from the modified. In Polish, the modifier must be identified before the modification relationship. I assume that Russian occupies an intermediate position between these two languages and that its semantic dominant may therefore, for the time being, be considered unmarked as to the characteristics of the Serbocroatian and Polish semantic dominants. Only much more extensive research will throw light on this problem. As far as the Serbocroatian and Polish semantic dominants are concerned, we may yet look at a few cases in which one Serbocroatian preposition, *u*, corresponds to two Polish prepositions, *w* and *u*, at a case in which two Serbocroatian prepositions, *s* and *iz*, correspond to one Polish preposition, *z*, at the relationship between Serbocroatian *od* and Polish *od*, and at Serbocroatian *pre* and *pri*, of which the Polish counterparts have not yet been investigated. There is some reason to believe that this material confirms the conclusions drawn thus far in my presentation.

Roughly speaking, the Serbocroatian preposition *u* followed by the locative or accusative corresponds to Russian *v* with the locative and accusative, respectively. In the relatively few instances in which Serbocroatian *u* followed by the genitive competes with Serbocroatian *kod* with the genitive (e.g., *u toga pisca jest svaka reč na svome mestu* or *u straha su velike oči*), the *u* construction seems to imply an integration of the modified into the modifier rather than a juxtaposition of the modified to the modifier, as implied by Serbocroatian *kod*, which is, *mutatis mutandis*, marked by the same features as Russian *u*: distinctness (duplication) and extension. As I have tried to argue when discussing the Serbocroatian prepositions *o* and *po*, which are marked by extension, Serbocroatian extension, given the semantic dominant of Serbocroatian, appears to emphasize the preexistence of the referent of the modifier. *Kod* is largely used to indicate location and not, as in Russian, to indicate possession. Distinctness and extension, as they cumulate in Serbocroatian *kod*, create on the one hand in Serbocroatian a referent which is set apart within the narrated situation with a sharper outline than *u* in Russian. On the other hand, the integrating variant of *u* (cf. *u toga pisca* ... and *u straha*), a weak version of which can be seen in Russian possessive *u*, is in Serbocroatian more strongly integrating than in Russian because it, too, is apparently influenced by the Serbocroatian dominant which presumably allows identification not before the modification relationship. This integrating type is represented by

Serbocroatian genitival *u*, which has lost its extension and distinctness features but has acquired dimensionality. Thus integration is conveyed by Serbocroatian *u* followed by the genitive in two ways: the modifier is a container (dimensionality) which can be identified only when the modification relationship has entered into force (the Serbocroatian semantic dominant) but is not marked, at that point, for distinctenss or extension.

The Serbocroatian preverb *u*- corresponds, roughly speaking, to Russian *v*- and partly to Russian *u*-; the two languages have the type SCr. *ugovoriti*, Russ. *ugovorit'* in common but Russian *uxodit'/ujti* corresponds to Scr. *odlaziti/odići*. In Russian, the meaning of the preposition–preverb *u* may be characterized as 'deviation.' Deviation can emphasize the final point which is to say, the result of the deviationary process, or it can emphasize the initial point from which the process is to deviate. In Russian the first type is represented by *ugovorit'*, the second type by *uxodit'/ujti*. The Slavic preverb indicates the result of the modification of the patient (or agent) by the lexical morpheme. The first Russian type means an integration into a point which can be identified only at the termination of the process. In this variant, Russian *u*- will be interpreted as giving the result of the verbal process. The Serbocroatian semantic dominant implies precisely this type of relationship, and, consequently, we find Scr. *ugovoriti* corresponding to Russ. *ugovorit'*. The second Russian type implies deviation from a starting point that has already been identified at the outset of the verbal process, in other words, at the outset of the modification relationship between the verbal lexical morpheme and the agent (or patient). This "point of departure" type is impossible in Serbocroatian unless we specify that the point of departure preexists (extension) and will be cancelled during the modification of the agent (or patient) by the verbal lexical morpheme, that is to say, during the verbal process. This is precisely what the preposition/preverb Russ. *ot*, Scr. *od* signifies. Since this "point of departure deviation" variant of *u*- cannot be created, under the Serbocroatian semantic dominant, by the cumulation of the Serbocroatian extension feature with the Serbocroatian distinctness feature, while in Russian this variant is created by the cumulation of Russian extension with Russian distinctness (duplication), we find that the point of departure variant of *u*- signified in Russian by the cumulation of Russian extension with Russian distinctness, corresponds to Serbocroatian *od*.

As regards Polish *w*, it seems that *w* also presents evidence for the characterization of the Polish semantic dominant as requiring identification of the referent before the narrated situation. For a moving into, Polish can use either *w* followed by the accusative or other constructions, among which *do* + gen. is the most common one; thus, for instance, *myśl przyszła w głowę* but *alkohol uderzał do głowy*. In the first sentence, the head (*głowa*) is, so to say, predestined to be the receptacle for the thought; it is identified beforehand. The relation between head and thought is natural. In the second sentence, the impression is conveyed by the use of the preposition *do*, which is marked for objectiveness and extension, that the relation between the head and the alcohol is less natural. The given head may be identified prior to the modification relationship, but this modification relationship affects that head minimally and within this relationship it remains potentially maximally distant from the modified, the alcohol. This difference in use between Polish *w* and Polish *do*, in translation both corresponding to English *to*, is quite normal and seems to give further evidence for the rule that in Polish the referent is preidentified.

A few words may be appropriate regarding the approximate correspondence of Polish *z* to Russian *s* and *iz*. The Russian preposition *s* is marked by extension, distinction and dimensionality, and one must assume that Polish *z*, *mutatis mutandis*, carries the same markings. Russian *iz* is marked for restrictedness, extension and dimensionality. Thus, *iz* and *s* have extension and dimensionality in common, but *iz* has restrictedness and lacks distinctness and *s* lacks restrictedness but does carry distinctness. If Polish *z*, along with Russian *z*, is marked by distinctness but lacks restrictedness, then we must seek an explanation for the fact that Polish distinctness is capable of replacing Russian restrictedness and, in combination with Polish extension and dimensionality, is able to correspond, to a large extent, to Russian *iz*. Crudely speaking, Polish distinctness, when *z* is followed by the genitive, functions to replace Russian *iz*. The genitive is the case of remoteness, since it is marked (on the level of case) by objectiveness (Jakobson's quantification). On the prepositional level, extension, duplication and dimensionality all signalize the relative independence of the prepositional object from the narrated situation. Since all Polish features must be governed by the Polish semantic coefficient (which presumably says that identification of the denotatum, the given referent, must take place before the modification relationship), they tend to visualize the referent as a point of departure. Polish distinctness individualizes the referent with regard to the rest of the narrated situation. Moreover, under the Polish semantic coefficient, this individualization must presumably be effectuated before the rest of the narrated situation takes place. Thus the image of the referent of *z* as a point of departure is reinforced. Both Polish *z* and Russian *s* are unmarked for restrictedness. Thus, Polish *z* can imply restrictedness (and dimensionality) is marked by extension, which means that the cancelled point, in other words, the point of departure, is at the same time retained as a point of reference. It is evident that if the Polish semantic dominant means preidentification, the effect of preidentification on Polish extension (and dimensionality and distinctness) followed by the genitive will come rather close to the Russian cumulation of extension (and dimensionality) with restrictedness.

One seems to find a certain amount of confirmation of this state of affairs in the comparison between Polish *od* and Russian *ot*. They correspond to each other in a great majority of cases. However, when the point of departure remains in the narrated situation and is the mere beginning point of a line which stretches through the narrated situation, Polish can retain *od*, but Russian apparently tends to use a preposition which is not marked by cancellation of the initial point, that is a preposition which is not marked for restrictedness. Thus we find Polish *wiatr od morza*, Russ.: *veter s morja*; Polish *od rana do nocy,* Russian *s utra do večera*; Polish *kupić od*, Russian *kupit' u*; Polish *proszek od bolu głowy*, Russian *porošok protiv golovnoj boli*; Polish *nóżka od stołu*, Russian *nožka stola*. In these instances it seems that Russian cannot use restrictedness since the entire modification relationship is integrally within the narrated situation, whereas Polish presumably preidentifies the referent of the prepositional object, which automatically integrates the referent into the narrated situation; hence probably the need to emphasize the role of the referent as a mere starting point by giving it the marking of cancellation (restrictedness), besides the marking of extension.

If it is true that Serbocroatian identifies what may have preexisted as being at any distance only in the narrated situation, it will have a tendency to signalize incontestable preexistence. Thus, we find in Serbocroatian *od* followed by prepositional objects signifying enduringly existing materials or dominant characteristics: *sto od drveta, novac od zlata, čovek od reči, selo od pet kuća, jedan on njih, lepo od tebe, od dosade*. The fact that the identification also of this type of referent can be identified in turn only in the given narrated situation pulls, so to say, the referent back into the narrated situation as objectively existing with regard to that narrated situation. As soon as there is objective existence, *od* is used: *od kraja marta, osećanje poznato od 1941 godine*. If the point of departure is confined to the narrated situation, no restrictedness is necessary: *ide s koncerta*. Also, *iz* will be used when the referent of the prepositional object is implied to exist independently of the narrated situation: Scr. *seminar iz književnosti*, Russ. *seminar po literature*; Scr. *ispit iz istorije*, Russ. *èkzamen po istorii*; Scr. *iz navike* Russ. *po privyčke*.

The motif of independent existence returns in one form or another in two Serbocroatian prepositions the Polish counterparts of which have not yet been investigated in the framework followed so far. The Serbocroatian preposition *pri* is marked by Serbocroatian objectiveness. Objectiveness means that within the narrated situation the modifier can be anywhere with respect to the modified. Moreover, the Serbocroatian semantic dominant itself seems, on another, more general, level of modification to have the same meaning. The result is apparently heavy emphasis in Serbocroatian objectiveness, not on a spatial relationship, but on simultaneousness exclusively from a point of view of time: Scr. *pri svesti*, Russ. *v pamjati*, Scr. *pri snazi*, Russ. *v polnom razgare sil*, Scr. *biti pri razgovoru*, Scr. *pri piću*, Scr. *pri ruci*, Russ. *pod rukoj*, Scr. *pri stolu*. The preverb *pri-*, correspondingly, tends to indicate a relationship of synchronization, which emphasizes that the modifier is present while the relation of the modifier to it is being established: Scr. *prikazivati*, Russ. *pokazyvat'*; Scr. *prilagati*, Russ. *prinosit'*, where the Serbocroatian lexical morpheme implies a presence in space given beforehand; Scr. *prići*, Russ. *podojti*, both compounds indicating in their own way an approach from nearby, thus implying a preestablished presence. For 'coming from afar' Serbocroatian uses *doći*, Russ. *prijti*.

Serbocroatian *pre* is marked by restrictedness alone. It gives a transition from an initial *na* situation to an ensuing *na* situation. Under the Serbocroatian semantic dominant as I have described it, both *na* situations should be identifiable not before the narrated situation. The result is that in Serbocroatian *pre* the transition is immediately contiguous to the narrated situation: Scr. *pre zore*, Scr. *pre oluje*; Scr. *nisam čuo pre* 'before this moment'; Scr. *pre osam godine* 'the modified preceded immediately eight years.' As any Slavic preverb, the Serbocroatian preverb *pre-* indicates the situation of the agent of intransitive verbs and of the patient of transitive verbs at the end of the verbal process. In *pre-*, the initial *na* situation is immediately contiguous upon the second, final, *na* situation. The transition from the initial to the final situation is therefore quite often the situation through which the actant goes during the verbal process, and *pre-* quite often gives the impression of giving the two stages through which the verbal process goes instead of the stages that the actant goes through. For instance, Scr. *pretražiti* corresponds to Russian *pereryt'*, *issledovat'*, *razvedat'*; Scr. *prepatiti* to Russ. *perestradat'*, *perenesti*, *vynesti*; Scr. *presuditi* to Russ. *prigovorit'*; and Scr. *prevladati* to Russ. *poborot'*, *pobedit'*. In the last examples it is evident that the relation between preverb and verbal lexical morpheme in Serbocroatian is different than it is in Russian and may affect the choice of verbal lexical morphemes in both languages.

The above is no more than a sketchy attempt to indicate the problematics of the semantic dominant. While my conclusion is that from language to language there are different semantic dominants which permeate and determine the entire semantic structure of the individual languages, it may very well be that the tentative conclusions regarding the contents of the semantic dominants of Serbocroatian, Russian and Polish are to a certain extent incorrect and will need emendations. What I have wanted to demonstrate here is a promising approach to the semantic dominant rather than an undisputable formulation of the distinctions involved.

Indiana University and Informatica Humana Foundation

NOTES

[1] English version in R. Jakobson, *Selected Writings* I², The Hague, 1971, 231-233.
[2] R. Jakobson and M. Halle, *Fundamentals of Language*², The Hague, 1971, 43, and R. Jakobson and L. Waugh, *The Sound Shape of Language,* Bloomington, Indiana, 1971, 134.
[3] R. Jakobson, "Beitrag zur allgemeinen Kasuslehre," *Travaux du cercle linguistique de Prague* 6 (1936) 240-248 (= *Selected Writings* 2, The Hague, 1971, 23-71); idem, "Morfologičeskie nabljudenija nad slavjanskim skloneniem," *American Contributions to the Fourth International Congress of Slavicists, Moscow, September 1958,* The Hague, 1958, 127-156 (= *Selected Writings* 2, 154-183).
[4] C. H. van Schooneveld, *Semantic Transmutations* I, *The Cardinal Semantic Structure of Prepositions, Cases and Paratactic Conjunctions in Contemporary Standard Russian,* Bloomington, Indiana, 1978; idem, "A Semantic Approach to Word Formation in Contemporary Standard Russian," *American Contributions to the Eighth International Congress of Slavists,* Columbus, Ohio, 1978, 597-615; idem, "The Place of Gender in the Semantic Structure of the Russian Language," *Scandoslavica* 23, 1977, 129-138; idem, "By Way of Introduction: Roman Jakobson's tenets and their potential," *Roman Jakobson, Echoes of his Scholarship,* Lisse, 1977, 10; "Contribution à l'étude comparative des systèmes des cas, des prépositions et des catégories grammaticales du verbe en russe moderne," *Studia Slavica hierosolymitana* II, 1978, 41-50; "Programmatic Sketch of a Theory of Lexical Meaning," to appear in a special roundtable issue of *Quaderni di Semantica,* Bologna; "The Morphemic Structure of the Slavic Word and Greenberg's Twenty-eighth Universal," *Slavic Word,* ed. D. S. Worth, The Hague, 1978, 443-448; "The Extension Feature in Russian" (Postscript regarding agreement), to appear in *Slavic Linguistics and Poetics, Studies for Edward Stankiewicz on his 60th Birthday* (= *International Journal of Slavic Linguistics and Poetics* 25-26), 1982, 456-7.
[5] C. H. van Schooneveld, "Baudouin de Courtenay's Methodological Premises for the Investigation of Language and their Relation to Present-Day Linguistics," to appear in the Proceedings of the International Conference in Commemoration of the 50th Anniversary of Jan Baudouin de Courtenay's Death, Warsaw, September 1979, and idem, "Programmatic Sketch ...," *Quaderni di Semantica.*
[6] "Contribution to the Quest for Meaning in Language," forthcoming.
[7] "Agreement in Russian," to appear in the Festschrift for L. Matejka.
[8] C. H. van Schooneveld, "Contribution to the Quest for Meaning in Language," forthcoming.
[9] E. Husserl, *Logische Untersuchungen* II, pt. 1², Halle a.d.S., 1913, 264 ff.
[10] H. R. Maturana and F. J. Varela, *Autopoiesis and Cognition* (*Boston Studies in the Philosophy of Science,* 42), Dordrecht, 1980, p. xvii and passim.
[11] E.g., Maturana and Varela, *op. cit.,* 51.
[12] Maturana and Varela, *op. cit.,* 39, 23, 98, 29 and 41.
[13] Maturana and Varela, *op. cit.,* 133, 43-44, 46.
[14] C. H. van Schooneveld, *Semantic Transmutations* I, p. 47, and Chapter VII.
[15] Maturana and Varela, *op. cit.,* 127, 129.
[16] J. Levenberg, *A Semantic Analysis of Aspect in Russian and Serbocroatian,* Ann Arbor, Michigan, 1981.
[17] The Serbocroatian examples and a number of statements about them are from a manuscript comparing the Serbocroatian and Russian prepositional systems by S. Soudakoff. The Polish examples and a number of statements about them are from a manuscript comparing the Polish and Russian prepositional systems by D. Soudakoff. I have provided translations only in cases of possible misunderstanding.

The "Second South Slavic Influence" in the History of the Russian Literary Language
(Materials for a Discussion)

Dean S. Worth

The term "Second South Slavic Influence" has been in use at least since Speranskij 1929 and is best known from Lixačev's important article of 1958/1960 and Birnbaum's comprehensive survey of 1975.[1] However, in spite of an already massive bibliography (Iovine 1977 lists over 700 positions), there is still very little general agreement about this term's content or its appropriateness as a label for the cultural-historical events of the period (late fourteenth – sixteenth centuries). One widespread view, found in one variety or another not only in textbooks but also in such serious investigations as Ščepkin 1920/1967, Vzdornov 1968, and Filin 1981, claims that the Turkish conquest of the Balkans in the late fourteenth century provoked a massive emigration of Bulgarian and Serbian intellectuals to Russia, the only remaining independent Orthodox country; there, these intellectuals participated in the "ispravlenie knig," that is, in restoring the supposedly degenerate Russian books to a more pristine (sc. Bulgarian, to some extent partly Serbian) state, a task for which they were well suited because of their knowledge of similar reforms carried out earlier by Patriarch Euthymius of Trnovo and his Bulgarian and Serbian followers.[2] Both the extent of this influence and its Euthymian origins have been challenged, most notably by Talev 1973 (and cf. Issatschenko 1980: 211 ff.), and both Larin 1975 and Filin 1981 emphasize the internal, Russian components of the developments of that period. Indeed, neither the "massive" character of this emigration, nor its origin in the Turkish conquest, has been demonstrated. We know the names of exactly three Balkan men of letters who came to Russia at this time, not one of whom was fleeing the Turks: Kiprian in 1375 (N.B.: well *before* Kosovo Polje), Grigorij Camblak c. 1416, and Paxomij Logofet ("Serb") sometime before 1438, — surely one of the world's smallest mass immigrations. Nor do we know much about the actual activities of these three literati.[3]

It seems fair to say that most of the important cultural-historical problems of the "Second South Slavic Influence" are still to be solved.[4] For the linguist or the cultural historian interested in the development of the Russian literary language, two clusters of problems are especially important. The first is that of separating out the strictly linguistic components of the "Second South Slavic

Influence" from the rhetorical devices with which they are usually lumped together. The former are important for the creation of a standard literary language, the latter only for a single component of this standard language, the language of literature (historical stylistics). It is symptomatic that the standard textbook illustrations of this "Influence" are the rhetorical flourishes of Epifanij Premudryj, flourishes which have clear origins in the rhetoric of the Kievan period and which were elaborated by a talented writer who was, however, a native Russian with no South Slavic connections.[5]

The second set of problems involves untangling the various types of influence discernible in the texts of the period: autochthonous influences (archaizing imitations of the Kievan period) vs. foreign influence; within the latter, South Slavic (Bulgarian, Serbian) vs. Greek; within Greek, those currents which came directly from Constantinople vs. those mediated by the Mt. Athos and other monasteries and/or the Bulgarian and Serbian courts. These problems of what might be called the "cultural triangle" of Byzantium, Mt. Athos, and Russia (especially, as time goes on, Moscow) are complicated indeed, and it will surely be some time before one can hope to see things at all clearly.[6] In the meantime, one can only hope for an accumulation of individual studies of specific aspects of the "Second South Slavic Influence," studies which may perhaps serve as building-blocks for some future edifice, or, at the least, help in formulating the kinds of questions that should be asked.

The present report will deal only with the strictly linguistic aspects of the "Second South Slavic Influence," paying no attention to problems of Hesychasm, Paleologan influence on iconography, Serbian motifs in architecture, etc., or to the purely decorative aspects of manuscript production (*vjaz'*, the *voronka*, teratological vs. geometric ornamentation, etc.). Reserving comment on the rhetorical devices of the period for a later paper, we shall consider here only the graphic, phonological, morphological, syntactic and lexical facts which have been said to be typical of the period under consideration. Our list of linguistic features makes no pretense of originality; on the contrary, our purpose is to take a fresh look at the "received opinion" on these matters, and we have extracted linguistic features freely from such sources as Sobolevskij 1894, Ščepkin 1920/1967, Karskij 1928, Lixačev 1958/1960, Talev 1973, Birnbaum 1975, Issatschenko 1980, Filin 1981, et al. We have tried to be reasonably complete in listing these features, and we have tried — as far as we know, for the first time — to divide all known features into groups, according to their most probable origin. It should be emphasized that our listing of any given feature here does not imply that we ourselves accept it as such.

A few words of caution are in order before proceeding to the classification itself. In many cases, the features to be adduced here as typical of the "Second South Slavic Influence" period can also be found, though generally less frequently, in texts of earlier or much later periods (specifically, several salient features of the "younger" Russian demiuncial are also to be found in the older demiuncial; see Žukovskaja 1981, cited by Filin 1981: 287). In some cases it is not clear whether a given set of facts should be considered as a single feature, or as a set of related features. For example, the younger demiuncial shows a general tendency to lengthen vertical lines, especially to bring down to the line those elements which, in the older demiuncial, were raised above the line: ѣ, ъ, and т develop toward ҍ, ҍ, and ɯ respectively. Is this one feature or three? Similarly, if one observes a general tendency to tilt letters toward the right in the younger demiuncial, replacing ѣ by ѣ́ and ѡ by ѻ, are we dealing with one phenomenon or two? Furthermore, the linguistic phenomena themselves are of such disparate nature, ranging from paleographic trivia to major syntactic features like new embedding techniques, that it is artificial to treat them in identical fashion, and especially to count them, — which is, however, precisely what we have done here. The conclusions to be extracted from such a study, especially the numerical conclusions, are no more than a very coarse measure of the origins of the phenomena associated with the "Second South Slavic Influence," but they are still *a* measure, and even a rough first approximation is better than no measure at all.

In the following pages, we divide the linguistic features of the "Second South Slavic Influence" into six groups, according to their most likely source: Hellenisms, archaisms, South Slavic features, Glagolitic features, Russian innovations, and features of uncertain origin. Needless to say, the actual origin of one or another feature is often very difficult to ascertain (ultimately, most of them go back to Greek and first entered Slavic in the Cyrillo-Methodian period, but this genetic fact has nothing to do with the functional role of individual features centuries later). There is much that is debatable in the treatment below, which is offered not as a definitive study, but as the basis for further discussion. For ease of reference and cross-reference, we have numbered the features sequentially, preposing alphabetic mnemonics to mark the group to which each feature belongs.

HELLENISMS. Sixteen linguistic features of the "Second South Slavic Influence" are the result of Greek influence. These features, many of which can be traced back to changes in the Greek cursive of the time, presumably arose in the Slavic monastery workshops of Constantinople (sic; see Vzdornov 1968) and Mt. Athos, where the close contact of Greek and Slavic monks, and the cultural prestige of Greek, made their adoption by Slavic scribes inevitable. From the monasteries, these innovations spread to other centers of religious and secular culture, first in the Slavic South (Euthymian Trnovo, the court of Stefan Lazar) and, later, in the renascent East. The fact that some of these graphic innovations appear earlier in the South than in the East (a "fact" which is open to question; see Žukovskaja 1982) reflects the earlier revival of interest in literary culture in the South, but does not in itself prove any causal connection between the Bulgaro-Serbian and the Russian developments.[7] One cannot deny altogether the possibility that the South Slavic cultural centers mediated this Greek influence — in such matters as these, categorical declarations are quite out of place — but one must not fall into the "post hoc, ergo propter hoc" fallacy.

Sixteen linguistic features can be attributed to Greek influence:

(H-1) Introduction of the wide alpha α for older a, д, etc. (Karskij 1928: 181-182, Larin 1975: 238).

(H-2) Introduction of epsilon ε for older Є , Ԑ ; ε was retained throughout the younger demiuncial and into the cursive (Karskij 1928: 186, Ščepkin 1920/1967: 130, Larin 1975: 238); cf. U-85, U-86 below.

(H-3) The shape of *ižica* develops from y to ѵ toward that of upsilon υ, and (H-3A) υ is now used as a letter, not only as a numeral (400), as had been the case in the older demiuncial (Sobolevskij 1894: 3-4, Ščepkin 1920/1967: 130, Karskij 1928: 172, Larin 1975: 238-239).

(H-4) The single-legged "i desjateričnoe" i, which had been used rarely in older texts, mostly in numerals, at line-end, and in иисоусъ, is now (H-4A) also used as a letter, appearing regularly before other vowels (rather than after them); this reflects the fact that, in Greek, the diphthongs ιη and ηο, ηε, ηα were much more frequent than were ηι and οη, εη, αη; (H-4B = G-79) the older i is now written with the dieresis, a fact perhaps due partly to Glagolitic influence (see G-79 below) (Ščepkin 1920/1967: 131-132, Karskij 1928: 193, Tixomirov-Muravev 1966: 32, Larin 1975: 240, Talev 1973: 61-62).

(H-5) Omega, which had all but disappeared in the older demiuncial, is reintroduced in both Greek and Slavic words (Talev 1973: 61), changing its shape from that with a central bar of medium height ω to one of two extremes, either acquiring a prominent center ѿ, or losing its center bar nearly altogether, ѡ, (Ščepkin 1920/1967: 130, Speranskij 1932: 53*ff*., Larin 1975: 238-239). In Serbian, the same change was occurring at the same time, ω being characteristic of 14th-c. mss. and ѿ, ѡ of those from the 15th c. (Džordžić 1970: 109).

(H-6) The older angular ("lomanoe" or "ostroe") в is replaced by a rounded ("krugloe") ʙ derived from the Greek cursive (and retained until eliminated from the *graždanka* by a personal decision of Peter I in 1710 (Istrin 1961: 308); somewhat later, a rectangular ("četyrexugoľnoe") ᴅ appears, occasionally in the 15th, but frequently only in the 17th c. Both innovations are a matter of frequency more than of form, since, e.g., the rounded ʙ can be found in the older demiuncial as well as in the younger (Ščepkin 1920/1967: 129-130, Karskij 1928: 182-183, Speranskij 1932: 53*ff.*, Larin 1975: 239).

(H-7) The older, angular-headed ꙁ (the somewhat rounded tail of which goes back as far as the Undoľskij Fragments and which had become usual by the 13th c.; see Karskij 1928: 191-192) is replaced by the round-headed ᛉ, an imitation of the Greek cursive (Ščepkin 1920/1967: 130, Karskij 1928: 191-192, Speranskij 1932: 53*ff.*, Istrin 1961: 262).

(H-8) Fita, which had formerly been used only as a numeral (9), is now used as a letter as well; also (H-8A = G-80), its horizontal bar is extended (θ > ѳ), perhaps under Glagolitic influence, see G-80, perhaps merely as an archaism harking back to OCS (Sobolevskij 1894: 4, Ščepkin 1920/1967: 130, Karskij 1928: 172).

(H-9) The digraph кс is replaced by the Greek ξ, at least in Greek names (Talev 1973: 62), which had formerly served only as a numeral (60) (Ščepkin 1920/1967: 130, Larin 1975: 239, Issatschenko 1980: 215).

(H-10) Similarly, the digraph пс is replaced by Greek ψ, at least in Greek names (Talev 1973: 62, Larin 1975: 239, Issatschenko 1980: 215).

(H-11) The cluster /ng/ is now spelled in the Greek manner, with гг rather than нг, in imitation of the Greek, e.g. ἄγγελλος (Sobolevskij 1894: 5).

(H-12) The progressive voicing assimilation /nt/ > /nd/ and /mp/ > /mb/ of Byzantine Greek is reflected in such spellings as анδонıн, олѵмвъ (Sobolevskij 1894: 5).

(H-13) Superscript *t* is written as ⸯ , ᴣ (Speranskij 1932: priloženie).

(H-14) A large number of ligature spellings are introduced at this time, with the second letter often written not above, but below the first, e.g. ᚛ = да, ᚜ = ащс, etc. (Speranskij 1932:63 and priloženie).

(H-15) The entire script grows rounder, imitating the Greek cursive; this affects letters discussed above, as well as some discussed elsewhere (υ, в, ҙ ; see U-94 (Speranskij 1932: *passim*).

(H-16) The only non-graphic phenomenon which can be attributed directly to Greek influence is the exclamatory genitive, e.g. оле вѣръı добръıа!, patterned directly on the Greek, e.g. Ὦ Πόσειδον, τῆς τέχνης! (Issatschenko 1980: 221). The construction inhabited Russian grammars from Smotryc'kyj through Lomonosov (Kjellberg 1959).

In addition, Larin 1975: 238 mentions a change in shape of м and л under Greek influence, but gives no particulars; since no other sources mention these letters specifically, we assume that the changes are covered by the general tendency toward rounding given as feature H-15 above.

ARCHAISMS. The most salient characteristic of Russian texts of the "Second South Slavic" period is not their Bulgarianness or Serbianness, but the fact that they show a mass retreat to the phonological and morphological (and, to a lesser extent, the syntactic and lexical) norms of religious texts of the Kievan period. They try — not always successfully, of course — to ignore four centuries of phonological and morphological change, just as they try to ignore four centuries of Russification of the genetically South Slavic religious language imported to Rus' in that earlier period. It is important to recognize, as Larin (1975: 240-241) has done, that the "Second South Slavic Influence" in Russia affected primarily religious documents and princely decrees, but not the great bulk of secular writing. Scholars argue about the autochthonous vs.

imported origin of literary Russian (the so-called Šaxmatov–Obnorskij controversy; for a different view, see Worth 1983b), but everyone agrees that by the latter 14th c. a considerable amalgamation and stabilization had taken place. In the case of religiously-oriented genres, this meant a considerable degree of penetration of East Slavic elements into what had originally been a much more markedly South Slavic language. It also meant, of course, that most of the specifically South Slavic elements, those which were specifically alien to the East Slavic scribes, had been removed from or adapted to, the vernacular (връхъ > вьрхъ or верхъ; врѣмя > время; рождьство > рожьство or рожество, etc.). This brings us to one of the central arguments of this paper, namely: even a massive increase in such "Slavonisms" as *trat* or *trъt* forms, щ instead of ч for *tj, *kti, gen. sing. *ja*-stems in я instead of ѣ, etc., etc. need not be seen as an imitation of South Slavic texts of the preceding period (13th and 14th cc.). From the point of view of the 15th-c. Russian scribe, these forms were nothing other than an attempt to return to the higher and more correct standards of his own, native past. That the normative language of religious literature in Kievan Rus' was, *genetically,* a South Slavic import, was of little importance even then, given its supranational character (Tolstoj 1961, Picchio 1963, Meščerskij 1975), and was certainly of no importance at all to a scribe of the 15th c. This Middle Russian scribe, after a four-century-long tradition, had every right to regard the language of Nestor and Ilarion as that of his own intellectual ancestors. As far as I know, there is not a shred of evidence that Russian scribes thought that the written language of the eleventh century, or of the fifteenth, was anything but their own; that is, they were happily ignorant of its South Slavic origins (indeed, the South Slav Konstantin Kostenečki even thought that Cyril and Method had relied primarily on *Russian* in their creation of OCS! (Jagić 1896: 108, Worth 1983a). In changing время to врѣмя or вьрхъ to връхъ, the Russian scribe was travelling not to Euthymian Bulgaria, but into his own, Russian past.

There are thirty-one identifiable archaisms of this sort. Two thirds of them are strictly indigenous, that is, they do not involve even genetic differences between the Eastern and the Southern Slavs. The other third involve differences which are genetically (but, in our view, quite irrelevantly) South Slavic. To simplify discussion, especially for those who may not share this point of view, we shall adduce these two groups separately. Since most of these features are well known from the standard literature (Sobolevskij 1907/1962, Borkovskij-Kuznecov 1963, Filin 1972, etc.), no attempt is made to provide complete documentation here.

EAST SLAVIC ARCHAISMS

(A-17) Etymological *ě and *e, which had fallen together in Moscow by the 16th c., were deliberately distinguished in pronunciation and writing, thanks to a combination of ecclesiastic and of dialectal influence (Uspenskij 1968: *passim*, Larin 1975: 244-245).

(A-18) Similarly, the Southwestern tendency to write *e in new closed syllables as ѣ is suppressed in the 15th c.

(A-19) The 14th-15th c. development of stressed *é* to *ó* when not followed by a soft consonant (or the graphic manifestation of more complex changes) is ignored or suppressed.

(A-20) Akanje spellings are excluded, perhaps under North Great Russian dialectal influence (Larin 1975: 245).

(A-21) Apocope of -*i* in the second person singular ending -ши is not reflected in texts (Larin 1975: 245).

(A-22) Similarly, texts ignore apocope of unstressed infinitival -ти.

(A-23) The spellings кы, гы, хы, which had long since given way to ки, ги, хи, are restored (Issatschenko 1980: 216).

(A-24) In the nom. sing. long-form adjective, the Great Russian tense-jer reflexes ои, еи are replaced by the -ыи, -ии common to all other Slavic languages; this is one of the few lasting changes of this period.

(A-25) Final clusters of obstruent stop + liquid are retained (вѣтръ, угль, etc.) without loss of the liquid or introduction of a svarabhakti vowel; this archaism, although eliminated later in some words (ветер, et al.), was responsible for the preservation of such clusters in other cases (рубль vs. dialectal рубель or рупь).

(A-26) Closely related to the above, but with additional morphological motivation, is the preservation of final -лъ in the masc. past tense (пеклъ, моглъ, везлъ, etc.).

(A-27) The *k* - *c, g* - *z, x* - *s* alternations resulting from the second velar palatalization are restored, as in Epifanij Premudryj's в тузѣ, мнозѣ, стисѣ (Larin 1975: 248, Issatschenko 1980: 221).

(A-28) The older *o*-stem oblique plural endings -омъ, -ы, -ѣхъ, which were beginning to give way to the *a*-stem endings -амъ, -ами, -ахъ during this period are preserved in their original form, partly, perhaps, under the influence of the chancery language, which tended to preserve the original *o*-stem endings.

(A-29) The old genitive plural ending ъ is restored, replacing the innovative овъ which had developed out of the reevaluated *u*-stem formant -ov- (Issatschenko 1980: 221).

(A-30) The completely artificial *ū*-stem nom. sing. ending -ы is reintroduced, e.g. in любы (Epifanij; Larin 1975: 248).

(A-31) The pronominal accusatives мене, тебе, себе are restored, driving out меня, тебя, себя.

(A-32) The directional clitics мя, тя, ся and ми, ти, си, which had dropped out of use (or, in the case of ся, been reevaluated as a verbal particle), are restored; in addition, (A-32A) the full form ся is maintained where the spoken language had reduced it to /s'/ (Larin 1975: 246).

(A-33) The supine, an artificial form even before the "Second South Slavic" period, is reintroduced at that time (Issatschenko 1980: 220).

(A-34) The imperfect tense, which had never been frequent and which had become quite artificial by the 15th c., is restored; Epifanij uses it correctly (желаше, вхожаше), even in the third plural (быва́ху, моляхуся, etc.; Larin 1975: 248).

(A-35) The dative absolute, the syntax of which was degenerate even in the Kievan period, is reintroduced at this time and perseveres, at least in the imagination of grammarians, until Lomonosov.

(A-36) The second accusative (постави мя попа), which began to give way to the instrumental toward the end of the period that concerns us (постави мя попомъ), was artificially maintained (Larin 1975: 246).

(A-37) Many Old Russian vocabulary items had disappeared by this time (Larin 1975: 246), but texts of the "Second South Slavic" period tend to archaize their vocabulary; chronicle texts, for example, substitute archaic Slavonisms for vernacular words (умре > преставися, успѣ; порты > ризы; прозвашася > нарекошася; речи, молвити > глаголати, etc.; Filin 1949: 38-56).

GENETICALLY SOUTH SLAVIC, FUNCTIONALLY EAST SLAVIC ARCHAISMS

(A-38) *tort groups are spelled trat, except for such Russisms as верещати, солома; trat forms are 2½ times more frequent in the 16th than in the 14th c. (Vinokur 1971: 76), and include such artificial creations as клаколъ, млание (Ščepkin 1920/1967: 130, Meščerskij 1978: 29-30, 47, cited in Meščerskij 1981: 109-110, Issatschenko 1980: 223).

(A-39) *tŭrt groups are spelled тръt (плъкъ, or, in the Serbian manner, плъкь, cf. S-48, instead of полкъ, пълкъ; this change is not carried out consistently, e.g., свершенъ, чернеческыя in the Житие святого отца Варлаама Пустынника, Larin 1975: 250 (Sobolevskij 1894: 5, Ščepkin 1920/1967: 130, Tixomirov–Murav'ev 1966: 32, Talev 1973: 61, Larin 1975: 239-240, Issatschenko 1980: 215).

(A-40) *telt groups are written in the OCS rather than in the Russian Church Slavonic manner (древо > дрѣво, etc.); this archaism, which was not carried through consistently, was soon eliminated, except for the persistent плѣнъ for older полонъ (Šaxmatov 1941: 74) (Larin 1975: 240, 249, Issatschenko 1980: 216).

(A-41) The increase in forms with щ rather than ч from *tj, *kti is a purely Russian archaism, unlike the corresponding voiced жд for ж from *dj; cf. S-59 (Larin 1975: 240, Issatschenko 1980: 223).

(A-42) The South Slavic spelling я < *ę is restored in the ja-stem gen. sing., nom.-acc. plur., *jo-stem acc. plur., and corresponding pronominal and adjectival forms, replacing both the older East Slavic forms (nominal ѣ, pron. and adj. оѣ) and the innovating Russian ои.

(A-43) In the gen. sing. masc. and neut. adjective, -аго replaces pronominal -ого, a change which lasted until 1917 (Issatschenko 1980: 221).

(A-44) Comparative adjectives in -аиш-, -еиш- are introduced.

(A-45) The single-negative sentence, e.g. и никого же видѣ instead of ... не видѣ is reintroduced (Issatschenko 1980: 221).
(A-46) Periphrastic "past progressive" forms consisting of finite verb and dependent active participle, e.g. бѣ крьстя (Issatschenko 1980: 220) or и бяше умѣя глаголати тремя языки (Larin 1975: 249), are reintroduced at this time. Like most of the archaisms adduced here, this goes back genetically via OCS to Greek (ἡ διδάσκαλων, etc.).
(A-47) The use of genetically OCS adverbs such as вельми, присно, зѣло increases during this period, along with the general archaization of the vocabulary referred to under A-37 above (Larin 1975: 248).

Several of the archaisms listed above had a lasting effect on literary Russian. Resistance to akanje, the e > o and ě > < e changes were important for Russian rhyme into the 19th c. *Tort > trat developments added a variety of stylistic doublets to the language, and the large number of *trat* forms, especially in compounds and suffixed formations, led to the productive use of *trat* forms in modern Russian derivational patterns (Ožegov defines вратарь as the one who защища[ет] ворота). Adjectival ои and ыи are still evident in Russian spelling rules, and affected rhyme through Pushkin's time (gen. sing. fem. нѣжной rhyming with acc. sing. masc. мятёжный, etc.). In general, the archaisms listed in this section, in spite of a certain number of ephemeral features (dative absolute, second palatalization, etc.), are the most important of all the features of the "Second South Slavic Influence" for the subsequent evolution of literary Russian.

SOUTH SLAVIC FEATURES. As explained above, we consider as evidence of South Slavic influence only those features whose appearance in Russian can most convincingly be explained as imitations of developments which had taken place in South Slavic texts of the immediately preceding period; other genetic South Slavonisms (*$tj > šč$, etc.), which had long since been incorporated into the Russian genre system, are treated here as purely Russian archaisms. This view is assumed to represent that of the 15th c. Russian scribe, who was surely better acquainted with major works of the Kievan period (Ilarion's *Slovo,* the *Life* of Feodosij Pečerskij, the *Čtenie* account of Boris and Gleb, et al.) than with the literary production of Euthymian Trnovo. In other words, to use Avanesov's term (1973), only those features which were *functionally* as well as genetically South Slavic will be attributed to the "Second South Slavic Influence". There are twenty-six such features.

(S-48) ъ is replaced by ь in auslaut. The use of a single jer (ъ or ь, depending on the orthographic school) was typical of Bulgaria (Karskij 1928: 203), and, as is well known, medieval Serbian texts tended to use only ь. The tendency to opt for final ь ran counter to the archaizing, and genetically South Slavic, use of тъ instead of Russian ть in the third pers. verb endings (except есть, нѣсть; Issatschenko 1980: 216), and was counter-phonetic in the then-hardening instr. sing. masc.-neut. (Sobolevskij 1894: 5, Ščepkin 1920/1967: 130, Tixomirov-Muravev 1966: 32).

(S-49) On the contrary, ъ replaces ь, and sometimes vocalized e, in inlaut (Sobolevskij 1894: 5), and, in particular, on the prefix boundary, where its use has been maintained until the present (Issatschenko 1980: 216). Karskij 1928: 317-318 attributes this distribution (ь in auslaut, ъ in inlaut) to the Euthymian reforms.

(S-50) In a related development, *jery* is now spelled as ы instead of older ъı, surely because of the Serbian replacement of both ъ and ь by ь. Larin considered this change "лишенное всякого оправдания" (1975: 239), unlike Ščepkin, who thought it a useful innovation (1920/1967: 131). The matter is rather complex, because, on the one hand, ъı was by no means unknown in South Slavic texts, esp. up to the 14th c. (Karskij 1928: 203-240) and, on the other, ы can be found in certain Old Russian mss. of the 12th and 13th cc., including the *Izbornik* of 1076 (Sobolevskij 1908: 52, Karskij *ibid.*), so that the ъı > ы change could have been motivated, at least in part, by the native archaizing tendency as well as by South Slavic developments; still, the dominant influence would seem to have been Serbian (Sobolevskij 1894: 4, Karskij 1928: 172, Tixomirov-Muravev 1966: 31).

(S-51) The phonetically unexpected vocalization of weak jer to *e* in the suffixes *$\overline{i}sk$ and *$\overline{i}stv$, attested since the 13th c., becomes regular in the more Slavonic layers of the vocabulary from the 15th c. (человѣческии, существо, etc.). Issatschenko 1980: 219-220 considers this part of the "Rebulgarisierung der Hochsprache," but adduces no firm evidence that this development is specifically South Slavic, rather than merely Slavonic.

(S-52) Jotated ѩ disappears, being replaced by a or я. This is actually two developments: (S-52A) the graphic change, namely the replacement of ѩ by я, at least in inlaut (Karskij 1928: 206); (S-52B) the phonetic dejotation of /aja/ to /aa/, which originated in Bulgarian dialects (Ščepkin 1920/1967: 130), and which is reflected orthographically in such spellings as своа, долгаа, etc. (Sobolevskij 1894: 5, Tixomirov-Muravev 1966: 32, Talev 1973: 60-61, Issatschenko 1980: 215). The spelling without jotation is extended to forms like всеа, which Bulgarian had never spelled with ѩ or a, cf. OCS вьсеѩ, later Bulgarian вьсеѧ, вьсеѫ, вьсеѭ and East Slavic вьсеѣ (Ščepkin, *ibid.*), thus creating a hybrid form (всса) unrelated to either East or South Slavic. Larin 1975: 240 calls such spellings as своа "совершенно чужд[ые] русскому произношению," which is somewhat exaggerated, in view of the well-known North Russian dialectal contractions of the type [dóbrā žoná].

(S-53A) The reintroduction of ѫ, especially in Southwestern and Western mss., more rarely and ephemerally in Moscow (Sobolevskij 1908: 55, Ščepkin 1920/1967: 131), has obvious Bulgarian origins and cannot be considered an East Slavic archaism, since both ѫ and ѭ, which had been used, albeit rarely, in some 11th and early 12th c. texts (Sobolevskij 1908: 52), had virtually disappeared by the 13th c. (Larin 1975: 239). The ѫ had become widespread in Middle Bulgarian, partly because of that language's confusion of ѫ and ѧ (Sobolevskij 1894: 6) and, in Russian, was then used in roots and in auslaut, regardless of etymology (**богородицѫ**, but also **сынѫ**, **смѫ**), — as one scribe put it, "красоты ради, а не истины" (Ščepkin 1920/1967: 130, Larin, *ibid.*). The graphic development (S-53B) is less clear: the younger Russian demiuncial ж has a larger head than the older, and shows the generally "lowered center of gravity" typical of this period (see U-87-92 below); however, the Bulgarian developments seem to have proceeded in the opposite direction, with the head growing smaller or even disappearing altogether (Karskij 1928: 208), so that feature (S-53B) should perhaps better be considered a Russian innovation rather than a South Slavic feature.

(S-54) The increased use of the old front nasal letter Ѧ, replacing ѩ (see S-52 above), is partly due to the widespread confusion of Ѧ and ѫ in Bulgarian of the preceding period (see S-53 above) (Karskij 1928: 206). Paleographically, the development of ѩ to ѩ shows the "lowered center of gravity" just mentioned (Larin 1975: 239). For Ѧ as a first pers. verb ending, see S-64 below.

(S-55) Connected with the two features just discussed, and originating in the Middle Bulgarian confusion of Ѧ and ѫ, is the confusion of я (Ѧ) and ю noted at this same period in Russian (Sobolevskij 1894: 6).

(S-56) The "*o očnoe*" Ѳ and its doubled variant ѲѲ appear at this time, primarily in iconic spellings like ѳкѳ, ѳѳчи. The graph Ѳ originated in Greek, and was used in older South Slavic mss. (Budilovič 1871, cited by Karskij 1928: 196), ѲѲ is attested from the 14th c. Kostenečki used Ѳ for the singular ѳкѳ, and ѲѲ for the plural ѳѳчи, similar to his use of o and ω in вода, вωды (Jagić 1896/1968: 120, Worth 1983a) (Karskij 1928: 195-197, Talev 1973: 61, Issatschenko 1980: 215).

(S-57) Etymological **ja* is spelled ѣ, originally a Bulgarian dialect development (Sobolevskij 1894: 5-6).

(S-58) Ю replaces y in anlaut, reflecting the Southern rather than the Eastern reflex of **jeu* et al. To some extent, this may be an archaizing development, since Ю and its mirror Ю were no rarity in older Russian mss. (Karskij 1928: 205-206, citing Sreznevskij 1885: 113). Paleographically, the development from 13th c. ГО to late 14th c. Ю shows the "lowered center of gravity" typical of the "Second South Slavic" period, but in the case of Ю, this could also be considered an archaism, since the raised horizontal bar of ГО was an innovation of the older demiuncial.

(S-59) The reflex of **dj* is introduced in its South Slavic form жд, rather than the ж, which had been characteristic of even purely religious texts in the older period. It is not clear that **dj* > жд is really a South Slavic feature, and not a purely internal Russian development. On the one hand, internal jer loss had created the cluster /žd/ in жьдати > ждати and тришьды > трижди, generally assumed to be a precondition of the appearance of жд, but on the other hand this жд is by no means uniformly characteristic of even the most elaborately Slavonized texts of this period (Epifanij, for example, has преже, рассужая, заблужаяся and the II Sofijsk. Chronicle has чюжимъ, чюжие, etc.; Larin 1975: 242-243) and became really frequent only during the 16th c., too late to be attributed directly to South Slavic influence (as opposed to the archaizing tendency, which lasted into the 17th c.) (Larin 1975: 240, Issatschenko 1980: 223).

(S-60) The *u*-stem formant -ов- is extended to the oblique cases of the plural (сыновомъ, сыновѣхъ for older сынъмъ, сынъхъ); this is a Bulgarian development (Sobolevskij 1894: 6, Talev 1973: 63), probably abetted by the strong Russian tendency toward stem levelling.

(S-61) Masculine personal names acquire the Bulgarian nom. sing. ending -ие, e.g. Василие (Sobolevskij 1903: cited by Talev 1973: 63).

(S-62) Numerals acquire the Bulgarian ending -х in the gen.(-loc.) plural, e.g. триехъ, пятихъ for older три(и), пятъ (Sobolevskij 1894: 6, Talev 1973: 63).

(S-63) The possessive pronominal substantives его, того acquire the Bulgarian formant в, becoming еговъ, тоговъ (Sobolevskij 1894: 6, Talev 1973: 63). However, this development may be due in part to the purely Russian tendency to adjectivalize all possessors, as in substandard ихний, егоный, etc.

(S-64) The first pers. sing. present tense appears with the endings - ѧ, - ѩ, instead of -ю, -у in the Russian version of Kostenečki's grammatical treatise (бїа́сѧ̃, бїе́шнсѧ̃, ..., see Worth 1983a). This goes back to the Bulgarian confusion of ѧ and ѫ (see S-53–55 above), as, for example, in the so-called "Eight Parts of Speech": творѧ́, твориши, ...;бїа́сѧ, бїе́шнсѧ; Worth 1983a), but whether this oddity ever escaped from grammars into real texts cannot yet be determined.

(S-65) Similarly, medieval grammatical treatises going back to the "Eight Parts of Speech" distinguish between a regular, unmarked future tense with the auxiliary нмамь + infinitive, and a special, marked "proximate future" (по малѣ бывающе) with хощу + infinitive, but it is unclear whether these forms were ever distinguished in practice (Worth 1983a).

(S-66) Closely related to the above is the distinction adduced by Talev 1973: 8 between an affirmative future in хотѣти and a negative future in не имѣти. One suspects that all three of these features (S-64, 65, 66) are grammatical ghosts of no real importance.

(S-67) The increased use of participial clauses, one of the two major embedding techniques characteristic of this and subsequent periods, is typical of the *izvitie sloves* which came from the South Slavic area, apparently having originated in Euthymian Trnovo. To a substantial extent, however, the rhetorical devices of this period, including participial embedding, could be seen as an elaboration of Kievan rhetoric, and it remains unclear, to what extent the increasingly elaborate constructions of the 15th and 16th cc. can be traced to specifically Bulgarian and Serbian models (Ivanov 1958: *passim*, Larin 1975: 248).

(S-68) The second principal embedding technique consists of subordinate clauses introduced by Slavonic иже, the increased use of which at this time was noted by Issatschenko 1980: 221. This, like S-67, may represent in part a return to the (Russian) Church Slavonic rhetoric of the Kievan period. A subtype of these constructions, however, (S-68A), in which the combination of иже and a past active participle together function like a finite subordinate clause (кый тъ есть младеньць, иже гласомъ проверещавый Issatschenko 1980: 221, ублажають тѣхъ, иже тогда умръшихъ Sofijsk. I Chr., Larin 1975: 243) would seem to be more a Greek calque than a South Slavic construction.

(S-69) Another syntactic feature of the "Second South Slavic" period, adduced by Issatschenko 1980: 221 as an example of "Rebulgarisierung," is the nominalization of singular participles, e.g. трепещу, не вѣдущи бываемаго (*ibid.*), but no South Slavic prototypes are provided.

(S-70) The replacement of infinitival clauses by personal forms introduced by да appears to have been motivated by this Balkan development, perhaps aided by archaizing reminiscences of similar OCS clauses.

(S-71) Among lexical features of this period, the greatly increased use of compounds has been attributed to the South Slavic "пристрасти[е] к сложным словам" (Larin 1975: 247, cf. Issatschenko 1980: 221-222), but this development might equally well represent a return to the translation techniques of the Kievan period (cf., for example, Istrin 1922).

(S-72) Bulgarian прѣзъ is substituted for Russian Church Slavic чрезъ, чрѣзъ (Sobolevskij 1894:6, Talev 1973: 63).

(S-73) Similarly, the Bulgarian first pers. sing. цъфту is substituted for Russian цвьту (Sobolevskij 1894: 6, Talev 1973: 63), but, like S-72, this is not a very important innovation.

Of the twenty-six features which did originate (or which may have originated) in preceding South Slavic developments, only ten had any lasting effect, and several of these were only marginal to the subsequent development of the Russian literary language. These ten are (S-49) ъ used on the prefix boundary; (S-50) ъı > ы, (S-51) stylistic doublets arising from different treatments of weak jer in -*īsk*-, -*īstv*- (дурацкий vs. гносеологический, etc.); (S-54) increased use of ѧ, which > я; (S-58) anlaut ю- in юноша, юг, etc.; (S-59) stylistic doublets arising from Southern vs. Eastern reflexes of *dj (возбудить/возбуждённый vs. перебудить/перебу́женный, etc.); (S-60) the -*ov*- formant in сыновья, кумовья, unless this is a Russian stem levelling (cf. dialectal дядьевья etc.); (S-62) -х in the numerals двух, трех, etc.; (S-67) participial subordination, an important aspect of all scientific prose; (S-71) compounding, of increasing importance in the scientific and technical vocabulary. Of these ten features, only the last two (S-67, participial subordination, and S-71, compounding) were of major and lasting importance for the development of literary Russian, and these two features are not unequivocally of South Slavic origin.

GLAGOLITIC FEATURES. One of the most intriguing, but also one of the most elusive aspects of the younger Russian demiuncial is the possibility that certain features developed wholly or partly under the influence of the Glagolitic alphabet. In the case of Э, it is generally agreed that this letter goes back to Glagolitic Э (Ščepkin 1920/1967: 131, Karskij 1928: 186-187; see G-74 below), but just why Glagolitic should have influenced the graphic practices of the 15th c. is never explained; further, Э is only one of more than half a dozen cases where Glagolitic influence may be suspected.

Glagolitic, usually of the rounded, "Bulgarian" type, had been used occasionally in Kievan Rus' in mss. and epigraphy (Vysockij 1966, Medynceva 1978), but it had gone out of use by the 14th c. In the late 15th and early 16th cc. Glagolitic reappears, this time as a cryptographic device, alongside Greek, Latin, and the Permian alphabet (Speranskij 1929: 58*ff.*, 65). Speranskij (*ibid.*) attributes the reemergence of Glagolitic to South Slavic influence. This view can neither be confirmed nor be denied, but it is in any case not firmly supported by the chronology, since Glagolitic reappears among the Russians only a century or more after the arrival of Kiprian in Moscow. One might equally well look to the monasteries of Mt. Athos for the source of renewed interest in this archaic script, especially because of the otherwise rather puzzling mixture of rounded, "Bulgarian," and angular Croatian elements that seem to have influenced the younger demiuncial in Russia. For now, the matter must remain in the area of conjecture, but it is, at the least, not entirely unreasonable to assume that Glagolitic was partially revived, and doubtless itself affected by the developing Greek cursive, in the Athonite monasteries and other monasteries on South Slavic territory, whence it spread to the secular centers of Orthodox culture, reaching Russia both directly and via South Slavic mediation (since Glagolitic had never died out entirely in the South, in Bulgaria as well as — notably — in Croatia). Be all this as it may, we should like to suggest here that the influence of Glagolitic on the younger Russian demiuncial may have been somewhat stronger than has yet been recognized. (Note: the following discussion is highly speculative; it is important to note that, even if Glagolitic provenance of some of these features is disproved, they will remain not specifically South Slavic, but rather in the uncertain group.)

Thirteen features of the younger demiuncial can be related to Glagolitic. Of these, some form of more or less direct influence seems likely in seven cases and these are counted as independent features below (G-74 to G-80). In the other six cases, the likelihood of such influence ranges from modest to minimal, and these cases have therefore not been counted as independent features, but are referred to by the alphanumeric notation under which they are discussed elsewhere in this paper, and enclosed in square brackets instead of parentheses.

(G-74) The Э ("оборотное") introduced at this time, primarily in Western and Southwestern mss. (Ščepkin 1920/1967: 131), obviously originates in Glagolitic Э, Э, the single-crossbar variant of which goes back as far as section B of the Prague Fragments (Vajs 1932: 80); it came to Western Russia from Serbia in the 16th c. and was first used in foreign words to mark non-palatalizing /e/ (Karskij 1928: 186-187, Larin 1975: 239).

(G-75) The extension of the vertical bars of T to form the new ⱀ had begun with an elongated left bar as early as the *Izbornik* of 1076, but was completed and usual only from the 15th c. (Ščepkin 1920/1967: 130, Karskij 1928: 198-199, Tixomirov-Murav'ev 1966: 31, Larin 1975: 238), at the same time that it became dominant in Serbia (Džordžić 1970: 109). On the one hand, this development is part of the general tendency at that time to extend vertical lines down to the line (cf. ъ > n, ѣ > rb), but on the other hand, it can hardly be mere coincidence that the new "трехногое" Ш so closely resembles Glagolitic ⵞ, especially in the latter's angular Croatian variant ⵞ (Vajs 1932: 91-92). The inference of such influence is not vitiated by the fact that it was primarily the rounded Bulgarian type of Glagolitic that affected Russian graphics, since there is some evidence that Croatian Glagolitic may have been known in the Bukovina in the 14th – 16th cc. (Speranskij 1929: 8), and since both types are found, mixed together, in at least one Croatian ms. of the 15th c.(*ibid.*).

(G-76) The numeral 900, which had been rendered by ҄ in older Russian mss., is expressed by Ц in the younger demiuncial. This usage first appears in a South Russian gospel text of 1427, copied from a South Slavic original (Karskij 1928: 216-217, cf. Ščepkin 1920/1967: 131, Tixomirov-Muraev 1866: 31). That this change had its origin in Glagolitic Ύ = 900 (Diels 1932: 23) can hardly be denied.

(G-77) The letter *dzelo*, which in the Russian uncial and older demiuncial had been used only to represent the numeral 6, and which in the older demiuncial had been written like a cursive Ꙁ , is reintroduced as Ѕ and used as both number and letter in the younger demiuncial. Karskij 1928: 172 attributes this to South Slavic influence, but as Džordžić (1970: 113) shows, the Serbian development was simultaneous with the Russian, which renders a causal connection uncertain. Karskij (1928: 189) derived the cursive *dzelo* Ꙁ from Glagolitic Ⰷ (cf. also Sobolevskij 1894: 4, 8 f.n. 1, Ščepkin 1920/1967: 130).

(G-78) The younger demiuncial introduced a different distribution of letters representing /u/, replacing У and sometimes ОУ by a curved digraph *uk* ȣ, which is almost identical to one variety of Glagolitic *u* (Vajs 1932: 93). What is typical of the younger demiuncial is not the mere appearance of *uk*, since the letter itself appears from the earliest mss., as a space-saver at line-end, or in musical texts, to avoid a two-note interpretation of oy (Karskij 1928: 199-200), but rather its high frequency and distribution (oy in anlaut and elsewhere). One can assume that Glagolitic cursive Ⱛ (Vajs *ibid.*) was one, but not the only factor which intensified the use of *uk* (Sobolevskij 1894: 3-4, Ščepkin 1920/1967: 130, Karskij 1928: 172, Tixomirov--Muraev 1966: 31-32).

(G-79) The dieresis which appears on the single-legged ї at this time may well have originated in the double circles at the top of Glagolitic Ⱛ (Vajs 1932: 83); furthermore, since the single-legged i was itself rare in older mss. (Karskij 1928: 193, Larin 1975: 24), there is some reason to think that the renewed use of two positionally alternant *i* letters represented a return to the graphic system of Glagolitic, which had distinguished *iže* Ⱛ from *i* Ⰹ .

(G-80) The long horizontal bar of *fita* (ѳ replacing the older θ), is too reminiscent of Glagolitic *fert* ⰼ to be due entirely to chance (Vajs 1932: 93).

The following features, although perhaps suggestive in their totality, cannot be taken as evidence of Glagolitic influence on the younger demiuncial on a letter-by-letter basis:

[U-87] The lowering of the left bar of ѣ to form the newer rѣ is reminiscent of the cursive Glagolitic ⱚ, angular ⱚ (Vajs 1932: 99).

[H-15] The general tendency toward rounding evident in the younger demiuncial, although due primarily to the Greek cursive (Speranskij 1932: *passim*), may have gained some secondary support from the cryptographic use of the rounded Bulgarian-type Glagolitic beginning in the late 15th–16th cc. (Speranskij 1929: 58*ff.*); since the Glagolitic itself was heavily dependent on the Greek cursive (Vajs 1932: 37*ff.*), one might regard this as evidence of indirect Hellenization.

[H-14] Increased use of space-saving devices such as abbreviations and ligatures was characteristic of later Glagolitic mss., e.g., $\overset{\text{дѕ}\dagger}{\underset{}{\text{о}\perp\text{о}}}$ = Cyrillic $\overset{\text{ш}}{\text{м}}$а = маша (= мьша?), *misa* (Vajs 1932: 108), as it was of some Russian mss. of the 15th, and especially of the 16th cc. (Speranskij 1932: 63 and *priloženie*; see H-14 above). The proliferation of ligatures in Croatian Glagolitic is well known. However, this coincidence of Russian and Croatian developments is more likely to be a simultaneous manifestation of Athonite practices than to result from any causal connection.

[U-95] The development of the "cup-type" ("чаша") Ү, Y to the one-sided ("получаша" or "одностороннее") Ч (Karskij 1928: 201-202 et al.; see U-95 below) is not dissimilar to some of the late Glagolitic letters adduced by Vajs 1932: 96: Ꙋ, Ꙋ. However, since the "half-cup" Ч had already begun to develop in the older demiuncial (Karskij 1928: 201-202), there is no reason to attribute this change to Glagolitic.

[H-5] The penstrokes necessary to produce the newly-introduced omega for /o/ are almost necessary to those required for Glagolitic Ә (with 90% rotation), but this connection is tenuous.

[G-77] Similarly, the Russian cursive ⱬ, used for *dzelo* in the older demiuncial (see G-77 above) is not unlike Glagolitic Ỷ etc. (Vajs 1932: 79), but this is unlikely to be more than coincidental.

One can conclude that Glagolitic influence on the younger demiuncial, though neither pervasive nor, with the exception of ⱔ, Ә, and Ї, lasting, was more substantial than has heretofore been recognized. This influence may have come to Russia via the Southern Slavs, but may equally well have emanated directly from Mt. Athos.

RUSSIAN INNOVATIONS. In a few cases, features specific to the period of "Second South Slavic Influence" seem to be Russian innovations. This is not to say that such features are entirely independent of developments elsewhere in the Slavic world, but only that their specific form, or the importance they assume for literary Russian, is unique to this territory. In all cases but the first, these developments could, almost equally well, be classified as archaisms, and in the case of -тельн-, as a South Slavic feature.

(R-81) The South Russian and/or Ukrainian lenited pronunciation of *g as /γ/ or [h] is adduced by Larin 1975: 245 as a "South Slavic Influence" feature. However, it is not clear whether there is any preference of /γ/ over [g] as early as the 15th c.

(R-82) The archaic pronunciation of weak jers in prefixes led to the development of an independent prefix co-, equivalent to Greek συν-, Larin *con-, co-* (Issatschenko 1980: 217), which in turn made possible lexical doublets like сбор/ собор (Meščerskij 1981: 109).

(R-83) Similarly, an independent prefix воз arises at the same time, and for the same reason. In both cases, one can assume that the rise of such independent prefixes was connected with the new, morpheme-by-morpheme translation technique (Keipert 1977: 84*ff.*, with further literature).

(R-84) The extraordinary expansion of adjectives in -тельн-, now independent of substantives in -тель, is described in convincing detail by Keipert 1977 *passim*. These adjectives are in many cases calqued on the Greek (землемерительнъ < γεωμετρικός, обоежительнъ < ἀμφίβιος, нестрадательнъ < ἀπαθής), but the emergence of independent -тельн-, of obviously great importance for the subsequent history of literary Russian, seems to have been primarily a Russian phenomenon.

These few Russian innovations were of considerable importance for the lexicon of the Russian literary language.

FEATURES OF UNCLEAR PROVENANCE. Finally, we are left with a baker's dozen of features, mostly paleographic, the sources of which are uncertain. They do not seem to depend directly on developments in Greek or the Balkan languages, although it would be incautious to exclude any such influence a priori. Overall, they represent a development in the direction of the cursive script that was to follow, and could for this reason perhaps be classified as Russian innovations.

(U-85), The most complex of these features of uncertain provenance is a group of
(U-86) developments connected with the graphic expression of /e/ and /je/. The most usual summary of these developments is that (U-85A) jotated ѥ disappears and (U-85B) is replaced by the so-called broad Є ("большое"). At the same time, (U-86A) the left-tilted "anchor" ("якорное") ҿ disappears, being (U-86B) replaced by the right-tilted "overturned" ("опрокинутое") ҿ. The actual facts, to the limited extent that one can extract them from the secondary literature, are more complex. The oldest texts use broad Є and narrow Ҁ interchangeably, the former sometimes representing /je/, especially in South Slavic mss. Broad Є becomes more frequent from the late 13th c., a century before the onset of the "Second South Slavic Influence"; this broad Є sometimes tilts to the left ҿ, driving out jotated ѥ, which, however, never disappears entirely, being found in mss. up to the 18th c. In Serbian mss., jotated ѥ is preserved until the 17th c., which means that the (partial) loss of ѥ in the younger Russian demiuncial could hardly have had

Serbian origins. This picture is complicated by the fact that a Greek-type ε (see G-2) and also the "оборотное" Э seem both to have been used as facultative substitutes for both broad Є and narrow Ԑ , representing /e/. All of these developments await a clearer exposition. From our present viewpoint, it suffices to say that they do not appear to have resulted from an external impetus (Sobolevskij 1894: 3, Ščepkin 1920/1967: 129, Karskij 1928: 172, 184-187, Tixomirov–Murav'ev 1966: 31, 91, Larin 1975: 239).

A second cluster of developments may be called the "lowering of the center of gravity" of graphic signs. As a general phenomenon this was first identified by Larin 1975: 239. The phenomenon has two concrete manifestations, a lowering of verticals to meet the line, and a change in the relative heights of the left and right ends of horizontal or quasi-horizontal elements.

(U-87) The left vertical bar of ъ is lowered to the line, creating њ.
(U-88) Older ѣ develops a similar left vertical, becoming њ (see Glagolitic features, p. 115 above).
G-75 The Glagolitic-influenced development of T to ɰ is of course part of this same general tendency.
(U-89) The change from H toward И, which had begun as early as 1220 (and is therefore not specific to the "Second South Slavic" period, is completed. In Serbian mss., H predominates in the 14th c. and И is rare until the 15th and becomes dominant only in the 16th, a chronology which would seem to exclude South Slavic influence on the Russian development (Ščepkin 1920/1967: 130, Karskij 1928: 192-193, Larin 1975: 239, Džordžić 1970: 109).
(U-90) The high horizontal bar of ГО, itself an innovation of the 13th c. older demiuncial, is lowered to Ю (Ščepkin 1920/1967: 130).
(U-91) Identically, the horizontal bar of older ГА is lowered to ІА (to the limited extent that this jotated letter is used at all).
(U-92) The diagonal cross bar of older N is raised toward the middle, giving modern H; this development had, however, begun in the 13th c. and is therefore not specific to the younger demiuncial (Ščepkin 1920/1967: 130, Karskij 1928: 195).

The remaining five features cannot be subsumed under any larger rubric.

(U-93) Jat' tilts to the right, becoming the so-called "lame jat'" ("хромой") ѣ, much as the change from ѡ to ѡ in U-86AB above (Ščepkin 1920/1967: 129, Larin 1975: 239).
(U-94) The redistribution of graphs representing /u/ may well be due to the preoccupation with such matters evident in the work of Kostenečki, but there is no direct evidence of Serbian influence on this aspect of the younger demiuncial. The oldest mss. use ОУ everywhere, the older demiuncial has ОУ in anlaut and У or its replacement ȣ (see G-78) elsewhere. Uk, which had been used as a space-saver at line end and in musical texts to mark monosyllabic /u/ (to be sung with a single note), becomes more frequent in the younger demiuncial, often replacing ОУ (Sobolevskij 1894: 3-4, Ščepkin 1920/1967: 130, Karskij 1928: 199-200, Tixomirov–Murav'ev 1966: 31-32).

(U-95) The vertical lines of Ж continue to spread farther apart, to Ж; this development had begun as early as the 11th c. In the "Second South Slavic" period, the small "head" of Ж, itself a 13th c. innovation, returned to "normal" size, a fact which Karskij 1928: 188-189 thinks may be due to South Slavic influence.

(U-96) The older symmetrical "чаша" Y or Y continues to develop toward the asymmetrical "получаша" Ч. The latter shape can, in fact, be found as early as the 1097 *Minei* (Sreznevskij 1885: 122, cited by Karskij 1928: 201-202), and had become increasingly frequent during the 14th c., occasionally losing its "leg" altogether (v); in Serbian, Y becomes asymmetrical only in the 15th c., a chronology which excludes any substantial South Slavic influence (Ščepkin 1920/1967: 130-131, Karskij 1928: 201-202, Tixomirox–Murav'ev 1966: 31, Larin 1975: 239, Džordžić 1970: 109-110).

(U-97) The only non-paleographic feature among those of uncertain origin is the spelling of the past passive participle with double -NN-, a feature attributed to the "Second South Slavic Influence" by Issatschenko 1980: 215, without, however, adducing direct evidence of its South Slavic origin.

Several of these features of unclear provenance left their traces on the graphics and orthography of literary Russian (Щ, Ч, the double-*n* participles), but the features themselves are rather on the periphery of the literary language system.

CONCLUSIONS. The linguistic features discussed above total ninety-seven. This number could, of course, be expanded or contracted somewhat, by separating features into their components or by grouping them into larger thematic units ("rounding", "tilting", etc.). Such expansion or contraction might change some details, but is unlikely to affect the overall distribution of features by group of origin. Similarly, there are a good many features whose origin can be determined only with a degree of uncertainty; to classify some features differently might also change details, but is unlikely to alter the general picture which emerges from this study.

The distribution by origin of the linguistic features of the "Second South Slavic Influence" is as follows:

Generic group and feature numbers	*No. of features*	*% of total*
Hellenisms (1-16)	16	16.5
Archaisms (17-47)	31	31.9
South Slavisms (48-73)	26	26.8
Glagolitisms (74-80)	7	7.2
Russianisms 81-84)	4	4.1
Unclear origin (85-97)	13	13.4

As these figures make clear, barely one fourth of the linguistic features associated with the "Second South Slavic Influence" are in fact "South

Slavic," if this term is taken to refer to Bulgarian and Serbian developments of the 13th and 14th cc. In a broader sense, of course, nearly every aspect of written Russian can be traced back to the "South Slavic" of the Cyrillo-Methodian period, but such a purely genetic view cannot contribute much to our understanding of the specific events of the 15th c. We conclude, therefore, that what was happening in the "Second South Slavic" period was not at all a slavish imitation of earlier developments in Bulgaria or Serbia, but a largely autochthonous development. This development, a response to the newly-won freedom from Tatar domination and to the increasing ascendency of Moscow ("the Third Rome"), was part of the quest for historical legitimacy typical of newly founded states. Moscow was turning to its own cultural past far more than to foreign models. Looking toward Kiev and Byzantium, rather than toward Bulgaria or Serbia, the young Muscovite state and its cultural leaders were engaged in a complex, largely artificial and archaizing search for spiritual legitimacy. In this search, the South Slavic world played only a minor role.

University of California, Los Angeles

POSTSCRIPT: I am grateful to my colleagues Professors Henrik Birnbaum and Michael Flier for discussion (at times, spirited) of many of the issues raised in this paper. Their attention has helped me to eliminate several obvious errors, without, however, dissuading me from certain admittedly rather risky proposals.

NOTES

[1] The oldest attestation I have found is in Speranskij 1929: 65 ("v svjazi s tak naz. «vtorym» jugoslavjanskim vlijaniem v russkoj pis'mennosti"); he repeats it, again with "jugo-", in Speranskij 1932: 59. The fact that in both cases Speranskij refers to the "so-called" Second South Slavic Influence implies he was not the first to use the term. The slightly revised "vtoroe južno-slavjanskoe vlijanie" was apparently first used by Lixačev 1958/1960: *passim.*
[2] For example: "Imenno s ètogo vremeni [the 1390s, DSW] načalas' massovaja èmigracija južnyx slavjan, pričem v pervuju očered' bežali, konečno, ljudi umstvennogo i vooblšče tvorčeskogo truda" (Vzdornov 1968: 171); "Konec XIV v. i pervye desjatiletija XV oznamenovany v Rossii naplyvom jugoslavjanskix vyxodcev" (Ščepkin 1920/1967: 129); "V svjazi s ètim [the Turkish conquest, DSW] uže s konca XIV i v načale XV v. v Rossiju napravilos' značitel'noe količestvo èmigrantov iz slavjanskix stran Balkanskogo poluostrova ... Mnogie iz èmigrantov zanjali v Russkom gosudarstve vidnoe položenie v kačestve ierarxov i izvestny kak političeskie dejateli i dejateli feodal'noj kul'tury" (Čerepnin 1956: 213); Filin 1981: 286 speaks of a "pritok bolgarskix i serbskix duxovnyx dejatelej ... [which arose because of the] zavoevanie Balkan turkami"; there are similar formulations in most textbooks, e.g., Kovalevskaja 1978: 104. Only Levin 1964 is more circumspect: "v èto vremja v svjazi s tureckimi zavoevanijami ... v Rossiju pereselilis' *nekotorye* [my emphasis, DSW] vysokoodarennye južnoslavjanskie pisateli."

³ Filin 1981:286 adds Maksim Grek, who was, however, born a quarter-century after the fall of Constantinople and who arrived in Moscow only in 1518. Maksim's arrival was certainly a major event in the long history of Hellenization (Metropolitan Feognost 1328, Feofan Grek 1378, Metropolitan Fotij 1410, Metropolitan Isidor 1436, Ivan III's marriage to Sophia Paleolog 1472, etc.), but there is no reason to connect it to the Turkish conquest of the Balkans.

⁴ Lixačev 1948/1960: 95-96, Larin 1975: 237, Filin 1981: 287.

⁵ The unthinking acceptance of Epifanij as a representative precisely of the "Second South Slavic Influence" is all the more strange in view of the fact that the always-cited *Life* of Stefan of Perm was written by Epifanij alone, whereas the much less "typical" *Life* of Sergij of Radonež was retouched by the genuinely South Slavic Paxomij Logofet (P. Serb). Surely Larin 1975: 248 is correct in referring to Epifanij as an archaist and not as an example of South Slavic influence.

⁶ What is needed, above all, are detailed studies of the textual material: which features actually appear, and when, and in which combinations, and with what frequency, etc. One suspects that a detailed textual study would bring many surprises. As an example of what might be found, let us look at the brief parallel texts from a *Služebnik* of Patriarch Euthymius and the *Trebnik* No. 376, copied directly from a text of Kiprian's. These texts were published by Ivanov 1958, who shows that Kiprian simply copied the *Trebnik* word for word from the Euthymian text. These parallel texts indeed provide some impressive evidence of "South Slavic Influence," but not at all of the sort one might expect: Kiprian, in fact, rather consistently modernizes and Russifies his protoype. For example, Kiprian regularly substitutes ү and оү for Euthymius' ѫ (бѫтвънѫѫ >
бѫтве́ноую, слѹжьѫ > слоѹьѹ, силоѫ > силою, дроугоуѫ просфорѫ > дрѹгѹю просфо́рѹ.

He occasionally omits Euthymius' (sometimes incorrect) jers (възємъ > вẓсᴹ, въсѣкомь >
всѧкоᴹ) or corrects them (g.pl. ктиторь > ктиторъ). In a *Služebnik* attributed to Kiprian, although not directly dependent on a Bulgarian model, one encounters a mixture of older Russian Church Slavonic and Russian innovations, but no consistent attempt to Bulgarize or archaize the text (Ivanov 1958: 58-59); the text has such Russianisms as достоить, будеть, etc.; пре́жє;

память прєбл҃гн҃ѣи вл҃ѵци нашєи бц҃и; ѿставлєнии грѣхо́въ; свершати, etc. Although this small amount of evidence is only anecdotal, it suggests the importance of looking closely at the texts themselves.

⁷ Especially since Russian contacts with the Greeks became more intense in the late 14th and 15th cc.: Greeks appear in Moscow and the Troice-Sergievskaja Lavra, Russians on Mt. Athos and in Constantinople (Speranskij 1932: 60-61).

REFERENCES

Avanesov, R. I.
1973 "K voprosam periodizacii istorii russkogo jazyka," *Slavjanskoe jazykoznanie. VII Meždunarodnyj s"ezd slavistov, Varšava, avgust 1973 g. Doklady sovetskoj delegacii,* Moscow, 5-24.
Bartoszewicz, A.
1979 *Istorija russkogo literaturnogo jazyka,* Warsaw.
Birnbaum, H.
1958 *Untersuchungen zu den Zukunftsumschreibungen mit dem Infinitiv im Altkirchenslavischen* (= *Acta Universitatis Stockholmiensis, Études de philologie slave,* 6), Stockholm.
1975 "On the significance of the Second South Slavic Influence for the evolution of the Russian literary language," *International journal of Slavic linguistics and poetics,* 21, 23-50.

Borkovskij, V. I., P. S. Kuznecov
1963   Istoričeskaja grammatika russkogo jazyka, Moscow.
Budilovič, A. S.
1871   Issledovanie jazyka drevneslavjanskogo perevoda XIII slov Grigorija Bogoslova, po rukopisi Imp. Publ. Biblioteki XI v., St. Petersburg.
Čerepnin, L. V.
1956   Russkaja paleografija, Moscow.
Diels, P.
1932   Altkirchenslavische Grammatik, I (= Sammlung slavischer Lehr- und Handbücher, hg. von A. Leskien und E. Berneker, I, 6), Heidelberg.
Džordžić, P.
1970   Istorija srpske ćirilice. Paleografsko-filološki prilozi, Belgrade.
Filin, F. P.
1949   Leksika drevnerusskogo literaturnogo jazyka drevnekievskoj èpoxi (po materialam letopisej) (= Leningradskij gos. ped. institut im. A. I. Gercena, Učenye zapiski, 80, Kafedra russkogo jazyka), Leningrad.
1972   Proisxoždenie russkogo, ukrainskogo i belorusskogo jazykov. Istoriko-dialektologičeskij očerk, Leningrad.
1981   Istoki i sud'by russkogo literaturnogo jazyka, Moscow.
Gorškov, A. I.
1969   Istorija russkogo literaturnogo jazyka. Moscow.
Grigorjan, V. M.
1976   "Vtoroe južnoslavjanskoe vlijanie i nekotorye voprosy literaturnogo processa na rubeže XV-XVI vv.," Slavia, 45, 151-158.
Iovine, M. S.
1977   The history and the historiography of the Second South Slavic Influence (Ph.D. dissertation, Yale University), Ann Arbor, Michigan.
Issatschenko, A. V.
1980   Geschichte der russischen Sprache. 1 Band. Von den Anfängen bis zum Ende des 17. Jahrhunderts, Heidelberg.
Istrin, V. A.
1961   "Vozniknovenie i razvitie slavjano-russkogo pis'ma," chapter 4 of his Razvitie pis'ma, Moscow, 258-318.
Istrin, V. M.
1922   Knigy vremen'nyja i obraznyja Georgija Mnixa. Xronika Georgija Amartola v drevnem slavjanskom perevode. Tekst, issledovanie i slovar'. Petrograd.
Ivanov, J.
1958   "Bŭlgarskoto knižovno vlijanie v Rusija pri mitropolit Kiprian (1375-1406)," Izvestija na Instituta za bŭlgarska literatura, 6, 25-79.
Jagić, V.
1896/1968   Codex slovenicus rerum grammaticarum. Rassuždenija južnoslavjanskoj i russkoj stariny o cerkovno-slavjanskom jazyke (= Slavische Propyläen, 25), Munich, 1968 (photomechanic reprint of the first edition, Berlin, 1896).
Karskij, E. F.
1928   Slavjanskaja kirillovskaja paleografija, Leningrad.
Keipert, H.
1977   Die Adjektiva auf -teľnъ. Studien zu einem kirchenslavischen Wortbildungstyp. I Teil (= Veröffentlichungen der Abteilung für slavische Sprachen und Literaturen des Osteuropa-Instituts [Slavisches Seminar] an der Freien Universität Berlin, 34), Wiesbaden.

Kjellberg, L.
1959 "L'interjection *o* + génitif, un calque du grec dans la langue russe," *Scando-Slavica*, 5, 121-131.
Kovalevskaja, E. G.
1978 *Istorija russkogo literaturnogo jazyka*, Moscow.
Larin, B. A.
1975 *Lekcii po istorii russkogo literaturnogo jazyka (X - seredina XVIII v.)*, Moscow.
Levin, V. D.
1964 *Kratkij očerk istorii russkogo literaturnogo jazyka*. 2nd ed., Moscow.
Lixačev, D. S.
1958/1960 "Nekotorye voprosy izučenija vtorogo južnoslavjanskogo vlijanija v Rossii," *Issledovanija po slavjanskomu literaturovedeniju i fol'kloristike. Doklady sovetskix učenyx na IV. Meždunarodnom s"ezde slavistov*, Moscow, 95-151 (first published as separately paginated brochure, Moscow, 1958).
Lunt, H. G., II
1949 *The orthography of eleventh century Russian manuscripts* (Columbia University dissertation), Ann Arbor, Michigan.
Medynceva, A. A.
1975 *Drevnerusskie nadpisi Novgorodskogo Sofijskogo sobora XI - XIV veka*, Moscow.
Meščerskij, N. A.
1975 "Drevneslavjanskij - obščij literaturno-pis'mennyj jazyk na rannem ètape kul'turno-istoričeskogo razvitija slavjan," *Vestnik Leningradskogo universiteta*, 1975, No. 8, 132-140.
1978 *Istočniki i sostav drevnej slavjano-russkoj perevodnoj pis'mennosti*, Leningrad. Not available to me.
1981 *Istorija russkogo literaturnogo jazyka*, Leningrad.
Picchio, R.
1963 "A proposito della Slavia Ortodossa e della comunità linguistica slava ecclesiastica," *Ricerche slavistiche*, 11, 105-127.
Sobolevskij, A. I.
1894 *Južno-slavjanskoe vlijanie na russkuju pis'mennost' v XIV - XV vekax. Reč', čitannaja na godičnom akte Arxeologičeskogo Instituta 8 maja 1894 goda*. St. Petersburg.
1903 *Perevodnaja literatura Moskovskoj Rusi*. Moscow.
1907/1962 *Lekcii po istorii russkogo jazyka*, Moscow, 1907. Reprinted (= *Slavistic printings and reprintings*, 37), 's-Gravenhage, 1962.
1908 *Slavjano-russkaja paleografija. Lekcii A. I. Sobolevskogo. S 20 paleografičeskimi tablicami*. 2nd ed., St. Petersburg.
Speranskij, M. N.
1929 *Tajnopis' v jugo-slavjanskix i russkix pamjatnikax pis'ma* (= *Ènciklopedija slavjanskoj filologii*, 4.3), Leningrad.
1932 "'Grečeskoe' i 'ligaturnoe' pis'mo v russkix rukopisjax XV - XVI vekov," *Byzantino-slavica*, 4, 55-64.
1960 "Iz nabljudenij nad složnymi slovami (composita) v stile literaturnoj russkoj školy XV - XVI vv. (iz istorii vizantijsko-jugoslavjansko-russkix svjazej)" in his *Iz istorii russko-slavjanskix literaturnyx svjazej*, Moscow, 160-197.
Sreznevskij, I. I.
1885 *Slavjano-russkaja paleografija XI - XIV vv. Lekcii, čitannye v Imp. S.-Peterburgskom universitete v 1865-1880 gg*. St. Petersburg.
Šaxmatov, A. A.
1941 *Očerk sovremennogo russkogo literaturnogo jazyka*, 4th ed., Moscow.

Ščepkin, V. N.
1920/1967   Russkaja paleografija, Moscow, 1967 (first published, 1918-1920).
Talev, I.
1973   Some problems of the Second South Slavic influence in Russia (= Slavistische Beiträge, 67), Munich.
Tixomirov, M. N., A. V. Muravev
1966   Russkaja paleografija, Moscow.
Tolstoj, N. I.
1961   "K voprosu o drevneslavjanskom jazyke kak obščem literaturnom jazyke južnyx i vostočnyx slavjan," Voprosy jazykoznanija, No. 1, 52-66.
Uspenskij, B. A.
1968   Arxaičeskaja sistema cerkovnoslavjanskogo proiznošenija (Iz istorii liturgičeskogo proiznošenija v Rossii), Moscow.
Vajs, J.
1932   Rukověť hlaholské paleografie. Uvedení do knižního písma hlaholského (= Rukověti slovanského Ústavu v Praze, II), Prague.
Vinokur, G. O.
1971   The Russian language. A brief history, Cambridge (translation of his Russkij jazyk, Moscow, 1945).
Vysockij, S. A.
1966   Drevnerusskie nadpisi Sofii Kievskoj XI - XIV vv., vyp. I, Kiev.
Vzdornov, G. I.
1968   "Rol' slavjanskix monastyrskix masterskix pis'ma Konstantinopolja i Afona v razvitii knigopisanija i xudožestvennogo oformlenija russkix rukopisej na rubeže XIV - XV vv.," Literaturnye svjazi drevnix slavjan (= Trudy otdela drevnerusskoj literatury, XXIII), Leningrad, 171-198.
Worth, D. S.
1983a   The origins of Russian grammar. Notes on the state of Russian philology prior to the advent of printed grammars (= UCLA Slavic Studies, 4), Columbus, Ohio. In press.
1983b   "Toward a social history of Russian," Medieval Russian culture, ed. H. Birnbaum and M. S. Flier (= California Slavic Studies, XII). In press.
Žukovskaja, L. P.
1963   Razvitie slavjanorusskoj paleografii (v dorevoljucionnoj Rossii i v SSSR), Moscow.
1982   "K voprosu o južnoslavjanskom vlijanii na russkuju pis'mennosť (Žitie Anisi po spiskam 1282-1632 gg.)," Istorija russkogo jazyka. Issledovanija i teksty, Moscow, 277-287.

В защиту запретных деепричастий

Ольга Йокояма

1. *Введение.* Доклад посвящается деепричастным оборотам (ДО) типа *Слушая его, у меня горели глаза и щеки.* Основываясь на данных нескольких живых и мертвых языков, мы попытаемся защитить нашу гипотезу о том, что ДО этого типа представляют собой явление систематическое, подчиняющееся определенным, весьма возможно, что универсальным, правилам на функциональном уровне языка.

Мы будем называть ДО названного типа «запретными» (З) ввиду того, что они запрещаются нормативными грамматиками большей части европейских языков. Существование нормативной грамматики оправдывается социо-лингвистическим аспектом языка и оспаривать ее значение отнюдь не входит в задачи теоретической лингвистики. Для нас ЗДО представляют языковое явление, нуждающееся в адекватном лингвистическом описании, к тому же, по всей вероятности, явление универсальное. На универсальность этого явления указывает в первую очередь существование его во многих языках: мы располагаем примерами из русского языка, сербо-хорватского языка, из моравских диалектов, из английского, французского, санскритского и японского языков. При том следует заметить, что в тех языках, где грамматическая традиция преимущественно описательная, а не нормативная, подобные ДО не подвергаются запрету. Второе доказательство универсальности ЗДО — это то, что несмотря на вековое осуждение их нормативными грамматиками, носители языка — от детей и до мастеров словесного творчества — продолжают порождать их (при определенных условиях, формулировке которых частично посвящена эта работа). Повидимому, в языке существует что-то, что вызывает их порождение. Наше третье доказательство — диахронное, из истории русского языка.

Утверждение о том, что ЗДО — явление универсальное, конечно, предполагает определенный анализ их структуры, а последний предполагает определенный лингвистический подход, в данном случае — с точки зрения порождающей-функциональной грамматики.[1] Приступим же к нашему анализу.

2. *Синхронный анализ.* Представим процесс порождения предложений с ДО упрощенно следующим образом (морфологические детали опускаются). На входе задается: *Она$_i$ сед- к столу, она$_i$ задума-*. Знак *i*

означает идентичность имен. На выходе получаем[2]: $\emptyset_i$ *Сев к столу, она$_i$ задумалась.* Трансформация, связывающая вход и выход, грубо говоря, следующая: подлежащее главного предложения, при условии идентичности его с подлежащим подчиняемого предложения, как бы «выбивает» подлежащее подчиняемого предложения, далее глаголу «выбитого» подлежащего придается деепричастная форма, а глаголу главного предложения — форма, согласующаяся с его подлежащим.

При наличии идентичности обоих подлежащих ДО считаются вполне приемлемыми. Необходимое условие для всех вообще опущений в языке — восстановимость их слушающим, и это условие тут соблюдено.

Если же подлежащие главного и подчиненного предложения неидентичны и опущение одного из них невосстановимо, то подлежащее подчиненного предложения не может быть «выбито». Так предложения ... *разбойники$_i$ приеха- с добычи, он$_j$ их$_i$ встрети-* ... ($i \neq j$ указывает на неидентичность подлежащих) при попытке породить ДО дает неприемлемый выход: $\emptyset_i$ *Приехав с добычи, он$_j$ их$_i$ встретил.* (При неидентичности двух подлежащих и невосстановимости одного из них в случае опущения подчинение одного их них другому происходит без опущения невосстановимого: ср. оригинал начала 18 века *Разбойники приехавше с добычи, и он их встретил* и его современный перевод *Когда разбойники приехали с добычи, он их встретил.*)

И вот, тем не менее, существуют многочисленные примеры, где $i \neq j$ и где подлежащее подчиняемого предложения все же опускается без видимого ущерба, т.к. оно восстановимо. Это-то и есть т.н. ЗДО. Очевидно, необходимым условием для опущения является не идентичность опускаемого подлежащего с подлежащим главного предложения, а восстановимость опущенного подлежащего. Что же обусловливает восстановимость?

Поставив вопрос таким образом, мы уже выходим за рамки предложения, т.к. восстановимость — понятие, не вмещающееся в рамки грамматического строя предложения; скорее, это понятие функциональное, т.е. контекстуальное или конситуационное. Для того, чтоб ответить на наш вопрос, обратимся к примерам[3]:

(1) В такую ночь, $\emptyset_i$ проходя по цепям, $\emptyset_i$ шагая через головы спящих красноармейцев, густо мозги$_j$ наливаются думами. (Фурманов)
(2) Strah$_j$ me$_i$ obuzima, $\emptyset_i$ pomišljauči na povratak. (Stevanović)
(3) $\emptyset_i$ Ayant couru à toute haleine, mon$_i$ coeur$_j$ se mit à battre.[4]
(4) After $\emptyset_i$ watching the Cubs in spring training, it$_j$ is the opinion of many observers$_i$ that ... (The Sporting News, 1978)
(5) tám$_i$ $\emptyset_i$ ha͜enam$_j$ dr̥ṣṭvá bhīr$_k$ viveda. (поздний ведийский, Шатапатха-брахмана) 'Того$_i$, $\emptyset_i$ увидев его$_j$, охватил страх$_k$.'

(6) Ø$_i$ Viňďa ze sklepa, ujely ím$_i$ na slínovém bahnisku nohy$_j$. (Galuška)[5]
(7) Еще Ø$_i$ подходя к игорной зале, ... со мною$_i$ почти делаются судороги$_j$. (Достоевский)

Все эти примеры объединяются тем, что подлежащее главного предложения в них обозначает либо часть тела (мозги, coeur, nohy), либо физическое или психическое состояние (судороги, strah, opinion, bhîr) лица, являющегося подлежащим подчиненного предложения. Можно сказать, что хотя $i \neq j$, i и j находятся в своего рода метонимической связи, т.е. $i \supset j$.

Подобная метонимическая связь наблюдается во многих ЗДО, но ею явление ЗДО однако не исчерпывается. Суть дела глубже. Обратите внимание на слова, помеченные i в главных предложениях примеров (1) - (7). Эти слова, обозначающие обладателя данной части тела, или переживающего данное физическое или психическое состояние, несут в себе все известные признаки темы: а именно, они безударны или слабо ударяемы, они прономинализированы или по крайней мере имеют при себе определенный артикль, а в примере (1) поссессивное прилагательное даже опущено (что обычно в славянских языках при наименовании частей тела и, конечно, при условии восстановимости обладателя, т.е. опять-таки при условии его тематичности). Заметьте также, что в языках, допускающих перестановку слов, перемещение этих слов на конец предложения в ударную позицию, т.е. рематизация их, приводит к неприемлемости выходного предложения: *Strah obuzima mene, pomišljajući na povratak; *... подходя к игорной зале, ... судороги делаются со мною. Значит, на основании примеров (1) - (7) можно сделать вывод, что ЗДО характеризует 2 фактора: 1) Метонимичность главного подлежащего по отношению к «выбиваемому» целому и 2) тематичность самого целого в главном предложении.

Естественным образом возникает вопрос: независимые ли это факторы, в равной степени необходимые при порождении ЗДО, или же это факторы, связанные один с другим, и, следовательно, один из них вытекает из другого? В связи с этим весьма показательны данные японского языка. В японском языке тематические и нетематические имена различаются при помощи частиц: частица *wa* ставится после тематического, а частица *ga* — после нетематического имени. Таким образом, два возможных перевода словосочетания *мои ноги,* (a) *boku no asi wa* и
я   посс. ноги тем.ч.
(b) *boku wa asi ga*, отличаются тем, что в первом темой
я   тем.ч. ноги нетем.ч.
является все словосочетание *мои ноги,* а во втором темой является слово *я, ноги* же нетематичны. Если мы теперь составим предложение, подлежащим которого является словосочетание *мои ноги,* то из двух

названных вариантов в сочетании с ДО оказывается приемлемым лишь второй:

'Поневоле просидев целый час на пятках, у меня сильно затекли ноги.'
(8) $\emptyset_i$ Iti zikan mo seiza saserarete, boku$_i$
$\begin{Bmatrix} \text{(a)* no asi}_j \text{ wa} \\ \text{(b) wa asi}_j \text{ ga} \end{Bmatrix}$ hidoku sibiretesimatta.

О чем же это говорит? Очевидно, синекдохичности *ног* самой по себе еще не достаточно; только выявив тематичность целого, т.е. обладетеля, при помощи специальной морфемы, мы получаем возможность «выбить» то имя в подчиненном предложении, которое соответствует теме главного предложения.[6]

Об относительной несущественности метонимичности говорит и следующая группа ЗДО:

(9) $\emptyset_i$ Пройдя калитку, Пьера$_i$ обдало жаром. (Толстой)
(10) Upon $\emptyset_i$ awakening next morning, the somber knell$_j$ of church bells reached our$_i$ ears.[7]
(11) $\emptyset_i$ Ayant lu la lettre, tout$_j$ me$_i$ sembla très difficile.
(12) $\emptyset_i$ stríyam dr̥ṣṭváya kitavám̐ tatāpa. (Ригведа 10.34.11) 'Увидя женщину, игрока ранило, т.е. Увидев женщину, игроку стало больно.'
(13) $\emptyset_i$ Prebirajući ključeve, učini mu$_i$ se da čuje svoje ime. (Petrović)

В то время как в предыдущей группе примеров можно было указать на два фактора — метонимичность и тематичность, из которых последний, очевидно, был существеннее, во второй группе примеров метонимичности вовсе не наблюдается. На месте ее мы видим другой общий семантический признак: содержание главного предложения говорит о том, что чувствует или переживает лицо, обозначенное «выбитым» подлежащим ДО, при том что это лицо не является формальным подлежащим главного предложения. Заметим, что тематичность этого лица в главном предложении сохранена в этой группе так же, как и в первой.

Далее приступим к последней группе примеров из тех же языков.

(14) $\emptyset_i$ Возвращаясь домой, нас$_i$ застала в роще гроза$_j$.
(15) $\emptyset_i$ Vraćajući se uveče, dočekala me$_i$ je mlaka crvenokasta svetlost$_j$. (Petrović)
(16) ?$\emptyset_i$ Turning around the corner, somebody$_j$ clubbed me$_i$ over the head.
(17) ? En $\emptyset_i$ montant les escaliers, on$_j$ m$_i$'attrapa la jambe.
(18) $\emptyset_i$ Doňďa zpátky, už tam byli ludé$_j$. (Galuška)

Семантического признака, характеризующего все главные предложения в этих примерах, не имеется. Можно было бы, пожалуй, говорить о тематичности имен, идентичных выбитым подлежащим, т.к. имена, помеченные *i* в этих примерах, (обозначим их N$_i$) явно тематичны. Единственное затруднение представляет пример (18): в главном предложении *už tam byli ludé* N$_i$ не только не имеется, но нет и следов его.

Пример (18), как кажется на первый взгляд, противоречит обобщению, сделанному нами выше по поводу предложения *разбойники$_i$ приеха- с добычи, он$_j$ их$_i$ встрети-*, а именно тому, что при неидентичности двух подлежащих и невосстановимости одного из них в случае опущение последнее не осуществляется. Тем не менее, писатель это предложение написал. Что же могло допустить его порождение? При рассмотрении контекста оказывается, что контекст удовлетворяет главному условию, необходимому для порождения ЗДО, а именно условию восстановимости опущенного подлежащего деепричастия. Контекст таков: *Nikdo tam nebyl, tož sem si pověsil kabát k oknu, balík sem dál na lavku, a šel sem si pro noviny. Doňďa zpátky, už tam byli ludé...* Из приведенного ясно, что тема предшествующего ДО контекста — *я*, то самое *я*, которое опущено в данном ДО. На фоне контекста, подсказывающего нам тему, опущенное подлежащее ЗДО в примере (18) вполне восстановимо, что и является главным условием при порождении ДО.

Таким образом, по рассмотрении трех групп ЗДО — группы с метонимичными подлежащими в главном предложении, группы с семантикой переживания в главном предложении, и группы без видимого общего семантического признака в главном предложении — оказывается, что все эти группы примеров объединяет одно: тематичность N_i. Самого N_i следует искать или в главном предложении по признакам, свойственным тематическим элементам (безударность, позиция в начале предложения, определенность, прономинализация), или же в предыдущем контексте, в особенности, когда главное предложение его не содержит.

Итак, когда подлежащее главного предложения N_i является одновременно и его темой, и темой предыдущего контекста, дело обстоит проще всего: так порождаются «законные» ДО типа *Сев к столу, она задумалась*. При условии же несовпадения подлежащего главного предложения с его темой возникает как бы конкуренция на роль «выбивателя». Примеры (16) и (17) помечены вопросительным знаком, который означает не полную приемлемость этих примеров, т.к. вне контекста они в какой-то степени могут даже означать, что опущенными подлежащими ДО являются англ. *somebody* или франц. *on*. Такая неоднозначность этих предложений объясняется конкуренцией на роль «выбивателя» между рематическим подлежащим и тематическим неподлежащим. Чем четче выражена тематичность неподлежащего в предыдущем контексте (как, например, обстояло дело с (18) и его контекстом), тем больше шансов, что ЗДО будет приемлемым, однозначным и что он пройдет незамеченным нормативным рекадтором, потому что он оправдан функциональным уровнем языка. В контексте в примерах (16) и (17) N_i, который несет в себе несколько признаков, говорящих в его пользу при конкуренции с N_j

(ср. N_i: $\begin{bmatrix} \text{+ 1-е лицо} \\ \text{+тема контекста} \\ \text{+определен. имя} \end{bmatrix}$ и N_j: $\begin{bmatrix} \text{-1-е лицо} \\ \text{-тема контекста} \\ \text{-определен. имя} \end{bmatrix}$),

одерживает верх над N_j, несмотря на то, что N_j имеет по крайней мере один признак, говорящий в его пользу (ср. N_i : [-подлежащее] и N_j : [+подлежащее]). Набор положительных и отрицательных знаков в матрице тематических признаков ведет к потенциальной неоднозначности ЗДО, и чем ближе «соперники» по количеству плюсов и минусов, тем более неоднозначен ЗДО. Этим и объясняется шкала премлемости ЗДО, именно шкала, потому что граница между приемлемыми и неприемлемыми ЗДО размыта. Интересно заметить, что решение конкуренции в пользу подлежащего N_j при явной тематичности N_i дает также не вполне приемлемые результаты (хотя в нормативной грамматике правил, осуждающих такие предложения, не имеется):

(19) ? $\emptyset_i$ Заметив ... машину, нам$_i$ стали махать какие-то люди$_j$. (Симонов; пример взят из Nichols, Rappaport and Timberlake 1980, *вопросительный знак и многоточие* наши)

3. *Диахронный анализ русских ДО*. Итак, мы охарактеризовали ЗДО как те случаи, когда подлежащее и тема главного предложения не совпадают, т.е. когда матрицы тематических признаков подлежащего и темы состоят из разнозначных признаков. Мы также предположили, что подлежащее ДО «выбивается» или темой-подлежащим или темой-неподлежащим, причем последняя или присутствует в главном предложении в каком-либо косвенном падеже, или же присутствует в предыдущем контексте. Такой анализ объясняет не только сам факт порождения ЗДО в разных языках, рассмотренных нами, но также и потенциальную двузначность некоторых ЗДО и связанную с ней шкалу приемлемости. Теперь нам остается еще объяснить, почему же в частности в современном русском литературном языке предложения типа восточноморавского (18) все-таки не порождаются.

Как было уже указано, пример (18) отличается от всех других тем, что в главном предложении «выбивателя» нет и следа; выбиватель имеется лишь в предыдущем контексте. Другими словами, «выбивание» подлежащего ДО совершается как бы из-за границы, через стык двух предложений. Этот факт существеннен, т.к. именно он объясняет, почему предложения типа (18) не существуют в современном русском литературном языке, несмотря на то, что раньше подобные предложения в нем встречались, например:

(20) И после того подьячей$_i$ из судного дела выпишет коротко, ... и $\emptyset_i$ выписав, по которому делу мочно судьям$_j$ указ чинить ... и они$_j$ то дело вершат. (Котошихин)

Оставим на время ДО и обратимся к вопросу «выбивания через стык» вообще. Опущение подлежащего, как известно, было общепринятым явлением в древнерусском языке и вплоть до начала 18 века, конечно, при условии восстановимости. Нередки были случаи, когда за первым упоминанием тематического подлежащего следовало до 20-30 глаголов, не сопровождаемых подлежащим. Т.е., говоря нашими словами, до середины 18 века выбиватель мог действовать на очень дальнем расстоянии. Не касаясь спорного вопроса о том, исчезновение ли связки вызвало распространение личных местоименных подлежащих в русском языке, или же наоборот, распространение личных местоимений сделало связку ненужной (ср. Соболевского 1907, Истрину 1921 и др. с Борковским 1952 и Ломтевым 1956), мы можем просто констатировать факт, что «выбивание на дальнем расстоянии», как правило, перестало совершаться где-то во второй половине 18 века, даже в тех случаях, когда условие восстановимости было удовлетворено: *Сей вельможа имеет горячку величаться своей породою. Он производит свое поколение от начала вселенной* (Трутень). В границах же одного предложения выбивание в современном языке не только допустимо, но и обязательно: *Он величается своей породой и *он/∅ производит свое поколение от начала вселенной.* Установившееся по каким бы то ни было причинам ограничение «выбивательной силы» на расстоянии распространялось, конечно, и на ДО. Таким образом, выбивание подлежащего ДО из-за стыка, возможное в примере (20), а также в восточноморавском примере (18), подпало под общее новое ограничение в русском литературном языке: выбивание подлежащего из-за стыка предложений воспрещается. Отсюда и исчезновение подобных примеров из современного русского литературного языка.

Что же касается всех остальных случаев ЗДО, которые в современном русском литературном языке составляют по нашему подсчету около 6% всех ДО[8], то употребление их встречается как до, так и после ограничения «выбивательной силы» на расстоянии, т.е. как до, так и после исчезновения случаев типа (20). Приведем примеры метонимической темы, темы, обозначающей переживающее лицо, и тем разнообразной семантики. Примеры 17 века:

(21) ... а ∅$_i$ лежа, на ум$_j$ взбрело ... (Аввакум)
(22) ... и ∅$_i$ поскочивши от ложе своего, нападе на них$_i$ страх$_j$ велик. (Сказание о явлении Унженского креста)
(23) ... ∅$_i$ прошед Попову гору, в лесу полские люди$_j$ его$_i$ ограбили. (Письма и бумаги Петра Великого)

Примеры 18 века:

(24) ... ∅$_i$ рассматривая здесь обои, воображение$_j$ мечтало сие, ... (Державин)

(25) ... ∅ᵢ Смотря на всех животных, кажется намᵢ, что онаⱼ ... (Зритель)
(26) ∅ᵢ Возвратясь из церкви, посетил меняᵢ доктор Штендерⱼ. (Фонвизин)

Подобных примеров и до и после 18 века можно привести множество.[9] Все это говорит об извечном бытовании ЗДО этого типа в русском языке. В сущности, тому же принципу тематичности выбивателя обязано и опущение подлежащего в примере из Лаврентьевской летописи, на несколько веков предшествующем появлению деепричастий как таковых: *Бысть радость велика въ Володимери градѣ видяще у собѣ великого князя всея Ростовьскыя земли*, и опущение подлежащего в стихе Мандельштама: *Немного красного вина, Немного солнечного мая, И, тоненький бисквит ломая, Тончайших пальцев белизна.*[10]

4. *Заключение.* Мы предложили вашему вниманию анализ ДО типа *Слушая его, у меня горели глаза и щеки* в рамках порождающей-функциональной грамматики. В результате анализа мы установили, что подобные ДО порождаются в результате несовпадения подлежащего главного предложения и его темы, причем именно тема оказывается идентичной с опущенным подлежащим ДО. Как сам факт порождения таких ДО, так и систематичность процесса их порождения свидетельствуют о тесном взаимодействии грамматических и функциональных процессов в языке.

Гарвардский университет

ПРИМЕЧАНИЯ

[1] При этом «порождающая грамматика» понимается нами широко, как теория, предполагающая разные уровни порождения предложения, связанные трансформациями; под «функциональной» же грамматикой подразумевается все привносимое в структуру предложения контекстом, конситуацией, прагматикой и речевым актом.
[2] На выходе можно получить и *Она села к столу и задумалась*, но обсуждение этого и других возможных выходов в этой работе производиться не будет.
[3] За неимением места, я буду по возможности ограничиваться в этом докладе минимальным числом примеров. Следует указать, однако, что русские примеры выбраны из 5500 ДО, найденных в источниках от XVII до XX века включительно; в это число входит более 2000 ДО рассмотренных в Gladney 1966. Примеры из других языков или взяты из источников или основываются на показаниях информантов.
[4] Приносим благодарность Joëlle Cabot за помощь в составлении французских примеров.
[5] Приносим благодарность Иосифу Сташеку, предоставившему нам материалы, написанные на восточноморавском наречии.
[6] В сущности, выделение обладателя при помощи специальной морфемы в японском примере соответствует ярко тематической русской конструкции *у меня* (т.е. *у* + родительный), которая нередко встречается как раз в главных предложениях с подчиненным ЗДО (вспомните пресловутый пример *Подъезжая к станции, у меня слетела шляпа*).

[7] Приносим благодарность Бренту Вайну за помощь в составлении английских примеров.
[8] В корпус вошло более 3500 ДО из русской литературы, прессы, эпистолярной и канцелярской прозы начиная от второй половины XVIII века и до наших дней; подсчет производился вручную.
[9] По нашим подсчетам выходит, что частотность их даже возросла с тех пор, как выбивание на расстоянии прекратилось, с 3% до 6%; корпус XVII — начала XVIII века состоит из более чем 2000 ДО.
[10] Выражаем благодарность проф. К. Ф. Тарановскому за указание этого примера.

СПИСОК РАБОТ, УПОМЯНУТЫХ В ТЕКСТЕ

Борковский, В. И.
 1952 «Исторические справки по синтаксису русского языка», *Русский язык в школе* I, 13-30.
Gladney, Frank Y.
 1966 *Observations on the syntax of gerunds in 17th-century Russian*. Ph.D. dissertation, Harvard University.
Истрина, Е. С.
 1919-1921 «Синтаксические явления Синодального списка I Новгородской летописи», *Известия отделения русского языка и словесности*, т. XXIV, кн. 2, 1-172; т. XXVI, 207-239.
Ломтев, Т. П.
 1956 *Очерки по историческому синтаксису русского языка*. Москва.
Nichols, Johanna, G. Rappaport, and A. Timberlake
 1980 "Subject, topic, and control in Russian," *Proceedings of the Sixth Annual Meeting of the Berkeley Linguistics Society*, ed. by Bruce R. Caron et al. Berkeley.
Соболевский, А. И.
 1907 [1962] *Лекции по истории русского языка*. The Hague.

Other Books From
Slavica Publishers, Inc.
PO Box 14388
Columbus, Ohio 43214

American Contributions to the Eighth International Congress of Slavists Vol. 1: Linguistics & Poetics; Vol. 2: Literature.

P. M. Arant: **Russian for Reading.**

H. I. Aronson: **Georgian A Reading Grammar.**

Balkanistica: Occasional Papers in Southeast European Studies, Vol. III; Vol. IV; Vol. V; Vol. VI.

H. Birnbaum: **Common Slavic Progress and Problems in Its Reconstruction.**

H. Birnbaum: **Lord Novgorod the Great Essays in the History and Culture of a Medieval City-State, Part I The Historical Background.**

H. Birnbaum & T. Eekman, eds.: **Fiction and Drama in Eastern and Southeastern Europe.**

K. L. Black, ed.: **A Biobibliographical Handbook of Bulgarian Authors.**

M. Bogojavlensky: **Russian Review Grammar.**

R. C. Botoman: **Imi place limba Romana/ A Romanian Reader.**

E. B. Chances: **Conformity's Children An Approach to the Superfluous Man in Russian Literature.**

C. V. Chvany & R. D. Brecht, eds.: **Morphosyntax in Slavic.**

F. Columbus: **Introductory Workbook in Historical Phonology.**

R. G. A. de Bray: **Guide to the South Slavonic Languages.**

R. G. A. de Bray: **Guide to the West Slavonic Languages.**

R. G. A. de Bray: **Guide to the East Slavonic Languages.**

B. L. Derwing & T. M. S. Priestly: **Reading Rules for Russian.**

D. Disterheft: **The Syntactic Development of the Infinitive in Indo-European.**

J. S. Elliott: **Russian for Trade Negotiations with the USSR.**

J. M. Foley, ed.: **Oral Traditional Literature A Festschrift for Albert Bates Lord.**

Folia Slavica, a journal of Slavic, Balkan, and East European linguistics, 1977 ff.

R. Freeborn, ed.: **Russian and Slavic Literature.**

V. A. Friedman: **The Grammatical Categories of the Macedonian Indicative.**

Other Books From
Slavica Publishers, Inc.

C. E. Gribble, ed.: *Medieval Slavic Texts, Vol. I, Old and Middle Russian Texts.*
C. E. Gribble: *Reading Bulgarian Through Russian.*
C. E. Gribble: *Russian Root List with a sketch of word formation, second edition.*
C. E. Gribble: *Slovarik russkogo jazyka 18-go veka/ A Short Dictionary of 18th-Century Russian.*
C. E. Gribble, ed.: *Studies Presented to Professor Roman Jakobson by His Students.*
G. J. Gutsche & L. G. Leighton, eds., *New Perspectives on Nineteenth-Century Russian Prose* (J. T. Shaw festschrift).
W. S. Hamilton: *Introduction to Russian Phonology and Word Structure.*
P. R. Hart: *G. R. Derzhavin: A Poet's Progress.*
M. Heim: *Contemporary Czech.*
M. Hubenova and others: *A Course in Modern Bulgarian, Part 1; Part 2.*
International Journal of Slavic Linguistics and Poetics.No. 23 1981 ff.
R. Jakobson: *Brain and Language.*
R. Katzarova-Kukudova & K. Djenev: *Bulgarian Folk Dances.*
A. Kodjak ed.: *Alexander Pushkin Symposium II.*
A. Kodjak: *Pushkin's I. P. Belkin.*
A. Kodjak, ed.: *Structural Analysis of Narrative Texts.*
D. J. Koubourlis, ed.: *Topics in Slavic Phonology.*
M. Launer: *Elementary Russian Syntax.*
R. Leed & A. & A. Nakhimovsky: *Beginning Russian, Vol. 1; Vol. 2.*
R. L. Lencek: *The Structure and History of the Slovene Language.*
J. F. Levin: *Reading Modern Russian.*
M. I. Levin: *Russian Declension and Conjugation: A Structural Description with Exercises.*
A. Lipson: *A Russian Course, Part 1; Part 2; Part 3.*
H. G. Lunt: *Fundamentals of Russian.*
P. Macura: *Russian-English Botanical Dictionary.*
T. F. Magner, ed.: *Slavic Linguistics and Language Teaching.*
M. Matejic & D. Milivojevic: *An Anthology of Medieval Serbian Literature in English.*

Other Books From
Slavica Publishers, Inc.

A. Nakhimovsky & R. Leed: *Advanced Russian.*

L. Newman, ed.: *The Comprehensive Russian Grammar of A. A. Barsov.*

F. J. Oinas, ed.: *Folklore, Nationalism & Politics.*

H. Oulanoff: *The Prose Fiction of Veniamin A. Kaverin.*

J. L. Perkowski: *Vampires of the Slavs.*

S. J. Rabinowitz: *Sologub's Literary Children: Keys to a Symbolist's Prose.*

L. A. Rice: *Hungarian Morphological Irregularities.*

D. F. Robinson: *Lithuanian Reverse Dictionary.*

R. A. & H. Rothstein: *Polish Scholarly Prose A Humanities and Social Sciences Reader.*

D. K. Rowney, ed.: *Russian and Slavic History.*

E. Scatton: *Bulgarian Phonology.*

W. R. Schmalstieg: *Introduction to Old Church Slavic.*

M. Shapiro: *Aspects of Russian Morphology, A Semiotic Investigation.*

O. E. Swan: *First Year Polish.*

C. E. Townsend: *Continuing With Russian, corrected reprint.*

C. E. Townsend: *Czech Through Russian.*

C. E. Townsend: *The Memoirs of Princess Natal'ja Borisovna Dolgorukaja.*

C. E. Townsend: *Russian Word-Formation, corrected reprint.*

D. C. Waugh: *The Great Turkes Defiance On the History of the Apocryphal Correspondence of the Ottoman Sultan in its Muscovite and Russian Variants.*

S. Wobst: *Russian Readings and Grammatical Terminology.*

J. B. Woodward: *The Symbolic Art of Gogol Essays on His Short Fiction.*

D. S. Worth: *Bibliography of Russian Word-Formation.*

M. T. Znayenko: *Gods of the Ancient Slavs Tatischev and the Beginnings of Slavic Mythology.*